The Waite Group's
C Programming
Using
Turbo C++®

The Waite Group's
C Programming Using
Turbo C++®

Robert Lafore
The Waite Group, Inc.

HOWARD W. SAMS & COMPANY
Macmillan Computer Publishing

This book is dedicated to Mitch Waite

International Standard Book Number: 0-672-22737-1
Library of Congress Catalog Card Number: 90-61922

From the Waite Group, Inc:
Development Editor: *Mitchell Waite*
Editorial Director: *Scott Calamar*
Editorial Coordinator: *Joel Fugazzotto*

From Sams:
Development Editor: *James Rounds and Greg Croy*
Acquisitions Editor: *James S. Hill*
Manuscript Editors: *Don MacLaren and Andy Saff*
Illustrators: *William D. Basham, Tom Emrick and Ralph E. Lund*
Cover Illustration: *Ron Troxell*
Indexer: *Joelynn Gifford*
Compositor: *Shepard Poorman Communications Corp.*

Printed in the United States of America

Trademark Acknowledgments

Contents

Tables

Format Specifiers	p 36, 44
Escape Sequences	p 46
Operators	p 53, 56, 49
Extended Key Codes	p 280
ANSI.SYS Codes	p 284
Precedence	p 119
logical operators	p 116
file types	p 541
system level of flags	p 577
bitwise operators	p 365
attribute byte	p 388

About the Author

Robert Lafore has been associated with the computer industry since 1965, when he learned assembly language on the DEC PDP-5. He holds degrees in mathematics and electrical engineering; founded Interactive Fiction, a computer game company; and has served as managing editor of The Waite Group. Mr. Lafore is author or co-author of the computer books *Soul of CP/M*, which describes assembly language in the CP/M environment; *Microsoft Macinations*, a Microsoft BASIC tutorial for the Macintosh; *Assembly Language Primer for the IBM PC and XT*, a 100,000-copy bestseller; *Microsoft C Programming for the PC*, a Microsoft C Tutorial for the PC; *Peter Norton's Inside OS/2*, and *OS/2 Presentation Manager Programming Primer*. Mr. Lafore has also been a petroleum engineer in Southeast Asia, a systems analyst at the Lawrence Berkeley Laboratory, and has sailed his own boat to the South Pacific.

Acknowledgments

I'd like to thank Mitchell Waite of The Waite Group for his dedicated and painstaking editing (complete with humorous asides and subliminal suggestions) and Harry Chesley, co-author of *Supercharging C* (Addison-Wesley), for his expert advice.

I am also indebted to the following individuals at Sams: Jim Hill for having the faith to buy this book idea, Damon Davis for publishing it, Jim Rounds for nursing it into the system, and Wendy Ford and Don Herrington for overseeing its production.

I would also like to thank Doug Adams for his technical edit, Bruce Webster of *Byte* magazine, Ray Duncan, and Herbert Schildt for reviewing the final manuscript, Harry Henderson for checking the final manuscript, and Don MacLaren of BooksCraft for his painstaking and skilled copy editing. In addition, thanks to Allen Holub for his editing of the revised edition.

Foreword

by Ray Duncan

In just a decade, C has made the transition from an obscure Bell Laboratories house language to the programming language of choice for professionals. C has been used successfully for every type of programming problem imaginable—from operating systems to spreadsheets to expert systems—and efficient compilers are available for machines ranging in power from the Apple to the Cray. On the new wave of the windowing, graphics-intensive 68000-based personal computers such as the Macintosh, Amiga, and Atari, C is the de facto standard for serious developers.

Why has C met with such success when other languages, born in the same time frame and designed with similar objectives, have gained only limited acceptance or have faded from view altogether? C's intimate association with UNIX, and the penetration into academia that was made possible by Bell Laboratory's broadminded licensing plans for universities, must be partly responsible. But the largest measure of C's success seems to be based on purely practical considerations: the portability of the compiler; the standard library concept; a powerful and varied repertoire of operators; a spare, elegant syntax; ready access to the hardware when needed; and the ease with which applications can be optimized by hand-coding isolated procedures.

The increasing dominance of C for both systems and applications programming has created a tremendous market for C books. I must confess that I am a compulsive buyer of computer books of every sort: an addiction based on curiosity, on a desire to learn from the approaches and styles of other authors, and on a continual search for excellent new books to recommend to readers of my column in *Dr. Dobb's Journal*. While indulging this pleasant but somewhat expensive habit over the last few years, I have built up quite a collection of C tutorials and reference works, but I have found nearly all of the introductory C books to be unsatisfying. The authors either have difficulty discussing C without blurring the issues with UNIX-specific details, or they succumb to a fascination with clever C tricks, or they simply progress so quickly from elementary concepts to lengthy, complex example programs that they leave the reader behind.

When Mitchell Waite asked me if I would like to review Robert Lafore's manuscript for this book, I was surprised but gratified. I have long considered Robert's *Assembly Language Primer for the IBM PC and XT* New American Library, 1985) to set the standard of quality in its category, and I hoped that his C primer would be equally well organized, lucid, and complete. I certainly was not disappointed! I believe the book you are holding in your hands is the most accessible book on C that has yet been published. The material is presented in Robert's usual clear, forthright style, and the pace is steady but not intimidating. Best of all, the example programs are short but interesting, clearly demonstrate the concepts under discussion, and are relevant to everyday programming problems on the IBM PC—you don't need to speak UNIX or buy your own VAX to reap their benefits.

Ray Duncan is a software developer and columnist for Dr. Dobb's Journal. *He is also author of* Advanced MS-DOS.

Introduction

This book has two interconnected goals: to teach the C programming language, and to show how C can be used to write applications for PC-type computers (the IBM PC, AT, and PS/2 series, and compatibles).

Borland's Turbo C++ provides the best platform yet devised for learning C. Its Integrated Development Environment (IDE) combines all the features needed to develop a C program —editor, compiler, linker, debugger and help system—into a single, easy-to-use screen display. This enables you to develop programs far more simply and conveniently than you can using the traditional command-line compiler system. Turbo C++ is also very fast and surprisingly inexpensive.

Incidentally, don't be confused by the product name. Borland calls it "Turbo C++," but it is really the lastest version of Turbo C, with C++ capabilities added on. You don't need to know anything about C++ to use this product for C programming.

With this book and Turbo C++, you'll be taking an easy and effective path to mastery of the C language and the ability to write PC applications.

What's Different About This Book?

Many introductory books on C present the language either in a UNIX-based environment or in a theoretical context, ignoring the machine the language is running on. This book takes a different approach: it teaches C in the context of PC computers and the MS-DOS operating system. There are several advantages to this approach.

First, focusing on a specific computer platform makes learning the language easier and more interesting. Many UNIX environments have no access to a standardized graphics system, or to other hardware-related peripherals. Programming examples must therefore concentrate on simple text-based interaction. In the PC world, on the other hand, we can make use of such features as graphics characters, program control of the cursor, and bit-mapped color graphics—capabilities which can enliven program examples and demonstrations.

Also, as we move on to more complex aspects of the language, we can explain Turbo C++ constructs that might otherwise seem theoretical and mysterious—such as pointers and unions—by relating them to actual applications on the IBM hardware.

Finally, if your goal is to write programs specifically for PC-type computers, then learning C in the MS-DOS environment, with examples that address specific aspects of PC hardware, will give you a head start in creating your own programs for this environment.

Learn by Doing

This book uses a hands-on appoach. We believe that trying things out yourself is one of the best ways to learn, so examples are presented in the form of complete working programs, which can be typed in and executed. In general, we show what the output from the examples looks like, so you can be sure your program is functioning correctly. Very short examples are used at the beginning of the book, working up toward longer and more sophisticated programs toward the end.

Illustrations and Exercises

We have also tried to make this a very visual book. Many programming concepts are best explained with pictures, so wherever possible we use figures to support the text.

Each chapter ends with a set of questions to test your general understanding of the material covered, and programming exercises to ensure that you understand how to put the concepts to work. Answers to both questions and exercises are provided in the back of the book.

Why Use C?

In the last decade, the C programming language has become the overwhelming choice of serious PC programmers. Why? C is unique among programming languages in that it provides the convenience of a higher-level language such as BASIC or Pascal, but at the same time allows much closer control of a computer's hardware and peripherals, as assembly language does. There are very few operations that can be performed on the PC in assembly language, that cannot be accomplished—usually far more conveniently—in C. This is probably the principle reason for C's popularity on the PC.

But C has other advantages as well. The better C compilers can now generate amazingly fast code. This code is so efficient that it is often difficult to produce significant speed increases by rewriting it in assembly language. C is also a well-structured language: its syntax makes it easy to write programs that are modular and therefore easy to understand and maintain. The C language includes many features that are specifically designed to help create large or complex programs. Finally, C is portable: it is easier to convert a C program to run on a different machine than it is to convert programs written in most other languages.

What You Should Know Before You Read This Book

Before you read this book you should probably have at least some experience with a higher-level language such as Pascal or BASIC. It is certainly possible to learn C as a first computer language. However, C is geared more toward the experienced programmer than the beginner. Its syntax is not—at least at first glance—as easy to understand as BASIC, and it incorporates some concepts that a beginning programmer might find difficult. For these reasons it is advantageous (although not essential) to be familiar with such concepts as variables, looping, conditional statements, and functions (subroutines) before beginning your study of C.

You should be familiar with the MS-DOS operating system. You should be able to list directories, and create, excute, copy and erase files. You should also be familiar with tree-structured directories and how to move about in them.

What Equipment You Need to Use This Book

You can use this book with a variety of different hardware and software configurations. Here's what you'll need.

Hardware

You should have access to an IBM PC, XT, AT, PS/2, or compatible. These machines use 8088, 8086, 80286, 80386, or 80486 microprocessors. In general, any machine that can run Version 2.0 or later of MS-DOS or PC DOS is appropriate. It should have at least 640K of memory.

Either a monochrome or color 80-column monitor will work fine for most of the book. However, Chapters 11 and 12, on color graphics, require the use of a color display. (Also, the Turbo C IDE looks better in color.) You can use a CGA, EGA, or VGA adaptor. It's preferable to have EGA or VGA capability, because Chapters 11 and 12 describe EGA and VGA modes not available on the CGA; but much of these two chapters applies to all three of these graphics systems. If your system does not include color graphics, it's not a catastrophe; everything in the book but these two chapters works fine in monochrome.

Turbo C++ now requires a hard (fixed) disk drive. If you're still using a floppy-only system, this should motivate you to upgrade. You'll also need a 5-1/4-inch floppy drive.

A mouse is convenient (and fun) for operating Turbo C's Integrated Development Environment, which features pull-down menus, resizable windows, and other features of a typical graphics user interface. However, you can do everything from the keyboard if you don't have a mouse.

Finally, although it's not absolutely essential, you'll probably want a printer to generate program listings and record program output.

Software

You should use the MS-DOS (or PC DOS) operating system with a version number of 2.0 or greater.

If you're using the OS/2 operating system, you'll be happy to know that you can also run Turbo C++ in the OS/2 compatibility box. Turbo C works just the same as it does in MS-DOS. All the example programs in this book also run in the compatibility box.

Of course, you'll need Borland's Turbo C++ compiler, which is widely available at computer stores. It can also be ordered directly from Borland International, 1700 Green Hills Road, Scotts Valley, CA 95067; phone 1-800-331-0877. You can also use the older Turbo C product, Version 2.0 or later. Most of the book will work with these older compilers, with the notable exception of Chapter 16, on C++ programming.

That's all you need. There is no need for a separate program editor, or a separate debugger, as there is with many other C compilers.

ANSI-Standard C

The C language has recently undergone a transition. C was created by Dennis Ritchie at Bell Laboratories in the early 1970s. (C's predecessor was a language called B). In 1978 Brian Kernighan and Dennis Ritchie published a book, *The C Programming Language*, which until recently served as an effective definition of C.

In 1989 a new version of the language emerged from the American National Standards Institute: ANSI-standard C. This version includes many features (such as type void and function prototyping) that were not present in the "traditional" Kernighan and Richie C. Turbo C, and this book, have been revised to conform to the new ANSI-standard C.

The C++ Extension to C

Turbo C is really a double-barreled product: you can use it to create programs in the C++ programming language as well as in normal C. C++ is an extension to C: it uses all the syntax of C, but adds new features, notably those that facilitate object-oriented programming. Object-oriented programming (OOP) is essentially a new way to organize programs. Turbo C implements the AT&T Version 2.0 of C++, the current standard.

Chapter 16 provides an easy-to-understand introduction to OOP and C++.

Because C++ presupposes an understanding of C syntax, and because object-oriented programming deals with program organization on a fairly sophisticated level, we strongly recommend that you become comfortable in C before digging into C++. Attempting to learn both at the same time may lead to a desire to give up programming for something simple, like quantum theory.

The Turbo C documentation tends to mix C and C++, but you should treat them as separate languages, which they are. If you're writing in C, you don't want C++ features creeping in. Even if they compile on your system, they will make your programs less portable to other systems and less readable to C programmers.

After you have a firm grasp on C, you can move on to C++. This language is on its way to becoming the most widely used for OOP, and object-oriented programming itself will become increasingly important in the years ahead. But until you know C, we recommend that you ignore C++.

Typographical Conventions

In the text sections of this book (as opposed to program listings), all C-language keywords, such as **if**, **while**, and **switch**, are shown in bold to better distinguish them from the ordinary English-language usage of these words. Likewise, all C functions, including user-written functions and library functions such as **printf()** and **gets()**, are in bold, as are variable names.

When string constants such as "Good morning" and "Fatal error" are used in the text, they are set off by double quotes, just as they are in the C language itself. Character constants are set off by single quotes, again following the convention of the C language: 'a' and 'b' are characters.

Operators, which often consist of a single character such as (+) and (\ ), are often surrounded by parentheses for clarity. Keyboard keys, such as [Ctrl], [Del], and [Z], are enclosed in square brackets.

Program names are not in bold, but include their file extensions, such as .c in myprog.c and .obj in myprog.obj.

Good Luck, Lieutenant

This book covers a lot of ground—from simple one-line programs to complex graphics and database applications. Our intention is to make the exploration of this territory as easy and as interesting as possible, starting slowly and working up gradually to more challenging concepts. We hope we've succeded, and that you have as much fun reading this book as we had writing it.

The Turbo C Programming Environment

- Setting up the Turbo C System
- Why C uses so many files
- Program creation in the IDE
- Writing a very simple Turbo C program
- Structure of C programs
- The **printf()** function

1

This chapter launches you on your C programming career. It has two goals. First we discuss how to set up the Turbo C++ development system, the directories, and files used by the system, and how you use Turbo C++ to create programs. Second, we present your first C program. From this program you'll learn about the organization of C programs in general, and about the **printf()** function in particular.

Setting Up the Turbo C Development System

In this section, we briefly introduce the components of the Turbo C development system, and make some suggestions for setting it up so you can compile the example programs in this book.

There are actually two development systems in Turbo C, the first of which will be important to us in this book. Let's see what they are.

The Integrated Development System (IDE)

Turbo C features an Integrated Development Environment, or IDE. (It's also referred to as the Programmer's Platform.) Users of Turbo Pascal or Turbo BASIC will already be familiar with the major features of the IDE. It is a screen display with windows and pull-down menus. The program listing, its output, error messages, and other information are displayed in separate windows. You use menu selections (or key combinations) to invoke all the operations necessary to develop your program, including editing, compiling, linking, and program execution. You can even debug your program within the IDE. An on-line help facility is available through menu selections. You can choose options (such as compiler optimization and memory model) from menus; gone are the days of trying to remember obscure command-line switches.

All this operates very smoothly and rapidly. It's also surprisingly easy to learn. In fact, the IDE provides an almost ideal environment for learning C; it's the system used in this book.

The Command-Line Development System

You should be aware that there is another, completely different way to develop C programs in Turbo C. This is a traditional command-line system, in which editing, compiling, linking, debugging, and executing are invoked from the DOS command line as separate activities, performed by separate programs. This system is relatively difficult to learn and complex to operate (although to some extent it can be automated with batch files). Although this system must be used in certain complex situations, it isn't necessary for the example programs in this book.

The Install Program

The two Turbo C development systems—IDE and command line—are loaded into the same directory of your hard disk. This directory is divided into several subdirectories, some of which contain a great many files. Fortunately, the creation of this directory structure and the loading of the files from the distribution disks are completely automated by an install program.

Before you start to set up your system, you should back up the distribution diskettes with the DISKCOPY utility. Use the backups to load the system.

Setting up the system is easy. Put disk 1 into the A: drive, and enter

```
C>a:install
```

You'll be asked to approve various default values already supplied by the INSTALL program. These cover such things as the names of the directories where the system will be installed, and what memory models you want to use. The screens are largely self-explanatory, and a status line at the bottom of the screen tells you what keys to press. If you accept the default values, you won't have much thinking to do. However, you may want to consider some options.

Directories

Unless you tell it otherwise, the INSTALL program puts all the subdirectories and files in a directory called TC. If you don't like this name, or already have a directory called TC, you must type in new pathnames in the appropriate places. Don't change the names of the subdirectories, like BIN, INCLUDE, LIB, and so on.

Hard Disk Space

Some versions of the INSTALL program say that the system requires 6M of hard disk space. You can reduce this to about 4M by changing some of the default values.

INSTALL normally loads example programs and a tutorial program called TOUR. If you want to save disk space, you can change the default "Yes" answers to "No" for these options.

Memory Models

An important question asked by INSTALL concerns *memory models*. There are five memory models: Small/Tiny, Compact, Medium, Large, and Huge. In the Small model (which is included in the Small/Tiny option) your program can have up to 64K of code and 64K of data storage. In the Medium model the program code can exceed this 64K limit, but the data is still restricted to 64K. Other models offer different arrangements of memory space.

Chapter 14 explores memory models more thoroughly. At this point, what you need to know is that each memory model requires a separate library file, and each library file takes up space on your hard disk. All the programs in this book can be compiled with the Small memory model. If you want to save disk space, you should tell INSTALL that you don't need the other memory models. Change the default "Yes" answers to "No" for all but the Small/Tiny options.

When you've set the options to your satisfaction, select the Start Installation option. INSTALL will create the necessary directories, and unpack and install the appropriate files. You will be asked periodically to place the various disks in the source drive.

The AUTOEXEC.BAT and CONFIG.SYS Files

After all the files have been loaded, you'll need to modify the PATH command in your AUTOEXEC.BAT file so that Turbo C's executable files are available from any directory. These files are in the TCBIN directory, so the command should look something like this:

```
PATH=C:\TC\BIN
```

Also, the CONFIG.SYS file should be modified to include the line FILES=20. Don't forget to reboot after changing the CONFIG.SYS file.

Files Used in C Program Development

Now that you've installed your system, you may be eager to start programming. First, however, let's examine the results of the installation process. If you're used to a simple language such as Pascal or BASIC, you may be surprised by the sheer number of files that came with the Turbo C system. At this point, it is difficult to understand exactly what all these files do, but you should have a rough idea before plunging into your first C program.

Executable Files

Executable files are stored in the subdirectory BIN. The most important executable—for this book, at least—is TC.EXE. Executing this program places the IDE on your screen.

The BIN directory also contains programs for the command-line development process previously mentioned, and utility programs for use in specialized situations. Here are some of them:

TCC	Command-line compiler
TLINK	Command-line linker
MAKE	File-management program
GREP	Searches for strings in groups of files
TOUCH	Updates file date and time
CPP	Preprocessor utility
TCINST	Customizes Turbo IDE
TLIB	Library file manager
UNZIP	Unpacks .ZIP (compressed) files
OBJXREF	Object file cross-reference utility
THELP	Popup utility to access help file

You'll use a few of these programs in later chapters, but none of them is necessary for developing simple programs. The IDE in the TC.EXE file does everything you need.

Library and Run-Time Files

Various files are combined with your program during linking. These files contain routines for a wide variety of purposes. There are library files, run-time object files, and math library files. They are all stored in the LIB directory.

Library Files

Library files are groups of precompiled routines for performing specific tasks. For example, if a programmer uses a function such as **printf()** (which is described later in this chapter) to display text on the screen, the code to create the display is contained in a library file. A library file has a unique characteristic: only those parts of it that are necessary will be linked to a program, not the whole file. If this weren't true, every program would be enormous.

C is especially rich in the number and variety of its library routines. Many processes which in other languages are built into the definition of the language (such as input/output statements) are handled in C by library functions.

As was mentioned earlier, there is one library file for each memory model. The files are called cs.lib, cc.lib, cl.lib, cm.lib, and ch.lib. The cs.lib file is used with the Small and Tiny models, cc.lib is used with the Compact model, cl.lib is used with the Large model, and so on. The INSTALL program installs one library file in LIB for each memory model you specify. If you request only the Small model, only cs.lib will be installed.

Another library file, graphics.lib, is linked with your program if you use the Turbo C graphics library functions (which are covered in Chapter 12).

Math Libraries

If you're going to use floating point arithmetic in your programs (as many examples in this book do), you'll need another library file. Each memory model has one such file, named maths.lib, mathc.lib, and so on. As with library files, the IDE selects the correct floating point file for your program, depending on the memory model you specify.

For floating point math you'll also need either fp87.lib or emu.lib. The first of these files is used if you have a math coprocessor chip (such as an 8087 or 80287) installed in your computer. The second is used if you don't have a math coprocessor, and must "emulate" its function in software. You can select one of these options from a menu in the IDE, but emu.lib is the default selection; it works whether you have a math coprocessor or not.

Run-Time Object Files

In addition to needing library files, each program must be linked with a *run-time* library object file. Again, each memory model has such a file, with names like c0s.obj, c0c.obj, and so on. These files contain the code to perform various functions after your program is running, such as interpreting command-line arguments (discussed in Chapter 8).

Header Files

The subdirectory called INCLUDE contains *header files*. These files (also called "include" files) are text files, like the ones you generate with a word processor or the Turbo C Editor. Header files can be combined with your program before it is compiled, in the same way that a typist can insert a standard heading in a business letter. Each header file has a .h file extension.

Header files serve several purposes. You can place statements in your program listing that are not program code but are instead messages to the compiler. These messages, called *compiler directives*, can tell the compiler such things as the definitions of words or phrases used in your program. Some useful compiler directives have been grouped together in header files, which can be included in the source code of your program before it goes to the compiler.

Header files also contain *prototypes* for the library functions. Prototypes provide a way to avoid program errors. Chapter 5 covers header files and prototypes in more detail.

Programmer-Generated Files

You can place the programs that you write in any subdirectory you choose; for instance, a subdirectory under TC. Whatever subdirectory you are in when you invoke TC is usually where the source files you type in, the executable file created by the system, and any other files generated by the system are placed.

Files and More Files

Why does C use so many different files? Dividing the various aspects of the language into separate files gives the language more flexibility. By keeping the input/output routines in separate library files, for instance, it's easier to rewrite C to work on a different computer: all that needs to be changed are the files containing input/output functions; the language itself remains the same.

The multiplicity of different library files also means that the routines used with a particular program can be custom tailored to that program's needs: if you don't need the "huge" memory model, for example, you don't need to use the larger and slower routines that go with it. You can add routines for floating point math or file I/O if you need them; if you don't, they don't take up space in your finished program.

Try not to feel overwhelmed by the complexity of the development system. As you learn more about C, the purposes of the various files will become clearer.

Using the Integrated Development Environment

This section shows how to use the IDE to write, compile, link, and run a simple Turbo C program. Later we'll examine in detail the syntax of the program itself.

Invoking the IDE

Change to the subdirectory where you want to develop your program. To activate the IDE, all you need to do is type "tc" at the DOS prompt (don't type "tcc", which is the name of the command-line compiler):

```
C>tc
```

That's all there is to it. The IDE screen, which initially displays only a menu bar at the top of the screen and a status line below, will appear.

The menu bar displays the menu names File, Edit, Search, Run, and so forth. The status line tells you what various function keys will do.

Using Menus

When you first invoke the IDE, the menu bar will be active. If it isn't, you can make it active by pressing the [F10] function key. When it's active, one name on the menu bar is highlighted. To select different menus, move the highlight left and right with the cursor (arrow) keys.

To cause a highlighted menu to drop down, so you can see its contents, press the down cursor key. Another approach to viewing a menu is to press the [Alt] key and the first letter of the menu name. Thus, to activate the Search menu, you would type [Alt] [S]. If you have a mouse, you can view the contents of a menu simply by clicking on the desired menu name. ("Click on" means to move the mouse pointer to the desired location and briefly press the left mouse button.) To move up and down the menu, use the up and down cursor keys. To close a menu and return to the menu bar, press [Esc].

As you move through the items on a menu, the status line changes to provide a description of the selected item. To activate a particular selection, press [Enter] while it is highlighted, or click on it with the mouse. The action specified will be carried out.

Opening an Edit Window with File/New

To type in your first program you'll need to open an Edit window. To do this, activate the File menu by clicking on the word "File" with the mouse, or by moving the menu-bar highlight to it and pressing [Enter]. Select New from this menu, either by clicking on "New" with the mouse or by moving the highlight down the menu with the cursor key and pressing [Enter]. (Selecting New from the File menu in this way is often abbreviated as *File/New*.)

You'll see a *window* appear on the screen. It's colored differently than the screen background, and has a double-lined border, as shown in Figure 1-1.

You can expand this window to fill the screen by clicking on the arrow in the upper right corner, or by selecting Zoom from the Window menu. If the listing is too large to fit in the window, you can scroll the window contents with the up and down cursor keys. To return to the menu bar from the window, press [F10] again. Now exit to DOS by selecting Quit from the File menu.

Opening an Edit Window from the Command Line

We've seen one way to open an edit window for a new program. Another approach is to supply the name of the file to be opened on the command line

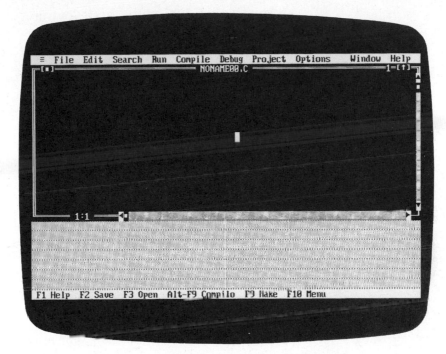

Figure 1-1. The IDE Screen with Edit Window

when TC is first invoked. In our case, we want to create a file called oneline.c, so at the DOS prompt, we type

```
C>tc oneline.c
```

This causes the IDE to be displayed on the screen as before. However, the Edit window will be automatically opened and given the name ONELINE.C. The oneline.c program doesn't exist yet, so this window will be empty. Later, a file called oneline.c will be created. (If this file existed already, it would be opened and its contents displayed in the Edit window.)

Now, with a blank Edit window awaiting us, we're ready to type in our first program.

Writing a Program

The Edit window should be active, with the cursor flashing at the upper right corner. Type in the program oneline.c, as follows:

```
void main(void)
{
    printf("I charge thee, speak!");
}
```

9

Type as you would on a typewriter. Characters will appear where the cursor is positioned. Press [Enter] to move the cursor to the beginning of the next line. Use the cursor keys to reposition the cursor anywhere on the screen. If you make a mistake, use the [Backspace] key to delete the character to the left of the cursor, or the [Del] key to delete the character under the cursor. You can delete an entire program line by positioning the cursor on it and pressing the [Ctrl] [Y] key combination.

We won't go into further detail here on using the Turbo Editor. We've explained enough here to get you started typing in simple programs. Appendix F describes additional Editor features, and Borland's Turbo C documentation covers the Editor and other IDE features in detail.

Be careful to enter the program exactly as shown, paying attention to the parentheses after the word "main", to the braces (not brackets) above and below the **printf()** statement, and to the semicolon at the end of this statement. At this point, don't worry about what the program does (although you can probably guess this), or why it's written the way it is. We'll show how to get it running first, and then go back and explain its syntax.

Saving the Program

After you've typed in the source file for the program, you should save it on your disk. To do this, select Save from the File menu. You can accomplish the same effect simply by pressing the [F2] function key. Many actions can be activated by using either the menu system or the function keys. The function keys are harder to learn, but faster once you know them.

If you invoked TC with the name oneline.c on the command line, then the file you are typing has already been given this name, as you can see at the top of the Edit window. In this case, the file will be saved to disk immediately when you select File/Save.

On the other hand, if you opened the Edit window by selecting File/New, then the file will have the temporary name NONAME00.C. When you select File/Save, a dialog box will appear. (A dialog box is a temporary window where you enter additional information.) At the top of this dialog box is a field called Save Editor File As. Type in the name oneline.c and press [Enter]. The file will be saved under this name.

Saving the source file is not necessary before compiling and running your program, but it's a good idea. There's always a small chance that executing the program will crash the system; if your source file isn't saved, it's gone forever.

Making an .exe File

After you've written the source file for your program, you need to turn it into an executable file. This is called "Making" the .exe file. Let's examine what this means in a general sense before we see how to carry out the task.

Compiling

The version of the program you typed in is understandable to human beings (at least if they know C). However, it is not understandable to the microprocessor in your computer. A program that is to be executed by the microprocessor must be in the form of a *machine language* file. Thus there must be two versions of the program: the one you type in, which is called the *source file,* and the machine-language version, which is called the *executable* (or sometimes *binary* file).

The *compiler*, which is a part of the IDE, translates this source code into another file, consisting of machine language.

Linking

The process would be conceptually simple if compiling were the end of the story, and you simply executed this new compiler-generated file to run your program. However, there's another step in most compiled languages, including Turbo C: a process called *linking*.

Linking is necessary for several reasons. First, your program may (and in fact almost certainly will) need to be combined with various library routines. As we noted, these are functions that perform tasks such as input/output. Library routines are stored in files with the .lib extension. Second, you may not want to compile all of your program at the same time. Larger C programs commonly consist of several separate files, some of which may already be compiled. The linker combines these files into a single executable file.

Like the compiler, the linker is built into Turbo C's IDE.

> The text editor produces .c source files, which go to the compiler, which produces .obj object files, which go to the linker, which produces .exe executable files.

The compiler generates an intermediate kind of file called an object file. The linker then links all the necessary object files together to produce a final, executable program. The relationship of the compilation process to the linking process is shown schematically in Figure 1-2.

In Turbo C (and most other versions of C), the source file you type in is given the .c file extension (as in "myprog.c"). The intermediate object files are automatically given the extension .obj by the compiler (myprog.obj), and the executable program files are given the extension .exe by the linker (myprog.exe). The operating system recognizes files with the extension .exe as executable files, so you can run them directly, like other application programs.

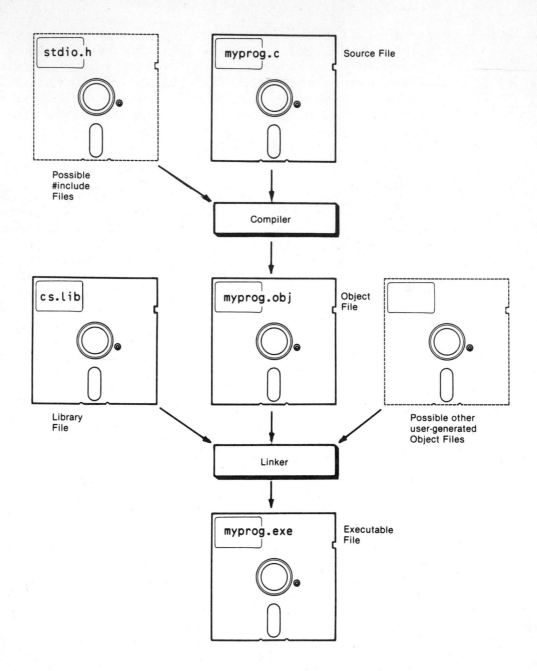

Figure 1-2. Relationship of Compiler and Linker

Compiling and Linking in the IDE

In the Turbo C IDE, compiling and linking can be performed together in one step. There are two ways to do this: you can select Make EXE File from the Compile menu, or you can press the [F9] key.

A great many things happen when you initiate the Make process. As you learned earlier, the compiler first transforms your source file, oneline.c, into an object file, oneline.obj. The linker then combines this file with various other files and parts of files. The resulting file is called oneline.exe. However, the IDE does not apply this process blindly.

Project/Make

Before compiling and linking a file, a part of the IDE called Project/Make checks the time and date on the file you're compiling. (This data is stored in each file.) Why is this a good idea? In complex programs, with many source files, checking the time and date of file creation can avoid unnecessary compilation of source files. Chapter 13 discusses this, and the other capabilities of Project/Make, in greater detail. For now, the important thing to know is that pressing [F9] causes the program in the Edit window to be compiled and linked.

If you want, you can perform compiling and linking separately. To do this, you'll need to see more menu options than you can when Turbo C is first started. Select Full Menus from the Options menu. It will toggle to On. This causes more selections to be displayed under each menu. Looking under the Compile menu, you'll find separate selections for Compile to OBJ and for Link EXE File. You can select these separately.

Screen Display for Compiling and Linking

While compiling is taking place, you'll see a window appear in the middle of the screen with the legend "Compiling" at the top. This window contains a variety of information: the name of the file being compiled, the number of lines compiled, the number of warnings, the number of errors, and the available memory. If your program was written correctly, this window will hardly be on the screen long enough to see, because Turbo C compiles so quickly. But if you've made a typing mistake, you'll have plenty of time to examine this window. In the "Correcting Syntax Errors" section, we'll explore the possibility that you made a typing error.

While linking is taking place, a different window appears. It looks much the same as the Compiling window, but with the legend "Linking" at the top. If you look closely you'll see file names flash by in the Linking field. These are files, such as emu.lib, maths.lib, c0s.obj, and cs.lib, that are being linked with the oneline.obj file. When the linking process terminates, the screen appears as shown in Figure 1-3 (if no mistakes were made when you wrote your program).

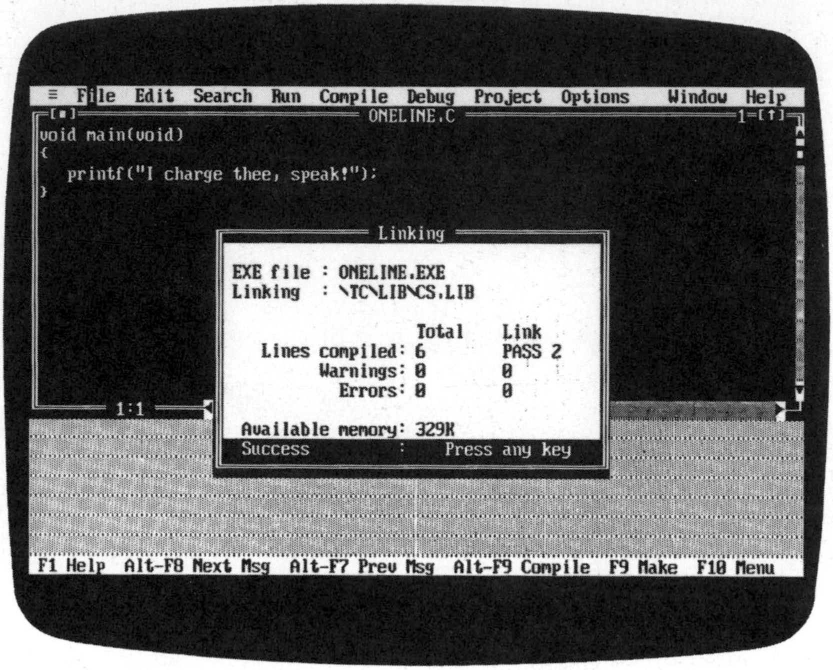

```
 ≡  File  Edit  Search  Run  Compile  Debug  Project  Options    Window  Help
┌─[■]─────────────────────────── ONELINE.C ─────────────────────────1═[↑]─┐
│void main(void)                                                          ▲
│{                                                                        ▓
│   printf("I charge thee, speak!");                                      █
│}                                                                        ▓
│             ┌──────────────────── Linking ────────────────────┐        ▓
│             │                                                  │        ▓
│             │  EXE file : ONELINE.EXE                          │        ▓
│             │  Linking  : \TC\LIB\CS.LIB                       │        ▓
│             │                                                  │        ▓
│             │                      Total     Link              │        ▓
│             │     Lines compiled: 6          PASS 2            │        ▓
│             │          Warnings: 0           0                 │        ▓
│             │            Errors: 0           0                 │        ▓
│├─ 1:1 ──────┤                                                  ├────────┤▼
│             │  Available memory: 329K                          │
│             │  Success          :     Press any key            │
│             └──────────────────────────────────────────────────┘
│
│
│
│
├─ F1 Help  Alt-F8 Next Msg  Alt-F7 Prev Msg  Alt-F9 Compile  F9 Make  F10 Menu ┤
```

Figure 1-3. A Successful Link

Compiling and Linking from the Command Line

We mentioned that there is a second development system in Turbo C. As a beginner in C, you will have little need to use the system, but we'll mention how it works.

To compile and link with the command-line system, you must first generate a source (.c) file using some kind of program editor. You can use the editor built into the IDE, or any other editor.

Compiling and linking takes place from DOS, and uses the program TCC.EXE. To compile and link the oneline.c program, you would enter the following:

```
C>tcc oneline.c
```

This produces the oneline.obj and oneline.exe files just as the IDE does. Any errors are printed out to the screen. Program development is much less convenient from the command line than in the IDE because you must constantly shift between your editor and tcc. Error correction is also clumsy.

Executing a Program

If there were no errors in the compiling or linking process, you're now ready to run the program. You can do this from the IDE by selecting Run from the Run menu, or by pressing the [Ctrl] [F9] key combination.

When you run the program you'll see the screen flicker briefly. The program has written a message to the screen, but not to the IDE screen. To see the program's output, select User Screen from the Window menu, or press [Alt] [F5]. You'll see the normal DOS screen, which should look like this:

```
C>tc
I charge thee, speak!
```

The first line is what you typed to invoke TC. The second line is the output from the program. Pressing any key takes you back to the IDE screen.

Sometimes you may find the output from one program appearing on the same line of the output screen as output from another program or from DOS. To avoid visual confusion, you can guarantee that output starts on a new line by selecting DOS Shell from the File menu before running your program. At the resulting DOS prompt, type "exit" to return to the IDE. Program output then starts on the line below "exit".

Correcting Syntax Errors

It is quite likely that your first attempt to compile a program will not be successful. If you have made an error typing in your program, the compiler will recognize this and let you know about it in the Compiler window. You'll see that the number of errors is not listed as 0, and the word "Errors" appears instead of the word "Success" in the bottom of the window.

When this happens, press any key to remove the compiler window. You'll see the Edit window with your program, with one line and one character in the line highlighted in different colors. Another window, called the Message window, will appear at the bottom of the screen. It will contain one or more error messages, one of which will be highlighted.

For example, suppose you left out the closing quotes after the phrase "I charge thee, speak!" in oneline.c. In the Edit window the opening quote will be highlighted, and in the message window the phrase "Error: Unterminated string or character constant in function main" is highlighted. This situation is shown in Figure 1-4.

One error often confuses the compiler into thinking there are other errors as well, and that's true in this case. Because the string is never terminated, the compiler assumes all the rest of the program is part of the string. The compiler thus does not recognize the closing parenthesis, so it displays another message: "Error: Function call missing) in function main."

To correct the error, you must edit the program. You activate the Edit window by pressing [F6]. The cursor is conveniently situated on the line con-

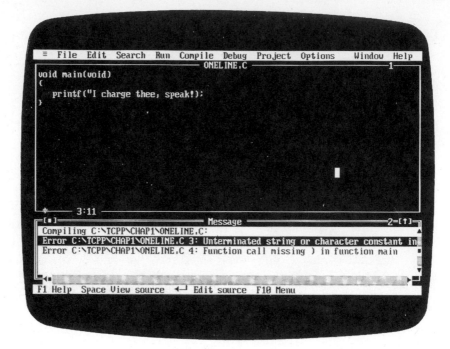

Figure 1-4. Compiler Error

taining the error. Now the appropriate correction can be made to the program; in this case, the missing quote is inserted.

If more than one error needs to be corrected, you can repeatedly move back and forth between the Error window and the Edit window by pressing [F6]. To view each error in turn, use the cursor keys to move the highlight in the Message window.

The linker displays errors in much the same way that the compiler does, but for different reasons. For example, if you misspell **printf()** as **printx()**, your program will compile correctly, but the linker will signal an error, because it won't be able to find a **printx()** function to link to your program.

When all the errors are corrected, press [F2] to save the source file, and then [F9] to compile and link again (or you can make the corresponding menu selections to carry out these actions).

The ease with which errors can be identified and corrected is one of Turbo C's most pleasing features. In the process of learning C you are likely to have more than one opportunity to try out this process.

Correcting Logical Errors

When you start writing more complex programs, you will often find that a program compiles and links without errors, but nevertheless fails to operate as intended. In such situations you will probably want to use Turbo C's debugger features to analyze what's going on. You can single step through a program, watch variables change as each statement is executed, and perform other activities to help you analyze your program's aberrant behavior.

Appendix G introduces Turbo C's debugging features. You probably p 723 don't need to know the details of debugging now, but you might want to skim through this appendix so you'll have an idea what features are available. Then you can put them to use when you need them.

Exiting the IDE

Before you exit the IDE, you may want to close the Edit window that contains your source file. If you don't close it, the IDE will automatically open an Edit window on this same program when you invoke it again from DOS. If this is what you want, that's fine, but you may find multiple unclosed Edit windows accumulating in the IDE, taking excessive screen space.

After you make the Edit window active, you can close it in three different ways. You can click on the small square in the upper left corner, you can select Close from the Window menu, or you can press the [Alt] [F3] key combination.

To exit from the IDE, select Quit from the File menu, or press the [Alt] [X] key combination. This takes you back to DOS.

From DOS you can see that the files oneline.c, oneline.bak, oneline.obj, and oneline.exe have been created. The .bak file, which is a backup for the .c file, is created automatically by the editor. This backup file can be useful if the original of your source file becomes corrupted. For simple programs, the .obj file can be erased after the .exe file is created. (When you develop multifile programs, you should keep the .obj files to facilitate the Make process, as we'll see in Chapter 13.)

You can execute your .exe file directly from DOS. Simply type the file's name at the DOS prompt:

```
C>oneline
```

You should see the same output phrase as before. Because most programs eventually run as stand-alone applications, this is the most realistic way to view your program's output. However, during program development it is not as convenient as executing from within the IDE.

Now that you understand the mechanics of creating a working Turbo C program, let's look at the syntax of the program itself.

The Basic Structure of C Programs

When they first encounter a C program, most people find it as complicated as an algebra equation. It seems densely packed with obscure symbols and long program lines and they think, uh-oh, I'll never be able to understand this. However, most of this apparent complexity is illusion. A program written in C is really not much more difficult to understand than one written in any other language, once you've gotten used to the syntax. Learning C, as is true with any language, is largely a matter of practice. The more you look at C programs, the less complex they appear, until at some point you wonder why you ever thought they looked complicated.

In the balance of this chapter, and the ones that follow, we'll introduce you to C in a carefully graded progression, so that each example is as simple as possible. We want to avoid the situation where you are suddenly confronted with a program so complicated that it looks like the chalkboard scribblings of a mad scientist. If the examples seem *too* simple, don't worry; they won't stay that way long.

Let's investigate the various elements of oneline.c.

```
void main(void)
{
    printf("I charge thee, speak!");
}
```

Function Definition

First, note the name "main." All C programs are divided into units called "functions." A function is similar to a subroutine in BASIC or a function in Pascal. We'll have more to say about functions in Chapter 5; for now, note that **main()** is a function. Every C program consists of one or more functions; this program has only one. No matter how many functions there are in a C program, **main()** is the one to which control is passed from the operating system when the program is run; it's the first function executed.

The word "void" preceding "main" specifies that the function **main()** will not return a value. The second "void," in parentheses, specifies that the function takes no arguments. We won't worry about either of these issues until Chapter 5.

C programs consist of functions. The **main()** function is the one to which control is passed when the program is executed.

Thus our program begins the way all C functions do: with a name, followed by parentheses. This signals the compiler that a function is being defined.

Delimiters

Following the function definition are braces which signal the beginning and end of the body of the function. The opening brace ({) indicates that a block of code that forms a distinct unit is about to begin. The closing brace (}) terminates the block of code. Braces in C perform a function similar to BE-GIN and END statements in Pascal. In our program there is only one statement between the braces: the one beginning with "printf".

Braces are also used to delimit blocks of code in situations other than functions; they are used in loops and decision-making statements, for example. We'll find out more about that in the next few chapters.

Although these elements may seem straightforward, we'll bet that at some point in your programming career you'll (1) forget the parentheses after **main** or (2) forget one or both of the braces that delimit the program.

Statement Terminator

The line in our program that begins with the word "printf" is an example of a *statement*. A statement in C is terminated with a semicolon. Note that a semicolon does not *separate* statements, as it does in Pascal. Also note (especially if you're a BASIC programmer) that the semicolon terminates the line, not the carriage return you type afterwards. C pays no attention to carriage returns in your program listing. In fact, the C compiler pays no attention to any of the so-called "whitespace" characters: the carriage return (newline), the space, and the tab. You can put as many or as few whitespace characters in your program as you like; they are invisible to the compiler.

While we're on the subject of semicolons, we'll make another bet: At some point you'll forget to use one at the end of a C statement.

Figure 1-5 shows the points of program structure we've discussed so far.

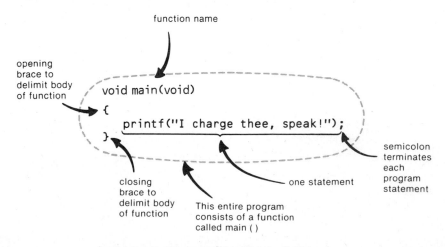

Figure 1-5. Structure of a Simple C Program

Program Style, Round One

Since you can put as many whitespace characters as you want in your program, it is almost a universal practice to use these characters to make the program easier to read. This is done by conforming more or less to the style guidelines used by Kernighan and Ritchie in *The C Programming Language* (see the Bibliography), as we did in our example. It would also be perfectly permissible to write the oneline.c program as

```
void main(void){printf("I charge thee, speak!");}
```

The compiler wouldn't know the difference. However, stretching the code out vertically makes for a more comprehensible program, and aligning matching braces makes it easier to ensure that each opening brace has a closing brace.

> The whitespace characters (space, tab, newline) are invisible to the compiler.

Indentation of blocks of code enclosed in braces is an important aspect of making C programs readable. In this example the program line is indented three spaces (our standard indent throughout this book). Indenting the line of code isn't critical in this short example, but when there are many sets of nested braces in a program, indentation becomes increasingly important.

The *printf()* Function

The program line

```
printf("I charge thee, speak!");
```

causes the phrase in quotes to be printed on the screen. The word **printf** is actually a function name, just as "main" is a function name. Since "printf" is a function, it is followed by parentheses. In this case, the parentheses contain the phrase to be printed, surrounded by quotes. This phrase is a function *argument*—information passed from **main()** to the function **printf()**. We won't dwell too much on arguments and the formal aspects of functions at this point; we'll save that for Chapter 5. Note however that when we mention function names such as **printf()** and **main()** in the text we'll usually include the parentheses following the name just to make it clear that we're talking about a function and not a variable or something else.

"I charge thee, speak!" is an example of a *string* of characters. In C, string constants such as this are surrounded by quotes; this is how the compiler recognizes a string. We'll be using strings as we go along, and we'll dig into their complexities in Chapter 6.

Notice that we have used the function **printf()** in our program. That is, we have called it just as we would call a subroutine in BASIC or a procedure in Pascal. But there is no code for this function in our program. Where is **printf()** stored? It's in the cs.lib library file. When compiling the program, the compiler realizes that **printf()** is not a function included in the oneline.c source file, so it leaves a message to that effect for the linker. The linker looks in cs.lib (since we're using the small memory model), finds the section of this file containing **printf()**, and causes this section to be linked with our **oneline.c** program. A similar process is followed for all C library functions.

One other aspect of our sample C program deserves mention: except for some letters in the string in quotes, it's written entirely in lowercase. Unlike some programming languages, C distinguishes between uppercase and lower-case letters. Thus the functions **PRINTF()** and **Printf()** are not the same as the function **printf()**. A convention often followed in C is to keep pretty much everything in lowercase (except constants, which we'll look at later) for ease of typing. Some programmers, however, use both lowercase and upper-case when naming functions and variables.

> C distinguishes between uppercase and lowercase.

Exploring the *printf()* function

The **printf()** function is actually a powerful and versatile output function. We're going to spend the remainder of this chapter exploring it. The **printf()** function is important because it is the workhorse output statement in C.

Printing Numbers

The **printf()** function uses a unique format for printing constants and variables. For a hint of its power let's look at another example:

```
void main(void)
{
    printf("This is the number two: %d", 2);
}
```

Invoke the IDE and a new file called printwo.c. Type this program in, and link and compile it as described earlier. Can you guess what message will be printed when you run it? Here's the output:

```
This is the number two: 2
```

Why was the digit 2 printed, and what effect does the %d have? The function **printf()** can be given more than one argument. In the oneline.c example we gave it only one: the string "I charge thee, speak!" Now we're giving it two: a string ("This is the number two: %d") on the left and a value (the number 2) on the right. These two arguments are separated by a comma. The **printf()** function takes the value on the right of the comma and plugs it into the string on the left. Where does it plug it in? Where it finds a *format specifier* such as %d.

Format Specifiers

The format specifier tells **printf()** where to put a value in a string and what format to use in printing the value. In this example, the %d tells **printf()** to print the value 2 as a decimal integer. Other specifiers could be used for the number 2. For instance, %f would cause the 2 to be printed as a floating point number, and %x would print it as a hexadecimal number. We'll explore these possibilities later.

Why not simply put the number 2 into the original string?

```
printf("This is the number two: 2");
```

In this example it wouldn't make any difference in what is printed out, since 2 is a constant. However, as we'll see in Chapter 2, variables can also be used in the **printf()** function, giving it the capability of changing what it prints while the program is running.

Printing Strings

Using format specifiers we can print string constants as well as numbers. Here's an example that shows both a string and a number being printed together:

```
void main(void)
{
    printf("%s is %d million miles\nfrom the sun.", "Venus", 67);
}
```

Type in this program (call it venus.c), compile, link, and execute it. The output will be:

```
Venus is 67 million miles
from the sun.
```

The **printf()** function has replaced the %s symbol with the string "Venus" and the %d symbol with the number 67, as shown in Figure 1-6.

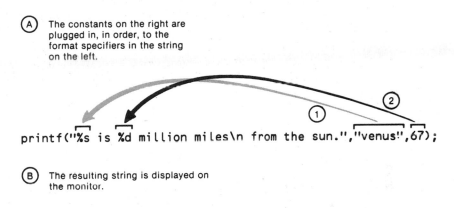

(A) The constants on the right are plugged in, in order, to the format specifiers in the string on the left.

```
printf("%s is %d million miles\n from the sun.","venus!",67);
```

(B) The resulting string is displayed on the monitor.

Figure 1-6. The **printf()** Function

This example also includes a new symbol, the '\n'. In C this means "newline" and stands for a single character that, when inserted in a string, has the effect of a carriage return and linefeed: that is, following a '\n' character, printing is resumed at the beginning of the next line. (The newline character is stored in memory as a single character—a linefeed—but it has the effect of both a carriage return and linefeed.)

Printing Characters

In our final example in this chapter we'll show how **printf()** can be used to print a single character.

You might think that a character is simply a string with only one character in it, but this is not the case in C; characters and strings are distinct entities. Here's a program, called sayjay.c, that prints a character and a string:

```
void main(void)
{
    printf("The letter %c is ", 'j');
    printf("pronounced %s.", "jay");
}
```

Here we've made two different program lines, each with a **printf()** function. The output of this program will be:

```
The letter j is pronounced jay.
```

In this program 'j' is a character and "jay" is a string. Notice that 'j' is surrounded by single quotes (actually apostrophes), while "jay" is surrounded by double quotes. This is how the compiler tells the difference between a character and a string.

Also note that even though the output is printed by two separate program lines, it doesn't consist of two lines of text. That's because **printf()** doesn't automatically print a newline character at the end of a line; if you want one, you must explicitly insert it.

Summary

In this chapter you've learned how to set up the Turbo C IDE to create, compile, link, and run C programs. To this end, you've learned about the organization of the various files provided with Turbo C. You've learned what simple C programs look like and that even the main part of a C program is a function. You know some of the potential of the **printf()** function, including how to print number, character, and string constants. You know how to use format specifiers, and the purpose of the newline character. At this point you should be able to write one- or two-line C programs that print out various phrases on the screen.

In Chapter 2 we'll continue our exploration of the **printf()** function and we'll look at other input and output functions. We'll also examine two other important C building blocks: variables and operators.

Questions

1. A compiled language runs more quickly than an interpreted one because the compiler translates each program statement into machine language
   a. never
   b. only once
   c. each time the program is executed
   d. each time the statement is executed

2. After the source file for a C program has been written, it must be c_____, l_____, and e_____.

3. The library files that come with the C programming system contain
   a. functions that perform input and output
   b. a text editor for program development

    c. functions for advanced math and other purposes

    d. the compiler and linker

4. The executable files that come with the C programming system include a program to a _____ the different phases of the compilation process.

5. What is the purpose of the parentheses following the word **main** in a C program?

6. The braces that surround the code in a C program
    a. delimit a section of code
    b. show what code goes in a particular function
    c. separate the code from the constants
    d. separate the source file from the object file

7. True or false: a carriage return must be used at the end of every C program statement.

8. What's wrong with the following C program?

```
void main
(
print"Oh, woe and suffering!"
)
```

9. What two sorts of things can go in the parentheses following the function **printf()**?

10. What is the output of the following program?

```
void main(void)
{
printf("%s\n%s\n%s", "one", "two", "three");
}
```

Exercises

1. Write a two-statement program that will generate the following output:

```
Mr. Green is 42,
Mr. Brown is 48.
```

Use string constants to represent the names and integer constants to represent the ages.

2. Write a program that will print the phrase

   `a, b, and c are all letters.`

   Use character constants to represent the letters.

2

C Building Blocks

- Variable types
- The **printf()** output function
- The **scanf()** and **getche()** input functions
- Special characters
- Arithmetic operators
- Relational operators

2

Before you can begin to write interesting programs in C you need to know at least some of the fundamentals of the language. In this chapter we present a selection of these basic building blocks.

Three important aspects of any language are the way it stores data, how it accomplishes input and output, and the operators it uses to transform and combine data. These are the three kinds of building blocks we'll discuss in this chapter. Of course, in a single chapter we can't present every aspect of each of these topics; much will remain to be said in later chapters. However, what we cover here will be enough to get you off the ground.

In the following chapters we'll put these building blocks to use exploring the control statements of the language: loops, decisions, and functions.

Variables

Variables may be the most fundamental aspect of any computer language. A variable is a space in the computer's memory set aside for a certain kind of data and given a name for easy reference.

Variables are used so that the same space in memory can hold different values at different times. For instance, suppose you're writing a program to calculate someone's paycheck. You'll need to store at least the hourly rate and the hours worked. If you want to do the calculation for more than one employee, you will need to use the same program and the same spaces in memory to store similar data for additional employees. A variable is a space in memory that plays the same role many times, but may contain a different value each time.

What different kinds of variables does the language recognize? How is this data stored? How do you tell the computer what sort of data you want to store? These are the questions we'll be exploring in this section.

Constants and Variables

In Chapter 1 we showed how the **printf()** function can be used to print constant numbers, strings, and characters. For example, this program

```
void main(void)
{
    printf("This is the number two: %d", 2);
}
```

printed the constant 2, plugging it into the format specifier, %d:

```
This is the number two: 2
```

Of course this is not very useful, since we could more easily have written:

```
void main(void)
{
    printf("This is the number two: 2");
}
```

to achieve the same result. The power of the **printf()** function—indeed, the power of computer languages in general—comes from the ability to use variables—which can hold many different values—in program statements. Let's rewrite the program above to use a variable instead of a constant:

```
void main(void)
{
    int num;

    num = 2;
    printf("This is the number two: %d", num);
}
```

This program, which we'll call var.c, gives the same output as before, but it has achieved it in quite a different way. It creates a variable, **num**, assigns it the value 2, and then prints out the value contained in the variable.

This program contains several new elements. In the first program statement,

```
int num;
```

a variable is declared: it is given a name and a type (type **int**, which we'll examine soon).

In the second statement,

```
num = 2;
```

the variable is assigned a value. The assignment operator (=) is used for this purpose. This operator has the same function as the (=) operator in BASIC or the (:=) operator in Pascal. (We'll have more to say about assignment operators in the last section of this chapter.)

In the third statement of the program, the variable name, **num**, is used as one of the arguments of the **printf()** statement, replacing the constant 2 used in the example in Chapter 1.

Variable Definitions

The statement

```
int num;
```

is an example of a *variable definition*. If you're a Pascal programmer you'll be familiar with this sort of statement; BASIC doesn't use (or at least doesn't need to use) variable definitions. The definition consists of the *type* name, **int**, followed by the name of the variable, **num**. In a C program all variables must be defined. If you have more than one variable of the same type, you can define them all with one type name, separating the variable names with commas:

```
int apples, oranges, cherries;
```

Defining a variable tells the compiler the *name* of the variable and the *type* of variable. Specifying the name at the beginning of the program enables the compiler to recognize the variable as "approved" when you use it later in the program. This is helpful if you commit the common error of misspelling a variable name deep within your program; the compiler will flag the error, whereas BASIC would simply assume you meant a different variable. Defining variables also helps you organize your program; collecting the variables together at the beginning of the program helps you grasp the overall logic and structure of your program.

> All variables must be defined to specify their name and type and set aside storage.

When you define a variable, the compiler sets aside an appropriate amount of memory to store that variable. In the present case we've specified an integer variable, so the compiler will set aside two bytes of memory. This is large enough to hold numbers from −32,768 to 32,767. Actually, the amount of memory used for an integer (and other variable types) is not defined as part of the C language; it is dependent on the particular computer system and compiler being used. However, Turbo C operates with two-byte integers, so we'll assume that's the case here. Figure 2-1 shows how an integer looks in memory.

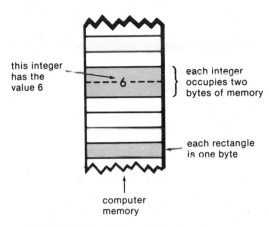

this integer has the value 6

each integer occupies two bytes of memory

each rectangle is one byte

computer memory

Figure 2-1. An Integer in Memory

Defining and Declaring

Although the difference won't be important until later, we should point out a subtle distinction between the words "definition" and "declaration" used in reference to variables. We've been discussing variable *definitions*, which specify the name and type of a variable, and also set aside memory space for the variable. A variable *declaration*, by contrast, specifies the variable's name and data type, but doesn't set aside any memory for the variable. Variable declarations are important in multifile programs, where a variable that is defined in one file must be referred to in a second file. The second file uses a declaration for this purpose, as we'll see in Chapter 14.

The Turbo C++ documentation prefers to call definitions "defining declarations," and declarations "referencing declarations." In most cases the word "declaration" is used for both meanings. We prefer the more consistent approach of distinguishing between the meanings, as is done by Kernighan and Ritchie (see Bibliography) and by other compiler vendors.

Variable Types

There are, of course, other types of variables besides integers, which is the only type we've seen so far. We'll summarize them here and then give examples of the uses of the more common types.

Most variable types are numeric, but there is one that isn't: the *character* type. You've already met character constants; you know that they consist of a letter or other character surrounded by single quotes. A character variable is a one-byte space in memory in which the character constants, such as 'a' or 'X', can be stored. The type name for a character is **char**. Thus, to declare two character variables, called **ch1** and **ch2,** you would use the statement:

```
char ch1, ch2;
```

There are also several different kinds of numerical variables. We'll look at them briefly now. Later we'll learn more about them when we use them in actual programs.

You already know about integers (type **int**). For situations when the normal integer is too small, the *long integer* (type **long** or **long int**) can be used. It occupies *four* bytes of memory and can hold integers from −2,147,483,648 to 2,147,483,647. This is a useful data type for numbers like the purchase price of a home in Marin County, California.

There are also two kinds of *floating point* variables. Floating point numbers are used to represent values that are *measured*, like the length of a room (which might have a value of 145.25 inches) as opposed to integers, which are used to represent values that are *counted*, like the number of rooms in a house. Floating point variables can be very large or small. One floating point variable, type **float**, occupies four bytes and can hold numbers from about 10^{38} to 10^{-38} with between six and seven digits of precision. (Precision means how many digits can actually be used in the number; if you attempt to store a number with too many digits, such as 2.12345678, in a floating point variable, only six digits will be retained: 2.12345.)

A *double-precision* floating point variable, type **double**, occupies eight bytes and can hold numbers from about 10^{308} to 10^{-308} with about 15 digits of precision. (The slight vagueness in specifying these limits of precision arises from the fact that variables are actually stored in the computer in binary, which does not represent an integral number of decimal digits.) Type **double** is the most commonly used floating point variable. There is also a larger **long double** type. It occupies 10 bytes and holds numbers from 10^{-4932} to 10^{4932}.

Figure 2-2 shows some of these variable types as they would look in the computer's memory.

Another variable type, **short**, is often used in C programs on other computers, where it has a different size from type **int**. (On the IBM system 370, for example, it is half the size of an integer.) However, in Turbo C, type **short** is a two-byte integer just like type **int** and therefore is seldom used.

The character type and the integer types also have **unsigned** versions (type **unsigned char**, **unsigned int**, and **unsigned long)** which change the range of numbers the type can hold. For instance, the **unsigned int** type holds numbers from 0 to 65,535, rather than from −32,768 to 32,767 as the regular **int** type does. These unsigned types can be useful in special circumstances, but are not used as often as the signed versions.

You may be wondering why we haven't mentioned a string type. The reason is simple: there is no string variable type in C. Instead, strings are

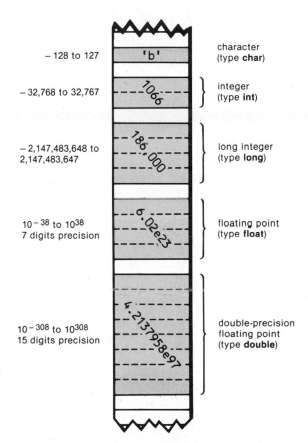

Figure 2-2. Variable Types in Memory

represented by arrays of characters. We've shown some examples of string constants already. For string variables, we'll have to wait until Chapter 6.

Let's look at a program that uses character, floating point, and integer variables. We'll call this program event.c.

```c
void main(void)
{
    int event;
    char heat;
    float time;

    event = 5;
    heat = 'C';
    time = 27.25;
    printf("The winning time in heat %c", heat);
```

```
      printf(" of event %d was %f.", event, time);
   }
```

Here's the output of this program:

```
The winning time in heat C of event 5 was 27.250000.
```

This program uses three common variable types: **int**, **char**, and **float**. You'll notice that we've used a new format specifier, %f, to print out the floating point number. We'll discuss this and other format specifiers soon, in the section on input/output. For now, remember that %f is used to print floating point numbers the same way that %d is used to print integers and %c is used to print characters.

Floating Point Variables

Floating point numbers are different from integers in that they are stored in memory in two parts, rather than one. These two parts are called the "mantissa" and the "exponent." The mantissa is the value of the number, and the exponent is the power to which it is raised.

Scientists and engineers use a similar technique for representing numbers: it's called "exponential notation." For example, in exponential notation the number 12,345 would be represented as 1.2345e4, where the number 4, following the e, is the exponent—the power of 10 to which the number will be raised—and 1.2345 is the value of the number. The exponent can also be negative: .0098765 is represented in exponential notation as 9.8765e−3. The idea in exponential notation is to transform every number, no matter how large or how small, into a value with only one digit to the left of the decimal point, followed by the appropriate power of 10. In effect, the exponent represents how many places you need to move the decimal point to transform the number into this standard form.

Exponential notation permits the storage of far larger and far smaller numbers than is possible with integer data types. However, arithmetic and other operations are performed more slowly on floating point numbers, so an integer variable is preferable unless the larger capacity of floating point numbers is necessary.

In Turbo C++, a floating point number of type **float** is stored in four bytes: one for the exponent, and three for the value of the number, as shown in Figure 2-3.

The format is actually not quite the same as the exponential notation used by humans, since the value of the number and the exponent are stored in the computer's memory in binary rather than decimal. However, the effect is the same. The one-byte exponent is large enough to hold exponents between 38 and −38. For instance, the number 123,456,000,000,000,000,000,000, 000,000,000,000,000.0 (which has 38 digits following the 1) is close to the

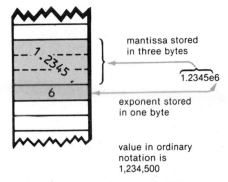

Figure 2-3. Floating Point Variable

largest number that can be stored; it would be represented in exponential notation as 1.23456e38.

Since only three bytes are available for holding the value of the number, only six or seven digits of precision are available in floating point variables. Thus, you can write numbers like 4345345.8476583746123, but the computer will store only 4.345345e6.

Just because a floating point variable is stored in the computer in exponential notation doesn't mean it must print out that way or that you need to type it in using exponential notation. In the event.c program shown earlier, the %f format specifier causes the number to be printed in the normal way with a decimal point. However, as we'll see in the next section, you can force **printf()** to print in exponential notation or even to make a choice between decimal and exponential.

Initializing Variables

It's possible to combine a variable definition with an assignment operator so that a variable is given a value at the same time it's defined. For example, the event.c program could be rewritten, producing event2.c:

```
void main(void)
{
    int event = 5;
    char heat = 'C';
    float time = 27.25;

    printf("The winning time in heat %c", heat);
    printf(" of event %d was %f.", event, time);
}
```

The output is just the same, but we've saved some program lines and simplified the program. This is a commonly used approach.

Input/Output

It's all very well to store data in the computer and make calculations with it, but you also need to be able to type new data into the computer and print out the results of your calculations. In this section we'll continue our examination of the ouput function **printf()**, and we'll introduce two input functions: **scanf()**, a versatile function that can handle many different kinds of input, and **getche()**, a specialized input function that tells your program which character you've typed, the instant you type it.

The *printf()* Function

We've been using **printf()** up to now without too much explanation of all its possibilities. Let's take a closer look.

Format Specifiers

As we've seen, a format specifier (such as %d or %c) is used to control what format will be used by **printf()** to print out a particular variable. In general, you want to match the format specifier to the type of variable you're printing. We've already used four of the format specifiers available with **printf()**: %d to print integers, %c to print characters, %s to print strings, and %f to print floating point numbers. While these are by far the most commonly used, there are others as well. Here's a list of the format specifiers for **printf()**:

%c   single character
%s   string
%d   signed decimal integer
%f   floating point (decimal notation)
%e   floating point (exponential notation)
%g   floating point (%f or %e, whichever is shorter)
%u   unsigned decimal integer
%x   unsigned hexadecimal integer (uses "abcdef")
%o   unsigned octal integer
 l   prefix used with %d, %u, %x, %o to specify long integer (for example %ld)

Field-Width Specifiers

The **printf()** function gives the programmer considerable power to format the printed output. Let's see how this is done.

In our event.c program the floating point variable **time** was printed out with six digits to the right of the decimal, even though only two of these digits were significant:

p 34

```
The winning time in heat C of event 5 was 27.250000.
```

It would be nice to be able to suppress these extra zeros, and **printf()** includes a way to do just that. We'll rewrite the event.c program, inserting the string ".2" (period 2) between the '%' character and the 'f' in the second **printf()** statement:

```
void main(void)
{
    int event = 5;
    char heat = 'C';
    float time = 27.25;

    printf("The winning time in heat %c", heat);
    printf(" of event %d was %.2f.", event, time);
}
```

Here's the output of this program, which is called event3.c:

```
The winning time in heat C of event 5 was 27.25.
```

As you can see, a number *following* the decimal point in the field-width specifier controls how many characters will be printed following the decimal point.

A digit *preceding* the decimal point in the field-width specifier controls the width of the space to be used to contain the number when it is printed. Think of this field width as an imaginary box containing the number. An example (with integer values) is shown in Figure 2-4.

Specifying the field width can be useful in creating tables of figures, as the following program, field.c, demonstrates.

```
void main(void)
{
    printf("%.1f %.1f %.1f\n", 3.0, 12.5, 523.3);
    printf("%.1f %.1f %.1f\n", 300.0, 1200.5, 5300.3);
}
```

Here's the output:

```
3.0 12.5 523.3
300.0 1200.5 5300.3
```

Even though we used spaces in the format strings to separate the numbers (the spaces in the format string are simply printed out as spaces in the output) and specified only one decimal place with the ".1" string, the num-

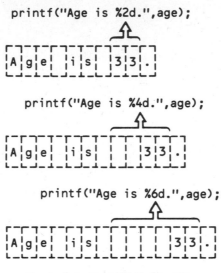

Figure 2-4. Field-Width Specifier

bers don't line up and so are hard to read. However, if we insert the number 8 before the decimal place in each field-width specification we can put each number in a box eight characters wide. Here's the modified program, field2.c:

```c
void main(void)
{
    printf("%8.1f%8.1f%8.1f\n", 3.0, 12.5, 523.3);
    printf("%8.1f%8.1f%8.1f\n", 300.0, 1200.5, 5300.3);
}
```

We should acknowledge the cluttered appearance of the **printf()** statements. Instant legibility is not one of C's strong points (at least not until you've been programming in it for a while). Although you know the purpose of all the elements in these statements, your eye may have trouble unraveling them. It may help to draw lines between the individual format specifiers to clarify what's happening. Figure 2-5 shows this format string dissected.

The format specifier in **printf()** determines the interpretation of a variable's type, the width of the field, the number of decimal places printed, and the justification.

Here's the output of the program, showing that, although the format specifiers may be hard to read, the output is a model of organization:

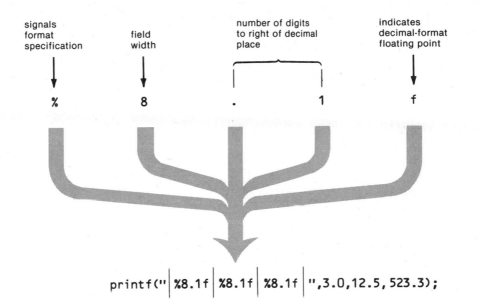

```
printf(" %8.1f %8.1f %8.1f ",3.0,12.5,523.3);
```

Figure 2-5. *printf()* Format String

```
    3.0     12.5     523.3
  300.0   1200.5    5300.3
```

A <u>minus sign preceding the field-width specifier</u> will put the <u>output</u> on the <u>left side of the field</u> instead of the right. For instance, let's insert minus signs in the field-width specifiers in the preceding program to create field3.c:

```
void main(void)
{
    printf("%-8.1f%-8.1f%-8.1f\n", 3.0, 12.5, 523.3);
    printf("%-8.1f%-8.1f%-8.1f\n", 300.0, 1200.5, 5300.3);
}
```

The output will be lined up on the *left* side of the fields, like this:

```
3.0     12.5     523.3
300.0   1200.5   52300.3
```

This format may be useful in certain circumstances, especially when printing strings.

The various uses of the format specifier are summarized in Appendix A.

Escape Sequences

We saw in Chapter 1 how the newline character, '\n', when inserted in a **printf()** format string, would print the carriage return-linefeed combination. The newline character is an example of something called an "escape sequence," so called because the backslash symbol (\ ) is considered an "escape" character: it causes an escape from the normal interpretation of a string, so that the next character is recognized as having a special meaning. Here's an example called tabtest.c that uses the newline character and a new escape sequence, '\t', which means "tab."

```
void main(void)
{
    printf("Each\tword\tis\ntabbed\tover\tonce");
}
```

Here's the output:

```
Each    word    is
tabbed  over    once
```

Turbo C tabs over eight characters when it encounters the '\t' character; this is another useful technique for lining up columns of output. The '\n' character causes a new line to begin following "is."

The tab and newline are probably the most often used escape sequences, but there are others as well. The following list shows the common escape sequences.

\n   Newline
\t   Tab   8 characters
\b   Backspace
\r   Carriage return
\f   Formfeed
\'   Single quote
\"   Double quote
\\   Backslash
\xdd ASCII code in hexadecimal notation (each d represents a digit)
\ddd ASCII code in octal notation (each d represents a digit)

The first few of these escape sequences are more or less self-explanatory. The newline, which we've already seen, has the effect of both a carriage return and linefeed. Tab moves over to the next eight-space-wide field. Backspace moves the cursor one space left. Formfeed advances to the top of the next page on the printer.

Characters that are ordinarily used as delimiters—the single quote, double quote, and the backslash itself—can be printed by preceding them with the backslash. Thus, the statement

```
printf("Dick told Spot, \"Let's go!\"\n");
```

will print

```
Dick told Spot, "Let's go!"
```

Printing Graphics Characters

What's the purpose of those last two escape sequences, \xdd and \ddd?

As you probably know, every character (letters, digits, punctuation, and so forth) is represented in the computer by a number. True ASCII (an acronym for American Standard Code for Information Interchange) codes run from 0 to 127 (decimal). These cover the upper- and lowercase letters, digits from 0 to 9, punctuation, and control characters such as linefeed and backspace.

PC computers use an additional 128 characters, with codes running from 128 to 255. These additional characters consist of foreign-language symbols and graphics characters. IBM has also redefined a few characters below ASCII code 32 to be graphics characters. The entire set of IBM character codes is listed in Appendix D.

p 699

We've already seen how to print ordinary ASCII characters on the screen using characters or strings in **printf()**. We also know how to print certain special characters with a backslash escape sequence. But graphics and other nonstandard characters require a different approach; they can only be printed by sending the backslash and the number representing their character code.

The number can be represented in either octal or hexadecimal notation. Traditionally, octal has been used in UNIX-based systems, and to some extent this has carried over into C implementations on PC computers. However, the rest of the PC world, including all operating system and assembly language programming, speaks hexadecimal; so that's what we'll do in this book. There is no way to use decimal numbers as part of escape sequences—evidence of C's genesis in the world of systems programmers, who tend to think in terms of octal or hexadecimal, rather than decimal. (If you're not familiar with the hexadecimal system, consult Appendix B.)

Let's look at a program, charbox.c, that prints a simple graphics character, a small rectangle:

```
void main(void)
{
```

```
        printf("Here's the character: \xDB");
}
```

The output of this program is shown in Figure 2-6.

Here is the character: ■

Figure 2-6. Printing a Graphics Character

We've used the hexadecimal number DB (219 in decimal), which represents a solid rectangle.

Here's another example of the use of graphics characters:

```
void main(void)
{
    printf("\xC9\xCD\xBB\n");
    printf("\xC8\xCD\xBC\n");
}
```

This program, called box6char.c, which prints nothing but graphics characters, displays a box on the screen, as shown in Figure 2-7.

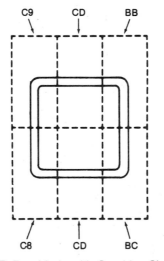

Figure 2-7. Box Made with Graphics Characters

Graphics characters are printed using their hex code in an escape sequence, such as '\xB0'.

These graphics characters are specific to the PC world, so programs using them cannot be ported to UNIX or other systems without modification. However, graphics characters offer an easy way to create graphics images on the PC screen. Programs using this form of graphics can be run on any PC system, even those without color graphics capabilities, making this the most universal form of graphics in the PC world. While not as versatile as color graphics, graphics characters can be used in many applications where simple graphics are required. One example is the Turbo C IDE itself.

We'll use other examples of graphics characters in programming examples in later chapters.

The *scanf()* Function

You already know about C's most-used *output* statements, **printf()**. In this section we're going to introduce an important *input* function, **scanf()**. C has a bewilderingly large collection of input and output functions, but **printf()** and **scanf()** are the most versatile in that they can handle all of the different variables and control their formatting.

Here's a program that uses **scanf()**. You can give it the filename age.c:

```
void main(void)
{
    float years, days;

    printf("Please type your age in years: ");
    scanf("%f", &years);
    days = years * 365;
    printf("You are %.1f days old.\n", days);
}
```

Besides **scanf()**, this program introduces two new symbols: the arithmetic operator for multiplication (*), and the address operator, represented by the ampersand (&). We'll talk about both of these later in the chapter. For the moment, simply note the surprising fact that **scanf()** requires the use of an ampersand before the variable name.

A typical interaction between the program and a precocious youngster might look like this:

```
Please type your age in years: 2
You are 730.0 days old.
```

Since we're using floating point we can also input decimal fractions:

```
Please type your age in years: 48.5
You are 17702.5 days old.
```

As you can see, the format for **scanf()** looks very much like that for **printf()**. As in **printf()**, the argument on the left is a string that contains format specifiers. In this case there is only one, %f. On the right is the variable name, **&years**.

The format specifiers for **scanf()** are similar to those for **printf()**, but there are a few differences. The following table shows them side-by-side for comparison:

Format	printf()	scanf()
single character	%c	%c
string	%s	%s
signed decimal integer	%d	%d
floating point (decimal notation)	%f	%f or %e
floating point (exponential notation)	%e	%f or %e
floating point (%f or %e, whichever is shorter)	%g	
unsigned decimal integer	%u	%u
unsigned hexadecimal integer (uses "ABCDEF")	%x	%x
unsigned octal integer	%o	%o

As we noted earlier, the first four type characters are the most commonly used.

In **scanf()** (unlike the **printf()** function) %e can be used in place of %f; they have the same effect. You can type your input using either exponential or decimal notation; either format is accepted by both %e and %f. The %g specifier, which allows **printf()** to choose exponential or decimal notation, whichever is shorter, is not necessary with **scanf()**, because the user makes the decision.

The l prefix is used before d, o, u, and x to specify type **long int**. Before e and f, it specifies type **double**. The L prefix before e and f specifies type **long double**.

The **scanf()** function can accept input to several variables at once. To demonstrate this, let's revise our event.c program to use input from the user, rather than assigning values to the variables within the program. This is event4.c:

```
void main(void)
{
    int event;
    char heat;
    float time;

    printf("Type event number, heat letter, and time: ");
    scanf("%d %c %f", &event, &heat, &time);
```

```
        printf("The winning time in heat %c", heat);
        printf(" of event %d was %.2f.", event, time);
    }
```

Here's the output:

```
    Type event number, heat letter, and time: 4 B 36.34
    The winning time in heat B of event 4 was 36.34.
```

How does **scanf()** know when we've finished typing one value and started another? Let's look at the process. As we type our three input values, 4, 'B', and 36.34, we separate them by spaces. The **scanf()** function matches each space we type with a corresponding space between the conversion type characters in the **scanf()** format string "%d %c %f". If we had tried to separate the values with another character—a dash or comma, for example—this would not have matched the space in the format string. The space we type serves as a delimiter because it matches the space in the format string. This process is shown in Figure 2-8.

Actually, we can use any whitespace character (space, newline, or tab) as a delimiter when we type in our input values; each will match the space in the format string. Here's a sample using the [Return] key:

```
    Type event number, heat letter, and time:
    7
    A
    49.2
    The winning time in heat A of event 7 was 49.20.
```

And here's an example using the [Tab]:

```
    Type event number, heat letter, and time: 3      A        14.7
    The winning time in heat A of event 3 was 14.70.
```

There are other, more complex ways of handling the formatting of input to **scanf()**, but we won't be concerned about them now.

The Address Operator (&)

The **scanf()** function in the age.c and event4.c programs used a new symbol: the ampersand (&) preceding the variable names used as arguments.

```
    scanf("%f", &years);
    scanf("%d %c %f", &event, &heat, &time);
```

What is its purpose? It would seem more reasonable to use the name of

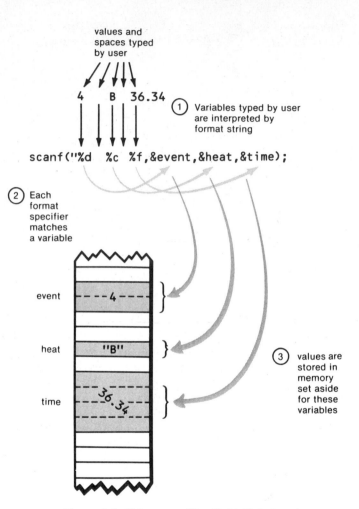

Figure 2-8. Using *scanf()* with Multiple Inputs

the variable without the ampersand, as we did in **printf()** statements in the same programs. However (for reasons that will become clear later), the C compiler requires the arguments to **scanf()** to be the *addresses* of variables, rather than the variables themselves. This peculiarity of **scanf()** is one of C's least user-friendly characteristics; it is close to certain you will forget the ampersands before the variables in **scanf()** at least once. However, the idea of *addresses* is the key to one of C's most powerful and interesting capabilities, so let's explore it further.

The memory of your computer is divided into bytes, and these bytes are numbered, from 0 to the upper limit of your memory (655,359, if you have 640K of memory). These numbers are called the "addresses" of the bytes. Every variable occupies a certain location in memory, and its address is that of

the <u>first byte it occupies</u>. Figure 2-9 shows an integer with a value of 2 at *ll*
address 1367.

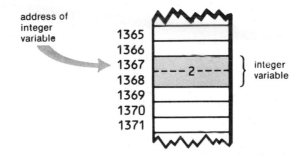

Figure 2-9. Address of Variable

Suppose we have declared an integer variable, **num**, in a program, and
assigned it the value 2. If the program later refers to the name of the variable,
num, the compiler will give the *value* stored in that variable, or 2. However, if
you refer to the name of the variable preceded by the ampersand, **&num**, the
compiler will give the *address* where **num** is stored.

Here's a program, addrtest.c, that demonstrates this operation:

```
void main(void)
{
    int num;

    num=2;
    printf("Value=%d, address=%d", num, &num);
}
```

And here's the output:

```
Value=2, address=3536
```

On our particular computer, the address where the variable **num** is stored is
3536. In another computer it would almost certainly be different, because of
variations in the size of the operating system and other factors. In any case,
knowing where a variable is stored will turn out to be very important in C
programming, as we'll learn when we get to the chapter on pointers.

In the meantime, all you need to remember about the address operator is
that in using **scanf()** you need to precede variable names with the ampersand
(except in the case of strings, which we're coming to soon).

The *getche()* Function

For some situations, the **scanf()** function has one glaring weakness: you need to type a [Return] before the function will digest what you've typed. But we often want a function that will read a single character the instant it's typed, without waiting for [Return]. For instance, in a game we might want a spaceship to move each time we pressed one of the cursor-control (arrow) keys; it would be awkward to type [Return] each time we pressed an arrow key.

We can use the **getche()** function for this purpose. The "get" means it gets something from the outside world; in other words, it's an input function. The "ch" means it gets a character, and the "e" means it echoes the character to the screen when you type it. (There is a similar function, **getch()**, which does not echo the typed character to the screen.) Another function, **getchar()**, is better known to programmers working on UNIX systems, but in Turbo C **getchar** is *buffered*, which means it doesn't pass the character typed by the user to the program until the user hits [Return].

Here's a simple program, gettest.c, that uses **getche()**:

```c
void main(void)
{
   char ch;

   printf("Type any character: ");
   ch = getche();
   printf("\nThe character you typed was %c.", ch );
}
```

And here's a sample interaction:

```
Type any character: T
The character you typed was T.
```

If you run this program, you'll notice that the phrase "The character you typed was" is printed immediately when you press any character key; you don't have to press the [Return] key.

Another point to notice is that the function itself takes on or "returns" the value of the character typed. It's almost as if the function were a variable that assigned itself a value; the function becomes the character typed. This is considerably different from the technique used in **scanf()**, where the value returned was placed in a variable that was one of **scanf()**'s arguments. Figure 2-10 shows the operation of the **getche()** function.

There is a downside to using **getche()**; if you make a mistake, you can't backspace to correct it, since as soon as you type a character, it's gobbled up by your program.

We'll see how useful **getche()** can be in the next chapter, when we learn such skills as how to count characters in phrases typed in by the user.

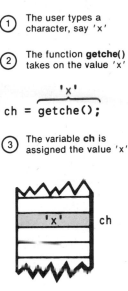

Figure 2-10. Operation of *getche()*

There is more to say about input/output, and we'll be returning to the topic throughout the book.

Operators

Operators are words or symbols that cause a program to do something to variables. For instance, the arithmetic operators (+) and (−) cause a program to add or subtract two numbers. There are many different kinds of operators; to list them all here would be to invite debilitating ennui. Instead we'll mention the most common: arithmetic and relational operators, and the less well-known (to non-C programmers) increment/decrement operators and arithmetic assignment operators. (Operators are summarized in Appendix A.) p689

Arithmetic Operators

In the age.c program we used the multiplication operator (*) to multiply two numbers together. C uses the four arithmetic operators that are common in most programming languages, and one, the remainder operator, which is not so common.

+   addition
−   subtraction

```
*    multiplication
/    division
%    remainder
```

Here's a program, ftoc.c, that uses several arithmetic operators. It converts temperatures in Fahrenheit to centigrade.

```
void main(void)
{
    int ftemp, ctemp;

    printf("Type temperature in degrees fahrenheit: ");
    scanf("%d", &ftemp);
    ctemp = (ftemp-32) * 5 / 9;
    printf("Temperature in degrees centigrade is %d", ctemp);
}
```

Here's some sample interaction with the program:

```
Type temperature in degrees fahrenheit: 32
Temperature in degrees centigrade is 0

Type temperature in degrees fahrenheit: 70
Temperature in degrees centigrade is 21
```

This program uses the standard formula for converting degrees Fahrenheit into degrees centigrade: subtract 32 from the Fahrenheit temperature and multiply the result by five-ninths.

```
ctemp = (ftemp-32) * 5 / 9;
```

There are several things to note about this statement. First, you'll see that we've surrounded some of the operators, the (*) and the (/), with spaces but have not used spaces around the minus sign. The moral here is that the C compiler doesn't care whether you use spaces surrounding your operators or not, so you're free to arrange your expressions however they look best to you. If you don't like the way the spaces are arranged in the example, you can arrange them another way when you type in the program.

Operator Precedence

The second point to notice about the ftemp.c program is that we've used parentheses around (ftemp−32). For those of you who remember your algebra the reason will be clear; we want the 32 subtracted from **ftemp** *before* we multiply it by 5 and divide by 9. Since multiplication and division are normally carried out before addition and subtraction, we use parentheses to ensure that the subtraction is carried out first.

The fact that (*) and (/) are evaluated before (+) and (−) is an example of *precedence*; we say that (*) and (/) have a higher precedence than (+) and (−). We'll be returning to this idea of precedence when we discuss different kinds of operators.

The Remainder Operator

The remainder operator (sometimes called the modulo operator) may be unfamiliar to you; it is used to find the remainder when one number is divided by another. For example, in the statement below, the variable **answer** will be assigned the value 3, since that's the remainder when the 13 is divided by 5.

```
answer = 13 % 5;
```

We'll find uses for all the arithmetic operators as we go along, but the remainder operator is useful in unexpected ways.

Expressions Versus Variables

Where can you use expressions containing arithmetic operators? We've already shown examples of their use in assignment statements, such as

```
days = years * 365;
```

It's also possible to include expressions involving arithmetic operators (and other kinds of operators as well) directly into **printf()** and other kinds of statements. For example, the following usage is just fine:

```
void main(void)
{
    int num = 2;

    printf("Number plus four is %d.", num + 4);
}
```

When this program, called exptest.c, is executed, the following phrase will be printed out:

```
Number plus four is 6.
```

Instead of a constant or a variable, **printf()** has printed out the value of the expression

```
num + 4
```

An "expression" is simply a combination of constants, variables, and operators that can be evaluated to yield a value. Since the variable **number** has the value 2, the expression evaluates to 6, and that's what is printed out. So you can use an expression almost anyplace you can use a variable. This is done more often in C than it is in most languages; we'll see examples as we go along.

> An entire expression can be used almost anyplace a variable can be used.

While we're on the subject of arithmetic operators, we should mention two kinds of operators that you may not have encountered before in other languages: arithmetic assignment operators and increment/decrement operators. Both are widely used in C, and both help to give C source listings their distinctive appearance.

Arithmetic Assignment Operators

If you compare a C program with a program with a similar purpose written in another language, you may well find that the C source file is shorter. One reason for this is that C has several operators that can compress often-used programming statements. Consider the following statement:

```
total = total + number;
```

Here the value in **number** is added to the value in **total**, and the result is placed in **total**. In C this statement can be rewritten:

```
total += number;
```

The effect is exactly the same, but the expression is more compact, as shown in Figure 2-11.

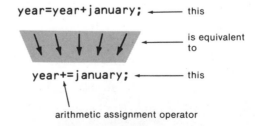

Figure 2-11. The Arithmetic Assignment Operator

Here's a program, assign.c, that makes use of this "plus-equal" operator:

```c
void main(void)
{
    int total = 0;
    int count = 10;

    printf("Total=%d\n", total);
    total += count;
    printf("Total=%d\n", total);
    total += count;
    printf("Total=%d\n", total);
}
```

And here's the output, showing the results of repeatedly adding the value of **count**, which is 10, to **total**.

```
Total=0
Total=10
Total=20
```

All the arithmetic operators listed earlier can be combined with the equal sign in the same way:

+=   addition assignment operator
−=   subtraction assignment operator
*=   multiplication assignment operator
/=   division assignment operator
%=   remainder assignment operator

There are assignment versions of some other operators as well, such as logical operators and bit-wise operators, which we'll encounter later.

The Increment Operator

C uses another operator that is not common in other languages: the increment operator. Consider the following program, incop.c:

```c
void main(void)
{
    int num=0;

    printf("Number=%d\n", num);
    printf("Number=%d\n", num++);
    printf("Number=%d\n", num);
}
```

Here's the output:

```
Number=0
Number=0
Number=1
```

How did the variable **num** get to be 1? As you can guess by examination of the program, the (++) operator had the effect of incrementing **num**; that is, adding 1 to it. The first **printf()** statement printed the original value of **num**, which was 0. The second **printf()** statement also printed the original value of **num**; then, *after* **num** was printed, the (++) operator incremented it. Thus the third **printf()** statement printed out the incremented value. The effect of **num(++)** is exactly the same as that of the statement

num ++

```
num = num + 1;
```

However, **num (++)** is far more compact to write, as shown in Figure 2-12. It also compiles into more efficient code.

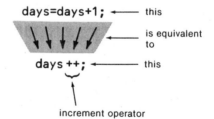

Figure 2-12. The Increment Operator

Let's rewrite the program, making a subtle change and producing incop2.c:

```
void main(void)
{
    int num=0;

    printf("Number=%d\n", num);
    printf("Number=%d\n", ++num);
    printf("Number=%d\n", num);
}
```

What did we do? We moved the (++) operator to the *beginning* of the **num** variable. Let's see what effect this has on the output:

```
Number=0
Number=1
Number=1
```

Now the variable **num** in the second **printf()** statement is incremented *before* it is printed.

Since there's an increment operator you can guess there will be a decrement operator as well. Let's modify our program again, using (−−), the decrement operator, and producing decop.c:

```
void main(void)
{
    int num=0;

    printf("Number=%d\n", num);
    printf("Number=%d\n", num--);
    printf("Number=%d\n", num);
}
```

Now instead of being incremented, the **num** variable is decremented: reduced by 1.

```
Number=0
Number=0
Number=-1
```

The effect is just the same as executing the statement

```
num = num - 1;
```

The (++) and (−−) operators can increment and decrement a variable without the need for a separate program statement.

The ability to increment (or decrement) a variable deep within an expression, and to control whether it will be incremented before or after it is used, is one of the features that makes a single line of code so powerful in C. We'll see many examples of these operators as we go along.

Relational Operators

In the next two chapters we'll be dealing with loops and decisions. These constructs require the program to ask questions about the relationship between variables. Is a certain variable greater than 100? If so, stop looping. Is the character the user just typed equal to a space? If so, increment the count of the number of words.

Relational operators are the vocabulary the program uses to ask questions about variables. Let's look at an example of a relational operator, in this case the "less than" (<) operator. This program is called lessthan.c:

```
void main(void)
{
    int age;

    age = 15;
    printf("Is age less than 21? %d\n", age < 21 );
    age = 30;
    printf("Is age less than 21? %d\n", age < 21 );
}
```

The output from this program looks like this:

```
Is age less than 21? 1
Is age less than 21? 0
```

In this program the **printf()** statements take the whole expression

```
age < 21
```

and print out its value. What is its value? That depends on the value of the variable **age.** When **age** is 15, which *is* less than 21, a 1 is printed out. When **age** is 30, which is *not* less than 21, a zero is printed. It would seem that 1 stands for true, and 0 stands for false. This turns out to be the case. In C, true is represented by the integer 1, and false is represented by the integer 0. In some languages, such as Pascal, true and false values are represented by a special variable type called "boolean." In C, there is no such data type, so true and false values are represented by integers. The operation of the relational expression is shown in Figure 2-13.

The relational operators in C look much like those in other languages. There are six of them:

<	less than
>	greater than
<=	less than or equal to
>=	greater than or equal to
==	equal to
!=	not equal to

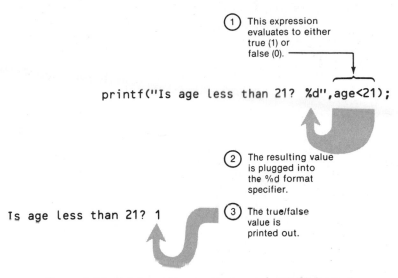

Figure 2-13. Relational Expression in a **printf()** Statement

Note that the relational operator "equal to" is represented by *two* equal signs. A common mistake is to use a single equal sign as a relational operator. For reasons that we'll learn later, the compiler doesn't notice that this is an error, so it can be a particularly frustrating bug to track down.

Here's an example using the equal-to (==) operator (sometimes called the "equal-equal" operator).

```
void main(void)
{
    int speed;

    speed = 75;
    printf("Is speed equal to 55? %d\n", speed == 55 );
    speed = 55;
    printf("Is speed equal to 55? %d\n", speed == 55 );
}
```

Here's the output of the equalto.c program:

```
Is speed equal to 55? 0
Is speed equal to 55? 1
```

Note again how the expression

```
speed == 55
```

evaluates to either a false (0) or a true (1) value.

An interesting point to notice about true and false values is that, although C will generate a 1 when it means true and a 0 when it means false, it will recognize *any* nonzero value as true. That is, there are a lot of integers that C thinks of as true, but only one—0—it thinks of as false. We'll make use of this fact in later programs.

Precedence, Round II

What will be printed out if you execute the following program? Remember that **true** is the integer 1 and **false** is the integer 0. These values can be used just like any other integer values, as shown by the prec.c program:

```
void main(void)
{
    printf("Answer is %d", 2+1 < 4 );
}
```

If you guessed "Answer is 1" you're right. First 2+1 is evaluated to yield 3, then this is compared with 4. It's less, so the expression

```
2+1 < 4
```

is true. True is 1, so that's what's printed.

Now watch closely: we're going to try something a little tricky. What will this program, prec2.c, print?

```
void main(void)
{
    printf("Answer is %d", 1<2 + 4 );
}
```

Did you guess "Answer is 5"? If so, you probably decided that 1<2 would evaluate to true, or 1, and 1 added to 4 would give 5. Sorry, this is plausible but incorrect. We misled you with the use of spaces in the expression 1<2 + 4. Here's how we should have written it:

```
1 < 2+4
```

There are two lessons here. First, as we mentioned before, the compiler doesn't care where you put spaces; both forms of the expression compile into the same program. Second, arithmetic operators have a *higher precedence* than relational operators. That is, in the absence of parentheses, the arithmetic operators are evaluated *before* the relational operators. In the expression above, the arithmetic operator (+) is evaluated first, yielding a value of 6 from the expression 2+4. Then the relational operator ($<$) is evaluated. Since 1 is less than 6, the value of the entire expression is true. Thus, the output of this program will be

```
Answer is 1
```

> Arithmetic operators have a higher precedence—that is, are evaluated before—relational operators.

All operators in C are ranked according to their precedence. We have not encountered many of these operators yet, so we won't pursue the subject of precedence further here. It will, however, arise from time to time as we learn more about C. Precedence is a more important issue in C than it is in some languages because of the complexity of the expressions that are routinely created. Appendix A includes a table showing the precedence of all the C operators.

p 690

Comments

It's helpful to be able to put comments into the source code file that can be read by humans but are invisible to the compiler. Here's a revision of our age program, with comments added. It's called agecom.c:

```c
/* agecom.c */
/* calculates age in days */
void main(void)
{
    float years, days;                    /* initialize variables */

    printf("Please type your age in years: ");  /* print prompt */
    scanf("%f", &years);              /* get age in years from user */
    days = years * 365;                  /* calculate age in days */
    printf("You are %.1f days old.\n", days);    /* print result */
}
```

A comment begins with the two-character symbol slash-asterisk (/*) and ends with an asterisk-slash (*/). These two-character symbols may seem awkward to type, especially in comparison to BASIC, where a single apostrophe (') at the beginning of the comment is all that's necessary. It also doesn't contribute to fast typing that the slash is lowercase while the asterisk is uppercase. As with other endeavors, however, if you type enough comments, it will start to seem easy.

In this example we've used two full-line comments to name the program and to say what it does. We've also placed comments on the lines with the program code. The only problem with comments that share lines with code is that it's easy to run out of space. C's long program statements, and the fact that they are indented, combine to reduce the number of character spaces available on a line.

Although a lot of comments are probably not necessary in this program, it is usually the case that programmers use too few comments rather than too many. Comments should be added anyplace there's a possibility of confusion. We'll refrain from repeating the standard lecture on how an adequate number of comments can save hours of misery and suffering when you later try to figure out what the program does.

Since C ignores whitespace characters, it's perfectly possible for comments to flow over two or more lines:

```
/*
This is
a multiline
comment
*/
```

Often asterisks are placed at the beginning of each line in a multiline comment. This is for aesthetic reasons; the asterisks are not comment symbols themselves and are ignored by the compiler.

```
/* This is a fancier
 * multiline
 * comment
 */
```

This is a common usage in C.

It is usually illegal to *nest* comments. That is, you can't say

```
/* Outer comment /* inner comment */ more outer comment */
```

This restriction can be annoying when you're debugging a program and you want to cause part of it to be invisible to the compiler by "commenting it out" (surrounding it with comment symbols). If the section of code you're commenting out contains comments, you'll get an error message. (However, Turbo C provides a command-line option that will make nested comments legal.)

It's easy to make errors with comment symbols, and the results of such errors can be particularly baffling to debug. For instance, if you forget the close-comment symbol (*/) at the end of a comment, the compiler will assume that your entire program from then on is a comment. It will not compile it and it also won't issue any error messages, or at least any messages that relate specifically to comments. Tracking down this sort of bug can be a major inconvenience, so be careful that every begin-comment symbol is matched with a close-comment symbol.

Summary

In this chapter we've introduced some of the more fundamental parts of C: variables, input/output, and operators.

You've learned that there are six major variable types in C: character, integer, long integer, floating point, double-precision floating point, and long double-precision floating point. You've learned how to declare and initialize variables and how to use them in assignment and other kinds of statements.

Concerning input/output functions, you've learned about format and field-width specifiers in the **printf()** function, about escape sequences, and about how to print graphics characters. You've been introduced to the **scanf()** and **getche()** input functions, and seen how **scanf()** is good for a variety of input and can handle multiple variables, while **getche()** returns any character typed in.

We've covered two major categories of operators, arithmetic operators and relational operators, and mentioned two less important but very "C-like" operators, the arithmetic assignment statement and the increment/decrement operator. We've also discussed comments and operator precedence.

With these fundamentals under your belt, you should be ready to wade into the next few chapters, where we discuss program structures such as loops, decisions, and functions.

Questions

1. Declaring variables is advantageous because it
   a. helps organize the program
   b. helps the compiler work efficiently
   c. avoids errors from misspelled variable names
   d. simplifies the writing of very short programs

2. The five major data types in C are
   c_____

i_____
f_____
l_____
d_____

3. Which of these C statements are correct?
    a. int a;
    b. float b;
    c. double float c;
    d. unsigned char d;

4. True or false: two variables can be declared in one statement.

5. Type **float** occupies _____ times as many bytes of memory as type **char**.

6. Type **int** can accommodate numbers from _____ to _____.

7. Which of the following is an example of initializing a variable?
    a. num=2;
    b. int num;
    c. num < 2;
    d. int num=2;

8. True or false: type **long** variables can hold numbers only twice as big as type **int** variables.

9. Floating point variables are used instead of integers to
    a. avoid being too specific about what value a number has
    b. make possible the use of large numbers
    c. permit the use of decimal points in numbers
    d. conceal the true value of the numbers

10. What do the escape sequences '\x41' and '\xE0' print?

11. Express the following numbers in exponential notation:
    a. 1,000,000

     b. 0.000,001

     c. 199.95

     d. −888.88

12. Express the following numbers in decimal notation:

     a. 1.5e6

     b. 1.5e−6

     c. 7.6543e3

     d. −7.6543e−3

13. What's wrong with this program?

```
/* age.c */
/* calculates age in days */
void main(void)
{
    float years, days;

    printf("Please type your age in years: ");  /* print prompt */
    scanf("%f", years);                          /* get input */
    days = years * 365;                          /* find answer */
    printf("You are %f days old.\n", days);      /* print answer */
}
```

14. A field-width specifier in a **printf()** function:

     a. controls the margins of the program listing

     b. specifies the maximum value of a number

     c. controls the size of type used to print numbers

     d. specifies how many character positions will be used for a number

15. True or false: a function can have a value.

16. Which of the following are arithmetic operators?

     a. +

     b. &

     c. %

     d. <

17. Rewrite the following statement using the increment operator:

```
number = number + 1;
```

18. Rewrite the following statement using arithmetic assignment statement:

    ```
    usa = usa + calif;
    ```

19. What is the meaning of the characters '\t' and '\r'?

20. The function **scanf()** reads
    a. a single character
    b. characters and strings
    c. any possible number
    d. any possible variable type

21. True or false: you need to press [Return] after typing a character in order for **getche()** to read it.

22. A relational operator is used to:
    a. combine values
    b. compare values
    c. distinguish different types of variables
    d. change variables to logical values

23. Are the following expressions true or false?
    a. 1 > 2
    b. 'a' < 'b'
    c. 1 = = 2
    d. '2' = = '2'

24. Precedence determines which operator:
    a. is most important
    b. is used first
    c. is fastest
    d. operates on the largest numbers

25. Is the following a correctly formed comment?

    ```
    /* This is a
    /* comment which
    ```

```
/* extends over several lines
*/
```

Exercises

1. Modify the age.c program to print the age in minutes instead of days.

2. Write a program that prints the square of a number the user types in. (The square is the number times itself.) Use floating point.

3. Rewrite the box.c program so it draws a similar box, but one that is four characters wide and four characters tall.

3

Loops

- **for** loop
- **while** loop
- **do while** loop
- nested loops
- values of functions and assignment expressions
- **break** and **continue** statements

3

In the last chapter we introduced variables, input/output functions, and operators. With these programming elements we wrote programs that were almost useful: converting from Fahrenheit to centigrade, for example. However, the programs were limited because, when executed, they always performed the same series of actions, in the same way, exactly once.

Almost always, if something is worth doing, it's worth doing more than once. You can probably think of several examples of this from real life, such as going to the movies and eating a good dinner. Programming is the same; we frequently need to perform an action over and over, often with variations in the details each time. The mechanism that meets this need is the "loop," and loops are the subject of this chapter.

There are three major loop structures in C: the **for** loop, the **while** loop, and a cousin of the **while** loop called the **do** loop (or **do while** loop). We'll discuss each of these in turn. We're going to start with the **for** loop because it has close analogies in both BASIC and Pascal, whereas—at least in old-style BASIC—there is no equivalent to the **while** loop. Also, the **for** loop is conceptually easy to understand, although the details can get complicated. This is true because all its elements are stated explicitly at the beginning of the loop. In the other loops, the elements are scattered throughout the program.

The *for* Loop

It is often the case in programming that you want to do something a fixed number of times. Perhaps you want to calculate the paychecks for 120 employees or print out the squares of all the numbers from 1 to 50. The **for** loop is ideally suited for such cases.

Let's look at a simple example of a **for** loop:

```
/* forloop */
/* prints numbers from 0 to 9 */
void main(void)
{
    int count;

    for (count=0; count<10; count++)
        printf("count=%d\n", count);
}
```

Type in the program (forloop.c) and compile it. When executed, it will generate the following output:

```
count=0
oount=1
count=2
count=3
count=4
count=5
count=6
count=7
count=8
count=9
```

This program's role in life is to execute a **printf()** statement 10 times. The **printf()** function prints out the phrase "count=" followed by the value of the variable **count**. Let's see how the **for** loop causes this to happen.

Structure of the *for* Loop

The parentheses following the keyword **for** contain what we'll call the "loop expression." This loop expression is divided by semicolons into three separate expressions: the "initialize expression," the "test expression," and the "increment expression."

Expression	Name	Purpose
count=0	Initialize expression	Initializes loop variable
count<10	Test expression	Tests loop variable
count++	Increment expression	Increments loop variable

Figure 3-1 shows the structure of the **for** loop.

The variable **count** occupies a key role in this **for** loop. In conjunction

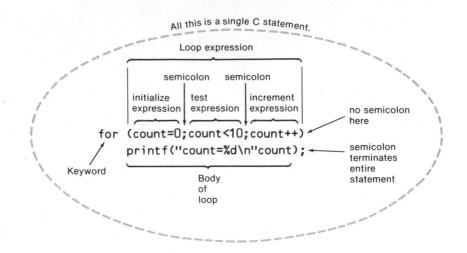

Figure 3-1. Structure of the *for* Loop

with the three parts of the loop expression, **count** is used to control the operation of the loop. Specifically, it keeps track of how many times we've been through the loop.

Let's look in more detail at the three parts of the loop expression and how they operate on the variable **count**.

The Initialize Expression

The initialize expression, **count=0**, initializes the **count** variable. The initialize expression is always executed as soon as the loop is entered. We can start at any number; in this case we initialize **count** to 0. However, loops are often started at 1 or some other number.

The Test Expression

The second expression, **count<10**, tests each time through the loop to see if **count** is less than 10. To do this, it makes use of the relational operator for "less than" (<). If the test expression is true (**count** *is* less than 10), the body of the loop (the **printf()** statement) will be executed. If the expression becomes false (**count** is 10 or more), the loop will be terminated and control will pass to the statements following the loop (in this case, there aren't any, so the entire program terminates).

The Increment Expression

The third expression, **count++**, increments the variable **count** each time the loop is executed. To do this, it uses the increment operator (++), described in the last chapter.

The loop variable in a **for** loop doesn't have to be increased by 1 each time through the loop. It can also be decreased by 1, as we'll see later on in this chapter, or changed by some other number, using an expression such as:

```
count = count + 3
```

In other words, practically any expression can be used for the increment expression.

The Body of the for Loop

Following the keyword **for** and the loop expression is the body of the loop: that is, the statement (or statements) that will be executed each time round the loop. In our example, there is only one statement:

```
printf("count=%d\n", count);
```

Note that this statement is terminated with a semicolon, whereas the **for** with the loop expression is not. That's because the *entire combination* of the **for** keyword, the loop expression, and the statement constituting the body of the loop are considered to be a single C statement.

> In a **for** loop, don't place a semicolon between the loop expression and the body of the loop, since the keyword **for** and the loop expression don't constitute a complete C statement.

Operation of the for Loop

Let's follow the operation of the loop, as depicted in Figure 3-2. First the initialization expression is executed, then the test condition is examined. If the test expression is false to begin with, the body of the loop will not be executed at all. If the condition is true, the body of the loop is executed and, following that, the increment expression is executed. This is why the first number printed out by our program is 0 and not 1; printing takes place *before* **count** is incremented by the (++) operator. Finally the loop recycles and the test expression is queried again. This will continue until the test expression becomes false—**count** becomes 10—at which time the loop will end.

We should note here that C permits an unusual degree of flexibility in the writing of the **for** loop. For instance, if separated by commas, more than one expression can be used for the initialize expression and for the increment expression, so that several variables can be initialized or incremented at once. Also, none of the three expressions actually needs to refer to the loop variable;

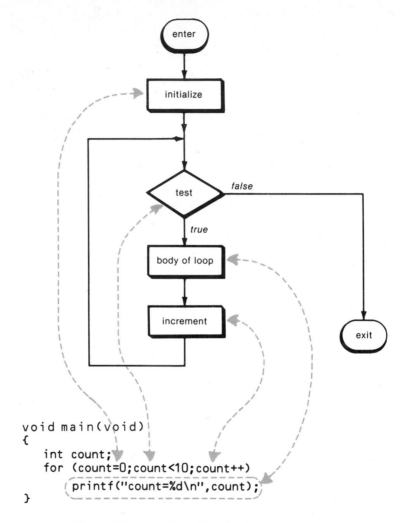

```
void main(void)
{
    int count;
    for (count=0;count<10;count++)
        printf("count=%d\n",count);
}
```

Figure 3-2. Operation of the *for* Loop

a loop variable isn't even essential. In many cases, the **for** loop is used roughly as we've shown it in the example, but we'll see an instance of multiple initialization in the next example.

Multiple Statements in Loops

The preceding example used only a single statement in the body of the loop. Two (or more) statements can also be used, as shown in the following program:

```
/* forloop2 */
/* prints numbers from 0 to 9, keeps running total */
void main(void)
{
    int count, total;

    for (count=0, total=0; count<10; count++)
        {
        total = total + count;
        printf("count=%d, total=%d\n", count, total);
        }
}
```

Type the program in (call it forloop2.c) and compile it. This program not only prints the numbers from 0 to 9, it also prints a running total:

```
count=0, total=0
count=1, total=1
count=2, total=3
count=3, total=6
count=4, total=10
count=5, total=15
count=6, total=21
count=7, total=28
count=8, total=36
count=9, total=45
```

Truly, a performance to make any power user envious.

The most important new feature of this program is the use of braces ({ and }) to encapsulate the two statements that form the body of the loop:

```
{
total = total + count;
printf("count=%d, total=%d\n", count, total);
}
```

There are two points to remember about this multistatement loop body. The first is that the whole package—the opening brace, the statements, and the closing brace—is treated as a single C statement, with the semicolon understood. This is often called a "compound statement" or "block." Thus, you don't need to type a semicolon after the last brace. The second point is that each statement within the block is also a C and must be terminated with a semicolon in the usual way. Figure 3-3 shows the operation of the **for** loop with multiple statements in the loop body. This figure is similar to that for the single-statement loop body; we've included it here partly to facilitate comparison with the operation of the **while** loop in the next section.

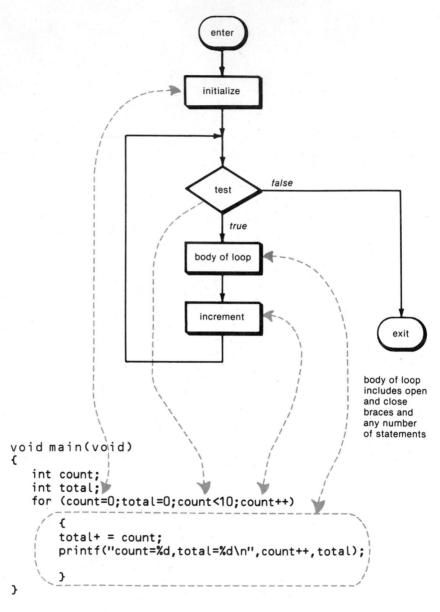

```
void main(void)
{
    int count;
    int total;
    for (count=0;total=0;count<10;count++)

        {
        total+ = count;
        printf("count=%d,total=%d\n",count++,total);

        }
}
```

Figure 3-3. Multiple Statements in *for* Loop

Note that we could have used the (+=) arithmetic assignment operator to add the value of **count** to the value of **total** in the expression:

```
total += count;
```

As we saw in Chapter 2, this is equivalent to:

```
total = total + count;
```

Loop Style Note

Many C programmers, including the venerable Kernighan and Ritchie (referred to in Chapter 1), handle braces in a somewhat different way than we've shown above. They put the opening brace on the same line as the loop expression:

```
for (count=0, total=0; count<10; count++) {
    total = total + count;
    printf("count=%d, total=%d\n", count, total);
}
```

This has the advantage of saving a line in the listing. However, the compiler doesn't care which way you choose, and we feel that aligning the matching braces vertically makes it easier to ensure that each opening brace is matched by a closing brace and helps to clarify the structure of the program. Both approaches are common. For ease of learning we'll use the one-brace-per-line approach for most of this book, but in the final chapters we'll show some examples of the more compact format.

Multiple Initializations in the *for* Loop

Another subtlety we've introduced into the forloop2.c program is that the initialization expression in the **for** loop contains *two* statements, separated by a comma: **count=0** and **total=0**. As we mentioned, this is perfectly legal syntax.

```
for (count=0, total=0; count<10; count++)
```

In this particular program we didn't really need to put the initialization of **total** within the loop; we could also have said:

```
total = 0;
for (count=0; count<10; count++)
```

but we wanted to show how two (or more) statements can be used in the initialization expression, and we saved a line of code—a desirable end in the eyes of most C programmers.

As we noted, multiple statements can also be used in this way in the increment expression; that is, you can increment two or more variables at the same time. However, only one expression is allowed in the test expression, since a single condition must determine when the loop terminates.

The use of multiple statements in the initialization expression also demonstrates why semicolons are used to separate the three kinds of expressions in the **for** loop. If commas had been used (as commas are used to separate the arguments of a function, for example), they could not also have been used to separate multiple statements in the initialization expression without confusing the compiler. The comma is sometimes called the "sequential evaluation operator," since it separates a list of similar items that will be evaluated in turn. Items separated by commas are evaluated from left to right.

An ASCII Table Program

Here's a program that uses a **for** loop to print out a table of ASCII codes. As you learned in Chapter 2, in the PC family, each of the numbers from 0 to 255 represents a separate character. From 0 to 31 are control codes (such as the carriage return, tab, and linefeed) and some graphics characters; from 32 to 127 are the usual printing characters; and from 128 to 255 are graphics and foreign language characters.

```
/* asctab */
/* prints table of ascii characters */
void main(void)
{
   int n;

   for (n = 1; n < 256; n++)        /* codes from 1 to 255 */
      printf ("%3d=%c\t", n, n); /* print as number and as char */
}
```

A section of the output is shown below:

```
41=)   42=*   43=+   44=,   45=-   46=.   47=/   48=0   49=1   50=2
51=3   52=4   53=5   54=6   55=7   56=8   57=9   58=:   59=;   60=<
61==   62=>   63=?   64=@   65=A   66=B   67=C   68=D   69=E   70=F
71=G   72=H   73=I   74=J   75=K   76=L   77=M   78=N   79=O   80=P
81=Q   82=R   83=S   84=T   85=U   86=V   87=W   88=X   89=Y   90=Z
91=[   92=\   93=]   94=^   95=_   96='   97=a   98=b   99=c  100=d
101=e 102=f 103=g 104=h 105=i 106=j 107=k 108=l 109=m 110=n
111=o 112=p 113=q 114=r 115=s 116=t 117=u 118=v 119=w 120=x
```

This program uses the tab character ('\t') in the **printf()** statement. This causes the next item printed to start eight spaces from the start of the last item. In other words, it divides the screen into columns eight characters wide. On an 80-column screen then, we have room for 10 items. (In the listing above the columns are actually only six spaces wide; we compressed it so the printout would fit on the page.) The **printf()** function also uses a field-width specifier of 3 so that each number is printed in a box three characters wide, even if it has only two digits.

The printf() *Function as a Conversion Device*

The **printf()** statement in our asctab.c program is performing a complex task with a minimum of fuss: printing both the character and its ASCII code. In most languages, this would require a separate conversion function to change the number **n** into the character whose ASCII value is **n.**

In C, we can use the same variable, **n**, for both number and character; only the format specifier changes: %c prints the character, while %d prints the number.

```
printf ("%3d=%c\t", n, n);
```

Format specifiers can interpret the same variable in different ways.

What's actually stored in the computer's memory is an integer, **n**, as specified in the type declaration statement. The %d format specifier prints the decimal representation of **n**, while the %c format specifier prints the character whose ASCII code is **n.** p 36

Drawing a Line with a Graphics Character

In Chapter 2 we introduced a graphics character representing a rectangle (ASCII code DB hexadecimal). Let's use this character and a **for** loop to draw p 42 a line across the screen. Here's the program:

```
/* line.c */
/* draws a solid line using rectangular graphics character */
void main(void)
{
    int cols;

    for (cols=1; cols<40; cols++)
        printf("%c", '\xDB');
}
```

Each time through the loop another rectangle is printed, creating a solid line of rectangles. The process is shown in Figure 3-4.

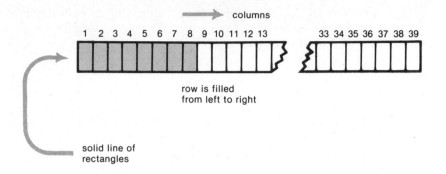

Figure 3-4. Operation of the line.c Program

Nested *for* Loops

It is possible to nest one **for** loop inside another. To demonstrate this structure, we'll concoct a program that prints out the multiplication table:

```
/* multab */
/* generates the multiplication table */
void main(void)
{
    int cols, rows;

    for(rows=1; rows < 13; rows++)        /* outer loop */
        {
        for(cols=1; cols < 13; cols++)    /* inner loop */
            printf( "%3d ", cols*rows );
        printf("\n");
        }
}
```

When you run this program, you'll get the following output:

```
 1   2   3   4   5   6   7   8   9  10  11  12
 2   4   6   8  10  12  14  16  18  20  22  24
 3   6   9  12  15  18  21  24  27  30  33  36
 4   8  12  16  20  24  28  32  36  40  44  48
 5  10  15  20  25  30  35  40  45  50  55  60
 6  12  18  24  30  36  42  48  54  60  66  72
 7  14  21  28  35  42  49  56  63  70  77  84
 8  16  24  32  40  48  56  64  72  80  88  96
 9  18  27  36  45  54  63  72  81  90  99 108
10  20  30  40  50  60  70  80  90 100 110 120
11  22  33  44  55  66  77  88  99 110 121 132
12  24  36  48  60  72  84  96 108 120 132 144
```

In this program the inner loop steps through 12 *columns*, from 1 to 12, while the outer loop steps through 12 *rows*. For each row, the inner loop is cycled through once; then a newline is printed in preparation for the next row. Each time through the inner loop—that is, at each intersection of a column and a row—the product of the row number (**rows**) and the column number (**cols**) is printed by the **printf** function. For instance, if the variable **cols** was 8, meaning we're on the eighth column, and **rows** was 4, meaning we're on the fourth row, then the program multiplies 8 by 4 and prints the product at the intersection of this row and column. Since we used the "less than" operator (<), the loop variables **cols** and **rows** never reach the limit of 13; the loops both terminate at 12.

To ensure that the columns line up, we use a field-width specifier of 4 in the **printf()** function.

Indentation and Nesling

As you can see, the body of the outer **for** loop is indented, and the body of the inner **for** loop (in this case a single line) is further indented. These multiple indentations make the program easier to read and understand. Although invisible to the compiler, some form of indentation is employed by almost all C programmers for nested loops.

The actual multiplication of **cols** times **rows** takes place inside the **printf()** function:

```
printf( "%4d", cols * rows );
```

We could have used another variable, say **product** (which would need to be defined), and written the inner loop:

```
{
product = rows * cols;
printf ( "%4d", product );
}
```

However, as we've noted, C programmers usually try to telescope statements in order to achieve compactness and eliminate unnecessary variables.

The fill.c Program

Here's another example of the nested **for** loop construction. This one looks like the multiplication table example, but instead it fills a box-shaped area of the screen with a solid color. It's actually an extension of the line.c program: *p 77* fill.c repeatedly prints lines of rectangles to create a solid area. Here's the listing:

```
/* fill.c */
/* fills square area on screen */
void main(void)
{
    int cols, rows;

    for (rows=1; rows<=22; rows++)
        {
        for (cols=1; cols<=40; cols++)
            printf("\xDB");
        printf("\n");
        }
}
```

p 40

As in the multab.c program, fill.c uses an outer **for** loop to control the rows and an inner **for** loop to control the columns. That is, the inner loop cycles through the columns to write a single row of rectangles, then the outer loop increments to go on to the next row. Figure 3-5 shows what the output of the program looks like while the program is in progress.

We've used a new relational operator in this program, the (<=) operator, meaning "less than or equal to." This means that the numbers used in the test expressions in the **for** loops, 22 and 40, are actually reached by the variables, as shown in Figure 3-5. In earlier programs the variables stopped one short of these limits, because the "less than" (<) operator was used.

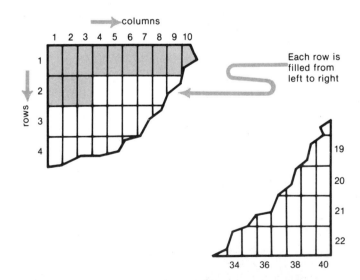

Figure 3-5. Output of the fill.c Program

Notice also that since '\xDB' is a character, and a character can be part of a string, we've put '\xDB' directly into the **printf()** format string, making it a one-character string. We could have written

p 40

```
printf("%c", '\xDB');
```

as we did in the line.c program, but the representation used in fill.c is simpler.

The *while* Loop

The second kind of loop structure available in C is the **while** loop. Although at first glance this structure seems to be simpler than the **for** loop, it actually uses the same elements, but they are distributed throughout the program.

Let's try to compare, as directly as possible, the operation of the **for** loop and the **while** loop. The following program uses a **while** loop to reproduce the operation of our earlier forloop2.c program, which printed the numbers from 0 to 9 and gave a running total.

p 73

```
/* wloop */
/* prints numbers from 0 to 9, keeps running total */
void main(void)
{
    int count = 0;
    int total = 0;

    while ( count < 10 )
        {
        total = total + count;
        printf("count=%d, total=%d\n", count++, total);
        }
}
```

As before, this program produces the following table:

```
count=0, total=0
count=1, total=1
count=2, total=3
count=3, total=6
count=4, total=10
count=5, total=15
count=6, total=21
count=7, total=28
```

```
count=8, total=36
count=9, total=45
```

Certainly the expression in parentheses following the keyword **while** is simpler than the three-part expression in the **for** loop. It dispenses with the initialization and increment expressions, retaining only the test expression:

```
count < 10;
```

The resulting structure is shown in Figure 3-6.

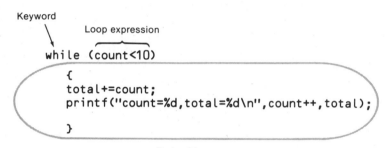

Figure 3-6. Structure of the *while* Loop

If the expressions that initialize and increment the counting variable are not in the **while** loop expression itself, where did they go?

The initialization step is now included in a variable declaration:

```
int count = 0;
```

The incrementing of the count variable can be seen in the **printf()** statement, which includes, instead of the variable **count** you might expect, the expression **count++** instead. This means that, as soon as **count** is printed, it is incremented.

Notice how easily we were able to increment the variable. In most other languages we would have needed a separate statement:

```
count = count + 1;
```

following the **printf()** statement; in C the expression **count++** has the same effect.

The operation of the **while** loop is shown in Figure 3-7.

The loop variable **count** is initialized outside the loop in the declaration **int count=0**. When the loop is first entered, the condition **count<10** is tested. If it's false, the loop terminates. If it's true, the body of the loop is

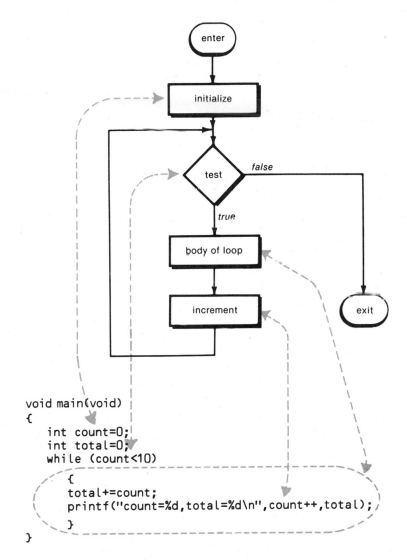

```
void main(void)
{
    int count=0;
    int total=0;
    while (count<10)
    {
    total+=count;
    printf("count=%d,total=%d\n",count++,total);
    }
}
```

Figure 3-7. Operation of the *while* Loop

executed. The increment expression is buried in the body of the loop. When the **printf()** statement that forms the loop body has finished printing, **count** is incremented by the (++) operator.

The Unexpected Condition

In situations where the number of iterations in a loop are known in advance, as they are in the wloop.c example, **while** loops are actually less appropriate. *p 81*

In this case the **for** loop is a more natural choice, since we can use its explicit initialize, test, and increment expressions to control the loop. So, when is the **while** loop the appropriate choice?

The **while** loop shines in situations where a loop may be terminated unexpectedly by conditions developing within the loop. As an example, consider the following program:

```
/* charcnt */
/* counts characters in a phrase typed in */
void main(void)
{
   int count=0;

   printf("Type in a phrase:\n");
   while ( getche() != '\r' )
      count++;
   printf("\nCharacter count is %d", count);
}
```

p 48, p 56, 40

This program invites you to type in a phrase. As you enter each character it keeps a count of how many characters you've typed, and when you hit [Return] it prints out the total. Here's how it looks in operation:

```
Type in a phrase:
cat
Character count is 3

Type in a phrase:
Knowledge rests not upon truth alone, but also upon error.
Character count is 58
```

(This last phrase is from Carl Jung, and considering that it was written before the invention of computers, it is surprisingly applicable to the art of programming.)

> **While** loops are more appropriate than **for** loops when the condition that terminates the loop occurs unexpectedly.

Why is the **while** loop more appropriate in charcnt.c than a **for** loop? The loop in this program terminates when the character typed at the keyboard is the [Return]character. There's no need for a loop variable, since we don't have to keep track of where we are in the loop, and thus no need for initialize or increment expressions, since there is no loop variable to initialize or increment. Thus the **while** loop, consisting only of the test expression, is the appropriate choice.

Let's look more closely at the loop expression in the **while** loop:

```
( getche() != '\r' )
```

This incorporates the function **getche()**, which, as we saw in Chapter 2, returns the value of a character the instant the character is typed. As you also learned, this function takes on or "returns" the value of the character typed, so the function can be treated like a variable and compared with other variables or constants. In this program we compare it with the constant '\r', the carriage return character that **getch()** will return when the user presses the [Return] key. The evaluation of the loop expression is shown in Figure 3-8.

p 48

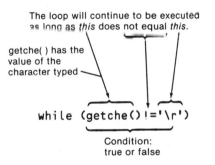

Figure 3-8. A Function Has a Value

Since we use the "not equal" operator (!=), the **while** loop will continue to be executed as long as it does *not* encounter a '\r'. When it does encounter it, the loop will terminate and the total number of characters typed will be printed out.

p 56
p 40

Using Functions as Elements in Expressions

Putting the **getche()** function into the **while** loop expression certainly makes for unusual looking syntax (at least that's how it strikes non-C programmers). Do we really need to do this? Doesn't it complicate things unnecessarily? As Will Rogers said when someone complained of the evils of old age, consider the alternative. We'll rewrite the program to use an explicit variable, **ch**, in the **while** expression, instead of the **getche()** function:

p 48

p 84

```
/* charcnt2.c */
/* counts characters in a phrase typed in */
void main(void)
```

```
{
    int count = -1;
    char ch = 'a';

    printf("Type in a phrase:\n");
    while ( ch != '\r' )
        {
        ch = getche();
        count++;
        }
    printf("\nCharacter count is %d", count);
}
```

Now the **while** loop expression is simplified, but look at the effect of this change on the rest of the program. We now have an extra variable **ch**. We need to initialize **ch** to avoid the possibility (remote though it may be) that it would start out with the value '\r'. We have an extra statement in the body of the **while** loop. Also, **count** must be initialized to an odd-looking −1 value because the program now checks which character is read *after* the loop is entered instead of before. Altogether, it appears that including the **getche()** function in the **while** expression is a good idea. It's also a very popular sort of construction in C.

ASCII Revisited

Here's a situation where it makes sense to use a separate **ch** variable, since we need it later in the program:

```
/* ascii.c */
/* finds ascii code of a character */
void main(void)
{
    char ch = 'a';

    while ( ch != '\r' )
        {
        printf("Enter a character: \n");
        ch=getche();
        printf("\nThe code for %c is %d.\n", ch, ch);
        }
}
```

This program asks the user to type a character and then prints out the ASCII code for the character. It will do this over and over. It's sort of a shorthand version of the asctab.c program shown earlier, but it's more useful when you

p76

only want to check the ASCII codes for one or two keyboard characters without looking at the entire table. Here's some sample output:

```
Enter a character:
a
The code for a is 97.
Enter a character:
b
The code for b is 98.
Enter a character:
A
The code for A is 65.
```

We can't put **getche()** in the **while** loop because we want to print a prompt to the user before invoking it. Since the **getche()** function is no longer included in the **loop** test expression, it has become part of an assignment statement:

```
ch = getche();
```

The **printf()** function, as in the asctab.c program, prints both the character version of **ch** and the numeric version, using the %c and %d format specifiers. Note that we can print a numerical value of **ch** even though at the start of the program it was declared a variable of type **char**. This demonstrates a useful feature of C: Character variables can be interpreted as *either* characters or numerical values (with a range of −128 to 127).

Typing [Return] terminates the program.

Nested *while* Loops

Just as **for** loops can be nested, so can **while** loops. The following program shows a **while** loop nested within a **for** loop.

```
/* guess.c */
/* lets you guess a letter */
void main(void)
{
    int j;
    char ch = 'a';

    for(j=0; j<5; j++ )
        {
        printf("\nType in a letter from 'a' to 'e':\n");
        while ( (ch=getche()) != 'd' )
```

```
        {
        printf("\nSorry, %c is incorrect.\n", ch);
        printf("Try again.\n");
        }
    printf("\nThat's it!\n");
    }
  printf("Game's over!\n");
}
```

This program lets you guess a lowercase letter from 'a' to 'e' and tells you if you're right or wrong. The outer **for** loop lets you play the game exactly five times. The inner **while** loop determines whether your guess is correct. If not, it loops again, asking you to try again. When you do guess correctly (which should take you no more than five tries, if you're on your toes) the inner loop terminates. The correct answer is always 'd' (unless you modify the program).

Here's a sample interaction:

```
Type in a letter from 'a' to 'e':
a
Sorry, a is incorrect.

Try again.
c
Sorry, c is incorrect.

Try again.
d
That's it!
```

As in the nested **for** loop example, each of the loops is indented to help clarify the operation of the program.

Assignment Expressions as Values

The most radical aspect of the guess.c program is the use in the inner **while** loop test expression of a complete *assignment expression* as a value:

see p 104

```
while ( (ch=getche()) != 'd' )
```

In the charcnt.c program we saw that a *function* could be used as if it were a variable; here the idea is carried to even greater lengths. How is this loop expression interpreted? First the function **getche()** must return a value. Say it's the character 'a'. This value is then assigned to the character variable **ch**. Finally, the entire assignment expression

```
ch=getche()
```

takes on the value of **ch**, which is 'a'. This value can then be compared with the character 'd' on the right side of the not-equal relational operator (!=). Figure 3-9 shows this process. The use of assignment expressions as values is a common idiom in C.

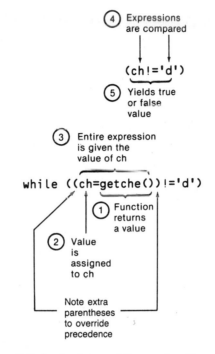

Figure 3-9. An Assignment Expression Has a Value

Precedence: Assignment Versus Relational Operators

Note that there is an extra set of parentheses around the assignment expression in the test expression of the inner **while** loop discussed above.

```
while ( (ch=getche()) != 'd' )
```

If the parentheses weren't there, the compiler would interpret the expression like this:

```
while ( ch = (getche() != 'd') )
```

This of course isn't what we want at all, since **ch** will now be set equal to the results of a true/false expression. The reason we need the parentheses is that the precedence of the relational operator (!=) is greater than that of the assignment operator (=). (This is shown in the table of operator precedence

p 690

in Appendix A.) So unless parentheses tell the compiler otherwise, the relational operator (!=) will be evaluated first. By inserting the parentheses, we ensure that the expression is evaluated correctly.

A Mathematical *while* Loop

Before we leave the subject of **while** loops, let's look at one more example. This one calculates the factorial of a number. As you no doubt remember from Mr. Klemmer's high-school math class, the factorial of a number is the number multiplied by all the numbers smaller than itself. Thus the factorial of 4 is 4*3*2*1, or 24.

Here's the listing:

```
/* factor */
/* finds factorial of number typed in */
void main(void)
{
    long number=1;
    long answer;

  while ( number != 0 )
      {
      printf("\nEnter a number: ");
      scanf("%ld", &number);
      answer = 1;
      while ( number > 1 )
         answer = answer * number--;
      printf("Factorial is: %ld\n", answer);
      }
}
```

Here's a sample of interaction with the program:

```
Type number: 3
Factorial is: 6

Type number: 4
Factorial is: 24

Type number: 7
Factorial is: 5040

Type number: 16
Factorial is: 2004189184
```

This program uses an outer **while** loop to recycle until a 0 value is entered. The inner loop uses the decrement operator to reduce the variable **number**—which starts out at the value typed in by the user—by 1 each time through the loop. When **number** reaches 1, the loop terminates.

A new wrinkle in this program is the use of long integers. Because factorials grow so rapidly, even an initial value of 8 would have exceeded an integer variable's capacity of 32,767. Long integers provide an improvement in that they can hold numbers up to 2,147,483,647, as you learned in Chapter 1. To accommodate long integers, we have used the variable type **long** in the declaration statement, and used the format specifier "ld" in the **printf()** and **scanf()** functions.

Using *while* Loops and *for* Loops

Now that we know how to write two different kinds of loops, how do we decide which one to use in a given situation?

Generally speaking, if at the time you enter the loop you already know how many times you want to execute it, you're probably better off with the **for** loop. If, on the other hand, the conditions for terminating the loop are imposed by the outside world, such as the user typing a certain character, then you're better off with the **while** loop.

We'll use numerous examples of both kinds of loops throughout this book.

The *do while* Loop

The last of the three loops in C is the **do while** loop. This loop is very similar to the **while** loop—the difference is that in the **do** loop the test condition is evaluated *after* the loop is executed, rather than before.

Here's our familiar program, which prints the numbers from 0 to 9 and a running total, revised to use a **do** loop:

p 81

```
/* doloop */
/* prints numbers from 0 to 9, keeps running total */
void main(void)
{
    int count = 0;
    int total = 0;

    do
      {
      total = total + count;
      printf("count=%d, total=%d\n", count++, total);
```

```
        }
    while ( count < 10 );
}
```

The output is the same as in previous versions of the program:

```
C>doloop
count=0, total=0
count=1, total=1
count=2, total=3
count=3, total=6
count=4, total=10
count=5, total=15
count=6, total=21
count=7, total=28
count=8, total=36
count=9, total=45
```

The **do** loop, unlike the other loops we've examined, has *two* keywords: **do** and **while**. The **do** keyword marks the beginning of the loop; it has no other function. The **while** keyword marks the end of the loop and contains the loop expression, as shown in Figure 3-10.

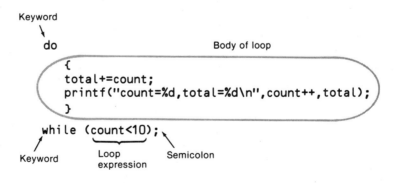

Figure 3-10. Structure of the *do* Loop

An important detail to note is that this loop, unlike the **for** and **while** loops, is terminated with a semicolon; that is, the test condition in the parentheses following **while** ends with a semicolon.

The operation of the **do** loop is sort of an upside-down version of the **while** loop. The body of the loop is first executed, then the test condition is checked. If the test condition is true, the loop is repeated; if it is false, the loop terminates, as can be seen in Figure 3-11. The important point to notice is

that the body of the loop will always be executed at least once, since the test
condition is not checked until the end of the loop.

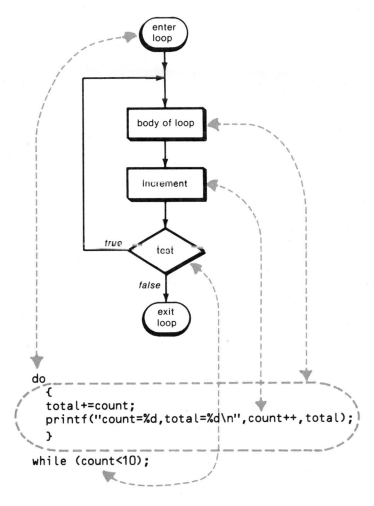

Figure 3-11. Operation of the *do* Loop

Pascal programmers might want to note that the **do** loop is similar to the
"repeat until" loop in Pascal, except that it continues to loop *while* the test
condition is true, while "repeat until" loops *until* the test condition is true.

When would you use a **do loop**? Any time you want to be sure the loop
body is executed at least once. This situation is less common than that where
the loop might not be executed at all, so the **do** loop is used less often than
the **while** loop. When in doubt, use the **while** loop; the operation of the
program is clearer if the test condition is set forth at the beginning of the loop.

If you find yourself writing a lot of **do** loops, you might want to try restructuring your program to turn some of them into **while**s.

Revised Guessing Game

Here's an example of a situation that calls for a **do** loop. Suppose we want to revise our guess-the-letter game so that instead of assuming you want to play a fixed number of times, it asks whether you want to play again after each game. To achieve this effect, we can rewrite the program as follows:

```c
/* guessdo */
/* lets you guess a letter */
/* uses do loop to ask if new game wanted */
void main(void)
{
    char ch;

    do
        {
        printf("\n\nType in a digit from 'a' to 'e':\n");
        while ( (ch=getche()) != 'c' )
            {
            printf("\nSorry, %c is incorrect.\n", ch);
            printf("Try again.\n");
            }
        printf("\nThat's it!\n");
        printf("\nPlay again? (Type 'y' or 'n'): ");
        }
    while ( getche() == 'y');
    printf("\nThanks for playing!");
}
```

Here's a sample session with the guessdo.c program:

```
Type in a digit from 'a' to 'e':
b
Sorry, b is incorrect.
Try again.
c
That's it!

Play again? (Type 'y' or 'n'): y

Type in a digit from 'a' to 'e':
d
```

```
Sorry, d is incorrect.
Try again.
c
That's it!

Play again? (Type 'y' or 'n'): n
Thanks for playing!
```

Notice that the body of the **do** loop will always be executed once. If you called up the program in the first place, we can assume that you want at least one game. After the first game, we ask if you want to continue. It is this situation, in which something must be done once before we ask if it should be done again, that is properly implemented with a **do** loop.

> The **do** loop is useful when the body of a loop will always be executed at least once.

The *break* and *continue* Statements

To round out our discussion of loops we should mention that C has two statements which can be used with any of the loops described above: **break** and **continue**.

The **break** statement bails you out of a loop as soon as it's executed. It's often used when an unexpected condition occurs; one that the loop test condition is not looking for. We'll see examples of this statement later.

The **continue** statement is inserted in the body of the loop, and, when executed, takes you back to the beginning of the loop, bypassing any statements not yet executed. **Continue** is a bit suspect in that it can make a program difficult to read and debug by confusing the normal flow of operations in the loop, so it is avoided by C programmers whenever possible.

Summary

This chapter has focused on the three C loops: **for, while,** and **do while.** You've learned how to create these and use them in a variety of situations. You've also learned how to nest one loop inside another, and how to use variables, functions, and assignment statements with relational operators in the loop expression. In short, you're ready to do things again and again.

Questions

1. The three parts of the loop expression in a **for** loop are
   the i_____ expression
   the t_____ expression
   the i_____ expression.

2. A single-statement **for** loop is terminated with a
   a. right bracket
   b. right brace
   c. comma
   d. semicolon

3. A _____ is used to separate the three parts of the loop expression in a **for** loop.

4. A multiple-statement **while** loop is terminated with a
   a. right bracket
   b. right brace
   c. comma
   d. semicolon

5. Multiple increment expressions in a **for** loop expression are separated by _____.

6. A **while** loop is more appropriate than a **for** loop when
   a. the terminating condition occurs unexpectedly
   b. the body of the loop will be executed at least once
   c. the program will be executed at least once
   d. the number of times the loop will be executed is known before the loop is executed

7. True or false: the initialize expression and increment expression are contained in the loop expression in a **while** loop.

8. An expression contains relational operators, assignment operators, and arithmetic operators. In the absence of parentheses, they will be evaluated in the following order

a. assignment, relational, arithmetic

b. arithmetic, relational, assignment

c. relational, arithmetic, assignment

d. assignment, arithmetic, relational

9. The more deeply a loop is nested, the more _____ it should be indented.

10. An assignment statement itself can have a _____ , just like a variable.

11. The advantage of putting complete assignment statements inside loop expressions is

a. to avoid awkward program constructions

b. to simplify the flow of control in the program

c. to reduce the number of program statements

d. to clarify the operation of the program

12. True or false: in almost every case where a variable can be used, an increment or decrement operator can be added to the variable.

13. A **do while** loop is useful when

a. the body of the loop will never be executed

b. the body of the loop will be executed at least once

c. the body of the loop may never be executed

d. the body of the executed loop was found by the butler

14. The **break** statement is used to exit from which part of a loop?

a. beginning

b. middle

c. end

d. none of the above

15. True or false: a **continue** statement causes an exit from a loop.

Exercises

1. Write a program that prints the squares of all the numbers from 1 to 20. (Perhaps you can adapt a similar exercise from the last chapter.)

2. Rewrite the charcnt.c program so that it counts characters until a period (.) is typed, rather than [Return].

3. Write a program that repeatedly calculates how many characters separate two letters typed in by the user until it is terminated with [Return]. For instance, there are *two* characters ('b' and 'c') between 'a' and 'd'. Take advantage of the fact that the arithmetic operators work on character variables just as well as they do on numbers.

4

Decisions

- The **If** statement
- The **if-else** statement
- The **else-if** construct
- The **switch** statement
- The conditional operator

4

We all need to be able to alter our actions in the face of changing circumstances. If the forecast is for rain, then I'll take my raincoat. If the freeway is under construction, then I'll take the back road. If, when I propose, she says yes, I'll buy her a ring; if she says no, I'll start dating Gladys.

Computer languages, too, must be able to perform different sets of actions depending on the circumstances. C has three major decision-making structures: the **if** statement, the **if-else** statement, and the **switch** statement. A fourth, somewhat less important structure, is the **conditional operator**. In this chapter we'll explore these four ways a C program can react to changing circumstances.

The *if* Statement

Like most languages, C uses the keyword **if** to introduce the basic decision-making statement. Here's a simple example:

```
/* testif */
/* demonstrates if statement */
void main(void)
{
    char ch;

    ch = getche();
    if ( ch == 'y' )
        printf("\nYou typed y.");
}
```

You can no doubt guess what will happen when this program is executed:

```
y
You typed y.
```

If you type 'y', the program will print "You typed y." If you type some other character, such as 'n', the program doesn't do anything.

Figure 4-1 shows the structure of the **if** statement. This structure is surprisingly similar to that of the **while** statement described in Chapter 3. The keyword is followed by parentheses, which contain a conditional expression using a relational operator. Following this, there is the body of the statement, consisting of either a single statement terminated by a semicolon, or (as we'll see shortly) multiple statements enclosed by braces. In fact, the only difference between the structure of the **if** statement and that of the **while** is that the words "if" and "while" are different.

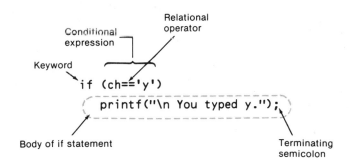

Figure 4-1. Structure of the *if* Statement

Notice too that there is no "then" keyword following the conditional expression, as there is in Pascal and usually is in BASIC.

There is no "then" keyword in C.

The **if** statement is similar to the **while** statement in operation as well as format. In both cases the statements making up the body of the statement will not be executed at all if the condition is false. However, in the **while** statement, if the condition is true, the statement (or statements) in the body of the loop will be executed over and over until the condition becomes false; whereas in the **if** statement they will be executed only once. Figure 4-2 shows the operation of the **if** statement.

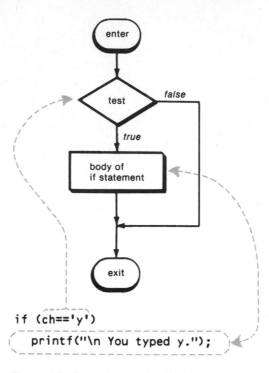

Figure 4-2. Operation of the *if* Statement

A Word-Counting Program

In the last chapter we included a program, charcnt.c, which counted the number of characters in a phrase typed by the user. Here's a slightly more complex program that counts not only the number of characters, but the number of words as well:

```
/* wordcnt */
/* counts characters and words in a phrase typed in */
void main(void)
{
    int charcnt=0;
    int wordcnt=0;
    char ch;

    printf("Type in a phrase:\n");
    while ( (ch=getche()) != '\r' )
        {
        charcnt++;
        if ( ch == ' ' )
```

```
        wordcnt++;
    }
  printf("\nCharacter count is %d", charcnt);
  printf("\nWord count is %d", wordcnt+1);
}
```

This program figures how many words there are by counting the number of spaces. (It could be fooled by multiple spaces between words, but we'll ignore that possibility.) Here's some sample interaction with the program:

```
Type in a phrase:
cat and dog
Character count is 11
Word count is 3

Type in a phrase:
This sentence actually uses nine words and sixty-five characters.
Character count is 65
Word count is 9
```

A tip of the hat to Douglas Hofstadter and his book *Metamagical Themas* (Basic Books, 1985) for the second phrase, which is the sort of example that is hard to type correctly the first time.

This program is similar to the charcnt.c program. The major addition is the **if** statement:

```
if ( ch == ' ' )
    wordcnt++;
```

This statement causes the variable **wordcnt** to be incremented every time a space is detected in the input stream. There will always be one more word than there are spaces between them (assuming no multiple spaces), so we add 1 to the variable **wordcnt** before printing it out. (We could also have used **++wordcnt**.)

Multiple Statements with *if*

As in the case of the various loop statements, the body of the **if** statement may consist of either a single statement terminated by a semicolon (as shown in the example above) or by a number of statements enclosed in braces. Here's an example of such a compound statement:

```
/* testif2.c */
/* demonstrates multiple statements following if */
void main(void)
```

```
{
    char ch;

    ch = getche();
    if ( ch == 'y' )
        {
        printf("\nYou typed y.");
        printf("\nNot some other letter.");
        }
}
```

In both testif.c programs we could have embedded the **getche()** function in the **if** expression, as we did in similar situations with the **while** loop in Chapter 3:

```
if ( getche() == 'y' )
```

This is more C-like, but we thought using it would make what the **if** statement was doing a bit less clear. However, in this next example, which is a program that reads two characters from the keyboard, we'll use this more compact construction.

Nested *if* Statements

Like the loop statements of the last chapter, **if** statements can be nested. Here's a simple example:

```
/* nestif.c */
/* demonstrates nested if statements */
void main(void)
{
    if ( getche() == 'n' )
        if ( getche() == 'o' )
            printf("\nYou typed no.");
}
```

Nesting here means that one **if** statement is part of the body of another **if** statement. In the example above, the inner **if** statement will not be reached unless the outer one is true, and the **printf()** statement will not be executed unless both **if** statements are true, as the following interaction with the program shows:

x   ← a non 'n' to start with terminates the program

nx   ← a non 'o' as the second letter does likewise

```
no                    ← only 'n' followed by 'o' gets to the printf( )
You typed no.
```

The operation of nested **if** statements is shown in Figure 4-3.

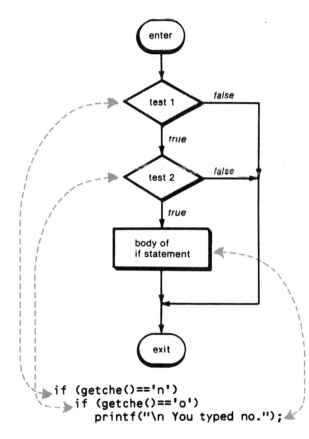

Figure 4-3. Nested *if* Statements

The *if-else* Statement

The **if** statement by itself will execute a single statement, or a group of statements, when the test expression is true. It does nothing when it is false. Can we execute a group of statements if and only if the test expression is *not* true? Of course. This is the purpose of the **else** statement, which is demonstrated in the following example:

```
/* testelse.c */
/* demonstrates if-else statement */
void main(void)
{
    char ch;

    ch = getche();
    if ( ch == 'y' )
        printf("\nYou typed y.");
    else
        printf("\nYou didn't type y.");
}
```

Typing 'y' elicits one response, while typing *anything else* elicits a different response.

```
y
You typed y.

n
You didn't type y.
```

Figure 4-4 shows the structure of the **if-else** statement and Figure 4-5 flowcharts its operation.

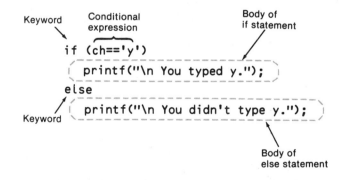

Figure 4-4. Structure of the *if-else* Statement

Notice that the **else** is indented to line up with the **if**. This is a formatting convention, which, if consistently followed, will enable you to better understand the operation of your program.

For clarity, each **else** should be indented the same amount as its matching **if**.

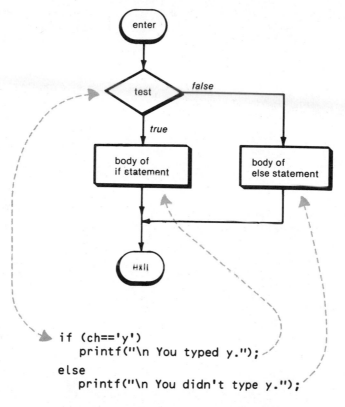

Figure 4-5. Operation of the *if-else* Statement

Character Graphics and the Checkerboard

As an example of the **if-else** statement at work, consider the following program, which prints a checkerboard on the monochrome screen.

```
/* checker */
/* draws a checkerboard on the screen */
void main(void)
{
    int x, y;

    for (y=1; y<9; y++)             /* stepping down */
        {
        for (x=1; x<9; x++)         /* stepping across */
            if ( (x+y) % 2 == 0 )   /* even numbered square? */
                printf("\xDB\xDB"); /* print filled square */
            else
```

p 40,704

```
        printf("  ");          /* print blank square */
    printf("\n");              /* new line */
    }
  }
```

Try out the program so you can see what it does. Figure 4-6 shows roughly what you'll see.

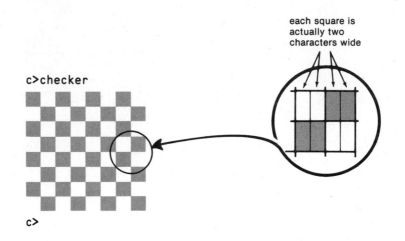

each square is
actually two
characters wide

c>checker

c>

Figure 4-6. Output of the checker.c Program

p77,79

This program is similar to those in Chapter 3 that drew a line and a rectangle, in that it uses the graphics character '\xDB' and nested loops to scan part of the screen. Here, however, the **if-else** construction gives the program the power to alter its operation, depending on which part of the screen it's about to write on.

How does this program work? The outer **for** loop (the variable **y**) moves down the screen one row at a time. That is, **y** marks what row we're on, starting at **y**=1 for the top row, and moving down to **y**=8. The inner loop (the variable **x**) moves across the screen one column at a time. That is, **x** marks what column we're on, starting at **x**=1 for the left-most column and moving across until **x**=8.

Actually, each of the columns pointed to by **x** is two characters wide. This glitch in the program is necessary because the characters on the PC screen are about twice as high as they are wide, so to create a correctly proportioned checkerboard each square must consist of two characters side-by-side: either two spaces or two solid rectangles. The purpose of the two **printf()** functions is just this: one prints two spaces, the other prints two solid rectangles using the '\xDB' character.

Getting Even with the Remainder Operator

How does the program decide when to print a square and when not to? In effect, the program numbers the squares and then colors only the even-numbered squares, leaving the odd-numbered squares blank. It determines whether a square is odd or even in the statement:

```
if ( (x+y) % 2 == 0 )
```

Each square is numbered, as shown in Figure 4-7. The number is obtained by adding the **x** and **y** coordinates of the square: **x+y**.

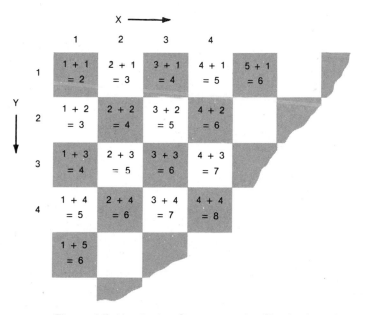

Figure 4-7. Numbering Squares on the Checkerboard

These numbers are not unique (more than one square has the same number) but they do exhibit the desired alternation between odd and even.

How then does the statement shown above reveal when a number is odd and when it is even? The remainder operator (%), which we mentioned in Chapter 1, is used for this purpose. With a divisor of two, the remainder will be 0 if the dividend is even, and 1 if the dividend is odd. The **if-else** statement can then determine whether to print two colored rectangles or two spaces for a given square (that is, for a particular value of **x** and **y**).

Drawing Lines

For another example of character graphics and the **if-else** statement, let's look at a pair of programs that draw lines on the monochrome screen. Actually, "line" may be too strong a word; it's really more of a diagonal "staircase" pattern.

Here's the first program:

```c
/* lines.c */
/* prints diagonal line on screen */
void main(void)
{
    int x, y;

    for (y=1; y<24; y++)        /* step down the screen */
      {
      for (x=1; x<24; x++)    /* step across the screen */
         if ( x == y )        /* are we on diagonal? */
            printf("\xDB");   /* yes, draw dark rectangle */
         else
            printf("\xB0");   /* no, draw light rectangle */
      printf("\n");           /* next line */
      }
}
```

This program is similar to the checkerboard program, except that instead of printing on even-numbered squares, it prints wherever the **x** coordinate and the **y** coordinate are equal. This will create a diagonal line extending from the upper left corner of the screen, where **x**=1 and **y**=1, down to the bottom of the screen, where **x**=23 and **y**=23.

Where the line is *not* drawn, the background is filled in with a light gray. For this purpose the program uses another graphics character, '\B0'. This is the same size as the solid rectangle created by '\DB', but consists of a pattern of tiny dots, creating a gray effect. Part of the output of the program is shown in Figure 4-8.

In this program we have not attempted to compensate for the aspect ratio of the characters on the screen as we did in the checkerboard program. As a consequence, each of the rectangles making up the line is twice as high as it is wide, and the line, which should appear to be at a 45-degree angle, actually slopes downward more steeply than that.

Nested *if-else* Statements

It is perfectly possible to nest an entire **if-else** construct within either the body of an **if** statement or the body of an **else** statement. The latter construction, shown in the following example, is quite common.

```c
/* lines2.c */
/* prints two diagonal lines on screen */
```

```
void main(void)
{
    int x, y;

    for (y=1; y<24; y++)                /* step down the screen */
        {
        for (x=1; x<24; x++)            /* step across the screen */
            if ( x == y )               /* NW-SE diagonal? */
                printf("\xDB");         /* print solid color */
            else
                if ( x == 24 - y )      /* SW-NE diagonal? */
                    printf("\xDB");     /* print solid color */
                else
                    printf("\xB0");     /* print gray */
        printf("\n");                   /* next line */
        }
}
```

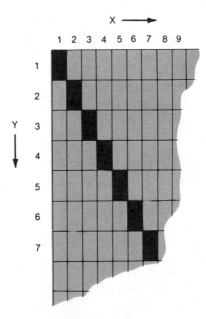

Figure 4-8. Output of the lines.c Program

This program is similar to the last one, except that it draws two lines on the screen, as shown in Figure 4-9. The first line is the same as in the last program. The second line goes in the opposite direction, from upper right to lower left. Thus the two lines create a dark X shape in the middle of a gray rectangle.

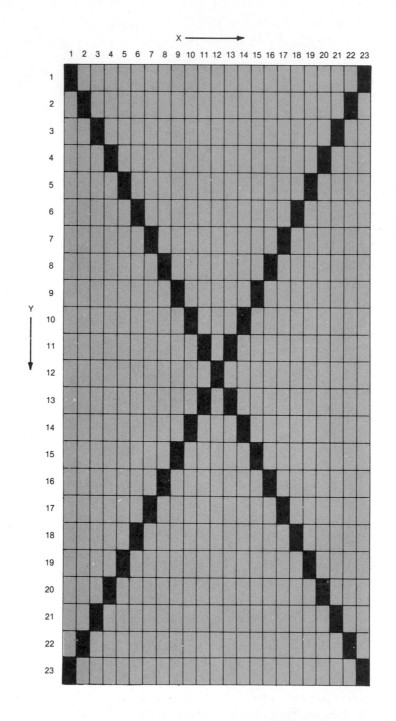

Figure 4-9. Output of the lines2.c Program

Note how the second **if-else** construction, which draws the second line, is nested inside the first **else** statement. If the test expression in the first **if** statement is false, then the test expression in the second **if** statement is checked. If it is false as well, the final **else** statement is executed. The process is shown in Figure 4-10.

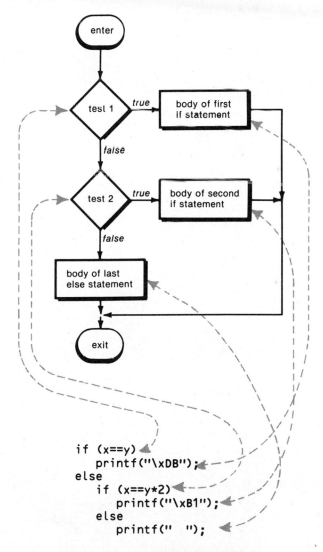

```
if (x==y)
    printf("\xDB");
else
    if (x==y*2)
        printf("\xB1");
    else
        printf(" ");
```

Figure 4-10. Nested *if-else* Statements

You can see in the listing that each time a structure is nested in another structure, it is also indented for clarity. This is similar to the way nested loops are indented.

There are several alternatives to this nested **if-else** structure. One involves a format change, one involves a new C statement, **switch**; and the third involves *logical operators*. We'll look at this last alternative in a moment. First, however, let's examine a possible pitfall in the use of nested **if-else** statements.

Which *if* Gets the *else*?

Consider the following program, which looks as if it would respond with an appropriate comment when the user types in the temperature (in degrees Fahrenheit).

```
/* temper.c */
/* makes remark about temperature */
void main(void)
{
    int temp;

    printf("Please type in the temperature: ");
    scanf("%d", &temp);
    if ( temp < 80 )
       if ( temp > 60 )
          printf("Nice day!");
    else
       printf("Sure is hot!");
}
```

Suppose **temp** is 32. What will be printed when this program is executed? Would you guess nothing at all? That seems reasonable: the first **if** condition (temp < 80) will be true, so the second **if** condition (temp > 60) will be evaluated. It will be false, so it looks as if the program will exit from the entire nested **if-else** construct.

However, we have attempted to mislead you by altering the indentation. You may have been fooled, but the compiler won't be. Here's what happens:

```
Please type in the temperature: 32
Sure is hot!
```

The problem is that the **else** is actually associated with the **if** immediately preceding it, not the first **if,** as the indentation would lead you to believe. The rule is that an **else** is associated with the last **if** that doesn't have its own **else**. Here's a modified version of the program which will operate correctly:

```
/* temper2.c */
/* makes remark about temperature */
void main(void)
```

```
{
    int temp;

    printf("Please type in the temperature: ");
    scanf("%d", &temp);
    if ( temp < 80 )
        if ( temp > 60 )
            printf("Nice day!");
        else
            printf("Sure is chilly!");
    else
        printf("Sure is hot!");
}
```

Here the inner **else** is paired with the inner **if**, and the outer **else** is paired with the outer **if**. The indentation in this case is not misleading.

An **else** is associated with the last **if** that doesn't have its own **else**.

If you want to ensure that an **else** goes with an earlier **if** than the one it would ordinarily be matched with, you can use braces to surround the intervening **if** structure. Surrounding the **if** with braces makes it invisible to the **else**, which then matches up with the earliest nonbraced **if**. We've modified the example to show how this looks (note that this program doesn't print anything if the temperature is colder than 60).

```
/* temper3.c */
/* makes remark about temperature */
void main(void)
{
    int temp;

    printf("Please type in the temperature: ");
    scanf("%d", &temp);
    if ( temp < 80 )
        {                                /* these braces make */
        if ( temp > 60 )                 /* this "if" */
            printf("Nice day!");         /* invisible */
        }                                /* to */
    else                                 /* this else */
        printf("Sure is hot!");
}
```

Logical Operators

p111

We can simplify the lines2.c program from earlier in this chapter by using an operator we have not yet encountered: the *logical operator*. Logical operators are a powerful way to condense and clarify complicated **if-else** structures (and other constructions as well). Let's see what effect a logical operator, in this case the OR operator, represented by two vertical bars (¦¦), will have on the program. Then we'll explore logical operators in general.

```
/* lines3.c */
/* prints two diagonal lines on screen */
void main(void)
{
    int x, y;

    for (y=1; y<24; y++)
       {
       for (x=1; x<24; x++)
       if ( x==y || x==24-y )   /* if either condition */
          printf("\xDB");       /* is true, print solid box */
       else                     /* otherwise */
          printf("\xB0");       /* print gray box */
       printf("\n");
       }
}
```

This program yields the same output as the previous example—a pair of crossed diagonal lines—but does so in a more elegant way. The logical OR operator (¦¦) means if *either* the expression on the right side of the operator (x==24−y), *or* the expression on the left (x==y) is true, then the entire expression (x==y ¦¦ x==24−y) is true.

Note that the logical operator (¦¦) performs an *inclusive* OR. That is, if either the expression on one side of the operator, or the expression on the other, or *both* expressions are true, then the entire expression is true. (An *exclusive* OR, by contrast, would provide a *false* result if the expressions on both sides were true; C does not have an exclusive OR operator.)

There are three logical (sometimes called "Boolean") operators in C:

¦¦   logical OR
&&   logical AND
!   logical NOT

Here's a program that uses the logical AND operator (&&):

```
/* digitcnt.c */
/* counts characters and numerical digits in a phrase */
void main(void)
{
    int charcnt=0;
    int digitcnt=0;
    char ch;

    printf("Type in a phrase:\n");
    while ( (ch=getche()) != '\r' )
       {
       charcnt++;
       if ( ch > 47 && ch < 58 )
          digitcnt++;
       }
    printf("\nCharacter count is %d", charcnt);
    printf("\nDigit count is %d", digitcnt);
}
```

This program is a modification of our earlier charcnt.c and wordcnt.c programs. In addition to counting the characters in a phrase, it also counts any of the numeric digits 0 through 9 which are part of the phrase. Here's an example:

```
C>digitcnt
Type in a phrase:
He packed 4 socks, 12 shirts, and 1,000 hopes for the future.
Character count is 61
Digit count is 7
```

The key to this program is the logical AND operator (&&). This operator says: if *both* the expression on the left (ch>47) and the expression on the right (ch<58) are true, then the entire expression (ch>47 && ch<58) is true. This will only be true if **ch** is between 48 and 57; these are the ASCII codes for the digits from 0 to 9.

There are several things to note about these logical operators. Most obviously, they are composed of double symbols: (¦¦) and (&&). Don't use the single symbols: (¦) and (&). These single symbols also have a meaning (they are bitwise operators, which we'll examine later), but it isn't the meaning we want at the moment.

Perhaps it is not so obvious, though, that the logical operators have a lower precedence than the relational operators, such as (==). It's for this reason that we don't need to use parentheses around the relational expressions x == y, ch > 47, and so on. The relational operators are evaluated first,

p 119

then the logical operators. (We'll summarize operator precedence in a moment.)

> Logical operators have lower precedence than relational operators.

Although we don't make use of the fact here, you should know that logical operators are always evaluated from left to right. Thus, if you have a condition such as:

```
if ( a<b && b<c )
```

you know that (a<b) will be evaluated first. Also, in this case, C is smart enough to know that if the condition to the left of the && is false, then there's no point in evaluating the rest of the expression, since the result will be false anyway.

The third logical operator is the NOT operator, represented by the exclamation point (!), and sometimes called the "bang" operator. This operator reverses the logical value of the expression it operates on; it makes a true expression false and a false expression true.

The NOT operator is a unary operator: that is, it takes only one operand. In this way it's similar to the negative sign in arithmetic: the $(-)$ in -5 also takes only one operand.

Here's an example of the NOT operator applied to a relational expression.

```
!(x < 5)
```

This means "not **x** less than five." In other words, if **x** is less than 5, the expression will be false, since (x < 5) is true. We could express the same condition as (x >= 5).

The NOT operator is often used to reverse the logical value of a single variable, as in the expression

```
if( !flag )
```

This is more concise than the equivalent

```
if( flag==0 )
```

Operator Precedence, Revisited

Since we've now added the logical operators to the list of operators we know how to use, it is probably time to review all of these operators and their precedence. Table 4-1 summarizes the operators we've seen so far. The higher an operator is in the table, the higher its precedence. (A more complete precedence table can be found in Appendix A.)

p690

Table 4-1. *Operator Order of Precedence*

Operators	Type
! −	unary: logical NOT, arithmetic minus
* / %	arithmetic (multiplicative)
+ −	arithmetic (additive)
< > <= >=	relational (inequality)
== !=	relational (equality)
&& ||	logical AND and OR
= += −= *= /= %=	assignment

Unary operators—those which act on only one value—have the highest priority. Then come arithmetic operators; here multiplication and division have higher precedence than addition and subtraction. Similarly, those relational operators that test for inequality have a higher precedence than those that test for equality. Next come the logical operators and finally the assignment operators. As you know, parentheses can be used to override any of these precedence relations.

The *else-if* Construct

We've seen how **if-else** statements can be nested. Let's look at a more complex example of this arrangement:

```
/* calc.c */
/* four-function calculator */
void main(void)
{
    float num1=1.0, num2=1.0;
    char op;

    while ( !(num1==0.0 && num2==0.0) )
        {
        printf("Type number, operator, number\n");
        scanf("%f %c %f", &num1, &op, &num2);
        if ( op == '+')
            printf(" = %f", num1 + num2);
        else
```

```
        if (op == '-')
            printf(" = %f", num1 - num2);
        else
            if (op == '*')
                printf(" = %f", num1 * num2);
            else
                if (op == '/')
                    printf(" = %f", num1 / num2);
    printf("\n\n");
    }
}
```

This program gives your computer, for which you spent thousands of dollars, all the raw power of a four-function pocket calculator. You first type a number, then an operator—which can be any of the arithmetic operators (+), (−), (*), or (/)—and finally a second number. The program then prints out the answer.

Entering zero values for both numbers terminates the program (no matter what value you use for the operator). This is handled by the logical expression in the **while** statement. Notice the use of the logical NOT operator (!). When both **num1** and **num2** are zero, then the expression

```
!(num1==0.0 && num2==0.0)
```

is false, so the loop terminates. This expression is equivalent to

```
num1 !=0.0 !! num2 != 0.0
```

If either variable is non-zero, the loop continues.

Here we've used **scanf()** to read in the first number, the operator, and the second number in a single statement. As we discussed in Chapter 1, the white spaces between the variables in the format string in the **scanf()** statement permit you to separate the variables you type in with any sort of whitespace characters: spaces, tabs, or newlines. Actually, it's not even necessary to type any whitespace character in this example. **scanf()** will know we've finished typing the first number when it sees a non-numeric character, and it will then wait for the second number. Here are examples of different approaches used with the calc.c program:

```
Type number, operator, number
3 + 3                              ← separated by spaces
 = 6.000000
Type number, operator, number
1                                  ← separated by newlines
/
3
```

```
  = 0.333333
Type number, operator, number
1000*1000                                    ← no separation
  = 1000000.000000
Type number, operator, number
1000000/3
  = 333333.333333
```

Structurally, the important point to notice about this program is how the **if-else** constructs are nested. Since there are so many, the nesting and the resulting indentation gets quite deep, making the program difficult to read. There's another way to write, and think about, this situation. This involves the creation of a sort of imaginary construct called "else-if." We reformat the program, but not in a way the compiler will notice:

```c
/* calc2.c */
/* four-function calculator */
void main(void)
{
    float num1=1.0, num2=1.0;
    char op;

    while ( !(num1==0.0 && num2==0.0) )
        {
        printf("Type number, operator, number\n");
        scanf("%f %c %f", &num1, &op, &num2);
        if ( op == '+')
            printf(" = %f", num1 + num2);
        else if (op == '-')
            printf(" = %f", num1 - num2);
        else if (op == '*')
            printf(" = %f", num1 * num2);
        else if (op == '/')
            printf(" = %f", num1 / num2);
        printf("\n\n");
        }
}
```

This operates exactly as before, but we've rearranged the whitespace to make the program easier to read. By simply deleting spaces and the newline, each **if** is moved up next to the preceding **else**, thus making a new construction: **else-if**. We think of **else-if** as meaning, "if the test expression that follows is true, execute the statement in the body of the **else-if** (in this case a **printf()** statement) and go to the end of the entire **else-if** chain; otherwise, go to the next **else-if** statement in the chain." Figure 4-11 shows this process in a flowchart.

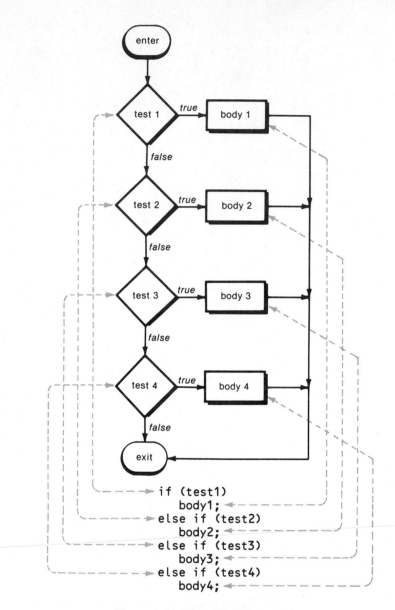

Figure 4-11. The *else-if* Construct

The **else-if** construction is a reformatting of nested **if-else** statements.

The *break* Statement

In the next section we'll look at the **switch** statement, which provides an alternative to the **else-if** construct. However, the **switch** statement relies on another statement, **break**. So we'll digress briefly to see how **break** is used to escape from a loop; then we'll go on to explore the role it plays in the **switch** statement.

We'll demonstrate **break** with a guessing game program. In this game the user picks a number between 1 and 99 and the program tries to guess what it is. The user replies to the computer's guesses by saying whether the guess is higher or lower than the number the computer is thinking of. Here's the listing:

```
/* numguess.c */
/* program guesses number user is thinking of */
void main(void)
{
   float guess, incr;
   char ch;

   printf("Think of a number between 1 and 99, and\n");
   printf("I'll guess what it is.  Type 'e' for equals,\n");
   printf("'g'for greater than, and 'l' for less than.\n");
   incr = guess = 50;             /* two assignments at once */
   while ( incr > 1.0 )           /* while not close enough */
      {
      printf("\nIs your number greater or less than %.0f?\n",
                              guess);
      incr = incr / 2;
      if ( (ch=getche()) == 'e' ) /* if guessed it already */
         break;                   /* escape from loop */
      else if (ch == 'g')         /* if guess too low */
         guess = guess + incr;    /*    try higher */
      else                        /* if guess too high */
         guess = guess - incr;    /*    try lower */
      }
   printf("\nThe number is %.0f.  Am I not clever?", guess);
}
```

The strategy employed by numguess.c is to ask questions that cut in half the range in which the number might lie. Thus the program first asks if the number is greater or less than 50. If the number is greater than 50, the program asks if the number is greater or less than 75, while if it's less than 50 the program asks if it's greater or less than 25. The process continues until the program deduces the number. Here's a sample interaction, with the user thinking of the number 62:

```
Think of a number between 1 and 99,
  and I'll guess what it is. Type 'e' for equals,
  'g' for greater than, and 'l' for less than.

Is your number greater or less than 50?
g
Is your number greater or less than 75?
l
Is your number greater or less than 63?
l
Is your number greater or less than 56?
g
Is your number greater or less than 59?
g
Is your number greater or less than 61?
g
The number is 62. Am I not clever?
```

The test expression in the **while** loop waits for the variable **incr** (for increment)—which is added to or subtracted from **guess** and then divided by 2 each time through the loop—to become 1. At that point the program knows that the number has been guessed, so it prints out the guess. However, there is the possibility the program will actually print the number the user is thinking of when it's trying to narrow down the range; it might ask if the number is greater or less than 75, for example, when in fact the user is thinking of 75. At this point, the honorable user will type 'e'. Now the program knows it can stop trying to guess the number, so it needs to get out of the loop right away. The **break** statement is used for this purpose.

Break is often useful when a condition suddenly occurs that makes it necessary to leave a loop before the loop expression becomes false. And, as we'll see next, it is essential in the **switch** statement.

Several other points about numguess.c should be noted. First, the following statement is written on two lines:

```
printf("\nIs your number greater or less than %.0f?\n",
                                           guess);
```

This linebreak was necessary because the one line exceeded the width of the page. The C compiler doesn't mind if you break a line in the middle this way, as long as you <u>don't break it in the middle of a string.</u>

Second, in the statement

```
incr = guess = 50;
```

we've assigned two variables a value using only one statement. This is possible because an assignment statement itself has a value (as we mentioned in Chapter 3). In this case, the statement

```
guess = 50;
```

takes on the value 50, and the variable **incr** can then be set equal to this value.

The *switch* Statement

Now that we know how the **break** statement works, we're ready to move on to **switch**. The **switch** statement is similar to the **else-if** construct but has more flexibility and a clearer format. It is analogous to the **case** statement in Pascal. Let's rewrite our calc2.c program to use **switch**:

p 121

```c
/* calc3.c */
/* four-function calculator */
void main(void)
{
    float num1=1.0, num2=1.0;
    char op;

    while ( !(num1==0.0 && num2==0.0) )
        {
        printf("Type number, operator, number\n");
        scanf("%f %c %f", &num1, &op, &num2);
        switch ( op )
            {
            case '+':
                printf(" = %f", num1 + num2);
                break;
            case '-':
                printf(" = %f", num1 - num2);
                break;
            case '*':
                printf(" = %f", num1 * num2);
                break;
            case '/':
                printf(" = %f", num1 / num2);
                break;
```

```
        default:
            printf("Unknown operator");
        }
    printf("\n\n");
    }
}
```

Structurally, the statement starts out with the keyword **switch**, followed by parentheses containing an integer or character variable which we'll call the "switch variable" (although it can also be an expression, like a+b). The structure of the **switch** statement is shown in Figure 4-12.

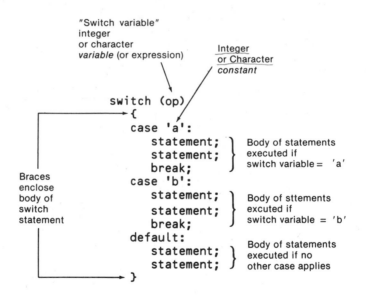

Figure 4-12. The Structure of the *switch* Statement

Following each of the **case** keywords is an integer or character *constant*. (It can be a constant expression, like 'a' + 2, but it must evaluate to a constant; variables are not allowed here.) This constant is terminated with a colon (not a semicolon). There can be one or more statements following each **case** keyword. These statements need not be enclosed by braces, although the entire body of the **switch** statement—all the **case**s—is enclosed in braces.

When the **switch** is entered, the switch variable should already have been set to some value, probably the value of one of the integer or character constants that follow the **case** keywords. If so, control is immediately transferred to the body of statements following this particular **case** keyword. The operation of the **switch** statement in the calc3.c program is shown in Figure 4-13.

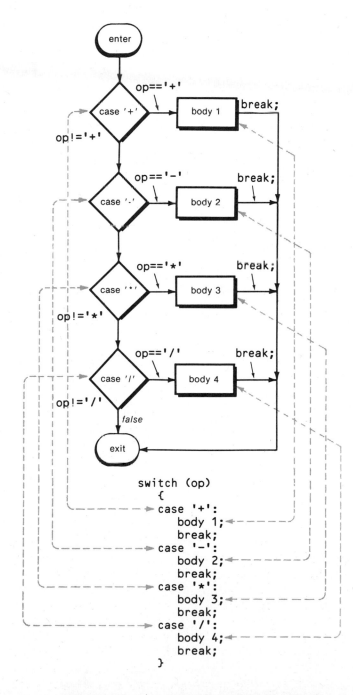

Figure 4-13. Operation of the *switch* Statement

If the **switch** variable does not match any of the case constants, control goes to the keyword **default**, which is usually at the end of the switch statement. Using the **default** keyword can be a great convenience; it acts as a sort of master **else** statement, saying in effect, "if none of the above, then do this." (If there is no **default** keyword, the whole **switch** statement simply terminates when there is no match.) In the example above, if the user has typed a character that isn't one of the four for which there is a **case** constant, then control will pass to the statements following the **default** keyword. Here's how that possibility looks in operation when an illegal operator symbol is typed:

```
Type number, operator, number
2 q 2
Unknown operator
```

The **break** statements are necessary to terminate the **switch** statement when the body of statements in a particular case has been executed. As it did in the numguess.c example earlier, the **break** statement has the effect of immediately taking the program out of the structure it finds itself in: a loop in numguess.c and a **switch** here.

> If no **break** statement is used following a **case**, control will fall through to the next **case**.

Without the **break**, the program will execute not only the statements for a particular case, but all the statements for the following cases as well. (This is unlike the operation of the Pascal **case** statement.) Needing to write all the **breaks** may sound like an inconvenience, but it actually makes for a more flexible construction, as shown in the following variation of the calc3.c program:

```
/* calc4.c */
/* four-function calculator */
void main(void)
{
    float num1=1.0, num2=1.0;
    char op;

    while ( !(num1==0.0 && num2==0.0) )
        {
        printf("Type number, operator, number\n");
        scanf("%f %c %f", &num1, &op, &num2);
        switch ( op )
```

```
          {
          case '+':
             printf(" = %f", num1 + num2);
             break;
          case '-':
             printf(" = %f", num1 - num2);
             break;
          case '*':
          case 'x':
             printf(" = %f", num1 * num2);
             break;
          case '/':
          case '\\':  ←
             printf(" = %f", num1 / num2);
             break;
          default:
             printf("Unknown operator");
          }
       printf("\n\n");
       }
   }
```

This program tries to be a little more friendly to the user by dealing with the instances when the user types an 'x' instead of a '*' to mean multiply, or a '\' instead of a '/' to mean divide. Since control falls right through one **case** to the **case** below in the absence of a **break** statement, this construction makes it easy for several values of the **switch** variable to execute the same body of code.

Note that, since the backslash is already the escape character, we must type '\\' to indicate the backslash itself.

Here's what happens when you type the new operators:

```
C>calc4

Type number, operator, number
2 \ 3
 = 0.666667

Type number, operator, number
10 x 10
 = 100.000000
```

The Conditional Operator

We'll finish off this chapter with a brief look at one of C's stranger constructions, a decision-making operator called the "conditional operator." It consists of two symbols used on three different expressions, and thus it has the distinction of being the only ternary operator in C. (Ternary operators work on three variables, as opposed to the more common binary operators, such as (+), which operate on two expressions, and unary operators, such as (!), which operate on only one.) The conditional operator has the form: *condition ? expression1 : expression2.*

The conditional operator consists of both the question mark and the colon. *Condition* is a logical expression that evaluates to either true or false, while *expression1* and *expression2* are either values or expressions that evaluate to values.

Here's how it works. The condition is evaluated. If it's true, then the entire conditional expression takes on the value of *expression1*. If it's false, the conditional expression takes on the value of *expression2*. Note that the entire conditional expression—the three expressions and two operators—takes on a value and can therefore be used in an assignment statement.

Here's an example:

```
max = (num1 > num2)   ?   num1 : num2;
```

The purpose of this statement is to assign to the variable **max** the value of either **num1** or **num2**, whichever is larger. First the condition **(num1>num2)** is evaluated. If it's true, the entire conditional expression takes on the value of **num1**; this value is then assigned to **max**. If **(num1>num2)** is false, the conditional expression takes on the value of **num2**, and this value is assigned to **max**. This operation is shown in Figure 4-14.

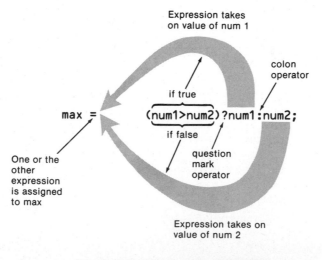

Figure 4-14. The Conditional Operator

This expression is equivalent to the **if-else** statement:

```
if (num1 < num2)
    max = num2;
else
    max = num1;
```

But it is more compact than the **if-else;** since the entire statement takes on a value, two separate assignment statements are not needed. This operator can be used very elegantly in the right sort of situation.

Here's another example:

```
abs = (num < 0) ? -num : num;
```

This statement evaluates to the absolute value of **num**, which is simply **num** if **num** is greater than zero, but **-num** if **num** is less than zero.

Summary

You now know a good deal about the major elements of decision-making in C. You've learned about the three major decision-making statements—**if, if-else,** and **switch**. You've seen how **if** statements and **if-else** statements can be nested and how a series of **if-else** statements can be transformed into the **else-if** construction. You've learned the elements of the **switch** statement: the switch variable, switch constants, and the **case** and **default** keywords. You've also learned about the three logical operators—NOT (!), OR (¦¦), and AND (&&)—and about the **break** statement, which causes an immediate exit from a loop or **switch** structure. Finally, you learned about the conditional operator, which returns one or the other of two values, depending on whether a condition is true or false.

Questions

1. In a simple **if** statement with no **else**, what happens if the condition following the **if** is false?
   a. the program searches for the last **else** in the program
   b. nothing
   c. control "falls through" to the statement following the **if**
   d. the body of the **if** statement is executed

2. Is the following a correct C program?

```
void main(void)
{
   if ( getche() == 'a' ) then
      printf("\nYou typed a.");
}
```

3. True or false: nesting one **if** inside another should be avoided for clarity.

4. The main difference in operation between an **if** statement and a **while** statement is

   a. the conditional expression following the keyword is evaluated differently

   b. the **while** loop body is always executed, the **if** loop body only if the condition is true

   c. the body of the **while** statement may be executed many times, the body of the **if** statement only once

   d. the conditional expression is evaluated before the **while** loop body is executed but after the **if** loop body

5. The statements following **else** in an **if-else** construction are executed when

   a. the conditional expression following **if** is false

   b. the conditional expression following **if** is true

   c. the conditional expression following **else** is false

   d. the conditional expression following **else** is true

6. Is this C program correct?

```
void main(void)
{
   if(getch()=='a') printf("It's an a"); else printf("It's not");
}
```

7. True or false: the compiler interprets **else-if** differently than it does an equivalent **if-else**.

8. The statements following a particular **else-if** in an **else-if** ladder are executed when

a. the conditional expression following the **else-if** is true and all previous conditions are true

b. the conditional expression following the **else-if** is true and all previous conditions are false

c. the conditional expression following the **else-if** is false and all previous conditions are true

d. the conditional expression following the **else-if** is false and all previous conditions are false

9. Which **if** in a program does an **else** pair up with?

   a. the last **if** with the same indentation as the **else**

   b. the last **if** not matched with its own **else**

   c. the last **if** not enclosed in braces

   d. the last **if** not enclosed in braces and not matched with its own **else**

10. The advantage of a **switch** statement over an **else-if** construction is

    a. a default condition can be used in the **switch**

    b. the **switch** is easier to understand

    c. several different statements can be executed for each case in a **switch**

    d. several different conditions can cause one set of statements to be executed in a **switch**

11. Is this a correct **switch** statement?

```
switch(num)
   {
   case 1;
      printf("Num is 1");
   case 2;
      printf("Num is 2");
   default;
      printf("Num is neither 1 nor 2");
   }
```

12. True or false: a **break** statement must be used following the statements for each **case** in a **switch** statement.

13. Is this a correct **switch** statement?

```
switch (temp)
   {
```

```
        case temp<60:
           printf("It's really cold!");
           break;
        case temp<80:
           printf("What charming weather!");
           break;
        default:
           printf("Sure is hot!);
        }
```

14. The purpose of the conditional operator is to
    a. select the highest of two values
    b. select the more equal of two values
    c. select one of two values alternately
    d. select one of two values depending on a condition

15. If num is −42, what is the value of this conditional expression?

    ```
    ( num < 0 ) ? 0 : num*num;
    ```

Exercises

1. Write a program that will ask the user how fast he or she drives, and then print out what response a police officer would make to the following speed ranges: >75, >55, >45, <45. Use nested **if-else** statements.

2. Modify the checker.c program to draw a checkerboard where each square, instead of being one row high and two columns wide, is three rows high and six columns wide.

3. Modify the lines2.c program to draw four lines, the first two the same as in lines2.c, the third a vertical line passing through the center of the rectangle (where the first two lines cross), and the fourth a horizontal line passing through the center of the rectangle. The effect is something like a British flag. Use logical operators.

5

Functions

- Functions
- Returning a value from a function
- Sending values to a function
- Arguments
- External variables
- Preprocessor directives

5

No one can perform all of life's tasks personally. You may ask a repairperson to fix your TV set, hire someone to mow your lawn, or rely on a store to provide fresh vegetables rather than growing your own. A computer program (except for a very simple one) is in much the same situation; it cannot handle every task alone. Instead, it calls on other programlike entities—called "functions" in C—to carry out specific tasks. In this chapter we'll explore the topic of functions. We'll look at a variety of ways functions are used, starting with the simplest case and working up to examples that demonstrate some of the power and versatility of functions in C.

At the end of the chapter we'll explore another area of C that ties into the idea of functions in several ways: that of "preprocessor directives."

What Do Functions Do?

As we noted in Chapter 1, a function in C serves a similar purpose to a subroutine in BASIC and to functions or procedures in Pascal. Let's examine in more detail why a function is used.

Avoiding Unnecessary Repetition of Code

Probably the original reason functions (or subroutines, as they were first known) were invented was to avoid having to write the same code over and over. Suppose you have a section of code in your program that calculates the square root of a number. If, later in the program, you want to calculate the square root of a different number, you don't want to have to write the same instructions all over again. Instead, in effect, you want to jump to the section of code that calculates square roots and then jump back again to the normal program flow when you're done. In this way, a single section of code can be used many times in the same program. The saving of code is depicted in Figure 5-1.

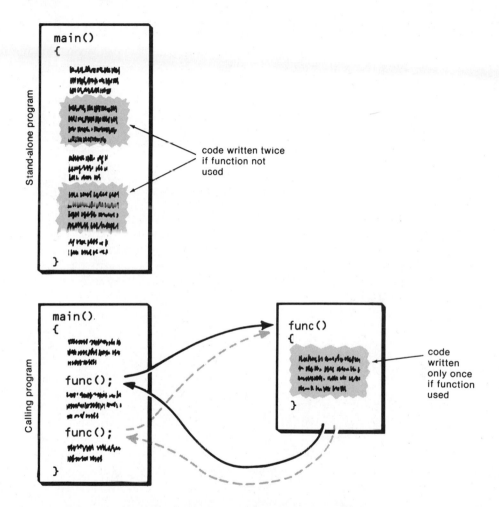

Figure 5-1. Code Savings Using Function

Program Organization

This is all the early subroutines did. However, over the years it was found that using the subroutine idea made it easier to organize programs and keep track of what they were doing. If the operation of a program could be divided into separate activities, and each activity placed in a separate subroutine, then each subroutine could be written and checked out more or less independently. Separating the code into modular functions also made programs easier to design and understand.

Independence

As this idea took hold, it became clear that there was an advantage in making subroutines as independent from the main program and from one another as possible. For instance, subroutines were invented that had their own "private" variables; that is, variables that could not be accessed from the main program or the other subroutines. This meant that a programmer didn't need to worry about accidentally using the same variable names in different subroutines; the variables in each subroutine were protected from inadvertent tampering by other subroutines. Thus it was easier to write large and complex programs. Pascal and most other modern programming languages make use of this independence, and C does too, as we'll find out soon.

C Functions and Pascal Procedures and Functions

For Pascal programmers, we should mention at this point a difference between C and Pascal that might cause some initial confusion. In Pascal, functions and procedures are two separate entities. A function in that language returns a value, whereas a procedure carries out a task or returns data via arguments. In C these two constructs are combined: a C function can return data via arguments and can also return a value. We'll note other differences between C and Pascal as we go along.

Simple Functions

As we noted, using a function is in some ways like hiring someone to perform a specific job for you. Sometimes the interaction with such a person is very simple; sometimes it's more complex. Let's start with a simple case.

Suppose you have a task which is always performed in exactly the same way—mowing your lawn, say. When you want it done, you get on the phone to the lawn person and say, "It's time, do it now." You don't need to give instructions, since that task is *all* the person does. You don't need to be told when the job is done. You assume the lawn will be mowed in the usual way, the person does it, and that's that.

Let's look at a simple C function that operates in the same way. Actually, we'll be looking at two things: a program that "calls" or activates the function (just as you call the lawn person on the phone) and the function itself. Here's the program:

```
/* textbox.c */
/* puts box around text */
void line(void);               /* prototype for line() */
```

```
void main(void)
{
    line();                                /* draw line */
    printf("\xDB TITUS ANDRONICUS \xDB\n"); /* message */
    line();                                /* 2nd line */
}



/* line() -- this is function definition */
/* draws solid line on screen */
void line(void)                 /* function declarator */
{
    int j;                      /* counter */

    for (j=1; j<=20; j++)       /* print block 20 times */
        printf("\xDB");         /* solid block */
    printf("\n");               /* print carriage return */
}
```

This program draws a box around the words "TITUS ANDRONICUS" (one of the lesser known Roman emperors). Figure 5-2 shows what the output looks like.

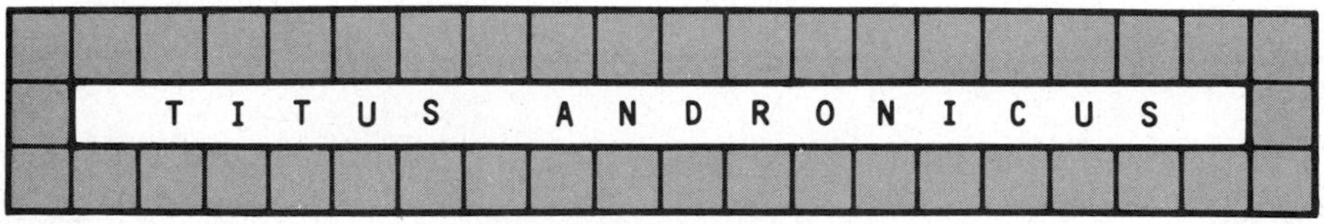

Figure 5-2. Output of textbox.c

To achieve this effect we've first drawn a line of rectangles across the screen (using the graphics character '\xDB'), then printed the emperor's name—preceded and ended by a rectangle to form the ends of the box—and finally drawn another line. However, instead of writing the code to draw the line twice, we made it into a function, called **line**.

The Structure of Functions

The textbox.c program looks almost like two little programs, but actually each of these "programs" is a function. As we mentioned in Chapter 1, **main()** is a function, so it's not surprising that **line()**, which is also a function, looks like it. The only thing special about **main()** is that it is always executed first. It doesn't even matter if **main()** is the first function in the listing; you can place other functions before it and **main()** will still be executed first.

In this example, **main()** calls the function **line()**. "Calls" means "to cause to be executed." To draw the two lines of boxes, **main()** calls **line()** twice.

There are three program elements involved in using a function: the function *definition*, the call to the function, and the function *prototype*. Let's look at each of these in turn.

The Function Definition

The function itself is referred to as the function definition. The definition starts with a line that includes the function name, among other elements:

```
void line(void)    /* note: no semicolon */
```

This line is the *declarator* (a name only a lexicographer could love). The first **void** means that **line()** doesn't return anything, and the second means that it takes no arguments. We'll examine return values and arguments later in the chapter.

Note that the declarator does not end with a semicolon. It is not a program statement, whose execution causes something to happen. Rather, it tells the compiler that a function is being defined.

The function definition continues with the *body* of the function: the program statements that do the work. Figure 5-3 shows the declarator and the function body that make up the function definition.

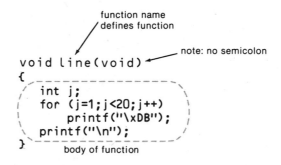

Figure 5-3. Function Definition

The body of the function is enclosed in braces. Usually these braces are placed at the left margin, as we've already seen in numerous examples of the function **main()**.

Calling the Function

As with the C library functions we've seen, such as **printf()** and **getche()**, our user-written function **line()** is called from **main()** simply by using its name, including the parentheses following the name. The parentheses let the compiler know that you are referring to a function and not to a variable or something else. Calling a function like this is a C statement, so it ends with a semicolon.

```
line();   /* function call -- note semicolon */
```

This function call causes control to be transferred to the code in the definition of **line()**. This function draws its row of squares on the screen, and then returns to **main()**, to the statement immediately following the function call.

Function Prototype (Declaration)

There's a third function-related element in the textbox.c example. This is a line before the beginning of **main()**:

```
void line(void);   /* function prototype -- note semicolon */
```

This looks very much like the declarator line at the start of the function definition, except that it ends with a semicolon. What is its purpose?

You've already seen many examples of *variables* in C programs. All the variables were defined by name and data type before they were used. A *function* is declared in a similar way at the beginning of a program before it is called. The function declaration (or prototype—the terms mean the same thing) tells the compiler the name of the function, the data type the function returns (if any), and the number and data types of the function's arguments (if any). In our example, the function returns nothing and takes no arguments; hence the two **voids**.

Notice that the prototype is written *before* the **main()** function. This causes the prototype to be visible to all the functions in a file. You'll learn more about this when we discuss external veriables later in this chapter.

The key thing to remember about the prototype is that the data type of the return value must agree with that of the declarator in the function definition, and the number of arguments and their data types must agree with those in the function definition. In this case, both the return value and the arguments are **void**, but you'll soon see examples of other data types. If the data types don't agree, you'll get unhappy messages from the compiler.

> A *prototype* declares a function
> A *function call* executes a function
> A function *definition* is the function itself

Local Variables

The variable **j** used in the **line()** function is known only to **line()**; it is invisible to the **main()** function. If we added this statement to **main()** (without declaring a variable **j** there):

```
printf("%d", j);
```

we'd get a compiler error because **main()** wouldn't know anything about this variable. We could declare another variable, also called **j**, in the **main()** function; it would be a completely separate variable, known to **main()** but not to **line()**. This is a key point in the writing of C functions: variables used in a function are unknown outside the function. The question of which functions know about a variable and which don't is called the "visibility" of the variable. A local variable will be visible to the function it is defined in, but not to others.

A local variable used in this way in a function is known in C as an "automatic" variable, because it is automatically created when a function is called and destroyed when the function returns. The length of time a variable lasts is called its "lifetime." We'll have more to say about visibility and lifetime in Chapter 14, when we discuss storage types.

A Sound Example

Let's reinforce our understanding of functions with another example. This one uses the special character '\x7', which is called BELL in the standard ASCII code. On the PC, printing this character, instead of ringing a bell, causes a beeping sound. Here's the program:

```
/* beeptest.c */
/* tests the twobeep function */
void twobeep(void);          /* function prototype */

void main(void)
{
    twobeep();               /* function call */
    printf("Type any character: ");
    getche();                /* wait for keypress */
    twobeep();               /* function call */
}

/* twobeep() function definition */
/* beeps the speaker twice */
void twobeep(void)           /* function declarator */
```

```
{
    long j;

    printf("\x7");            /* first beep */
    for (j=1; j<100000; j++)  /* delay */
        ;                     /* (null statement) */
    printf("\x7");            /* second beep */
}
```

This program first calls a subroutine, **twobeep()**, which does just what its name says: it sounds two beeps separated by a short silent interval. Then the program asks you to strike a key; when you do, it sounds the two beeps again.

Note how the delay is constructed: A **for** loop is set up to cycle 100,000 times. However, there is no body of program statements in this loop. Instead, there is a statement consisting of only the semicolon. This constitutes a "null" statement: a statement with nothing in it. It's only role is to terminate the **for** loop. If you are using a slower computer with an 8088 or 8086 micro-processor, you may want to decrease the delay by making the constant smaller: 20,000 or even 5,000.

Functions That Return a Value

Let's look at a slightly more complicated kind of function: one that returns a value. An analogy can be made here with hiring someone to find out something for you. In a way, you do this when you dial 767-8900 to find out what time it is. You make the call, the person (or computer) on the other end of the line gives you the time, and that's that. You don't need to tell them what you want; that's understood when you call that number. No information flows from you to the phone company, but some flows from it back to you.

A function that uses no arguments but returns a value performs a similar role. You call the function, it gets a certain piece of information and returns it to you. The function **getche()** operates in just this way; you call it—without giving it any information—and it returns the value of the first character typed on the keyboard.

Suppose we wanted a function that returned a character as **getche()** does, but that also automatically translated any uppercase characters into lowercase. Such a function, with a calling program that uses a **switch** statement to create a rudimentary menu program, is shown below:

```
/* getlow.c */
/* tests getlc function */
char getlc(void);    /* function prototype */

void main(void)
```

```
{
   char chlc;           /* char returned */

   printf("Type 'a' for first selection, 'b' for second: ");
   chlc = getlc();    /* get converted character */
   switch (chlc)       /* print msg, depending on char */
      {
      case 'a':
         printf("\nYou typed an 'a'.");
         break;
      case 'b':
         printf("\nYou typed a 'b'.");
         break;
      default:
         printf("\nYou chose a non-existent selection.");
      }
}


/* getlc */
/* returns character */
/* converts to lowercase if in uppercase */
char getlc(void)
{
   char ch;                 /* char from keyboard */

   ch = getche();           /* get character */
   if ( ch>64 && ch<91 )    /* if it's uppercase, */
      ch = ch + 32;         /* add 32 to convert to lower */
   return (ch);             /* return character to caller */
}
```

Our new function, **getlc()** (for "get lowercase"), returns a value of type **char**. The return type is no longer **void** as in previous examples. Notice that both the prototype and the declarator in the function definition begin with **char** to reflect this fact. The **getlc()** function is called from the main program with the statement:

```
chlc = getlc();
```

Just as in the case of **getche()**, the function itself appears to "take on the value" it is returning. It can thus be used as if it were a variable in an assignment statement, and the value returned (a lowercase character) will be assigned to the variable **chlc**, which is then used in the **switch** statement to determine which message will be printed. Here are examples of output from the program:

```
Type 'a' for first selection, 'b' for second: a
You typed an 'a'.

Type 'a' for first selection, 'b' for second: A
You typed an 'a'.

Type 'a' for first selection, 'b' for second: c
You chose a nonexistent selection.
```

Notice how the capital 'A' typed by the user is successfully converted to lowercase. (We should mention that Turbo C includes library functions for case conversion: **toupper()** and **tolower()**.)

The *return* Statement

In the textbox.c and beeptest.c programs shown earlier, the functions returned (jumped back to) the calling program when they encountered the final closing brace (}) which defined the end of the function. No separate "return" statement was necessary.

This approach is fine if the function is not going to return a value to the calling program. In the case of our menu.c program, however, we want to return the value of the character read from the keyboard. In fact, we want to return one of two possible values: the character itself, if it is in lowercase already, or a modified version of the character, if it is in uppercase. So we use the **if** statement to check if **ch** is in uppercase (uppercase letters run from ASCII 65 to 90). If so, we add 32 (the difference between ASCII's 'A' = 65 and 'a' = 97) to **ch**. Finally, we return to the calling program with the new value of the character, by placing the variable name between the parentheses following **return()**.

The **return()** statement has two purposes. First, executing it immediately transfers control from the function back to the calling program. And second, whatever is inside the parentheses following **return** is returned as a value to the calling program.

Figure 5-4 shows a function returning a value to the calling program.

The **return** statement need not be at the end of the function. It can occur anywhere in the function; as soon as it's encountered, control will return to the calling program. For instance, we could have rewritten the **getlc()** function like this:

```
/* getlc() */
/* returns character */
/* converts to lowercase if in uppercase */
char getlc(void)
{
    char ch;                /* char from keyboard */
```

```
ch = getche();          /* get character */
if ( ch>64 && ch<91 )   /* if it's uppercase, */
    return(ch + 32);    /* add 32 to convert to lower */
else
    return (ch);        /* return character to caller */
}
```

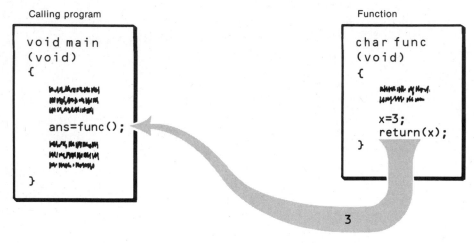

Figure 5-4. Function Returning a Value

Here different **return** statements will be used depending on whether **ch** is uppercase or not.

The **return** statement can also be used without the parentheses. When this is the case, no value is returned to the calling program.

Returning Type *int*

Here's another example of a function that returns a value, this time of type **int**. This example, called **getmins()**, gets a time in hours and minutes from the user. The main program uses this function to calculate the difference in seconds between two times:

minute

```
/* intimes.c */
/* calculates difference between two times */
int getmins(void);                       /* func prototype */
```

```
void main(void)
{
   int mins1, mins2;                     /* minutes */

   printf("Type first time (form 3:22): ");
   mins1 = getmins();                    /* get minutes */
   printf("Type second (later) time: ");
   mins2 = getmins();                     /* get minutes */
                                  /* find difference */
   printf("Difference is %d minutes.", mins2-mins1 );
}

/* getmins() */
/* gets time in hours:minutes format */
/* returns time in minutes */
int getmins(void)
{
   int hours, minutes;

   scanf("%d:%d", &hours, &minutes);  /* get user input */
   return ( hours*60 + minutes );     /* convert to minutes */
}
```

Essentially, what the function **getmins** does is accept a time in hours and minutes from the user and convert it into minutes by multiplying the hours by 60 and adding the minutes. There is one new wrinkle in the use of the **scanf()** function, however.

New Wrinkle in scanf()

If you are very attentive you may have noticed something new in the **scanf()** statement: there is a *colon* between the two format specifiers, %d and %d, rather than a space as in the past.

```
scanf("%d:%d", &hours, &minutes);
```

This has the effect of requiring the user to type a colon between the two numbers for the two %d's, rather than permitting only whitespace characters (space, tab, newline). Thus, the user can type the time in standard hours and minutes format, using a colon to separate them. Here's a sample session with intimes.c:

```
Type first time (form 3:22): 6:00
Type second (later) time: 7:45
Difference is 105 minutes.
```

You may notice that **scanf()** is not a very forgiving function; if you type anything but a colon, **scanf()** will terminate immediately without waiting for the minutes to be typed and without giving you any warning that it's doing so. A truly user-friendly program would add some code to give better feedback to the user.

Returning Type *float*

Here's an example in which a function returns type **float**.

In this program, the **main()** function asks the user for the radius of a sphere, and then calls a function named **area()** to calculate the area of the sphere. The **area()** function returns the area of the sphere in the form of a floating point value.

```
/* sphere.c */
/* calculates area of a sphere */
float area(float);     /* prototype */

void main(void)
{
    float radius;

    printf("Enter radius of sphere: ");
    scanf("%f", &radius);
    printf("Area of sphere is %.2f", area(radius) );
}

/* area() */
/* returns area of sphere */
float area(float rad)
{
    return( 4 * 3.14159 * rad * rad );
}
```

Let's take a look at a sample of interaction with the sphere.c program:

```
Enter radius of sphere: 10
Area of sphere is 1256.64

Enter radius of sphere: 4000
Area of sphere is 201061760.00
```

The last example calculates the approximate surface area of the earth: a little over 200 million square miles. With so much space available, it's surprising people are willing to pay such high prices for land in Manhattan.

Limitation of *return()*

Before we move on to other things, you should be aware of a key limitation in the use of the **return()** statement: you can only use it to return *one value*. If you want your function to return two or more values to the calling program, you need another mechanism. In the following sections we'll see how, using arguments, it's possible to pass more than one piece of information *to* a function. However, getting more than one piece of information back will be a topic for a later chapter, since it requires a knowledge of the concepts of addresses and pointers.

> Using a **return** statement, only one value can be returned by a function.

Using Arguments to Pass Data to a Function

So far the functions we've used haven't been very flexible. We call them and they do what they're designed to do, either returning a value or not. Like our lawn person who always mows the grass exactly the same way, we can't influence them in the way they carry out their tasks. It would be nice to have a little more control over what functions do, in the same way it would be nice to be able to tell the lawn person, "Just do the front yard today, we're having a barbecue out back."

The mechanism used to convey information to a function is the *argument*. You've already used arguments in **printf()** and **scanf()** functions; the format strings and the values used inside the parentheses in these functions are arguments.

Here's an example of a program in which a single argument is passed to a user-written function:

```
/* bargraph.c */
/* draws bargraph, demonstrates function arguments */
void bar(int);            /* function prototype */

void main(void)
{
    printf("Terry\t");        /* print name */
    bar(27);                  /* draw line 27 chars long */
    printf("Chris\t");        /* print name */
    bar(41);                  /* draw line 41 chars long */
    printf("Reggie\t");       /* and so on */
```

```
        bar(34);
        printf("Cindy\t");
        bar(22);
        printf("Harold\t");
        bar(15);
    }

/* bar() */
/* function draws horizontal bar, 'score' characters long */
void bar(int score)          /* function declarator */
{
    int j;

    for(j=1; j<=score; j++)    /* draw 'score' number of */
        printf("\xCD");        /* double-line characters */
    printf("\n");              /* newline at end of bar */
}
```

This program generates a bargraph of names and bars representing, say, the scores in a spelling test. The output of the program is shown in Figure 5-5.

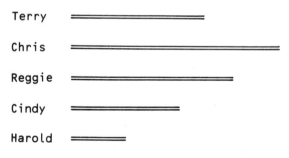

Figure 5-5. Output of the bargraph.c Program

In this program the purpose of the function **bar()** is to draw a horizontal line, made up of the double-line graphics character ('\xCD') on the screen. For each person (Terry, Chris, etc.), the main program prints the name and then calls the function, using as an argument the score received by that person on the test.

Structure of a Function Call with Arguments

There are a number of things to notice about this program. First, in the main program, the number we want to pass to the function **bar()** is included in the parentheses following "bar" in the function call:

```
    bar(27);
```

We could have used a variable name instead of the constant 27; we'll see an example of this shortly.

In the function definition, a variable name **score** is placed in the parentheses following "bar":

```
void bar(int score)
```

This ensures that the value included between parentheses in the main program is assigned to the variable between parentheses in the function definition. This is shown schematically in Figure 5-6. Notice that the data type of **score** is also specified in the function definition. This constitutes a definition of the argument variable, setting aside memory space for it in the function.

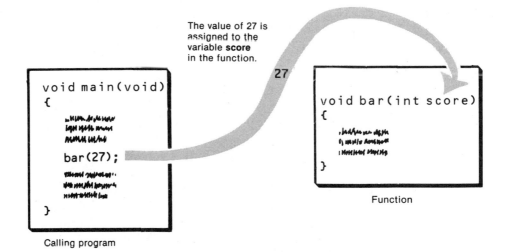

Figure 5-6. Passing a Value to a Function

The structure of a function with an argument is shown in Figure 5-7 on the next page.

Passing Variables as Arguments

In the example above we passed *constants* (such as the number 27) as an argument to the function **bar()**. We can also use a *variable* in the calling program, as this variation on the bargraph.c program demonstrates:

```
/* bargr2.c */
/* draws bargraph, demonstrates function arguments */
void bar(int inscore);              /* function prototype */
                                    /*    with identifier */
```

151

```
void main(void)
{
    int inscore=1;

    while ( inscore != 0 )        /* exit on zero score */
        {
        printf("Score=");         /* prompt the user */
        scanf("%d", &inscore);    /* get score from user */
        bar(inscore);             /* draw line */
        }
}


/* bar */
/* function to draw horizontal bar */
void bar(int score)
{
    int j;

    for(j=1; j<=score; j++)    /* draw 'score' number of */
        printf("\xCD");        /*     double-line character */
    printf("\n");             /* newline at end of bar */
}
```

```
                    Formal
                    argument                    Function
                       \                        declarator
                        \                      /
        void bar(int score)
            {
             ┌─ int j; ─────────────────────────┐
             │  for (j=1;j<=score;j++)           │
             │      printf("\xCD");              │
             │  printf("\n");                    │
            }└──────────────────────────────────┘
                         Body of
                         function
```

Figure 5-7. Function Definition with Argument

In this program the function **bar()** is the same as before. However, the main program has been modified to accept scores from the keyboard. Figure 5-8 shows a sample of interaction with the program. Entering 0 terminates it.

Since the scores we pass to **bar()** are no longer known in advance, we must use a variable to pass them to the **bar()** function. We do this in the statement:

```
bar(inscore);
```

```
Score=20
```

```
Score=30
```

```
Score=15
```

```
Score= 5
```

Figure 5-8. Output of the bargr2.c Program

Now, whatever value the user types is recorded by **scanf()** and assigned to the variable **inscore**. When **bar()** is called, this is the value passed to it as an argument. Figure 5-9 shows this process.

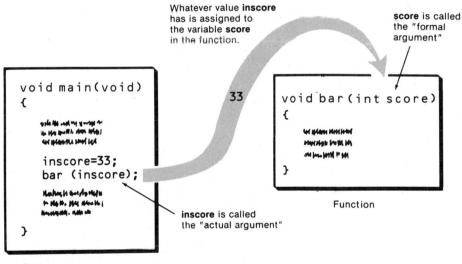

Figure 5-9. Variable Used as Argument

Different names have been assigned to the arguments in the calling and called functions: **inscore** in the calling program and **score** in the function. Actually, we could have used the same name for both variables; since they are in different functions, the compiler would still consider them to be separate variables.

Note that the argument in the calling program is referred to as the "actual argument," while the argument in the called function is the "formal argument." In this case, the variable **inscore** in the calling program is the actual argument, and the variable **score** in the function is the formal argument. Knowing these terms will not help you program better, but it may impress people at parties.

Passing Multiple Arguments

We can pass as many arguments as we like to a function. Here's an example of
a program that passes two arguments to a function, **rectang()**, whose purpose
is to draw variously sized rectangles on the screen. The two arguments are the
length and width of the rectangle, where each rectangle represents a room in a
house.

```c
/* roomplot.c */
/* tests the rectang() function */
void rectang(int, int);            /* function prototype */

void main(void)
{
    printf("\nLiving room\n");     /* print room name */
    rectang(22,12);                /* draw room */
    printf("\nCloset\n");          /* etc. */
    rectang(4,4);
    printf("\nKitchen\n");
    rectang(16,16);
    printf("\nBathroom\n");
    rectang(6,8);
    printf("\nBedroom\n");
    rectang(12,12);
}


/* rectang() */
/* draws rectangle of length, width */
/* length goes across screen, width goes up-and-down */
void rectang(int length, int width)
{
    int j, k;

    length /= 2;                   /* horizontal scale factor */
    width /= 4;                    /* verical scale factor */
    for (j=1; j<=width; j++)       /* number of lines */
       {
       printf("\t\t");             /* tab over */
       for (k=1; k<=length; k++)   /* line of rectangles */
          printf("\xDB");          /* print one rectangle */
       printf("\n");               /* next line */
       }
}
```

This program prints the name of a room and then draws a rectangle representing the dimensions of the room. A sample of the output from the program is shown in Figure 5-10.

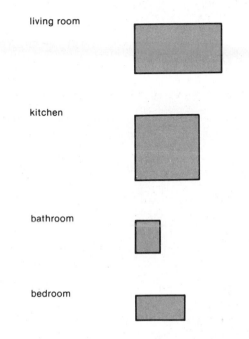

living room

kitchen

bathroom

bedroom

Figure 5-10. Output of the roomplot.c Program

The operation of the function is very much like that of the rectangle-drawing program in Chapter 3. Our new wrinkle here is the use of scale factors. These are necessary so the room dimensions can be expressed in feet. The function divides the length (the horizontal dimension on the screen) by 2 and the width (the vertical dimension) by 4. This makes it possible for a series of typical rooms to fit on the screen, and also compensates for the fact that a character on the screen is twice as high as it is long. To make a square room look square, we must divide its vertical dimension by twice as much as its horizontal dimension. The division operation for the scale factors is carried out using an assignment operator. As we saw in Chapter 2, the statement

```
length /= 2;
```

is equivalent to

```
length = length / 2;
```

The process of passing two arguments is similar to passing one. The value of the first actual argument in the calling program is assigned to the first

p 53

155

formal argument in the function, and the value of the second actual argument is assigned to the second formal argument, as shown in Figure 5-11.

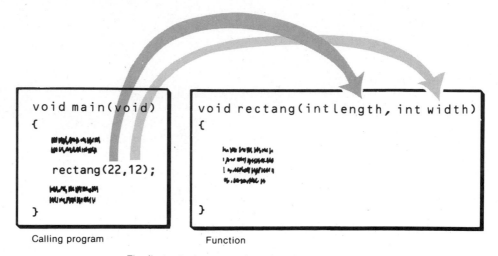

Calling program   Function

The first actual argument is assigned
to the first formal argument; the
second actual argument is assigned
to the second formal argument.

Figure 5-11. Multiple Arguments Passed to Function

Of course, three or more arguments could be used in the same way.

Using More Than One Function

You can use as many functions as you like in a program, and any of the functions can call any of the other functions. There is an important difference here between C and Pascal. In Pascal, a function (or a procedure), call it Alpha, can be defined *inside* another function, Beta, so that it is not visible to other functions, like Gamma, that are not in Beta. In C, however, all functions are visible to all other functions. This situation is shown in Figure 5-12.

In this respect, C is more like BASIC, where it is impossible to nest or "hide" one subroutine inside another.

In C, all functions, including **main()**, have equal status and are visible to all other functions.

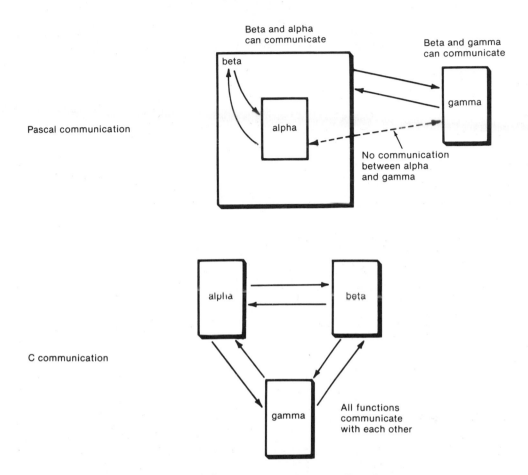

Figure 5-12. Communication Between Functions

Which approach is better? Being able to nest functions, as in Pascal, does provide some added flexibility in certain situations—you could use the same function name for two different functions, for example, which might be advantageous in large programs. However, the C approach—all functions are equal—is conceptually easier and usually doesn't result in any inconvenience to the programmer.

Let's look at a program involving several functions. This program calculates the sum of the squares of two integers typed in by the user. The program actually uses three functions as well as **main()**. The first function does the actual calculation, while **main()** simply gets the numbers from the user and prints out the result. The second function returns the square of a number (the number multiplied by itself), and the third function returns the sum of two numbers.

```
/* multifun.c */
/* tests sumsqr() function */

int sumsqr(int, int);              /* function prototypes */
int sqr(int);
int sum(int, int);

void main(void)
{
    int num1, num2;                /* user-supplied values */

    printf("Type two numbers: ");   /* gets two numbers, */
    scanf("%d %d", &num1, &num2);   /* prints sum of squares */
    printf("Sum of the squares is %d", sumsqr(num1,num2) );
}

/* sumsqr function */
/* returns sum of squares of two arguments */
int sumsqr(int j,int k)
{
    return( sum( sqr(j), sqr(k) ) );
}

/* sqr function */
/* returns square of argument */
int sqr(int z)
{
    return(z * z);
}

/* sum function */
/* returns sum of two arguments */
int sum(int x, int y)
{
    return(x + y);
}
```

Notice that none of the functions is nested inside any other. In Pascal, we could have placed, for instance, the **sum()** and **sqr()** functions inside the **sumsqr()** function. In C, all the functions are visible to all other functions. The main program, for instance, could call **sum()** or **sqr()** directly if it needed to.

Another point to note is that functions can appear in any order in the program listing. They can be arranged alphabetically, in the order in which they are called, by functional group, or any other way the programmer wishes.

Arranging the functions in an order that makes them easier to refer to can be a real advantage for the programmer, especially in larger programs with dozens of functions. Note too that the **main()** function does not need to be the first one in the program, although it usually is.

External Variables

So far, the variables we have used in our example programs have been confined to the functions using them; that is, they have been "visible" or accessible only to the function in which they were declared. Such variables, which are declared inside a particular function and used only there, are called "local" (or "automatic") variables. While local variables are preferred for most purposes, it is sometimes desirable to use a variable known to *all* the functions in a program rather than just one. This is true when many different functions must read or modify a variable, making it clumsy or impractical to communicate the value of the variable from function to function using arguments and return values. In this case, we use an "external" variable (sometimes called a "global" variable).

Here's an example of a program that uses an external variable:

```
/* extern.c */
/* tests use of external variables */
void oddeven(void);                /* function prototypes */
void negative(void);

int keynumb;                       /* external variable */

void main(void)
{
    printf("Type keynumb: ");
    scanf("%d", &keynumb);
    oddeven();                     /* function call */
    negative();                    /* function call */
}

/* oddeven() */
/* checks if keynumb is odd or even */
void oddeven(void)
{
    if ( keynumb % 2 )             /* reference external var */
        printf("Keynumb is odd.\n");
    else
        printf("Keynumb is even.\n");
```

```
}

/* negative() */
/* checks if keynumb is negative */
void negative(void)
{
    if ( keynumb < 0 )                 /* reference external var */
        printf("Keynumb is negative.\n");
    else
        printf("Keynumb is positive.\n");
}
```

In this program, **main()** and two other functions, **oddeven()** and **negative()**, all have access to the variable **keynumb**. To achieve this new global status for **keynum**, it was necessary to declare it *outside* of all of the functions, including **main()**. Thus it appears following the two title comment lines, but before the definition of **main()**.

Here's a sample interaction with the program:

```
Type keynumb: -21
Keynumb is odd.
Keynumb is negative.


Type keynumb: 44
Keynumb is even.
Keynumb is positive.
```

As you can see, **main()** is able to place a value in the variable **keynumb**, and both **oddeven()** and **negative()** are able to read the value of the variable.

There is more to be said about the visibility of variables to various functions and the related question of how long a variable lasts: its *lifetime*. These questions relate to another important topic: C's capability of combining separately compiled object files together at link time into a single executable program. We'll return to these topics in Chapter 15.

We should, however, point out the dangers of indiscriminate use of external variables. It may seem tempting to simplify things by making all variables external; BASIC programmers in particular tend to fall victim to this practice. However, there are several reasons why it is not a good idea. First, external variables are not protected from accidental alteration by functions that have no business modifying them. Second, as we'll see in Chapter 15, external variables use memory less efficiently than local variables. The rule is that variables should be local unless there's a very good reason to make them external.

Prototype Versus Classical K and R

When Kernighan and Ritchie defined the C language in their 1978 book (see the bibliography), they did not include function prototypes. Prototypes are a refinement introduced by the recent ANSI standard, and should be used in all new programs. However, many existing programs were written using the older K and R approach, so you should be familiar with it. Also, comparing the prototype system with the classical K and R approach helps to clarify the advantages of prototypes.

Examples of the Two Approaches

Let's look at two versions of a single program. The first uses the prototype approach:

```
/* proto.c */
/* uses prototyping */
void func(int);                  /* function prototype */

void main(void)                  /* return type for main() */
{
   int actarg = 1234;

   func(actarg);                 /* function call */
}

/* func() */
/* function prints out value of argument */
void func(int formarg)           /* function declarator */
{                                /*    and variable declaration */
   printf("Argument is %d", formarg);
}
```

There should be no surprises here. The **main()** function passes a value to **func()**, which prints it out.

Now let's look at the K and R approach, without prototypes:

```
/* noproto.c */
/* program doesn't use prototyping */
main()                                   /* no prototype */
{
   int actarg = 1234;
   func(actarg);                         /* function call */
}
```

```
/* func() */
/* function prints out value of argument */
func(formarg)                           /* function declarator */
int formarg;                            /* declare argument */
{
    printf("Argument is %d", formarg);
}
```

Although it uses the obsolete format, this program will still compile and run in Turbo C++. The ANSI standard, to which Turbo C++ adheres, allows the old-style approach so that older source files can be compiled. Turbo C++ does generate warning messages to let you know if you're not ANSI compatible.

There are two major differences between nonproto.c and proto.c. First, as its name implies, noproto.c does not use a prototype for the function. This works, provided that the function returns a value of type **int**. If the function returns any other type, such as **float**, then it must have a prototype. However, the prototype need not include the data types of the arguments. To be ANSI compatible, the prototype must include the data types of the arguments.

The second major difference is that the function declarator and the definition of the function parameters are on separate lines. This has the same effect as the single-line ANSI approach, but it is not so intuitive, and it doesn't match the format of the prototype (if there is one).

Advantages of Prototyping

Why were prototypes adopted for the ANSI standard? Their major advantage is that the data types of a function's arguments are clearly specified at the beginning of a program. A common error in K and R programs was to call a function using the wrong data type for an argument; **int**, for example, instead of **long**. If the function call and the function definition were in different files, this lead to program failure in a way that was very difficult to debug, because there was no warning from the compiler. When a prototype is used, however, the compiler knows what data types to expect as arguments for the function, and is always able to flag a mismatch as an error. Also—as in declaring variables—the prototype clarifies for the programmer and anyone else looking at the listing what each function is and what its arguments should be.

The ANSI standard introduced type **void** for functions that didn't return anything. Previously, a function that didn't return anything was considered to be type **int** by default, an inconsistent and potentially confusing approach. This is why Turbo C++ generates warning messages for noproto.c: in the absence of prototypes, it assumes **main()** and **func()** are type **int**, but sees that they don't return a value of this (or any) type.

ANSI also introduced **void** as meaning that the function takes no arguments, thus removing a another potential source of confusion.

Argument Names in the Declarator

ANSI C makes another service available to the programmer. Argument names can be used in the prototype as a reminder of what the function arguments are. So far we've shown prototypes without these names. For instance, in the roomplot.c example, the prototype is

```
void rectang(int, int);
```

This conforms to ANSI C, in that it tells the compiler the data types of the arguments. However, a human being reading the source code may be confused as to which argument is which, because they both have the same data type. This can be inconvenient, especially when the prototypes and the functions are in different files, and the function itself may not be readily accessible. To clarify the situation, the prototype can be changed to

```
void rectang(int length, int width);
```

Not only is this clearer, it also matches exactly the declarator in the function definition. You may want to use this approach all the time; you certainly should use it in multifile programs with functions taking multiple arguments of the same data type.

What About *main()*?

Although prototypes are specified for all functions, we don't use one for **main()**. You can do this if you want, but, because **main()** is a special case, it's not necessary. Turbo C doesn't generate error messages if you neglect a prototype for **main()**.

You can also leave out the **void** used to specify the arguments to **main()** without eliciting any error messages. In subsequent programs, however, we will use arguments to **main()**, so inserting the **void** makes it clear that we didn't just forget the arguments; we are deliberately not using them.

Preprocessor Directives

At this point, we'll shift gears a little and explore a topic which at first glance might not seem to have much to do with functions: the use of *preprocessor directives*. Preprocessor directives form what can almost be considered a language within the language of C. This is a capability that does not exist in many other higher-level languages (although there are similar features in assembly language).

To understand preprocessor directives, let's first review what a compiler does. When you write a line of program code

```
num = 44;
```

you are asking the compiler to translate this code into machine-language instructions that can be executed by the microprocessor chip in the computer. Thus, most of your listing consists of instructions to the microprocessor. Preprocessor directives, on the other hand, are instructions *to the compiler itself*. Rather than being translated into machine language, they are operated on directly by the compiler before the compilation process even begins; hence the name *pre*processor.

> Normal program statements are instructions to the microprocessor; preprocessor directives are instructions to the compiler.

Here we'll examine two of the most common preprocessor directives, **#define** and **#include**. There are others, some of which we'll look at in Chapter 14.

Preprocessor directives always start with a number sign (#). The directives can be placed anywhere in a program, but are most often used at the beginning of a file, before **main()**, or before the beginning of particular functions.

The #define Directive

The simplest use for the **define** directive is to assign names (DAYS_YEAR or PI, for instance) to constants (such as 365 or 3.14159). As an example, let's modify the sphere.c program from earlier in the chapter. In its original incarnation, the constant 3.14159 appeared in this program in the **area()** function in the line

```
return( 4 * 3.14159 * rad * rad );
```

Here's the modified program:

```
/* sphere2.c */
/* calculates area of a sphere */

#define PI 3.14159                    /* #define directive */
```

```
float area(float);                    /* prototype */

void main(void)
{
   float radius;

   printf("Enter radius of sphere: ");
   scanf("%f", &radius);
   printf("Area of sphere is %.2f", area(radius) );
}

/* area() */
/* returns area of sphere */
float area(float rad)
{
   return( 4 * PI * rad * rad );    /* use of identifier */
}
```

In this new version, the preprocessor first looks for all program lines beginning with the number sign (#). When it sees the **#define** directive, it goes through the entire program, and at every place it finds PI it *substitutes* the phrase 3.14159. This is a mechanical process: simply the substituting of one group of characters, "3.14159," for another, "PI." It's very much like a word processsor's "global search and replace." Figure 5-13 shows the structure of the **#define** directive.

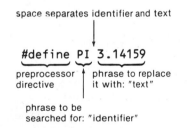

Figure 5-13. Structure of the **#define** Directive

The phrase on the left (PI), which will be searched *for*, is called the "identifier." The phrase on the right (3.14159), which will be substituted for it, is called the "text." A space separates the identifier from the text. By convention, the identifier (in this case, PI) is written in all caps. This makes it easy when looking at the listing to tell which parts of the program will be altered by **#define** directives.

Why Use #define?

Perhaps you wonder what we've gained by substituting PI for 3.14159 in our program. Hopefully, we've made the program easier to read. Although such a common constant as 3.14159 is easily recognized, there are many instances where a constant does not reveal its purpose so readily. For example, as we'll find out later, the phrase "\x1B[C" causes the cursor to move one space to the right. But which would you find easier to understand in the middle of your program, "\x1B[C", or "CURSOR_RIGHT"? Thus, we would use the **#define** directive

```
#define CURSOR_RIGHT "\x1B[C"
```

Then whenever CURSOR_RIGHT appeared in the program, it would automatically be replaced by "\x1B[C" before compilation began.

There is another, perhaps more important reason for using the **#define** directive in this way. Suppose a constant like 3.14159 appears many times in your program. Further suppose that you now decide you want an extra place of precision; you need to change all instances of 3.14159 to 3.141592. Ordinarily, you would need to go through the program and manually change each occurrence of the constant. However, if you have defined 3.14159 to be PI in a **#define** directive, you only need to make one change, in the **#define** directive itself:

```
#define PI 3.141592
```

The change will be made automatically to all occurrences of PI before compilation begins.

Why Not Use Variable Names?

Couldn't we use a variable like **int** or **float** for the same purpose as a **#define** directive? A variable could also provide a meaningful name for a constant, and permit one change to effect many occurrences of the constant. It's true, a variable can be used in this way. However, there are at least three reasons why it's a bad idea. First, it is inefficient, since the compiler can generate faster and more compact code for constants than it can for variables. Second, using a variable for what is really a constant encourages sloppy thinking and makes the program more difficult to understand: if something never changes, it is confusing to make it a variable. And third, there is always the danger that a variable will be altered inadvertently during execution of the program, so that it is no longer the "constant" you think it is.

In other words, using **#define** can produce more efficient and more easily understood programs. It is used extensively by C programmers—you'll see many examples as we go along.

The const *Modifier*

The new ANSI standard C defines a modifier, **const**, that can be used to achieve almost the same effect as **#define** when creating constants. Here's how it looks:

```
const float PI = 3.141592;
```

This statement creates a variable of type **float** and gives it the value 3.141592, similar to a normal function declaration. However, the **const** tells the compiler not to permit any changes to the variable. So if you try to modify **PI** you'll get an error message from the compiler. This approach is gaining in popularity.

Macros

The **#define** directive is actually considerably more powerful than we have shown so far. This additional power comes from **#define**'s ability to use *arguments*. Before we tackle this, let's look at one more example of **#define** without an argument to make the transition clearer. In this example we show that **#define** can be used, not only for constants, but to substitute for any phrase we like. Suppose your program needs to print the message "Error" at several places in the program. You use the directive:

```
#define ERROR printf("\nError.\n");
```

Then if you have a program statement such as

```
if (input > 640)
    ERROR
```

it will be expanded into

```
if (input > 640)
    printf("\nError.\n");
```

by the preprocessor before compilation begins. The moral here is that an identifier defined by **#define** can be used as an entire C statement.

Now let's look at an example of **#define** with an argument. If you've ever thought that the **printf()** function makes you go to a lot of trouble just to print a number, consider this alternative:

```
/* macroprn.c */
/* demonstrates macros, using printf() statements */

#define PR(n) printf("%.2f\n", n);  /* macro definition */
```

```
void main(void)
{
   float num1 = 27.25;
   float num2;

   num2 = 1.0 / 3.0;
   PR(num1);                              /* calls to macro */
   PR(num2);
}
```

Here's the output of the program:

```
C>macroprn
27.25
0.33
```

You can see that our abbreviated version of the **printf()** statement, **PR(n)**, actually prints out the two numbers.

In this program, whenever the preprocessor sees the phrase "PR(n)" it expands it into the C statement:

```
printf("%.2f\n",n);
```

A **#define** directive can take arguments, much as a function does.

However, that's not all it does. In the **#define** directive, the **n** in the identifier **PR(n)** is an *argument* that matches the **n** in the **printf()** statement in the text. The statement **PR(num1)** in the program causes the variable **num1** to be substituted for **n**. Thus, the phrase **PR(num1)** is equivalent to:

```
printf("%.2f\n", num1);
```

Figure 5-14 shows how this process works.

A **#define** directive that uses arguments in this way is called a "macro." Macros have some of the characteristics of functions, as will be made clearer in the next example.

Syntax note: Whenever you use a **#define** directive, you shouldn't use any spaces in the identifier. For instance,

```
#define PR (n) printf("%.2f\n",n);
```

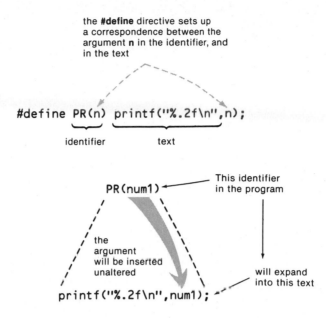

Figure 5-14. Arguments Used in the **#define** Directive

would not work, because the space between PR and (n) would be interpreted as the end of the identifier.

Macros and Functions

Macros and functions can actually perform many of the same tasks. For instance, let's modify our sphere.c program from earlier in the chapter to use a macro, instead of the function **area()**, to do the actual calculation of the area of a sphere. Here's the revised program:

```
/* sphereM.c */
/* calculates area of a sphere */
/* uses a macro */
#define PI 3.14159               /* definition of PI */
#define AREA(X) (4 * PI * X * X)  /* macro for area of sphere */

void main(void)
{
    float radius;

    printf("Enter radius of sphere: ");
    scanf("%f", &radius);
    printf( "Area of sphere is %.2f", AREA(radius) );
}
```

Here the preprocessor will substitute the text

```
(4 * 3.14159 * radius * radius)
```

for the identifier AREA(radius). Note that we've used an identifier within an identifier: AREA(radius) is expanded, and the PI within it is changed to 3.14159.

Use of Parentheses in Macros

Liberal use of parentheses in a macro can save considerable grief. Why? Suppose your program contains the following lines:

```
#define SUM(x,y) x + y
- - - - -
ans = 10 * SUM(3,4)
```

What value will **ans** be given when you run the program? You might think 3 would be added to 4, giving 7, and that result, when multiplied by 10, would yield 70. Wrong. Look at the expansion of the assignment statement. **SUM(3,4)** turns into simply **3 + 4**. Thus, the entire statement becomes:

```
ans = 10 * 3 + 4
```

Multiplication has a higher precedence than addition, so the result will be 30 + 4, or 34. This is different enough from the correct answer of 70 to suggest that we have a problem. The solution is to put parentheses around the entire text part of the **#define** directive:

```
#define SUM(x,y) (x + y)
```

Now the assignment statement is expanded into

```
ans = 10 * (3 + 4)
```

which yields the correct result.

Even enclosing the entire text in parentheses, however, does not solve all possible problems. Consider a macro that does multiplication:

```
#define PRODUCT(x,y) (x * y)
- - - - -
ans = PRODUCT(2+3,4)
```

Here the programmer was rash enough to use an expression, 2+3, as an argument for the macro. One might hope that this would yield an answer of 20 (2+3 is 5, multiplied by 4). However, look what happens in the expansion:

```
ans = (2+3*4).
```

The multiplication will be done first, so we'll have 2 + 12, or 14. Here, the solution is to enclose *each argument* in parentheses. For clarity, we did not do this in the examples above, but we should have. Suppose in the sphereM.c program we had used an expression such as **rad+3** as an argument to the AREA(radius) macro. It would have been expanded to (4 * PI * rad + 3 * rad + 3) or (4*PI*rad + 3*rad + 3), which is no way to calculate the area of a sphere of radius **rad+3**.

> For safety's sake, put parentheses around the entire text of any define directive that uses arguments and also around each of the arguments.

Thus, to be sure your macros will do what you want, enclose the entire text expression in parentheses and each variable in the text expression, as well.

When to Use Macros

Macros often can be used more conveniently than functions, as our example above demonstrates. Of course, the task to be carried out by the macro should not be too complex, as macros are essentially single statements. Assuming a fairly simple task, however, when should you use a macro and when a function?

Each time a macro is invoked, the code it generates is actually inserted in the executable file for the program. This leads to multiple copies of the same code. The code for a function, however, only appears once, so using a function is more efficient in terms of memory size. On the other hand, no time is wasted calling a macro; whereas, when you call a function, the program has to arrange for the arguments to be transferred to the function and jump to the function's code. So a function takes less memory but is slower to execute, while a macro is faster but uses more memory. You have to decide which approach suits your particular program better.

> A macro generates more code but executes more quickly than a function.

Excessive use of macros can also make a program difficult to read, since it requires constant reference back and forth between the **#define** directives at the beginning of the program and the identifiers in the program body. Deciding when to use a macro and when not to is largely a matter of style.

The *#include* Directive

The second preprocessor directive we'll explore in this chapter is **#include**. The **#include** directive causes one source file to be included in another.

Here's an example of why you might want to do such a thing. Suppose you write a lot of math-oriented programs that repeatedly refer to formulas for calculating areas of different shapes. You could place all these formulas, as macros, in a single separate source file. Then, instead of having to rewrite all the macros every time you wrote a program that used them, you could insert them into the .c source file using the **#include** directive.

Such a separate source file might look like this:

```
#define PI 3.14159
#define AREA_CIRCLE(radius) (PI*radius*radius)
#define AREA_SQUARE(length,width) (length*width)
#define AREA_TRIANGLE(base,height) (base*height/2)
#define AREA_ELLIPSE(radius1,radius2) (PI*radius1*radius2)
#define AREA_TRAPEZOID(height,side1,side2) (height*(side1+side2)/2)
```

This is not something you would want to type over and over again if you could avoid it. Instead, you type it in once with your word processor and save it as a file. You might call the file areas.h. The .h extension is commonly used for "header" files, which this is: a group of statements that will go at the head of your program.

When you write your source file for a program that needs to use these formulas, you simply include the directive

```
#include "areas.h"
```

at the beginning of your program. All the statements shown above will be added to your program as if you had typed them in.

This is very similar to a word processor or editor being used to read, say, a standard heading into a business letter. In fact in this particular instance you could have used your word processor to read the file areas.h into your source file; the effect would have been similar.

There are actually two ways to write **#include** statements. The variation in format tells the preprocessor where to look for the file you want included.

The variation shown above

```
#include "areas.h"
```

shows the filename surrounded by quotes. This causes the preprocessor to start searching for the areas.h file in the directory containing the current source file. If it doesn't find it there, it will look in other directories.

The other approach is to use angle brackets:

```
#include <areas.h>
```

This format causes the preprocessor to start searching in the standard header directory, which we'll discuss next.

Standard Header Files

The C language comes with a number of *standard header files*. These files contain definitions and macros that may be useful to a programmer in certain circumstances. They are usually grouped in a single directory called the INCLUDE directory. Although we mentioned the existence of this directory in Chapter 1, we haven't made use yet of any header files from it. However, there are many situations where it's necessary.

For instance, some quite common C library "functions" are actually macros that are defined in header files. Two examples are **getchar()** and **putchar()**, which are actually macros derived from two other functions, **getc()** and **putc()**. The file stdio.h in the INCLUDE directory contains these definitions:

```
#define  getchar()   getc(stdin)
#define  putchar(c)  putc((c),stdout)
```

We needn't concern ourselves at this point with exactly what this means; we'll learn more about *stdin* and *stdout* when we investigate files. However, if you needed to use either of these "functions" in your program, you would use the preprocessor directive:

```
#include <stdio.h>
```

Header Files and Prototyping

Another reason to use header files is to provide prototypes of library functions.

As we saw earlier in this chapter, prototypes can provide a means of avoiding type mismatches between actual arguments and formal arguments when a user-written function is called. Header files can give this same protection for library functions.

Each library function provided with Turbo C is associated with a header file: that is, a file with the extension .h that is kept in the \INCLUDE directory. The prototype for the function is part of the corresponding header file.

For example, the prototype for the **printf()** function is stored in the file studio.h (along with the prototypes for many other functions).

Thus, to ensure that you have not inadvertently called a library function using arguments of the wrong data type, you need only **#include** the appropriate header file for the function at the start of the program. The Turbo C++ library documentation, under the heading for each library function, tells which header file contains the prototype for the function.

For simplicity and compactness, we do not show **#includes** for every library function used in the example programs in this book. However, you definitely should; you will save yourself a great deal of debugging time. Do as we say, not as we do.

For example, if you use **printf()** and **getche()** in a program, include the header files STDIO.H and CONIO.H, as shown in the following listing:

```
/* header.c */
/* demonstrates correct use of header files */

#include <stdio.h>      /* for printf() */
#include <conio.h>      /* for getche() */

void main(void)
{
   printf("Type 'y' or 'n': ");
   getche();
}
```

Although you can get away with not using a prototype for library functions that return type **int**, the header file (or a handwritten prototype) must be supplied when you use library functions that return other types. This includes most of the arithmetic functions, such as **sqrt()** and **sin()**, which return type **double**. As we mentioned, errors that occur from failure to include prototypes are not flagged by the compiler and are notoriously difficult to find.

Summary

In this chapter you've learned how to use functions: how to write them, how to use them to return values, and how to send them information using arguments. You've learned that a function commonly uses local variables which are visible only within the function itself and not to other functions. You've learned, too, to use external variables, which are visible to all functions. Finally you've learned about the preprocessor directives **#define**, which can be used to give names to constants or even whole C statements, creating a functionlike capability, and **#include**, which causes one source file to be included in another.

Questions

1. Which of these are valid reasons for using functions?
   a. they use less memory than repeating the same code
   b. they run faster
   c. they keep different program activities separate
   d. they keep variables safe from other parts of the program

2. True or false: a function can still be useful even if you can't pass it any information and can't get any information back from it.

3. Is this a correct call to the function **abs()**, which takes one argument?

   ```
   ans = abs(num)
   ```

4. True or false: to return from a function you must use the keyword **return**.

5. True or false: you can return as many data items as you like from a function to the calling program, using the keyword **return()**.

6. Is this a correctly written function?

   ```
   abs(num);
   {
       int num;
       if ( num<0 )
           num = -num;
       return(num);
   }
   ```

7. Which of the following are differences between Pascal and C?
   a. Pascal uses functions and procedures, C only functions
   b. there is no way to return from a Pascal function as there is in C
   c. functions can be nested in Pascal but not in C
   d. Pascal functions are all of type **int**

8. True or false: the variables commonly used in C functions are accessible to all other functions.

9. Which of the following are valid reasons for using arguments in functions?

a. to tell the function where to locate itself in memory
b. to convey information to the function that it can operate on
c. to return information from the function to the calling program
d. to specify the type of the function

10. Which of the following can be passed to a function via arguments?
    a. constants
    b. variables (with values)
    c. preprocessor directives
    d. expressions (that evaluate to a value)
    e. functions (that return values)

11. Is the following a correctly structured program?

```
void main(void)
{
    int three=3;
    type(three);
}
void type(float num)
{
    printf("%f",num);
}
```

12. Which of the following is true?
    a. C functions are all equal
    b. C functions can be nested within each other
    c. C functions are arranged in a strict hierarchy
    d. C functions can only be called from **main()**

13. External variables can be accessed by _____ function(s) in a program.

14. An external variable is defined in a declaration
    a. in **main()** only
    b. in the first function that uses it
    c. in any function that uses it
    d. outside of any function

15. An external variable can be referenced in a declaration
    a. in **main()** only
    b. in the first function that uses it
    c. in any function that uses it
    d. outside of any function

16. What is a preprocessor directive?
    a. a message from the compiler to the programmer
    b. a message to the linker from the compiler
    c. a message from the programmer to the compiler
    d. a message from the programmer to the microprocessor

17. The **#define** directive causes one phrase to be ___ _____ for another.

18. Is this a correctly formed **#define** statement?

    `#define CM PER INCH 2.54`

19. In this **#define** directive, which is the identifier and which is the text?

    `#define EXP 2.71828`

20. What is a macro?
    a. a **#define** directive that acts like a function
    b. a **#define** directive that takes arguments
    c. a **#define** directive that returns a value
    d. a **#define** directive that simulates **scanf()**

21. A variable should not be used to store values that never change because
    a. the program will run more slowly
    b. the program will be harder to understand
    c. there is no such data type
    d. the value of the "constant" might be altered

22. Will the following code correctly calculate postage that is equal to a fixed rate times the sum of the combined girth and height of a parcel?

    ```
    #define SUM3(length,width,height) length + width + height
    - - -
    postage = rate * SUM3(l,w,h)
    ```

23. The **#include** directive causes one source file to be _____ in another.

24. A header file is
    a. a file which must precede all source code files
    b. a source code file
    c. a file that can be **#include**d in other source code files
    d. a source code file containing various definitions and macros

25. Standard header files can be found in the _____directory.

Exercises

1. Write a program that prints out the larger of two numbers entered from the keyboard. Use a function to do the actual comparison of the two numbers. Pass the two numbers to the function as arguments, and have the function return the answer with **return()**.

2. Rewrite the intimes.c program from this chapter so that instead of working only with hours and minutes, it works with hours, minutes, and seconds. Call this program times.c

3. Rewrite the times.c program from exercise 2 to use a macro instead of a function. Getting the data from the user must take place in the main program, but the conversion from hours-minutes-seconds to seconds should take place in the macro.

6

Arrays and Strings

- Arrays
- Initializing arrays
- Multidimensional arrays
- Arrays as function arguments
- Strings
- String functions

6

You might wonder why we have placed the topics of arrays and strings together in one chapter. The answer is simple: strings *are* arrays: arrays of type **char**. Thus to understand strings we need to understand arrays. In this chapter we'll cover arrays first and then move on to strings.

We should note that, in many C books and courses, arrays and strings are taught at the same time as pointers. We feel it is clearer to introduce these topics separately. Pointers will be a new concept for many readers, and it seems unfortunate to complicate the discussion of arrays and strings, which are not that different from their counterparts in other languages, by introducing pointers at the same time. We'll get to pointers soon enough: they're the subject of Chapter 7.

Arrays

If you have a collection of similar data elements, you may find it inconvenient to give each one a unique variable name. For instance, suppose you wanted to find the average temperature for a particular week. If each day's temperature had a unique variable name, you would end up reading in each value separately:

```
printf("Enter Sunday temperature: ");
scanf("%d", &suntmp);
printf("Enter Monday temperature: ");
scanf("%d", &montmp);
- - - - -
```

and so on, for each day of the week, with an expression for the average such as this:

$$(suntmp + montmp + tuestmp + wedtmp + thutmp + fritmp + sattmp)/7$$

This is an altogether unwieldy business, especially if you want to average the temperatures for a month or a year.

Clearly we need a convenient way to refer to such collections of similar data elements. The array fills the bill. It provides a way to refer to individual items in a collection by using the same variable name, but differing *subscripts*, or numbers. Let's see how we'd solve our problem of averaging the temperatures for a week using arrays:

```c
/* temp.c */
/* averages one week's temperatures */
void main(void)
{
   int temper[7];                /* array definition */
   int day, sum;

   for (day=0; day<7; day++)     /* put temps in array */
      {
      printf("Enter temperature for day %d: ", day);
      scanf("%d", &temper[day]);
      }

   sum = 0;                      /* calculate average */
   for (day=0; day<7; day++)
      sum += temper[day];
   printf("Average is %d.", sum/7);
}
```

This program reads in seven temperatures, stores them in an array, shown symbolically in Figure 6-1, and then, to calculate an average temperature, reads them back out of the array, adding them together, and dividing by 7. Here's a sample run:

```
Enter temperature for day 0: 74
Enter temperature for day 1: 76
Enter temperature for day 2: 77
Enter temperature for day 3: 77
Enter temperature for day 4: 64
Enter temperature for day 5: 66
Enter temperature for day 6: 69
Average is 71.
```

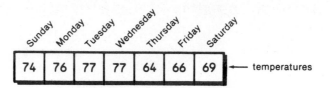

Figure 6-1. Symbolic Representation of an Array

(Meteorology buffs will notice that temperatures rose slowly during the first part of this particular week in August and that a cold front passed through on Wednesday night.)

There's a lot of new material in this program, so let's take it apart slowly.

Array Definition

An array is a collection of variables of a certain type, placed contiguously in memory. Like other variables, the array needs to be defined, so the compiler will know what kind of array, and how large an array, we want. We do that in the example above with the line:

```
int temper[7];
```

Here the **int** specifies the type of variable, just as it does with simple variables, and the word **temper** is the name of the variable. The [7], however, is new. This number tells *how many* variables of type **int** will be in our array. (Each of the separate variables in the array is called an "element.") The brackets tell the compiler that we are dealing with an array. Figure 6-2 is a schematic representation of what the array looks like.

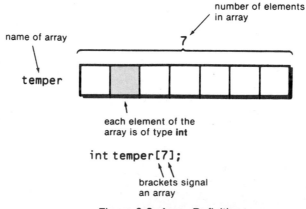

Figure 6-2. Array Definition.

Referring to Individual Elements of the Array

Once the array has been established, we need a way to refer to its individual elements. This is done with subscripts, the numbers in brackets following the array name. Note, however, that this number has a different meaning when *referring* to an array element than it does when *defining* the array, when the number in brackets is the size of the array. When referring to an array element, this number specifies the element's position in the array. All the array elements are numbered, starting at 0. The element of the array with the number 2 would be referred to as:

```
temper[2]
```

Note that, because the <u>numbering starts with 0</u>, this is *not* the second element of the array, but the third. Thus, the last array element is one less than the size of the array. This arrangement is shown in Figure 6-3.

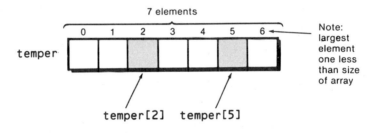

Figure 6-3. Array References

In our program we are using an integer *variable*, **day**, as a subscript to refer to the various elements of the array. This variable can take on any value we want and so can point to the different array elements in turn. This ability to use variables as subscripts is what makes arrays so useful.

```
temper[day]
```

Entering Data into the Array

Here's the section of code that places data into the array:

```
for (day=0; day<7; day++)        /* put temps in array */
   {
   printf("Enter temperature for day %d: ", day);
   scanf("%d", &temper[day]);
   }
```

The **for** loop causes the process of asking for and receiving a temperature from the user to be repeated seven times. The first time through the loop, **day** has the value 0, so the **scanf()** statement will cause the value typed in to be stored in array element **temper[0]**, the first element of the array. This process will be repeated until **day** becomes 6. That is the last time through the loop, which is a good thing, because there is no array element **temper[7]**.

> The first element in an array is numbered 0, so the last element is 1 less than the size of the array.

This is a common idiom in C for dealing with arrays: a **for** loop that starts with 0 and goes up to, but does not include (note the "less-than" sign), the size of the array.

In the **scanf()** statement, we've used the address operator (&) on the element of the **&temper[day]** array, just as we've used it earlier on other variables (**&num**, for example) to be read in by the **scanf()** function. In so doing, we're passing the *address* of this particular array element to the function, rather than its value; this is what **scanf()** requires.

Reading Data from the Array

The balance of the program reads the data back out of the array and uses it to calculate an average. The **for** loop is much the same, but now the body of the loop causes each day's temperature to be added to a running total called **sum**. When all the temperatures have been added up, the result is divided by 7, the number of data items.

```
sum = 0;                        /* calculate average */
for (day=0; day<7; day++)
    sum += temper[day];
printf("Average is %d.", sum/7);
```

Using Different Variable Types

Although the example above used an array of type **int**, an array can be of any variable type. As an example, let's rewrite temp.c to be of type **float**:

```
/* fltemp.c */
/* averages one week's temperatures */
void main(void)
{
    float temper[7];            /* array definition */
```

```
float sum;
int day;

for (day=0; day<7; day++)        /* put temps in array */
   {
   printf("Enter temperature for day %d: ", day);
   scanf("%f", &temper[day]);
   }

sum = 0;                          /* calculate average */
for (day=0; day<7; day++)
   sum += temper[day];
printf("Average is %.1f", sum/7.0);
}
```

This program operates in much the same way as temp.c, except that now it can accept numbers with decimal fractions as input and so can calculate a more precise average. Here's a sample run:

```
Enter temperature for day 0: 80.5
Enter temperature for day 1: 78.2
Enter temperature for day 2: 67.4
Enter temperature for day 3: 71.4
Enter temperature for day 4: 74.6
Enter temperature for day 5: 78.3
Enter temperature for day 6: 80.1
Average is 75.8
```

We had a cooling trend in the middle of the week, with ideal beach temperatures on the weekends.

We've changed the array (and the variable **sum**) to type **float**, and we've altered the format specifiers in the **scanf()** and **printf()** statements accordingly.

Reading in an Unknown Number of Elements

So far we've worked with a fixed amount of input, requiring a data item for each of the days of the week. What if we don't know in advance how many items will be entered into the array? Here's a program that will accept any number of temperatures—up to 40—and average them:

```
/* fltemp2.c */
/* averages arbitrary number of temperatures */
void main(void)
```

```
{
    float temper[40];                  /* array definition */
    float sum=0.0;
    int num, day=0;

    do                                 /* put temps in array */
        {
        printf("Enter temperature for day %d: ", day);
        scanf("%f", &temper[day]);
        }
    while ( temper[day++] > 0 );

    num = day-1;                       /* number of temps entered */
    for (day=0; day<num; day++)        /* calculate average */
        sum += temper[day];
    printf("Average is %.1f", sum/num);
}
```

Here's a run in which only three temperatures are entered:

```
Enter temperature for day 0: 71.3
Enter temperature for day 1: 80.9
Enter temperature for day 2: 89.2
Enter temperature for day 3: 0
Average is 80.5
```

As you can see, we've replaced the **for** loop with a **do while** loop. This loop repeatedly asks the user to enter a temperature and stores the responses in the array **temper**, until a temperature of 0 or less is entered. (Clearly, this is not a program for cold climates.) When the last item has been typed, the variable **day** will have reached a value 1 greater than the total number of items entered. This is true because it counts the 0 (or negative number), which the user entered to terminate the input. Thus to find the number of items entered, **num**, we subtract 1 from **day**. The variable **num** is then used as the limit in the second **for** loop, which adds up the temperatures, and it's also used as the divisor of the resulting sum.

There's another change in the program as well. We've used a **#define** directive to give the identifier LIM the value of 40:

```
#define LIM 40
```

We then used LIM in the array definition. Using a **#define**d value as an array size is common in C. Later, if we wish to change the size, all we need do is change the 40 in the **#define** statement, and the change will be reflected anywhere this value appears. In this particular program, the number is only used once, but we'll soon see examples in which the array dimension occurs repeatedly in the program, making the use of the **#define** directive a real convenience.

Bounds Checking

We've made the size of the array to be 40 in the **#define** directive. This is large enough to hold one month's temperatures, with some left over. But suppose a user decided to enter *two* months worth of data? As it turns out, there probably would be Big Trouble. The reason is that in C there is no check to see if the subscript used for an array exceeds the size of the array. Data entered with too large a subscript will simply be placed in memory *outside the array*: probably on top of other data or the program itself. This will lead to unpredictable results, to say the least, and there will be no error message from the compiler to warn you that it's happening.

> C does not warn you when an array subscript exceeds the size of the array.

The solution, if there's the slightest reason to believe the user might enter too many items, is to check for this possibility in the program. For instance, we could modify the **do-while** loop as follows:

```
do
   {
   if ( day >= LIM )              /* beyond array end? */
      {
      printf("Buffer full.\n");
      day++;                      /* won't be incremented later */
      break;                      /* exit loop */
      }
   printf("Enter temperature for day %d: ", day);
   scanf("%f", &temper[day]);
   }
while ( temper[day++] > 0 );
```

Now if the loop is entered with **day** equal to 40, which is 1 past the end of the buffer at 39, the message "Buffer full" will be printed and the **break** statement will take us out of the loop to the second part of the program. (We need to increment **day** since the **while** statement won't be executed.) Here's a run showing the last few lines before the user oversteps the bounds:

```
Enter temperature for day 38: 73.4
Enter temperature for day 39: 62.2
Buffer full.
Average is 75.1
```

As you can see, the temperature for day 39 is accepted, but then the program realizes that one more item would be one too many, prints the message, and **break**s out of the loop.

Initializing Arrays

So far, we've shown arrays that started life with nothing in them. Suppose we want to compile our program with specific values already fixed in the array? This is analogous to initializing a simple variable:

```
int george = 45;
```

Here's a program demonstrating the initializing of an array. The program makes change; you type in a price in cents, and the program tells you how many half-dollars, quarters, dimes, nickels, and pennies it takes to make up this amount.

```
/* change.c */
/* program to make change */

#define LIM 5
int table[LIM] = { 50, 25, 10, 5, 1 };

void main(void)
{
    int dex, amount, quantity;

    printf("Enter amount in cents (form 367): ");
    scanf("%d", &amount);
    for (dex=0; dex<LIM; dex++)
        {
        quantity = amount / table[dex];
        printf("Value of coin=%2d, ", table[dex] );
        printf("number of coins=%2d\n", quantity );
        amount = amount % table[dex];
        }
}
```

Here's a sample run:

```
Enter amount in cents (form 367): 143
Value of coin=50, number of coins= 2
Value of coin=25, number of coins= 1
Value of coin=10, number of coins= 1
Value of coin= 5, number of coins= 1
Value of coin= 1, number of coins= 3
```

The program has figured out that $1.43 is two half-dollars, one quarter, one dime, one nickel, and three pennies. This is smarter than some checkout people.

The program works by taking the value of the largest coin, 50, and dividing it into the amount typed in (the variable **amount**). It prints out the answer, which is the number of half-dollars necessary, and then it performs the same division but this time with the remainder operator (%). This remainder, in turn, is used as the new amount, which is divided by the next smallest size of coin, 25. The process is repeated five times, once for each coin.

The array is used to hold the values, expressed in cents, of the various coins. Here's the statement that initializes the array to these values:

```
int table[LIM] = { 50, 25, 10, 5, 1 };
```

The list of values is enclosed by braces, and the values are separated by commas. The values are assigned in turn to the elements of the array, so that table[0] is 50, table[1] is 25, and so on, up to table[4], which is 1.

Storage Classes and Array Initialization

You may be wondering why we put the array declaration outside of the **main()** function, thus making it an external variable. The reason is that you can't initialize an array that is a local (automatic) variable. Why not? Because C doesn't create such an array until the function containing it is called, and by then it's too late to put initial values in it.

> You can't initialize a local (automatic) array.

Thus if you want to initialize an array, it must use a variable that stays in existence for the life of the program. There are two classes of variables that do this. One is the **external** storage class, which we've used in the example above. The other is the **static** class. Unlike external variables, **static** variables are not visible outside the function in which they're declared, but like external variables, they don't disappear when the function terminates. As we noted in Chapter 5, how long a variable lasts is called its "lifetime." Lifetime, and the related idea of visibility, are characteristics of a variable's *storage class*. We'll discuss storage classes in more detail in Chapter 15.

Here's the change.c program rewritten to use a **static** variable class for the array **table**[ ]:

```
/* change2.c */
/* program to make change */
#define LIM 5

void main(void)
{
   static int table[] = { 50, 25, 10, 5, 1 };
   int dex, amount, quantity;

   printf("Enter amount in cents (form 367): ");
   scanf("%d", &amount);
   for (dex=0; dex<LIM; dex++)
      {
      quantity = amount / table[dex];
      printf("Value of coin=%2d, ", table[dex] );
      printf("number of coins=%2d\n", quantity );
      amount = amount % table[dex];
      }
}
```

This is similar to the first version, but the array definition has been moved inside the function **main()** and the word "static" has been added to it. The two programs operate in exactly the same way, but if there were other functions in the program, they would be able to access the external array in change.c, while the static array in change2.c would be invisible to them.

Array Size and Initialization

We've made another kind of change in the array definition between change.c and change2.c.

The change.c program used the value LIM (which was **#defined** as 5) in the array declaration:

```
int table[LIM] = { 50, 25, 10, 5, 1 };
```

But in change2.c this number is simply left out, leaving an empty pair of brackets following "table":

```
static int table[] = { 50, 25, 10, 5, 1 };
```

p 188

How can we get away with this? The answer is that if no number is supplied for the size of the array, the compiler will very kindly count the number of items in the initialization list and fix that as the array size.

What happens if a number *is* supplied, but it does not agree with the actual number of items on the list? If the number is larger than the number of items, the extra spaces in the array will be filled in with zeros. If the number is too small, the compiler will complain (as well it might; where could it put the leftover values?).

Array Contents and Initialization

You should also know what the initial values of array elements will be if they are not initialized explicitly. In other words, if we execute an array declaration inside the function, like this:

```
main()
{
    int array[10];
    - - - - -
```

and then, without putting anything into the array, we say

```
printf("Array element 3 has the value %d", array[3]);
```

what value will be printed out? Would you guess 0? That's close, but not right. In fact, what you'll get is a garbage number: whatever value was sitting in that particular part of memory before the function was called and the array declared. At least that's true in the case of the automatic variable declaration shown. However, if the array was declared as an external or static variable, it *will* be initialized to 0.

The lesson is that if you want your array initialized to all zeros, but don't want to do it yourself, make sure it's external or static.

More Than One Dimension

So far we've looked at arrays with only one dimension: that is, only one subscript. It's also possible for arrays to have two or more dimensions. This permits them to emulate or "model" multidimensional objects, such as graph paper with rows and columns, or the computer display screen itself.

Here's a sample program that records, not one list of data as our previous programs have, but two lists side-by-side. This program stores the travel expenses for a number of secret agents who are known only by their code numbers.

191

```
/* travel.c */
/* stores list of secret agents' travel expenses */
#define ROWS 10        /* number of rows in array */
#define COLUMNS 2      /* number of columns in array */

void main(void)
{
    float agents [ROWS] [COLUMNS];
    float number, expenses;
    int index=0, outdex;

    printf("Enter 3-digit agent numbers,\n");
    printf("then travel expenses (007 1642.50)\n");
    printf("Enter 0 0 to quit.\n");

    do                      /* get list of agents and expenses */
        {
        printf("Agent's number and expenses: ");
        scanf( "%f %f", &number, &expenses );
        agents[index][0] = number;
        agents[index][1] = expenses;
        }
    while ( agents[index++][0] != 0 );

    for (outdex=0; outdex<index-1; outdex++)  /* print list */
        {
        printf("Agent %03.0f ", agents[outdex][0] );
        printf("spent %7.2f.\n", agents[outdex][1] );
        }
}
```

There are two parts to the program: a **do-while** loop that gets the data from the user and stores it in the two-dimensional array *table*[ ][ ], and a **for** loop that prints out the contents of the array. Here's a sample run:

```
Enter 3-digit agent numbers,
then travel expense (007 1642.50)
Enter 0 0 to quit.
Agent's number and expenses: 101 2331.50
Agent's number and expenses: 007 8640
Agent's number and expenses: 901 123.25
Agent's number and expenses: 904 500.6
Agent's number and expenses: 0 0
Agent 101 spent 2331.50.
```

```
Agent   7 spent 8640.00.
Agent 901 spent  123.25.
Agent 904 spent  500.60.
```

The **do-while** loop is similar to that in the fltemp3.c program which obtained the temperature from the user. However, instead of getting only one piece of data each time through the loop, we get two; placing them in the variables **agents[index][0]** and **agents[index][1]** with the **scanf()** statement:

```
scanf( "%f %f", &agents[index][0], &agents[index][1] );
```

The first subscript is the row number, which changes for each agent. The second subscript tells which of two columns we're talking about: the one on the left, which contains the agent numbers, or the one on the right, which lists expenses for a particular month. Each subscript goes in its own set of brackets following the variable name. The array arrangement is shown in Figure 6-4.

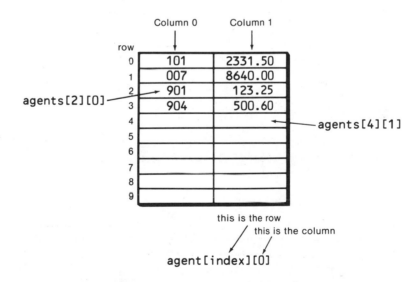

Figure 6-4. Array Used in travel.c Program

Notice that the entire array is of type **float**. We've tried to disguise this by not printing out decimal places with the agent numbers, but in reality the agent numbers are of type **float** just as the expenses are. We chose **float** because we wanted to use dollars and cents for the expenses. The ideal arrangement would be to have the agent numbers be of type **int** and the expenses of type **float**, but arrays must be of a single data type. This is an important limitation of arrays. In Chapter 9 we'll see how something called a "structure" will permit the use of multiple types in an array.

Here's a program that plots a two-dimensional grid on the screen. Initially, the grid is filled with dots (periods). But after the grid is drawn, the program then cycles through a loop asking the user for a pair of coordinates. When the user types the two coordinates (separated by a comma), the program draws a gray box at the corresponding location on the screen (or a light green or light amber box, depending on the color of your monitor).

Using this program provides a visual way to understand how a two-dimensional coordinate system works. Try typing in pairs of numbers. Where will 0,0 be plotted? How about 5,0? Or 0,5? Remember that the horizontal, or x-coordinate, is typed in first, then the vertical, or y-coordinate. Here's the listing:

```
/* plot.c */
/* plots coordinates on screen */
#define HEIGHT 5
#define WIDTH 10

void main(void)
{
   char matrix [HEIGHT] [WIDTH];
   int x,y;
                               [x]
   for(y=0; y<HEIGHT; y++)         /* fill matrix with periods */
     for(x=0; x<WIDTH; x++)
        matrix[y][x] = '.';
   printf("Enter coordinates in form x,y (4,2).\n");
   printf("Use negative numbers to quit.\n");

   while ( x >= 0 )                /* until neg coordinates */
     {
     for(y=0; y<HEIGHT; y++)     /* print matrix */
       {
       for(x=0; x<WIDTH; x++)
          printf("%c ", matrix[y][x] );
       printf("\n\n");
       }
     printf("Coordinates: ");
     scanf("%d,%d", &x, &y);     /* get coordinates */
     matrix[y][x]='\xB1';        /* put gray box there */
     }
}
```

Figure 6-5 shows a sample of interaction with the program. The user has previously entered the coordinates 2,1; on this turn, the coordinates are 5,2. The program has plotted both pairs on the screen.

coordinates:5,2

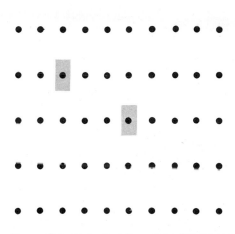

Figure 6-5. Output of the plot.c Program

Remember that the results of typing coordinates that exceed the bounds of the array can be disastrous. Don't type an x-coordinate greater than 9, nor a y-coordinate greater than 4. (You probably will anyway. The worst that can happen is a system crash.) Alternatively, you could modify the program to trap out-of-bounds entries, as we did earlier; for simplicity, we have not done this here.

Initializing Two-Dimensional Arrays

We've learned how to initialize a one-dimensional array; what about two dimensions? As an example, we'll modify the plot.c program to play the game of battleship. In this game one player (the computer) has concealed a number of ships at different locations in a 10-by-5 grid. The other player (the human) tries to guess where the ships are by typing in coordinates. If the human guesses right, a hit is scored, and the coordinates on the grid are marked with a solid rectangle. If the human guesses wrong, the coordinates are marked with a light gray rectangle, making it easier to remember what areas have already been tested.

There are five ships concealed in the grid: one battleship 4 units long, two cruisers 3 units long, and two destroyers 2 units long. They are all placed either horizontally or vertically (not diagonally). In the program a ship will be represented by the number 1, and coordinates where there is no ship by the number 0.

We get the ships into the array by initializing the array when we write the program. Note that even though this is a character array (to save memory space), we use numbers as values:

```c
/* bship.c */
/* plays battleship game */
#define HEIGHT 5
#define WIDTH 10

char enemy [HEIGHT] [WIDTH] =
   { { 0, 0, 0, 0, 0, 0, 0, 0, 0, 0 },
     { 0, 1, 1, 1, 1, 0, 0, 1, 0, 1 },
     { 0, 0, 0, 0, 0, 0, 0, 1, 0, 1 },
     { 1, 0, 0, 0, 0, 0, 0, 1, 0, 0 },
     { 1, 0, 1, 1, 1, 0, 0, 0, 0, 0 }   };

void main(void)
{
   char friend [HEIGHT] [WIDTH];
   int x,y;

   for(y=0; y<HEIGHT; y++)          /* fill array with periods */
      for(x=0; x<WIDTH; x++)
         friend[y][x] = '.';
   printf("Enter coordinates in form x,y (4,2).\n");
   printf("Use negative numbers to quit.\n");

   while ( x >= 0 )                 /* until neg coordinates */
      {
      for(y=0; y<HEIGHT; y++)       /* print array */
        {
        for(x=0; x<WIDTH; x++)
           printf("%c ", friend[y][x] );
        printf("\n\n");
        }
      printf("Coordinates: ");
      scanf("%d,%d", &x, &y);       /* get coordinates */
      if ( enemy[y][x]==1 )         /* if it's a hit */
         friend[y][x]='\xDB';       /* put solid box there */
      else                          /* otherwise */
         friend[y][x]='\xB1';       /* gray box */
      }
}
```

The ships are located in the array initialization at the start of the program. You should be able to see the battleship on the left, oriented horizontally, in the second row down. A sample run is shown in Figure 6-6.

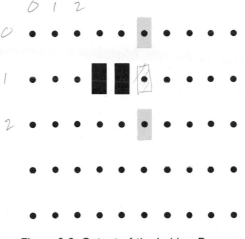

Figure 6-6. Output of the bship.c Program

In this figure the user tried 4,0, which was a miss, and then 4,1, which was a hit. Then, thinking the ship might be located vertically, the user tried 4,2 to no avail. Trying 5,1 proved that the ship didn't extend to the right. The next choice, 3,1, was a hit, so now the user will see how big a ship it is by going further left. The other ships still lurk in the darkness, waiting to be discovered.

(It would be fun to modify the program so that two people could compete, but that would take us too far afield.)

Notice the format used to initialize the array: an outer set of braces, and then 5 inner sets of braces, each with 10 members separated by commas. The inner sets of braces are separated from each other by commas as well.

We can conclude that lists go in braces, and that the elements of the list are separated by commas, whether the members of the list are composed of numbers or other lists.

> The values used to initialize an array are separated by commas and surrounded by braces.

Initializing Three-Dimensional Arrays

We aren't going to show a programming example that uses a three-dimensional array. However, an example of initializing a three-dimensional array will consolidate your understanding of subscripts:

```
int threed[3][2][4] =
    {   {   { 1, 2, 3, 4 },
            { 5, 6, 7, 8 },  },
        {   { 7, 9, 3, 2 },
            { 4, 6, 8, 3 },  },
        {   { 7, 2, 6, 3 },
            { 0, 1, 9, 4 }   }    };
```

This is an array of arrays of arrays. The outer array has three elements, each of which is a two-dimensional array of two elements, each of which is a one-dimensional array of four numbers.

Quick now, how would you address the array element holding the only 0 in this declaration? The first subscript is [2], since it's in the third group of three two-dimensional arrays; the second subscript is [1], since it's in the second of two one-dimensional arrays; and the third subscript is [0], since it's the first element in the one-dimensional array of numbers. We could say, therefore, that the expression

```
threed[2][1][0] == 0
```

is true.

Arrays as Arguments

We've seen examples of passing various kinds of variables as arguments to functions. Is it also possible to pass an *array* to a function? The answer is, sort of. Let's see what this means.

Here's a program that uses a function called **max()** to find the element in an array with the largest value:

```
/* maxnum.c */
/* tells largest number in array typed in */
#define MAXSIZE 20              /* size of array */
int max(int[], int);           /* prototype */

void main(void)
{
    int list[MAXSIZE];
    int size = 0;              /* start at element [0] */
    int num;                   /* temp storage */
    do                         /* get list of numbers */
        {
        printf("Type number: ");
        scanf("%d", &list[size]);
        }
    while ( list[size++] != 0 ); /* exit loop on 0 */
```

```
    num = max(list,size-1);         /* get largest number */
    printf("Largest number is %d", num);     /* print it */
}

/* max() */
/* returns largest number in array */
int max(int list[], int size)
{
    int dex, max;
    max = list[0];                  /* assume 1st element largest */
    for (dex=1; dex<size; dex++)    /* check remaining elements */
       if ( max < list[dex] )       /* if one bigger, */
          max = list[dex];          /*   make it the largest */
    return(max);
}
```

The user types in a set of numbers (no more than 20) and the program prints out the largest one. Here's a sample run:

```
    Type number: 42
    Type number: 1
    Type number: 64
    Type number: 33
    Type number: 27
    Type number: 0
    Largest number is 64
```

The first part of this program should look familiar: it's our usual **do-while** loop for reading in a list of numbers. The only new element here is the statement:

```
    num = max(list,size);
```

This is the call to the function **max()**, which returns the largest number. There are two arguments to the function: the first is the array **list**, the second is the variable **size**.

The critical thing to notice here is how we pass the array to the function: we use the name of the array, all by itself. We've seen array elements, which look like **list[index]**, before, but what does the array name mean without any brackets? It turns out that the array name used alone is equivalent to the *address* of the array. Actually, it's equivalent to the address of the first element in the array, which is the same thing.

Thinking about addresses and values can become confusing, so let's recapitulate what we know about the addresses of simple variables. Let's imagine an integer variable **num** with a value of 27. Perhaps it has been initialized like this:

```
int num = 27;
```

Figure 6-7 shows how this variable looks in memory.

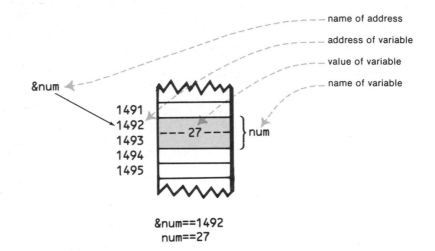

&num==1492
num==27

Figure 6-7. The Address and Value of a Simple Variable

There are four things to know about the variable: its name (**num**), its value (27), its address (which happens to be 1492, although this will vary from program to program and system to system), and—watch closely—the name of the address, which is **&num**.

Now let's see what a similar representation looks like for an array.

> An array is referred to by its address, which is represented by the name of the array, used without subscripts.

Figure 6-8 shows the array **list**[ ], which in this instance is located in memory starting at address 1500. Note the value of a typical element in the array (64), the name of this element (**list[2]**), the address of the array (1500), and the name of this address (**list**). Why isn't the address of the array called something like **&list**? This would be consistent with the way the addresses of variables are named, but it would leave the word "list," which isn't used to name anything else about the variable, going begging. Thus **list** refers to an address if **list** is an array, but would refer to a value if **list** were a simple variable.

Incidentally, can you think of another way to represent the address **list**? How about this?

```
&list[0]
```

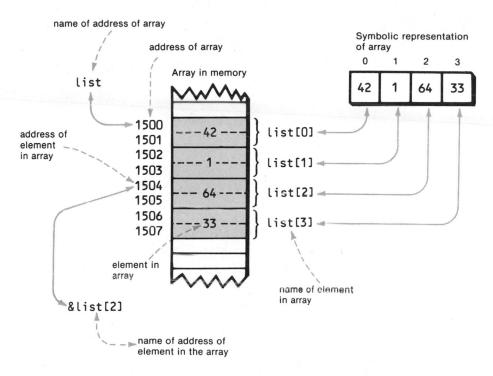

Figure 6-8. The Address and Elements of an Array

Since **list**[O] is the first element of the array, it will have the same address as the array itself. And since **&** is the address operator, **&list[O]** gives the address of the first element of the array. In other words,

```
list == &list[O]
```

An understanding of addresses will become increasingly important as we move on to the study of pointers in the next chapter, since addresses are closely related to pointers.

To summarize, to tell the compiler we want to talk about the address of an array, we use the name of the array, with no brackets following it. Thus (to return to the maxnum.c program), our call to the function **max()** passes the address of the array, represented by the word **list**, to the function.

Addresses of Things Versus Things

It's important to realize that passing the *address* of something is not the same thing as passing the something. When a simple variable name is used as an argument passed to a function, the function takes the *value* corresponding to this variable name and installs it as a new variable in a new memory location created by the function for that purpose.

But what happens when the address of an *array* is passed to a function as an argument? Does the function create another array and move the values into it from the array in the calling program? No. Since arrays can be very large, the designers of C determined that it would be better to have only *one* copy of an array no matter how many functions wanted to access it. So instead of passing the *values* in the array, only the *address* of the array is passed. The function then uses the address to access the *original* array. This process is shown in Figure 6-9. Thus, in the **max()** function, when we reference elements of the array, as in the statement

```
max = list2[dex];
```

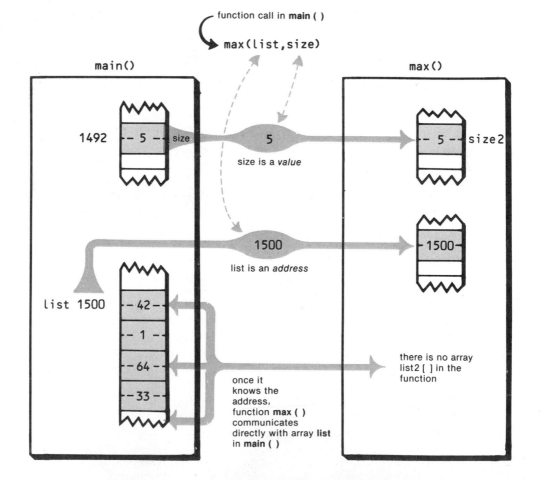

Figure 6-9. Passing a Value and an Array Address to a Function

references to the array **list2**[ ] are actually references to the array **list**[ ]. We can give the array any name we want in the function, but all we are doing is telling the function where the original array, **list**[ ], is. There *is* no array **list2**[ ]: this is simply the way the function refers to the array **list**[ ].

> Passing an array name to a function does not create a new copy of the array.

Sorting an Array

Before we go on to strings, let's look at a function that sorts the values in an array. Sorting is an important task in many applications, particularly database programs, in which a user wants to rearrange a list of items in numerical or alphabetical order. Here's the listing:

```c
/* sortnum.c */
/* sorts numbers typed in to array */
#define MAXSIZE 20               /* size of buffer */
void sort(int[], int);           /* prototype */

void main(void)
{
    static int list[MAXSIZE];    /* buffer for numbers */
    int size = 0;                /* size 0 before input */
    int dex;                     /* index to array */

    do                           /* get list of numbers */
        {
        printf("Type number: ");
        scanf("%d", &list[size]);
        }
    while ( list[size++] != 0 ); /* exit loop on 0 */
    sort(list,--size);           /* sort numbers */
    for (dex=0; dex<size; dex++) /* print sorted list */
        printf("%d\n", list[dex]);
}

/* sort() */
/* sorts array of integers */
void sort(int list[], int size)
{
    int out, in, temp;
```

p 189

```
for (out=0; out<size-1; out++)      /* for each element */
    for (in=out+1; in<size; in++)   /* look at those lower */
        if (list[out] > list[in])   /* if element greater than */
            {                       /*   any lower down, */
            temp = list[in];        /* swap them */
            list[in] = list[out];
            list[out] = temp;
            }
}
```

And here's an example of the program at work:

```
Type number: 46
Type number: 25
Type number: 73
Type number: 58
Type number: 33
Type number: 18
Type number: 0
18
25
33
46
58
73
```

The program first asks for a list of numbers (as you can see from the array definition, you shouldn't type more than 20). As the user types in the numbers, they are placed in the array **list[ ]**. Once the user terminates the list by typing 0 (which is not placed on the list), the program then calls the **sort()** function, which sorts the values in the list.

The overall structure of the program is similar to that of maxnum.c. It first gets a series of numbers from the user and puts them in an array, **list[ ]**. Then it calls the **sort()** function, and finally it prints out the contents of the newly sorted array.

In this program we've used the same name, **list[ ]**, for the array in the function as in the calling program. A different name could be used to refer to the array; either way, it's the same array.

The Bubble Sort

The sorting process used in the **sort()** function may require a word of explanation. The function starts off thinking about the first array variable, **list[0]**. The goal is to place the smallest item on the list in this variable. So the function goes through all the *remaining* items on the list, from list[1] to list[size-1], comparing each one with the first item. Whenever it finds one that is smaller than the first item, it swaps them. This will put the smallest item in **list[0]**.

Once the smallest item is dealt with, the function wants to put the next smallest item in **list[1]**. So it goes through all the remaining items, from **list[2]** on, comparing them with **list[1]**. Whenever it finds one that is smaller, it swaps them. This will end up with **list[1]** containing the second smallest item. This process is continued until the entire list is sorted. This approach is called the "bubble sort," because the smaller values bubble up through the list. Figure 6-10 shows how it works. (We should note that the bubble sort, while easy to program, is less efficient than many other sorting algorithms.)

The outer loop, with the variable **out**, determines which element of the array will be used as the basis of comparison (as **list[0]** is the first time through the loop). The inner loop, with the variable **out**, steps through the remaining items, comparing each one with the first (from **list[1]** to the end of the list, the first time through). When the comparison of two items shows they are out of order, they're swapped.

The swapping process requires us to put the value of the first variable, **list[in]**, in a temporary location; put the second value, **list(out)**, in the first variable; and finally return the temporary value (originally from **list[in]** to **list[out]**).

Remember that all this swapping and rearranging of values takes place in the original array, **list[ ]**, in the calling program. The **sort()** function finds out where the array is (from the address passed to it) and manipulates it by "remote control," without having to drag all the values from the array into the function.

Two-Dimensional Arrays as Arguments

We've seen how to pass a one-dimensional array as an argument, but what about a two-dimensional array? As an example, we'll blend our travel.c program, which recorded the travel expenses for a list of secret agents, and our maxnum.c program, which figured out the largest element in an array. The resulting program will print out the agent number and the amount spent by the agent with the highest travel expenses.

p 192

p 198

Here's the program listing:

```
/* highex.c */
/* stores list of secret agents' travel expenses */
/* reports number of agents with highest expenses */
#define ROWS 10       /* number of rows in array */
#define COLUMNS 2      /* number of columns in array */
int maxex(float[][COLUMNS], int);  /* prototype */

void main(void)
```

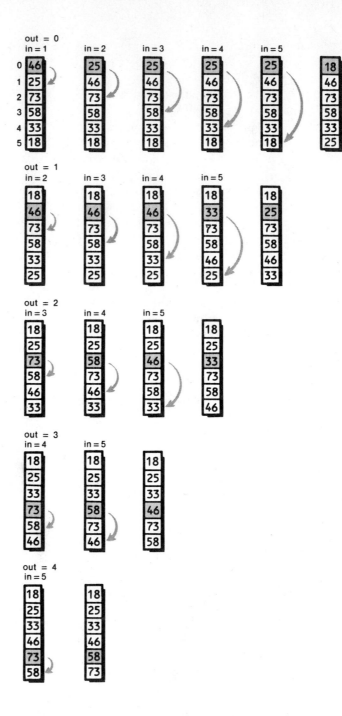

$$\frac{(n-1)(n-2)}{2} \ passes$$

Figure 6-10. Bubble Sort

```
{
    float agents [ROWS] [COLUMNS];
    float number, expenses;
    int index=0;

    printf("Enter 3-digit agent numbers,\n");
    printf("then travel expenses (007 1642.50)\n");
    printf("Enter 0 0 to quit.\n");

    do                      /* get list of agents and expenses */
        {
        printf("Agent's number and expenses: ");
        scanf( "%f %f", &number, &expenses);
        agents[index][0] = number;
        agents[index][1] = expenses;
        }
    while ( agents[index++][0] != (float)0.0 );
    index--;                /* restore to size of array */

    index = maxex(agents, index);    /* find agent's index */
    printf("Agent with highest expenses: %03.0f. ",
                            agents[index][0] );
    printf("Amount: %.2f.", agents[index][1] );
}

/* maxex() */
/* returns array index to largest amount in column 1 */
int maxex(float list[][COLUMNS], int size)
{
    int dex, maxdex;
    float max;
    max = list[0][1];               /* assume 1st element largest */
    maxdex = 0;                     /* save its index */
    for (dex=1; dex<size; dex++)    /* check remaining elements */
        if ( max < list[dex][1] )   /* if one bigger, */
            {
            max = list[dex][1];     /* make it the largest */
            maxdex = dex;           /* save its index */
            }
    return(maxdex);                 /* return index */
}
```

Here's a sample run. Now we've typed in a list of agent numbers and expenses, and the program has figured out the agent with the highest expenses and printed out the number and the amount.

```
Enter 3-digit agent numbers,
then travel expenses (007 1642.50)
Enter 0 0 to quit.
Agent's number and expenses: 901 645.25
Agent's number and expenses: 801 784.50
Agent's number and expenses: 302 112.95
Agent's number and expenses: 007 9456.99
Agent's number and expenses: 405 298.60
Agent's number and expenses: 006 5019.00
Agent's number and expenses: 0 0
Agent with highest expenses: 007. Amount: 9456.99.
```

In many ways, passing a two-dimensional array to a function is similar to passing an array of one dimension, but there is at least one surprise.

The method of passing the address of the array to the function is identical no matter how many dimensions the array has, since all we pass is the address of the array (in this case, **agents**):

```
index = maxex(agents, index);
```

However, the declaration of the array in the function may look a bit mysterious:

```
float list[][COLUMNS];
```

We don't need to tell the function how many *rows* there are. Why not? Because the function isn't setting aside space in memory for the array. All it needs to know is that the array has two columns; this permits it to reference accurately any array variable. For instance, to find the space in memory where **agents**[3][1] is stored, the function multiplies the row index (3) by the number of elements per row (COLUMNS, which is 2), and then adds the column index (which is 1). The result is 3 * 2 + 1 = 7, as shown in Figure 6-11.

We've had to modify the function **max()** from our earlier program in order to return the row index of the agent in question, rather than a numerical quantity as before. This involves saving the index whenever we save a new maximum.

At this point you should be starting to feel comfortable with arrays. You know how to define arrays of differing sizes and dimensions, how to initialize arrays, how to refer to particular array elements, and how to pass an array to a function. With this under your belt, you should be ready to handle strings, which are simply a special kind of array.

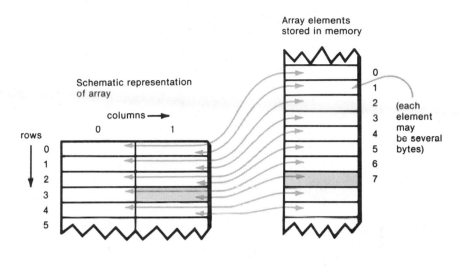

agents [3] [1] correspond to
array element 7 in memory

Figure 6-11. Two-Dimensional Array Stored in Memory

Strings

Strings are the form of data used in programming languages for storing and manipulating text, such as words, names, and sentences. In C, a string is not a formal data type as it is in some languages (e.g., Pascal and BASIC). Instead, it is an array of type **char**. When you think about it, this makes a good deal of sense; a string is a series of characters, and that's just what an array of type **char** is. Most languages actually treat strings as arrays of characters, but conceal this fact from the programmer to varying degrees. BASIC, for example, never lets on that strings are arrays, but Pascal, although treating strings as a separate data type, does permit you to reference individual string characters as array members.

String Constants

We've already seen examples of strings, as in the statement:

```
printf("%s", "Greetings!");
```

"Greetings!" is a string constant. That means that the string itself is stored someplace in memory, but that it cannot be changed (just as your program cannot change the 3 in the expression **x = 3;**). Figure 6-12 shows what this string constant looks like stored in memory.

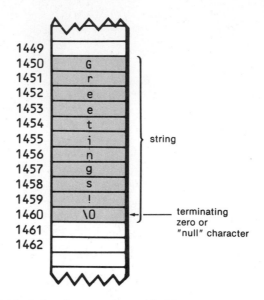

Figure 6-12. String Constant Stored in Memory

Each character occupies one byte of memory, and the last character of the string is the character '\0'. What character is that? It looks like two characters, but it's actually an escape sequence, like '\n'. It's called the "null character," and it stands for a character with a value of 0 (zero). Note that this is not the same as the character 0.

— AscII —

Hex 00

> All strings must end with a null character, '\0', which has a numerical value of 0.

The terminating null ('\0') is important, because it is the only way functions that work with the string can know where the end of the string is. In fact, a string not terminated by a '\0' character is not really a string at all, but merely a collection of characters.

String Variables

We've looked at a string constant, now let's see what a string variable looks like. Here's an example program that reads in a string from the keyboard, using **scanf()**, and prints it out as part of a longer phrase:

```
/* ezstring.c */
/* reads string from keyboard and prints it */
```

```
void main(void)
{
    char name[81];

    printf("Enter your name: ");
    scanf("%s", name);
    printf("Greetings, %s.", name);
}
```

And here's a sample run:

```
Enter your name: Hieronymous
Greetings, Hieronymous.
```

Before a string can be read into a program, some space in the computer's memory must be set aside for it. This shouldn't be too surprising; after all, memory must also be set aside before a simple variable can be stored in a program. For instance, before we can successfully execute the line

```
scanf("%d", &num);
```

we need to declare the variable **num**, causing the compiler to set aside an appropriately sized chunk of memory to store the value the user enters.

The situation is similar for strings, except that, since there is going to be a *series* of characters arriving, a series of bytes must be set aside for them. In ezstring.c, we've declared an array of 15 characters. This should be enough for names 15 characters long, right? Well, not quite. Don't forget the terminating null character '\0'. When **scanf()** gets the name from the keyboard, it automatically includes the '\0' when it stores the string in memory; thus, if your array is 15 characters long, you can only store strings of 14 characters.

The operation of ezstring.c is shown in Figure 6-13.

The warning applied to arrays in general applies to strings: don't overflow the array that holds the string. If the user of ezstring.c typed a name of more than 14 characters, the additional characters would be written over other data or the program itself. Perhaps a better choice for the array definition would have been:

```
char fname[81]
```

This would permit a name to go all the way across the screen: 80 characters. Hardly anyone's name is that long!

You may have noticed something odd about the **scanf()** statement in the ezstring.c program. That's right; there's no address operator (&) preceding the name of the string we're going to print:

```
scanf("%s", fname);
```

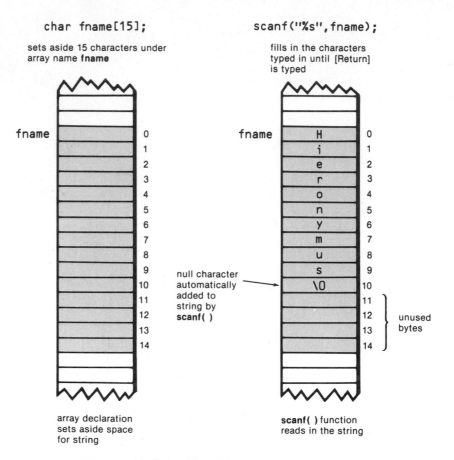

Figure 6-13. String Placed in Memory by *scanf()*

This is because **fname** is an *address*. We need to preface numerical and character variables with the **&** to change values into addresses, but **fname** is already the name of an array, and therefore it's an address and does not need the &.

> Since a string name is an address, no address operator need precede it in a **scanf()** function.

The String I/O Functions *gets()* and *puts()*

There are many C functions whose purpose is to manipulate strings. One of the most common is used to input a string from the keyboard. Why is it needed? Because our old friend, the **scanf()** function, has some limitations when it comes to handling strings. For example, consider the following trial run with the ezstring.c program:

```
Enter your name: Genghis Khan
Greetings, Genghis.
```

The program has suddenly adopted an informal style, dropping the last name (something it might be unwise to do unless you knew Genghis very well). Where did the second word of our string go? Remember that **scanf()** uses *any* whitespace character to terminate entry of a variable. The result is that there is no way to enter a multiword string into a single array using **scanf()** (at least without a lot of trouble).

The solution to this problem is to use another C library function: **gets()**. The purpose of **gets()** is, as you may have guessed, to GET a string from the keyboard. It is not as versatile an input function as **scanf()**; it specializes in doing one thing: reading strings. It is terminated *only* when the [Return] key is struck; so spaces and tabs are perfectly acceptable as part of the input string.

The **gets()** function is part of a matching pair; there is a function to *output* strings as well: **puts()** (for PUT String).

Here's a revised version of our ezstring.c program that makes use of both of these functions:

```
/* getput.c */
/* reads string and prints string using gets() and puts() */
void main(void)
{
    char name[81];

    puts("Enter your name: ");
    gets(name);
    puts("Greetings, ");        ——— includes line feed
    puts(name);
}
```

Let's see what happens when our favorite Mongol warrior tries this new version of the program:

```
Enter your name:
Genghis Khan
Greetings,
Genghis Khan
```

Now the program remembers the entire name and there's less chance of Genghis being offended. The **gets()** function has done just what we wanted.

The **puts()** function is a special-purpose output function specializing in strings. Unlike **printf()**, it can only output one string at a time and, like **gets()**, it has no ability to format a string before printing it. The syntax of **puts()** is simpler than **printf()**, however, so it's the function to use when you want to output a single string.

Initializing Strings

Just as arrays can be initialized, so can strings. Since a string is an array of characters, we can initialize one in exactly that way, as the following example demonstrates:

note

```
char feline[] = { 'c', 'a', 't', '\0' } ;
```

However, C concedes that strings are a special kind of character array by providing a shortcut:

static
```
char feline[] = "cat" ;
```

As you can see, this is considerably easier to write (and read); but it means the same thing to the compiler. Notice that while the individual characters were surrounded by single quotes, the string is surrounded by double quotes. Notice too that we don't need to insert the null character '\0'. Using the string format causes this to happen automatically.

Let's look at a variation on the last program, making use of an initialized string:

```
/* strinit.c */
/* reads string and prints string, shows string initialization */

void main(void)       note
{
   static char salute[] = "Greetings,";
   char name[81];

   puts("Enter your name: ");
   gets(name);
   puts(salute);
   puts(name);
}
```

The output will be exactly the same as before (assuming the same name is typed in). However, "Greetings," is no longer printed as a string constant in the **puts()** function; instead, it's included in the array declaration. The **puts()** function can then print it out using the array address as an argument.

salute

We've had to give the array **name**[ ] in this program the storage class **static**. As you'll remember from our discussion of arrays, only external arrays or arrays given the class **static** can be initialized.

| p189

Here's a sample run with strinit.c:

```
Enter your name:
Cato the Elder
Greetings,
Cato the Elder
```

So we see that our initialization process works just fine. However, the format of the output could be improved: it would have been nicer if the name was on the same line as the salutation:

```
Greetings, Cato the Elder
```

What's happened is that the **puts()** function automatically replaces the null character at the end of the string with a newline character as it prints the string, so that all strings printed by **puts()** end with a newline. So, sometimes **puts()** is not the ideal choice for outputting strings, and **printf()** must be used instead.

Examining a String

We've told you how a string looks in memory, but you shouldn't take our word for it; you can write a program to investigate this for yourself. The following program examines each memory location occupied by a string and prints out what it finds there. In the process it demonstrates a new C library function, **strlen()**:

```
/* strexam.c */
/* looks at string in memory */
void main(void)
{
    char name[81];
    int dex;

    puts("Enter your name: ");
    gets(name);
    for (dex=0; dex < strlen(name)+4; dex++)
        printf("Addr=%5u char='%c'=%3d\n",
                        &name[dex], name[dex], name[dex] );
}
```

Here's an example of the output:

```
Enter your name:
Plato
Addr= 3486 char='P'= 80
Addr= 3487 char='l'=108
Addr= 3488 char='a'= 97
Addr= 3489 char='t'=116
Addr= 3490 char='o'=111
Addr= 3491 char=' '=  0
Addr= 3492 char='<'= 60
Addr= 3493 char='#'= 35
Addr= 3494 char='u'=117
```

To show what happens after the end of the string, we've printed out four characters beyond the end of the string that was typed in. First there's the terminating null character, which prints as a space but has the value 0. Then there are garbage characters, which have whatever values were in memory before this part of memory was declared to be an array. If we had declared a **static** or **external** array, these spaces would all have been 0 instead of garbage characters.

We've used the address operator (&) to get the address of each of the characters that make up the string:

```
&name[dex]
```

We've also used our old trick of printing the characters in two different formats: once as a character and once as a number. The last new thing in this program is the use of the new string function, **strlen()**. We use the value returned by this function to tell us how many characters to print out from the **for** loop.

```
for (dex=0; dex < strlen(name)+4; dex++)
```

Let's examine the **strlen()** function and string-handling functions in general.

String Functions

In keeping with its philosophy of using a small language kernel and adding library functions to achieve greater power, C has no special string-handling operators. In BASIC you can assign a value to a string with an equal sign, and in Pascal you can compare two strings with a less-than sign. But in C, which thinks of strings as arrays, there are no special operators for dealing with them.

However, C does have a large set of useful string-handling library functions. We've used one of the most common in the strexam.c program: the **strlen()** function. This function returns the length of the string whose address is given to it as an argument. Thus in our program, the expression

```
strlen(name)
```

will return the value 5 if the string name has the value "Plato". (As you can see, **Strlen()** does not count the terminating null character.)

An Array of Strings

Earlier in the chapter we saw several examples of two-dimensional arrays. Let's look now at a similar phenomenon, but one dealing with strings: an array of strings. Since a string is itself an array, an array of strings is really an array of arrays, or a two-dimensional array.

Our example program asks you to type in your name. When you do, it checks your name against a master list to see if you're worthy of entry to the palace (or perhaps it's only an "in" restaurant on the Upper East Side). Here's the listing:

```
/* compare.c */
/* compares word typed in with words in program */
#define MAX 5
#define LEN 40   -10

void main(void)
{
   int dex;
   int enter=0;
   char name[40];
   static char list[MAX][LEN] =
                  { "Katrina",
                    "Nigel",
                    "Alistair",
                    "Francesca",
                    "Gustav"     };
   printf("Enter your name: ");                    /* get name */
   gets(name);
   for (dex=0; dex<MAX; dex++)                      /* go thru list */
      if( strcmp(&list[dex][0],name)==0 )           /* if match */
         enter = 1;                                 /* set flag */
   if ( enter == 1 )                                /* if flag set */
      printf("You may enter, oh honored one."); /* one response */
   else                                            /* otherwise */
      printf("Guards! Remove this person!");    /* different one */
}
```

(handwritten annotations: "no. items", "1 + longest string")

There are two possible outcomes when you interact with this program. Either your name is on the list:

```
Enter your name: Gustav
You may enter, oh honored one.
```

or it isn't:

```
Enter your name: Robert
Guards! Remove this person!
```

p196

Notice how our array of strings is initialized. Because a phrase in quotes is already a one-dimensional array, we don't need to use braces around each name as we did for two-dimensional character arrays. We do need braces around all the strings, however, since this is an array of strings. As before, the individual elements of the array—strings in this case—are separated by commas.

The order of the subscripts in the array declaration is important. The first subscript, MAX, gives the number of items in the array, while the second subscript, LEN, gives the length of each string in the array. Having a fixed length array for each string, no matter how long it actually is, can lead to a considerable waste of space. (In Chapter 7, when we explore pointers, we'll show how to avoid this problem.)

We've used another string function, **strcmp()**, in this program, in the expression

```
strcmp( &list[dex][0], name ) == 0
```

The **strcmp()** function compares two strings and returns an integer value based on the comparison. If we assume that **string1** is on the right side within the parentheses and **string2** is on the left

```
strcmp(string2,string1)
```

then the value returned will have the following meanings:

Returned Value	Meaning
less than zero	string1 less than string2
zero	string1 identical to string2
greater than zero	string1 greater than string 2

In this context, "less than" and "greater than" mean that if you put **string1** and **string2** in alphabetical order, the one that appeared first (closer to the A's) would be considered "less than" those following. However, we don't make use of the "less than" and "greater than" capabilities of the function in this program; here we only need to know when the the strings are identical, which is true when the function returns a value of 0.

A further wrinkle in this program is the use of a "flag" to remember whether there has been a match. The flag, a variable that remembers a condition for a short time, is called **enter**, and it is set to 1 (true) if any of the names match, and remains 0 if there are no matches at the end of the loop. The **if-else** statement then queries the flag to find out what to print.

Deleting Characters

It's often useful to be able to delete a character from the middle of a string (if you're writing a word processing program or text editor, for example). There are no library functions to do this in Turbo C, so we'll develop a routine to perform this function.

Here's a program that demonstrates **strdel()**, our homemade STRing DELete function:

```
/* delete.c */
/* deletes a character from a string */
void strdel(char str[], int n);   /* prototype */

void main(void)
{
    char string[81];                /* buffer for string */
    int position;                   /* position of character */

    printf("Type string [Return], position\n");
    gets(string);                   /* get string */
    scanf("%d", &position);         /* get character */
    strdel(string,position);        /* delete character */
    puts(string);                   /* print new string */
}

/* strdel() */
/* deletes character from string */
void strdel(char str[], int n)    /* buffer, size of buffer */
{
    strcpy(&str[n], &str[n+1] );   /* move 2nd part of string */
}                                  /* one space to left */
```

This program asks for a string and for the position in the string of the character to be deleted (remember that the first character is 0). Then the program calls the **strdel()** function to delete the character at that position. Here's a sample interaction:

```
Type string [Return], position
```

```
cart
2
cat
```

The program has deleted character number 2, 'r', from the string "cart."

The **strdel()** function works by moving one space to the left all characters that are to the right of the character being deleted. This is shown in Figure 6-14.

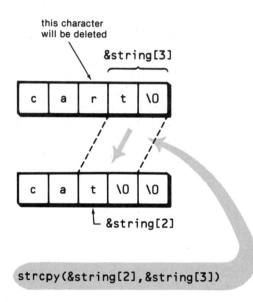

Figure 6-14. Operation of the *strdel()* Function

To move the characters, the function makes use of the **strcpy** library function. This function simply copies one string to another. For instance, if a program included the following statements:

```
char buffer[10];
- - - - -
strcpy(buffer, "Dante");
```

the string "Dante" would be placed in the array **buffer**[ ]. The string would include the terminating null, which means that six characters in all would be copied.

If you're a BASIC programmer, you may be wondering why we can't achieve the same effect more simply by saying:

```
buffer = "Dante";      /* illegal construction */
```

We can't do this because C treats strings far more like arrays than BASIC does. Since it is impossible to set one array equal to another with an assignment statement, it is also impossible to set one string equal to another in this way. A function must be used instead.

Now let's look closely at which string is being copied and where it's being copied to. Two arguments are needed by the **strcpy()** function: the string to be copied is the second argument and the place it will be copied to is the first argument.

We want to move one space to the left the string following the character being deleted. In the "cart" to "cat" example, the string we want to copy has only two characters: 't' and the null character '\0'. But what is the name of this string? How do we represent it as an argument to **strcpy()**? Remember that we identify an array by the address where it begins. The same is true of strings. In this case, the string we want to move begins at the letter 't'. What's the address of this character? It's **&string[3]**, which is also the address of the string we want to move, so this is the second argument we give **strcpy()**.

Now we want to move this string one character to the left. That means putting it at the address of the 'r', which is the character we want to delete. The address of the 'r' is **&string[2]**, since the 'r' is in position 2 in the string.

Thus, assuming that n has the value 2, the statement

```
strcpy(&str[n], &str[n+1] );
```

will copy the string "t\0" to position &str[2], blotting out the character 'r' as it does so.

The Turbo C compiler comes with many more string functions than we've shown here, including functions to duplicate a string, concatenate (put together) two strings, find a character in a string, convert a string to all lower- or all uppercase, and so on. Using some of these string operations requires an understanding of pointers, which will be our topic in Chapter 7.

Summary

In this chapter we've learned how to handle arrays in a variety of forms. We've learned how to declare arrays, how to access their elements, and how to give them initial values when the program is compiled. We've covered one- and two-dimensional arrays and even taken a peek at initializing a three-dimensional array. We've learned that the addresses of arrays can be passed to functions, so that functions can access the elements of the array.

Next, we looked at strings, which are simply arrays of type **char**. We've seen how to initialize strings and how to use two new I/O functions: **gets()** and **puts()**. We've also examined a trio of string functions: **strlen()**, which returns the length of a string; **strcmp()**, which compares two strings; and **strcpy()**, which copies one string into the space occupied by another.

Questions

1. An array is a collection of variables of
   - a. different data types scattered throughout memory
   - b. the same data type scattered throughout memory
   - c. the same data type placed next to each other in memory
   - d. different data types placed next to each other in memory

2. Why is a string like an array?
   - a. They are both character arrays
   - b. An array is a kind of string
   - c. They both access functions the same way
   - d. A string is a kind of array

3. An array declaration specifies the t_____, n_____, and
   s_____ of the array.

4. Is this a correct array declaration?

   ```
   int num(25);
   ```

5. Which element of the array does this expression reference?

   ```
   num[4]
   ```

6. What's the difference between the 3s in these two expressions?

   ```
   int num[3];
   num[3] = 5;
   ```

   - a. first is particular element, second is type
   - b. first is size, second is particular element
   - c. first is particular element, second is array size
   - d. both specify array elements

7. What does this combination of statements do?

   ```
   #define LIM 50
   char collect[LIM];
   ```

   - a. makes LIM a subscript
   - b. makes LIM a variable of type **float**

   c. makes **collect**[ ] an array of type LIM

   d. makes **collect**[ ] an array of size LIM

8. If an array has been defined this way:

```
float prices[MAX];
```

is the following a good way to read values into all the elements of the array?

```
for(j=0; j<=MAX; j++)
    scanf("%f", prices[j]);
```

9. Is this a correct way to initialize a one-dimensional array?

```
int array = { 1, 2, 3, 4 };
```

10. What will happen if you try to put so many variables into an array when you initialize it that the size of the array is exceeded?

   a. nothing

   b. possible system malfunction

   c. error message from the compiler

   d. other data may be overwritten

11. What will happen if you put too few elements in an array when you initialize it?

   a. nothing

   b. possible system malfunction

   c. error message from the compiler

   d. unused elements will be filled with 0s or garbage

12. If you want to initialize an array it must be a _____ or a _____ array.

13. What will happen if you assign a value to an element of an array whose subscript exceeds the size of the array?

   a. the element will be set to 0

   b. nothing, it's done all the time

   c. other data may be overwritten

   d. possible system malfunction

14. Can you initialize a two-dimensional array this way?

```
int array[3][3] = {  { 1, 2, 3 },
                     { 4, 5, 6 },
                     { 7, 8, 9 }  };
```

15. In the array in question 14, what is the name of the array variable with the value 4?

16. If an array had been defined like this:

```
int array[12];
```

the word **array** represents the a _____ of the array.

17. If you don't initialize a **static** array, what will the elements be set to?

    a. 0

    b. an undetermined value

    c. a floating point number

    d. the character constant '\0'

18. When you pass an array as an argument to a function, what is actually passed?

    a. the address of the array

    b. the values of the elements in the array

    c. the address of the first element in the array

    d. the number of elements in the array

19. True or false: a function operates on an integer array passed to it as an argument by placing the values of that array into a separate place in memory known only to the function.

20. A string is

    a. a list of characters

    b. a collection of characters

    c. an array of characters

    d. an exaltation of characters

21. "A" is a _____ while 'A' is a _____ .

22. What is the following expression?

    `"Mesopotamia\n"`

    a. a string variable
    b. a string array
    c. a string constant
    d. a string of characters

23. A string is terminated by a _____ character, which is written _____.

24. The function _____ is designed specifically to read in one string from the keyboard.

25. If you have declared a string like this:

    `char name[10];`

    and you type in a string to this array, the string can consist of a maximum of _____ characters.

26. True or false: the function **puts()** always adds a '\n' to the end of the string it is printing.

27. Which is more appropriate for reading in a multiword string?
    a. **gets()**
    b. **printf()**
    c. **scanf()**
    d. **puts()**

28. Assuming the following initialization:

    `char string[] = "Blacksmith";`

    how would you refer to the string "smith" (the last five letters of the string)?

29. What subtle format problem does this statement exhibit?

    `name = "George";`

30. What expression would you use to find the length of the string **name**?

Exercises

1. Modify the temp.c program so that it not only accepts seven temperatures and calculates the average but also prints out the temperatures that have been read in.

2. Modify the fltemp2.c program to use a **while** loop instead of a **do-while** loop.

3. Write a function, and a program to test it, that will insert a character anywhere in a string. The call to the function should have the form

   ```
   strins(string, character, position);
   ```

   Before writing this function, ask yourself which end of the string **strcpy()** starts copying from.

7

Pointers

- Pointers
- Returning multiple values from functions
- Pointers and arrays
- Pointer arithmetic
- Pointers and strings
- Double indirection
- Pointers to arrays

7

Pointers are regarded by most people as one of the most difficult topics in C. There are several reasons for this. First, the concept behind pointers—indirection—may be a new one for many programmers, since it isn't commonly used in such languages as BASIC or Pascal. And second, the symbols used for pointer notation in C are not as clear as they might be; for example, the same symbol is used for two different but related purposes, as we'll see.

Conceptually, however, pointers aren't really that obscure, and with a little practice the symbols start to make a sort of sense. In other words, pointers may be difficult, but they aren't *too* difficult. Our goal in this chapter is to demystify pointers, to explain as clearly as possible what they're for and how they work. To this end we start slowly, in an attempt to ensure that the groundwork is laid carefully before we go on to use pointers in more advanced situations.

Pointer Overview

Before we show programming examples that demonstrate the use of pointers, we're going to discuss generally what pointers are and why they're used.

What Is a Pointer?

A pointer provides a way of accessing a variable (or a more complex kind of data, such as an array) without referring to the variable directly. The mechanism used for this is the *address* of the variable. In effect, the address acts as an intermediary between the variable and the program accessing it. There is a somewhat analogous mechanism in the spy business, in which an agent in the field might leave his or her reports in a special place (a post office box or a hollow tree) and have no direct contact with the other members of the network. Thus if captured, there is very little information the agent can be forced to reveal about the organization. We can say that the agent has only *indirect* access to those for whom the information is intended.

In a similar way, a program statement can refer to a variable *indirectly*, using the address of the variable as a sort of post office box or hollow tree for the passing of information.

Why Are Pointers Used?

Pointers are used in situations when passing actual values is difficult or undesirable. (It's seldom the case that an enemy program will force a function to reveal the names of variables in the calling program!) Some reasons to use pointers are:

1. to return more than one value from a function
2. to pass arrays and strings more conveniently from one function to another
3. to manipulate arrays more easily by moving pointers to them (or to parts of them), instead of moving the arrays themselves
4. to create complex data structures, such as linked lists and binary trees, where one data structure must contain references to other data structures
5. to communicate information about memory, as in the function **malloc()**, which returns the location of free memory by using a pointer.

We'll explore some of these uses for pointers in this chapter. We'll save the use of pointers with structures, linked lists, and **malloc()** for Chapter 9.

Another reason sometimes given for using pointers is that pointer notation compiles into faster or more efficient code than, for example, array notation. It's not clear that this is actually a major factor for modern compilers; probably many programmers become enamored of pointer notation and grasp at any excuse to use it.

You've Already Used Pointers

If you think that reason 2—passing arrays more conveniently from one function to another—sounds familiar, that's because it is; in Chapter 6 you used pointers to pass arrays and strings to functions. Instead of passing the array itself, you passed the *address of the array*. This address is an example of a pointer *constant*. There are also pointer variables; it's the interplay between pointer constants and pointer variables that gives pointers such power. We'll see further examples of pointers used with arrays later in this chapter.

> A pointer constant is an address; a pointer variable is a place to store addresses.

Returning Data from Functions

We're going to start our examination of pointers by finding out how functions can return multiple values to the program that called them. You've already seen that it's possible to pass many values to a function and return a single value from it, but what happens when you want to return more than one value from a function to the calling program? Since there is no mechanism built into functions to do this, we must rely on pointers. Of the many ways pointers can be used, this is perhaps the simplest; at the same time, it is a technique that accomplishes an essential task. There are many situations in which a function must communicate more than one value to the calling program.

Review: Passing Values to a Function

Before we show how this works, let's review what happens when we pass values *to* a function. (You've already seen examples of such functions in Chapter 5—the function that adds two numbers, for example.) Here's a very simple program that passes two values, the integers 4 and 7, to a function called **gets2()**:

```
/* values.c */
/* tests function which accepts two values */
void gets2(int, int);           /* prototype */
void main(void)
{
   int x=4, y=7;                 /* intialize variables */

   gets2(x, y);                  /* pass vars to function */
}

/* gets2() */
/* prints out values of two arguments */
void gets2(int xx, int yy)
{
   printf("First is %d, second is %d", xx, yy);
}
```

This is not an enormously useful function: it simply prints out the two values passed to it. However, it demonstrates an important point: the function receives the two values from the calling program and stores them—or rather, stores duplicates of them—in its own private memory space. In fact, it can even give these values different names, known only to the function: in this case, **xx** and **yy** instead of **x** and **y**. Figure 7-1 shows how this looks. The function then can operate on the new variables, **xx** and **yy**, without affecting the original **x** and **y** in the calling program.

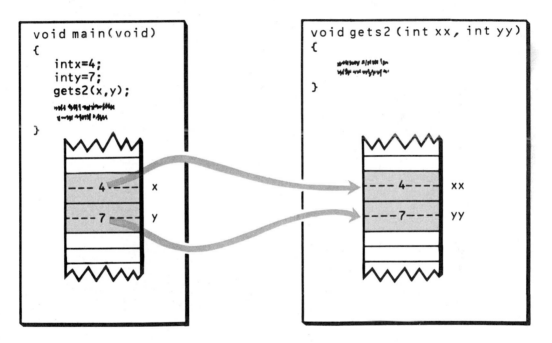

Values are passed to function
and duplicated in the function's;
memory space.

Figure 7-1. Values Duplicated in Function's Memory

Passing Addresses to a Function

Now let's look at the reverse situation: passing two values from the function back to the calling program. How do we do this? A two-step process is used. First, the calling program, instead of passing *values* to the function, passes it *addresses*. These addresses are where the calling program wants the function to place the data it generates; in other words, they are the addresses of the variables in the calling program where we want to store the returned values. Here's the program:

```
/* passback.c */
/* tests function that returns two values */
void rets2(int *, int *);  /* prototype */

void main(void)
{
   int x, y;                 /* variables */

   rets2( &x, &y );          /* get values from function */
   printf("First is %d, second is %d", x, y);
}

/* rets2() */
/* returns two numbers */
void rets2(int *px, int *py)
{
   *px = 3;                  /* set contents of px to 3 */
   *py = 5;                  /* set contents of py to 5 */
}
```

address of y (handwritten annotation)

address of integer value (handwritten annotation)

And here's what happens when you run the program:

```
First is 3, second is 5.
```

This program again doesn't do anything very useful. The calling program, **main()**, calls the **rets2()** function, which supplies two values, 3 and 5, to the calling program. The calling program then prints out the values. While it may not be useful, the program is crammed with new ideas. Let's take it apart step-by-step.

First, notice that the calling program itself never gives any values to the variables **x** and **y**. And yet, when the program is run, these variables have values; they are printed out by the calling program, as we can see from the output. We can infer that the **rets2()** function must somehow have supplied these values to the calling program.

The calling program told **rets2()** where to put the values by passing it addresses. It did this using the address operator **&**. The expression

```
rets2( &x, &y );
```

causes the addresses of **x** and **y** to be passed to the function and stored in the function's private memory space. These addresses have been given names by the function: **px** and **py**. That's how the function can refer to them, just as if they were any other kind of variables (of course we could have used any names we wanted here, like the more descriptive but longer **ptr_to_x** and **ptr_to_y**).

Defining Pointer Variables

As with any variables, the places set aside for these addresses, **px** and **py**, must be *defined*, so the compiler will know how large a memory space to allot for them and what names we want to give them. Since we are storing addresses, or pointer constants, you might expect a whole new data type here, something along the lines of:

```
ptr px, py;      /* not exactly how pointers are defined */
```

where **ptr** might be the data type for pointers. After all, addresses are all the same size, and we want to set aside enough memory to hold an address. Ordinarily, two bytes will hold an address. (When memory models other than "small" are used, this may not be true; however, the small model is used for all programs in this book. We'll have more to say about memory models in Chapter 14.)

Defining a pointer variable does in fact set aside two bytes of memory, but there is an added complexity. For reasons which we'll explain later, the compiler needs to know, not only that we're defining a pointer, but also *to which kind of data item the pointer points*. In other words, every time we set aside space to store the address of a variable, we need to tell the compiler the data type of the variable. This information must be communicated to the compiler, along with the fact that we're defining a pointer. Let's make a second guess at what such a definition might look like:

```
int_ptr px, py;    /* still not how pointers are defined */
```

where **int_ptr** is the data type for pointers that point to integer variables. We're getting closer. However, C is a concise language, so instead of using the word "ptr", C uses the asterisk (*). The asterisk is used differently from the words representing simple data types (e.g., **int** and **float**); the asterisk is used immediately before *each* variable, rather than being used once at the beginning of the definition. Thus, the real definition for two integer pointers is:

```
int *px, *py;      /* correct definition of two pointers */
```

The definition sets aside two bytes in which to store the address of an integer variable and gives this storage space the name **px**. It also sets aside another two bytes in which to store the address of another integer variable and gives this space the name **py**. The asterisks tell the compiler that these variables will contain *addresses* (not values), and the **int** tells it that the addresses will point to integer variables. Note that the definition itself doesn't say anything about what will be placed in these variables.

The format of this definition is shown in Figure 7-2.

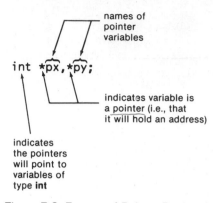

Figure 7-2. Format of Pointer Declaration

(Note that the asterisk as it's used here is a *unary* operator: it operates on only one variable (such as **px** in ***px**). Thus, the compiler cannot confuse it with the same symbol used for multiplication, which is a **binary** operator, operating on two variables.)

The concise nature of this definition format is one of the causes of confusion about pointers, so we'll reiterate what's happening: for each variable name (**px** and **py** in this case) the definition causes the compiler to set aside a two-byte space in memory into which an address can be placed, as shown in Figure 7-3.

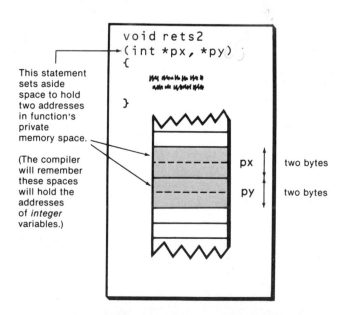

Figure 7-3. Operation of Pointer Declaration

In addition, the compiler is aware of the type of variable the address refers to; in this case, integers.

Supplying Values to Pointer Variables

Now, when the function is called by the calling program with the statement

```
rets2( &x, &y );
```

the two addresses provided by the calling program, **&x** and **&y**, are placed in the spaces provided by the definition in the function. Thus, control is passed to the function, but also these two addresses (which, in this case, might be 1310 and 1312) are placed in the space set aside for **px** and **py**. This process is shown in Figure 7-4.

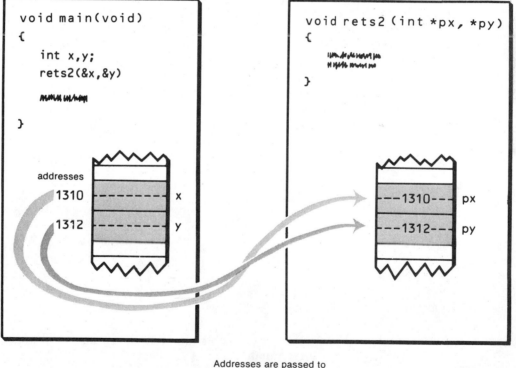

Addresses are passed to
function, and stored
in the function's memory
space.

Figure 7-4. Addresses Stored in Function's Memory

Let's examine this process carefully to make sure we've got the terms straight. We can say that **px** and **py** are pointer _variables_, and that the addresses 1310 and 1312 are <u>pointer</u> *constants*. Figure 7-5 shows a closeup view of these variables being assigned these constant values.

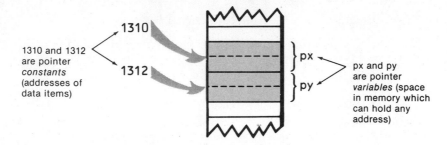

1310 and 1312 are pointer *constants* (addresses of data items)

px and py are pointer *variables* (space in memory which can hold any address)

Figure 7-5. Pointer Constants Placed in Pointer Variables

The Indirection Operator

The function now knows the addresses of the variables into which the calling program wants values placed. The big question is, how does the function *access* these variables? (To return to our spy analogy: how does the spy go about leaving a message in the hollow tree?)

Think about this question for a moment, because in the answer lies the key to what pointers really are. If the function knew the names for **x** and **y** (if they were external variables, for example), it could simply say:

```
x = 3;
y = 5;
```

But it doesn't know the names of the variables; all it knows are the addresses where these variables are stored. We want a new kind of operator, something like **variable_pointed_to_by**, so we can make such assignment statements as:

```
variable_pointed_to_by_px = 3;    /* not really how it's done */
variable_pointed_to_by_py = 5;
```

As you might expect, C uses a much more concise format for this operator. Here's how pointers are actually used:

```
*px = 3;
*py = 5;
```

It's our old friend the asterisk again. However—and herein lies the source of much confusion—it's used in a slightly different way here than it is in pointer definitions. In a definition it means "<u>pointer data type</u>," just as **int** means

p233

"integer data type." Here it means something else: "variable pointed to by." So the first statement above translates into "assign the variable pointed to by **px** the value of 3," and the second, "assign the variable pointed to by **py** the value 5." Figure 7-6 shows the effect.

> In a definition the (*) symbol means "pointer type"; in other statements it means "variable pointed to by."

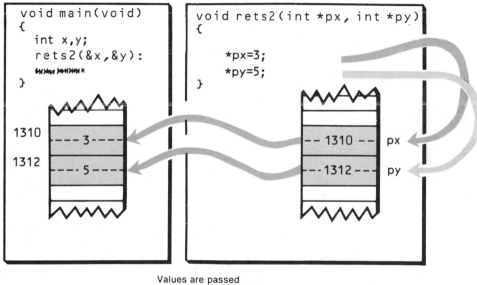

Values are passed
indirectly into **main ( )**'s
memory space.

Figure 7-6. Values Returned to Calling Program

The function has *indirectly* passed the values 3 and 5 to the variables **x** and **y**. It's indirect because the function didn't know the names of the variables, so it used their addresses (which were stored in the function, having been passed to it from the calling program), along with the indirection operator (*), to achieve the same effect. Figure 7-7 shows the structure of an assignment statement using the indirection operator.

We can conclude that the **main()** program has one way of accessing the variables **x** and **y**, while **rets2()** has another. **Main()** calls them **x** and **y**, while **rets2()** calls them *px and *py. This situation is depicted somewhat fancifully in Figure 7-8.

So now, finally, we know how a function can return values to the calling program.

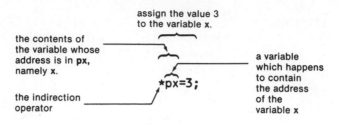

Figure 7-7. The Indirection Operator

main()   rets2()

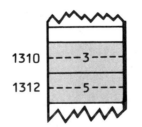

Figure 7-8. Different Perspectives

Going Both Ways

Once a function knows the addresses of variables in the calling program, it not only can place values in these variables, it can also take values out. That is, pointers can be used not only to pass values from a function to the calling program, but also to pass them from the program to the function. Of course, we've seen in earlier chapters that values can be passed directly to a function, but once pointers are being used to go one way, they can easily be used to go the other.

Consider the following function, which adds a constant to two values in the calling program. The function reads the value from the calling program's address space, adds the constant to it, and returns the result to the same spot.

```
/* addtotwo.c */
/* tests function that adds constant to two values */
void addcon(int *px, int *py);   /* prototype */

void main(void)
{                                      address of y
    int x=4, y=7;                      /* initialize variables */

    addcon(&x, &y);                    /* add 10 to both variables */
    printf("First is %d, second is %d", x, y);
}

/* addcon() */                         pointer px
/* adds constant to values in calling program */
void addcon(int *px, int *py)
{
    *px = *px + 10;                    /* add 10 to contents of px */
    *py = *py + 10;                    /* add 10 to contents of py */
}                     contents at address px
```

When the program is run, it prints out:

```
First is 14, second is 17.
```

Here the values 4 and 7 are stored in the variables **x** and **y** in the calling program. The calling program passes the addresses of these variables to the function **addcon()**, which adds the constant 10 to them.

This program looks much like passback.c, except for the assignment p 232 statements in the function:

```
*px = *px + 10;
*py = *py + 10;
```

Here the indirection operator has been used on both sides of the equal sign. The first statement means that we get the contents of the variable pointed to by **px** (this is **x**, whose value is 4), add 10 to it, and return the result to the same place (the variable pointed to by **px**—which is still **x**, but whose value will now be 14). In a similar way the second statement will cause the variable **y** to end up being 17.

In other words, we can use the symbol *px, where **px** is a variable containing the address of **x**, almost exactly as we could have used the variable **x** itself, had it been accessible to us.

Pointers Without Functions

Our examples so far have dealt with pointers that store addresses passed to functions. This is a common use for pointers, and an easy one to implement, but it may tend to obscure some of the operation of pointers. The reason for this is that the function-call mechanism itself takes over the task of assigning an address to the pointer variable. That is, when we call a function with the statement

```
addcon(&x, &y);
```

then the function **addcon()**, which starts with the declarator

```
void addcon(int *px, int *py)
```

will *automatically* assign the addresses of **x** and **y** to the pointer variables **px** and **py**.

Let's look at an example in which we need to perform this assignment "by hand" in the program itself, rather than using a call to a function to do it for us.

The following program carries out the same task as did the addtotwo.c program. However, instead of calling a function to add a constant to the two variables, it does so directly in the program.

p 239

```
/* addin.c */
/* shows use of pointers within program */
/* uses scaling factors */
void main(void)
{
   int x=4, y=7;
   int *px, *py;                  /* pointer variables */

   printf("\nx is %d, y is %d\n", x, y);
   px = &x;                       /* put addresses of numbers */
   py = &y;                       /*    in pointers */
   *px = *px + 10;                /* add constant to contents */
   *py = *py + 10;                /*    of pointers */
```

```
    printf("x is %d, y is %d\n", x, y);
}
```

We use a **printf()** statement to print out the values of **x** and **y**, then add 10 to them, then use another **printf()** statement to print out the new values. Here's the output:

```
x is 4, y is 7.
x is 14, y is 17.
```

Of course all this could have been handled much more easily with the statements

```
x = x + 10;
y = y + 10;
```

However, directly assigning values to the variables would not reveal nearly as much about pointers. (Actually, as battle-scarred C programmers, we should be using

```
x += 10;
y += 10;
```

but this tends to obscure the details of the operation for those not entirely comfortable with arithmetic assignment statements.)

The new elements in the program are the assignment statements

```
px = &x;
py = &y;
```

These statements take the addresses of the variables **x** and **y** and put them in the pointer variables **px** and **py**. This is what the function call **addcon(&x, &y)** did automatically in the addtotwo.c program. The statements

```
*px = *px + 10;
*py = *py + 10;
```

work just as they did in addtotwo.c; in fact, the output of the program is identical. The operation of the program is shown in Figure 7-9. *p239*

An important lesson can be learned by imagining what would happen if the statements **px = &x** and **py = &y** were left out of the program. Would it still work? No, because then there would be no address or at least not a correct address in the variables **px** and **py**. So the references to ***px** and ***py** would refer not to **x** and **y**, but to whatever was located in the addresses that happened to be in **px** and **py**. Since these addresses could point to the program itself, or to the operating system, disaster could swiftly follow.

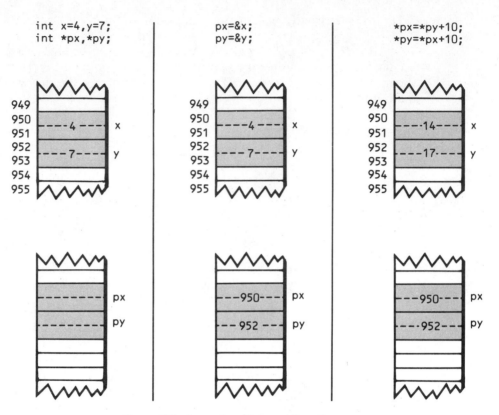

Figure 7-9. Operation of the addin.c Program

The moral is, make sure you <u>assign a pointer variable</u> an appropriate <u>address</u> before you use it.

> ***ptr**   is the <u>contents</u> of **ptr**
> **&var**   is the <u>address</u> of **var**

Pointers and Arrays

In Chapter 6 we explored arrays and saw examples of array notation: how to reference array elements with such statements as **table[x][y]**. As it turns out, this array notation is really nothing more than a thinly disguised form of pointer notation. In fact, the compiler translates array notation into pointer notation when compiling, since the internal architecture of the microprocessor understands pointers but does not understand arrays.

To make clearer the relationship between pointers and arrays, let's look at a simple program, expressed first in <u>array notation</u> and then in pointer notation.

Here's the array version:

```
/* array.c */
/* prints out values from array */
void main(void)
{
    static int nums[] = { 92, 81, 70, 69, 58 };
    int dex;

    for (dex=0; dex<5; dex++)
        printf("%d\n", nums[dex] );
}
```

And here is the output—it should not come as a surprise to anyone:

```
92
81
70
69
58
```

This is a straightforward program. Array notation is used to access individual elements of the array in the expression **nums[dex].**

Now let's see how this program would look using <u>pointer notation</u>:

```
/* parray.c */
/* uses pointers to print out values from array */
void main(void)
{
    static int nums[] = { 92, 81, 70, 69, 58 };
    int dex;

    for (dex=0; dex<5; dex++)
        printf("%d\n", *(nums+dex) );
}
```

This version is identical to the first, except for the expression ***(nums+dex)**. What does it mean? Its effect is exactly the same as that of **nums[dex]** in the earlier example; in other words, it accesses that element of the array **nums** whose subscript is contained in the variable **dex**. (Thus, if **dex** is 3, we'll get element **nums[3]**, which is 69.)

How do we interpret ***(nums+dex)**? First, as we know, **nums** is the address of the array. Now if we add, say, the number 3 to this address, what will we get? In other words, if **dex** is 3, what is **nums+dex**? Would you guess the result would be an address three bytes from the start of the array? If so, you have not counted on the extreme cleverness of the designers of C.

After all, what we want is not an address three bytes from the start of the array, but the address of *element number 3* in the array. If each element of the array is an integer, it takes up two bytes, so we want to look at the address *six* bytes from the start of the array. As shown in Figure 7-10, if the array **nums** starts at 1400, then when **dex** is 3 we want **nums+dex** to have the value 1406—which is the address of **nums[3]**—not the value 1403 (which is the second half of **nums[1]** and meaningless).

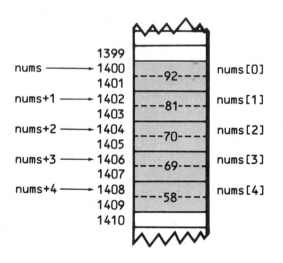

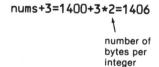

Figure 7-10. Pointer Addition

In other words, if we say **nums+3**, we don't mean three *bytes*, we mean three *elements of the array*: three integers if it's an integer array, three floating point numbers if it's a floating point array, and so on.

And that's exactly what the C compiler delivers. It looks at the context of the plus sign, and if we're adding 3 to a pointer, it doesn't add 3, it adds 3 *times* however many bytes each element of the array occupies. How does it know how many bytes per element? In this case, since we're adding something to an address at the start of an array, **nums[ ]**, it looks at the array declaration, finds out it's an array of type **int**, and, since there are two bytes per integer, multiplies by 2.

Now that you know this, you should be able to figure out the meaning of the expression

```
*(nums+dex)
```

If **dex** is 3, then this expression means "the contents of element 3 of the array **nums[ ]**"; this value is 69. Thus, as we've noted, ***(nums+dex)** is the same thing as **nums[dex]**. They are both ways of referring to the contents of an array element.

> ***(array+index)** is the same as **array[index]**

There are also two ways to refer to the *address* of an array element. We can say **nums+dex** in pointer notation, and **&nums[dex]** in array notation. These relationships are shown in Figure 7-11.

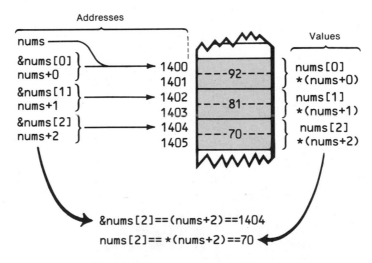

Figure 7-11. Addresses and Values

What do we gain by using pointer notation as opposed to array notation? Probably not very much in this context. However, pointer notation is commonly used with arrays in this way, so it's good to be familiar with it. More important, similar notation is used in many other instances where array notation would not work at all, as we'll see directly.

Return of the Killer Averages

p 184

As another example of the equivalence of array and pointer notation, we're going to translate the temperature-averaging program fltemp2.c from Chapter 6 into pointer notation. We'll use this program, and a variant of it, to demonstrate some important aspects of pointer variables and constants. You might want to refer back to fltemp2.c before looking at this modified version:

```
/* ptrtemp.c */
/* averages arbitrary number of temperatures */
/* uses pointer notation */
void main(void)
{                          a pointer constant
    float temper[40];                  /* array declaration */
    float sum=0.0;
    int num, day=0;

    do                                 /* put temps in array */
        {
        printf("Enter temperature for day %d: ", day);
        scanf("%f", temper+day);
        }
    while ( *(temper+day++) > 0 );

    num = day-1;                       /* number of temps entered */
    for (day=0; day<num; day++)        /* calculate average */
        sum += *(temper+day);
    printf("Average is %.1f", sum/num);
}
```

This works as it did in Chapter 5; you type in an arbitrary number of temperatures, and the program prints out the average. We've modified three different expressions in this program, with the goal of changing the address **&temper[day]** into **temper+day** and the value stored there from **temper[day]** into ***(temper+day)**. Here are the three lines affected:

```
scanf("%f", temper+day);
- - - -
while ( *(temper+day++) > 0 );
- - - -
sum += *(temper+day);
```

What we've done here is perform almost a literal translation from array notation to pointer notation. However, such a literal translation does not yield the most efficient or elegant programming.

Pointer Constants and Pointer Variables

Is there any way to simplify these three unwieldy expressions? In each, we're using the expression **temper+day** as a way to reference individual items of the array by varying the value of **day**. Could we get rid of **day** by using the increment operator on the address itself, instead of using the variable **day**? For example, can we use an expression like this?

```
while ( *(temper++) > 0 );   /* can't do this */
```

The answer is no, and the reason is that **temper** is a pointer constant. It is not a variable. It is the address of the array **temper**, and this value will not change while the program is running. The linker has decided where this array will go—say address 810—and that's where it will stay. So trying to increment this address has no meaning; it's like saying

```
x = 3++;   /* can't do this either */
```

Since you can't increment a constant, the compiler will flag this as an error.

> You can't change the value of a pointer constant, only of a pointer variable.

So we've run into a problem. It would be nice to use a statement as clear as *(temper++), but we can't increment a constant. However, we *can* increment *variables*. This is one of the real strengths of the C language: the ability to use pointer variables. So let's rewrite the program to make use of such variables.

```
/* ptrtemp2.c */
/* averages arbitrary number of temperatures */
/* uses pointer variables */
void main(void)
{
    float temper[40];              /* array declaration */
    float sum=0.0;
    int num, day=0;
    float *ptr;                    /* pointer variable */
```

```
        ptr = temper;                   /* set pointer to array */
        do                              /* put temps in array */
           {
           printf("Enter temperature for day %d: ", day++);
           scanf("%f", ptr);
           }
        while ( *(ptr++) > 0 );

        ptr = temper;                   /* reset pointer to array */
        num = day-1;                    /* number of temps entered */
        for (day=0; day<num; day++)     /* calculate average */
           sum += *(ptr+day);
        printf("Average is %.1f", sum/num);
        }
```

The strategy here is to place the address **temper** (say it's 810) into a pointer variable called **ptr**. Now we can refer to **ptr** in much the same way we refer to **temper**. We can use **ptr** as an address that will point to an array element, and we can use ***ptr** as the contents of that address. Moreover, since **ptr** is a variable, we don't need to add something to it to point to each element of the array in turn; all we need to do is increment it:

```
   ptr++
```

We set **ptr** equal to the address **temper** before we enter the loop to read in the temperatures, and we reset it again before we enter the loop to average them. Then in both these loops we increment **ptr** with the (++) operator so that it points to each array element in turn. (Because **ptr** points to an array of type **float**, the (++) operator causes it to be incremented by four bytes.) The process is shown in Figure 7-12.

By using pointer variables we have simplified the program and made it run faster, since only one variable, **ptr**, must be referenced each time through the loop, instead of both **temper** and **dex**.

Pointers to Arrays in Functions

We started this chapter by learning how pointers can be used for communication among functions, and then we examined how pointers can be used to reference array elements. Let's combine these two techniques to see how a function can use pointers to access elements of an array whose address is passed to the function as an argument.

As an example, we'll modify our program addtotwo.c, which adds a constant to two variables in the calling program, to add a constant to all the elements in an array. This is a function that might prove useful in a variety of circumstances. Here's the listing:

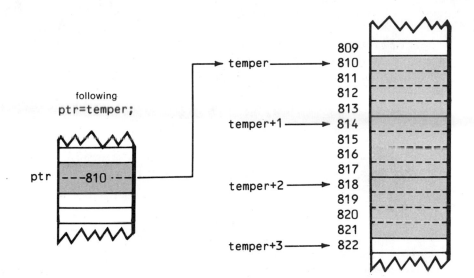

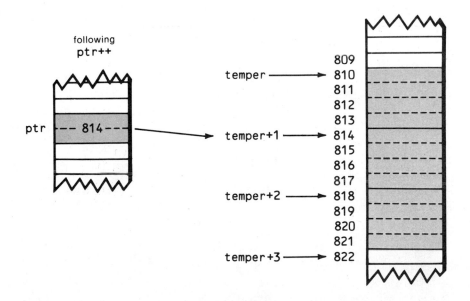

Figure 7-12. Incrementing a Pointer Variable

```
/* addarray.c */
/* tests function to add constant to array values */
#define SIZE 5                    /* size of array */
void addcon(int *, int, int);     /* prototype */
```

pointer const points to 1st element

```
void main(void)
{
    static int array[SIZE] = { 3, 5, 7, 9, 11 };
    int konst = 10;                 /* constant to be added */
    int j;

    addcon(array, SIZE, konst);    /* call funct to add consts */
    for (j=0; j<SIZE; j++)          /* print out array */
        printf("%d  ", *(array+j) );
}

/* addcon() */
/* adds constant to each element of array */
void addcon(int *ptr, int size, int con)
/* arguments: array, array size, constant */
{
    int k;
    for(k=0; k<size; k++)           /* add const to each element */
        *(ptr+k) = *(ptr+k) + con;
}
```

pointer variable

Here the calling program supplies the address of the array, **array**; the size of the array, SIZE (which is **#define**d to be 5); and the constant to be added to each element, **konst** (which is assigned the value 10).

The function assigns the address of the array to the pointer **ptr**, the size to the variable num, and the constant to the variable **con**. Then a simple loop serves to add the constant to each element of the array.

The output of this program shows the new contents of the array to verify that the function has done its work. Here's what it looks like:

```
13  15  17  19  21
```

size

Pointers and Strings

Let's turn now to the relationship of pointers and strings. Since strings are arrays and arrays are closely connected with pointers, you might expect that strings and pointers are closely related, and this is correct.

String Functions and Pointers

Many of the C library functions that work with strings do so by using pointers. As an example, let's look at an example of a string function that returns a pointer. The function is **strchr()**, which returns a pointer to the first occurrence of a particular character in a string. If we say

```
ptr = strchr(str, 'x');
```

then the pointer variable **ptr** will be assigned the address of the first occurrence of the character 'x' in the string **str**. Note that this isn't the *position* in the string, which runs from 0 to the end of the string, but the *address*, which runs from 2343—or wherever the string happens to start—to the end of the string.

Here is the function **strchr()** used in a simple program that allows the user to type in a sentence and a character to be searched for. The program then prints out the address of the start of the string, the address of the character, and the character's position relative to the start of the string (0 if it's the first character, 1 if it's the second, and so forth). This relative position is simply the difference between the two addresses.

```
/* search.c */
/* searches string for a given character */
void main(void)
{
    char ch, line[81], *ptr, *strchr();

    puts("Enter the sentence to be searched: ");      p 215
    gets(line);                                        p 213
    printf("Enter character to search for: ");
    ch = getche();

    ptr = strchr(line,ch);      /* return pointer to char */
    printf("\nString starts at address %u.\n", line);
    printf("First occurrence of char is address %u.\n", ptr);
    printf("This is position %d (starting from 0)", ptr-line);
}
```

Here's a sample run:

```
Enter the sentence to be searched:
The quick brown fox jumped over the lazy dog.
Enter character to search for: x
String starts at address 3610.
First occurrence of character is address 3628.
This is character position 18.
```

In the declaration statement, we've set aside a pointer variable, **ptr**, to hold the address returned by **strchr()**. Since this is the address of a character, **ptr** is of type **char***. Once the function has returned this address, we can print it out and use it to calculate the position of the character in the string: the value **ptr—line**.

Are you wondering what the expression ***strchr()*** is doing in the declaration statement? As we discussed in Chapter 5, any function that doesn't return an integer value must be declared. The **strchr()** function returns a pointer to a character, so it must be declared to be of this type. We could have left this declaration out if we'd included the preprocessor statement

```
#include <string.h>
```

at the beginning of the program. This would work just as well (and is generally the preferred approach), since the header file string.h contains prototypes for the string handling functions.

Strings Initialized as Pointers

We showed an example of initializing a string as an array in the program strinit.c in Chapter 6. Our next example shows how this program can be modified so that the string is initialized as a pointer. Here's the listing:

```
/* strinit.c */
/* shows string initialization */
/* uses pointers */
void main(void)
{
    static char *salute = "Greetings,";
    char name[81];

    puts("Enter your name: ");
    gets(name);
    puts(salute);
    puts(name);
}
```

Here, to initialize the string, we've used the statement

```
char *salute = "Greetings,";
```

instead of

```
static char salute[] = "Greetings,";
```

These two forms appear to have much the same effect in the program. Is there a difference? Yes, but it's quite a subtle one. The array version of this statement sets aside an array with enough bytes (in this case 10) to hold the word, plus one byte for the '\0' (null) character. The address of the first character of the array is given the name of the array, in this case, **salute**. In the pointer version, an array is set aside in the same way, but a *pointer variable* is also set aside; it is this pointer that is given the name **salute**. Figure 7-13 shows how this looks.

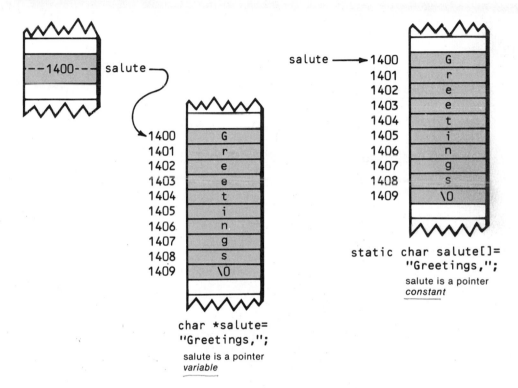

Figure 7-13. String Array Versus String Pointer

In the array style of initialization, **salute** is a pointer constant, an address which cannot be changed. In the pointer style, **salute** is a pointer variable, which can be changed. For instance, the expression

```
puts(++salute);
```

would print the string starting with the second character in the string:

```
reetings,
```

The added flexibility of the pointer approach can often be used to advantage, as we'll see shortly.

Initializing an Array of Pointers to Strings

There's another difference between initializing a string as an array or as a pointer. This difference is most easily seen when we talk about an array of strings (or if we use pointers, an array of pointers to strings).

In Chapter 6 we showed how to initialize an array of strings in the program compare.c. In the following example we'll modify this program so that the strings are initialized as pointers.

p217

```
/* comparep.c */
/* compares word typed in with words in program */
/* uses pointers */
#define MAX 5
void main(void)
{
    int dex;
    int enter=0;
    char name[40];
    static char *list[MAX] =
                    { "Katrina",
                      "Nigel",
                      "Alistair",
                      "Francesca",
                      "Gustav"     };
    printf("Enter your name: ");                    /* get name */
    gets(name);
    for (dex=0; dex<MAX; dex++)                      /* go thru list */
       if( strcmp(list[dex],name)==0 )              /* if match */
          enter = 1;                                /* set flag */
    if ( enter == 1 )                               /* if flag set */
       printf("You may enter, oh honored one.");    /* one response */
    else                                            /* otherwise */
       printf("Guards! Remove this person!");       /* different one */
}
```

pointer to a pointer

p218

What does the expression **char *list[MAX]** mean? Such complex expressions are generally deciphered from right to left, so, as shown in Figure 7-14, this one means an array of pointers to characters.

In the array version of this program, the strings were stored in a rectangular array with 5 rows and 10 columns. In the new version, the strings are stored contiguously in memory; they don't form an array, so there is no wasted space between them. However, an array of *pointers to* these strings has been created. Figure 7-15 shows the differences between these two approaches.

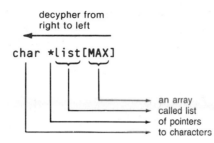

Figure 7-14. Declaration of Array of Pointers

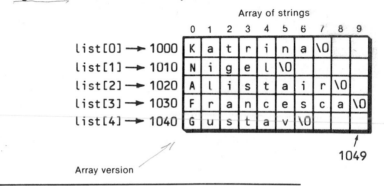

Figure 7-15. Array of Strings Versus Array of Pointers

As you can see, the pointer version takes up less space in memory; it ends at 1038, while the array version ends at 1049. Thus, one reason to initialize strings as pointers is to use memory more efficiently. Another reason is to obtain greater flexibility in the manipulation of the strings in the array, as the next example will show.

> Initializing a group of strings using pointer notation uses less memory than initializing them as a two-dimensional array.

Lvalue and Rvalue   *Left value , Right value*

Occasionally, when experimenting with pointers and strings, you may receive error messages from the compiler that use the term *lvalue*, as in "lvalue required." What does this mean?

Essentially, an lvalue is a variable, as opposed to an rvalue which is a constant. The terms arose from the left-right positions in a typical assignment statement:

```
var = 3;
```

An expression that can appear on the left side of an assignment statement is a variable and is called an "lvalue." An expression that must remain on the right side of the equal sign because it is a constant is called an "rvalue." If you attempt to use a constant on the left side of the equal sign in the assignment statement, the compiler will flag it as an error.

Manipulating Pointers to Strings

As you know, when an array is passed as an argument to a function, it is not actually the array that is passed, but only its address. The array itself does not move. The same is true of strings: when we pass a string to a function, we are passing only its address. This ability to reference strings by addresses can be very helpful when we want to manipulate a group of strings. In the following example we will sort an array of strings, using an approach similar to that of the sortnum.c program in Chapter 6. However, we won't move the strings themselves around in the array; instead, we'll sort an array of pointers to the strings.

p263

This program accepts a series of names typed in by the user, places them in an array, and sorts the pointers to the array so that, in effect, the names are rearranged into alphabetical order. Then, the resulting sorted list is printed out. Here's the program:

```c
/* sortstr.c */
/* sorts list of names typed in to array */
#define MAXNUM 30            /* maximum number of names */
#define MAXLEN 81            /* maximum length of names */
void main(void)
{
    static char name[MAXNUM][MAXLEN];    /* array of strings */
    char *ptr[MAXNUM];              /* array of pntrs to strings */
    char *temp;                    /* extra pointer */
    int count = 0;                 /* how many names */
    int in, out;                   /* sorting indexes */

    while ( count < MAXNUM )       /* get names */
       {
       printf("Name %d: ", count+1);
       gets(name[count]);
       if ( strlen(name[count])==0 )
          break;                   /* quit if no name */
       ptr[count++] = name[count]; /* each ptr points to name */
       }

                               /* sort the pointers */
    for (out=0; out<count-1; out++)    /* for each string */
       for (in=out+1; in<count; in++) /* look at those smaller */
          if ( strcmp(ptr[out],ptr[in]) > 0 )  /* compare */
             {                       /* if any smaller, */
             temp = ptr[in];         /* swap pointers */
             ptr[in] = ptr[out];
             ptr[out] = temp;
             }

    printf("\nSorted List: \n");
    for (out=0; out<count; out++) /* print sorted list */
       printf("Name %d: %s\n", out+1, ptr[out]);
}
```

bubble sort (handwritten)

p 218 (handwritten)

And a sample run:

```
Name 1: Thomas        ← typed in by user
Name 2: Cummings
Name 3: Sandburg
Name 4: Masefield
Name 5: Shelley
Name 6: Auden
Name 7:
```

```
Sorted list:
Name 1: Auden          ← printed out by program
Name 2: Cummings
Name 3: Masefield
Name 4: Sandburg
Name 5: Shelley
Name 6: Thomas
```

This program uses both an array of strings and an array of pointers. The pointers occupy the array declared by the expression:

```
char *ptr[MAXNUM];
```

The strings occupy a two-dimensional array:

```
static char name[MAXNUM][MAXKEN];
```

Because we don't know in advance how long they will be, we must use a rectangular array to hold the strings that are typed in (rather than initializing them as pointers to strings). We use rows 81 characters long; these will hold names extending across the entire screen.

As the strings are read in, the statement

```
ptr[count++] = name[count];
```

assigns the address of each string, which is stored in the array **name[ ][ ]**, to an element of the pointer array **ptr[ ]**. Then this array of pointers is sorted. Finally, the strings are printed out in alphabetical order, using the array of pointers as a reference. Figure 7-16 shows how the pointers look before and after sorting. The array **name[ ][ ]** itself remains unchanged; only the pointers to the elements of the array have been rearranged.

There is a subtle aspect to this program that may have slipped your notice. Let's take a closer look.

Parts of Arrays Are Arrays

The C language embodies an unusual but powerful capability: it can treat parts of arrays *as arrays*. More specifically, each row of a two-dimensional array can be thought of as a one-dimensional array. This can be very useful if one wishes to rearrange the rows of a two-dimensional array, as we just did in the sortstr.c example.

Do you see anything unusual about the following statement from sortstr.c?

```
ptr[count++] = name[count];
```

That's right: although the array **name[ ][ ]** is a two-dimensional array, we use only one subscript when we refer to it in this statement: **name[count]**. What does **name[count]** mean, if **name[ ][ ]** is a two-dimensional array?

Remember that we can think of a two-dimensional array as an array of arrays. In this case, the definition

```
static char name[MAXNUM][MAXLEN];
```

can be thought of as setting up a one-dimensional array of MAXNUM elements, each of which is a one-dimensional array MAXLEN characters long. In other words, we have a one-dimensional array of MAXNUM strings. We refer to the elements of a one-dimensional array with a single subscript, as in **name[count]**, where **count** can range up to MAXNUM. More specifically, **name[0]** is the address of the first string in the array, **name[1]** is the address of the second string, and so forth. Thus the expression **name[count]** makes sense and simplifies the coding of the program.

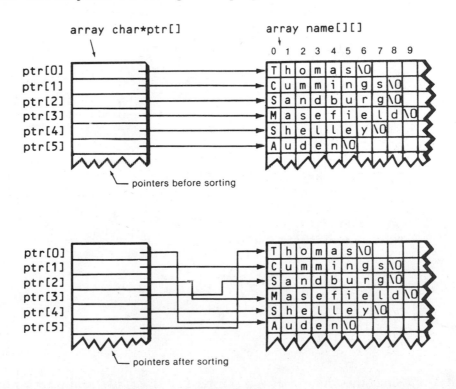

Figure 7-16. Sorting Pointers to Strings

Double Indirection: Pointers to Pointers

The ability of the C language to treat part of an array as an array is actually a disguised version of another C topic, double indirection, or pointers that point to pointers. Being able to reference a pointer with a pointer gives C enormous power and flexibility in creating complex arrangements of data. As a hint of what's involved, let's look at an example of double indirection, derived from a two-dimensional array.

p257

In the sortstr.c program, we dealt with parts of arrays as strings. This was in some ways easier than dealing with parts of arrays as arrays, which we will now look at in a two-dimensional array of numbers.

We'll start off with a simple program that takes an existing two-dimensional array, adds a constant to each element, and prints out the result. We'll use normal array notation for this program, so it should hold no surprises:

```
/* double.c */
/* shows use of 2-dimensional arrays */
#define ROWS 4
#define COLS 5

void main(void)
{
   static int table[ROWS][COLS] =
                   { { 13, 15, 17, 19, 21 },
                     { 20, 22, 24, 26, 28 },
                     { 31, 33, 35, 37, 39 },
                     { 40, 42, 44, 46, 48 }  };
   int j, k;

   for(j=0; j<ROWS; j++)       /* add constant to each element */
      for(k=0; k<COLS; k++)
        table[j][k] = table[j][k] + 10;

   printf("\n");
   for(j=0; j<ROWS; j++)       /* print out array */
      {
      for (k=0; k<COLS; k++)
         printf("%d ", table[j][k] );
      printf("\n");
      }

}
```

Since the program adds a constant 10 to each element, the output looks like this:

```
23 25 27 29 31
30 32 34 36 38
41 43 45 47 49
50 52 54 56 58
```

Now, suppose we rewrite this program to use pointer notation instead of array notation. The question is, how do we write the expression **table[j][k]** in pointer notation? To do this, we make use of the fact that a two-dimensional array is an array of one-dimensional arrays as shown in Figure 7-17.

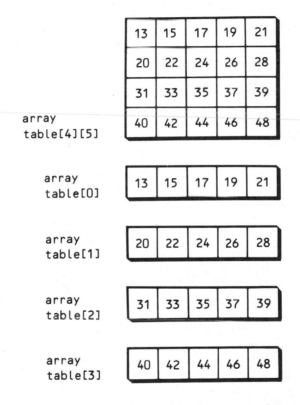

array
table[4][5]

array
table[0]

array
table[1]

array
table[2]

array
table[3]

row ordered

Figure 7-17. Each Row of an Array Is an Array

Let's figure out how to use pointers to refer to the fourth element in the third row of the array, or **table[2][3]**, which is 37 (before the 10 is added).

First, the address of the entire array is **table**. Let's assume the array starts at address 1000 in memory, so **table==1000**. It's an integer array, so each element takes two bytes. There are five elements in each row, so each row takes 10 bytes. Thus each row starts 10 bytes further along than the last one. And, since each row is a one-dimensional array, each of these one-dimensional arrays starts 10 bytes further along than the last one, as shown in the top part of Figure 7-18.

The compiler knows how many columns there are in the array, since we specified this in the array declaration. So it knows how to interpret the expression **table+1**; it takes the address of **table** (1000), and adds the number of bytes in a row (5 columns times 2 bytes per column, equaling 10 bytes). Thus **table+1** is interpreted as the address 1010. This is the address of the second one-dimensional array in the array, **table+2** is the address of the third such array, and so on. We're looking for an item in the third row, whose address is **table+2**, or 1020.

Now, how do we refer to the individual elements of a row? We've mentioned before that the address of an array is the same as the address of the first element in the array. For example, in the one-dimensional array **list[SIZE]**, **list** is the same as **&list[0]**. Again referring to Figure 7-18, we've already determined that the address of the array formed by the third row of **table[ ][ ]** is **table[2]**, or **table+2** in pointer notation. The address of the first element of this array is **&table[2][0]**, or ***(table+2)** in pointer notation. Both pointer expressions, **table+2** and ***(table+2)**, refer to the contents of the same address, 1020. Why use two different expressions for the same thing? The difference between ***(table+2)** and **table+2** is in the units of measurement. If you add 1 to **table+2** you get **table+3**, or the address of the fourth row of **table[ ][ ]**; you've added 10 bytes. But if you add 1 to ***(table+2)**, you get the address of the next element in the row; you've added 2 bytes.

> An element of a two-dimensional array can be referenced with a pointer to a pointer.

So the address of the fourth element is ***(table+2)+3**. And, finally, the *contents* of that element is ***(*(table+2)+3)**, which is 37. This expression is a pointer to a pointer.

In other words,

```
table[j][k] == *(*(table+j)+k)
```

We've figured out how to translate two-dimensional array notation into pointer notation. Now we can rewrite our program, incorporating this new notation:

```
/* double2.c */
/* shows use of pointers on 2-dimensional arrays */
#define ROWS 4
#define COLS 5
```

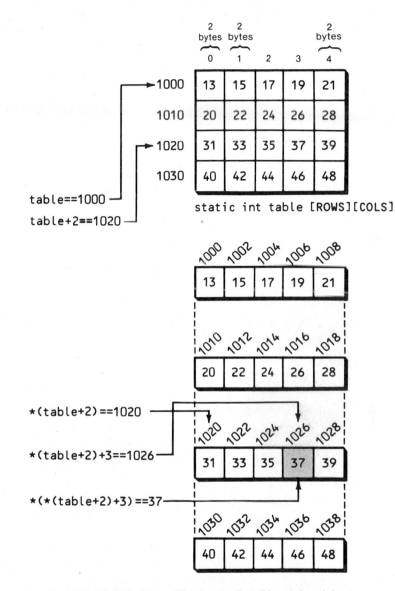

Figure 7-18. Pointing to Element in Two-Dimensional Array

```
void main(void)
{
    static int table[ROWS][COLS] =
                    { { 13, 15, 17, 19, 21 },
                      { 20, 22, 24, 26, 28 },
                      { 31, 33, 35, 37, 39 },
```

```
                              { 40, 42, 44, 46, 48 } };
        int j, k;

        for(j=0; j<ROWS; j++)       /* add constant to each element */
           for(k=0; k<COLS; k++)
             *(*(table+j)+k) = *(*(table+j)+k) + 10;

        printf("\n");
        for(j=0; j<ROWS; j++)        /* print out array */
           {
           for (k=0; k<COLS; k++)
              printf("%d ", *(*(table+j)+k) );
           printf("\n");
           }

     }
```

This version of the program will work just the same as the old one did.

The Rocketship Program

Let's look at a slightly more ambitious example that incorporates double indirection. This program models a very crude rocketship taking off. As a spectacular graphics display, the program leaves something to be desired (especially since we haven't learned how to clear the screen between pictures), but it does demonstrate how to manipulate array elements using pointers.

The program consists of a large loop. To cycle once through the loop, press any key. Each time through the loop, the program draws a line, representing the ground, consisting of five double lines (graphics character '\xCD'). It then draws the rocketship, defined in the program as four elements of a character array: a main body ('\DB'), a nose cone, and two engines ('\x1E'). After drawing the rocket, the rows of the array that contain the rocket are, in effect, rotated; each row moves up one character, and the top row is placed on the bottom. (Actually we don't rotate the array itself, as we'll see in a moment.) Then the array is printed again. The effect is of the rocketship rising from the ground, as shown in Figure 7-19. Here's the listing for the program:

```
/* move.c */
/* moves image on screen */
#define ROWS 10
#define COLS 5
#define HEIGHT 25     /* height of screen in rows */

void main(void)
```

```
{
    int count, j, k;
    char *ptr[ROWS];                        /* pointers to rows */
    char *temp;                             /* pointer storage */


    static char pict[ROWS][COLS] =          /* rocketship */
            {  { 0,       0,       0,       0,       0       },
               { 0,       0,       0,       0,       0       },
               { 0,       0,       0,       0,       0       },
               { 0,       0,       0,       0,       0       },
               { 0,       0,       0,       0,       0       },
               { 0,       0,       0,       0,       0       },
               { 0,       0,       0,       0,       0       },
               { 0,       0,       0,       0,       0       },
               { 0,       0,       '\x1E', 0,       0       },
               { 0,       '\x1E', '\xDB', '\x1E', 0       }  };

    static char gnd[] =                     /* ground line */
            { '\xCD', '\xCD', '\xCD', '\xCD', '\xCD', 0 };


    for(count=0; count<ROWS; count++)       /* set up pointers */
        *(ptr+count) = *(pict+count);


    for(count=0; count<ROWS-1; count++)
        {
        for(j=0; j<HEIGHT-ROWS; j++)        /* print blank lines */
        printf("%c", '\n');
        for(j=0; j<ROWS; j++)               /* print rocket */
            {
            for(k=0; k<COLS; k++)
                printf("%c", *(*(ptr+j)+k) );
            printf("%c", '\n' );
            }
        printf("%s\n", gnd);                /* print ground */


        temp = *ptr;                        /* rotate pointers */
        for(j=0; j<ROWS-1; j++)
            *(ptr+j) = *(ptr+j+1);
        *(ptr+ROWS-1) = temp;
        getch();                            /* wait for keypress */
        }
}
```

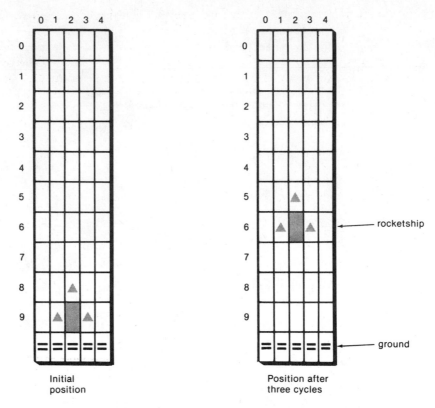

Figure 7-19. Rocketship Rising from the Ground

Here's how the program works. We declare an array of pointers to characters.

```
char *ptr[ROWS];
```

In each of the elements of this array, we place the address of one row of the array **pict[ ][ ]** using the loop:

```
for(count=0; count<ROWS; count++)
  *(ptr+count) = *(pict+count);
```

We print out the elements of the array as individual characters using two nested loops, a process we used in Chapter 6. In this case, however, we use pointer notation to refer to individual elements of the array, in the expression

```
printf("%c", *(*(ptr+j)+k) );
```

Notice that we don't actually refer to the array **pict[ ][ ]** itself, but rather to the array of pointers, **ptr[ ]**, that point to it.

To make the rocket appear to rise off the ground line, we in effect move the elements in each row of the array **pict[ ][ ]**, upward one row at a time. If we actually moved all the array elements we would need to move all 50 characters in memory, and this would be time consuming. So instead of moving the rows of the array, we simply move the pointers that point to these rows. There are only 10 pointers, so this is a much faster operation than moving 50 characters. (If we were trying to move an object wider than five characters, the speed advantage would be greater still.)

The pointers are rotated in the array **ptr[ ]**: each element moves up one location, and the top element goes to the bottom. We store the top row, **ptr[0]**, in the pointer variable **temp**, then use a loop to move the contents of each row to the row whose subscript is one less than where it came from, and finally we insert the top element, stored in **temp**, back into the bottom row. (This is like the technique employed for sorting strings earlier in this chapter.) Figure 7-20 shows the pointers after three cycles through the loop; each pointer has moved up three rows in the array ***pict[ROWS]**.

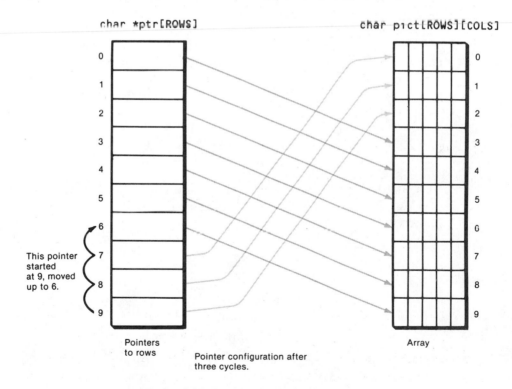

Figure 7-20. Rocketship Pointer Configuration

Now when we print out the array, we'll see that the rocket appears to have risen one character from the ground line each time through the loop.

Actually, the array **pict[ ][ ]** remains unaltered, with the rocket still in the lowest position. However, by printing out the rows of the array in a different order, the rocket appears to move.

Our method of clearing the screen is to print enough newlines to scroll the picture off the top. We'll see a better way to clear the screen in the next chapter.

Summary

This chapter has introduced the subject of pointers and has covered some of the less complex ways pointers can be used. We've seen how to declare pointer variables with such statements as **int *ptr2**; and we've learned how to refer to the values pointed to by pointers, using such expressions as ***ptr2** (the asterisk having a different meaning in the two cases). We've used pointers to return multiple values from a function to the calling program and to permit a function to modify values contained in the calling program, with the use of expressions like ***ptrx=*ptfx+10**.

The second major topic we covered in the chapter was the relationship of pointers to arrays. We saw how to reference individual array elements using pointer notation and how to perform arithmetic on pointers. We've seen that pointer variables can be modified, but that pointer constants—the addresses of data structures—cannot.

We've investigated the use of pointers with strings, seeing how some string library functions return pointers and the uses that can be made of such functions. We've also learned how to initialize strings using pointers instead of arrays and the benefits of this approach.

Finally we've learned how to use pointer notation to refer to the elements of a two-dimensional array, and we've seen how this relates to the idea of a pointer to a pointer.

Questions

1. Why are pointers sometimes found to be difficult to understand?
   a. They point to data beyond our control.
   b. They use the same symbol to refer to two different things.
   c. The idea of indirection is not used in some languages.
   d. They require a knowledge of quantum mechanics.

2. Which of these are reasons for using pointers?
   a. To manipulate parts of arrays

    b. To refer to key words such as **loop** and **if**

    c. To return more than one value from a function

    d. To refer to particular programs more conveniently

3. True or false: the address of an array is a pointer constant.

4. True or false: passing the addresses of arrays to functions is beyond the scope of this book.

5. True or false: passing a value to a function places the address of that value in the function's private memory space.

6. For a function to return more than one value, it must first be passed the addresses of the variables to be returned. This is because

    a. The function must always contain the same amount of numbers, whether addresses or values.

    b. The addresses are actually a code that is deciphered into values by the function.

    c. The function needs to know where to find library routines.

    d. The function needs to know where to put the values it returns.

7. If we call a function with the statement **blotch(&white,&black)**, what purpose do **&white** and **&black** serve?

    a. They are integer values we're passing to the function.

    b. They are the addresses of the function and the calling program.

    c. They are the addresses of the variables where we want values returned or modified in the calling program.

    d. They are the addresses of library routines needed by the function.

8. To return more than one value from a function, we must pass the function the _____ of the values we want returned; then, in the function, we must first _____ pointers to hold these values, and finally we access the values using _____ .

9. Which is the correct way to define a pointer?

    a. int_ptr x;

    b. int *ptr;

    c. *int ptr;

    d. *x;

10. Which are correct ways to refer to the variable **ch**, assuming the address of **ch** has been assigned to the pointer **fingerch**?

    a. *fingerch;

    b. int *fingerch;

    c. *finger;

    d. ch

    e. *ch

11. In the expression **float *fptr;** what has type float?

    a. The variable **fptr**

    b. The address of **fptr**

    c. The variable pointed to by **fptr**

    d. None of the above

12. Assuming that the address of the variable **var** has been assigned to the pointer variable **pointvar**, write an expression that does not use **var** and that will divide **var** by 10.

13. Assuming that the address of **vox** has been assigned to the pointer variable **invox**, which of the following expressions are correct?

    a. vox == &invox

    b. vox == *invox

    c. invox == *vox

    d. invox == &vox

14. When a function is called using **&x** as a parameter, where is the value of **&x** placed?

15. What statement must be added to the following program to make it work correctly?

```
void main(void)
{
    int j, *ptrj;
    *ptrj = 3;
}
```

16. Assuming we want to read in a value for **x**, and the address of **x** has been assigned to **ptrx**, does this statement look all right?

```
scanf("%d", *ptrx);
```

17. Assuming that **spread[]** is a one-dimensional array of type int, which of the following refers to the value of the third element in the array?

   a. *(spread+2)

   b. *(spread+4)

   c. spread+4

   d. spread+2

18. Suppose an array has been defined as

```
int arr[3];
```
Can you use the expression **arr++**?

19. What will the following program do when executed?

```
void main(void)
{
    static int arr[] = { 4, 5, 6 };
    int j;
    for(j=0; j<3; j++)
        printf("%d  ", *(arr+j) );
}
```

20. In the program above, the plus sign in the expression **arr+j** means to add j times _____ bytes, to **arr**.

21. What will the following program do when executed?

```
void main(void)
{
    static int arr[] = { 4, 5, 6 };
    int j;
    for(j=0; j<3; j++)
        printf("%d  ", arr+j );
}
```

22. What will the following program do when executed?

```
void main(void)
{
    static int arr[] = { 4, 5, 6 };
    int j, *ptr;
    ptr = arr;
```

```
        for(j=0; j<3; j++)
            printf("%d  ", *ptr++ );
}
```

23. Are the following statements equivalent?

```
char errmsg[] = "Error!";
char *errmsg = "Error!";
```

24. One difference between using array notation to define a group of strings and using pointer notation is that in array notation each string occupies _____ of memory, but when pointer notation is used each string occupies _____ of memory.

25. Given the declaration

```
static char s7[] = "I come not to bury Caesar";
```

what will the following statements cause to be printed?

```
printf("%s", s7 );
printf("%s", &s7[0] );
printf("%s", s7+11 );
```

26. When you declare a string using pointer notation, and the string is 10 characters long, ____ bytes are set aside in memory. (Note: this isn't as easy as it looks.)

27. True or false: every column of a two-dimensional array can be considered to be another two-dimensional array.

28. Given the following array definition:

```
static int arr7[2][3] = {  { 10, 11, 12 },
                           { 13, 14, 15 }  };
```

refer to the element occupied by the number 14 in array notation and then in pointer notation.

29. If you want to exchange two rows in a two-dimensional array, the fastest way is to:

   a. exchange the elements of the two rows

   b. exchange the addresses of each element in the two rows

c. set the address of one row equal to the address of the other, and vice versa

d. store the addresses of the rows in an array of pointers and exchange the pointers

30. How do you refer to **arr7[x][y]** using pointer notation?

Exercises

In the following exercises, use pointer notation wherever possible.

1. Write a function, and a program to test it, that will place a zero in each of three variables in the calling program.

2. Write a function, and a program to test it, that will place a zero in each element of an array passed to it from the calling program.

3. Write a function, and a program to test it, that will change a string to the null string. The string is defined in the calling program.

Keyboard and Cursor

- Extended keyboard codes
- ANSI.SYS cursor control
- Key reassignment
- Command-line arguments
- Redirection of input and output

8

In this chapter we're going to change our focus from the C language itself to C's interaction with the PC computer. This doesn't mean that we've covered everything there is to know about C; we'll take up other important aspects of the language in later chapters. You now know enough, however, to begin exploring some of the features of the PC computer family in order to put C to work in real-world situations.

We'll cover two major topics in this chapter: first, the IBM extended character codes, which enable a program to read the function keys, cursor control keys, and special key combinations and second, the ANSI.SYS control functions, which give the programmer control over where the cursor is on the screen and permit other operations as well. Almost all applications programs—word processors, database programs, and even games—need to make use of these capabilities to provide a more sophisticated level of interaction with the user.

At the end of the chapter we'll explain command-line arguments: arguments typed in the command line when you call your program from DOS. We'll show an example that uses the ANSI.SYS routines and command-line arguments to redefine the PC's function keys. We'll show how redirection can be used to give even simple programs the ability to read and write files. As we go along, we'll also discuss several new C library functions.

The material in this chapter, besides extending your capability to write interesting and powerful programs, also serves as an introduction to directly accessing the character display memory, a topic we'll return to in Chapter 10.

Extended Keyboard Codes

We've already seen that the keyboard generates the usual ASCII codes for letters, numbers, and punctuation. Such keys all generate one-byte ASCII codes.

However, there are a great many keys and key combinations not represented by this one-byte character set. For instance, the function keys, F1 to F10, are not represented, nor are the cursor control keys on the numeric keypad. How does a program determine when these keys are being pressed?

The PC provides a second set of 256 keys and key combinations by using an *extended code*. This code consists of *two* bytes; the first byte is 0 and the second byte is a number indicating the particular key or key combination. When a key that is not in the normal character set—the F1 key, for example—is pressed, it first sends a 0 to the keyboard buffer and then the specific code. (The keyboard buffer is a temporary storage area where characters typed at the keyboard are stored until they are read by a program.) A program that expects to read extended codes checks for a character with the value 0. If it finds one, it knows the next character will be an extended code, with a completely different interpretation than the normal code.

> Extended keyboard codes use two characters, the first of which has an ASCII value of 0.

Because no character is represented by 0 in the normal IBM character set, there is no confusion when this character is received; it always indicates an extended code will follow. Figure 8-1 shows the format of the extended code.

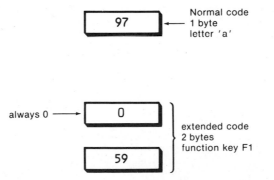

Figure 8-1. Normal and Extended Codes

Exploring the Extended Codes

Here's a program that enables us to explore these extended keyboard codes:

```
/* kbdtest.c */
/* prints code of keyboard key */
void main(void)
{
   unsigned char key, key2;

   while ( (key=getch()) != '\r' )   /* read keyboard */
      if( key == 0 )                  /* if extended code, */
         {
         key2 = getch();             /* read second code */
         printf("%3d %3d\n", key, key2);
         }
      else
         printf("%3d\n", key);       /* not extended code */
}
```

This program prints out the code for any key typed: either the normal one-byte IBM character code or the two-byte extended code. We don't want to echo the character typed, since there is no printable equivalent for the extended codes, so we use the function **getch()**, which works just like **getche()**, except that the character is not printed on the screen.

In the **while** test expression, the program reads the first code. If it's 0, the program knows it's dealing with an extended code, so it reads the second part of the code, using **getch()** again, and prints out the numerical value of both parts. If the first part is *not* 0, the program concludes that it is simply a normal character, and prints out its value. Note that type **unsigned char** is needed to hold values greater than 127. Press [Enter] to exit the program.

Here's a sample run:

```
  0  59
 97
  0  75
```

The first code shown here results from pressing function key [F1], the second is simply a lowercase 'a', and the third is the left arrow (on the number 4 of the numeric keypad). Typing in this program and experimenting with it will provide a variety of insights about the extended codes available.

Table 8-1 shows the extended codes that can be obtained by typing a single key. The table shows the second byte of the code; the first byte is always 0. Many more codes can be accessed by using the [Alt], [Ctrl], or [Shift] keys in combination with another key, as shown in Table 8-2. These two-key codes are used less often than the single-key variety, but they do provide an amazing variety of choices for programs that need them. These two tables are found on page 276.

Interpreting the Extended Codes

A common approach to writing C functions to interpret the extended codes is
to use the **switch** statement, as we do in the following demonstration:

p 125

```
/* extend.c */
/* tests extended codes */
void main(void)
{
    unsigned char key, key2;

    while ( (key=getch()) != '\r' )   /* read keyboard */
        if( key == 0 )                /* if extended code, */
          {
          key2 = getch();             /* read second code */
          switch (key2)
             {
             case 59:
                printf("Function key 1\n"); break;
             case 60:
                printf("Function key 2\n"); break;
             case 75:
                printf("Left arrow\n"); break;
             case 77:
                printf("Right arrow\n"); break;
             default:
                printf("Some other extended code\n");
             }
          }
      else
          printf("Normal code: %3d=%c\n", key, key);
}
```

This program is similar to kbdtest.c, but it uses **switch** to analyze and print p 278
out interpretations of some of the codes. We'll be using this same format in a
variety of programs later in this chapter.

Notice that we've placed more than one statement on the same line in
this program:

```
printf("Function key 1\n"); break;
```

It is generally easier to read a C program when only one statement is used per
line, but in the **switch** construct, statements are often doubled up this way to
save space and provide a cleaner format.

Now that we've introduced the extended keyboard codes, let's see how
they're used in a typical situation: for cursor control.

Cursor Control and ANSI.SYS

The PC family of computers comes with a system for directly controlling the position of the cursor on the screen. However, this capability is not built into the PC's read-only memory (ROM) as are the normal routines for accessing I/O devices. Rather it is contained in a separate file called the ANSI.SYS file.

Table 8-1. *One-Key Extended Codes*

Second Byte (Decimal)	Key That Generates Extended Code
59	F1
60	F2
61	F3
62	F4
63	F5
64	F6
65	F7
66	F8
67	F9
68	F10
71	Home
72	Up arrow
73	PgUp
75	Left arrow
77	Right arrow
79	End
80	Down arrow
81	PgDn
82	Ins
83	Del

Table 8-2. *Two-Key Extended Codes*

Second Byte (Decimal)	Keys That Generate Extended Code
15	Shift Tab
16 to 25	Alt Q, W, E, R, T, Y, U, I, O, P
30 to 38	Alt A, S, D, F, G, H, J, K, L
44 to 50	Alt Z, X, C, V, B, N, M
84 to 93	Shift F1 to F10
94 to 103	Ctrl F1 to F10
104 to 113	Alt F1 to F10
114	Ctrl PrtSc (start and stop printer echo)
115	Ctrl left arrow

Table 8-2. (cont.)

Second Byte (Decimal)	Keys That Generate Extended Code
116	Ctrl right arrow
117	Ctrl End
118	Ctrl PgDn
119	Ctrl Home
120 to 131	Alt 1, 2, 3, 4, 5, 6, 7, 8, 9, 0, -, =
132	Ctrl PgUp

ANSI stands for American National Standards Institute, and the ANSI.SYS file provides a standardized set of codes for cursor control. This file is actually an example of an *installable device driver*: a section of code written to control an I/O device, which is added to the operating system (DOS) after DOS is installed.

Once placed in DOS, ANSI.SYS intercepts all the numeric codes being sent to the screen for printing. If any of these codes contains a special *escape code* (a special sequence of characters), the ANSI.SYS file deals with the code itself, moving the cursor or performing other functions. If the code arriving is a normal character, it is simply passed to the regular video routines in ROM, which display it on the screen in the usual way.

As we'll see later, ANSI.SYS not only allows control of the cursor, it also lets us redefine keys on the keyboard; thus it also intercepts the code for any key typed and checks to see if any special action is necessary. We'll look at key redefinitions later in the chapter.

Installing ANSI.SYS

Since ANSI.SYS is an optional part of DOS, it must be installed each time you power up your computer. Fortunately, using the CONFIG.SYS file, this job is automated, so that once you've got your system set up, you don't need to worry about it again. Here's how it's done.

> To use ANSI.SYS, the ANSI.SYS driver must be installed in the operating system.

CONFIG.SYS File Must Be Present

You must have a CONFIG.SYS file in your root directory. The operating system examines this file when the system is first powered up and makes any changes or additions to the operating system this file requests.

CONFIG.SYS File Must Refer to ANSI.SYS

To use ANSI.SYS, the CONFIG.SYS file must contain a line like this:

```
DEVICE=C:\ANSI.SYS
```

This tells DOS where to look for the ANSI.SYS file so it can incorporate it into the operating system.

ANSI.SYS File Must Be Present

ANSI.SYS is a file that comes with your operating system. It must be available somewhere in your disk system, so that the operating system can find it when it's told to do so by the CONFIG.SYS file, but it need not be in the main directory.

Once it is installed, ANSI.SYS is actually incorporated into the operating system, so DOS will be increased by the size of ANSI.SYS: about 1,600 bytes.

Cursor Control with ANSI.SYS

Cursor control is achieved with ANSI.SYS using escape sequences: a string of several special characters. ANSI.SYS looks for this escape sequence, which can be transmitted as part of a string in a **printf()** function, and interprets the commands that follow it. The escape sequence is always the same: the nonprinting character, '\x1B' (sometimes called the "escape character"), followed by a left bracket, '['. After the escape sequence comes either a single letter or a more complex set of characters. Using such sequences, the cursor can be moved up or down and left or right, or it can be positioned at a specific row or column.

Here's a simple program that demonstrates the use of a cursor control sequence. The sequence involved is **"\x1B[B"**; in other words, the normal escape sequence '\x1B' and '[', followed by a capital 'B', as shown in Figure 8-2.

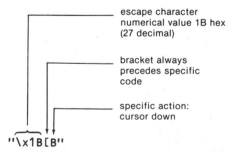

escape character
numerical value 1B hex
(27 decimal)

bracket always
precedes specific
code

specific action:
cursor down

``"\x1B[B"``

Figure 8-2. Format of ANSI.SYS Escape Sequence

The effect of this sequence is to move the cursor down one line, keeping its horizontal position unaltered. The example program will print whatever you type at the keyboard, but it will do so diagonally; that is, the letters will go down at the same time they're going across. Here's the program:

```
/* diag.c */
/* moves cursor diagonally */
void main(void)
{
   while ( getche() != '\r')      /* print character */
      printf("\x1B[B");           /* cursor down */
}
```

Before running this program, make sure the cursor is at the top of the screen. Exit to DOS (or use Dos Shell) and enter the CLS command. Type a short message, terminated by [Enter]. Here's some sample output:

```
H
 a
  c
   k
    e
     r
      s
       .
```

Using #define with Escape Sequences

The escape sequence, "\x1B[B", is cryptic and difficult to read. As we get into more complicated programs it will be useful to use mnemonics to represent the sequences so our **printf()** statements won't look like an alchemist's equations. We can do this easily with the **#define** directive, as the following rewrite of diag.c shows:

```
/* diag2.c */
/* moves cursor diagonally */
#define C_DOWN "\x1B[B"          /* move cursor down */
void main(void)
{
   while ( getche() != '\r')      /* print character */
      printf( C_DOWN );           /* cursor down */
}
```

Here **#define** lets us substitute the easily understandable identifier C_DOWN for the obscure "\x1B[B". We'll make extensive use of **#define** in the rest of the programs in this chapter.

Cursor Command Summary

Of course moving the cursor down is only one of the possible commands we can give. Table 8-3 lists the most common ones. We'll explore many of them in this chapter.

Table 8-3. *ANSI.SYS Cursor Control Codes*

Code	Effect
"[2J"	Erase screen and home cursor
"[K"	Erase to end of line
"[A"	Cursor up one row
"[B"	Cursor down one row
"[C"	Cursor right one column
"[D"	Cursor left one column
"[%d;%df	Cursor to row and column specified
"[s"	Save cursor position
"[u"	Restore position
"[%dA"	Cursor up number of rows specified
"[%dB"	Cursor down number of rows specified
"[%dC"	Cursor right number of columns specified
"[%dD"	Cursor left one row number of columns specified

* All codes must be preceded by the character '\x1B'. The symbol '%d' is a placeholder for a number, to be filled in by a **printf** argument.

Cursor Control from the Keyboard

Now that we know about extended character codes and cursor control, we can put both ideas together to control the cursor with the arrow keys.

Here's a program that enables you to draw simple designs on the screen:

```
/* draw.c */
/* moves cursor on screen, leaves trail */
#define CLEAR  "\x1B[2J"
#define C_LEFT "\x1B[D"
#define C_RITE "\x1B[C"
#define C_UPUP "\x1B[A"
#define C_DOWN "\x1B[B"
#define L_ARRO 75
#define R_ARRO 77
#define U_ARRO 72
#define D_ARRO 80
#define ACROSS 205
#define UPDOWN 186
```

```
void main(void)
{
    int key;

    printf(CLEAR);
    while ( (key=getch() ) == 0 )
        {
        key=getch();
        switch (key)
            {
            case L_ARRO : printf(C_LEFT); putch(ACROSS);
                break;
            case R_ARRO : printf(C_RITE); putch(ACROSS);
                break;
            case U_ARRO : printf(C_UPUP); putch(UPDOWN);
                break;
            case D_ARRO : printf(C_DOWN); putch(UPDOWN);
                break;
            }
        printf(C_LEFT);
        }
}
```

This program waits for you to press any of the four arrow keys. (These keys share the number keys 8, 4, 6, and 2 on the numeric keypad, so the [NumLock] key must be toggled appropriately for the program to work.)

The program begins by clearing the screen, using the escape sequence "\x1B[2J". This also puts the cursor in the "home" position: the upper left corner of the screen.

> All ANSI.SYS commands begin with the escape sequence, "\x1B[".

The **while** loop then waits for an extended code. If a normal key is pressed, the program exits, but pressing any of the cursor keys will cause the cursor to move in the appropriate direction (down if the down-arrow is pressed, etc.). If the direction is up or down, the vertical double-line character is printed; if left or right, the horizontal double-line character is printed. The result is a crude line-drawing capability that generates what looks like piping diagrams for nuclear reactors. Figure 8-3 shows a sample drawing session.

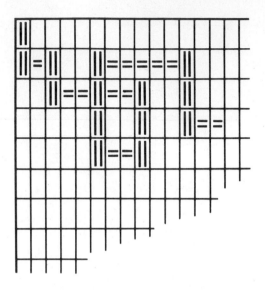

Figure 8-3. Session with draw.c

This program uses a **switch** statement to interpret the key being pressed. For each of the four cursor control keys, the cursor is first moved in the corresponding direction using a **printf()** statement; then the appropriate graphics character is printed using the **putch()** function. This function is analogous to the **getch()** function we've used before, except that it prints a character on the screen, rather than reading a character from the keyboard.

Notice that we've used **#define** directives not only for the cursor escape sequences, but also for the values of the cursor control keys and graphics characters. This not only clarifies the program, it provides a convenient way, using comments following the directives, to explain what the codes mean.

Printing a character causes an automatic right shift of the cursor. We must return the cursor to its position under the last character printed, so after any character is printed, we need to move the cursor back to the left.

Moving the Cursor to an Arbitrary Position

Besides moving the cursor one row or column at a time, we can also move it directly to any location on the screen using a somewhat more complex escape sequence. This sequence starts with the usual escape character, '\x1B', followed by the left bracket. Then there is a number representing the *row* we want the cursor to move to, then a semicolon, then another number representing the *column* we want to move to, and finally a lowercase 'f'. Figure 8-4 shows the format of this sequence.

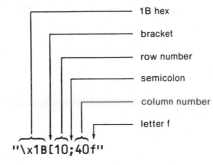

Figure 8-4. Format of Cursor-Positioning Sequence

The following program demonstrates this sequence in use:

```
/* position.c */
/* demonstrates cursor position command */
#define CLEAR "\x1B[2J"              /* clear screen */
#define ERASE "\x1B[K"              /* erase line */
void main(void)
{
    int row=1, col=1;

    printf(CLEAR);
    while ( row != 0 )
        {
        printf("\x1B[23;1f");        /* cursor at row=23, col=1 */
        printf(ERASE);               /* erase line */
        printf("Type row and column number (form 10,40): ");
        scanf("%d,%d", &row, &col);     /* get coordinates */
        printf("\x1B[%d;%df", row, col); /* position cursor */
        printf("*(%d,%d)", row, col);    /* print coordinates */
        }
}
```

This program clears the screen with the sequence "\x1B[2J" and cycles in the **while** loop, waiting for the user to type a pair of coordinates. The prompt to the user is always printed low on the screen, at row 23, so it won't interfere with the coordinates to be plotted; this is accomplished with the statement:

```
printf("\x1B[23;1f");
```

Another escape sequence, "\x1B[K", then erases from the cursor position to the end of the line; finally the prompt itself is printed, inviting the user to type in the row and column numbers, separated by a comma. When the coordinates are typed in, the program moves the cursor to this location, prints an asterisk, and labels the location with the coordinates.

Here's a sample session:

```
                                            *(2,35)
                    *(3,15)
                                                    *(4,40)
            *(5,5)
                                        *(6,30)
                            *(7,20)

                *(9,10)
        *(10,1)
```

Lower down on the screen is the prompt:

```
Type row and column number (form 10,40): 10,1
```

which will remain in the same place while the program is running. Enter a row coordinate of zero to terminate the program.

Writing Anywhere on the Screen

Here's another program that uses the cursor-positioning sequence. This program prints two menus, positioning them along the top of the screen as does Turbo C's IDE. Here's the listing:

```
/* putmenus.c */
/* demonstrates placing text on screen */
#define SIZE1 5                 /* items on menu1 */
#define SIZE2 4                 /* items on menu2 */
#define CLEAR "\x1B[2J"         /* clears screen */
void display(char *arr[], int size, int hpos);  /* prototype */

void main(void)
{
    static char *menu1[] =      /* first menu */
                { "Open",
                  "Close",
                  "Save",
                  "Print",
                  "Quit", };
    static char *menu2[] =      /* second menu */
```

```
                { "Cut",
                  "Copy",
                  "Paste",
                  "Reformat", };
      printf(CLEAR);                /* clear screen */
      display(menu1,SIZE1,20);      /* display first menu */
      display(menu2,SIZE2,40);      /* display second menu */
      getch();                      /* exit on any keystroke */
   }


   /* display() */
   /* displays menu at given column number */
   /* arr=menu array, size=size of array, hpos=column number */

   void display(char *arr[], int size, int hpos)
   {
      int j;
      for(j=0; j<size; j++)       /* for each menu item */
         {
         printf("\x1B[%d;%df", j+1, hpos); /* position cursor */
         printf("%s\n", *(arr+j) );        /* print item */
         }
   }
```

The items for each menu are stored as an array of pointers to strings. The program then uses a function to display the menus. The function positions the cursor using the ANSI.SYS cursor-positioning sequence, taking the row number from the number of the item on the menu and the column number passed from the main program. The menu item is then printed out at that location.

The output of the program looks like this:

```
            Open          Cut
            Close         Copy
            Save          Paste
            Print         Reformat
            Quit
```

In a larger program, a similar function could be used to print as many menus as desired or to print text in columns.

We will soon show a more sophisticated version of this menu program, but first we need to explore another aspect of the ANSI.SYS file: the ability to change character *attributes*.

Character Attributes

Every character displayed on the screen is stored in the computer's memory as two bytes. One byte contains the normal code for the character, while the other byte contains the character's attribute. The "attribute" of a character describes its appearance: blinking, printed in bold (intensified), underlined, or printed in reverse video (black on white instead of the normal white on black).

> Every character is stored in the display memory as two bytes: one for the ASCII code of the character and one for the attribute.

The attribute of a character or string can be set using an ANSI.SYS escape sequence. The sequence, following the usual escape character and bracket, consists of a number, followed by the letter 'm'. Here's a list of the numbers that produce effects in the monochrome display:

0   Turns off attributes: normal white on black
1   Bold (high intensity)
4   Underline
5   Blinking
7   Reverse video: black on white
8   Invisible: black on black

Figure 8-5 shows the format for the sequence to turn on blinking characters.

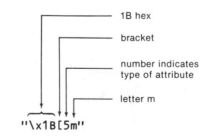

"\x1B[5m"

Figure 8-5. Format of Attribute Control Sequence

These sequences are sent during the printing process. Once a particular attribute has been turned on, all characters printed from then on will have this attribute. The attribute will remain in effect until turned off with another escape sequence.

Here's a program that demonstrates the character attributes:

```c
/* attrib.c */
/* changes graphics attributes */
#define NORMAL  "\x1B[0m"
#define BOLD    "\x1B[1m"
#define UNDER   "\x1BL4m"
#define BLINK   "\x1B[5m"
#define REVERSE "\x1B[7m"

void main(void)
{
    printf("Normal %s Blinking %s Normal\n\n", BLINK, NORMAL);
    printf("Normal %s Bold %s Normal\n\n", BOLD, NORMAL);
    printf("Normal %s Underlined %s Normal\n\n", UNDER, NORMAL);
    printf("Normal %s Reversed %s Normal\n\n", REVERSE, NORMAL);
    printf("%s %s Reversed and blinking %s", BLINK, REVERSE, NORMAL);
}
```

Figure 8-6 shows what the output looks like, although of course the blinking attribute cannot be effectively rendered on paper. (If you're using a color monitor, underlining may be shown by a different color.)

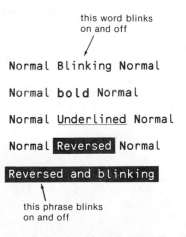

Figure 8-6. Output of the attrib.c Program

As you can see from the last line of the program, attributes can be combined: you can use any combination you like as long as it's logically consistent (you can't combine reverse video and invisible, or reverse video and underlining).

Selectable Menu

Now that we know something about operating the ANSI.SYS file, we can put this knowledge to work in a more sophisticated program: a "selectable menu," like the menus in Turbo C's IDE.

When it is first started, the program displays a menu with five items: Open, Close, Save, Print, and Quit. By operating the up-arrow and down-arrow keys, the user can cause any of these items to be displayed in reverse video. If the user presses the [Enter] key while a particular item is highlighted, an action corresponding to that item will be performed. In this particular program, the action on four of the items is the same: the name of the item selected is printed out. Of course in a real application program, more substantive actions would follow from the menu selections. The fifth item, Quit, behaves just as it does in more serious programs; selecting it causes the program to terminate and control to return to the operating system.

Here's the listing:

```c
/* menu.c */
/* demonstrates simple menu */
#define TRUE 1
#define NUM 5                    /* number of menu items */
#define CLEAR "\x1B[2J"          /* clear screen */
#define ERASE "\x1B[K"           /* erase line */
#define NORMAL "\x1B[0m"         /* normal attribute */
#define REVERSE "\x1B[7m"        /* reverse video attribute */
#define HOME "\x1B[1;1f"         /* cursor to top left */
#define BOTTOM "\x1B[20;1f"      /* cursor to lower left */
#define U_ARRO 72                /* up-arrow key */
#define D_ARRO 80                /* down-arrow key */
#define INSERT 82                /* "Ins" key */
void action(int);               /* prototypes */
char getcode(void);
void display(char *arr[], int size, int pos);

int main(void)
{
   static char *items[NUM] =     /* menu items */
            { "Open",
              "Close",
              "Save",
              "Print",
              "Quit",  };
   int curpos;                   /* position of selected item */
   printf(CLEAR);                /* clear screen */
   curpos=0;                     /* select top of menu */
```

```
    while (TRUE)
       {
       display(items,NUM,curpos); /* display menu */
       switch ( getcode() )        /* act on key pressed */
          {
          case U_ARRO:
             if( curpos>0 ) --curpos; break;
          case D_ARRO:
             if( curpos<NUM-1 ) ++curpos; break;
          case '\r':
             action(curpos); break;
          }
       }
}


/* display() */
/* displays menu */
void display(char *arr[], int size, int pos)
{
   int j;

   printf(HOME);                    /* cursor to top left */
   for(j=0; j<size; j++)            /* for each menu item */
      {
      if(j==pos)                    /* if selected, */
         printf(REVERSE);           /* print in reverse video */
      printf("%s\n", *(arr+j) );    /* print item */
      printf(NORMAL);               /* restore normal attribute */
      }
   printf(BOTTOM);                  /* cursor to lower left */
}


/* getcode() */
/* gets keyboard code */
char getcode(void)
{
   int key;

   if( (key=getch()) == 0 )        /* if extended code */
      return( getch() );           /* return the code */
   else if ( key == '\r' )         /* if [Enter] */
      return(key);                 /* return it */
   else                            /* if anything else */
      return(0);                   /* return 0 */
}
```

```
/* action() */
/* performs action based on cursor position */
void action(int pos)
{
    printf(ERASE);                    /* erase lower line */
    switch(pos)
      {
      case 0:
        printf("Open"); break;        /* calls to routines */
      case 1:                         /* could be inserted here */
        printf("Close"); break;
      case 2:
        printf("Save"); break;
      case 3:
        printf("Print"); break;
      case 4:
        exit(0);                      /* exit from program */
      }
}
```

This program consists of a **main()** function and three other functions: one to display the menu, one to get the extended code from the keyboard, and one to take action depending on the menu item selected.

The **main()** function consists of a simple loop. In the loop, the menu is first displayed by calling **display()**, then the keyboard is checked by using **getcode()** to see if the user has pressed an up- or down-arrow or the [Enter] key. Moving up or down the menu with the arrows causes a variable, called **curpos** (for CURsor POSition), to be incremented (cursor going down) or decremented (cursor going up). If the [Enter] key is pressed, control goes to the **action()** function, which either prints the name of the menu item or exits from the program if Quit has been selected.

The exit() Function

Notice the use of the C library **exit()** function. This function immediately terminates the program and passes control back to the calling entity, in this case the PC DOS or MS-DOS operating system. It doesn't matter how deeply you're nested within functions; **exit()** still terminates the entire program.

If an argument is placed in the parentheses of the **exit()** function, it is returned to the operating system, where it is available to the ERRORLEVEL subcommand in the batch file processor. That is, you can put such commands as

```
IF ERRORLEVEL 1 GOTO ERR1
```

in a batch file to sample the value placed in the **exit()** function by the program. This gives the batch file the chance to change its operation depending on the results of the program.

A return value of 0 ordinarily indicates a normal termination, while a non-zero value may be used as an error code. Notice that the type of **main()** reflects the fact that a value is being returned.

The display() and getcode() Functions

The **display()** function uses the identifier HOME to position the cursor at row 1, column 1. Then it displays the menu by looping through each menu item, incrementing the row number so that each item is printed directly below the last. If the number of the row is the same as **curpos**, it means the menu item is selected (**curpos** keeps track of what's selected), and that item is printed in reverse video.

Figure 8-7 shows how the top part of the screen looks with the Save item selected. If an item is printed out, it is shown farther down the screen, on line 20.

```
Open
Close
Save
Print
Quit
```
The highlighting moves from item
to item in response to the cursor
control keys.

Figure 8-7. Operation of the menu.c Program

The menu.c program could be used as the basis for a more powerful menu-driven program. Menus could be added, and these could be made into "pull-down" menus; that is, their contents normally would be hidden, but a particular menu would be displayed when selected with the left or right arrow.

Function Key Assignment Using ANSI.SYS

Let's turn our attention to another capability of the ANSI.SYS file: assigning different strings to the function keys.

Assigning strings to function keys enables you to configure your keyboard for the kind of work you usually do. For instance, if you write a lot of C programs, you might want to list the C source files in a particular directory:

```
C>dir *.c
```

If you could assign this string to a function key, you could save yourself a lot of time printing this phrase. The convenience would be even greater for longer commands:

```
type \accounts\1987\march\receive.dat
```

Here's a program that performs just this sort of function key reassignment.

```
/* assign.c */
/* assigns function key to string typed by user */
void main(void)
{
    char string[81];
    int key;

    printf("Enter number of function key: ");
    gets(string);
    key = atoi(string);
    puts("Enter string to assign to that key:");
    gets(string);
    printf("\x1B[0;%d;\"%s\";13p", key+58, string);
}
```

Probably the most difficult part of this program to unravel is the escape sequence in the final **printf()** statement. The escape sequence for assigning a string to a function key is shown in Figure 8-8.

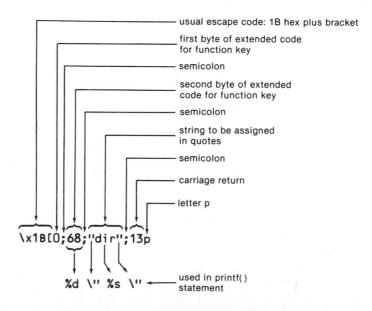

Figure 8-8. Format of Function Key Assignment Sequence

If this convoluted syntax isn't enough to make you abandon programming in favor of woodcarving, nothing will be.

Because quotes cannot be used in a string in C, they must be represented by backslash-quotes (\"). Since we want to use variables for the number of the function key and the string to be assigned to it, we represent these with the format specifiers %d and %s, which the function replaces with the variables **key+58** and **string**. The function obtains these values from the user, plugs them into the string, executes the **printf()** statement, and voilà, the function key is reassigned.

Avoiding scanf()

Perhaps you're wondering why the **gets()** and **atoi()** functions are used to read the function key number in the program, rather than a **scanf()**. The reason is that **scanf()** has a number of peculiarities, and one of them is that a newline character may be left, unread, in the keyboard buffer after **scanf()** has finished reading a number. For example, if we execute the statement

```
scanf("%d", &num);
```

the user will type a number, press [Return], and wait for **scanf()** to digest the number. The number will be read and removed from the buffer all right, but often (depending on the compiler) the newline character will be left in the buffer. If so, then the *next* input command (a **gets()**, for example) will read the newline. If the input command is looking for a string, it will see the newline and think the user has entered a string with no characters but the newline. Turbo C unfortunately leaves the newline in the buffer.

There are various ways around this problem. One that works on some systems is to include a newline in the format string of the **scanf()** function:

```
scanf("%d\n", num);
```

This should force **scanf()** to read the newline from the buffer, since any character in the format string matching one in the input string should be read and removed from the keyboard buffer. However, this does not work in Turbo C. In any case, **scanf()** is a rather large function in terms of the number of bytes it adds to your compiled program, so it's nice to have an alternative approach to reading variables. The **gets()** function is preferable for strings, but what about numbers?

The **scanf()** function is bulky and does not always behave as one would like.

In this program we use a combination of two functions to read the number representing the function key. The first function is **gets()**, which reads in the number *as a string*. The second function is **atoi()**, which stands for "ASCII to integer." This function takes a string as an argument and returns an integer with the same value. In other words, if the string was "21", the function would return the number 21. The resulting program, using **gets()** and **atoi()**, requires substantially less memory than if we had used **scanf()**.

Now our assign.c program works just as it's supposed to, assigning any phrase we like to any function key we like. However, we'd like to improve it; we'd like to be able to assign the function keys by using this program in a *batch file*. This way, many keys could be automatically assigned when we power up our system. Unfortunately, the present version of assign.c requires that its input come from the user and not from the parameters of a batch file. What can we do? To solve this problem, we need to know about command-line arguments.

Command-Line Arguments

You've used application programs (including Turbo C itself) in which, when you invoke the program from the operating system, you can type not only the name of the program, but various other items as well, such as the name of a file the application is to work on. A typical example might be

```
C>wordproc letter.txt
```

where wordproc is an application program and letter.txt is a file this application will open and process. Here the string "letter.txt" is used as a *command-line argument:* an argument that appears on the command line following the C> prompt.

Use of multiple arguments in the command line is clearly a useful feature. So how can we access these arguments from within the application?

Here's another question: Will we ever find anything besides **void** to put inside the parentheses of the **main()** function?

As you may have guessed, the answers to these seemingly unrelated questions are in fact two sides of a coin. By putting the right things inside the parentheses of **main()**, we can allow our program to read command-line arguments to its heart's content. C automatically adds the capability to read these arguments to all C programs. As programmers, all we need to do is make use of it. The following program shows how:

```
/* comline.c */
/* demonstrates command line arguments */

void main( int argc, char *argv[] )
```

```
{
    int j;

    printf("Number of arguments is %d\n", argc);
    for(j=0; j<argc; j++)
        printf("Argument number %2d is %s\n", j, *(argv+j) );
}
```

Here's a sample run with the program, in which we simply type the words "one", "two", and "three" as command-line arguments following the program name. It's easiest to use the program from DOS, so get out of Turbo C with [Alt][x] and type the following at the DOS prompt (you can also use the Arguments item in the IDE Run menu):

```
C>comline one two three
Number of arguments is 4
Argument number  0 is C:\TURBOC\COMLINE.EXE
Argument number  1 is one
Argument number  2 is two
Argument number  3 is three
```

The two arguments used in the parentheses following **main()** are **argc** and **argv**. The variable **argc** is the total number of command-line arguments typed; in this case, 4 (the pathname of the program itself is counted as the first argument).

> The arguments in **main(argc,argv)** are the number of command-line arguments and an array of pointers to the individual arguments.

The variable ***argv[]** represents an array of pointers to strings, where each string holds one command-line argument. The strings can be accessed by referring to them as ***(argv+1)**, ***(argv+2)**, and so on (or in array notation, **argv[1]**, **argv[2]**, etc.). The first string, ***(argv+0)**, is the full pathname of the program itself.

The names **argc** (for ARGument Count) and **argv** (for ARGument Values) are traditionally used in these roles, but any other name could be used instead (although you might confuse tradition-bound C programmers).

Assigning Function Keys with Command-Line Arguments

Now that we understand command-line arguments, we can incorporate them into the program described in the last section, which reassigns the function keys. We'll do this in two steps.

Here's the first version of the program:

```
/* funkey0.c */
/* assigns function key to string typed by user */
/* uses command-line arguments */

void main( int argc, char *argv[] )
{
    int key;

    if(argc != 3)
        {
        printf("example usage: C>funkey0 2 dir");
        exit();
        }
    key = atoi(argv[1]);
    printf("\x1B[0;%d;\"%s\";13p", key+58, argv[2]);
}
```

p 296

For simplicity, we've restricted this version of the program to one-word strings; in other words, you can assign the string "dir" to a function key, but you can't assign "dir *.c" because this string contains two words, and they will be treated as two separate command-line arguments. We'll first investigate this program and then expand it to handle multiword strings.

The funkey0.c program first checks to be sure the user has entered exactly three command-line arguments. The first is the program name itself, the second is the number of the function key to be assigned, and the third is the one-word string to be assigned to that key. Users who have entered the wrong number of arguments are shown an example of correct usage; then the program exits so they can try again. It is common practice in dealing with command-line arguments to perform some of this kind of checking to see if the user appears to know what to type in.

p 298

Assuming the number of arguments is correct, the program converts **argv[1]** (or ***(argv+1)** if you prefer) into a number, using the **atoi()** function. The **argv[2]** argument is the one-word string to be typed in. The number and the string are then incorporated into the escape sequence, which is transmitted to ANSI.SYS using the **printf()** statement.

Assigning Function Keys with Multiple Arguments

Although what we type into the command line appears to be a string of characters, the operating system interprets it as a series of separate variables, with each space signaling the end of a variable. To make it possible for our program to assign a string with multiple words ("dir *.c", for example) to a function key, we must combine the command-line arguments into a single string.

The following program does this, using the function **strcpy()** to place the first argument in the empty buffer **string**, and then using the function **strcat()**, which <u>concatenates</u> one string with another, to add a space, and then each argument in turn, to **string**. Here's the listing:

```
/* funkey.c */
/* assigns function key to string typed by user */
/* uses any number of command-line arguments */
void main( int argc, char *argv[] )
{
    int key, j;
    char string[80];

    if(argc < 3)                        /* if too few */
        {                               /* arguments, */
        printf("example usage: A>funkey 2 dir *.c");
        exit();                         /* then exit */
        }
    key = atoi(argv[1]);                /* funct key number */
    strcpy(string,argv[2]);             /* first word in line */
    for(j=3; j<argc; j++)               /* if more words, */
        {
        strcat(string," ");             /* add space */
        strcat(string,argv[j]);         /* add word */
        }
    if( strcmp(string, "null") == 0 )   /* if string is "null" */
        strcpy(string, "");             /* no string */
    printf("\x1B[0;%d;\"%s\";13p", key+58, string);
}
```
p 218

If we want to erase the string that has been assigned to a function key, we type "null" as our string; the null string will then be assigned to the function key.

Turbo C actually embodies a more elegant solution to the problem of multiple-word arguments. If <u>double quotes</u> are used to surround a string containing spaces, the entire string is interpreted as <u>one argument</u>. Thus, in funkey0.c, it would be possible to use the command-line argument

```
funkey0 1 "dir *.c"
```

However, this approach is not recognized by some other compilers, and so is less portable.

Before we leave the subject of the ANSI.SYS file, we should point out some of the pluses and minuses of using ANSI.SYS for cursor control. On the plus side, it's fairly easy to program the necessary escape sequences to move the cursor and perform the other functions of ANSI.SYS. However, it's not a particularly fast way to move the cursor, and it requires that the ANSI.SYS file be loaded into memory and that the CONFIG.SYS file be properly configured to reference it. For a commercial product this might present a problem, since some users would not want to go to the trouble of setting up these files. For less formal programs, and for exploring the capabilities of the system, ANSI.SYS provides a very convenient and powerful group of capabilities.

In later chapters we'll show how some of these capabilities can be handled in ways that are faster and more convenient for the user, although more difficult to program.

There is another programming technique that, like command-line arguments, lies in the gray area between C and MS-DOS. This is the process of *redirection*, which we'll examine now.

Redirection

The MS-DOS operating system incorporates (in Versions 2.0 and later) a powerful feature that allows a program to read and write files, even when this capability has not been built into the program. This is done through a process called "redirection."

Redirection provides an easy way to save the results of a program; its use is vaguely similar to that of the [Ctrl][PrtSc] key combination to save program output to the printer, except that the results can be sent to a disk file. This is often a more convenient and flexible approach than providing a separate function in the program to write to the disk. Similarly, redirection can be used to read information from a disk file directly into a program.

Ordinarily, a program derives its input from the "standard input device," which is assumed to be the keyboard, and sends its output to the "standard output device," which is assumed to be the display screen. In other words, DOS makes certain assumptions about where input should come from and output should go. Redirection enables us to change these assumptions.

> Output can be redirected to go to a file instead of the screen; input can be redirected to come from a file instead of the keyboard.

Redirecting Output

Let's see how we might redirect the output of a program, from the screen to a file. We'll start by considering the simple program shown below:

```
/* mirror.c */
/* echos typing to the screen */
void main(void)
```

```
{
    int ch=0;

    while( (ch=getch()) != '\r' )
        putchar(ch);
    putchar('\r');
}
```

The **putchar** function outputs one character to the standard output device. Ordinarily, when we run this program, **putchar()** will cause whatever we type to be printed on the screen, until the [Enter] key is pressed, at which point the program will terminate, as shown in this sample run:

```
C>mirror
All's well that ends well.
C>
```

(The programs in this section should be run directly from DOS, not from Turbo C's IDE.) Let's see what happens when we invoke the program from DOS in a different way, using redirection:

```
C>mirror >file.txt

C>
```

Now when we call the program and type the same phrase, "All's well that ends well.", nothing appears on the screen! Where did our typing go? We've caused it to be redirected to the file called file.txt. Can we prove that this has actually happened? Yes, by using the DOS command TYPE:

```
C>type file.txt
All's well that ends well.
```

There's the result of our typing, sitting in the file. The redirection operator, which is the "greater than" symbol (>), causes any output intended for the screen to be written to the file whose name follows the operator.

The data to be redirected to a file doesn't need to be typed by a user at the keyboard; the program itself can generate it. Any output normally sent to the screen can be redirected to a disk file. As an example, we could invoke the putmenus.c program, developed earlier in this chapter, and redirect its output to a file: *p 288*

```
C>putmenus >file.txt
                            ← type any character here
C>
```

Then if we were to examine file.txt with TYPE, we'd see that the output of putmenus.c had been written to the file. Even the cursor control commands are saved, so that using TYPE clears the screen before the menus are displayed.

This can be a useful capability any time you want to capture the output of a program on a file, rather than displaying it on the screen.

DOS predefines a number of filenames for its own use. One of these names is PRN, which stands for the printer. Output can be redirected to the printer by using this filename. For example, if you invoke the mirror.c program this way:

```
C>mirror >PRN
```

anything you type will be printed on the printer when you press [Enter].

Redirecting Input

We can also redirect *input* to a program so that, instead of reading characters from the keyboard, the program reads them from a file. Fortunately we can demonstrate this with the same program, mirror.c, we used to demonstrate redirection of output. This is because the program both accepts input from the keyboard and outputs it to the screen.

To redirect the input, we need to have a file containing something to be printed. We'll assume we've placed the message "The greatest of these is charity" in the file called file.txt using the Turbo C editor or redirecting the output of transfer.c. (Make sure to include [Enter] at the end.) Then we use the "less than" sign (<) before the file name:

```
C>mirror <file.txt
The greatest of these is charity.
C>
```

The phrase is printed on the screen with no further effort on our part. Using redirection, we've made our mirror.c program perform the work of the DOS TYPE command.

Figure 8-9 shows how redirected input and output look compared with normal input and output.

Both Ways at Once

Redirection of input and output can be used together; a program's input can come *from* a file via redirection, while at the same time its output is being redirected *to* a file. In DOS nomenclature, we can say the program acts as a *filter*.

To demonstrate this process, we'll use a slightly fancier program than before. Instead of simply storing and retrieving files in their original form, we'll develop a pair of programs, one to code a message and another to decode it.

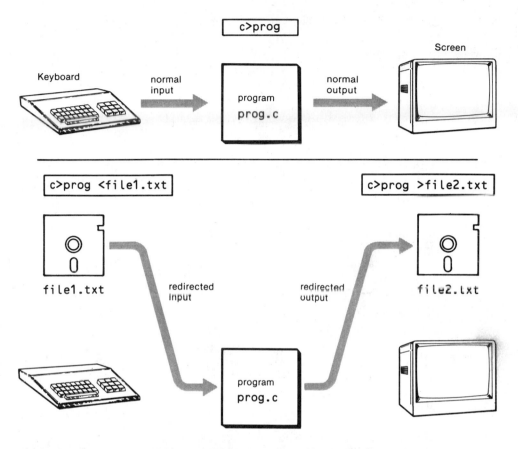

Figure 8-9. Normal and Redirected Input/Output

Here's the program that does the coding:

```
/* code.c */
/* encodes file */
/* to be used with redirection */
void main(void)
{
    char ch;

    while( (ch=getch()) != '\r' )
        putchar(ch+1);
    putchar('\r');
}
```

This program reads a character, either from the keyboard or—using redirection—from a file, and outputs it in coded form, either to the screen or to another file. The cipher is rudimentary; it consists of adding 1 to the ASCII code for the character. Of course any 10-year-old could break this code, but if you're interested you can probably think of ways to make it tougher.

Notice that we don't encode the '\r' character: that's why we leave the writing of this character outside the loop.

Let's assume you've generated a file, called file1.txt, which contains the message you wish to code. You can create this file using either the transfer.c program with redirection (although it's hard to use because the characters aren't echoed to the screen) or by using the Turbo C editor. If you use the editor, make sure to end the file with [Enter]. We can verify what's in the file this way:

```
C>type file1.txt
Meet me at the hollow tree.
```

To code this file, we redirect our input *from* file1.txt, to code.c, and also redirect it *to* a different file, file2.txt, like this:

```
C>code <file1.txt >file2.txt
```

Data will be read from file1.txt, coded, and written to file2.txt. Having done this, we can use TYPE to see what the coded file looks like.

```
C>type file2.txt
Nffu!nf!bu!uif!ipmmpx!usff/
```

To *decode* the file, we use a program that looks very much like code.c:

```
/* decode.c */
/* decodes file */
/* to be used with redirection */
void main(void)
{
    char ch;

    while( (ch=getch()) != '\r' )
        putchar(ch-1);
    putchar('\r');
}
```

This program subtracts 1 from the value of each character, thus reversing the coding process. We'll write the decoded results to file3.txt. Here's how we apply the program, again using double redirection, to our coded file:

```
C>decode <file2.txt >file3.txt
```

Finally, to prove that both the coding and decoding have worked correctly, we print out the file containing the decoded message:

```
C>type file3.txt
Meet me at the hollow tree.
```

A point to note about redirection: the output file is erased before it's written to, so don't try to send output to the same file from which you're receiving input.

The programs in this section use the '\r' character to signal end-of-file. In more general-purpose programs, you may want to use −1 or the '\x1A' character for this purpose.

Redirection can be a powerful tool for developing utility programs to examine or alter data in files.

Redirection is used to establish a relationship between a program and a file. Another DOS operator can be used to relate two programs directly, so that the output of one is fed directly into another, with no files involved. This is called "piping," and uses the bar character (|). We won't pursue this topic, but you can read about it in the DOS documentation.

Summary

You now can read the codes of the extended character set, so that your program can tell when such keys as the function and cursor-control keys are pressed. You've also learned how to use the ANSI.SYS file for clearing the screen, controlling the cursor, and assigning strings to the function keys.

You know how your program can interpret command-line arguments (words typed following a program name at the C> prompt), and you've seen how the input and output of a program can be redirected to come from and be sent to disk files, using the DOS redirection operators (<) and (>).

Finally, you've learned a handful of new functions: **exit()**, which permits a quick return from your program to DOS, **putchar()**, which writes a single character to the screen, **atoi()**, which converts from a string to a number, and **strcat()**, which attaches or concatenates two strings together.

In the next chapter, we'll look into structures, an important topic in the C language, and we'll see how they and their cousin, the union, can help access other important features of the PC.

Questions

1. The purpose of the extended keyboard codes is to
   a. read foreign language characters
   b. read letter keys typed with [Alt] and [Ctrl]
   c. read the function and cursor control keys
   d. read graphics characters

2. How many extended codes are there (including codes that are not used)?

3. How many bytes are used to represent an extended keyboard code?

4. True or false: extended keyboard codes represent only single keys such as F1.

5. Which of the following is the extended code for the F1 key?
   a. 97
   b. 1 78
   c. '\xDB'
   d. 0 59

6. ANSI.SYS is
   a. a rare nerve disease
   b. an installable device driver
   c. a file enabling expanded keyboard and cursor capability
   d. a file always searched for by DOS on startup

7. CONFIG.SYS is
   a. a file always searched for by DOS on startup
   b. a file containing instructions for modifying DOS
   c. a file that can tell DOS to install ANSI.SYS
   d. none of the above

8. Describe what needs to be in the system before ANSI.SYS can be used.

9. All ANSI.SYS "escape sequences" start with
   a. '\x['

    b. '['

    c. '\x1B'

    d. '\x1B['

10. Write the escape sequence to clear the screen: _____.

11. True or false: the cursor can be moved to any screen location, but only in increments of one row or column.

12. Write four character attributes:

    a. Bo _____

    b. Bl _____

    c. Un _____

    d. Re _____

13. Write the escape sequence to move the cursor right one column: _____.

14. True or false: the **exit()** function causes an exit from a function.

15. Write a statement that will transform the string **str** into a number **num**, assuming that **str** equals "122".

16. True or false: using ANSI.SYS escape sequences, an arbitrary string can be assigned to any function key.

17. Command-line arguments are:

    a. something that happens in the military

    b. additional items following the C> prompt and a program name

    c. the arguments **argc** and **argv**

    d. the arguments **argv[0]**, **argv[1]**, and so forth

18. Write two program statements that combine the word "steeple" with the word "chase" and leave the result in an array called **str[ ]**.

19. Redirection is

    a. sending the output of a program somewhere besides the screen

    b. getting a program from somewhere besides an .exe file

    c. getting input to a program from somewhere besides the keyboard

    d. changing the standard input and output devices

20. Write a DOS command that will cause a program called **prog1** to take its input from a file called **f1.c** and send its output to a file called **f2.c**

Exercises

1. Write a program that will enable the user to type in a phrase, echoing characters to the screen. If the user presses the left-arrow key (not the backspace), the program should erase the character to the left of the cursor, so that the whole phrase can be erased one character at a time. Use extended keyboard codes and ANSI.SYS cursor control.

2. Write a program that uses a command-line argument to perform decimal to hexadecimal conversion; that is, the decimal number will be typed on the command line, following the program name:

```
C>decihex 128
Hex=80
C>
```

Use unsigned integers so the program can convert values between 0 and 65535.

3. Write a program that will read a C source code file using redirection, and determine if the file contains the same number of left and right braces. This program can then be used to check for mismatched braces before compiling. Its operation should look like this in the cases where there are unequal numbers of braces:

```
C>braces <prog.c
Mismatched braces
C>
```

Use **getchar()** to read the characters, and terminate on the EOF character defined in the STDIO.H header file.

Structures, Unions, and ROM BIOS

- Structures
- Nested structures
- Arrays of structures
- Linked lists
- Unions
- ROM BIOS routines

9

In this chapter we explore C's most versatile device for representing data: the structure. We'll also describe another data storage mechanism that is in some ways similar to a structure, but in other ways is completely different: the union. Finally we'll put our knowledge of structures and unions together to find out how to access the family of powerful routines built into the PC's hardware: the Read-Only Memory Basic Input/Output System (ROM BIOS). Knowing how to use the ROM BIOS routines will be important when we investigate character and color graphics in following chapters.

Structures

We have seen how simple variables can hold one piece of information at a time and how arrays can hold a number of pieces of information of the same data type. These two data storage mechanisms can handle a great variety of situations. But we often want to operate on data items of different types together as a unit. In this case, neither the variable nor the array is adequate.

For example, suppose you want a program to store data concerning an employee in an organization. You might want to store the employee's name (a character array), department number (an integer), salary (a floating point number), and so forth. Perhaps you also have other employees, and you want your program to deal with them as elements of an array.

Even a multidimensional array will not solve this problem, since all the elements of an array must be of the same data type. You could use several different arrays—a character array for names, a floating point array for salaries, and so on—but this is an unwieldy approach that obscures the fact that you're dealing with a group of characteristics relating to a single entity: the employee.

To solve this sort of problem, C provides a special data type: the *structure*. A structure consists of a number of data items—which need not be of the same type—grouped together. In our example, a structure would consist of the employee's name, department number, salary, and any other pertinent information. The structure could hold as many of these items as we want. Figure 9-1 shows the differences among simple variables, arrays, and structures.

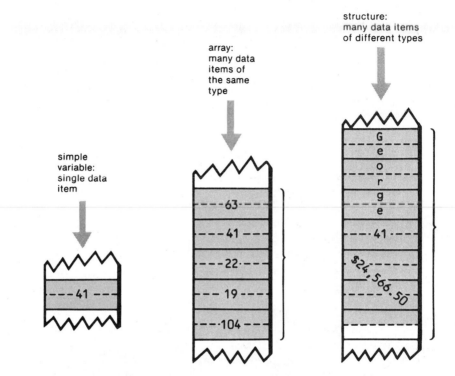

Figure 9-1. Simple Variables, Arrays, and Structures

Pascal programmers will recognize a C structure as similar to a *record*.

Structures are useful, not only because they can hold different types of variables, but also because they can form the basis for more complex constructions, such as linked lists. We'll provide an example of this later on.

A Simple Structure

Here's a program that uses a simple structure containing two data items: an integer variable **num** and a character variable **ch**. The data items in a structure are called *members*.

```
/* struct.c */
/* demonstrates structures */
void main(void)
```

```
{
    struct easy        /* defines data type 'struct easy' */
       {
       int num;        /* structure member */
       char ch;        /* structure member */
       };

    struct easy ez1;   /* declares 'ez1' to be */
                       /*    of type 'struct easy' */

    ez1.num = 2;       /* reference elements of 'ez1' */
    ez1.ch = 'Z';
    printf("ez1.num=%d, ez1.ch=%c\n", ez1.num, ez1.ch );
}
```

When run, this program will generate the following output:

```
ez1.num=2, ez1.ch=Z
```

This program demonstrates the three fundamental aspects of using structures: declaring the structure type, defining structure variables, and accessing members of the structure. We'll look at these three operations in turn.

Declaring a Structure Type

The fundamental data types used in C, such as **int** and **float**, are predefined by the compiler. Thus, when you use an **int** variable, you know it will always consist of two bytes (at least in Turbo C) and that the compiler will interpret the contents of these two bytes in a certain way. This is not true of structures. Since a structure may contain any number of elements of different types, the programmer must tell the compiler what a particular structure is going to look like before using variables of that type.

In the example program, the following statement declares the structure type:

```
struct easy
   {
   int num;
   char ch;
   };
```

This statement declares a new data type called **struct easy**. Each variable of this type will consist of two members: an integer variable called **num**, and a character variable called **ch**. Note that this statement doesn't define any variables, and so it isn't setting aside any storage in memory. It just tells the compiler what the data type **struct easy** looks like, conveying the *plan* for the structure. Figure 9-2 shows the format of a structure type declaration.

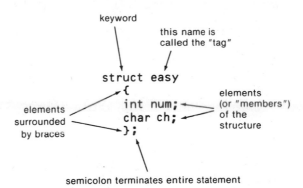

Figure 9-2. Format of a Structure Type Declaration

The keyword **struct** introduces the statement. The name **easy** is called the *tag*. It names the kind of structure being defined. Note that the tag is not a variable name, since we are not defining a variable; it is a *type* name. The members of the structure are surrounded by braces, and the entire statement is terminated by a semicolon.

> A structure is a data type whose format is defined by the programmer.

Defining Structure Variables

Once we've declared our new data type, we can define one or more variables to be of that type. In our program, we define a variable **ez1** to be of type **struct easy**:

```
struct easy ez1;
```

This statement *does* set aside space in memory. It establishes enough space to hold all the items in the structure: in this case, three bytes: two for the integer, and one for the character. (In some situations the compiler may allocate more bytes, so that the next variable in memory will come out on an even address.) The variable definition **struct easy ez1;** performs a function similar to such variable definitions as **float salary** and **int count;** it tells the compiler to set aside storage for a variable of a specfic type and gives a name to the variable. Figure 9-3 shows what the structure variable **ez1** looks like, first grouped together conceptually and then as the elements of the structure would look in memory.

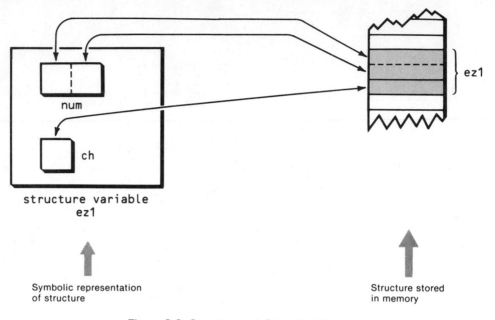

Figure 9-3. Structure *ez1* Stored in Memory

Accessing Structure Members

Now how do we refer to individual members of the structure? In arrays, we can access individual elements with a subscript: **array[7]**. Structures use a different approach: the "dot operator" (.), which is also called the "membership operator." Here's how we would refer to the **num** part of the **ez1** structure:

```
ez1.num
```

The variable name preceding the dot is the structure name; the name following it is the specific member of the structure. Thus the statements

```
ez1.num = 2;
ez1.ch = 'Z';
```

give a value of 2 to the **num** member of the structure **ez1** and a value of 'Z' to the **ch** member. Similarly, the statement

```
printf("ez1.num=%d, ez1.ch=%c\n", ez1.num, ez1.ch );
```

causes the values of these two member variables to be printed out.

> The <u>dot operator</u> (.) connects a structure variable name with a member of the structure.

The dot operator provides a powerful and clear way to specify members of a structure. An expression like **employee.salary** is more comprehensible than **employee[27]**.

Multiple Structure Variables of the Same Type

Just as there can be more than one **int** or **float** variable in a program, there also can be any number of variables of a given structure type. In the following program, for example, there are two variables, **ez1** and **ez2**, both of type **struct easy**:

```
/* struct2.c */
/* demonstrates structures */
/* uses two structure variables */
void main(void)
{
    struct easy        /* defines data type 'struct easy' */
        {
        int num;
        char ch;
        };

    struct easy ez1;  /* declares 'ez1' and 'ez2' to be */
    struct easy ez2;  /*   of type 'struct easy' */

    ez1.num = 2;       /* reference members of 'ez1' */
    ez1.ch = 'Z';
    ez2.num = 3;       /* reference members of 'ez2' */
    ez2.ch = 'Y';
    printf("ez1.num=%d, ez1.ch=%c\n", ez1.num, ez1.ch );
    printf("ez2.num=%d, ez2.ch=%c\n", ez2.num, ez2.ch );
}
```

Notice how the members of the two different structures are accessed: **ez1.num** gets **num** from the structure **ez1**, while **ez2.num** gets it from **ez2**.

Combining Declarations

You can combine in one statement the declaration of the structure type and the definition of structure variables. As an example, the easy2.c program can be rewritten like this:

```
/* struct2a.c */
/* demonstrates structures */
/* combines declaration and definition */
void main(void)
{
    struct easy         /* declares data type 'struct easy' */
        {               /* defines 'ez1' and 'ez2' to be */
        int num;        /*   of type 'struct easy' */
        char ch;
        } ez1, ez2;

    ez1.num = 2;        /* reference elements of 'ez1' */
    ez1.ch = 'Z';
    ez2.num = 3;        /* reference elements of 'ez2' */
    ez2.ch = 'Y';
    printf("ez1.num=%d, ez1.ch=%c\n", ez1.num, ez1.ch );
    printf("ez2.num=%d, ez2.ch=%c\n", ez2.num, ez2.ch );
}
```

The effect is the same as that provided by the separate statements, but the format is more compact (though perhaps less clear).

Entering Data into Structures

Let's examine a slightly more realistic programming example. This involves placing data into structures and reading it out again. This will be the first version of a program that will evolve throughout the chapter. Our goal, which will require several intermediate steps, is to develop a simple database program that will demonstrate one of the most useful ways data can be organized in C: as an array of structures.

In the following program, we construct a database for a typical employee category: the secret agent. If you're setting up a clandestine operation in a foreign country, the program will be right up your (dark) alley. If your needs are more pedestrian, you'll find the program is easily adaptable to other sorts of personnel.

In this program, the database stores two items of information about each secret agent: a name, represented by a character array, and a code number, represented by an integer. This information is entered into the program by the user and is then printed out again by the program. In this version of the program, there is space to store the data for only two agents; in later versions we'll show how to expand the program's capacity.

Here's the program:

```
/* twoagent.c */
/* stores and retreives data for two secret agents */
```

```
void main(void)
{
   struct personnel                    /* declare data structure */
      {
      char name [30];                  /* name */
      int agnumb;                      /* code number */
      };
   struct personnel agent1;            /* define a struct variable */
   struct personnel agent2;            /* define another one */
   char numstr[81];                    /* for number input */

   printf("\nAgent 1.\nEnter name: ");    /* get first name */
   gets(agent1.name);
   printf("Enter agent number (3 digits): "); /* get number */
   gets(numstr);
   agent1.agnumb = atoi(numstr);

   printf("\nAgent 2.\nEnter name: ");    /* get 2nd name */
   gets(agent2.name);
   printf("Enter agent number (3 digits): "); /* get number */
   gets(numstr);
   agent2.agnumb = atoi(numstr);

   printf("\nList of agents:\n" );
   printf("   Name: %s\n", agent1.name);     /* first agent */
   printf("   Agent number: %03d\n", agent1.agnumb);
   printf("   Name: %s\n", agent2.name);     /* second agent */
   printf("   Agent number: %03d\n", agent2.agnumb);
}
```

We declared a structure type called **personnel**, which will be used as the model for the structure variables that hold the data for the two agents. The structure variables **agent1** and **agent2** are then declared to be of type **struct personnel**.

Data is then placed into the appropriate structure elements using the statements

```
gets(agent1.name);
```

and

```
gets(numstr);
agent1.agnumb = atoi(numstr);
```

319

These statements are similar to those that we would use for simple variables, but the dot operator indicates that we're dealing with structure elements.

p298

We have used the **gets()** and **atoi()** combination, described in Chapter 8, to avoid a problem with **scanf()** and the keyboard buffer.

The four **printf()** statements print out the contents of our small database.

Here's a sample run:

```
Agent 1.
Enter name: Harrison Tweedbury
Enter agent number (3 digits): 102

Agent 2.
Enter name: James Bond
Enter agent number (3 digits): 007

List of agents:
   Name: Harrison Tweedbury
   Agent number: 102
   Name: James Bond
   Agent number: 007
```

Notice that we can print out leading zeros: this is accomplished by preceding the field width in the **printf()** statement with a zero: **%03d**.

Figure 9-4 shows how the structure variable **agent1** looks symbolically and how it looks stored in memory.

Let's look at some other structure operations that will be useful later on: initializing structures, passing their values in assignment statements, and using them as arguments to functions.

Initializing Structures

Like simple variables and arrays, structure variables can be initialized—given specific values—at the beginning of a program. The format used is quite similar to that used to initialize arrays.

Here's an example, using a modified version of our twoagent.c program. In this case the data on the two agents is contained in initialization statements within the program, rather than being input by the user:

```
/* initage.c */
/* demonstrates initialization of structures */

struct personnel              /* declares structure */
   {
   char name [30];            /* name */
```

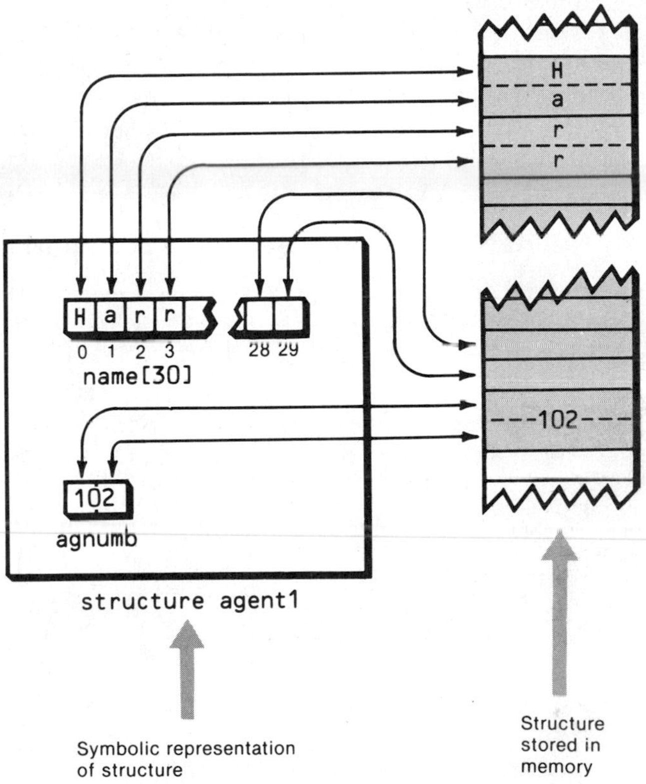

Figure 9-4. Structure *agent1* Stored in Memory

```
   int agnumb;                      /* code number */
   };

struct personnel agent1 =      /* initializes struct variable */
   { "Harrison Tweedbury", 012 };

struct personnel agent2 =      /* initializes another one */
   { "James Bond", 007 };

void main(void)
{
   printf("\nList of agents:\n" );
   printf("   Name: %s\n", agent1.name);     /* first agent */
   printf("   Agent number: %03d\n", agent1.agnumb);
   printf("   Name: %s\n", agent2.name);     /* second agent */
   printf("   Agent number: %03d\n", agent2.agnumb);
}
```

Here, after the usual declaration of the structure type, the two structure variables are defined and initialized at the same time. As with array initialization, the equal sign is used, followed by braces enclosing a list of values, with the values separated by commas.

When this program is executed, it will generate output similar to that of our previous example.

Assignment Statements Used with Structures

In the original version of C defined by Kernighan and Ritchie, it was impossible to assign the values of one structure variable to another variable using a simple assignment statement. In ANSI-compatible versions of C, including the Turbo C compiler, this is possible. That is, if **agent1** and **agent2** are structure variables of the same type, the following statement can be used: **agent2=agent1;**.

> The value of one structure variable can be assigned to another structure variable of the same type.

This is an important capability, so let's look at an example of its use. In this modification of our secret agent program, information is obtained from the user about one agent and is then assigned to a second structure variable, using an assignment statement:

```
/* twins.c */
/* demonstrates assignment of structures */
void main(void)
{
    struct personnel              /* declare data structure */
        {
        char name [30];           /* name */
        int agnumb;               /* code number */
        };

    struct personnel agent1;      /* define a struct variable */
    struct personnel agent2;      /* define another one */

    printf("\nAgent 1.\nEnter name: ");    /* get first name */
    gets(agent1.name);
    printf("Enter agent number (3 digits): "); /* get number */
    scanf("%d", &agent1.agnumb);
```

```
     agent2 = agent1;                    /* assigns one structure */
                                         /* to another */
     printf("\nList of agents:\n" );
     printf("   Name: %s\n", agent1.name);     /* first agent */
     printf("   Agent number: %03d\n", agent1.agnumb);
     printf("   Name: %s\n", agent2.name);     /* second agent */
     printf("   Agent number: %03d\n", agent2.agnumb);
}
```

When we run this program, data on two agents will be printed out as before, but it will be exactly the same data for both agents.

This is a rather amazing capability when you think about it: when you assign one structure to another, all the values in the structure are actually being assigned, all at once, to the corresponding structure elements. Only two values are assigned in this example, but there could be far more. Simple assignment statements cannot be used this way for arrays, which must be moved element by element.

Nested Structures

Just as there can be arrays of arrays, there can also be structures that contain other structures. This can be a powerful way to create complex data types.

For a simple example, imagine that our secret agents are sent out as a team, consisting of one "chief" and one "indian." The following program creates a structure with the tag **team**. This structure consists of two other structures of type **personnel**.

```
/* team.c */
/* demonstrates nested structures */

struct personnel                  /* declares structure */
   {
   char name [30];                /* name */
   int agnumb;                    /* code number */
   };

struct team                       /* declares structure */
   {                              /* whose members are */
   struct personnel chief;        /* themselves structures */
   struct personnel indian;
   };

struct team team1 =                       /* defines and */
   { { "Harrison Tweedbury", 012 },       /* initiailizes */
     { "James Bond",        007 } };      /* struct var 'team1' */
```

```
void main(void)
{
   printf("\nChief:\n" );
   printf("   Name: %s\n", team1.chief.name);
   printf("   Agent number: %03d\n", team1.chief.agnumb);
   printf("Indian:\n" );
   printf("   Name: %s\n", team1.indian.name);
   printf("   Agent number: %03d\n", team1.indian.agnumb);
}
```

Figure 9-5 shows the arrangement of nested structures.

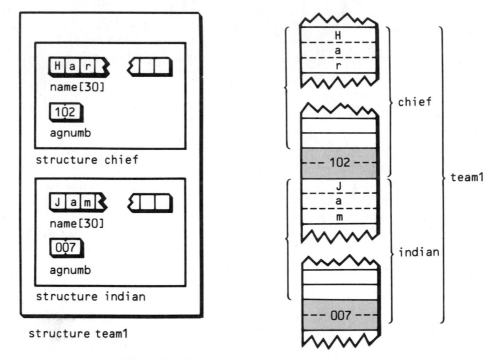

Figure 9-5. Structure *team1* Stored in Memory

Let's look at some details in this program.

First, we've defined a structure variable **team1**, which is of type **team**, and initialized it to the values shown. As when multidimensional arrays are initialized, nested braces are used to initialize structures within structures.

Second, notice the method we used to access the elements of a structure that is part of another structure. Here the dot operator is used *twice*, as in the expression

```
team1.chief.name
```

This refers to element **name** in the structure **chief** in the structure **team1**.

Of course, the nesting process need not stop at this level; we can nest a structure within a structure within a structure. Such constructions give rise to variable names that can be surprisingly self-descriptive, for instance:

```
triumph.1962.engine.carb.bolt.large
```

Passing Structures to Functions

In the same way that it can be passed in an assignment statement, the value of a structure variable can also be passed as a parameter to a function. This is a powerful feature that greatly simplifies the use of functions and thus the writing of well-constructed modular programs that use structures.

As an example, we'll rewrite our twoagent.c program to use functions to obtain the data about the agents from the user and to print it out. This is another step along the road to being able to access an array of structures, which is one of the most natural ways to model a database. Here's the program:

p 318

```
/* passtwo.c */
/* stores two agents */
/* demonstrates passing structures to functions */

struct personnel newname();      /* function prototypes */
void list(struct personnel);

struct personnel                 /* declare data structure */
   {
   char name [30];               /* agent name */
   int agnumb;                   /* agent number */
   };

void main(void)
{
   struct personnel agent1;      /* define structure variable */
   struct personnel agent2;      /* define another one */

   agent1 = newname();           /* get data for first agent */
   agent2 = newname();           /* get data for 2nd agent */
   list(agent1);                 /* print data for first agent */
   list(agent2);                 /* print data for 2nd agent */
}

/* newname() */
/* puts a new agent in the database */
```

```
struct personnel newname()
{
   char numstr[81];                /* for number */
   struct personnel agent;         /* new structure */

   printf("\nNew agent\nEnter name: ");        /* get name */
   gets(agent.name);
   printf("Enter agent number (3 digits): "); /* get number */
   gets(numstr);
   agent.agnumb = atoi(numstr);
   return(agent);                              /* return struct */
}

/* list() */
/* prints data on one agent */
void list(struct personnel age)    /* struct passed from main() */
{
   printf("\nAgent: \n");
   printf("   Name: %s\n", age.name);
   printf("   Agent number: %03d\n", age.agnumb);
}
```

Since both functions, as well as the main program, need to know how the structure type **personnel** is declared, this declaration is made global by placing it outside of all functions, before **main()**. The functions **main()**, **newname()**, and **list()** define their own internal structure variables, called **agent1** and **agent2**, **agent**, and **age**; to be of this type.

The function **newname** is called from the main program to obtain information from the user about the two agents. This function places the information in the internally defined structure variable, **agent**, and returns the value of this variable to the main program using a **return** statement, just as if it were returning a simple variable. The function **newname()** must be declared to be of type **struct personnel** in **main()**, since it returns a value of this type.

The main program assigns the values returned from **newname()** to the structure variables **agent1** and **agent2**. Finally **main()** calls the function **list()** to print out the values in **agent1** and **agent2**, passing the values of these two structures to the function as variables. The **list()** function assigns these values to an internal structure variable **age** and accesses the individual elements of this structure to print out the values.

Arrays of Structures

We now know enough to realize our goal of creating an array of structures, where each structure represents the data for one secret agent. This is a more ambitious program. We've provided a simple user interface, consisting of a choice of two single-letter selections. If the user types an 'e', the program will allow information on one agent to be entered. If the user types an 'l', the program will list all the agents in the database.

We've also added an additional item of information: the agent's height (a floating point variable), just to prove that structures can have more than two elements.

We want to use a floating point value for this number, and that requires the use of a new function, **atof()**, to convert from the input string to floating point. This function returns a double-precision floating point number, so we specify that in the structure at the start of the program. Since we are returning a noninteger value from a function, we need to provide the prototype for the function, which Turbo C requires to avoid becoming confused; hence the directive

```
#include <stdlib.h>
```

at the beginning of the program.

Here's the listing:

```
/* agent.c */
/* maintains list of agents in memory */
#include <stdlib.h>              /* for atof() */
#define TRUE 1
void newname(void);             /* prototypes */
void listall(void);

struct personnel               /* declare data structure */
   {
   char name [30];             /* name */
   int agnumb;                 /* code number */
   float height;               /* height in inches */
   };
struct personnel agent[50];     /* array of 50 structures */
int n = 0;                      /* number of agents listed */

void main(void)
{
   char ch;

   while ( TRUE )
      {
      printf("\nType 'e' to enter new agent,"); /* print */
      printf("\n   'l' to list all agents,");    /* selections */
      printf("\n   'q' to quit: ");
      ch = getche();                          /* get choice */
      switch (ch)
         {
         case 'e':                            /* enter new name */
```

```
                        newname(); break;
                case 'l':                           /* list entire file */
                    listall(); break;
                case 'q':
                    exit(0);
                default:                            /* user mistake */
                    puts("\nEnter only selections listed");
            }  /* end switch */
        }  /* end while */
}  /* end main */


/* newname() */
/* puts a new agent in the database */
void newname(void)
{
    char numstr[81];                            /* for number */

    printf("\nRecord %d.\nEnter name: ", n+1); /* get name */
    gets(agent[n].name);
    printf("Enter agent number (3 digits): "); /* get number */
    gets(numstr);
    agent[n].agnumb = atoi(numstr);
    printf("Enter height in inches: ");        /* get height */
    gets(numstr);
    agent[n++].height = atof(numstr);    /* convert to float */
}


/* listall() */
/* lists all agents and data */
void listall(void)
{
    int j;
    if (n < 1)                              /* check for empty list */
        printf("\nEmpty list.\n");
    for (j=0; j < n; j++)                   /* print list */
        {
        printf("\nRecord number %d\n", j+1);
        printf("   Name: %s\n", agent[j].name);
        printf("   Agent number: %03d\n", agent[j].agnumb);
        printf("   Height: %4.2f\n", agent[j].height);
        }
}
```

And here's a sample run:

```
Type 'e' to enter new agent        — "q" to quit;
  'l' to list all agents: e
Record 1.
Enter name: Harrison Tweedbury
Enter agent number (3 digits): 102
Enter height in inches: 70.5

Type 'e' to enter new agent
  'l' to list all agents: e
Record 2.
Enter name: Ursula Zimbowski
Enter agent number (3 digits): 303
Enter height in inches: 63.25

Type 'e' to enter new agent
  'l' to list all agents: e
Record 3.
Enter name: James Bond
Enter agent number (3 digits): 007
Enter height in inches: 74.3

Type 'e' to enter new agent
  'l' to list all agents: l

Record number 1
   Name: Harrison Tweedbury
   Agent number: 102
   Height: 70.50

Record number 2
   Name: Ursula Zimbowski
   Agent number: 303
   Height: 63.25

Record number 3
   Name: James Bond
   Agent number: 007
   Height: 74.30
```

Following this interaction we could then have continued by adding more agents, or listing the agents again, as the spirit moved us.

Defining an Array of Structures

Notice how the array of structures is defined:

```
struct personnel agent[50];
```

This statement provides space in memory for 50 structures of type **personnel**. This structure type is declared by the statement

```
struct personnel                   /* declare data structure */
   {
   char name [30];                 /* name */
   int agnumb;                     /* code number */
   float height;                   /* height in inches */
   };
```

Figure 9-6 shows conceptually what this array of structures looks like.

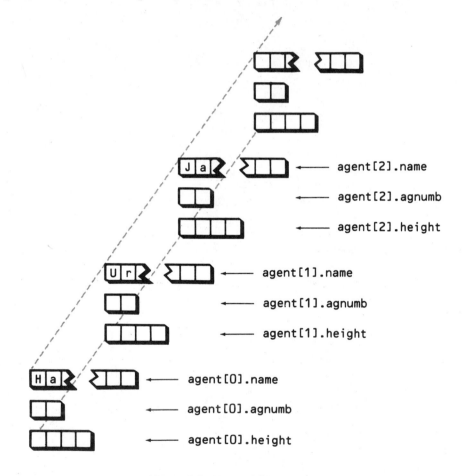

Figure 9-6. Array of Structures

For simplicity, we've defined the array of structures as a global variable, so that all the functions in the program can access it.

Accessing Members of Array of Structures

Individual members of a structure in our array of structures are accessed by referring to the structure variable name **agent**, followed by a subscript, followed by the dot operator, and ending with the structure element desired, as in this example:

```
agent[n].name
```

The balance of the program uses constructions we've discussed before.

> The expression **agent[n].name** refers to element **name** of the **nth** structure in an array of structures of type **agent**.

The overall scheme of this program can be applied to a wide variety of situations for storing data about particular entities. It could, for example, be used for inventory control, where each structure variable contained data about a particular item, such as the stock number, price, and number of items available. Or it could be used for a budgeting program, where each structure contained information about a budget category, such as name of the category, the budgeted amount, and the amount spent to date.

About the only thing lacking to make this program a useful database application is a way to store the data as a disk file, a topic we'll explore in Chapter 12.

Pointers and Structures: The Linked List

Before we leave structures, let's look at one more way that structures can be used: the linked list. The linked-list approach to storing data is useful in itself, and it also provides a background for further study of the use of pointers with functions. This example will give us some insight into how structures can be used to create a wide variety of complex data types.

A linked list consists of structures related to one another by pointers, rather than by being members of an array, as in the agent.c example. To demonstrate this construction, we'll rewrite our agent.c program to store data as a linked list. The basic idea is that each structure on the list contains a pointer that points to the next structure. The pointer in the last structure on the list doesn't point to anything, so we give it the value of 0, or null. Figure 9-7 shows how this looks.

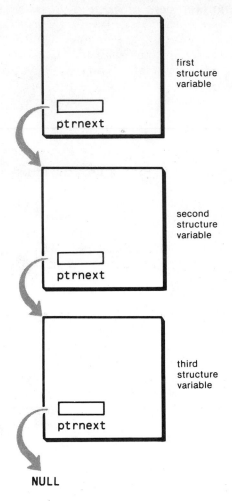

Figure 9-7. Linked List

Before we can understand the program that will create and manipulate our linked list, we need to explore some of the building blocks used in its operation. There are two new ideas: how structure elements can be accessed using pointers, and how an area of memory can be assigned to a variable using pointers and the **malloc()** function. Let's examine each of these in turn.

Accessing Structure Elements Using Pointers

Just as pointers can be used to contain the addresses of simple variables and arrays, they can also be used to hold the addresses of structures. Here's an example that demonstrates a pointer pointing to a structure:

```
/* ptrstr.c */
/* demonstrates pointers to structures */
void main(void)
{
    struct xx              /* declare structure type */
       {
       int num1;
       char ch1;
       };
    struct xx xx1;     /* define structure variable */
    struct xx *ptr;    /* define pointer to structure */

    ptr = &xx1;            /* assign address of struct to ptr */
    ptr->num1 = 303;    /* refer to members of structure */
    ptr->ch1 = 'Q';
    printf("ptr->num1=%d\n", ptr->num1 );
    printf("ptr->ch1=%c\n", ptr->ch1 );
}
```

Here we've declared a structure **xx** and defined a structure variable **xx1** of type **struct xx**. You've seen this before, but the next step is new: we define a variable of type "pointer to structure xx" in the statement:

```
struct xx *ptr;
```

Next we assign the address of the structure variable **xx1** to **ptr** using the line

```
ptr = &xx1;
```

Thus, if the structure **xx1** happened to be located at address 1000, the number 1000 would be placed in the variable **ptr**.

Now, can we refer to the members of the structure using the pointer instead of the structure name itself? As you've learned, if we know the name of a given structure variable, we can access its elements using this name and the dot operator. For instance, in the example above, the expression **xx.num1** refers to the element **num1** in the structure **xx**. Is there an analogous construction using **ptr** instead of **xx**? We can't use **ptr.num1** because **ptr** is not a structure but a pointer to a structure, and the dot operator requires a structure on the left side.

A literal approach would be to use the expression **(*ptr).num1**. Since we know that **ptr** points to **xx1**, it follows that ***ptr** is the contents of **xx1**. So substituting in the expression **xx1.num1** gives us **(*ptr).num1**. The parentheses are needed around ***ptr** because the dot operator has higher priority than the indirection operator. However, this is an unwieldy expression, so C provides a simpler approach: the two-part operator –> is used: a combination of the minus and less-than signs called the "arrow operator," as in the expression **ptr–>num1**. This has exactly the same effect as **(*ptr).num1**.

> The (.) operator connects a *structure* with a member of the structure; the (–>) operator connects a *pointer* with a member of the structure.

In the ptrstr.c program example above, we've used this construction to assign values to the members of the structure, as in the expression

```
ptr->num1 = 303;
```

Similar constructions are used to read those values back out again with **printf()** statements.

Allocating Memory: The malloc() Function

When we declare an array of structures, the compiler allocates enough memory to hold the entire array. This is not efficient if we don't come close to filling the entire array; in the agent.c example, for instance, we put 3 secret agents in an array that could hold 50, so the space for the 47 unused structure variables was wasted.

One of the advantages of using the linked-list approach (which we really will demonstrate soon) is that we use only as much memory as is needed to hold the data actually entered. Each time we decide to add an agent to the list, the program will acquire just enough memory to do the job. One mechanism for acquiring this memory is the C library function **malloc()**. A program can tell **malloc()** how much memory it needs, and **malloc()** will return a pointer to a space in memory just that large.

Let's look at a short example of the **malloc()** function at work:

```
/* maltest.c */
/* tests malloc() */
void main(void)
{
   struct xx              /* declare structure */
      {
      int num1;
      char ch1;
      };
   struct xx *ptr;        /* define pointer to structure */
   int j;
```

```
    printf("sizeof(struct xx)=%d\n", sizeof(struct xx) );
    for(j=0; j<4; j++)
        {
        ptr = (struct xx *) malloc( sizeof(struct xx) );
        printf("ptr=%x\n", ptr );
        }
    }
```

p336

This program declares a structure type called **xx**. It calls **malloc()** four times. Each time, **malloc()** returns a pointer to an area of memory large enough to hold a new version of the structure. Note that nowhere in the program do we define any structure variables. In effect, the structure variables are *created* by the function **malloc()**; the program does not know the *names* of these structure variables, but it knows where they are in memory because **malloc()** has returned pointers to them. These structure variables can therefore be accessed, using pointers, just as if they had been declared at the beginning of the program.

Here's the program's output:

```
sizeof(struct xx)=3
ptr=554
ptr=65e
ptr=564
ptr=56e
```

Each time we call **malloc()** we need to tell it the size of the structure we want to store. We could do this by adding up the bytes used by each of the elements in our structure, or we can turn the task over to a C library function called **sizeof()**. This function takes a *data type* as an argument and returns the size in bytes that the data type occupies. For instance, the expression

```
sizeof(float)
```

would return the value 4, since type **float** occupies four bytes in memory.

In our program we've used **sizeof()** in a **printf()** statement so we can see what value it returns for the size of the structure **xx**. Here it returns 3, since the structure consists of one character and one integer.

It's surprising that even though **malloc()** is told to return a memory area of three bytes, it spaces the starting addresses of these areas eight bytes apart. (We've used hexadecimal notation for the addresses, a common practice in C programming. If hexadecimal is unfamiliar to you, consult Appendix B.) The reason for this is less clear, but it doesn't matter too much if **malloc()** wastes a few bytes here and there, as long as it sets aside enough space for each structure variable.

The key statement in maltest.c is:

```
ptr = (struct xx *) malloc( sizeof(struct xx) );
```

This statement assigns the pointer value (the address) returned by **malloc()** to the pointer variable **ptr**. The argument taken by **malloc()**, sizeof(struct xx), is the size of the structure. What is the expression **(struct xx *)** that *precedes* **malloc()**? To understand the use of this expression, we need to know about a C feature called *typecasting*, so let's digress briefly to see what this means.

Typecasting

Sometimes we need to force the compiler to return the value of an expression as a particular data type. For example, suppose we've been using a floating point variable **flovar** in a program, and at some point we want to calculate the square root of its value. Turbo C contains a library routine **sqrt()**, which will return a square root, but the argument sent to this function must be of type **double**. If we send the function a variable of type **float**, it will return a nonsense result. So we need to convert our variable **flovar** to type **double**. To do this, we use the *cast* operator, which consists of putting parentheses around the name of the data type. In this example we would say:

```
answer = sqrt( (double)flovar );
```

The expression **(double)** causes **flovar** to be converted from type **float** to type **double** before it is used.

We need to perform a similar data conversion on the pointer returned by **malloc()**, although for a different reason. Remember that the compiler needs to know two pieces of information about every pointer: the address of the item pointed to and its data type. The **malloc()** function returns the address, but it conveys no information about the data type. In order to avoid confusing the compiler, we must ensure that the value returned by **malloc()** is of type **pointer to struct xx**. We do this by using a typecast: the name of the data type enclosed in parentheses, preceding the value being assigned. This forces the value to be of that type, and ensures that the compiler will assign a pointer of the correct size to the variable **ptr**.

> When **malloc()** returns a pointer to a structure, the compiler must be told the type of the structure pointed to.

Using malloc()

For a simple example of **malloc()** at work, we'll rewrite our ptrstr.c example, this time using a pointer value obtained from **malloc()**, rather than using the address operator on a declared structure variable.

p 333

```
/* ptrstr2.c */
/* demonstrates pointers to structures */
void main(void)
{
    struct xx              /* declare structure type */
        {
        int num1;
        char ch1;
        };
    struct xx *ptr;     /* define pointer to structure */

                        /* get address to hold structure */
    ptr = (struct xx *)malloc( sizeof(struct xx) );          p334

    ptr->num1 = 303;    /* refer to members of structure */    p334
    ptr->ch1 = 'Q';
    printf("ptr->num1=%d\n", ptr->num1 );
    printf("ptr->ch1=%c\n", ptr->ch1 );
}
```

Notice the similarities to the earlier version of ptrstr.c. Everything is the same, *p333*
except that the structure variable is not defined in the listing, it is created by
malloc() at run time.

With this background under our belts, it's time (finally) to take a look at
the linked-list version of agent.c.

The Agent Program Using Linked Lists

Here's the listing for the program. In many ways it is similar to the earlier
agent.c program that used an array of structures, but the differences are signif- *p327*
icant and will require some explanation.

```
/* agent2.c */
/* maintains list of agents */
/* uses linked list */
#include <stdlib.h>              /* for atof() */
#include <stdio.h>              /* for NULL, etc. */
#define TRUE 1
void newname(void);             /* prototypes */
void listall(void);

struct prs                      /* declare data structure */
    {
    char name [30];             /* agent's name */
    int agnumb;                 /* agent's number */
```

```
           double height;               /* height in inches */
  ──→      struct prs *ptrnext;         /* ptr to next structure */
           };
      struct prs *ptrfirst, *ptrthis, *ptrnew;  /* define pointers */
                                             /* to structure */
      void main(void)
      {
         char ch;

         ptrfirst = (struct prs *)NULL;            /* no input yet */
         while (TRUE)
            {
            printf("\nType 'e' to enter new agent"); /* print */
            printf("\n  'l' to list all agents,");   /* selections */
            printf("\n  'q' to quit: ");
            ch = getche();                       /* get choice */
            switch (ch)
               {
               case 'e':                          /* enter new name */
                  newname(); break;
               case 'l':                          /* list entire file */
                  listall(); break;
               case 'q':                          /* exit program */
                  exit(0);
               default:                           /* user mistake */
                  puts("\nEnter only selections listed");
               }   /* end switch */
            }   /* end while */
      }   /* end main */

/* newname() */
/* puts a new agent in the database */
void newname(void)
{
   char numstr[81];                        /* for numbers */
                                           /* get memory space */
   ptrnew = (struct prs *) malloc( sizeof(struct prs) );
   if(ptrfirst == (struct prs *)NULL )   /* if none already */
      ptrfirst = ptrthis = ptrnew;       /* save addr */
   else                                  /* not first item */
      {                                  /* go to end of list */
      ptrthis = ptrfirst;                /* (start at begin) */
      while( ptrthis->ptrnext != (struct prs *)NULL )
         ptrthis = ptrthis->ptrnext;     /* find next item */
      ptrthis->ptrnext = ptrnew;         /* point to new item */
```

p336

p334

```
        ptrthis = ptrnew;                       /* go to new item */
        }
    printf("\nEnter name: ");                    /* get name */
    gets(ptrthis->name);
    printf("Enter number: ");                    /* get number */
    gets(numstr);
    ptrthis->agnumb = atoi(numstr);
    printf("Enter height: ");                    /* get height */
    gets(numstr);
    ptrthis->height = atof(numstr);
    ptrthis->ptrnext = (struct prs *) NULL;      /* this is end */
}


/* listall() */
/* lists all agents and data */
void listall(void)
{
    if (ptrfirst == (struct prs *)NULL )          /* if empty list */
        { printf("\nEmpty list.\n"); return; }    /*    return */
    ptrthis = ptrfirst;                           /* start at first item */
    do
        {                                         /* print contents */
        printf("\nName: %s\n", ptrthis->name );
        printf("Number: %03d\n", ptrthis->agnumb );
        printf("Height: %4.2lf\n", ptrthis->height );
        ptrthis = ptrthis->ptrnext;               /* move to next item */
        }
    while (ptrthis != (struct prs *)NULL ); /* quit on null ptr */
}
```

In operation, this program is much like agent.c, except that it no longer prints record numbers; since we do not have an array subscript to work with, it complicates the program to keep track of the record numbers (although this capability could be easily added to the program if desired). Here's the sample interaction with the program:

p327

```
Type 'e' to enter new agent        'g' to quit
   'l' to list all agents: e
Enter name: George Smiley
Enter number: 999
Enter height: 64.3

Type 'e' to enter new agent
   'l' to list all agents: e
Enter name: James Bond
```

```
Enter number: 007
Enter height: 74.25

Type 'e' to enter new agent
   'l' to list all agents: e
Enter name: Mata Hari
Enter number: 121
Enter height: 58.75

Type 'e' to enter new agent
   'l' to list all agents: l
Name: George Smiley
Number: 999
Height: 64.30

Name: James Bond
Number: 007
Height: 74.25

Name: Mata Hari
Number: 121
Height: 58.75
```

The challenging part of understanding this program is following what happens to the pointers. As we've noted, the basic idea is that each structure variable contains a pointer to the next structure on the list; the pointer in the last structure contains the null pointer. These pointers are called **ptrnext**, since they point to the next structure. Figure 9-8 shows how this looks, assuming that the first structure is assigned the address 3000.

In addition to the **ptrnext** variable contained in each structure, the program also keeps track of three other pointers declared at the beginning of the program.

One of these pointers, called **ptrfirst**, will be used to hold the address of the first structure in the list. This is a key address, since it's how the program finds the list. The pointer is set to null at the beginning of the program by the statement:

```
ptrfirst = (struct prs *)NULL;
```

Let's look at this statement. First, NULL is **#define**d to be 0 in the file stdio.h; this is a standard definition used by C programmers, and since we had included the file anyway, to define "stdin," it's easy to use NULL instead of 0. Since this value is going to be assigned to a pointer, it must be typecast to the same type as the other pointers, namely **(struct prs *)**.

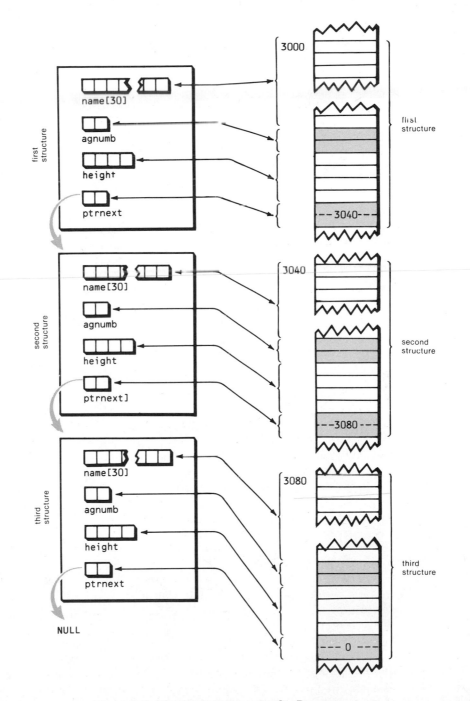

Figure 9-8. Structures in the agent2.c Program

The **main()** function is otherwise much the same as in agent.c; it consists mostly of a **switch** statement to route control to different functions. It's in the functions **newname()** and **listall()** that most of the pointer manipulation takes place.

Adding an Agent to the Database

If the user wants to add an agent to the database, the program calls on the function **newname()**. This function uses **malloc()** to get a pointer to a space big enough for the structure (40 bytes, as it turns out). This address is assigned temporarily to a pointer called **ptrnew**. If this is the first item to be placed on the list, the **ptrfirst** variable will still be set to null, as the program will discover with the statement

```
if(ptrfirst == (struct prs *)NULL )
```

The program then sets both **ptrfirst** and **ptrthis** to the new address in **ptrnew**. The individual items in the structure are then filled in by the user's replies, which are assigned to the variables **ptrthis−>name**, **ptrthis−>agnumb**, and so forth.

However, if this isn't the first item on the list, the program must work its way to the end of the list, so it can change the pointer **ptrnext** in the last element of the array from null to the address in **ptrnew**, thus linking the new item. The **while** loop in **newname()** is used to move to the end of the list. It starts by assigning **ptrfirst** to **ptrthis**. Then it looks to see if the expression

```
ptrthis−>ptrnext
```

(the pointer in the structure currently being looked at) is null. If so, the end of the list has been reached. If not, the **while** loop continues by assigning the address in **ptrthis−>ptrnext** to **ptrthis** and cycling through the **while** loop again. The operation of moving through the list and adding a new structure to the end is shown in Figure 9-9.

Displaying the Data on the List

Displaying the data on the list is a matter of following the chain of pointers from one structure to another. The function **listall()** first checks to see if the list is empty by checking **ptrfirst** to see if it is null. If not, it enters a **do while** loop that prints out the elements of the structure pointed to by **ptrthis**, gets the address of the next structure in line from **ptrthis−>ptrnext**, assigns this address to **ptrthis**, and repeats the process. The loop ends when **ptrthis−>ptrnext** turns out to be null.

There are many refinements that can be made when using linked lists. For instance, the address of the last item on the list is often stored (sometimes as a pointer in the first item of the list, which is then treated as a dummy item). Having this pointer available avoids having to read through the entire

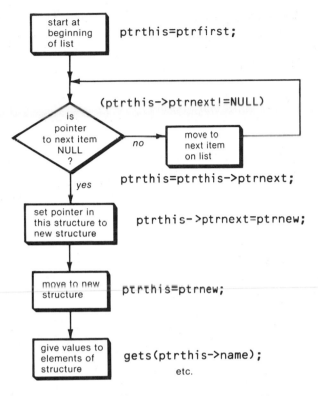

Figure 9-9. Adding a New Structure to the List

list to add a new item to the end; the program can go directly to the last item. This is a timesaver when the list becomes long. Also, lists can be linked backward as well as forward, as we've shown, or they can be circular.

Deleting an item from a linked list is fairly easy. Say the structure to be deleted is B. Then the pointer in the preceding structure, A, is changed to point to C rather than B. If it is desired to free the memory used by the deleted structure, a library function **free()** can be used. This function takes as an argument a pointer to the structure to be deleted. This technique can result in significant memory savings when many items are being added and deleted.

It is easy to search through linked lists for a particular name or other data item. The search program follows the chain of pointers, as in our example, and checks each structure to see if it contains the desired item.

> Very complex data organizations can be built on the idea of a structure containing a pointer.

Pointers to structures can be used for many other configurations besides the linked list we've shown here. For example, there is the tree structure, where each element points to two or more elements, each of which points to other elements, and so on. We'll leave these topics to other books.

Unions

Unions have the same relationship to structures that you might have to a distant cousin who resembled you but turned out to be smuggling contraband in a third-world country; they may look the same, but they are engaged in different enterprises.

Both structures and unions are used to group a number of different variables together. But while a structure enables us to treat as a unit a number of different variables stored at different places in memory, a union enables us to treat the same space in memory as a number of different variables. That is, a union is a way for a section of memory to be treated as a variable of one type on one occasion, and as a different variable, of a different type, on another occasion.

You might wonder why it would ever be necessary to do such a thing, but we'll be seeing a very practical application soon. First, let's look at a simple example:

```
/* union.c */
/* demonstrates unions */
void main(void)
{
    union intflo            /* declare union of type 'intflo' */
        {
        int intnum;         /*     integer member */
        float fltnum;       /*     floating point member */
        } unex;             /* define 'unex' to be type intflo */

    printf("sizeof(union inflo)=%d\n", sizeof(union intflo) );
    unex.intnum = 734;
    printf("unex.intnum=%d\n", unex.intnum );
    unex.fltnum = 867.43;
    printf("unex.fltnum=%.2f\n", unex.fltnum );
}
```

As you can see, we declare a union type (**intflo**) and a union variable (**unex**) in much the same way we declare structure types and variables. However, the similarity ends there, as we can see from the output of the program:

```
sizeof(union inflo)=4
unex.intnum=734
unex.fltnum=867.43
```

Although the union holds a floating point number (**fltnum**) and an integer (**intnum**), its size is only four bytes. Thus, it is big enough to hold one element or the other but not both at the same time. In the program we first give a value to the variable **unex.intnum** and read it out. Then we give a value to **unex.fltnum** and read it out. We can't give values to these two variables at the same time, because they occupy the same space in memory; if we assigned **unex.intnum** a value, and then tried to read out a value of **unex.fltnum,** we'd get nonsense because the program would try to interpret an integer as a floating point number. Figure 9-10 shows a conceptual view of the union **intflo** and its relationship to memory.

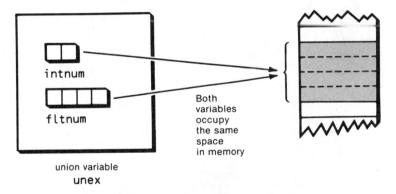

union variable
unex

Figure 9-10. Union Variable **unex** Stored in Memory

Why use unions? One reason is to use a single variable name to pass data of different types. We could rewrite the C library function **sqrt()**, for example, so that instead of requiring an argument of type **double**, it would accept any data type. A union could be used in the function to store the incoming data; any data type would be acceptable. The union might look like this:

```
union number
    {
    double dnum;
    float fnum;
    long lnum;
    int inum;
    char cnum;
    };
```

In this way the same function would serve for all data types. (The function would need to examine the data in the union to determine which type it was or it would need to be told the type via a second parameter.)

Another use for unions is to give the *same* data different names and treat it as different types, depending on the needs of the function using it. We'll see an example of this in the next section. But before we go on to that topic we need to be familiar with one more C construction.

> A union provides a way to look at the same data in several different ways.

Unions of Structures

Just as structures can be nested within each other, so too can unions be nested in unions, unions in structures, and structures in unions. Here's an example of a structure nested in a union:

```c
/* unistruc.c */
/* demonstrates union of structures */

void main(void)
{
    struct twoints          /* declare structure 'twoints' */
        {
        int intnum1;
        int intnum2;
        } stex;             /* 'stex' is type struct twoints */

    union intflo            /* declare union 'intflo' */
        {
        struct twoints stex; /* union contains a structure */
        float fltnum;
        } unex;             /* 'unex' is type union intflo */

    printf("sizeof(union intflo)=%d\n", sizeof(union intflo) );
    unex.stex.intnum1 = 734;
    unex.stex.intnum2 = -333;
    printf("unex.stex.intnum1=%d\n", unex.stex.intnum1 );
    printf("unex.stex.intnum2=%d\n", unex.stex.intnum2 );
    unex.fltnum = 867.43;
    printf("unex.fltnum=%.1f\n", unex.fltnum );
}
```

Here's the output of unistruc.c:

```
sizeof(union intflo)=4
unex.stex.intnum1=734
unex.stex.intnum2=-333
unex.fltnum=867.4
```

In this program we declare a structure type **twoints** and a structure variable **stex** of that type. The elements of the structure are two integers, **intnum1** and **intnum2**. We also declare a union type **intflo** and a union variable **unex** of that type. The elements of the union are the structure **stex** and a floating point variable **fltnum**.

As we do with nested structures, we access members of this union of structures using the dot operator twice. Thus,

```
unex.stex.intnum1
```

is the element **intnum1** in the structure **stex** in the union **unex**.

This configuration, the union of structures, will be important when we explore the ROM BIOS.

The ROM BIOS

As we noted at the beginning of this chapter, PC computers come with a set of built-in routines collectively called the ROM BIOS. These routines are a permanent part of the machine; in this sense, they are more hardware than software. Our C programs can make use of these routines to perform a variety of input/output activities. In the remainder of this chapter we'll explore the ROM BIOS and see how it can be accessed from C.

Advantages of Using ROM BIOS

As the name implies, the BIOS routines mostly handle input/output operations. Some of the routines duplicate C library functions. For example, there is a ROM BIOS routine to put a character on the screen, similar in operation to **putch()**, and another routine similar to **getche()**. For many of the routines built into ROM, however, there is no equivalent in C. The most important capability lacking in the C library is in graphics. For instance, to change graphics modes or to put a dot on the graphics screen requires a call to a ROM BIOS routine. As a consequence, if you want to exercise control over various graphics operations, it is important to know how to access the ROM BIOS.

Overview of the ROM BIOS Library

There are dozens of ROM BIOS routines. The exact number depends on which computer in the PC family you're using. The largest category of routines deals with the video display. There are routines to set the video mode, control the cursor size and position, read and write characters, and place dots on the color screen, among others. There are also ROM routines for other input/output devices, including the diskette drives, the serial port, the cassette reader (does anyone ever use this device?), joysticks, user-defined devices, the keyboard, and the printer.

We cannot cover all the ROM BIOS routines in this book; there are far too many. For a complete explanation of all the ROM BIOS routines, see the bibliography.

In this section we'll explore several ROM BIOS routines; we'll cover more graphics-oriented ROM routines in Chapters 10 and 11.

Accessing the ROM BIOS

The ROM BIOS routines are written in assembly language and were designed to be called by assembly language programs. As a consequence, calling them from C is not as simple as calling C library functions. C compilers working on the PC generally provide a method to access these routines, but using this method requires at least some understanding of the architecture of the microprocessor chip that powers the computer. This chip can be the 8086, 80286, 80386, or 80486, depending on the particular machine. For our discussion we will assume that all these chips operate in the same way.

Microprocessor Architecture for C Programmers

When we call a C function from a C program, we can pass values using arguments placed in the parentheses following the function name, as in the expression **strcat(s1,s2)**. These values (in this example the addresses of strings) are placed in an area of memory called the stack, where the function can find and operate on them.

When we use C to call a BIOS routine, the process is somewhat different. Instead of values being placed in an area of memory, they are placed in hardware devices called *registers*. These are somewhat like memory locations, but they have far more capabilities. Registers are the heart of the microprocessor; they are used to perform arithmetic and many other operations, but here we are concerned only with using them as locations for passing arguments to the BIOS.

There are a number of registers in the microprocessor; the ones we will be most concerned with are shown in Figure 9-11. As you can see, each of these four registers, AX, BX, CX, and DX, consist of two bytes. (Either upper- or lowercase may be used for register names, so they can be called ax, bx, cx, and dx as well.) In some ways the registers are like integer variables in C. They can hold two bytes of data, and we can put whatever values we like into them, just as we can assign whatever value we want to a variable. Unlike C variables, however, the registers are fixed; they are always there, and they always have the same names. They can be thought of as special-purpose permanent variables.

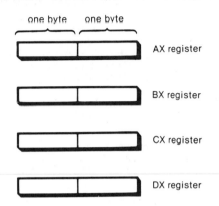

Figure 9-11. The Main 8086 Registers

The Dual Role of the Registers

Another difference between C variables and registers is that registers can be accessed in two different ways: either as four two-byte registers, or as eight one-byte registers, as shown in Figure 9-12.

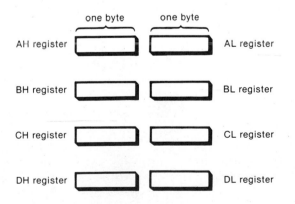

Figure 9-12. Registers as One-Byte Storage

In the one-byte interpretation each register is split into a high half (AH, BH, CH, and DH) and a low half (AL, BL, CL, DL). Although the register itself is the same physical object whether used as one two-byte device or two one-byte devices, the rest of the hardware in the chip interprets each differently, and so each must be accessed differently by the software.

The idea of using the same variable storage in two different ways should sound familiar; it is similar to our description of a union in the last section. In fact, a union is the mechanism used to communicate with the registers. But before we show an example of this, we need to explore one other idea.

Interrupt Numbers

The ROM BIOS routines are accessed through *interrupts*. We need not concern outselves with exactly how interrupts work; for our purposes an interrupt can be thought of as *a group of functions*. Each of these groups has its own *interrupt number*. For instance, all the routines that deal with the video display use interrupt number 10 (hex), and all those that deal with the disk drive use number 13 (hex). Thus, in order to call a ROM BIOS routine, we must first know its *interrupt number*.

> An interrupt provides access to a group of ROM BIOS routines.

To specify a routine within one of these groups, we place a value in the one-byte AH register. Various other registers may also hold values, depending on the specific function called.

The *int86()* Function

The mechanism used to access a ROM BIOS routine is a C library function called **int86()**. The "int" stands for "interrupt" and the "86" refers to the 80x86 family of chips. This function takes the interrupt number and two union variables as arguments. The first union represents the values in the registers being sent *to* the ROM routine, and the second represents the values in the registers being returned *from* the ROM routine to the C program. Figure 9-13 shows the format of this function. Notice that the function actually requires the *addresses* of the unions, not the unions themselves (in the same way **scanf()** requires the addresses of numerical variables).

Now, we're ready for an actual example of a program that accesses the ROM BIOS.

Finding the Memory Size

One of the routines built into the ROM BIOS will return the size of the RAM memory installed in the machine. This can be an interesting capability when

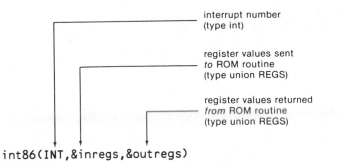

interrupt number
(type int)

register values sent
to ROM routine
(type union REGS)

register values returned
from ROM routine
(type union REGS)

int86(INT,&inregs,&outregs)

Figure 9-13. Format of the *int86()* Function

used in a stand-alone program, if you don't happen to know how much memory there is in the machine you're using. It can be even more useful to a program that uses large amounts of memory, runs on various computers that may have a variety of memory sizes, and needs a way to find out just how much memory is available.

The data required for this ROM BIOS routine is summarized in the box. We'll use similar boxes for other ROM BIOS routines as we go along.

ROM BIOS routine:	Memory size
Interrupt 12 hex:	Memory size
Input registers:	None
Output registers:	AX=memory size in Kbytes

Here there are only two pertinent items of data about the routine: we invoke it by calling interrupt 12 hex, and the memory size is read from the AX register. (Other ROM BIOS routines will use additional input and output parameters.)

Here's the program.

```
/* memsize0.c */                    interrupt
/* prints memory size */           12 hex
#define VIDEO 0x12  <              /* BIOS interrupt number */      p 691

void main(void)
{
    struct WORDREGS                /* registers as 16-bit words */
        {
        unsigned int ax;
        unsigned int bx;
```

```
                              unsigned int cx;
                              unsigned int dx;
                              unsigned int si;
                              unsigned int di;
                              unsigned int flags;
                              };

                       struct BYTEREGS            /* registers as 8-bit bytes */
                              {
                              unsigned char al, ah;
                              unsigned char bl, bh;
                              unsigned char cl, ch;
                              unsigned char dl, dh;
                              };

                       union REGS                 /* either bytes or words */
                              {
                              struct WORDREGS x;
                              struct BYTEREGS h;
                              };

                       union REGS regs;           /* regs to be type union REGS */
                       int size;

                       int86(VIDEO, &regs, &regs); /* call video interrupt */
                       size = regs.x.ax;           /* get value from AX register */
                       printf("Memory size is %d Kbytes", size );
                       }
```

declared in dos.h

And here's the output generated on a particular machine:

```
Memory size is 256 Kbytes
```

A Union of Structures

As you can see, the program uses two structures and a union. The first structure, whose tag is WORDREGS, consists of all the registers in their two-byte interpretation. (In assembly language a two-byte piece of data is called a "word," hence the name WORDREGS, for "word registers.") The data type used is **unsigned int**, since the numbers stored in the registers are not considered to be signed.

The structure declares the four two-byte registers we discussed: the AX, BX, CX, and DX registers. It also declares several registers we didn't mention: the SI, DI, and FLAGS registers. We don't need these registers in the ROM calls we use, but they must appear in the structure, since the **int86** function is expecting them.

The second structure, whose tag is BYTEREGS, consists of the same registers interpreted as eight one-byte registers.

The union consists of these two structures (a construction described in the last section). This union creates a set of variables that can be looked at either as four two-byte registers or as eight one-byte registers. The WORD-REGS structure is given the variable name **x** (since all the two-byte registers end in this letter), while the BYTEREGS structure is given the name **h** (since the high half of the registers end in this letter). The union variable declared to be of type REGS is called **regs**.

Thus to access a register we use the dot operator twice:

```
regs.x.bx
```

means the BX register, while

```
regs.h.cl
```

refers to the CL register.

In our program, we don't need to send any values to the routine, so nothing is placed in any of the registers before we call **int86()**. Interrupt number 12 (hex) is unusual in this respect; most interrupt numbers require more information, as we'll see. Since one argument is not used, we can use the same union variable, **regs**, for both the outgoing and incoming values:

— VIDEO or 0x12

```
int86(MEM, &regs, &regs);
```

On the return from **int86()** the memory size has been placed in the AX register, which we access in the expression

```
size = regs.x.ax
```

The data type of **size** agrees with that of **regs.x.ax** since they are both unsigned integers.

Using the Declarations in dos.h

Actually, in Turbo C the structures WORDREGS and BYTEREGS and the union REGS are already declared in a file called dos.h. Thus, if we **#include** this file in our program, we can dispense with the explicit declarations, as this version of the program shows:

) p 351 352

```
/* memsize.c */
/* prints memory size */
#include <dos.h>              /* declares REGS */
```

```
#define VIDEO 0x12                 /* BIOS interrupt number */

void main(void)
{
   union REGS regs;                /* regs to be type union REGS */
   int size;

   int86(VIDEO, &regs, &regs); /* call video interrupt */
   size = regs.x.ax;              /* get value from AX register */
   printf("Memory size is %d Kbytes", size );
}
```

p352

This is certainly a much handier format, although it does not reveal as much about what is going on.

Setting the Cursor Size

Let's look at an example that requires us to send values *to* a ROM routine. This program will call a ROM routine that changes the size of the cursor, so let's first examine how the cursor is created.

On the monochrome screen, the cursor consists of 14 short horizontal lines, numbered from 0 to 13 (reading from top to bottom), as shown in Figure 9-14. If you're using an EGA color display, there are only 9 lines, numbered from 0 to 8.

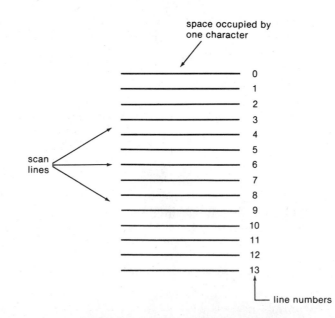

Figure 9-14. The Monochrome Cursor

The default cursor, the one you are most used to seeing, uses only two of these lines, 12 and 13, at the bottom of the character position (7 and 8 in EGA). To redefine the size of the cursor, we call the BIOS routine at interrupt 10 (hex), with the AH register containing 1.

ROM BIOS routine:	Set cursor size
Interrupt 10 hex:	Video
Input registers:	AH=01
	CH=starting scan line (0 to 13 dec)
	CL=ending scan line (0 to 13 dec)
Output registers:	None

We also place the starting cursor line number in the CH register, and the ending line number in the CL register.

Here's the program.

```
/* setcur.c */
/* sets cursor size */
#include "dos.h"        /* declares REGS */
#define CURSIZE 1       /* "set cursor size" service */
#define VIDEO 0x10      /* video BIOS interrupt number */

void main( int argc, char *argv[] )
{
   union REGS regs;
   int start, end;
   if (argc != 3)
      {
      printf("Example usage: C>setcur 12 13");
      exit();
      }
   start = atoi( argv[1] );    /* string to integer */
   end = atoi( argv[2] );
   regs.h.ch = (char)start;    /* starting line number */
   regs.h.cl = (char)end;      /* ending line number */
   regs.h.ah = CURSIZE;        /* service number */
   int86(VIDEO, &regs, &regs); /* call video interrupt */
}
```

In this example we make use of command-line arguments (described in Chapter 8) to get the starting and ending cursor lines numbers from the user. To cause the cursor to fill the entire character block, we would type:

```
C>setcur 0 13
```

(Do this from DOS, not Turbo C's IDE.) To return to the normal cursor, we would type:

```
C>setcur 12 13
```

Specifying a starting number greater than the ending number causes a two-part cursor, as you'll see if you try this:

```
C>setcur 12 1
```

Making the Cursor Disappear

You can make the cursor vanish if you set bit 5, in the byte placed in the CH register, to 1. What do we mean by bit 5? The bits in every byte are numbered from 0 to 7, with the least significant bit being 0, as shown in Figure 9-15. To set bit 5 on, we can place the hex number 20 in the CH register. Hex 20 is 00100000 in binary, which is just the bit configuration we need.

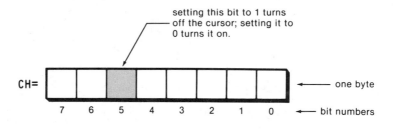

Figure 9-15. The Cursor On/Off Bit

The following program accomplishes the task:

```
/* curoff.c */
/* turns cursor off */
#include <dos.h>              /* declares REGS */
#define CURSIZE 1            /* "set cursor size" service */
#define VIDEO 0x10           /* video BIOS interrupt number */
#define STOPBIT 0x20         /* this bit turns cursor off */

void main(void)
{
   union REGS regs;
   regs.h.ch = STOPBIT;         /* turns cursor off */
   regs.h.ah = CURSIZE;         /* service number */
   int86(VIDEO, &regs, &regs); /* call video interrupt */
}
```

This program is similar to setcur.c, except that we don't need to put anything into the CL register. When you run it, the cursor will vanish (which can be unnerving).

To turn the cursor back on, use the setcur.c program. Since it sends a value in CH that includes a 0 value for bit 5, the cursor will reappear no matter which values you use for the starting and stopping lines (provided they're between 0 and 13).

There are many other ways to use ROM BIOS; we've only scratched the surface here. We'll return to the topic in Chapter 10.

Using Interrupts to Call DOS

In addition to the routines built into the ROM BIOS, there are also a number of routines in the MS-DOS operating system that can be called by a C program. In general, these "DOS call" routines are less useful for the C programmer. Many of them deal with disk input/output, which is already handled very well by normal C library functions, and we will not explore them in this book. However, the method of accessing these interrupt routines is very similar to that for accessing the ROM BIOS routines.

Summary

In this chapter we've covered the use of structures, which allow us to combine several variables of different types into a single entity, and unions, which allow one area of memory to be treated in several different ways. We've also explored the use of structures and unions in accessing the routines built into the ROM BIOS of the PC computer.

Questions

1. Array elements must all be of the _____
_____, whereas structure members can be of
_____ _____.

2. True or false: an appropriate use for a structure is to store a list of prices.

3. The purpose of declaring a structure type is to
   a. set aside the appropriate amount of memory
   b. define the format of the structure
   c. specify a list of structure elements

d. declare a new data type

4. Write a statement that declares a structure type consisting of two elements: a string of 10 characters and an integer.

5. How many structure variables of a given type can you use in a program?
   a. one
   b. none
   c. as many as you like
   d. as many as there are elements in the structure

6. Before you can access a member of a structure, you must

   (a) declare the structure _____,

   (b) define a structure _____,

   (c) give the item in step b a _____.

7. Write a statement that will define a structure variable **car** to be of structure type **vehicle**.

8. Assume the following statements have been made:
   ```
   struct body
      {
      int arms;
      int legs;
      };
   struct body jim;
   ```
   Write an assignment statement that will set the number of arms in jim's body equal to 2.

9. Is it possible to declare a structure type and define a structure variable in the same statement? If so, rewrite the example in question 8 to use this approach.

10. Assuming that **struct1** and **struct2** are structure variables of the same type, is the following statement possible?
    ```
    struct1 = struct2;
    ```

11. Given the statement

```
xxx.yyy.zzz = 5;
```

which of the following are true?

   a. Structure **zzz** is nested within structure **yyy**.

   b. Structure **yyy** is nested within structure **xxx**.

   c. Structure **xxx** is nested within structure **yyy**.

   d. Structure **xxx** is nested within structure **zzz**.

12. Write a statement that declares a structure of type **partners** containing two structures of type **body**.

13. True or false: it is possible to pass a structure to a function in the same way a simple variable is passed.

14. Write a statement that defines a pointer to type **struct book**.

15. If **temp** is a member of the structure **weather**, and the statement

```
addweath = &weather;
```

has been executed, then which of the following represents **temp**?

   a. weather.temp

   b. (*weather).temp

   c. addweath.temp

   d. addweath->temp

16. The function **malloc()** returns a pointer to _____.

17. One advantage a linked list has over an array is that the linked list can use less _____.

18. In a linked list, each structure on the list contains a pointer to the _____ _____.

19. True or false: the **sizeof()** function returns the size of a variable.

20. A union consists of a number of elements that

   a. all have the same type

   b. must be structures

   c. are grouped next to each other in memory

    d. all occupy the same space in memory

21. Write a statement that declares a union type with two elements: a string 10 characters long and an integer.

22. What does ROM BIOS stand for?

23. The routines in the ROM BIOS are located
    a. in the operating system
    b. in the C compiler
    c. in the C library
    d. in the hardware of the computer

24. True or false: the ROM BIOS consists mostly of routines that perform input/output operations.

25. The registers used in microprocessors
    a. are used to hold floating point numbers
    b. are used to hold addresses of I/O devices
    c. act somewhat like C functions
    d. act somewhat like C variables

26. Name the four main registers in the microprocessor of PC computers.

27. List eight other names that can be used for these four registers.

28. A union is used to represent the registers because
    a. there are so many registers
    b. the registers can hold either characters or integers
    c. the registers all have two names
    d. no one is sure what to call the registers

29. If one wants to put the value 3 in the DL register, which of the following statements is appropriate?
    a. regs.l.dl = 3;
    b. regs.x.dx = 3;
    c. regs.h.dx = 3;
    d. regs.h.dl = 3;

30. True or false: there is no way for a program to determine how large a memory it is running in.

Exercises

1. Write a short program that will: (a) set up a structure to hold a date (the structure will consist of three integer values, for the month, day, and year); (b) assign values to the members of the structure; and (c) print out the values in the format 12/31/88.

2. Modify the program of exercise 1 so that the date is printed out by a function. Pass the structure to the function.

3. There is a ROM BIOS routine that will set the position of the cursor. It uses interrupt number 0x10, with AH=2, DH=row number, and DL=column number (both of which start at 0, unlike the numbering for the ANSI.SYS command, in which numbering starts at 1). BH must contain 0. Modify the position.c program in Chapter 8 so that it performs in the same way, placing coordinates on the screen, but uses this ROM routine to position the cursor instead of the ANSI.SYS sequence.

10

Memory and the Character Display

- Bitwise operators
- Memory-mapped displays
- The PC character display
- The attribute byte
- Segment/offset addressing
- **Far** pointers
- Equipment list word

10

This chapter focuses on manipulating the character display using *direct memory access*. The character display places characters, as opposed to graphics, on the screen. It operates whether you have a monochrome or a color display adapter. In past chapters we've explored a variety of techniques to place characters on the screen, but all these techniques have made use of C library functions. Now we'll show how to access the screen directly, an approach that provides a much faster way to place characters on the screen and has other advantages as well. This chapter is a prerequisite for the next chapter, on color graphics, since an understanding of the techniques of direct memory access is important to working with the color graphics modes.

Getting the maximum utility out of direct memory access requires an understanding of the C *bitwise operators*, which permit individual bits in memory to be accessed and manipulated. Accordingly, we'll start this chapter with a discussion of the bitwise operators. Then we'll explore the concept of memory-mapped displays, and show how direct memory access can be used for a very simple word-processing program. This will involve the use of *far pointers*, a kind of pointer that can point to anyplace in memory. We'll also see how the attribute byte can be manipulated using the bitwise operators and look at a different way of operating on the bit level, using a construction called a "bit field." Finally, we'll explore a special area of the PC's memory where various kinds of data about the system are stored, and see how, using this area, a program can find out what sorts of equipment are connected to the computer.

This chapter requires some understanding of the hexadecimal and binary numbering systems. If these topics are unfamiliar to you, you should read Appendix B before continuing.

The Bitwise Operators

So far we've dealt with fixed types of data: characters, integers, and so forth. We haven't attempted to look *within* these data types to see how they are constructed out of individual bits and how these bits can be manipulated. Being able to operate on the bit level, however, can be very important in programming, especially when a program must interact directly with hardware. While programming languages are data-oriented, hardware tends to be bit-oriented; that is, a hardware device often requires input and output in the form of individual bits rather than in the form of byte-oriented data types such as characters and integers.

One of C's unusual features is a powerful set of bit-manipulation operators. These make it possible for the programmer to perform any desired manipulation of individual bits within a piece of data. In this section we'll explore these operators.

The Bitwise AND (&) Operator

C uses six bitwise operators, summarized in the following table:

Operation	Symbol
AND	&
Inclusive OR	¦
Exclusive OR (XOR)	^
Right shift	>>
Left shift	<<
Complement	~

These operators can be applied to characters and integers (signed and unsigned) but not to floating point numbers. Since the operators affect individual bits, it's important to know how to refer to the bits in a character or integer. The bits are numbered from right to left, as shown in Figure 10-1.

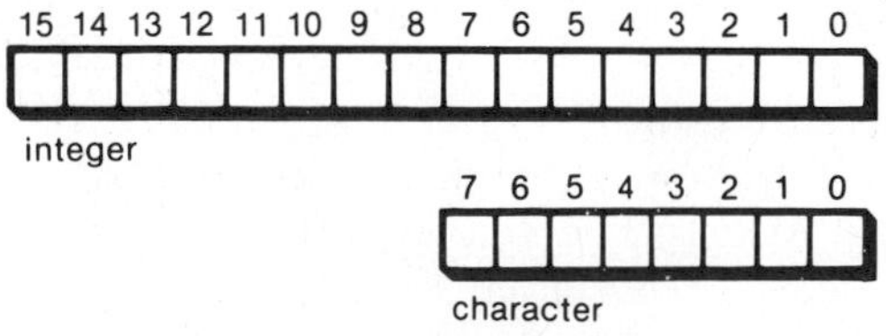

Figure 10-1. Bit Numbering

We'll start off by looking at just one of these operators in action, the bitwise AND operator. This operator is represented by the ampersand (&). Don't confuse this operator with the logical AND operator, represented by two ampersands (&&).

The bitwise AND operator takes two operands, which must be of the same type. The idea is that the two operands are compared on a bit-by-bit basis. If bit 0 of the first operand is a one *and* bit 0 of the second operand is also a one, then bit 0 of the answer is a one; otherwise bit 0 is a zero. This rule can be summarized as shown in Figure 10-2.

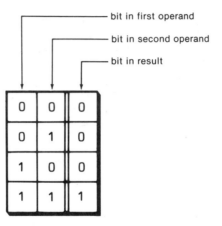

Figure 10-2. Rules for Combining Bits Using AND (&) Operator

The bitwise operators AND, OR, and XOR operate on a pair of bits to yield a third bit. The process is applied to each bit position of the operands in turn.

The rule is applied to all the bits of a data item in turn. Unlike operations involving normal arithmetic, each pair of corresponding bits is completely independent; there is no carry from one column to another. Figure 10-3 shows an example of two variables of type **char** being bitwise ANDed together.

A good way to become familiar with the logical operators is to write a program that allows experimentation with different inputs to see what results are produced by particular operators. The most convenient format for input and output is hexadecimal, since each hex digit corresponds to exactly four bits. Here's a simple program that permits testing of the AND operator, using hexadecimal character variables:

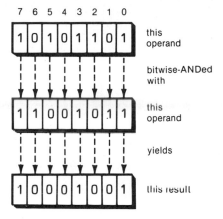

Figure 10-3. Example of Bitwise AND

```
/* andtest.c */
/* demonstrates bitwise AND operator */
void main(void)
{
    unsigned int x1, x2;

    while( x1 != 0 || x2 != 0 )    /* terminate on 0,0 */
        {
        printf("\nEnter two hex numbers (ff or less): ");
        scanf("%x %x", &x1, &x2);
        printf("%02x & %02x = %02x\n", x1, x2, x1 & x2 );
        }
}
```

This program uses the (&) operator in the expression

```
x1 & x2
```

to find the appropriate answer, which is then printed out by the **printf()** statement.

Here are some examples of the AND operator at work using the program:

```
Enter two hex numbers (ff or less): 1 0
01 & 00 = 00
```

and (with the prompt line and user input not shown):

```
00 & 01 = 00
```

```
01 & 01 = 01
```

For a more advanced example, here are the two hex digits c and 7 ANDed together:

```
0c & 07 = 04
```

The expansion of these hex digits into bits is shown in Figure 10-4.

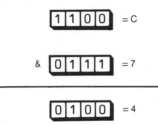

Figure 10-4. Two Hex Digits ANDed Together

The bitwise AND operator is often used to test whether a particular bit in a data item is set to 0 or 1. The testing process works because 0 ANDed with either 0 or 1 is still 0, while 1 ANDed with a bit is whatever the bit is. For example, to test if bit 3 of a character variable **ch** is 0 or 1, the following statement can be used:

```
bit3 = ch & 0x08;
```

Figure 10-5 shows this process in operation. Here if bit 3 of **ch** is 1, then the variable **bit3** will be assigned the value 1, otherwise 0 will be assigned.

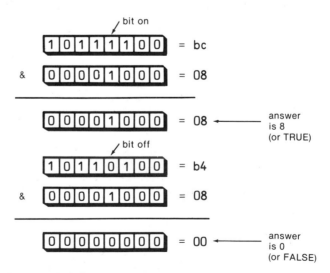

Figure 10-5. Bitwise AND Used for Test

We'll see an example of the bitwise AND used for testing bits in the program hextobin.c, coming up soon.

The Bitwise OR (¦) Operator

Another important bitwise operator is OR, represented by the vertical bar (¦). When two bits are ORed together, the resulting bit is 1 if either or both of the two operand bits is 1. If neither of the two bits is 1, the result is 0. This rule is shown in Figure 10-6.

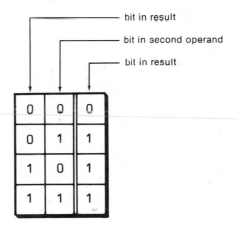

Figure 10-6. Rules for Combining Bits Using OR (¦) Operator

Here's a program that demonstrates the OR operator:

```
/* ortest.c */
/* demonstrates bitwise OR operator */
void main(void)
{
    unsigned int x1, x2;

    while( x1 != 0 ¦¦ x2 != 0 )    /* terminate on 0,0 */
        {
        printf("\nEnter two hex numbers (ff or less): ");
        scanf("%x %x", &x1, &x2);
        printf("%02x ¦ %02x = %02x\n", x1, x2, x1 ¦ x2 );
        }
}
```

And here's some sample output (without the prompt lines):

```
00 ¦ 01 = 01
01 ¦ 00 = 01
01 ¦ 01 = 01
0c ¦ 07 = 0f
ad ¦ cb = ef
```

If you're hazy about these results—or those in the last section on AND—you should verify that they're correct by expanding them into their binary form, performing the OR operation on each pair of corresponding bits, and translating them back into hexadecimal.

The bitwise OR operator is often used to combine bits from different variables into a single variable. For example, suppose we had two character variables, **ch1** and **ch2**, and suppose bits 0 through 3 of **ch1** contained a value we wanted, while bits 4 through 7 of **ch2** were the ones we wanted. Assuming the unwanted part of both variables was set to all 0s, we could then combine the two with the statement:

```
ans = ch1 ¦ ch2;
```

Figure 10-7 shows how this works, assuming that **ch1** is 0x07 and **ch2** is 0xd0.

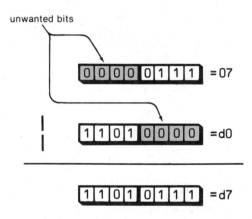

Figure 10-7. Bitwise OR Operator Used to Combine Values

The Bitwise Right-Shift (>>) Operator

Besides bitwise operators that operate on two variables, there are several bitwise operators that operate on a single variable. An example is the right-shift operator, represented by two "greater than" symbols (>>). This operator moves each bit in the operand to the right. The number of places the bits are moved is determined by the number following the operand. Thus, the expression

```
ch >> 3
```

causes all the bits in **ch** to be shifted right three places. Figure 10-8 shows an example of the hex value 72 being shifted right two places. Note that shifting right one bit is the same as dividing the operand by 2.

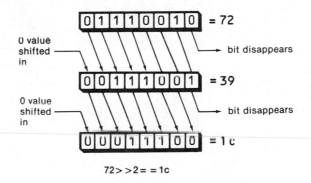

72>>2==1c

Figure 10-8. Example of Right-Shift Operator

Here's a program that demonstrates the right-shift operator:

```
/* shiftest.c */
/* demonstrates bitwise right shift operator */
void main(void)
{
    unsigned int x1, x2;

    while( x1 != 0 )          /* terminate on x1=0 */
        {
        printf("\nEnter hex number (ff or less) and number of bits ");
        printf("\nto shift (8 or less; example 'cc 3'): ");
        scanf("%x %d", &x1, &x2);
        printf("%02x >> %d = %02x\n", x1, x2, x1 >> x2 );
        }
}
```

Here's some sample output:

```
Enter hex number (ff or less) and number of bits
to shift (8 or less; example 'cc 3'): 80 1
80 >> 1 = 40
```

Here are some other, examples:

(handwritten: unsigned, with insertion mark)

```
80 >> 2 = 20
80 >> 7 = 01
f0 >> 4 = 0f
```

Again, if this isn't clear, translate the hex numbers into binary, shift them by hand, and translate back into hex to verify that the results are correct.

In the examples so far, zeros are inserted into the left-most bit. This is because the data type being shifted is **unsigned char**. However, this may not be the case if the data type is **char**, which is assumed to be signed, with the left-most bit being the sign bit. If the left-most bit of a type **char** variable starts out equal to 1, the number is considered negative. To maintain the sign of the number when it is right-shifted, 1s are inserted in the left-most bit. Thus the following statement will be true:

```
80 >> 2 == e0
```
(handwritten: ← signed)

If unsigned types are used, zero is always shifted in on the left, and if a signed number is positive, 0s are also shifted in. The same is true also of signed and unsigned integer types.

> If the sign bit is set in a signed operand, right shifts will cause 1s to be shifted in from the left.

Hexadecimal to Binary Conversion

We've mentioned several times that you might want to perform hex to binary conversions to verify our results. It would be nice if we could get the computer to do this, saving ourselves the trouble. As we've seen in the past, it's easy to perform conversion to and from hexadecimal in C by using the %x type specifier in **printf()** and **scanf()** functions. However, there is no corresponding specifier for binary, so let's write a program to carry out this conversion for us.

Here's the program:

```
/* hextobin.c */
/* converts hex number to binary */
void main(void)
{
    int j, num=1, bit;
    unsigned int mask;
    char string[10];
```

hex No.

FFFF or less

```
    while(num != 0)                          /* terminate on 0 */
      {
      mask = 0x8000;          hex          /* 1000000 binary */ ←
      printf("\nEnter number: ");                    + 7 2cros
      scanf("%x", &num);
      printf("Binary of %04x is:  ", num);
      for(j=0; j<16; j++)                   /* for each bit */
         {
         bit = (mask & num) ? 1 : 0;  /* bit is 1 or 0 */    p130
         printf("%d ", bit);              /* print bit */
         if(j==7)                          /* print dash between */
            printf("-- ");                 /*     bytes */
         mask >>= 1;                       /* shift mask to right */
         }
      }
    }
```

Here's some sample interaction:

```
Enter number: 1
Binary of 0001 is:  0 0 0 0 0 0 0 0--0 0 0 0 0 0 0 1
Enter number: 80
Binary of 0080 is:  0 0 0 0 0 0 0 0--1 0 0 0 0 0 0 0
Enter number: 100
Binary of 0100 is:  0 0 0 0 0 0 0 1--0 0 0 0 0 0 0 0
Enter number: f00
Binary of 0f00 is:  0 0 0 0 1 1 1 1--0 0 0 0 0 0 0 0
Enter number: f0f0
Binary of f0f0 is:  1 1 1 1 0 0 0 0--1 1 1 1 0 0 0 0
```

This program uses a **for** loop to go through all 16 bits of an integer variable, from left to right. The heart of the operation is contained in two statements that use bitwise operators:

```
bit = (mask & num) ? 1 : 0;
```

and

```
mask >>= 1;
```

In the first statement we make use of a mask. This is a variable that starts out with a single bit in the left-most position. The mask is then ANDed with the number that we want to express in binary, the variable **num**. If the result is nonzero (true), then we know the corresponding bit in **num** is 1; otherwise it's 0. The conditional statement assigns the value 1 to the variable **bit** if the bit being tested in **num** is 1, and 0 otherwise.

The left-shift statement then shifts the mask to the left, and the process is repeated for the next bit. The first time through the loop the mask will be 1000000000000000 binary, while the second time through it will be 0100000000000000, and so forth. Eventually all 16 bits will be printed out.

Other Logical Operators

There are six bitwise operators in all, of which we've now looked at three. We'll briefly review the remaining three and then show a six-function bitwise calculator which, if you type it in and compile it, will enable you to experiment with and learn more about the bitwise operators.

The Bitwise XOR (^) Operator

The ordinary bitwise OR operator (¦), discussed earlier, returns a value of 1 when either bit, or both bits, in the operand is 1. The bitwise *exclusive OR*, or XOR operator, by contrast, returns a value of 1 when either bit, but *not both* bits, is 1. This operator is represented by the caret (^). Figure 10-9 shows the rules for this operator.

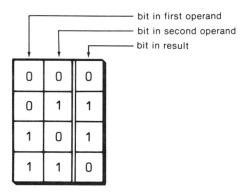

Figure 10-9. Rules for Combining Bits Using XOR Operator

The XOR operator can be useful for "toggling" a bit: that is, switching it back and forth between 0 and 1. This is true because a 1 XORed with 1 is 0, while a 1 XORed with a 0 is 1.

> An XOR operation applied twice to particular bits in an operand yields the original operand.

For instance, to toggle bit 3 in a variable **ch** of type **char**, we could use the statement:

```
ch = ch ^ 0x08;
```

Figure 10-10 shows how repeated application of this operation toggles bit 3 back and forth, while leaving the other bits unchanged. The variable **ch** is assumed to start out with the value 0xBC. We'll see an example of a bit being toggled to produce a useful result later on in the chapter.

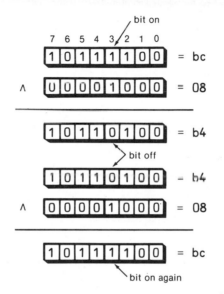

Figure 10-10. Bitwise XOR Operator Used as Toggle

The Bitwise Left-Shift Operator (<<)

The left-shift operator is, as you might guess, similar to the right-shift operator, except that bits are shifted left instead of right. The value of the bits inserted on the right is always 0, regardless of the sign or data type of the operand.

The Bitwise Complement Operator (~)

The bitwise complement operator (~) acts on a single operand; it takes every bit in the operand and makes it 1 if it was a 0 and 0 if it was a 1. For example, the following equalities are true:

```
~03 == fc
~ffff == 0
~cc == 33
~88 == 77
```

Complementing a number twice always returns the original number.

The Bitwise Calculator

Let's put all the bitwise operators together into one program. This program acts as a bitwise calculator, into which we type any suitable operand and a bitwise operator; it then displays the result. It is a useful program for exploring and learning about all the bitwise operations.

```c
/* bitcalc.c */
/* performs bitwise calculations */
void pbin(int);          /* prototypes */
void pline(void);

void main(void)
{
    char op[10];
    unsigned int x1, x2;

    while( x1 != 0 || x2 != 0 )  /* terminate on 0 op 0 */
        {
        printf("\n\nEnter expression (example 'ff00 & 1111'): ");
        scanf("%x %s %x", &x1, op, &x2);
        printf("\n");
        switch( op[0] )
            {
            case '&':
                pbin(x1); printf("& (and)\n"); pbin(x2);
                pline(); pbin(x1 & x2);
                break;
            case '|':
                pbin(x1); printf("| (incl or)\n"); pbin(x2);
                pline(); pbin(x1 | x2);
                break;
            case '^':
                pbin(x1); printf("^ (excl or)\n"); pbin(x2);
                pline(); pbin(x1 ^ x2);
                break;
            case '>':
                pbin(x1); printf(">> "); printf("%d\n", x2);
                pline(); pbin(x1 >> x2);
                break;
            case '<':
                pbin(x1); printf("<< "); printf("%d\n", x2);
                pline(); pbin(x1 << x2);
                break;
            case '~':
                pbin(x1); printf("~ (complement)\n");
```

```
            pline(); pbin(~x1);
            break;
        default: printf("Not valid operator.\n");
        }
    }
}


/* pbin */
/* prints number in hex and binary */
void pbin(int num)
{
    unsigned int mask;
    int j, bit;
    mask = 0x8000;                  /* one-bit mask */
    printf("%04x  ", num);          /* print in hex */
    for(j=0; j<16; j++)             /* for each bit in num */
        {
        bit = (mask & num) ? 1 : 0; /* bit is 1 or 0 */
        printf("%d ", bit);         /* print bit */
        if(j==7)                    /* print dash between */
            printf("-- ");          /*     bytes */
        mask >>= 1;                 /* shift mask to right */
        }
    printf("\n");
}


/* pline() */
void pline(void)
{
    printf("---------------------------------------\n");
}
```

As you can see, this program consists mostly of a large **switch** statement containing all the bitwise operations. The user types in an operand, a bitwise operator, and another operand. The program displays the result. The only anomaly is in the complement operator, which takes only one operand but requires a second operand to be typed after the operator (~) to satisfy the variable list in the **scanf()** statement (any number will do).

Here are some examples of interaction with the program. For brevity, the initial prompt is only shown on the first example:

```
Enter expression (example 'ff00 & 1111'): f0f0 | 3333
f0f0  1 1 1 1 0 0 0 0--1 1 1 1 0 0 0 0
| (incl or)
3333  0 0 1 1 0 0 1 1--0 0 1 1 0 0 1 1
```

```
-------------------------------------------
f3f3   1 1 1 1 0 0 1 1--1 1 1 1 0 0 1 1

f0f0   1 1 1 1 0 0 0 0--1 1 1 1 0 0 0 0
<< 2
-------------------------------------------
c3c0   1 1 0 0 0 0 1 1--1 1 0 0 0 0 0 0

f0f0   1 1 1 1 0 0 0 0--1 1 1 1 0 0 0 0
^ (excl or)
3333   0 0 1 1 0 0 1 1--0 0 1 1 0 0 1 1
-------------------------------------------
c3c3   1 1 0 0 0 0 1 1--1 1 0 0 0 0 1 1

f0f0   1 1 1 1 0 0 0 0--1 1 1 1 0 0 0 0
~ (complement)
-------------------------------------------
0f0f   0 0 0 0 1 1 1 1--0 0 0 0 1 1 1 1
```

p 372

This program makes use of the routine from the hextobin.c program, transformed into the function **pbin()**, to print out binary versions of the operands and results.

Now that you know how to manipulate bits, we're ready to explore memory-mapped graphics and see what role bit manipulation plays in influencing the display.

The Character Display Memory

When you attach a video monitor to your PC you must also install in the computer a printed circuit board called a graphics adaptor. This board has on it the circuitry necessary to convey information from the computer to the display. What does this hardware consist of, and how can we access it from our programs?

Communication between the adaptor and the computer takes place using a special section of memory as a sort of common ground. This section of memory is physically located on the adaptor board and can be accessed both by the microprocessor and by the display screen. The microprocessor can insert values into this memory and read them out just as it can with ordinary random-access memory (RAM). The display hardware continuously takes the values from this memory and places the corresponding character on the screen.

The normal character display consists of 25 lines of 80 characters each, for a total of 2,000 characters. Each of these characters is associated with a particular address in the display memory. Two bytes in the memory are used for each character: one to hold the extended ASCII character code, a value from 0 to 255 (0 to ff in hex), and one to hold the attribute. (We'll investigate the details of the attribute byte later in this chapter.) Thus 4,000 bytes of memory are needed to represent the 2,000 characters on the screen.

The monochrome memory starts at address B0000 (hex) and goes up to B0F9F (F9F hex is 3999 decimal). Figure 10-11 shows the relationship between this memory and the display.

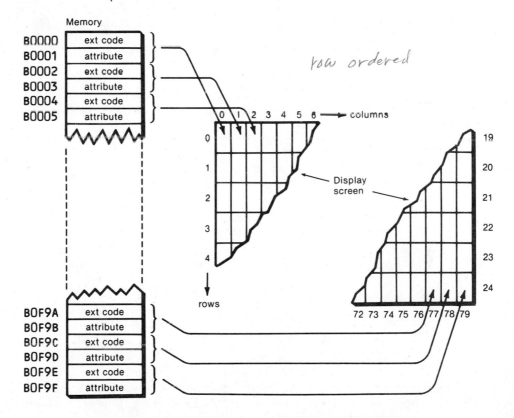

Figure 10-11. The Monochrome Display and MA Memory

If you have a color monitor attached to your computer and are using it for your text display, the text display memory occupies a different set of addresses. It starts at B8000 and runs up to B8F9F. Thus you should translate references to address B0000 in the text to address B8000.

When we call a C library routine to display a character on the screen, it calls a routine in ROM BIOS. The ROM BIOS routine puts the character on the screen by placing the values for the character's extended code and attribute byte in the appropriate address in the adaptor's memory. But we can take a shortcut. If our program inserts values for these bytes directly into memory, we can save a lot of time, because (among other reasons) we eliminate the overhead of calling one routine that calls another routine.

Far Pointers

When we know the address, the usual way we insert values into memory is to make use of pointers. Thus, you might expect that to place a character in the first location of the screen memory we might use statements such as the following:

```
int *ptr;              /* looks plausible */
- - - -
ptr = 0xB0000;         /* but */
- - - -
*(ptr) = ch;           /* won't work */
```

We first declare a pointer-to-int. We want to point to integers so we can treat the two-byte combination of extended character code and attribute together. We then set this pointer equal to the address of screen memory. Finally, we access this location using the indirection operator.

Unfortunately, we've made a mistake: the normal pointer variable type (no matter what data type it points to) consists of a *two*-byte quantity, while the address B0000 hex is a *two and one-half* byte (5-digit) number. No matter how hard we try, we can't cram this number into two bytes.

Segments

The reason for this embarrassing situation is that normal pointers are used to contain addresses in only one *segment*. In the 80x86 family of microprocessors (the 8088, 8086, 80286, 80386, and 80486) a segment is a section of memory containing 10000 (hex), or 65,536 (decimal) bytes. Within the segment, addresses run from 0 to FFFF hex. Ordinarily (at least in the small memory model, which we are using in this book) all the data in a C program is located in one segment. Thus the normal two-byte pointer works perfectly in most situations. To access addresses outside the segment, however, a different scheme must be used.

Internally, the 80x86 handles this situation with a special set of registers called *segment registers*. Addresses outside a segment are formed by combining the starting address of a segment, called the *segment address*, with the address within the segment, called the *offset address*. The starting address of the segment is placed in a segment register.

As an example, let's take an address half-way through the monochrome memory. This is the 1,000th character, which is 2,000 decimal bytes or 7d0 hex. The segment containing the monochrome memory can be assumed to start at the same place the memory starts: at address B0000. The segment register holds only the top four of these digits, or B000. This arrangement is shown in Figure 10-12.

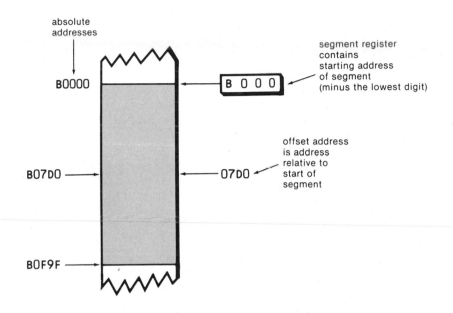

Figure 10-12. Segment Register and Video Memory

To obtain the absolute address, the address in the segment register is combined with the offset address. This combination takes place in a strange way; in effect, the contents of the segment register are shifted left four bits and then added to the offset address. Figure 10-13 shows how this looks in the case of the address in the middle of the display memory.

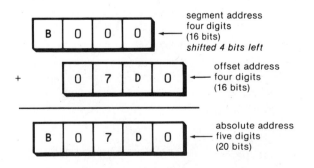

Figure 10-13. Combining Segment and Offset Addresses

In Figure 10-13 the segment address, B000, is shifted left four bits and then added to the offset address, 07D0. The result is the real or absolute memory address, B07D0.

> In the microprocessor the absolute address is obtained by shifting the segment address left four bits and then adding the offset address.

Using Segment-Offset Addresses in C

In C, an address that is outside of the program's normal data segment also makes use of this segment-plus-offset combination. However, the address is represented slightly differently. Instead of using the absolute address, C requires a 32-bit (four-byte, 8-hex digits) representation consisting of the four digits of the segment address followed by the four digits of the offset address. Thus, in C, the absolute address B07D0 is rendered as 0xB00007D0 (B000 followed by 07D0).

> In C, 32-bit pointers are calculated by shifting the segment address left 16 bits and then adding the offset address.

Since a normal pointer can't hold these 32-bit addresses, how do we make use of them? There are several approaches. One is to use the large memory model. This approach, which is intended to accommodate programs that use more data than can fit in a single segment, automatically makes all data references using the segment-offset combination. (We'll have more to say about memory models in Chapter 14). In the large model, all pointers become four-byte quantities, rather than two-byte. The disadvantage of the large memory model is that references to *all* data now will be made with four-byte pointers. This is inefficient, since it takes the computer longer to access memory using a four-byte pointer.

A better approach is to use the small memory model, but to declare a **far** pointer specifically in those cases when we need to point outside the normal data segment. A **far** pointer is one that holds a four-byte address, rather than the usual two-byte address. Thus it can hold the segment-offset combination. We declare a **far** pointer by inserting the **far** keyword just before the variable name. Our skeleton program can thus be rewritten like this:

```
int far *ptr;          /* declares far pointer */
- - - -
ptr = 0xB0000000;      /* segment B000 plus offset 0000 */
```

```
- - - -
   *(ptr) = ch;          /* now this will work */
```

Filling the Screen with a Character

Let's use the **far**-pointer approach to fill the screen with 2,000 copies of a single character. To show how rapid this approach is, compared with using such C library routines as **putch**, we'll make it possible to change the character by pressing a key. Each time the user presses a new key, the entire screen is filled, almost instantaneously, with the new character. The program terminates when the user types an [Enter]. Here's the listing:

```
/* dfill.c */
/* uses direct memory access to fill screen */
#define LENGTH 2000

void main(void)
{
   int far *farptr;
   int addr;
   char ch;

   printf("Type character to start, type again to change");
   farptr = (int far *) 0xB8000000;   /* B0000000 for mono */
   while( (ch=getche()) != '\r' )    /* terminate on [Enter] */
      for(addr=0; addr<LENGTH; addr++)
         *(farptr + addr) = ch | 0x0700;
}
```

Remember that if you are using a color monitor for text display, you should use the constant 0xB8000000. If you're using a monochrome monitor, use 0xB0000000 in dfill.c, since the text memory of the color display occupies a different space in memory. This is true of all programs in this chapter that directly address the display memory; if you're using monochrome, change the address.

This program uses a simple **for** loop, running from 0 to 2,000, to fill in all the memory addresses in the monochrome memory. The statement that does the job is

```
   *(farptr + addr) = ch | 0x0700;
```

This statement references each address in turn by adding the number **addr**, which runs from 0 to 1999, to the starting address of video memory, which we set **farptr** to before the loop.

On the right side of this assignment statement the variable **ch** is the character we want to place in memory; it was obtained from the keyboard. The constant 0x0700 is the attribute byte, shifted left one byte to place it on the left side of the two-byte (integer) quantity. This constant, 0x07, is the "normal" attribute; that is, the one that creates nonblinking, nonbold, white-on-black text. We'll see why soon.

Cycling through the loop 2,000 times inserts 2,000 integers in memory; the high byte of the integer is the extended character code and the low byte is the attribute.

Another statement that requires explanation is

```
farptr = (int far *) 0xB8000000;
```

What is the expression in parentheses, and why is it necessary? The problem here is that the constant 0xB8000000 and the variable **farptr** are of different types: the constant looks like a long integer, while **farptr** is a far pointer to *int*. To avoid a warning from the compiler, we force the constant to be a **far** pointer to **int**, by preceding it with the name of the type in parentheses. This is another example of "casting," mentioned in Chapter 9.

The attribute byte also requires more explanation; we'll further investigate its format later in this chapter. First, however, let's make a small change to the program.

```
/* dfill2.c */
/* uses direct memory access to fill screen */
#define ROMAX 25
#define COMAX 80
void main(void)
{
    int far *farptr;
    int col, row;
    char ch;

    printf("Type character to start, type again to change");
    farptr = (int far *)0xB8000000;   /* B0000000 for mono */
    while( (ch=getche()) != '\r' )
        for(row=0; row<ROMAX; row++)
            for(col=0; col<COMAX; col++)
                *(farptr + row*COMAX + col) = (int)ch | 0x0700;
}
```

In future programs, we'll make use of functions that accept as input the row and column number of a character and then display the character on the screen at the appropriate place using direct memory access. This program shows how it's done. In the last line, the variables **row** and **col** represent the row and column number of the character to be inserted. The corresponding memory address is found by multiplying the row number by the number of columns in a row, then adding the result and the column number to the starting address of the monochrome memory in **farptr**. Since we are now imagining the screen as a two-dimensional entity of rows and columns (rather than a one-dimensional group of memory addresses), we use two nested loops to insert the characters.

Speed Comparison

To get an idea of the speed advantage provided by direct memory access using **far** pointers, we'll rewrite dfill2.c to use the **putch()** library function. Here's the listing:

```
/* cfill.c */
/* uses putch() to fill screen */
#define ROMAX 25
#define COMAX 80
#define CLEAR "\x1B[2J"              p284
void main(void)
{
    int col, row;
    char ch;

    printf("Type character to start, type again to change");
    while( (ch=getche()) != '\r' )
       {
       printf(CLEAR);
       for(row=0; row<ROMAX; row++)
          for(col=0; col<COMAX; col++)
             printf("%c", ch);
       }
}
```

This program also fills the screen with a single character, but, at least on our system, it takes about *20 times longer* than dfill2.c.

One-Line Word Processor

To see how **far** pointers might be used in a somewhat more useful situation than filling the screen with a single character, let's create a very simple word processing program—one that is so simple it operates on only a single line of text. We'll do this in two steps. First we'll show a program which allows the user to type in a line of characters and to move the cursor back and forth along the line. Any character can be erased by moving the cursor to it and typing over it. Later, when we've learned more about attributes, we'll show an

improved model of the program that permits insertion, deletion, and underlining.

Here's the first version:

```
/* wpro1.c */
/* rudimentary word-processing program */
/* allows typing, cursor movement, and typeover */
#include "dos.h"              /* for REGS definition */
#define COMAX 80              /* max number of columns */
#define R_ARRO 77             /* right arrow */
#define L_ARRO 75             /* left arrow */
#define VIDEO 0x10            /* video ROM BIOS service */
#define CTRL_C '\x03'         /* [Ctrl] [C] */
int col=0;                    /* cursor position */
int far *farptr;              /* video memory pointer */
union REGS regs;              /* for ROM BIOS calls */
void cursor(void);            /* prototypes */
void insert(char);
void clear(void);


void main(void)
{
   char ch;
   farptr = (int far *)0xB8000000;   /* start of screen mem */
   clear();                          /* clear screen */
   cursor();                         /* position cursor */
   while( (ch=getch()) != '\r' )     /* exit on [Enter] */
      {
      if ( ch == 0 )                 /* if char is 0 */
         {
         ch = getch();               /* read extended code */
         switch(ch)
            {
            case R_ARRO: if(col<COMAX) ++col; break;
            case L_ARRO: if(col>0)     --col; break;
            }
         }
      else                           /* not extended code */
         if(col<COMAX)               /* print char at col */
            insert(ch);
      cursor();                      /* reset cursor */
      }
}


/* cursor() */
```

```
/* move cursor to row=0, col */
void cursor(void)
{
   regs.h.ah = 2;                 /* 'set cursor pos' service */
   regs.h.dl = col;               /* column varies */
   regs.h.dh = 0;                 /* always top row */
   regs.h.bh = 0;                 /* page zero */
   int86(VIDEO, &regs, &regs); /* call video interrupt */
}
```
p 350

```
/* insert() */                    writes (typeover)
/* inserts character at cursor position */
void insert(char ch)
{
   int j;
   *(farptr + col) = ch | 0x700;         /* insert char */
   ++col;                                /* move cursor right */
}
```
— p389

```
/* clear() */
/* clears screen using direct memory access */
void clear(void)
{
   int j;
   for(j=0; j<2000; j++)                 /* fill screen memory */
      *(farptr + j) = 0x0700;            /* with 0's (attr=07) */
}
```
p389

Almost everything in this program should already be familiar to you. The program first clears the screen, using a routine that fills the screen memory with 0s; this is the same approach we used to fill the screen with a character in dfill.c. Then the cursor is moved to the beginning of the single line (the top line of the screen) using the "Set cursor position" video ROM BIOS service, which we described in Exercise 3 in Chapter 9.

p 383

p 361

ROM BIOS routine:	Position cursor
Interrupt 10 hex:	Video
Input registers:	AH=02
	DH=row number
	DL=column number
	BH=page number (usually 0)
Output registers:	None

The **switch** statement approach to deciphering the cursor keys was used in Chapter 8. Pressing the appropriate cursor key increments or decrements the variable **col**, which indicates the column the cursor is on. A call to the **cursor()** function moves the cursor to this column.

If the character typed is not an extended character (namely a cursor key) it is inserted into the display at column **col** using the **insert()** subroutine, which should be familiar from the discussion of **far** pointers above. The **col** variable is incremented when a character is inserted so that the next character will be typed just to its right.

Now it's time to explore the oft-postponed subject of the attribute byte.

The Attribute Byte

As we've noted before, the location in the graphics memory corresponding to a single character position on the screen consists of two bytes: one to hold the extended code of the character, the other to hold its attribute. In Chapter 8 we discussed the attributes: underline, intensified, blinking, and reverse video. How do these relate to the attribute byte?

Figure 10-14 shows how the attribute byte is divided into sections. Two of these sections consist of a single bit. Bit 3 controls intensity, and bit 7 controls blinking. If one of these bits is set to 1, the corresponding attribute (blinking or intensified) is turned on; when the bit is set to 0, the attribute is off.

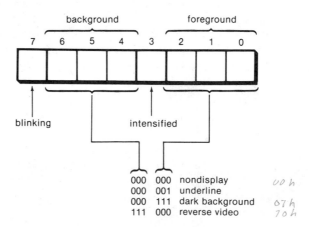

Figure 10-14. The Attribute Byte

The two other sections of the attribute byte consist of three bits each. Bits 0, 1, and 2 make up the "foreground color," while bits 4, 5, and 6 make up the "background color." (Of course in the monochrome display there is no color, but the same attribute byte format is used in the color display.) There are three choices for the monochrome display foreground color: black, white (or green or amber, depending on your display), and underline. The underline attribute is treated as a color, for some reason. For the background there are only two color choices: black or white. Figure 10-14 shows the four meaningful ways these "colors" can be combined, yielding nondisplay (invisible), underline, normal video (white on black), and reverse video (black on white).

p 384

Here's a revision of our dfill2.c program that fills the screen with characters all having the blinking attribute. The operating system won't reset the attribute bytes to normal when the program is done, so to make the screen stop blinking you'll need to use the DOS command CLS, which does reset the attribute bytes.

```
/* dfill3.c */
/* fills screen using blinking attribute */
#define ROMAX 25
#define COMAX 80
void main(void)
{
    int far *farptr;
    int col, row;
    char ch;

    printf("Type character to start, type again to change");
    farptr = (int far *) 0xB8000000;   /* B0000000 for mono */
    while( (ch=getche()) != '\r' )     /* terminate on [Enter] */
       {
       for(row=0; row<ROMAX; row++)
          for(col=0; col<COMAX; col++)
             *(farptr + row*COMAX + col) = ch | 0x8700;
       }
}
```

In the last program we used the attribute 07, which is 00000111 in binary. That is, the three bits of the foreground color are set to 1s, while everything else is a 0. To turn on blinking, we want to set bit 7 to 1, so we use the hex number 87, which is 10000111 in binary. This byte then is in effect shifted left eight bits, as described earlier, so it's on the left side of the integer which will be placed in memory.

The Attribute Fill Program

To get a better idea of the attributes and how they interact, type in and compile the following program. This is a variation of dfill.c, but it includes a **switch** statement that permits different attributes to be selected when the screen is filled. Besides demonstrating the attribute byte, this program also provides a good example of the bitwise operators at work.

```
/* attrfill.c */
/* uses direct memory access to fill screen */
#define ROMAX 25
#define COMAX 80
void fill(char, char);    /* prototype */

void main(void)
{
   char ch, attr;
   attr = 0x00;
   printf("Type 'n' for normal,\n");
   printf("     'u' for underlined,\n");
   printf("     'i' for intensified,\n");
   printf("     'b' for blinking,\n");
   printf("     'r' for reverse video,\n");
   while( (ch=getch()) != '\r')
     {
     switch (ch)
       {
       case 'n':
          attr = 0x07;         /* set to normal */
          break;               /* 0000 0111 */
       case 'u':
          attr = attr & 0x88;  /* set to underline */  1000 1000
          attr = attr | 0x01;  /* x000 x001 */
          break;
       case 'i':
          attr = attr ^ 0x08;  /* toggle intensified */
          break;               /* xxxx Txxx */
       case 'b':
          attr = attr ^ 0x80;  /* toggle blinking */
          break;               /* Txxx xxxx */
       case 'r':
          attr = attr & 0x88;  /* set to reverse */
          attr = attr | 0x70;  /* x111 x000 */
          break;
       }
     fill(ch,attr);
     }
}

/* fill() */
```

```
/* fills screen with character 'ch', attribute 'attr' */
void fill(char ch, char attr)
{
   int far *farptr;
   int col, row;

   farptr = (int far *) 0xB8000000;   /* B0000000 for mono */
   for(row=0; row<ROMAX; row++)
      for(col=0; col<COMAX; col++)
         *(farptr + row*COMAX + col) = ch | attr<<8;
}
```

When the screen is filled, using the **fill()** function, the variable **attr** is used for the attribute byte, rather than a constant as before. This value of **attr** is set by the various options in the **switch** statement.

Different options are handled in differing ways. Typing 'n' for normal always resets **attr** to 07 hex, which provides the standard attribute. The two one-bit attributes, blinking and intensified, can be toggled on and off, using the bitwise XOR operator on the appropriate bit. Reverse video and underline are set by masking off only the "color" attributes and resetting them without disturbing the one-bit attributes. Type [Enter] to exit the program.

In previous programs we placed the attribute in an integer: 0x0700. Here we use a character for the attribute, so we need to shift it left one byte before combining it with the character **ch**. We do this using the left-shift (<<) operator in the last statement in fill().

A style note: for clarity we've written the bitwise operations as separate statements. To achieve compactness, however, we could have combined them, so that, for example, these lines

```
attr = attr & 0x88;   /* set to underline */
attr = attr | 0x01;   /* x000 x001 */
```

would become

```
attr = (attr & 0x88) | 0x01;
```

Bit Fields

In the attrfill.c program we accessed individual bits and groups of bits using the bitwise operators. We can take an entirely different approach to accessing bits: the use of "bit fields." A bit field is a special kind of structure. Each of the members of such a structure occupies a certain number of bits. The number of bits each member occupies is specified following a colon in the structure declaration. The members of the structure then are packed into an integer. The members must all be of type **unsigned int**. Here's an example of a bit-field declaration:

```
struct bits ?
   {
   unsigned int twobits  : 2;   /* bits 0 and 1 */
   unsigned int sixbits  : 6;   /* bits 2 through 7 */
   unsigned int againsix : 6;   /* bits 8 through 13 */
   unsigned int onebit   : 1;   /* bit 14 */
   unsigned int extrabit : 1;   /* bit 15 */
   } sample;
```

Figure 10-15 shows how the integer represented by this structure looks.

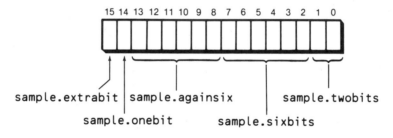

Figure 10-15. Bit Fields

Accessing the members of a field requires the same format as accessing members of other structures: the dot operator is used to connect the name of the structure variable with the name of the member, as in these examples:

```
sample.twobits = 3;
sample.sixbits = 63;
sample.onebit = 1;
```

Note that you can't give a field element a value that exceeds its capacity; a one-bit field can have only two values, 0 and 1, while a six-bit field can have values from 0 up to 63. Thus the values assigned above are all maximums.

The version of the attrfill.c program shown below uses bit fields to access the various parts of the attribute byte.

```
/* attrf2.c */
/* uses direct memory access to fill screen */
#define ROMAX 25
#define COMAX 80
void fill(char, unsigned int);
```

```
void main(void)
{
    struct bits                 /* bit fields */
        {
        unsigned int foregnd : 3;   /* bits 0, 1, 2 */
        unsigned int intense : 1;   /* bit 3 */
        unsigned int backgnd : 3;   /* bits 4, 5, 6 */
        unsigned int blinker : 1;   /* bit 7 */
        } b1;                       /* define struct variable */

    union                       /* declare union */
        {                       /* of */
        unsigned int attr;      /* unsigned int and */
        struct bits b1;         /* bitfield */
        } u1;                   /* define union variable */

    char ch;

    printf("Type 'n' for normal,\n");
    printf("     'u' for underlined,\n");
    printf("     'i' for intensified,\n");
    printf("     'b' for blinking,\n");
    printf("     'r' for reverse video,\n");
    while( (ch=getch()) != '\r')   /* terminate on [Enter] */
        {
        switch (ch)
            {
            case 'n':                   /* set to normal */
                u1.b1.foregnd = 7;
                u1.b1.backgnd = 0;
                break;
            case 'u':                   /* set to underline */
                u1.b1.foregnd = 1;
                break;
            case 'i':                   /* toggle intensity */
                u1.b1.intense = (u1.b1.intense==1) ? 0 : 1;
                break;
            case 'b':                   /* toggle blinking */
                u1.b1.blinker = (u1.b1.blinker==1) ? 0 : 1;
                break;
            case 'r':                   /* set to reverse */
                u1.b1.foregnd = 0;
                u1.b1.backgnd = 7;
                break;
            }
```

393

```
            fill(ch, u1.attr);
            }
    }


    /* fill() */
    /* fills screen with character 'ch', attribute 'attr' */
    void fill(char ch, unsigned int attr)
    {
        int far *farptr;
        int col, row;

        farptr = (int far *) 0xB8000000;   /* B0000000 for mono */
        for(row=0; row<ROMAX; row++)
            for(col=0; col<COMAX; col++)
                *(farptr + row*COMAX + col) = ch | attr<<8;
    }
```

Because the attributes must be accessed both as bit fields and as an integer, a union is used so that they can be referred to in either way.

To set foreground and background colors, the appropriate fields are assigned the desired values. To toggle the blinking and intensity attributes, the conditional operator is used to assign values to the appropriate bits.

> Bit fields provide an organized approach to accessing individual bits and groups of bits.

Using fields probably gives a cleaner-looking approach, while the bitwise operators, which closely mirror the underlying assembly language instructions, are faster.

Word Processing Revisited

Now that we know about attributes, we can expand our rudimentary word processing program. We'll give it the capability to underline words. To start underlining, the user types the [Alt] [u] key combination; to stop underlining, the user repeats the combination. (On a color display, underlining may show up as a color change.)

In addition to adding underlining, we'll also give the program the capability to insert and delete characters. To insert a character, the user simply moves the cursor to the desired spot and starts typing. The characters to the right will be shifted further right to make room. To delete, the user hits the backspace key; this deletes the character to the left of the cursor. Any characters to the right will be shifted left to fill in the space.

p386

Here's the listing:

```c
/* wpro2.c */
/* rudimentary word-processing program */
/* with delete, insert and underlining */
#include <dos.h>              /* for REGS definition */
#define COMAX 80              /* max number of columns */
#define R_ARRO 77             /* right arrow */
#define L_ARRO 75             /* left arrow */
#define BK_SPC  8             /* backspace */
#define ALT_U 22             /* [Alt] and [u] key combo */
#define VIDEO 0x10            /* video ROM BIOS service */
#define NORM 0x07            /* normal attribute */
#define UNDR 0x01            /* underline attribute */
void cursor(void);           /* prototypes */
void insert(char, char);
void delete(void);
void clear(void);

int col=0;                   /* cursor position */
int length=0;                /* length of phrase */
int far *farptr;             /* pointer to video memory */

void main(void)
{
   char ch, attr=NORM;

   farptr = (int far *) 0xB8000000; /* (B0000000 for mono) */
   clear();                         /* clear screen */
   cursor();                        /* position cursor */
   while( (ch=getch()) != '\r' )    /* exit on [Enter] */
      {
      if ( ch == 0 )                /* if char is 0 */
         {
         ch = getch();              /* read extended code */
         switch(ch)
            {
            case R_ARRO: if(col<length) ++col; break;
            case L_ARRO: if(col>0)      --col; break;
            case ALT_U: attr = (attr==NORM) ? UNDR : NORM;
            }
         }
      else
         switch(ch)
            {
```

```
                case BK_SPC: if(length>0) delete(); break;
                default: if(length<COMAX) insert(ch,attr);
                }
          cursor();
          }
}

/* cursor() */
/* move cursor to row=0, col */
void cursor(void)
{
   union REGS regs;

   regs.h.ah = 2;                 /* 'set cursor pos' service */
   regs.h.dl = col;               /* column varies */
   regs.h.dh = 0;                 /* always top row */
   regs.h.bh = 0;                 /* page zero */
   int86(VIDEO, &regs, &regs);    /* call video interrupt */
}

/* insert() */
/* inserts character at cursor position */
void insert(char ch, char attr)
{
   int j;

   for(j=length; j>col; j--)               /* shift chars left */
      *(farptr + j) = *(farptr + j - 1);   /*    to make room */
   *(farptr + col) = ch | attr<<8 ;        /* insert char */
   ++length;                               /* increment count */
   ++col;                                  /* move cursor right */
}

/* delete() */
/* deletes character at position one left of cursor */
void delete(void)
{
   int j;

   for(j=col; j<=length; j++)              /* shift chars right */
      *(farptr + j - 1) = *(farptr + j);
   --length;                               /* decrement count */
   --col;                                  /* move cursor left */
}

/* clear() */
```

```
/* clears screen by inserting 0 at every location */
void clear(void)
{
   int j;

   for(j=0; j<2000; j++)                      /* fill screen memory */
      *(farptr + j) = 0x0700;                 /* with 0's (attr=07) */
}
```

When the [Alt] [u] key combination is typed, the conditional expression at the end of the **switch** construct,

```
attr = (attr==NORM) ? UNDR : NORM;
```

toggles the **attr** variable back and forth between UNDR and NORM, which are the 07 (normal) and 01 (underline) attribute bytes.

The **insert()** function now sports a new **for** loop. This loop uses direct memory access and a **far** pointer to shift all the characters that are right of the cursor, one space to the right. This shifting process must start at the right-hand end of the existing phrase; if the shifting were to start on the left, the left-most character would overwrite the character next to it before it could be shifted. When all the characters have been shifted out of the way, the character typed by the user is inserted at the cursor position. Figure 10-16 shows this process.

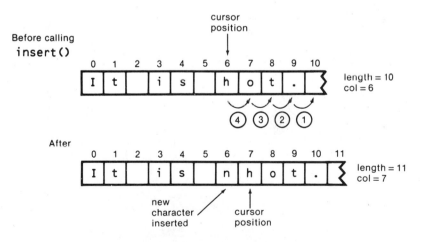

Figure 10-16. The *insert()* Function

Deletion is carried out in a similar way; all the characters to the right of the cursor are shifted left one space; the left-most character writes over the character to be deleted. In this case the shifting starts on the left-hand end.

This word processing program should give at least some idea of the possibilities of direct memory access.

The Equipment List Word

Before we leave this chapter, we will examine one other feature of the PC computer: the equipment list word. This is a two-byte area in low memory—absolute address 410 hex—that contains information about the equipment connected to the computer. When the PC is first turned on, the ROM BIOS startup routine examines the computer's various connectors to see what peripherals are in use and then sets the bits in this word accordingly.

This word can be useful in two ways. First, a program often needs to know if a certain piece of equipment is present. There's no use trying to print on the serial printer, for instance, if one isn't hooked up to the system. Second, as we'll see in Chapter 11, it's sometimes necessary to alter the settings in the equipment list word.

Figure 10-17 shows the layout of the equipment list word. To access the word, we use a **far** pointer, as we did with video memory. In this case, however, the pointer will point to segment 0000, offset address 0410 (hex), which is represented in C as 00000410 hex, or simply 0x410.

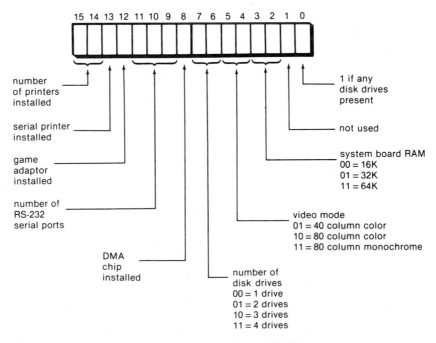

Figure 10-17. The Equipment List Word

To examine the individual bits and groups of bits in the word, we'll use the bitwise operators (we could also have used fields). In general, we'll shift the equipment list word to the right, to put the bits we want on the right of the word, and then we'll mask any unwanted bits on the left with the bitwise AND operator.

In addition to the equipment list word, we also read a word that contains the size of installed memory in Kbytes. We showed earlier how to check the memory size using a ROM BIOS routine; accessing this word directly is another, probably slightly faster method.   *p351*

The memory size word is located at absolute address 413 hex, so to access it we need to reset the variable **farptr** to point to this new address. Here's the listing:

```
/* eqlist.c */
/* lists equipment attached to computer */
#define EQLIST 0x410    /* location of equipment list word */
#define MEMSIZ 0x413    /* location of memory size word */
void main(void)
{
   int far *farptr;
   unsigned int eq, data;

   farptr = (int far *)EQLIST;
   eq = *(farptr);
   data = eq >> 14;                     /* printers */
   printf("Number of printers is %d.\n", data);
   if(eq & 0x2000)                      /* serial printer */
      printf("Serial printer is present.\n");
   data = (eq >> 9) & 7;                /* serial ports */
   printf("Number of serial ports is %d.\n", data);
   if(eq & 1)                           /* diskette drives */
      {
      data = (eq >> 6) & 3;
      printf("Number of diskette drives is %d.\n", data+1);
      }
   else
      printf("No diskette drives attached.\n");
   data = (eq >> 4) & 3;                /* video mode */
   switch (data)
      {
      case 1: printf("Video is 40 column color.\n"); break;
      case 2: printf("Video is 80 column color.\n"); break;
      case 3: printf("Video is 80 column monochrome.\n");
      }
   farptr = (int far *) MEMSIZ;
```

p372 (handwritten, next to `if(eq & 0x2000)` line: 100000--00000000)

```
        printf("Memory is %d Kbytes.\n", *(farptr) );
    }
```

And here's a sample run for a particular installation:

```
Number of printers is 1.
Number of serial ports is 1.
Number of diskette drives is 2.
Video is 80 column monochrome.
Memory is 256 Kbytes.
```

There's a variety of useful words and bytes stored in the data area from 400 to 600 hex. To learn more about this area, you can consult one of the books referred to in Appendix C.

Summary

This chapter has focused on the character display and its relation to a special area of memory. We've learned that, for each character on the screen, there corresponds a two-byte area of memory: one byte to hold the extended ASCII character code, the other byte to hold the attribute. To help manipulate such hardware-oriented data as attribute bytes, we learned about the bitwise operators: AND, OR, XOR, left shift, right shift, and complement. We explored a simple one-line word processing program, and finally we saw how to access various areas in low memory, specifically the equipment list word, which tells what equipment is connected to the computer.

In the next chapter we'll put what we've learned here to use in investigating color graphics on the PC.

Questions

1. Express the following hexadecimal values in binary:
   a. 0x01
   b. 0xf8
   c. 0x1234
   d. 0xfc0a

2. Numbers are represented internally in the computer as
   a. decimal
   b. binary

    c. hexadecimal

    d. none of the above

3. True or false: the bitwise operators treat all variables as true or false values.

4. Which of the following will be true if bit 5 of the character variable **ch** is a 1?

    a. (ch & 8)

    b. (ch & 10)

    c. (ch & 20)

    d. (ch & 40)

5. The bitwise AND operator is often used to _____ off unwanted bits.

6. What does the expression (0xff | 0x32) evaluate to?

    a. 0x32

    b. 0x00

    c. 0xff

    d. 0xcd

7. If **num** is of type **int**, what does (num >> 8) evaluate to when **num** has the value 0xf000?

    a. 0x000f

    b. 0x00f0

    c. 0xff00

    d. 0xfff0

8. The bitwise OR operator is often used to _____ different bits in different variables.

9. The 8086 family of chips uses a combination of two addresses to access data outside the normal segment. These addresses are called the _____ address and the _____ address.

10. A normal two-byte pointer cannot hold addresses outside a given segment because:

a. it can't get through the segment barrier

b. it isn't large enough

c. it doesn't know where other segments are

d. it's not a segment register

11. Before being added to the offset address, the value in the segment register is:

a. shifted left four bits

b. multiplied by 0x10

c. converted to decimal

d. complemented

12. When the segment address is combined with the offset address, the result is the _____ address.

13. A **far** pointer is a variable that can hold addresses _____ bytes long.

14. Suppose the segment address is A100 (hex) and the offset address is 1234 (hex). The resulting absolute address, expressed as a C **far** pointer constant, is

a. 0xA1234

b. 0xA234

c. 0xA2234

d. 0xA1001234

15. True or false: the following is a valid way to declare a **far** pointer:

```
char far *farptr;
```

16. One reason to use direct memory access to put characters on the screen, rather than going through C library routines, is to make the process _____.

17. The phrase "memory-mapped video" means that

a. the program must remember what it drew on the display

b. for each location on the screen there corresponds a location in memory

    c. the display is usually used for drawing maps

    d. display characters are mapped from ROM

18. True or false: the following is a valid way to assign a value to a **far** pointer:

```
farptr = 0xA1001234;
```

19. To use **far** pointers in a program, it is necessary to

    a. know the address of the segment to be used

    b. typecast the pointer addresses

    c. know the offset address of the data

    d. use the indirection operator

20. True or false: the following is a valid way to access the memory location pointed to by a **far** pointer:

```
value = *(farptr);
```

21. The attribute byte is located

    a. in low memory

    b. at the beginning of each segment

    c. after each character

    d. in the display memory

22. The intensity and blinking attributes are controlled by individual _____ in the attribute byte, while the foreground and background "colors" are controlled by _____.

23. Bit fields provide a way to

    a. access individual bits

    b. simplify access to arrays of data

    c. access groups of bits

    d. modify bits

24. The monochrome screen memory starts at absolute memory address _____ (hex) and ends at _____ (hex).

25. The equipment list word provides information about

a. the video display

b. the diskette drive

c. serial and parallel printers

d. serial ports

Exercises

1. Write a program that resembles ortest.c but which allows the user to play with the XOR bitwise operator rather than the OR bitwise operator.

2. Write a program that will allow the user to type a binary number (up to 16 1s and 0s) and that will then convert this number into both hexadecimal and decimal.

3. Write a program that in operation resembles the draw.c program from Chapter 8, which draws lines on the screen in response to the user pressing the cursor keys. But instead of using the ANSI.SYS codes to place each character, use direct access to the display memory (a **far** pointer). Note: when the character being placed on the screen is one of the extended character set (such as the cursor keys), a problem may arise because the character will be interpreted as being negative. Use bitwise operators to remove the offending bits.

11

Direct-Access Color Graphics

- Graphics modes
- ROM BIOS graphics routines
- Direct access to graphics memory
- CGA graphics modes
- EGA bit-plane graphics
- VGA bit-plane graphics

11

The ability to draw pictures—in color, in a fraction of a second—is one of the most fascinating capabilities of modern computers. Graphics can be used in almost any computer program; graphs can help the user make sense of the numbers produced in spreadsheet or database programs, most games rely heavily on graphics, the user interface to almost any program may use graphics, and now even entire operating systems such as Windows and the OS/2 Presentation Manager are using graphics-oriented user interfaces. The chances are that the program you're writing can profit from graphics, too.

In this and the next chapter we'll explore the various techniques a C programmer can use to produce graphic images on MS-DOS computers. This chapter explores the direct approach: using ROM BIOS routines and direct access to the video memory. These techniques are the fastest and most flexible. They will also work (with variations) with C compilers other than Turbo C, and they teach the most about using C and about PC architecture. In Chapter 12, we'll look at the special-purpose functions Turbo C makes available for graphics.

You'll need a graphics adaptor and a graphics display monitor to run the programs in this chapter; a character-only display won't work. The first part of this chapter is applicable to all graphics display adaptor standards: the Graphics Adaptor (CGA), the Enhanced Graphics Adaptor (EGA), and the Video Graphics Array (VGA) graphics standards. In the second part of this chapter, we'll explore some graphics features specific to the EGA and VGA.

Modes

Just as an artist can choose from a variety of media when creating a picture (oils, etching, watercolors, collage, and so forth), so a PC graphics programmer can choose from a variety of different modes, or formats. Each mode provides a different combination of graphics characteristics. These characteristics include the resolution, the number of possible colors, whether text or graphics are to be displayed, and other elements. Different modes require different hardware (monitors and adaptor boards), and different programming approaches. All this can be confusing for someone new to graphics, so in this section we'll briefly discuss the various graphics elements, and how they come together to make up each of the modes.

In the section following this we'll show how to change to the desired graphics mode, and then we'll finally get down to the business at hand: putting pixels on the screen.

Table 11-1 summarizes the available modes and the graphics characteristics of each one. We'll explain the elements of this table in the following sections.

Table 11-1. *IBM Color Graphics Modes*

Mode (dec)	Colors	Resolution	Adaptor	Monitor	Minimum Memory	Pages	Starting Address
0 text	16 grey	40x25*	CGA	CD	2K	8 (16K)	B8000
1 text	16	40x25*	CGA	CD	2K	8 (16K)	B8000
2 text	16 grey	80x25*	CGA	CD	4K	4 (16K)	B8000
3 text	16	80x25*	CGA	CD	4K	4 (16K)	B8000
4 grph	4	320x200	CGA	CD	16K	1 (16K)	B8000
5 grph	4 grey	320x200	CGA	CD	16K	1 (16K)	B8000
6 grph	2 (B&W)	640x200	CGA	CD	16K	1 (16K)	B8000
7 text	2 (B&W)	80x25*	MA	MD	4K	1 (4K)	B0000

Modes 8, 9, and 10 are for the PC jr.
Modes 11 and 12 are used internally by the EGA board.

Mode (dec)	Colors	Resolution	Adaptor	Monitor	Minimum Memory	Pages	Starting Address
13 grph	16	320x200	EGA	ECD	32K	2 (64K)	A0000
14 grph	16	640x200	EGA	ECD	64K	1 (64K)	A0000
15 grph	2 (B&W)	640x350	EGA	ECD	64K	1 (64K)	A0000
16 grph	16	640x350	EGA	ECD	128K	1(128K)	A0000
17 grph	2 (B&W)	640x480	VGA	VD	256K	4(256K)	A0000
18 grph	16	640x480	VGA	VD	256K	1(256K)	A0000
19 grph	256	320x200	VGA	VD	256K	4(256K)	A0000

*Characters. Other resolutions in pixels.

grph	= Graphics	MA	= Monochrome Adaptor
MD	= Monochrome Display	CGA	= Color Graphics Adaptor
CD	= Color Display	EGA	= Enhanced Graphics Adaptor
ECD	= Enhanced Color Display	VGA	= Video Graphics Array
VD	= VGA Display		

Resolution

Graphics images on a computer screen are composed of tiny dots called pixels, for "picture elements." (For some reason, IBM calls them "pels," but we'll stick with the more commonly accepted term.) Pixels are arranged on the screen in horizontal rows: there are a fixed number of rows, and each row contains a certain number of pixels. The number of pixels used on the screen is called the *resolution*. Each graphics mode uses a particular resolution. For example, mode 4 uses a resolution of 200 rows, each 320 pixels across. This is abbreviated 320 by 200, or 320x200.

Higher resolution means a sharper, clearer picture, with less pronounced "jaggies" (the stairstep effect on diagonal lines). On the other hand, higher resolution also uses more memory for the display, and so is more expensive.

Each pixel can appear in a variety of different colors (assuming the correct mode is set and the correct hardware is available). The arrangement of pixels on the screen is shown in Figure 11-1.

graphics display

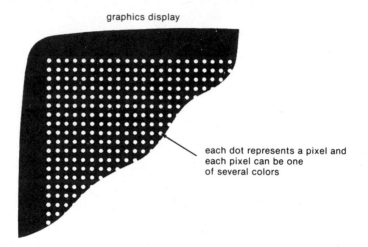

each dot represents a pixel and each pixel can be one of several colors

Figure 11-1. Graphic Images Are Made from Pixels

Text or Graphics

Some modes exist only to place text on the color screen, others are made for graphics.

In the graphics modes, each bit, or each group of bits, corresponds to a particular pixel (dot) on the screen. In the text modes, as we saw in Chapter 9, a group of bits (actually two bytes) corresponds to a character. In this chapter we'll be concentrating on the graphics modes; we've already covered many of the basic aspects of the text modes in Chapter 9.

Color

Some graphics modes provide more colors than others. Several modes provide only two colors: black and white (or perhaps black and green or amber, depending on your monitor). Other modes provide 4, 16, or 256 colors.

The situation is actually slightly more complicated than this. For example, a particular mode may allow only four colors on the screen, but it may be possible to switch to a second group of four colors (although the second group cannot appear on the screen at exactly the same time as the first). These groups of colors are called *palettes*.

Display Monitors

Different monitors are used for the different display modes. The simplest and least expensive is a text-only monitor. This can be used only with mode 7. The least expensive color monitor displays only the CGA modes: 0 through 6. An EGA-capable monitor can display additional modes, from 13 through 16, as well as the CGA modes. VGA monitors can display still more modes, from 17 to 19, as well as the CGA and EGA modes. Generally, the higher the mode number, the greater the resolution or number of colors displayed. Multisync monitors can be used with all standards. Monitors are made by a wide variety of manufacturers.

The Display Adaptor

In general (except for some IBM PS/2 series machines) PC computers don't come with the capability to send the signals necessary to generate text or graphics on the monitor. This is the function of a printed circuit board called a "display adaptor," which plugs into one of the slots inside the computer. There are display adaptors corresponding to the four graphics standards mentioned above: monochrome (text only), CGA, EGA, and VGA.

The CGA allows resolutions up to 640x200. At this resolution, two colors (black and white) are available. At a lower resolution, 320x200, four colors are available. The CGA also provides several text modes. The EGA adaptor increases resolution to 640x350 with 16 colors. VGA increases resolution again to 640x480 with 16 colors, and allows 256 colors, but at a lower resolution of 320x200.

> The greater the resolution of a graphics system, and the more colors, the more memory is required on the graphics adaptor.

Display Memory

As we described in Chapter 10, one of the key elements on any of the graphics adaptors is memory. This random access memory is similar to that in the computer, except that data placed in it causes an immediate change in the picture on the monitor.

Different display adaptors come with different amounts of memory. The monochrome adaptor has only 4K, enough for two bytes for each of 2000 characters (80 columns times 25 rows). The CGA has more memory, 16K, which is enough for 640x200 pixels if only two colors are used. In this case, each bit in memory corresponds to one pixel. The figure 16K is derived from the total number of pixels: 640 times 200 is 128,000 pixels. Because each pixel corresponds to one bit, we can divide by 8 bits per byte to arrive at 16,000 bytes (this is actually slightly less than 16K, which is 16,384 bytes).

If the resolution is cut in half, to 320x200, we can now use two bits for each pixel, and two bits can represent four colors. This is another mode available on the CGA.

In contrast, the EGA comes standard with 64K of memory. This allows 16 colors with a resolution of 640x200. (We can verify this by doing the arithmetic as shown above, remembering that 16 colors requires four bits per pixel.) Additional memory can also be added to the EGA to provide a total of either 128K or 256K. If 128K is available, another mode becomes possible: 640x350 with 16 colors. (Extending the memory to 256K makes possible additional pages, as is described next). VGA comes with 256K of memory, which provides 640x480 and 16 colors, or 320x200 with 256 colors.

The following table summarizes the amount of memory necessary to support different numbers of colors at different resolutions:

Resolution	2	Colors 4	16	256
320x200	8K	16K	32K	256 k
640x200	16K	32K	64K	
640x350	32K	64K	128K	

640 x 480   256 k

Pages

When enough graphics memory is available in the adaptor, it's possible to keep several screens of data in the memory at the same time. Thus, on the EGA board, mode 13 (320x200, 16 colors) requires only 32K, but 64K is available. The extra memory can be used to hold a second screen image. By switching from one page to another, very rapid changes can be made to the image on the screen.

Starting Address

As with other parts of RAM, a memory location in a graphics adaptor is identified by its address. We've already learned that the character memory for monochrome systems starts at absolute address B0000, while that for color systems starts at B8000. The graphics memory in the CGA modes starts at B8000, and in the EGA and VGA modes it starts at A0000. These addresses are important if we want to access the display memory directly from our program.

Using the Modes

In this chapter we'll mostly be concerned with mode 4, which is available for all graphics adaptors; mode 13, which works on EGA and VGA adaptors; and two VGA-specific modes: 18 and 19. We'll start with a look at mode 4, but before we do that, we need to know how to switch from one mode to another.

Setting Modes

If you're using the monochrome monitor and the monochrome adaptor, when you first turn on your computer, it will boot up in mode 7. If you're using a color display with the CGA, EGA, or VGA you'll probably boot up in mode 3, a text-only mode. Neither of these modes permits you to do graphics. To draw graphics on the color screen, you'll need to know how to switch from mode 7 (or mode 3) to a graphics mode.

The ROM BIOS Set Mode Command

To select the mode, we make use of a ROM BIOS routine called Set Video Mode. This involves putting 0 in the AH register, the desired mode number in the AL register, and executing an interrupt number 10 (hex).

ROM BIOS routine:	Set video mode
Interrupt 10 hex:	Video
Input registers:	AH=0
	AL=mode number
Output registers:	None

The setmode.c Program

Here's the program that lets us switch graphics modes. It reads the command-line argument to know which mode we want. Thus, to switch to mode 4 from DOS, we would type

```
C>setmode 4
```

Here's the program:

```
/* setmode.c */
/* sets graphics mode to value supplied */
#include <dos.h>          /* declares REGS */
#define SETMODE 0         /* "set video mode" service */
#define VIDEO 0x10        /* video BIOS interrupt number */

void main( int argc, char *argv[] )
{
    union REGS regs;
    int mode;

    if (argc != 2)
        { printf("Example usage: setmode 7"); exit(); }

    mode = atoi( argv[1] );    /* string to integer */
    regs.h.al = (char)mode;    /* mode number in AL register */
    regs.h.ah = SETMODE;       /* service # in AH register */
    int86(VIDEO, &regs, &regs); /* call video interrupt */
}
```

p 350

(Don't use this program within Turbo C's IDE although you can run it from a DOS shell invoked from the IDE). You need to be able to change modes before running the program. Switch to mode 4 by typing

```
C>setmode 4
```

The C> prompt should appear on the color display, but you won't see the flashing cursor: that's because the graphics modes don't support the cursor. Want to see the cursor? Switch to a text mode, say mode 3. There's the prompt with the cursor. Notice that switching modes clears the screen. This can be a useful (though slow) way to clear the screen, either by using setmode.c or by calling the Set Mode ROM routine from within a program.

Displaying Pixels with ROM Routines

Now that we know something about graphics, and have a way to change to a graphics mode, we're finally ready to put some pixels on the screen.

The simplest way to display graphics images is to use a ROM routine called Write Dot. The ROM routines for video displays are not especially fast, but they are easy to program. (We'll see how to speed things up later.)

The following program, cstripes.c, is designed for use with mode 4, which is available for all video adaptors. Before you execute this program, you must use the setmode.c program developed in the last section to switch to mode 4.

p 412

The cstripes.c program draws four vertical stripes on the screen, each in a different color, as shown in Figure 11-2.

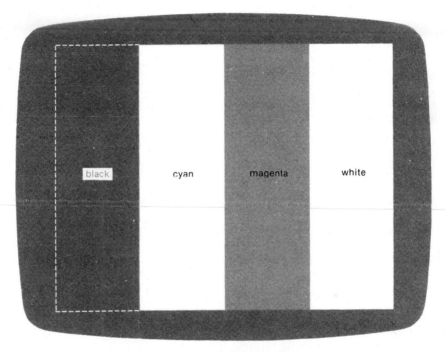

black   cyan   magenta   white

Figure 11-2. Output of the cstripes.c Program

This program shows all the colors that can be displayed at one time in this mode. (Later we'll see how to double the number of colors by changing palettes.) Here's the listing:

```
/* cstripes.c */
/* fills CGA screen with 4 color bars.  Use mode 4 (320x200) */
#include <dos.h>               /* to declare REGS */
#define MAXR 200               /* rows */
#define MAXC 320               /* columns */
#define VIDEO 0x10             /* video interrupt # */
#define WDOT 12                /* 'write dot' ROM BIOS */
void main(void)
{
    union REGS regs;
    int row, col;
```

```
for(row=0; row<MAXR; row++)
   for(col=0; col<MAXC; col++)
      {
      regs.h.ah = WDOT;       /* 'write dot' service */
      regs.x.dx = row;        /* row in DX */
      regs.x.cx = col;        /* column in CX */
      regs.h.al = col/80;     /* color change every 80 rows */   cols
      regs.h.bh = 0;          /* page number */
      int86(VIDEO, &regs, &regs); /* call video services */
      }
}
```

This program consists of an inner **for** loop to draw each row (in this mode each row has 320 pixels) and an outer loop to step through the 200 rows. For each pixel the program calls interrupt 10, the video services interrupt. The AH register contains 12 (dec) to specify the ROM BIOS Write Dot service; DX and CX contain the row and column; BH contains the page number, which must be 0 in this mode; and AL contains the color.

To run the program from DOS, set the mode to 4 first:

```
C>setmode 4
C>cstripes
```

ROM BIOS routine:	Write dot
Interrupt 10 hex:	Video
Input registers:	AH=0C hex *12 dec*
	CX=column number
	DX=row number
	AL=color
	BH=page number
Output registers:	None

The normal or "default" set of colors in this mode is as follows:

Palette 1	
Number	Color
0	black
1	cyan
2	magenta
3	white

To specify the color for a particular pixel, we simply put the appropriate color number, from 0 to 3, in the AL register when calling the Write Dot ROM BIOS routine. In the cstripes.c program, we want to create four vertical stripes, each of a different color. The column numbers (the variable **col**) run from 0 to 319, so we divide this number by 80 to arrive at color numbers that run from 0 to 3 across each row, using the statement:

```
regs.h.al = col/80;
```

This results in four vertical stripes being drawn. Since the first stripe is black, it will look as if nothing is being drawn in the left quarter of the screen.

We noted earlier that the Write Dot ROM BIOS routine is not too fast. How slow it is depends on which member of the PC computer family you're using. On the slowest machine, a PC or XT running at 4.77 megahertz, it takes 40 seconds to generate the display in cstripes.c. Even on a 386 machine it takes several seconds. We'll soon see how to speed this up.

Drawing Rectangles

Now that we know how to put a dot on the screen, we can create patterns other than stripes. The next program draws a series of concentric rectangles on the screen, as shown in Figure 11-3.

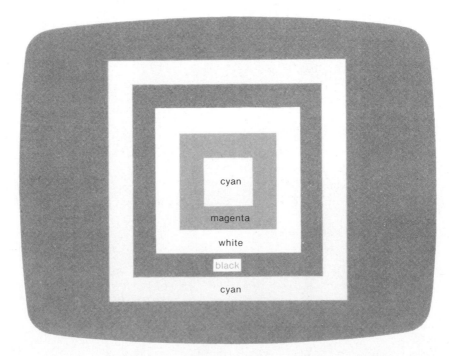

Figure 11-3. Output of the conrect.c Program

Here's the listing:

```
/* conrect.c */
/* draws concentric rectangle of different colors */
#include <dos.h>                        /* for REGS structure */
void rect(int, int, int, int, unsigned char);  /* prototypes */
void putpt(int, int, unsigned char);

void main(void)
{
   int z;

   for(z=50; z>=10; z-=10)                /* series of rectangles */
      rect(100-z, 100+z, 160-z, 160+z, (z/10)%4);
}

/* rect() */
/* draws rectangle on screen using putpt() */
void rect(int top, int bot, int left, int rite,
                                       unsigned char color)
{
   int x, y;

   for(y=top; y<=bot; y++)
      for(x=left; x<=rite; x++)
         putpt(x,y,color);
}

/* putpt() */
/* displays point at location col, row */
#define VIDEO 0x10
#define WDOT 0x0C
void putpt(int col, int row, unsigned char color)
{
   union REGS regs;

   regs.h.ah = WDOT;          /* 'write dot' service */
   regs.x.dx = row;           /* row in DX */
   regs.x.cx = col;           /* column in CX */
   regs.h.al = color;         /* color in AL */
   regs.h.bh = 0;             /* video page number */
   int86(VIDEO, &regs, &regs);  /* call video services */
}
```

step size (handwritten annotation)

mod (handwritten annotation)

We've broken the program into three parts: a function **putpt()**, which uses the ROM BIOS routine to put a point on the screen; a function **rect()**, which draws a rectangle, given the column numbers of the left and right sides of the rectangle and the row numbers of the top and bottom; and the **main()** program, which calls the **rect()** routine five times, asking for a smaller rectangle each time. The variable **color** cycles repeatedly through the series 0, 1, 2, 3, as each new rectangle is drawn.

Setting Color Palette and Background

As we've noted, we can choose a different set of four colors if we wish. Let's see how this is done.

In mode 4 there are two possible sets of colors or palettes. We've already seen the first one: black, cyan, magenta, and white. How do we switch to the second set? Once again, a ROM BIOS routine, this one called Set Color Palette, does the job.

ROM BIOS routine:	Set color palette
Interrupt 10 hex:	Video
Input registers:	AH=0B (hex)
	BH=1 (to change palette)
	BL=Palette number
Output registers:	None

Here's a program that allows you to switch to any desired palette. Like setmode.c, it uses a command-line argument to specify the palette. Here's the listing: p 412

```
/* setpal.c */
/* sets color palette to one of two values */
#include <dos.h>          /* declares REGS */
#define SETPAL 0x0B       /* "set color palette" service */
#define VIDEO 0x10        /* video BIOS interrupt number */
void main( int argc, char *argv[] )
{
   union REGS regs;
   int pal;                    /* palette number */

   if (argc != 2)
      { printf("Example usage: C>setpal 0"); exit(); }
   pal = atoi( argv[1] );      /* string to integer */
```

```
        regs.h.bh = 1;                /* BH=1 to set palette */
        regs.h.bl = pal;              /* palette # from user */
        regs.h.ah = SETPAL;           /* service # in AH register */
        int86(VIDEO, &regs, &regs);   /* call video interrupt */
}
```

p 416

To try out this program, first switch to mode 4, then run the conrect.c program. This will give you a picture of concentric rectangles on the screen, in the default palette, which is number 1. Then switch to the second palette.

```
C>setmode 4
C>conrect
C>setpal 0
```

Now you'll see the same pattern, but this time in the colors of the second palette.

Palette 0	
Number	*Color*
0	black
1	green
2	red
3	brown

The color black remains the same for both palettes; this is the background color—the color on the screen where nothing has been written.

Changing the Background

All the graphics adaptors are capable of generating 16 colors. Even in mode 4, which allows only 8 colors (two palettes of four colors each), we can see all 16 colors by changing the *background* color from black.

ROM BIOS routine:	Set background
Interrupt 10 hex:	Video
Input registers:	AH=0B (hex)
	BH=0 (to change background)
	BL=palette number
Output registers:	None

Here's a program that uses a variation of the Set Color Palette ROM routine to change the background. We specify that we want to change the background by placing a 0 in the BH register instead of a 1, as we do for changing the palette.

```c
/* setback.c */
/* sets color of background to one of 16 values */
#include <dos.h>          /* declares REGS */
#define SETPAL 0x0B       /* "set color palette" service */
#define VIDEO 0x10        /* video BIOS interrupt number */
void main( int argc, char *argv[] )
{
   union REGS regs;
   int pal;                           /* palette number */
   if (argc != 2)
      { printf("Example usage: C>setback 15"); exit(); }
   pal = atoi( argv[1] );      /* string to integer */
   regs.h.bh = 0;                /* BH=0 to set background */
   regs.h.bl = pal;             /* palette # from user */
   regs.h.ah = SETPAL;          /* service # in AH register */
   int86(VIDEO, &regs, &regs); /* call video interrupt */
}
```

Now when you invoke this program in mode 4, you have a choice of 16 possible colors. Table 11-2 lists them.

Table 11-2. *Available Colors*

Num	Color	Num	Color
0	Black	8	Grey
1	Blue	9	Light blue
2	Green	10	Light green
3	Cyan	11	Light cyan
4	Red	12	Light red
5	Magenta	13	Light magenta
6	Brown	14	Yellow
7	White	15	Intense white

You can use setback.c to experiment with colors. In graphics modes, the background and the border both change to the color specified. In the text modes, only the border (the area of the screen outside where printing can appear) changes. By changing the background color, you can alter the effective color of the pixels you put on the screen, making all 16 colors available in mode 4, although not at the same time.

Color Generation

Where do these 16 colors come from? The CGA, and the EGA and VGA in this mode, generate four signals that are sent to the display for each pixel. These signals are blue, green, red, and intensity.

These four signals can be combined in specific ways to produce the 16 colors shown in Table 11-2. First, any combination of blue, green, and red signals can be made to yield one of eight colors. Then, if the intensity signal is added, eight more colors (lighter versions of the first eight) are generated. Table 11-3 shows how the signals are combined to produce the colors. A 1 indicates that the signal is present and a 0 indicates it's not. Later we'll see how these combinations of signals can be represented as combinations of bits in the EGA-specific graphics modes.

Table 11-3. *Signal Combinations*

Num	Color	Components			
		Intensity	Red	Green	Blue
0	Black	0	0	0	0
1	Blue	0	0	0	1
2	Green	0	0	1	0
3	Cyan *blue, green*	0	0	1	1
4	Red	0	1	0	0
5	Magenta *red, blue*	0	1	0	1
6	Brown *red, green*	0	1	1	0
7	White	0	1	1	1
8	Grey	1	0	0	0
9	Light blue	1	0	0	1
10	Light green	1	0	1	0
11	Light cyan	1	0	1	1
12	Light red	1	1	0	0
13	Light magenta	1	1	0	1
14	Yellow *red, green*	1	1	1	0
15	Intense white	1	1	1	1

Direct Memory Access and the Graphics Display

So far we've used ROM routines to put pixels on the screen. As we've noted, this is easy but slow. Now let's look at an alternative method that is harder to program, but that can have a significant speed advantage: direct memory access to the display memory. We've already explored this topic as it relates to the memory in the character display (see Chapter 10), so you should understand the fundamentals of the process. The difference is that we will be accessing bits representing pixels, rather than bytes representing characters.

Memory Usage in Mode 4

Before we can manipulate the bits in the display adaptor's memory, we need to understand how these bits relate to the pixels on the screen.

In mode 4, two bits are used to represent each pixel, since there are four possible colors associated with the pixel. Figure 11-4 shows how these combinations look. Four of these two-bit combinations are placed in each byte of the screen memory, so that, for example, the top row of 320 pixels requires 320 divided by 4, or 80 bytes of memory.

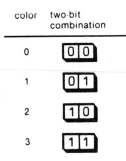

Figure 11-4. Two-Bit Combinations Used for Colors

There is an added complexity in the way the memory relates to the screen. The *even* rows of pixels go in one part of memory, while *odd* rows go in another. This scheme was designed to make the hardware more efficient, but it complicates life for the programmer. The part of the memory holding the even rows starts at B8000, while that for the odd rows starts at BA000. BA000 is B8000 plus 2000 hex; 2000 hex is 8192 decimal, and we need 8,000 decimal bytes to hold the information for all the even lines, since we have 80 bytes per row times 100 rows. We need another 8,000 bytes for odd lines.

In mode 4 memory, the even scan lines occupy a different area of memory than the odd lines.

Figure 11-5 shows how pixels on the screen relate to the display memory. A two-bit combination represents each pixel, so each byte represents four pixels.

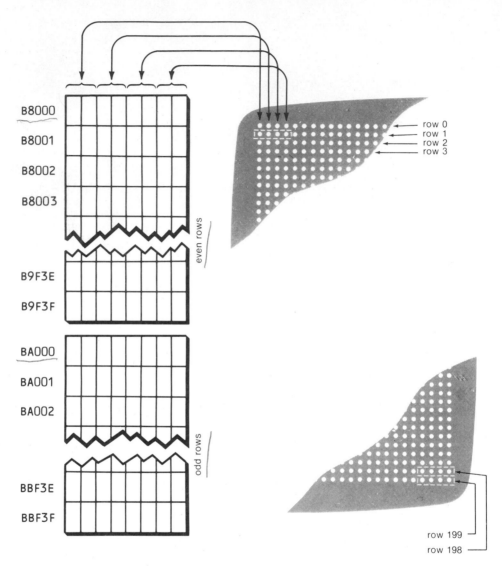

Figure 11-5. Memory Organization for Mode 4

Putting Bytes in Memory

For filling large patterns on the screen with color, it's more efficient to place whole bytes—each of which represents four pixels—in memory at once, rather than placing individual pixels. The following program imitates the behavior of the earlier cstripes.c program but operates more briskly: about 15 times faster. This speed increase is made possible by using direct memory access rather than a ROM routine and by putting four pixels on the screen at once, rather than one.

p 413

Here's the listing:

```
/* fstripes.c */
/* fills CGA screen with 4 color bars.  Use mode 4 (320x200) */
/* uses direct memory access */
#define MAXR 200                        /* rows */
#define MAXC 320                        /* columns */
#define MAXB (MAXC/4)                   /* bytes in a row (80) */
#define BPC (MAXB/4)                    /* bytes per color (20) */
char table[4] =
      { 0x00, 0x55, 0xAA, 0xFF };    /* color byte table */
void main(void)
{
    char color, far *farptr;
    int addr, index, row, col;

    farptr = (char far *)0xB8000000; /* set ptr to CGA mem */
    for(row=0; row<MAXR; row++)
      for (col=0; col<MAXB; col++)
        {
        index = (col/BPC) & 0x03;   /* clr chng evry 20 byts */
        color = table[index];       /* get color pattern */
        addr = row*(MAXB/2) + col;  /* address of byte */
        if(row & 1)                 /* if odd row number */
           addr += (8192-40);       /* use second bank */
        *(farptr + addr) = color;   /* set 4 pixls */
        }
}
```

As in cstripes.c, this program is built around two nested **for** loops; the inner loop moves across a row, while the outer loop steps down from row to row. There are several complexities in this program, though, that weren't present in cstripes.c.

First, because there are four pixels per byte, and we want to address each byte in turn rather than each pixel, the variable **col** actually counts across the 80 bytes in a row, rather than the 320 pixels. Thus, the limit in this loop is MAXB, the number of pixels in a row divided by the number of pixels in a byte.

The second complexity is that the program must calculate the memory address that corresponds to a particular group of four pixels. For even rows, this address will be the row number (the variable **row**) divided by 2 (since we're only counting the even rows) times the number of bytes per row, which is MAXB, all added to the column number (the number of bytes across). This is calculated in the line:

```
addr = (row/2)*MAXB + col;
```

423

For odd rows we must add a constant to this address. The constant is the number of bytes between B8000, where the section of memory for the even rows begins, and BA000, where the section of memory for the odd rows begins. This is 2000 hex, or 8,192 decimal. From this must be subtracted MAXB/2, because, although we're on row 1, for example, this is really row 0 in the second memory bank; the effect is the same as using row−1.

The third complexity is to figure out what color information to place in each byte before inserting it in memory.

In the fstripes.c program, all four pixels in each byte will be the same color, since the wide stripes we're drawing don't require fine detail. Thus, a byte can be configured in any of four possible ways, depending on the color being used. Each of these configurations can be represented by a hex number, as shown in Figure 11-6.

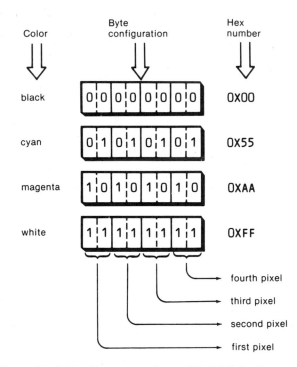

Figure 11-6. Hex Representations of Solid-Color Bytes

In fstripes.c these four bytes are stored in the array called **table**. The program selects which of these four representations to use by dividing the column number by the number of bytes to be devoted to each color stripe; in this case, MAXB divided by 4, or 20 bytes per stripe.

Finally, using a **far** pointer, the program inserts the correct byte into memory.

Try this program. You'll be amazed at the speed increase over cstripes.c.

p.422

Putting Single Pixels in Memory

Now that we know how to access a particular byte in the display memory, there is nothing to stop us getting at the individual bit-pairs that represent an individual pixel. This will give us the power to imitate the Write Dot ROM BIOS routine, using direct memory access. This is not only educational, in that it shows what Write Dot has to do to access a given pixel, it also provides us with a faster routine than Write Dot.

The following program uses a function called **putpt()** (for "put point") to emulate the operation of the Write Dot routine. To test this function, the main part of the program draws four lines, two diagonal—colored cyan and magenta—and one vertical and one horizontal—colored white—as shown in Figure 11-7.

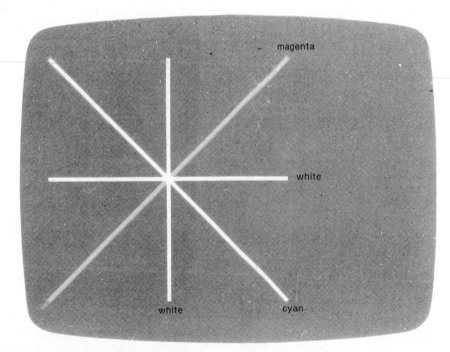

Figure 11-7. Output of the diagline.c Program

Here's the listing:

```
/* diagline.c */
/* draws diagonal lines on screen using putpt() */
#define CYAN 0x01
#define MAGENTA 0x02
#define WHITE 0x03
void putpt(int, int, unsigned char);      /* prototype */
```

```
void main(void)
{
   int x;

   for(x=0; x<200; x++)                /* draw all lines */
      {
      putpt(x,x,CYAN);                 /* diagonal line */
      putpt(x,199-x,MAGENTA);          /* diagonal line */
      putpt(x,100,WHITE);              /* horizontal  line */
      putpt(100,x,WHITE);              /* vertical line */
      }
}


/* putpt() */
/* displays point at location col, row */
#define BYTES 40                       /* (bytes per row) / 2 */
void putpt(int col, int row, unsigned char color)
{
   int addr, j, bitpos;
   int mask=0xFF3F;                    /* 11111111 00111111 */
   unsigned char temp;
   unsigned char far *farptr;          /* to hold screen address */

   farptr = (char far *)0xB8000000; /* set ptr to screen addr */


   /* calculate offset address of byte to be altered */
   addr = row*BYTES + (col >> 2);   /* calculate address */   rh bytes
   if(row & 1)                         /* if odd row number */
      addr += 8152;                    /* use 2nd memory bank */


   /* shift two-bit color & mask to appropriate place in byte */
   color <<= 6;                        /* put color on left */
   bitpos = col & 0x03;                /* get lower 2 bits */
   for(j=0; j<bitpos; j++)             /* shift mask & color */
      {                                /*    to right */
      mask >>= 2;                      /*    bitpos times */
      color >>= 2;
      }
   /* put two color bits in screen memory location */
   temp = *(farptr+addr) & (char)mask; /* and off color bits */
   *(farptr+addr) = temp | color;      /* or on new color */
}
```

In the following discussion, we make extensive use of the bitwise operators. If you're hazy on these, you may want to review the appropriate section of Chapter 10.

The **putpt( )** function has three parts. First it must find the address of the memory byte to be modified. This is handled in a way similar to that in the fstripes.c program, except that the variable **col** now actually represents a pixel location from 0 to 319. This column number must be divided by the number of pixels per byte before being used to calculate the address. For example, if we want to access a location on the screen 102 pixels from the left edge of the screen, this is 102/4 or the 25th byte from the start of the row.

Actually, instead of dividing by 4, we shift the column number to the right two bits, which has the same effect but is faster (since the shift instructions in the microprocessor are faster than the division instructions). This approach also emphasizes that the lower two bits of the column number have no effect on which byte we're addressing.

> The bitwise left-shift and right shift operators have the same effect and are faster than multiplying and dividing by powers of 2.

The second part of **putpt( )** positions the two color bits correctly so that they can be placed in the appropriate location within the byte whose address we've just calculated. This is done by starting with these two color bits (which are passed to **putpt( )** from the calling program) on the left side of the byte, and then shifting them right, as many times as is necessary to put them in the appropriate place in the byte. The number of times to shift is determined by the lower two bits of the column number: a value from 0 to 3, which is the position of the two color bits in the byte. This is found in the statement

```
bitpos = col & 0x03;
```

Thus, if our column number is 102, by masking off all but the lower two bits, we retain only the 2, which is assigned to **bitpos**. Now we know not only the address of the byte being accessed, but the position in the byte of the two bits representing the pixel.

There may be a color other than black already on the screen when we want to put our pixel there. If this is true, it's important that we don't change the six other bits in the byte we're addressing, otherwise we'd erase the underlying color. For this reason, we must first read the byte, then AND off (remove) the two bits we want to change, leaving the other six unaltered; then OR on (insert) the two color bits. We use a mask to AND off the appropriate bits. To create the mask, we start with the constant 0xFF3F, which is 11111111-00111111 binary. We then shift this constant to the right the same

p372

number of times we shift the two color bits. (We use an integer so we can guarantee 1s will be shifted in on the left.)

The shifting of the color bits and the mask can take place in the same loop, since they're shifted the same number of times. Figure 11-8 shows this process where the color bits are 01 (cyan) and the last two bits of the column number are the number 2, meaning that we must shift the color bits and the mask to the right twice (shifting two bits each time).

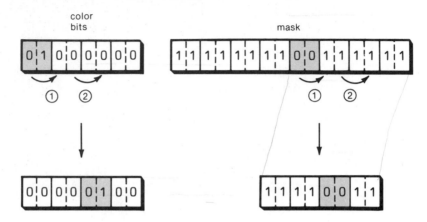

Figure 11-8. Shifting the Color Bits and Mask

Once we've got the color bits and the mask in the right place, we read the value of the byte from the video memory, AND it with the mask, OR on the color bits, and put it back into memory. This is the function of the statements in the third and final part of the program:

```
temp = *(farptr+addr) & (char)mask; /* AND off color bits */
*(farptr+addr) = temp | color;      /* OR on new color */
```

To prove that the **putpt()** function can write over other colors without disturbing them, run fstripes.c to put colored stripes on the screen, then run diagline.c to draw lines over it. You'll see that the colors in the background stripes remain undisturbed.

The Bouncing Ball

Besides drawing rectangles and lines on the screen, we can also draw other shapes. And we can make these shapes appear to move, by drawing and re-drawing them in different positions. In the following program we create a ball and set it in motion on the screen, at a 45-degree angle. Every time it hits the edge of the screen, it reflects or "bounces," like a ball on a pool table, so it ends up traversing a complicated pattern, as shown in Figure 11-9.

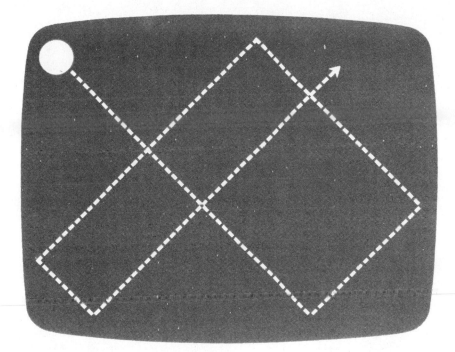

Figure 11-9. Bouncing Ball

```
/* bounce.c */
/* draws bouncing ball */
#define MAXC 320
#define MAXR 200
#define RED 2
#define BLACK 0
void drawball(int, int, unsigned char);      /* prototypes */
void putpt(int, int, unsigned char);

void main(void)
{
    int x=10, y=10, dx=4, dy=4;

    while( kbhit()==0 )              p432
        {
        x+=dx; y+=dy;
        if(x<10 || x>MAXC-20)  dx *= -1;
        if(y<10 || y>MAXR-20)  dy *= -1;
        drawball(x,y,RED);                  /* draw ball */
        drawball(x,y,BLACK);                /* erase ball */
        }
}
```

```
/* drawball() */                      diameter
/* draws ball, (radius) 16 pixels. Upper-left corner at col, row */
void drawball(int col, int row, unsigned char color)
{
   unsigned int mask;
   int x, y, dotpat;

   static int ball[16] =              /* picture of ball */
               { 0x07E0, 0x1FF8, 0x3FFC, 0x7FFE,
                 0x7FFE, 0xFFFF, 0xFFFF, 0xFFFF,
                 0xFFFF, 0xFFFF, 0xFFFF, 0x7FFE,
                 0x7FFE, 0x3FFC, 0x1FF8, 0x07E0 };
   for(y=0; y<16; y++)                /* each of 16 rows */
      {
      dotpat = ball[y];              /* pattern for this row */
      mask = 0x8000;                 /* one-bit mask on left */
      for(x=0; x<16; x++)            /* each of 16 columns */
         {
         if(mask & dotpat)           /* if part of pattern */
            putpt(col+x, row+y, color); /* draw dot */
         mask >>= 1;                 /* move mask right */
         }
      }
}


/* putpt() */
/* displays point at location col, row */
#define BYTES 40                      /* (bytes per row) / 2 */
#define BANK 8192-BYTES               /* 2nd bank - one row */
void putpt(int col, int row, unsigned char color)
{
   int addr, j, bitpos;
   int mask=0xFF3F;                   /* 11111111 00111111 */
   unsigned char temp;
   unsigned char far *farptr;         /* to hold screen address */

   farptr = (char far *) 0xB8000000;/* set ptr to screen addr */

   /* calculate offset address of byte to be altered */
   addr = row*BYTES + (col >> 2);   /* calculate address */
   if(row & 1)                        /* if odd row number */
      addr += BANK;                   /* use 2nd memory bank */
   /* shift two-bit color & mask to appropriate place in byte */
   color <<= 6;                       /* put color on left */
   bitpos = col & 0x03;               /* get lower 2 bits */
```

```
for(j=0; j<bitpos; j++)          /* shift mask & color */
   {                             /*    2 bits right */
   mask >>= 2;                   /*      bitpos times */
   color >>= 2;
   }
/* put two color bits in screen memory location */
temp = *(farptr+addr) & (char)mask; /* AND off color bits */
*(farptr+addr) = temp | color;      /* OR on new color */
}
```

This program uses the **putpt()** function from the last example. It also intro- p 42L
duces a new function, **drawball()**. This function uses a pattern, consisting of
an array of integers, to represent the ball. Each integer has 16 bits, and there
are 16 integers, so this array can define a rectangular object of 16 by 16 pixels.
The relationship between the hex numbers and the pattern is shown in Figure
11-10.

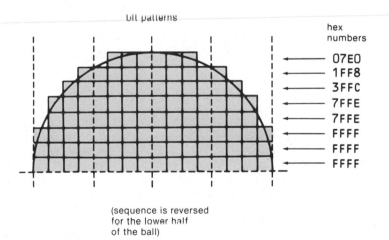

Figure 11-10. Hex Numbers Representing Ball

The **drawball()** function uses a **for** loop to go through each of the 16
integers in turn. For each number, an inner **for** loop uses a one-bit mask to
test each bit of the pattern word. If the bit is on, a dot is written to the screen
using **putpt()**. If it's not on, no bit is drawn. The result is a drawing of a ball,
reproduced on the screen.

To move the ball, the main program draws it, then erases it, then calculates the new location and draws it again. When the ball comes too close to
the edge of the screen, which is checked for by the **if** statements, the signs of
dy and **dx**—the increments by which the x and y coordinates of the ball are
increased—are reversed, thus reversing the ball's direction of motion.

Of course other patterns could be used here as well— spaceships, running men, icons representing disks or files, or whatever. The size of the pattern could also be changed: an array of type **char**, with 64 pixels, could be drawn faster than the present 256-pixel pattern.

The C library function **kbhit()** returns a 0 if no key was struck, and a 1 when the user hits any key.

The ball may look as if its two halves don't quite fit together. You can fix this by drawing only the even-numbered scan lines.

EGA-Specific Modes

The EGA (and VGA) adaptors make available several modes that don't exist on the CGA board. These modes use a different conceptual approach to putting colors on the screen than do the CGA modes, so in this section we'll explore a representative EGA-specific mode, number 13. Mode 13 provides a resolution of 320x200, with 16 colors (instead of the 4 colors provided by CGA mode 4). Mode 13 doesn't require the ECD monitor, but it can be used with this display, and the principles involved are the same for the higher-resolution modes 15 and 16, which do require the ECD.

ROM Routines and the EGA

As with the CGA modes, the simplest approach to putting color on the screen with the EGA modes is to use the Write Dot ROM BIOS routine. Here's an example that draws 16 differently colored vertical bars. The effect is shown in Figure 11-11. To run it, first change to mode 13, then run the program from DOS:

p 412

```
C>setmode 13
C>estripes
```

```
/* estripes.c */
/* fills EGA screen with 16 color bars.  Use mode 13 (320x200) */
#include <dos.h>                          /* to declare REGS */
#define MAXR 200                          /* rows */
#define MAXC 320                          /* columns */
#define VIDEO 0x10                        /* video interrupt # */
#define WDOT 12                           /* 'write dot' ROM BIOS */

void main(void)
{
   union REGS regs;
   int row, col;
```

```
for(row=0; row<MAXR; row++)
   for(col=0; col<MAXC; col++)
      {
      regs.h.ah = WDOT;              /* 'write dot' service */
      regs.x.dx = row;               /* row in DX */
      regs.x.cx = col;               /* column in CX */
      regs.h.al = col/20;            /* colr chng evry 20 rows */   cols
      regs.h.bh = 0;                 /* page number */
      int86(VIDEO, &regs, &regs);    /* call video services */
      }
}
```

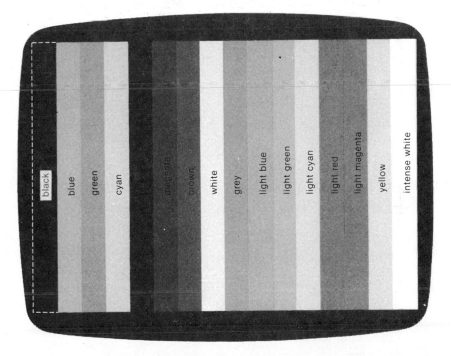

Figure 11-11. Output of the estripes.c Program

This program is similar to the cstripes.c program used for mode 4, except that *p4/3*
we can now display 16 colors (15 not counting black) instead of four. Thus we
must change colors every 20 columns.

 With the Write Dot routine we can do anything in mode 13 we did in
mode 4: draw rectangles, lines, bouncing balls, and so forth. As with the CGA
modes, however, the Write Dot routine is easy to program but slow. To speed
things up we can access the EGA memory directly, but to do that we need to
know something about how the EGA works with colors.

Bit Planes

Earlier we saw how the CGA board forms pixels of varying colors by combining two bits in all possible ways, yielding four colors. Each pixel is represented by two adjacent bits in a byte; so each byte can hold the information for four pixels. You might think that to achieve 16 colors we would use more bits; four bits would do the job, and we could pack two pixels in a byte. However, the EGA uses a different approach.

The EGA thinks of each color as occupying a separate area of memory. The 64K standard EGA memory is divided into four sections, or "planes," one for red, one for blue, one for green, and one for intensified. In any given plane, each bit represents one pixel, so eight blue pixels are packed into a byte in the blue plane, eight red pixels into a byte in the red plane, and so on. Figure 11-12 shows how this looks.

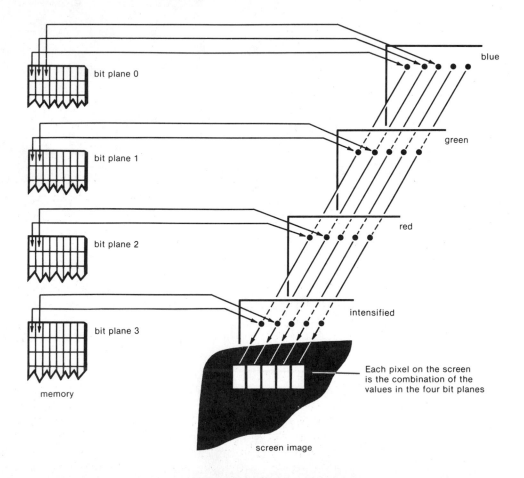

Figure 11-12. Bit Planes and Pixels

If you're only going to work with, say, blue pixels, then you can do all your work in bit plane 0. However, to combine colors, you'll need to work in several bit planes at the same time. For instance, to set a pixel to light cyan, you'll need to set the appropriate bit to 1 in plane 0 (blue), in plane 1 (green), and in plane 3 (intensified).

Now you might suppose that each of the four bit planes would occupy a different address space (range of addresses) in memory, so that accessing a particular byte in a particular bit plane would simply be a matter of figuring out the appropriate address. However, the designers of the EGA were more devious than that. Why? Suppose the bit planes were in separate address spaces (perhaps A000, A2000, A4000, and A6000). Then, to put a light cyan pixel on the screen, we'd need to put a bit in three different places in memory; this would require three separate write operations (using **far** pointers). Not very efficient.

Instead, the EGA is designed so that—hold onto your hat—*all four bit planes occupy the same address space*. They all start at address A0000 hex. In the case of mode 13, with 320 times 200—or 64,000—pixels, the amount of memory needed is 64,000 divided by 8 pixels per byte, which is 8,000 (dec) or 1F40 (hex) bytes. So all four bit planes start at A0000 and run up to A1F3F.

All four EGA bit planes occupy the same memory address space.

But if all the bit planes are in the same place in memory, how can we specify that we want to turn on a pixel in only one color—blue, say? It looks as if, to turn on one bit, we end up turning on four bits, one in each bit plane, at the same time. How can we select only the bit planes we want? To answer this question, we must know how to program something called the *map mask register*.

The Map Mask Register

The EGA board contains a custom integrated circuit chip called the *sequencer*. This device contains several registers, including the map mask register. By placing an appropriate value in the lower four bits of the map mask register, we can specify which of the four bit planes we want to write to. We can specify one plane or a group of planes. Figure 11-13 shows the map mask register in relation to the bit planes.

For a pixel to be set to a particular color, the bits in the correct bit planes must be turned on. For this to happen, the bit must be set to 1 in the byte sent from the CPU, *and* the bit in the map mask register at the position corresponding to the desired color must also be set to 1. Figure 11-14 shows a single bit being set to the color red. We could turn on several different bits at once and several different bit planes could be activated as well, so that the pixels could be colored with composite colors.

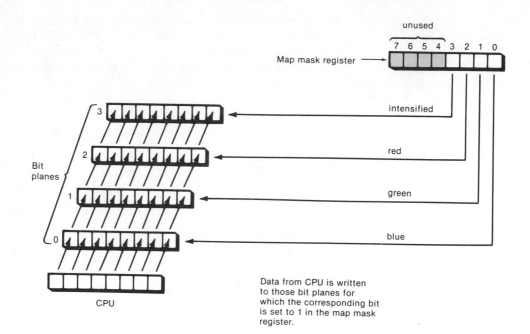

Figure 11-13. The Map Mask Register

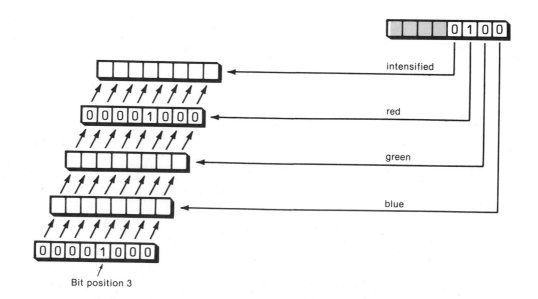

Figure 11-14. Turning on Red Bit at Bit Position 3

But how do we go about putting values into the map mask register? To answer this question, we need to know how to use C to communicate with a generalized set of I/O devices called *ports*.

Input/Output Ports

So far in this book we've learned to communicate with a variety of I/O devices: the character display, the keyboard, the printer, and, in this chapter, the color graphics display. Most of this communication has been performed by calling a C library routine, as when we print something on the screen using **printf()**, or a ROM BIOS routine, as when we put a dot on the screen using the Write Dot routine. Using ROM BIOS gets us closer to the hardware than do the routines in the C library, but sometimes we need an even closer connection between our program and the hardware. At the most fundamental level, hardware on the IBM is accessed through the medium of *input/output ports*.

A port is an eight-bit register. It can be accessed by software, but it is also physically connected to a hardware device; in fact, it is usually part of a hardware device. The IBM can have 65,536 ports connected to it; they are numbered from 0 to FFFF hex. However, only a small number of these addresses are actually used.

The ROM BIOS communicates with almost all I/O devices using ports. Usually we can use a ROM BIOS routine to access a device, so we don't need to know how the program accesses the ports. For some devices, though, there are no ROM BIOS routines available to our program. One example of this is the IBM's speaker; if we want our computer to make noise (other than a simple beep), we must use ports. Another instance where we may directly access ports is in programming the EGA.

How do we access a port using the C language? Turbo C provides two functions for this purpose: **outportb()**, which writes a byte to a port, and **inportb()**, which reads a byte from a port. Here's an example of the **inportb()** function. The statement

```
result = inportb(portno);
```

reads the byte from the port with the address **portno**. The variable **portno** must be an unsigned integer between 0 and FFFF hex, and the function returns an integer value (although only the lower byte contains information).

Similarly, the C statement

```
outportb(portno,value);
```

causes the information in **value** to be written to the port with the address **portno**. Here **portno** is an unsigned integer as before and **value** is also an integer, though it cannot have a value greater than FF (hex).

Thus, to output a value to an I/O port, all we need to know is the address of the port and the value to be sent to it; then we use **outportb()**.

Writing to the Map Mask Register

At this point we know almost everything necessary to put the appropriate bit plane value in the map mask register. However, there is one added complexity. There are several registers associated with the sequencer (a clocking mode register, a character map select register, a memory mode register, and so on) in addition to the one we want, the map mask register. To simplify the hardware, all these registers use the same port address: 3C5 hex. Therefore, we need to be able to specify which of these registers we want to access through the port. This is done with yet another register in the sequencer; this one is called the "address register," and its address is 3C4 hex. First we put an index number in the address register to tell it which register we want to refer to; for the map mask register, the index is 2. Then we put a number, representing the bit plane we want to reference, into 3C5.

> Accessing a register in the EGA generally requires writing to two ports: one to select the register, one to send it a value.

Writing Bytes to the EGA Memory

Now, finally, we're ready to write colors to the screen using EGA mode 13. The following program places 16 horizontal stripes on the screen, each one with a different color. Use setmode before running the program.

```
/* hstripes.c */
/* horizontal stripes.  Use mode 13 (320x200) */
/* (uses EGA write mode 0) */
#define MAXR 200                        /* rows */
#define MAXC 320                        /* columns */
#define MAXB (MAXC/8)                   /* bytes in a row */

void main(void)
{
    char far *farptr;
    int row, col;
    unsigned char color;

    farptr = (char far *) 0xA0000000;  /* set ptr to EGA mem */
    for(row=0; row<MAXR; row++)         /* draw rows of pixels */
        {
```

```
color = (row/12) & 0x0f;        /* colr chng evry 12 rows */
outportb(0x3C4,2);              /* set color to write */
outportb(0x3C5,color);          /*    in map mask register */
for (col=0; col<MAXB; col++)
   *(farptr + row*MAXB + col ) = 0xff; /* set 8 pixels */
}
}
```

Although hstripes.c is similar to the fstripes.c program for mode 4, changing colors in this program involves the two **outportb()** functions, and the stripes are drawn horizontally instead of vertically. Figure 11-15 shows how this looks.

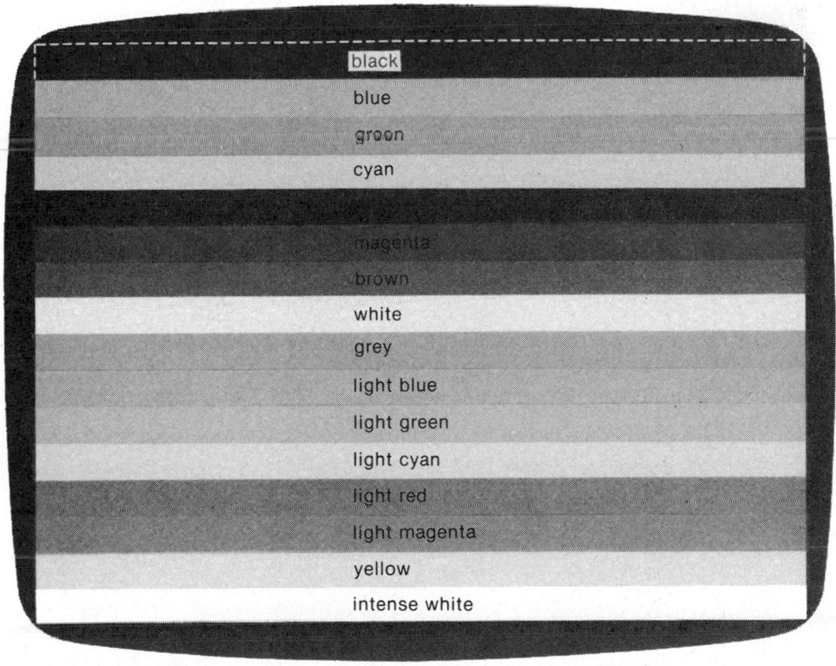

p 423

—red

Figure 11-15. Output of the hstripes.c Program

Because eight pixels are set with each memory access, it's a fast program, as you can see by comparing it with estripes.c.

Writing Bits to the EGA Memory

It's not necessary to display whole bytes at a time; we can also turn on individual bits. The following program draws 20 vertical lines on the screen. Each line is two pixels wide, so in the appropriate bytes, two bits are set to 1, while the remaining six are set to 0. Here's the listing:

```
/* vlines.c */
/* draws vertical lines.  Use mode 13 (320x200) */
/* (uses EGA write mode 0) */
#define MAXR 200                /* rows */
#define MAXC 320                /* columns */
#define PIX  8                  /* pixels per byte */
#define MAXB (MAXC/PIX)         /* bytes in a row */

void main(void)
{
    char far *farptr;
    int row, col, addr;
    unsigned char color, temp;

    farptr = (char far *) 0xA0000000;  /* set ptr to EGA mem */

    /* vertical lines, each two pixels wide */
    for(col=0; col<MAXC; col+=16)    /* space vertical lines */
       {                             /*   every 16 pixels */
       color = col/16;               /* change color every line */
       outportb(0x3C4,2);            /* set color to write */
       outportb(0x3C5,color);        /*   in map mask register */
       for(row=0; row<MAXR; row++)   /* draw one vertical line */
          {
          addr = row*MAXB + col/PIX;    /* calculate address */
          *(farptr+addr) = 0xC0;     /* send bits 7, 6 only */
          }
       }
}
```

p 437

The output of this program is shown in Figure 11-16.

For simplicity, the lines are separated by 16 pixels, or two bytes. Thus, the left-most two bits (numbers 7 and 6) of every other byte are set to the appropriate color, using the statement

```
*(farptr+addr) = 0xC0;
```

As before, the color is selected with the map mask register.

For some simple operations, the technique used in hstripes.c and vlines.c will suffice. However, when we try to use this technique in a more complicated situation, such as drawing one color on top of another, we run into trouble. To

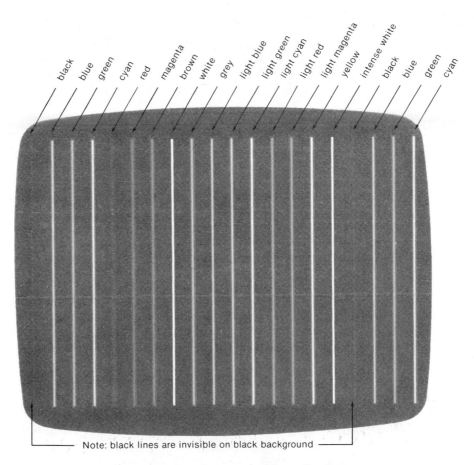

Figure 11-16. Output of the vlines.c Program

see the problem, clear the graphics screen (using the setmode.c program), run hstripes.c and then, without clearing the screen, run vlines.c:

```
C>setmode 13
C>hstripes
C>vlines
```

The vertical stripes will be drawn over the horizontal stripes. This is a rigorous test of a graphics system; if there is any inadequacy in the approach used, it will show up when one color is written on top of another. And, as it turns out, there is a problem; where a line crosses a stripe, in most cases there is an area to the right of the line where the stripe's color is changed or set to black, as shown in Figure 11-17.

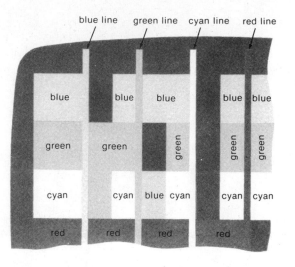

Figure 11-17. Incorrect Interaction of Stripes and Lines

The problem is that when a byte is written to a certain address on a given bit plane, those bits that are set to 1 are turned on, while those that are set to 0 are turned off. So, when we run vstripes.c, the two left-most bits in the byte being written to are set to the appropriate color, but the remaining six bits are turned off, causing a loss of that color in the six pixels to the right of each line.

In the CGA modes the solution to this problem was to *read* the contents of the existing byte from the CGA memory, OR on the appropriate bits, and rewrite the entire byte. This technique cannot be applied so simply in the EGA because there are four separate bit planes to read; doing four reads to achieve one write would not be very efficient. So the designers of the EGA provided another solution: a way to protect some bits from being changed.

Changing selected bits in a byte in the EGA bit planes requires protecting those bits that will not be changed.

The Bit Mask Register

We know that the map mask register can specify which bit planes are to be accessed when a byte is written to the EGA memory. In this case, those bit planes for which a bit is set to 1 in the map mask register can be written to, while those for which the bit is set to 0 will be unaffected by a write.

In a similar way it is possible to specify which bits in a byte (in all four bit planes) can be written to and which will be immune to change. The mechanism for this is the *bit mask register*. Figure 11-18 shows the relation of this register to the bit planes. To write to a certain bit in a particular bit plane, the corresponding bits in *both* the map mask register and the bit mask register must be set to 1.

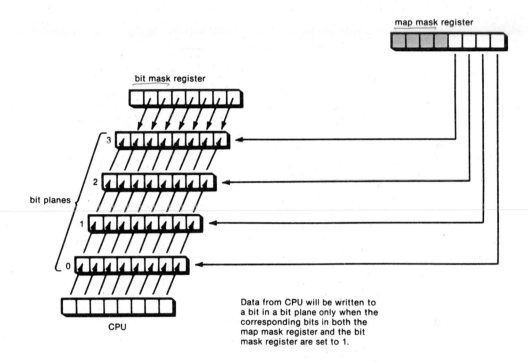

Figure 11-18. The Map Mask Register

When the EGA is first powered up, the bit mask register is set to all 1s, so all the bits can be written to. To protect a bit from being written to, we change this bit to 0. Like the map mask register, the bit mask register is accessed using I/O ports. And, again like the map mask register, it requires that an index number be sent to a different port before the register itself can be accessed. Here's what the necessary program statements look like:

```
outportb(0x3CE,8);    /* select the bit mask register */
outportb(0x3CF,0xC0); /* specify bits to be changed */
```

The bit mask register is part of a chip called the graphics controller register. To select the bit mask register, an 8 is sent to port 0x3CE. Then the desired bit configuration is sent to port 0x3CF.

443

The ecross.c Program

Now that we know how to prevent certain bits from being altered when we write to a byte in the EGA memory, we can solve the problem uncovered when we attempted to write vertical lines on top of horizontal stripes. The following program combines the earlier hstripes.c and vlines.c programs. The stripes part of the program is the same, but the line-drawing routine has been altered so that all but the left-most two bits of each byte being written to are rendered immune to change. This is done by setting the right-most six bits to 0 in the bit mask register. The appropriate constant is 0xC0, which is 11000000 in binary. Here's the listing:

```
/* ecross.c */
/* horizontal stripes, vertical lines.  Use mode 13 (320x200) */
/* (use EGA write mode 0) */
#define MAXR 200                 /* rows */
#define MAXC 320                 /* columns */
#define PIX  8                   /* pixels per byte */
#define MAXB (MAXC/PIX)          /* bytes in a row */

void main(void)
{
   char far *farptr;
   int row, col, addr;
   unsigned char color, temp;

   farptr = (char far *) 0xA0000000;  /* set ptr to EGA mem */
   /* horizontal stripes */
   for(row=0; row<MAXR; row++)    /* draw rows of pixels */
      {
      color = (row/12) & 0x0f;    /* colr chng evry 12 rows */
      outportb(0x3C4,2);          /* set color to write */
      outportb(0x3C5,color);      /*    in map mask register */
      for (col=0; col<MAXB; col++)
         *(farptr + row*MAXB + col ) = 0xff; /* set 8 pixels */
      }
   /* vertical lines, each two pixels wide */
   outportb(0x3CE,8);             /* select bit mask reg */
   outportb(0x3CF,0xC0);          /* change bits 7 and 6 only */
   for(col=0; col<MAXC; col+=16)  /* space vertical lines */
      {                           /*    every 16 pixels */
      color = col/16;             /* change color every line */
      outportb(0x3C4,2);          /* set color to write */
      outportb(0x3C5,color);      /*    in map mask register */
      for(row=0; row<200; row++)  /* draw one vertical line */
```

```
      {
      addr = row*MAXB + col/PIX; /* calculate address */
      temp = *(farptr+addr);     /* read byte into latches */   ←
      *(farptr+addr) = 0xFF;     /* send all bits */
      }
   }                             /* restore settings */
outportb(0x3CE,8);              /* select bit mask reg */
outportb(0x3CF,0xFF);          /* restore 'all bits' mode */   ←
}
```

There's another important addition to the ecross.c program, one that demonstrates how the bit mask register is used. Before writing the 0xC0 byte, the program *reads* the contents of the existing byte from EGA memory. However, the contents of this read, placed in **temp**, are never used. (This elicits a warning from the Turbo C compiler.) What then is the purpose of the read? To understand why reading is necessary before writing, you need to know about another set of EGA registers called the *latch registers*.

The Latch Registers

Our earlier diagrams of the bit planes simplified the situation; they showed data from the CPU going directly into the bit planes in EGA memory. Actually, there is another element in the data path between the CPU and the EGA memory: the latch registers. There is one latch register for each bit plane. When a byte is written by the CPU to the EGA, it actually goes to the latch registers first, then into memory. When it's read from memory, it goes to the latch registers on it's way to the CPU. This arrangement is shown in Figure 11-19.

The latch registers are important in the functioning of the bit mask register. Here's the sequence of events when a byte is written by the CPU to EGA memory. First, the byte arrives at the latch registers. (If some of the bit positions have been made immune to change by the bit mask register, though, the bits from the CPU will be blocked at these positions before they can get to the latch registers.) Finally, the contents of the latch registers are written into the EGA memory.

> The latch registers are an intermediate storage area between the CPU and the EGA memory.

The bits in the latch registers that did *not* receive CPU data are sent to memory as well. To ensure that these bits do not alter the data in memory, we read the data from memory into the latch registers before doing a write. Then when the write is performed, the new bits from the CPU are placed in the

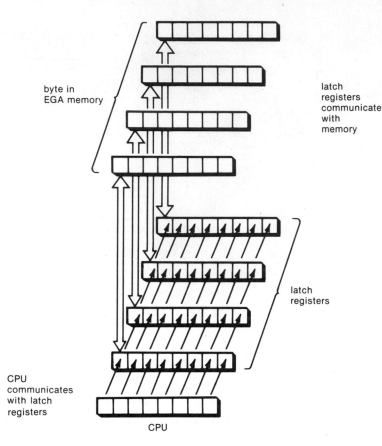

byte in
EGA memory

latch
registers
communicate
with
memory

latch
registers

CPU
communicates
with latch
registers

CPU

Figure 11-19. The Latch Registers

latches, the old bits remain as they were read from memory, and finally the complete contents of the latch registers are written back into memory. This process is shown in Figure 11-20. The figure shows only one of the four bit planes. However, a read or write operation transfers data between all four latch registers and all four bit planes simultaneously.

There is another detail to notice about the ecross.c program; it is necessary to restore the bit mask register to all 1s when the program is finished. If this is not done, only two bits in each byte can be written to by other programs accessing the EGA (including the operating system). This produces strange effects on the screen, so it's important for every program that uses the bit mask register to restore it before exiting.

The ecross.c program generates a much more pleasing picture on the screen than did the execution of hstripes.c followed by vlines.c. The lines no longer cause the unwritten pixels on their right to be destroyed. In fact, using the map mask register and the bit mask register as we've shown is a good way

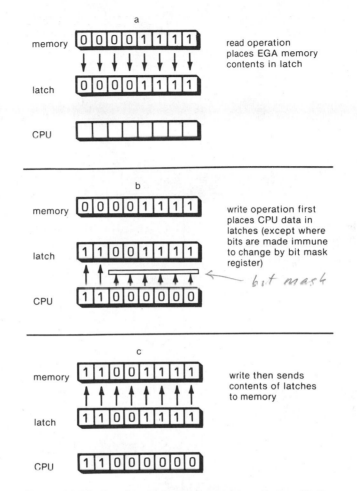

Figure 11-20. Reading Sets Latch Registers Before Writing

to handle a variety of situations, especially those involving complicated shapes. This system is, however, only one of three possible *write modes* available on the EGA; it is write mode 0.

In the following sections we'll examine the other two write modes. We'll start with write mode 2, which is more closely related to mode 0, and then we'll examine mode 1, which is used in special situations.

EGA Write Mode 2

The EGA write mode 0 provides good control of individual pixels, since a write operation can turn each one of eight pixels either on or off. It is thus suitable for operating on complex shapes. Write mode 2, on the other hand, puts its emphasis on fine control of color, at the expense of detailed shape manipulation. Let's look at the difference in operation of these two modes.

In EGA write mode 0, CPU data forms a pattern of bits; in write mode 2 it forms a color.

In write mode 0, the map mask register determined which bit planes could be changed, the bit mask register determined which bits could be changed, and the data from the CPU specified which bits in the bit planes would be set to 0 and which to 1 (the bit configuration). Write mode 2 uses a different approach. In mode 2, the data from the CPU determines the color instead of the bit configuration. This is effected by sending the CPU data directly to the map mask register rather than to the latches. The write operation, in addition to specifying the color, then automatically sets all the bits in the byte addressed to the color specified, unless they are protected by the bit mask register. Figure 11-21 shows how this looks.

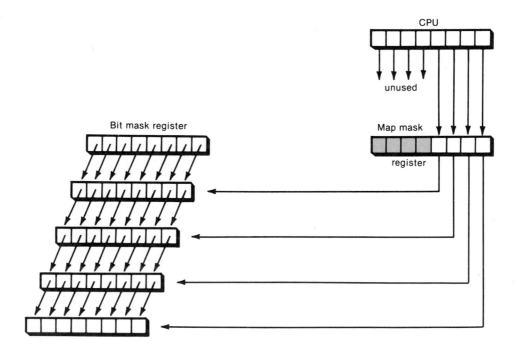

Figure 11-21. EGA Write Mode 2

The various write modes are selected by placing values in the *mode* register. This is another register in the graphics controller register. It's index number is 5, so the following **outportb()** statements change to write mode 2:

```
outportb(0x3CE,5);   /* select mode register */
outportb(0x3CF,2);   /* set to write mode 2 */
```

Here's a modification of the earlier ecross.c program, rewritten to work in write mode 2: p 444

```
/* ecross2.c */
/* horizontal stripes, vertical lines.  Use mode 13 (320x200) */
/* (uses EGA write mode 2) */
#define MAXR 200                 /* rows */
#define MAXC 320                 /* columns */
#define PIX  8                   /* pixels per byte */
#define MAXB (MAXC/PIX)          /* bytes in a row */
void main(void)
{
   char far *farptr;
   int row, col, addr;
   unsigned char color, temp;

   farptr = (char far *) 0xA0000000; /* set ptr to EGA mem */
   outportb(0x3CE,5);                /* select mode register */
   outportb(0x3CF,2);                /*    set to mode 2 */
   outportb(0x3C4,2);                /* select map mask register */
   outportb(0x3C5,0xF);              /* activate all bit planes */

   /* horizontal stripes */
   outportb(0x3CE,8);                /* select bit mask reg */
   outportb(0x3CF,0xFF);             /* make all bits writeable */
   for(row=0; row<MAXR; row++)
      {
      color = (row/12) & 0x0f;    /* colr chng evry 12 rows */
      for (col=0; col<MAXB; col++)
         *(farptr + row*MAXB + col ) = color; /* set 8 pixels */
      }
   /* vertical lines, each two pixels wide */
   outportb(0x3CE,8);                /* select bit mask reg */
   outportb(0x3CF,0xC0);             /* change bits 7 and 6 only */
   for(col=0; col<MAXC; col+=16)  /* vertical lines */
      {                           /*    every 16 pixels */
      color = col/16;             /* change color every line */
```

```
     for(row=0; row<200; row++)   /* draw vertical line */
        {
        addr = row*MAXB + col/PIX;   /* calculate address */
        temp = *(farptr+addr);   /* read byte into latches */
        *(farptr+addr) = color;   /* send color to address */
        }
     }                              /* restore settings: */
  outportb(0x3CE,8);               /* select bit mask reg */
  outportb(0x3CF,0xFF);            /* make all bits writeable */
  outportb(0x3CE,5);               /* select mode register */
  outportb(0x3CF,0);               /* set write mode 0 */
}
```

There are a number of things to note about this program. First, it's necessary to select the correct mode, as described earlier. Then, using the map mask register, all the bit planes must be made active so that subsequent writes will be accepted. This is accomplished with the statements

```
outportb(0x3C4,2);    /* select map mask register */
outportb(0x3C5,0xF);  /* activate all bit planes */
```

For the horizontal stripes, all eight bit positions in each byte must be writeable; the following statements do that:

```
outportb(0x3CE,8);     /* select bit mask register */
outportb(0x3CF,0xFF);  /* make all bits writeable */
```

The loops for writing both the stripes and the lines look much the same as in ecross.c, except that instead of being set to the bit configuration, the address pointed to is set to the _color_ in the statements

```
*(farptr + row*MAXB + col ) = color;
```

and

```
*(farptr+addr) = color;
```

At the end of the program, it's important to reset the write mode to 0 and make all bits writeable in the bit mask register, so other programs can use the EGA.

The screen image created by the ecross2.c program is much the same as that created by ecross.c. There is a difference, however, in the way colors interact when written over each other, which points out a difference in the operation of EGA write modes 0 and 2. The distinction is shown in Figures 11-22 and 11-23.

In write mode 0 (shown in Figure 11-22), when a color is written over another color, only those bit planes that are being turned on are affected. If other bit planes are already on, they remain on. This is because a single write operation will affect all four bit planes at a particular bit position the same way, turning them all either on or off (provided they are selected by the map mask register). Thus, where the blue line crosses the green stripe, the line appears cyan because the blue and the green are combined. Similar color mixtures appear at the other intersections.

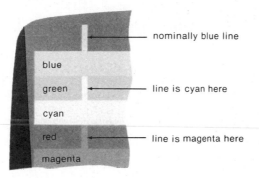

Figure 11-22. Section of Output of ecross.c Program   *mode 0*

The background could be set to black in write mode 0 by sending a 0 to all the bit planes and then, in a second write operation, sending the bit of the desired color. Write mode 2 is more efficient. In write mode 2 (shown in Figure 11-23), the values sent to the map mask register can turn bit planes off as well as on. Thus there is no mixing of colors at the intersections. This also means that it's possible to draw black images on a colored background, since all four bit planes can be turned off where black is desired.

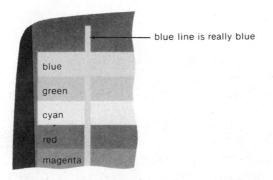

Figure 11-23. Section of Output of ecross2.c Program   *mode 2*

EGA Write Mode 1

EGA write mode 1 is a special write mode intended for rapidly copying an image from one part of the screen to another. This is useful in operations such as scrolling the screen, or scrolling parts of the screen. A read operation in mode 1 reads all four bit planes at a particular address into the latch registers. A write operation then writes all four bit planes into a different address. Thus a single read followed by a single write can transfer a byte in all four bit planes at the same time, allowing a far more efficient operation than if four separate reads and writes had to be made. Figure 11-24 shows the operation of write mode 1.

The program following uses write mode 1 to scroll the entire screen downward. Try executing hstripes.c before running this program, so you'll have something to scroll.

```
/* escroll.c */
/* scrolls entire screen downward.  Use mode 13 (320x200) */
/* (uses EGA write mode 1) */
#define MAXR 200                      /* rows */
#define MAXC 320                      /* columns */
#define MAXB (MAXC/8)                 /* bytes in a row */

void main(void)
{
   char far *farptr;
   register int addr;                 /* make it faster */

   farptr = (int far *)0xA0000000;  /* set ptr to EGA mem */
   outportb(0x3C4,2);               /* select map mask register */
   outportb(0x3C5,0xF);             /*    activate all planes */
   for(addr=0; addr<MAXB; addr++) /* erase top row by */
      *(farptr+addr) = 0;           /*    setting all bits to 0 */
   outportb(0x3CE,5);               /* select mode register */
   outportb(0x3CF,1);               /*    set write mode 1 */
   while ( !kbhit() )               /* until key pressed, */
      for(addr=MAXR*MAXB; addr>MAXB; addr--) /* move all bytes */
         *(farptr+addr) = *(farptr+addr-MAXB); /* down one row */
   outportb(0x3CE,5);               /* select mode register */
   outportb(0x3CF,0);               /*    set write mode 0 */
}
```

This program first erases the top row to avoid duplicating the line at the top of the screen. Then, using write mode 1, it shifts all the bytes in the EGA memory one row downward. The shifting process starts with the last address

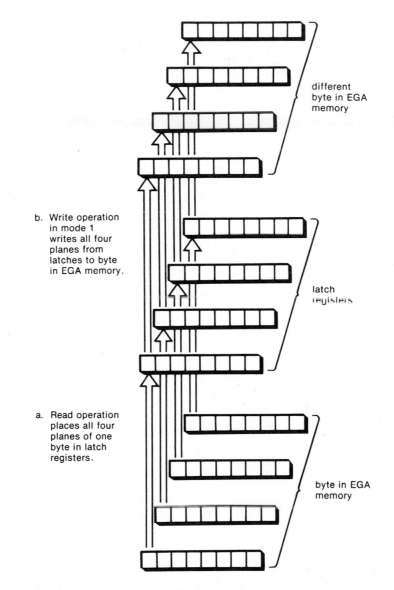

b. Write operation
in mode 1
writes all four
planes from
latches to byte
in EGA memory.

a. Read operation
places all four
planes of one
byte in latch
registers.

different
byte in EGA
memory

latch
registers

byte in EGA
memory

Figure 11-24. Write Mode 1

on the screen, which is MAXR*MAXB, and writes into it the contents of the
address one row up, which is the same address minus MAXB (the number of
bytes in a row). The shifting process then works its way up to the top of the
screen.

Similar uses of write mode 1 can quickly copy any area of memory to any
other area, making possible a variety of scrolling and animation effects.

VGA-Specific Modes

VGA offers all the modes of CGA and EGA graphics, as well as three new modes: 17, 18, and 19. Mode 17 is a black and white mode; we won't cover it here. Mode 18 provides the same 16 colors as EGA, but with higher resolution, and mode 19 permits the simultaneous display of 256 colors. We'll examine these two modes in turn.

VGA High Resolution

VGA mode 18 provides 640 by 480 resolution, using 16 colors. This mode operates in almost exactly the same way as EGA mode 13. It uses bit planes and registers (such as the map mask register and the bit mask register) in the same way the EGA does. Thus, programming mode 18 is almost identical to programming EGA mode 13, except that the vertical resolution for mode 18 must be changed to accommodate 480 lines instead of 350.

p 438

For example, here's the earlier hstripes.c program rewritten to run in VGA mode 18:

```
/* vgastrip.c */
/* horizontal stripes.  Use mode 18 (640x480) */
/* uses VGA write mode 0 */
#define MAXR 480                    /* rows */
#define MAXC 640                    /* columns */
#define MAXB (MAXC/8)               /* bytes in a row */
void main(void)
{
   char far *farptr;
   int row, col;
   unsigned char color;

   farptr = (char far *) 0xA0000000;  /* set ptr to VGA mem */
   for(row=0; row<MAXR; row++)        /* draw rows of pixels */
      {
      color = (row/30) & 0x0f;     /* color chng evry 30 rows */
      outportb(0x3C4,2);           /* set color to write */
      outportb(0x3C5,color);       /*    in map mask register */
      for (col=0; col<MAXB; col++)        /* across col */
         *(farptr + row*MAXB + col ) = 0xff; /* set 8 pixels */
      }
}
```

The effect is similar to that shown in Figure 11-15. This program uses write mode 0 to put the same 16 horizontal color bars on the screen as did hstripes.c, but does so with the higher resolution of mode 18. The other write modes can also be used in VGA mode 18.

VGA 256 Colors

VGA mode 19 can display 256 colors simultaneously, with a resolution of 320 by 200. (If you change palettes, you can access up to 262,144 colors, as we'll see in the next chapter.)

Mode 19 is conceptually the simplest of the graphics modes. There are 64,000 pixels on the screen (320 times 200). Each pixel is represented by one byte in memory, so each pixel can have up to 2^8, or 256 colors. The pixels are mapped onto the bytes in memory in the most straightforward way, starting with the upper-right pixel and scanning line by line down the screen. You don't need to set any registers, or worry about memory banks or bit planes.

The example program draws 256 boxes on the screen, each in a different color.

left

```
/* vga256.c */
/* draws 256 different colored squares.  Use VGA mode 19 */
#define MAXX 320           /* horizontal pixels */
#define MAXY 192           /* vert pixels (divisible by 16) */
#define PPBX (MAXX/16)     /* pixels per color box, horizontal */
#define PPBY (MAXY/16)     /* pixels per color box, vertical */

void main(void)
{
   char far *farptr;       /* pointer to video memory */
   int x, y;               /* pixel coordinates (0-319, 0-191) */
   int row, col;           /* color box coordinates (0-15) */
   unsigned char color;    /* color of box (0-255) */

   farptr = (char far *) 0xA0000000;   /* set ptr to VGA */
   for(y=0; y<MAXY; y++)               /* cycle down */
     for(x=0; x<MAXX; x++)             /* cycle across */
       {
       col = x/PPBX;                   /* find box coords */
       row = y/PPBY;
       color = col + row*16;           /* calculate color */
       *(farptr + y*MAXX + x) = color; /* set the pixel */
       }
}
```

Each color box is 20 pixels wide and 12 pixels high, and there are 256 boxes on the screen, in a 16 by 16 matrix, as shown in Figure 11-25.

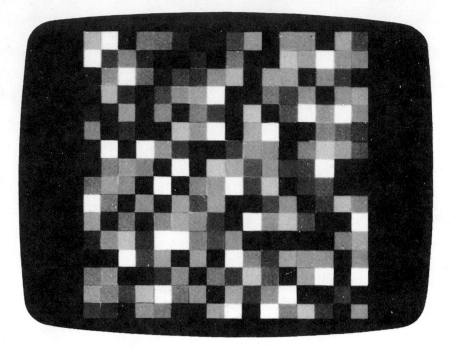

Figure 11-25 Output of the vga256.c Program

Each box has a different color, starting with color 0 at the upper left corner and continuing to color 255 at the lower right.

The program keeps track of two sets of coordinates: **x** and **y** specify the pixel location, and **col** and **row** specify the color box location. For each pixel location the program calculates the box location and colors the pixel accordingly. (There are faster ways to do this, but they complicate the program.) The first row of boxes displays the 16 EGA colors, the second row is a gray scale, and subsequent rows contain a variety of color blends.

Summary

Graphics is a complex topic, with an almost infinite number of possibilities. There is much more to know about the graphics adaptors than we have presented here. The EGA and VGA especially are complicated pieces of hardware, and a complete discussion of their features and the way they can be put to use would require a book in itself. However, we have at least had an introduction to graphics programming in C on the PC.

We've discussed the PC's graphics modes and the various characteristics that distinguish one mode from another: resolution, number of colors, text or graphics, type of display adaptor and monitor necessary, amount of graphics memory needed and its starting address, and number of pages. We've presented a program for switching from one mode to another by calling a ROM BIOS routine.

We've looked at mode 4, which is common to the CGA, EGA, and VGA adaptors, in some detail. We've shown how to use a ROM BIOS routine to write a pixel on the screen in this mode and used other ROM BIOS routines to change the color palette and background color. We've also seen how to address the graphics memory directly in this mode and developed programs to draw lines and bouncing balls.

As an example of an EGA-specific mode, we've looked at mode 13. We've seen that the Write Dot ROM BIOS routine works well for this mode, but that, as in other modes, direct memory access is faster. We've seen how direct memory access for the EGA modes differs from that for the CGA and how bit planes are used to store color data. Finally, we've looked at two VGA-specific modes.

Questions

1. List eight characteristics of a graphics mode.

2. In computer graphics, resolution is
   a. the clarity of the displayed image
   b. the number of bits per byte
   c. the number of colors per pixel
   d. the number of pixels in the display

3. Without counting palette changes, how many colors are there in mode 4? How many, if you count palette changes?

4. In mode 4, a pixel gets its color value from a combination of
   a. bit planes
   b. bits in a byte
   c. rows and columns
   d. text and graphics

5. From a programmer's viewpoint, the easiest way to put a pixel on the screen is to use a _____ _____. The fastest way to fill an area with color is to use _____ _____.

6. What four signals are combined to form background colors in the display monitor?

7. Which of the following is necessary for direct memory access?
   a. setting a pointer to the start of display memory
   b. calculating how far into the memory a pixel is
   c. using the indirection operator to access a byte
   d. modifying only those bits corresponding to the pixel

8. How many pixels per byte are there in mode 4?

9. The second memory bank in mode 4 is used for
   a. attributes
   b. unused in this mode
   c. the cyan and magenta pixels
   d. the odd-numbered rows

10. Mode 6 has a resolution of 640x200, with two colors: black and white. Which expression will find the address of the byte containing the pixel at **row** and **col**? (Ignore the memory bank correction.)
    a. addr = row*40 + col/16
    b. addr = row*80 + col/8
    c. addr = row*40 + col/4
    d. addr = row*60 + col/4

11. In mode 13 there are _____ colors.

12. One bit plane holds
    a. the information about a single color
    b. the even-numbered rows
    c. the color values for certain pixels
    d. the bits in certain positions in a byte

13. True or false: writing can take place to only one bit plane at a time.

14. To send information to a register in the EGA, one must use
    a. direct memory access
    b. the **outportb()** function

    c. a port

    d. a ROM BIOS routine

15. The map mask register is used to tell the EGA what _____ pixels we want to write.

16. Which of the following statements is appropriate for sending a value to a port?

    a. outportb(portno, value);

    b. value = inportb(portno);

    c. *(portno) = value;

    d. port(number, value);

17. In mode 13 how many pixels are there per byte?

18. What is the correct bit plane number for the color cyan?

    a. 0

    b. 1

    c. 2

    d. 3

19. The bit mask register is used to select which _____ will be written to.

20. The latch registers serve as an intermediate storage area between

    a. EGA memory and the bit map register

    b. the CPU and the map mask register

    c. the map mask register and the CPU

    d. EGA memory and the CPU

21. After the bit mask register has been set, a byte must be _____ to set the latch registers.

22. The mode register of the EGA board is used to

    a. switch the EGA to different graphics modes

    b. make sure certain bit planes are not used

    c. select an EGA write mode

    d. make sure certain bits are not used

23. True or false: in EGA write mode 0, any pixel in any bit plane can be turned either on or off by a single write operation.

24. In EGA write mode 2, the data from the CPU goes to
    a. the bit planes at the memory address specified
    b. the map mask register
    c. the bit mask register
    d. the latch registers

25. EGA write mode 1 is used to rapidly _____ a group of pixels.

Exercises

1. Write a program for mode 4 that will fill the screen with a color of the user's choice from palette 1.

2. Modify the conrect.c program to write concentric rectangles using direct memory access, rather than the ROM BIOS Write Dot routine. Speed it up by writing one byte at a time. Don't worry if the rectangles are not completely concentric.

3. Write a program that duplicates the action of the diagline.c program (drawing four lines of different colors that cross at the center of the screen) but uses graphics mode 13, direct memory access, and EGA write mode 2. Develop a **putpte()** function for this program that can be called with the arguments **row**, **column**, and **color**, and that puts the appropriate pixel on the screen.

12

Turbo C Graphics Functions

- Text windows
- Initializing graphics modes
- Rectangles, ellipses, and polygons
- Filling and patterns
- Bit images and animation
- Text fonts in graphics mode

12

The first Turbo C, Version 1.0, had no graphics functions. If you wanted to put graphics images on the screen, you had to use the ROM BIOS or direct memory access techniques described in the last chapter. Beginning with Version 1.5, Turbo C has remedied this oversight. Now you have access to library routines that create windows, draw graphics elements like circles and lines, use a variety of text fonts in different sizes, control the color of text and graphics elements, and much more. This chapter shows how these functions work.

The Turbo C graphics functions can be used for many of the effects that were demonstrated using direct memory access in the last two chapters. The Turbo C functions are well thought out and simple to use, so creating a graphics-oriented application is faster and easier than using the techniques discussed earlier. If this is true, why use direct memory access? In most cases direct access results in a faster-running program. So, to achieve the highest performance programs, this technique is preferable. Also, direct memory access provides capabilities which are unavailable with the Turbo C graphics functions. But to quickly put together a prototype program, or to create a program where the highest performance is not necessary, the Turbo C graphics functions are a great convenience. They're also fun to play with. There are no new C language concepts introduced in this chapter, so you can relax and enjoy making pictures!

There are close to 100 of these functions, so we can't cover them all in this chapter. However, we will cover the majority, concentrating on the most important functions. Appendix E lists the Turbo C graphics functions used in this book, and also shows some important definitions and structures used with these functions.

In general we'll show short, easy-to-follow examples of each function as it's introduced. At the end of the chapter there are several more ambitious examples that demonstrate some of the effects possible with the Turbo C graphcs functions. These include a presentation-quality bar-graph generator, a hypnotic kenetic painting, and a program that generates the extraordinary images of the Mandelbrot set.

Most of the example programs use CGA graphics. These examples can be used without modification on CGA, EGA, and VGA systems. In a few cases CGA is inappropriate, and we show examples using EGA graphics.

The graphics functions fall into two broad categories. First are those that operate on text using a text display (or the text mode on a graphics display). We'll call these *text-mode* functions. Second are functions that create pixel graphics images—such as lines and circles—on a graphics display. These are *graphics mode* functions. We'll look at text-mode functions first, since their setup is simpler and there are fewer of them.

Text-Mode Functions

The text functions described in this section operate in text mode. Thus a graphics display is not necessary; you can use either the monochrome display (mode 7), or the text mode on a graphics display (mode 3, for example). (See Chapter 11 for a discussion of video modes.)

Little preparation is necessary to use text-mode functions in your program (unlike the graphics-mode functions to be described later). You need only **#include** the header file conio.h at the beginning of your program.

A few computers have video adaptors which are not completely compatible with the IBM industry standard. If this is the case on your system, you may want to add another line to your program:

```
directvideo=0;    /* use ROM BIOS routines for screen access */
```

The **directvideo** variable determines whether the system writes directly to the video memory, which requires the display adaptors to be IBM compatible, or whether it writes to the screen using ROM BIOS routines. The ROM BIOS approach works on almost all machines, but is much slower, as we learned in the last chapter. The default setting, **directvideo=1**, causes the system to use direct access to video memory, so if this approach works on your computer—which it probably will—you don't need to worry about setting this variable. If you have trouble, set it to 0.

Windows

A major purpose of the Turbo C text-mode functions is to permit the use of *windows*. A window is simply a rectangular area of the screen that forms a boundary for video output. You've probably seen windows used in graphical interfaces such as the Macintosh and the OS/2 Presentation Manager. Turbo C itself uses windows in the IDE; there is typically an Edit window and a Message window on the screen at the same time.

The Turbo C graphics functions make it easy to manipulate text in a window instead of in the entire screen. For instance, if you're typing a line of text into a window, the cursor will be confined by the left and right edges of the window, rather than by the edges of the screen as it normally is.

Here's a short program that demonstrates a window, and introduces several text-mode functions. It sets up a window, and then repeatedly writes a word into the window until the window is full and additional words cause the window contents to scroll upward.

```c
/* window.c */
/* tests character graphics functions */
#include <conio.h>                       /* for text functions */
#define LEFT    10                       /* define window */
#define TOP      8
#define RIGHT   52
#define BOT     21
#define HEIGHT (BOT-TOP+1)

void main(void)
{
   int j;

   window( LEFT, TOP, RIGHT, BOT );     /* specify window */
   textcolor( RED );                    /* set text color */
   textbackground( GREEN );             /* set text background */
   for( j=0; j<100; j++ )               /* 100 words */
      {
      cputs( "Greetings " );            /* print word */
      delay( 100 );                     /* slow down the loop */
      }
   gotoxy( 15, 8 );                     /* go to window center */
   cputs( "   THE  END   " );           /* print phrase */
   gotoxy( 1, HEIGHT );                 /* cursor to bottom line */
   getche();                            /* wait for key press */
}
```

The **window()** function defines an area of the screen as the text window, using the left and right columns and the top and bottom rows as parameters. On an 80x25 screen, the columns run from 1 to 80, and the rows from 1 to 25.

Assuming you have a color display, the next two functions, **textcolor()** and **textbackground()** set the color of the characters to red, and each character's background color to green. The symbols RED and GREEN are defined in the file conio.h, so there is no need to define them in the program. There are 16 text colors and 8 background colors. The following table lists the colors and their numeric equivalents. (They're also listed in Appendix E.)

Define Text Window

```
void window( left, top, right, bottom )
int left;      /* coordinates of window */
int top;       /* on 80x25 screen, */
int right;     /* range is from 1 to 80 */
int bottom;    /* and 1 to 25 */
```

Number	Name	Foreground	Background
0	BLACK	X	X
1	BLUE	X	X
2	GREEN	X	X
3	CYAN	X	X
4	RED	X	X
5	MAGENTA	X	X
6	BROWN	X	X
7	LIGHTGRAY	X	X
8	DARKGRAY	X	
9	LIGHTBLUE	X	
10	LIGHTGREEN	X	
11	LIGHTCYAN	X	
12	LIGHTRED	X	
13	LIGHTMAGENTA	X	
14	YELLOW	X	
15	WHITE	X	

The functions used to specify these colors take only one parameter—the color itself. Either the name or numerical equivalent can be used.

Set Text Color

```
void textcolor( color )
int color;      /* from 0 to 15, or constants */
```

Define Text Window *Set Background Color*

```
void textbackground( color )
int color;      /* from 0 to 7, or constants */
```

The **textcolor()** function can specify the *blinking* attribute in addition to the color, if the number 128 is added to the numeric color value, or if the constant BLINK is added to the color constant, as in RED+BLINK.

Note that the graphics functions examined so far are of type **void**. Some graphics functions return an error code if they could not perform their mission, but these do not. If you give these functions an incorrect value, the operation is not carried out, but your program has no way to discover this.

Once the colors are specified, the program writes the word "Greetings" 100 times. Because a window has been defined, the **cputs()** function automatically starts at the top of the window rather than at the top of the screen. This function is similar to **puts()**, but works with windows. It starts each line at the left edge of the window and wraps to the next line when it reaches the right edge. When it reaches the bottom of the window, it scrolls the contents of the window upward. The delay caused by the **delay()** function, which pauses the program the number of milliseconds given it as a parameter, makes this action easier to see as the program runs. The output of the program is shown in Figure 12-1.

The cursor can be moved to any location in the window using the function **gotoxy()**. This function takes as parameters the column and row (x and

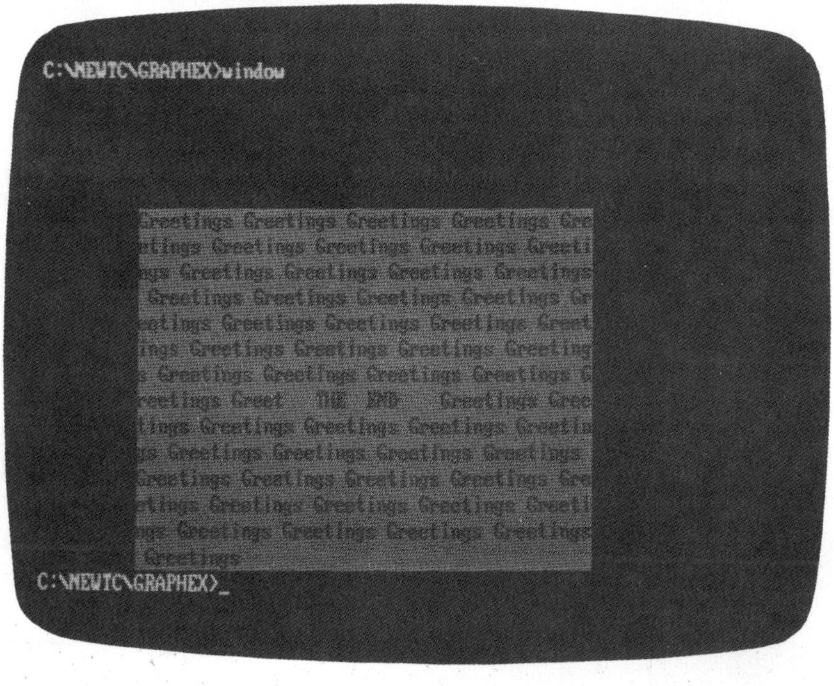

Figure 12-1. Output of the window.c Program

y) coordinates for the new cursor position. Note that these coordinates are
measured *relative to the window*, not to the screen. Thus the (15, 8) used in
the program means 15 columns from the left edge of the window, and 8 rows
down from the top of the window. This is roughly the middle of the window.
Once situated there, the program uses **cputs()** to write the phrase "THE
END."

Move Cursor

```
void gotoxy( x, y )
int x;     /* x coordinate of cursor */
int y;     /* y coordinate of cursor */
```

relative to window

If we left the cursor in the middle of the window when the program
terminated, the DOS prompt might overwrite part of the window, so the last
statement in the program moves the cursor to the bottom of the window.
What's the coordinate of the bottom of the window? It's not BOT (21) used
to define the window, since this is measured from the top of the screen.
Rather it's the height of the window, which is BOT−TOP+1. Confusion
between window and screen coordinates is a common source of errors in
graphics programs.

Moving Text

Another text-mode function, **movetext()**, copies a rectangular area of text
from one part of the screen to another. The next example program creates a
window, fills it with text, and then moves it to another location using this
function.

```
/* movetext.c */
/* moves text to memory and back */
#include <conio.h>
#define LEFT        26              /* define window */
#define TOP         7
#define RIGHT       65
#define BOT         20
#define DESLEFT     1               /* destination NW corner */
#define DESTOP      1
#define NUMCOLORS   16              /* number of text colors */
void main(void)
{
```

```
        int j;

        window( LEFT, TOP, RIGHT, BOT );      /* specify window */
        textbackground( GREEN );              /* set text background */
        for( j=0; j<98; j++ )                 /* 98 words */
           {                                  /* change color */
           textcolor( j % NUMCOLORS );        /*    every word */
           cputs( "Greetings " );             /* print word */
           }
        delay( 2000 );

                                              /* move window */
        movetext( LEFT, TOP, RIGHT, BOT, DESLEFT, DESTOP );
        getche();                             /* wait for keypress */
        }
```

Mod

The output of the program is shown in Figure 12-2. The move is successfully completed even though the source and destination rectangles overlap.

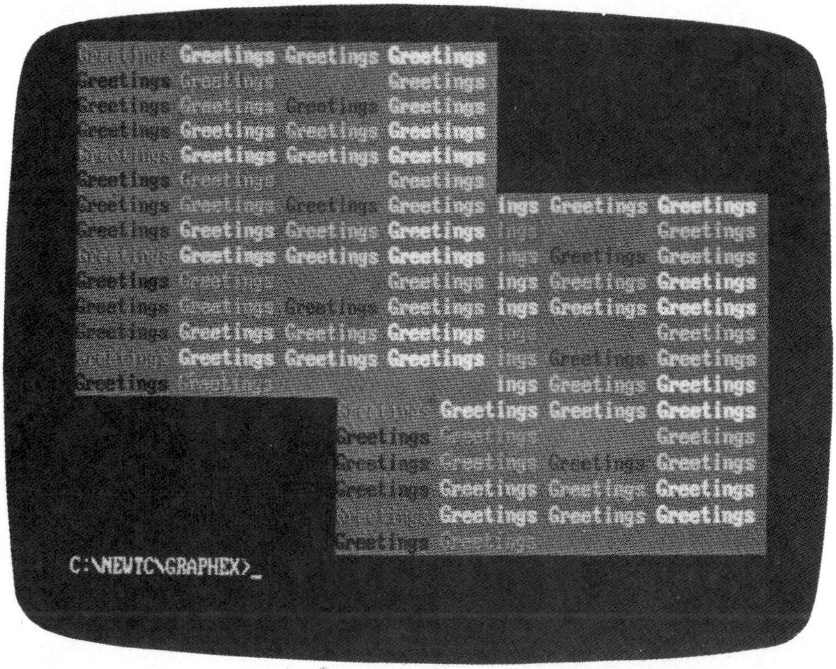

Figure 12-2. Output of the movetext.c Program

The **movetext()** function operates on absolute screen coordinates, not window coordinates. Although we don't make use of it in this program, the function returns a 0 value if the operation was not successful. This error return can be caused by using coordinates outside the window area. We don't check for the function's return value in the example, but a serious graphics program should do this. The program could then alert the user, or take whatever steps are appropriate.

Copy Text Rectangle to Different Screen Location

```
int movetext( left, top, right, bottom leftDest, topDest )
int left;              /* coordinates of rectangle to be moved */
int top;
int right;
int bottom;
int leftDest;          /* upper left corner of destination */
int topDest;
```

You might use **movetext()** to move a text-filled window around on the screen when the user wants to reposition it.

Saving and Restoring Screen Text

The text on a rectangular part of the screen can be saved in memory, and later restored to the same or a different location on the screen. This is useful in a variety of circumstances. You may want to put a small window on top of existing text on the screen and later remove it, restoring the existing text to its previous state. You may also have noticed how some applications, including Turbo C itself, save the existing screen before they begin, and restore it when the user exits. Our next example does the same thing, using the functions **gettext()** and **puttext()**.

```
/* savetext.c */
/* demonstrates saving and restoring screen text */
#include <conio.h>            /* needed for text functions */
#define LEFT    1             /* define entire screen */
#define TOP     1
#define RIGHT  80
#define BOT    25
int buff[80][25];            /* buffer for screen contents */

void main(void)
{
   int x, y, j;
                              /* save previous screen contents */
```

```
gettext( LEFT, TOP, RIGHT, BOT, buff );
x = wherex();              /* save previous cursor position */
y = wherey();
clrscr();                  /* clear screen */
for( j=0; j<300; j++ )     /* fill screen with text */
   cputs( "Turbo C  " );
getche();                  /* hold image until key press */
                           /* restore previous screen */
puttext( LEFT, TOP, RIGHT, BOT, buff );
gotoxy( x, y-1 );          /* restore cursor position */
}
```

This program first saves the contents of the entire screen to a memory buffer **buff**, using **gettext()**. The buffer requires two bytes for every screen character, so we use an integer data type, placing one character in each integer array element. We use a two-dimensional array, with the width and height of the entire screen as array dimensions. (A one-dimensional array 80x25, or 2000 integers, works just as well.)

The function takes as arguments the screen coordinates of the area to be saved, and the address in memory to store it.

Copy Text from Screen to Memory

```
int gettext( left, top, right, bottom, addr )
int left;       /* coordinates of rectangle to be copied */
int top;
int right;
int bottom;
void *addr;     /* address of buffer to hold text */
```

The program also clears the screen, using the graphics function **clrscr()**.

Clears Text Window

```
void clrscr( void )
```

This function takes no arguments and returns no value: it's all action.

The **puttext()** function is similar to **gettext()**, except that it moves text from memory back to the screen:

Copy Text from Memory to Screen

```
int puttext( left, top, right, bottom, addr )
int left;      /* coordinates of rectangle to be copied */
int top;
int right;
int bottom;
void *addr;    /* address of buffer holding text */
```

The type **void ***, used for the address of the data buffer, specifies a pointer of *any* kind of data. Thus your buffer can be of type **char**, or if you prefer, of type **int**.

The program also saves the location of the cursor, and, before exiting, restores it to its original position. The cursor location is obtained with the functions **wherex()** and **wherey()**. These record the x and y coodinates of the cursor.

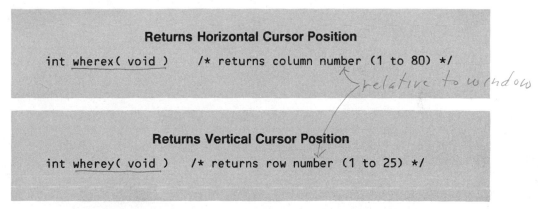

Returns Horizontal Cursor Position

```
int wherex( void )     /* returns column number (1 to 80) */
```

relative to window

Returns Vertical Cursor Position

```
int wherey( void )     /* returns row number (1 to 25) */
```

The type **void** means there are no arguments to these functions.

At the end of the program, the **gotoxy()** function restores the cursor to the previous position.

When the program runs, it fills the entire screen with the words "Turbo C." When the user presses a key, the program restores the previously saved screen contents using **puttext()**, and exits. Doing this lends a professional effect to any program.

Return of the Editor

Let's put the functions we've learned about so far, and some new ones, into a small application. This program is a variation of the wpro2.c editor from Chapter 10. Instead of working with only one line, it lets you edit all the text

p 394

that is in a window. The cursor control keys can position the cursor anywhere in the window, and text can be typed at that point.

The program introduces several new library functions. A new line can be inserted in a window at the current cursor position using **insline()**, and an existing line can be deleted using **delline()**. The keys [Ins] and [Del] are used to insert and delete lines.

Insert Text Line in Window

```
void insline( void )
```

Delete Text Line in Window

```
void delline( void )
```

Two other new functions used in the program are **highvideo()** and **lowvideo()**. The first sets the text to intensified, while the second restores it to normal. These options can be selected using the [Alt] [H] and [Alt] [L] key combinations.

Change to Intensified Text

```
void highvideo( void )
```

Change to Normal Text

```
void lowvideo( void )
```

We've also used the **gettext()** and **puttext()** functions to create an *undo* feature for our editor. Before a line is either inserted or deleted, the program saves the contents of the screen. Then, if the user decides that the insertion or deletion is a mistake, pressing the [Alt] [U] key combination restores the previous state of the screen.

Finally, if you're using a color display, you can change the text color by pressing [Alt] [C] followed by a single digit representing the color. (This gives you the first 9 of 15 colors.)

Here's the listing:

```
/* ezedit.c */
/* mini editor works in window */
#include <conio.h>                /* needed for text functions */
#define LEFT    10                /* left side of window */
#define TOP      8                /* top of window */
#define RIGHT   50                /* right side of window */
#define BOT     21                /* bottom of window */
#define WIDTH   (RIGHT-LEFT+1)    /* width of window */
#define HEIGHT  (BOT-TOP+1)       /* height of window */
#define TRUE     1
#define ESC     27                /* escape key */
#define L_ARRO  75                /* cursor control keys */
#define R_ARRO  77
#define U_ARRO  72
#define D_ARRO  80
#define INS     82                /* other extended code keys */
#define DEL     83
#define ALT_H   35
#define ALT_L   38
#define ALT_C   46
#define ALT_U   22
int buff [WIDTH] [HEIGHT];        /* buffer for undo */

void main(void)
{
   int x, y;
   char key;

   clrscr();                          /* clear entire screen */
   window( LEFT, TOP, RIGHT, BOT );   /* define window */
   x = 1; y = 1;                      /* position cursor */
   textbackground( RED );             /* set background color */

   while( (key=getch()) != ESC )      /* if [Esc], exit loop */
      {
      if( key == 0 )                  /* if extended code, */
         {
         switch( getch() )            /* read second character */
            {
            case L_ARRO:              /* move cursor left */
               if( x > 1 )
                  gotoxy( --x, y );
               break;
```

```
                 case R_ARRO:              /* move cursor right */
                    if( x < WIDTH )
                       gotoxy( ++x, y );
                    break;
                 case U_ARRO:              /* move cursor up */
                    if( y > 1 )
                       gotoxy( x, --y );
                    break;
                 case D_ARRO:              /* move cursor down */
                    if( y < HEIGHT )
                       gotoxy( x, ++y );
                    break;
                 case INS:                 /* insert new line */
                    gettext( LEFT, TOP, RIGHT, BOT, buff );
                    insline();
                    break;
                 case DEL:                 /* delete line */
                    gettext( LEFT, TOP, RIGHT, BOT, buff );
                    delline();
                    break;
                 case ALT_H:               /* intensified text */
                    highvideo();
                    break;
                 case ALT_L:               /* normal text */
                    lowvideo();
                    break;
                 case ALT_C:               /* change text color */
                    textcolor( getch()-'0' );
                    break;
                 case ALT_U:               /* undo: restore window */
                    puttext( LEFT, TOP, RIGHT, BOT, buff );
                    break;
                 } /* end switch */
              } /* end if */
           else                            /* not extended code */
              {
              putch( key );                /* print normal char */
              x = wherex();                /* update cursor */
              y = wherey();
              }
           } /* end while */
        }
```

p 465

p 394

The overall structure of the program is similar to that of wpro2.c in Chapter 10. If the user types a key with an extended code, the program uses a

switch statement to figure out what the code was and acts accordingly. However, because the program defines a window, all the screen output is confined to the window. The coordinates **x** and **y** measure the cursor's position relative to the window edges.

If a normal character (not an extended code) is typed, the **putch()** function will display it. However, in so doing it will move the cursor either one character to the right, or to the beginning of the next line. To make sure it keeps track of the cursor's location, the program reads its coordinates after every use of **putch()**, using the **wherex()** and **wherey()** functions.

Other Text-Mode Functions

We've covered almost all the text-mode functions. Others are **cprintf()**, which acts like **printf()** but writes to a window rather than the screen; **clreol()**, which clears to the end of the current line; **textattr()**, which sets both text and background colors at the same time; and **normvideo()**, which restores the previous intensity, whether high or low. Another function, **gettextinfo()**, reads several kinds of information into a structure: the video mode, the window postion and dimensions, the foreground and background colors, and the cursor position.

The **textmode()** function changes from one text mode to another. It takes one of the following values as an argument:

Value	Mnemonic	Change to
−1	LASTMODE	previous text mode
0	BW40	black and white, 40 columns
1	C40	color, 40 columns
2	BW80	black and white, 80 columns
3	C80	color, 80 columns
7	MONO	monochrome, 80 columns

This function should be used only to switch between text modes, and not from graphics to text mode.

The function **getche()**, like **putch()**, has been modified to echo input characters to the appropriate place in a window if one is active.

Note that the Turbo C window functions don't permit multiple windows to be active at the same time. Functions like **cputs()** relate only to the last window defined. However, you can create the effect of multiple windows by defining one window and writing to it, then defining another window and writing to it.

Graphics-Mode Functions

By far the largest number of graphics functions in Turbo C are for graphics mode, that is, putting pixels on a graphics screen to form lines, shapes, and patterns. In this section we'll look at these functions.

Initializing Graphics Mode

Before any of the graphics-mode functions can be used, the graphics system must be initialized by the function **initgraph()**. This function loads a graphics driver (like cga.bgi) from the disk and changes the display to the appropriate graphics mode.

Our next example uses **initgraph()** to initialize the system, and then draws a circle and a line. Here's the listing:

```
/* circline.c */
/* draws circle and line */
#include <graphics.h>
void main(void)
{
    int driver, mode;          /* graphics driver and mode */
    int x1=0, y1=0;            /* one end of line */
    int x2=199, y2=199;        /* the other end of line */
    int xC=100, yC=100;        /* center of circle */
    int radius=90;             /* radius of circle */

    driver = CGA;             /* CGA driver */
    mode = CGAC0;             /* palette 0 */

                              /* initialize graphics */
    initgraph( &driver, &mode, "c:\\tc\\bgi" );

    line( x1, y1, x2, y2 );    /* draw line */
    circle( xC, yC, radius );  /* draw circle */

    getche();                 /* keep picture until keypress */
    closegraph();             /* shut down graphics system */
}
```

p477

The **initgraph()** function is of type **void far**, and takes three arguments of type **int far ***. These are the addresses where the graphics driver and mode will be specified, and the address of a string holding the pathname to the graphics driver.

Initialize Graphics System

```
void far initgraph( addrDriver, addrMode, addrPath )
int far *addrDriver;   /* address holds driver number */
int far *addrMode;     /* address holds mode number */
int far *addrPath;     /* address of driver)path string */
```

Here are the choices for the graphics driver:

Value	Constant	Comment
0	DETECT	System detects highest graphics mode
1	CGA	
2	MCGA	
3	EGA	256K memory on EGA board
4	EGA64	64K memory on EGA board
5	EGAMONO	
6	IBM8514	
7	HERCMONO	Hercules
8	ATT400	
9	VGA	
10	PC3270	

The constants shown in the table are stored in graphics.h, so you can use either the constant or the value it represents as an argument.

For each driver there are several choices for the mode. For example, here are the modes for the CGA, EGA, and VGA drivers, as seen in the following table.

Driver	Value	Constant	Resolution	Pages	Colors
CGA	0	CGAC0	320x200	1	palette 0, 4 colors
	1	CGAC1	320x200	1	palette 1, 4 colors
	2	CGAC2	320x200	1	palette 2, 4 colors
	3	CGAC3	320x200	1	palette 3, 4 colors
	4	CGAHI	640x200	1	2 colors
EGA	0	EGALO	640x200	4	16 colors
	1	EGAHI	640x350	2	16 colors
VGA	0	VGALO	640x200	2	16 colors
	1	VGAMED	640x350	2	16 colors
	2	VGAHI	640x480	1	16 colors

The .BGI Files

The third argument to **initgraph()** is the pathname for the graphics driver. This driver is a file like cga.bgi or egavga.bgi. You would use the first of these to run programs in CGA modes, and the second for EGA or VGA modes. Other drivers are available for other display standards, such as Hercules and IBM 8514.

In the current version of Turbo C, these driver files are located in the subdirectory \TC\BGI, so this is the pathname used in the argument to **initgraph()**. Remember that in C the backslash is used as an escape character, so it must be doubled when used in an argument string. (You can substitute a forward slash (/), which MS-DOS interprets as a backslash; a forward slash does not need to be doubled.)

Because the graphics driver is a separate file, your program must be able to access it to run. Thus your program cannot run as a stand-alone application. The final section of this chapter, "Creating Stand-Alone Executables," shows how to circumvent this problem.

The graphics.h File

The graphics.h header file must be **#included** in every program that uses graphics functions (except the text mode functions). This file contains prototypes and constants for the graphics functions. The prototypes are essential because (among other reasons) the graphics functions return type **far**.

The graphics.lib file

The graphic.lib file contains the code for the graphics functions. If you use any of these functions in your program, the appropriate sections of this file are automatically linked with your program.

Lines and Circles

Once the circline.c program has initialized the graphics system, it draws a circle with a line through it, as shown in Figure 12-3.

The function that draws the line, **line()**, requires four parameters: the x and y coordinates of the start of the line, and the x and y coordinates of the end.

Draw Line Between Two Locations

```
void far line( x1, x2, y1, y2 )
int x1;    /* coordinates of one end of line */  pixels
int y1;
int x2;    /* coordinates of other end of line */
int y2;
```

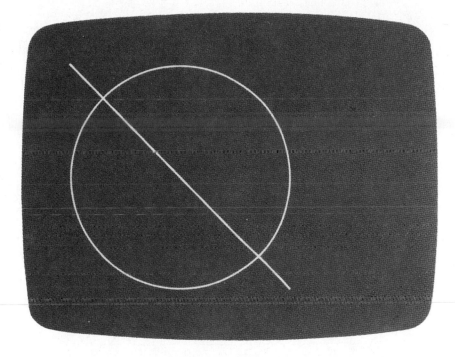

Figure 12-3. Output of circline.c Program

All these coordinates are expressed in pixels, measured from x=0 y=0 at the top lefthand corner of the screen. The arguments to the functions are of type **int** (as are the majority of arguments to graphics-mode functions).

The circle function requires the x and y coordinates of the center of the circle, and the circle's radius.

Draw Circle

```
void far circle( xC, yC, radius )
int xC;        /* center of circle (pixels) */
int yC;
int radius;    /* radius of circle */
```

Errors

If some functions—such as **initgraph()**—fail, they cause an error code to be generated in the graphics system. This error code can be queried with the function **graphresult()**.

Returns Error Code

```
int far graphresult( void )
```

The following example demonstrates the use of this function:

```
/* error.c */
/* draws circle and line */
#include <graphics.h>
void main(void)
{
    int driver, mode, error;
    char *errptr;                       /* pointer to error message */

    driver = CGA;                   /* CGA driver */
    mode = CGACO;                   /* palette 0 */
                                    /* bad path name */
    initgraph( &driver, &mode, "c:\\not\\here" );

    error = graphresult();          /* check for error */
    if( error )
       {
       printf("Error %d \n", error);    /* print error number */
       errptr = grapherrormsg( error ); /* get message ptr */
       puts( errptr );                  /* print message */
       }
    else
       puts("No error\n");
    getche();                       /* keep display until keypress */
    closegraph();                   /* shut down graphics system */
}
```

Once the error number has been discovered, it can be used as an argument to the function **grapherrormsg()**, which returns a pointer to a standard message.

Returns Error Message

```
char * far grapherrormsg( error )
int error;       /* error code */
```

The error.c program intentionally creates an error by using a pathname that does not contain the graphics driver. The program responds to this unfortunate mistake with the output:

```
Error -3
Device driver file not found (CGA.BGI)
```

A list of error messages can be found in the description of **graphresult()** in the Turbo C++ documentation.

Most of the example programs in this chapter do not include this sort of error-checking code. This makes the listings shorter and easier to understand. However, in a serious program, **graphresult()** should be employed whenever there is the slightest chance that a function might be improperly used. Examining the error code will make an application—and the program's user—aware of errors that might otherwise go undetected.

Autoinitialization

So far in this chapter we've explicitly told **initgraph()** what graphics driver and mode to use. This was done by giving values to the **driver** and **mode** arguments to this function. It is also possible to let the graphics system figure out for itself what graphics adaptor is connected to the computer, and use the "best" driver and mode—that is, the combination that gives the highest resolution.

There are two approaches to doing this. In the first, a special constant is used for the **driver** argument to **initgraph()**. This constant is defined in graphics.h as DETECT, which has a value of zero. Using this argument causes the system to choose the highest resolution adaptor and mode.

When DETECT is used, the program does not know in advance what mode will be used, and cannot assume anything about the screen resolution. To discover this, the **getmaxx()** and **getmaxy()** functions can be used. They return the pixel width and height of the screen.

The following program uses the DETECT argument to **initgraph()** to allow the system to choose the adaptor and mode. It then draws a border around the outside edge of the screen. To do this, it must know the screen dimensions, which it obtains with **getmaxx()** and **getmaxy()**.

```
/* border.c */
/* draws border around screen */
/* works with all graphics modes */
#include <graphics.h>
void main(void)
{
    int driver = DETECT;        /* auto-detect driver */
    int mode;                   /* use best mode */
```

```
    int maxx, maxy;            /* size of screen in pixels */
    int left, top, right, bot;  /* sides of rectangle */

    initgraph( &driver, &mode, "c:\\tc\\bgi" );
    maxx = getmaxx();          /* get screen dimensions */
    maxy = getmaxy();
    left = top = 0;            /* set rectangle sides */
    right = maxx;              /*    to edges of screen */
    bot = maxy;
    rectangle( left, top, right, bot );   /* draw rectangle */
    getche();                  /* wait for character */
    closegraph();              /* shut down graphics system */
}
```

The **getmaxx()** and **getmaxy()** functions are similar. They take no arguments, and return the appropriate dimension in pixels.

Returns Maximum Horizontal Screen Coordinate

```
int far getmaxx( void )
```

Returns Maximum Vertical Screen Coordinate

```
int far getmaxy( void )
```

The border is drawn with the function **rectangle()**. It takes four arguments that specify, in pixels, the the four edges of the rectangle to be drawn. As with other pixel-based graphics functions, the coordinate system starts at 0,0 in the upper left hand corner.

Draw Rectangle

```
void far rectangle( left, top, right, bottom )
int left;       /* edges of rectangle */  in pixels
int top;
int right;
int bottom;
```

In the second approach to autoinitialization, a function called **detect-graph()** returns values for the best driver and mode. These values can then be used as input to **initgraph()**.

In the following example, rather than sending the values to **initgraph()**, we print them out. This lets the user see what graphics adaptor is connected to the system, and what mode is the best available on the adaptor.

```
/* detect.c */
/* finds graphics driver and mode in use */
#include <graphics.h>
void main(void)
{
    int driver;                    /* graphics driver */
    int mode;                      /* graphics mode */
                                   /* find best driver and mode */
    detectgraph( &driver, &mode );
    if( driver == -2 )
        printf("No graphics hardware\n");
    printf("Driver = %d, mode = %d\n", driver, mode );
    getche();
}
```

p 477

The **detectgraph()** function takes as parameters two addresses into which the system can place the adaptor and mode numbers.

Returns Best Adaptor and Mode in System

```
void far detectgraph( addrDriver, addrMode )
int far *addrDriver;   /* address for driver number */
int far *addrMode;     /* address for mode number */
```

This function also returns an error number. If no graphics hardware at all is connected to the system, it will return −2, and place −2 in the **addrDriver** address.

The **detectgraph()** function is often used when the program (or the user) needs to make decisions based on the available graphics equipment. For example, an application might work with EGA and VGA graphics, but not work correctly using CGA. In this case the program could use **detectgraph()** to find out what adaptor was available, and send an error message or terminate the program if there was nothing better than CGA.

Line and Color

It's possible to vary the thickness of the lines used by the Turbo C graphics functions. This is done with the **setlinestyle()** function. The next example draws the same circle and line as did the circline.c program, but using thicker lines. Here's the listing:

p480

```
/* linetype.c */
/* draws circle and line with different line styles */
#include <graphics.h>
#define IGNORED  0
void main(void)
{
    int driver, mode;              /* graphics driver and mode */
    int x1=0, y1=0;                /* one end of line */
    int x2=199, y2=199;            /* the other end of line */
    int xC=100, yC=100;            /* center of circle */
    int radius=90;                 /* radius of circle */

    driver = CGA;                  /* CGA driver */
    mode = CGAC0;                  /* palette 0 */
                                   /* initialize graphics */
    initgraph( &driver, &mode, "c:\\tc\\bgi" );
                                   /* line pattern and thickness */
    setlinestyle( DASHED_LINE, IGNORED, THICK_WIDTH );
    line( x1, y1, x2, y2 );        /* draw line */
    circle( xC, yC, radius );      /* draw circle */

    getche();                      /* keep picture until keypress */
    closegraph();                  /* shut down graphics system */
}
```

p485

The result is shown in Figure 12-4.

An interesting aspect of the output is that the straight line is dashed, but the circle is not. The **setlinestyle()** function includes a parameter to specify different kinds of dotted lines (the line "style"), but this parameter applies only to straight lines, not to circles or other curved lines.

Specify Line Width and Style

```
void far setlinestyle( style, pattern, thickness )
int style;          /* solid, dotted, dashed, etc. */
unsigned pattern;   /* user-defined pattern
                       (when style=4) */
int thickness;      /* normal or thick */
```

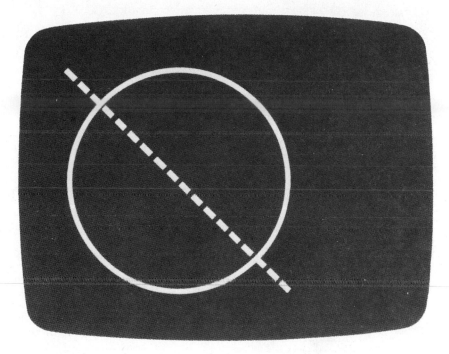

Figure 12-4. Output of the linetype.c Program

Here are the possible values for the **style** parameter.

Value	Constant
0	SOLID_LINE
1	DOTTED_LINE
2	CENTER_LINE
3	DASHED_LINE
4	USERBIT_LINE

A center line (used to indicate the center of objects in mechanical draw-ings) has a dot-dash, dot-dash pattern. If the USERBIT_LINE value is used for the **style** argument, then the **pattern** argument defines a 16-bit value, where each bit specifies whether a corresponding dot on a line section will be on or off. For example, a hex value of 0xFF00 would turn on the first half of the section and turn off the second, thus creating long dashes. 0xF0F0 would make shorter dashes, and 0xF6F6 provides a dash-dot dash-dot effect.

485

The **thickness** parameter has two possible values:

Value	Constant	Comment
1	NORM_WIDTH	1 pixel line width
3	THICK_WIDTH	3 pixels line width

p480

The **graphresult()** function will return −11 if improper arguments are used for **setlinestyle()**.

It is also possible to specify the color of lines, circles, and other graphics elements. This is effected with the **setcolor()** option. The next program draws the same line and circle as in previous examples, but colors the line light green and the circle light red.

```c
/* lincolor.c */
/* draws circle and line with different colors */
#include <graphics.h>
#define IGNORED  0
#define CGACO_LIGHTGREEN 1      /* CGA palette 0 colors */
#define CGACO_LIGHTRED   2
void main(void)
{
    int driver, mode;               /* graphics driver and mode */
    int x1=0, y1=0;                 /* one end of line */
    int x2=199, y2=199;             /* the other end of line */
    int xC=100, yC=100;             /* center of circle */
    int radius=90;                  /* radius of circle */

    driver = CGA;                   /* CGA driver */
    mode = CGACO;                   /* palette 0 */
                                    /* initialize graphics */
    initgraph( &driver, &mode, "c:\\tc\\bgi" );
                                    /* line pattern and thickness */
    setlinestyle( DASHED_LINE, IGNORED, THICK_WIDTH );

    setcolor( CGACO_LIGHTGREEN );   /* set color */
    line( x1, y1, x2, y2 );         /* draw line */
    setcolor( CGACO_LIGHTRED );     /* set color */
    circle( xC, yC, radius );       /* draw circle */

    getche();                       /* keep picture until keypress */
    closegraph();                   /* shut down graphics system */
}
```

p487

The **setcolor()** function takes only one argument: the color.

Specifies Color

```
void far setcolor( color )
int color;   /* color value for drawing operations */
```

The colors that can be used depend on what graphics mode is in use. In the present example we use CGA palette 0, which has four colors: black, light green, light red, and yellow. If we were using palette 1 we could select from black, light cyan, light magenta, and white. The colors for CGA are not defined in graphics.h, so we define our own constants using **#define** statements. Here are the CGA colors for different pallets:

Palette	Color 0	Color 1	Color 2	Color 3
CGAC0	BLACK	LIGHTGREEN	LIGHTRED	YELLOW
CGAC1	BLACK	LIGHTCYAN	LIGHTMAGENTA	WHITE
CGAC2	BLACK	GREEN	RED	BROWN
CGAC3	BLACK	CYAN	MAGENTA	LIGHTGRAY

In EGA and VGA graphics there are more color choices, which are defined in the graphics.h file. We've already seen the 16 constants for EGA graphics. (They're also listed in Appendix E.) For example, to modify the lincolor.c program to work in EGA and print the line in red and the circle in blue, we would change the driver and mode value to EGA and EGAHI:

p 465
p 710

```
driver = EGA;
mode = EGAHI;
```

p 477

Also, the parameters to **setcolor()** would be changed as shown:

p 465

```
setcolor( RED );          /* set EGA color */
line( x1, y1, x2, y2 );   /* draw line */
setcolor( BLUE );         /* set EGA color */
circle( xC, yC, radius ); /* draw circle */
```

No **#define** statements need be used, since the constants are already defined in graphics.h.

Ellipses and Polygons

Besides lines, circles, and rectangles, which we've encountered already, Turbo C also provides functions to create ellipses and polygons.

Here's a program that generates a series of nested ellipses.

```
/* ellipse.c */
/* draws nested ellipses */
#include <graphics.h>
void main(void)
{
    int driver, mode;               /* graphics driver and mode */
    int xE=150, yE=100;             /* center of ellipse */
    int xRad=150, yRad;             /* radii of ellipse */
    int stAngle=0, endAngle=360;    /* arc start and end angles */

    driver = CGA;                   /* CGA driver */
    mode = CGAC0;                   /* palette 0 */
                                    /* initialize graphics */
    initgraph( &driver, &mode, "c:\\tc\\bgi" );

                                    /* draw ellipses */
    for( yRad=0; yRad<100; yRad+=10 )       /* step thru y radii */
        ellipse( xE, yE, stAngle, endAngle, xRad, yRad );

    getche();                       /* keep picture until keypress */
    closegraph();                   /* shut down graphics system */
}
```

An ellipse has two radii, one in the x direction and one in the y direction. In this example, we vary the y radius so that 10 ellipses are drawn. The effect looks something like a watermelon, as shown in Figure 12-5.

The **ellipse()** function takes six arguments:

Draws Ellipse

```
void far ellipse( xE, yE, stAngle, endAngle, xRad, yRad )
int xE;             /* center of ellipse */
int yE;
int stAngle;        /* starting and ending angles */
int endAngle;
int xRad;           /* radii of ellipse */
int yRad;
```

The center of the ellipse corresponds to our intuitive idea of the center; it's not one of the focii used in geometry. If it is desired to draw only part of the ellipse—an elliptical arc— then the starting and ending angles can specify this arc. The angles are measured starting with 0 degrees at the 3 o'clock position, and increase counterclockwise, as they do on the coordinate plane.

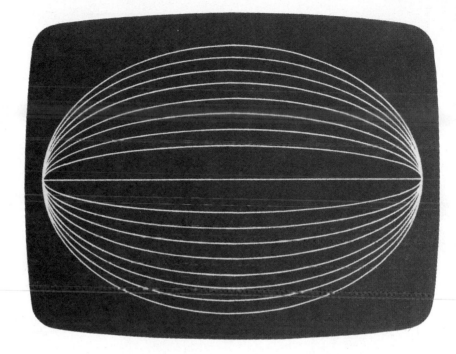

Figure 12-5. Output of the ellipse.c Program

The x and y radii correspond to the semimajor and semiminor axes used in geometry.

Polygons are figures consisting of an arbitrary number of straight line segments. Examples are triangles, rectangles, parallelograms (four-sided figures in which opposite sides are parallel but don't meet at right angles), trapezoids (four-sided figures in which only one pair of sides is parallel), pentagons (five-sided figures) and so forth. Actually, any connection of line segments is considered a polygon in Turbo C. The lines don't need to form a closed figure, and they can cross over each other.

In Turbo C the starting and ending point of each of these lines is placed on a list, and the function **drawpoly()** then creates the polygon from the list.

Here's an example that uses polygons to create the effect of a three-dimensional box. The front of the box consists of a rectangle, but the top and right side of the box are polygons, as shown in Figure 12-6.

The **drawpoly()** function takes only two parameters. The first is the number of points to connect with lines, and the second is the address of a list containing the points to connect.

The list of points is an array of integer values, with two values—the x coordinate first and then y—for each point. The **number** variable is the number of points, *not* the number of integers (since there are two integers per point).

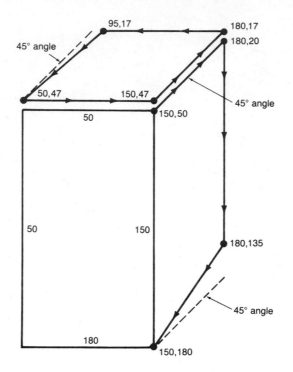

Figure 12-6. Output of the poly.c Program

Draws Polygon

```
void far drawpoly( number, addrList )
int number;          /* number of points */
int far *addrList;   /* address of list of points */
```

To form a complete four-sided polygon, *five* points must be specified; the first point must be repeated at the end of the list, since that's where the last line segment ends. We use five points for the top polygon. We've also moved the top polygon up three pixels to provide visual separation between it and the rest of the box. For the polygon on the right we specify only four points. This creates three lines. The missing line corresponds with the right hand line of the rectangle, so it doesn't need to be drawn.

In theory the top and side would be parallelograms (both pairs of sides equal, but to make the perspective convincing the lines that appear to go toward the back of the picture must converge on an imaginary single point. This is shown in the figure. The figure also uses arrows to show the order in which the points are placed on the lists.

Here's the listing:

```
/* poly.c */
/* draws polygons */
#include <graphics.h>
#define LEFT    50              /* coordinates for rectangle */
#define TOP     50
#define RIGHT   150
#define BOT     180

                               /* coordinates for polygons */
int rightpara[] = { 150,50, 180,20, 180,135, 150,180 };
int toppara[] = { 50,47, 150,47, 180,17, 95,17, 50,47 };

void main(void)
{
   int driver, mode;           /* graphics driver and mode */
   driver = CGA;               /* CGA driver */
   mode = CGAC0;               /* palette 0 */

                               /* initialize graphics */
   initgraph( &driver, &mode, "c:\\tc\\bgi" );
   rectangle( LEFT, TOP, RIGHT, BOT );
   drawpoly( 4, rightpara );
   drawpoly( 5, toppara );

   getche();                   /* keep figure until keypress */
   closegraph();               /* shut down graphics system */
}
```

Filling and Patterns

Turbo C can fill the outlines of graphics shapes with color by using several functions. One of the most useful functions is **fillpoly()**. This function is similar to **drawpoly()** in that it draws a polygon. However, it goes further by filling the inside of the polygon with the current fill pattern and fill color.

Draws and Fills Polygon

```
void far fillpoly( number, addrList )
int number;        /* number of points */
int far *addrList; /* address of list of points */
```

The current fill pattern and fill color are established by another function, **setfillstyle()**.

Set Fill Pattern and Color

```
void far setfillstyle( pattern, color )
int pattern;
int color;
```

The **pattern** variable can be one of the following, as is defined in graphics.h:

Name	Number	Result
EMPTY_FILL	0	sold background
SOLID_FILL	1	solid color
LINE_FILL	2	horiz lines
LTSLASH_FILL	3	///// thin lines
SLASH_FILL	4	///// thick lines
BKSLASH_FILL	5	\\\\\ thick lines
LTBKSLASH_FILL	6	\\\\\ thin lines
HATCH_FILL	7	light hatch
XHATCH_FILL	8	heavy cross-hatch
INTERLEAVE_FILL	9	interleaved lines
WIDE_DOT_FILL	10	wide-spaced dots
CLOSE_DOT_FILL	11	close-spaced dots
USER_FILL	12	user-defined pattern

We won't demonstrate the process, but you can create custom patterns by specifying the pattern with another function, **setfillpattern()**, and setting the **pattern** argument in **setfillstyle()** to USER_FILL.

The color is selected from the same list as it was for **setcolor()**. Invalid input to the function results in an error code of −11 being returned to **graphresult()**.

Here's an example program that draws the same three-dimensional box as drawpoly.c, and then fills the front of the box with one color and pattern, and the top and side with a different color and pattern, as shown in Figure 12-7.

```
/* fillpoly.c */
/* draws polygons, fills them with color */
#include <graphics.h>
#define CGA0_LIGHTRED   2       /* CGA palette 0 colors */
```

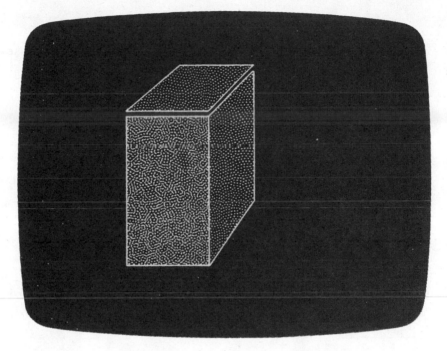

Figure 12-7. Output of the fillpoly.c Program

```
#define CGAO_YELLOW      3
                                     /* front rectangle */
int rect[] = { 50,50, 150,50, 150,180, 50,180, 50,50 };
                                     /* side (forth edge on rect) */
int sidepara[] = { 150,50, 180,20, 180,135, 150,180 };
                                     /* top (raised 3 pixels) */
int toppara[] = { 50,47, 150,47, 180,17, 95,17, 50,47 };

void main(void)
{
    int driver, mode;               /* graphics driver and mode */
    driver = CGA;                   /* CGA driver */
    mode = CGAC0;                   /* palette 0 */
                                    /* initialize graphics */
    initgraph( &driver, &mode, "c:\\tc\\bgi" );
                                    /* set fill for rectangle */
    setfillstyle( CLOSE_DOT_FILL, CGAO_YELLOW );
    fillpoly( 5, rect );            /* draw front rectangle */
                                    /* set fill for side and top */
    setfillstyle( SOLID_FILL, CGAO_LIGHTRED );
    fillpoly( 4, sidepara );        /* draw side polygon */
```

```
        fillpoly( 5, toppara );        /* draw top polygon */

        getche();                      /* keep picture until keypress */
        closegraph();                  /* shut down graphics system */
}
```

We use **fillpoly()** to draw and fill the front rectangle as well as the top and side polygons.

Another approach to filling areas is the **floodfill()** function. The advantage of this function is that it fills any arbitrary area, whether it's a polygon, a circle, an ellipse, or a series of unrelated lines or dots. The disadvantage is that it doesn't always work correctly in the CGA graphics modes.

Fill Any Bounded Area

```
void far floodfill( x, y, border )
int x;        /* x coordinate for fill start */
int y;        /* y coordinate for fill start */
int border;   /* color of border */
```

The **floodfill()** function needs to know the point where the fill begins. This point is called the *seed point*. The fill will spread outward from the seed point until it encounters a boundary with the color specified in the **border** parameter. The area either outside or inside a shape can be filled, depending where the seed point is located. If you try to fill an area that is not completely bounded, the fill will "escape" and cover the area outside as well as inside of the object.

Here's a program that fills a circle. It's intended to work with EGA graphics.

```
/* floodco.c */
/* fills circle with color using floodfill() */
#include <graphics.h>
#define XC       300
#define YC       175
#define RADIUS   150

void main(void)
{
    int driver, mode;        /* graphics driver and mode */

    driver = EGA;            /* CGA driver */
    mode = EGAHI;            /* palette 0 */
```

```
                           /* initialize graphics */
initgraph( &driver, &mode, "c:\\tc\\bgi" );
setcolor( RED );                    /* set line color */
circle( XC, YC, RADIUS );           /* draw circle */
setfillstyle( CLOSE_DOT_FILL, BLUE ); /* set fill pattern */
floodfill( XC, YC, RED );           /* fill circle */

getche();                           /* keep picture until keypress */
closegraph();                       /* shut down graphics system */
}
```

p492

The color used for fill may be the same or different from that used to outline the area. Note, however, that the color used in the **border** parameter to **floodfill()** must be the same as that used to draw the shape. In this case, the constant RED is used for both these arguments.

Graphs

Turbo C contains several functions that simplify the creation of graphs. These are **bar()**, **bar3d()**, and **pieslice()**. The first two are similar. Both draw a rectangle, and fill it with the current color and fill pattern, thus creating a bar suitable for use in a bar graph. The difference is that **bar3d()** also draws lines to the right and (optionally) above the bar to provide a 3-dimensional effect.

Draw 3-Dimensional Bar

```
void far bar3d( left, top, right, bottom, topflag )
int left;       /* coordinates of bar */
int top;
int right;
int bottom;
int depth;      /* "depth" of bar */
int topflag;    /* 0=no top on bar, !0=top */
```

Our next example uses **bar3d()** to create a simple graph. The result is shown in Figure 12-8.

The program could simply use 10 calls to **bar3d()**, each with different arguments. However, a program is easier to modify if it uses a loop to call the function repeatedly, changing the arguments each time to draw bars of different heights at different positions. Using **#define** statements, we can make it easy to change the number of bars, and their width, depth, separation, and other characteristics.

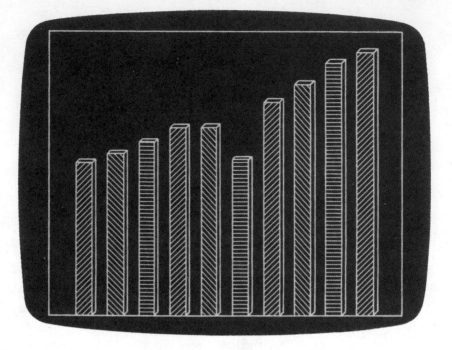

Figure 12-8. Output of the bargraph.c Program

```
/* bargraph.c */
/* generates bar graph */
#include <graphics.h>
#define N          10         /* number of values to graph */
#define BWIDTH     10         /* width of each bar */
#define SEP        12         /* separation between bars */
#define DI         (BWIDTH+SEP) /* distance from bar to bar */
#define SHFT       15         /* between border and 1st bar */
#define WIDTH   ( (N+1) * DI ) /* width of chart */
#define LEFT       5          /* left side of graph */
#define DEPTH      3          /* depth of bar */
#define TOPFLAG    1          /* put 3-D top on bar */
#define BOT        170        /* bottom of graph */
#define TOP        5          /* top of graph */
#define PPD (float)(BOT-TOP)/100   /* pixels per data unit */

void main(void)
{
    int driver, mode, error, j;
                                    /* data to display */
```

```
int data[N] = { 41, 47, 54, 62, 63, 59,
        75, 83, 89, 96  };
driver = CGA;                   /* initialize graphics */
mode = CGAC1;
initgraph(&driver, &mode, "\\tc\\bgi" );
                                /* draw border */
rectangle( LEFT, TOP, LEFT+WIDTH, BOT );

for( j=0; j<N; j++ )            /* draw bars */
   {
   setfillstyle( SOLID_FILL, 1+j%3 );   /* 3 colors */
   bar3d( LEFT+SHFT+j*DI,         BOT-data[j]*PPD,
         LEFT+SHFT+j*DI+BWIDTH, BOT, DEPTH, TOPFLAG );
   }
getche();
closegraph();
}
```

The program draws a border around the chart with **rectangle()**, then, in a loop, repeatedly sets the color of the bar with **setfillstyle()** and draws the bar with **bar3d**. Three CGA colors are used alternately (black is excluded because black bars don't stand out well).

We'll see a more sophisticated bar graph later in this chapter, when we've learned how to place text on a graphics image.

The function **pieslice()** draws an arc (a part of a circle). It also fills the arc with the current color and fill pattern. Like the ellipse, the angles of the arc are measured with 0 at the 3 o'clock position, running counterclockwise.

Draws and Fills Arc (for Pie Charts)

```
void far pieslice( xP, yP, stAngle, endAngle, radius )
int xA;          /* center of slice */
int yA;
int stAngle;     /* starting and ending angles */
int endAngle;
int radius;      /* radius of slice */
```

Repeated use of this function will generate a pie chart. Pie charts are typically used to show how a quantity is divided up— how the federal budget is spent, for example.

Our demonstration program creates a pie chart from six data items. The angle occupied by each item is calculated by adding all the items together, then dividing the value of each item by this total to find the fraction of the circle it occupies. The first slice begins at the 3 o'clock position, and each succeeding slice starts where the last one ended.

```
/* pie.c */
/* generates pie chart */
#include <graphics.h>
#define N         6              /* number of data items */
#define RADIUS   90              /* radius of pie */
#define X       100              /* center of pie */
#define Y       100
int data[N] = { 11, 19, 44, 32, 15, 7, };  /* data items */

void main(void)
{
   int driver, mode, j;
   float dataSum, startAngle, endAngle, relAngle;

   driver = CGA;                 /* initialize graphics */
   mode = CGAC0;
   initgraph(&driver, &mode, "\\tc\\bgi" );
                                 /* sum the data values */
   for( j=0, dataSum=0; j<N; j++ )
     dataSum += data[j];
   endAngle = 0;                 /* start at 3 o'clock angle */
   for( j=0; j<N; j++ )          /* draw slices */
      {
      startAngle = endAngle;    /* start at end of last slice */
      relAngle = 360 * (data[j] / dataSum); /* calculate angle */
      endAngle = startAngle + relAngle;   /* find end angle */
      setfillstyle( SOLID_FILL, j % 4 );  /* set fill, color */
                                          /* draw one slice */
      pieslice( X, Y, startAngle, endAngle, RADIUS );
      }
   getche();                     /* hold picture until keypress */
   closegraph();                 /* remove graphics system */
}
```

All four CGA colors are used, in order, for the slices.

Viewports

Viewports provide a way to restrict to an arbitrary size the area of the screen used for drawing. They are somewhat like windows in text mode. You can draw an image that would ordinarily occupy the entire screen, but if a viewport is in use, only part of the image will be visible. Note that viewports don't *scale* the image; that is, the image isn't compressed to fit the viewport. Rather, the parts of the image that don't fit in the viewport are simply not visible.

The following example is similar to the circline.c program from earlier in the chapter, except that a viewport is installed that is smaller than the image to be drawn. A rectangle is also drawn around the edge of the viewport so its location is more obvious. Figure 12-9 shows the resulting screen image.

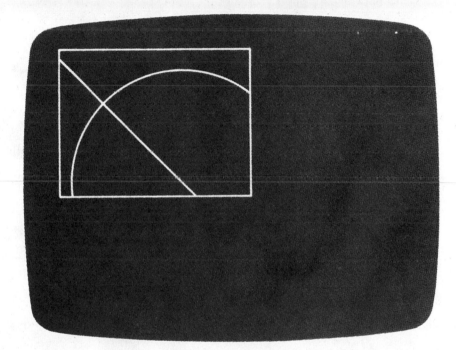

Figure 12-9. Output of the viewport.c Program

```
/* viewport.c */
/* draws circle and line within viewport */
#include <graphics.h>
void main(void)
{
    int driver, mode;              /* graphics driver and mode */
    int left=0, top=0, right=150, bot=100;  /* viewport */
    int clip=1;                    /* viewport clipping enabled */
    int x1=0, y1=0;                /* one end of line */
    int x2=199, y2=199;            /* the other end of line */
    int xC=100, yC=100;            /* center of circle */
    int radius=90;                 /* radius of circle */

    driver = CGA;                  /* CGA driver */
```

```
mode = CGAC0;                          /* palette 0 */
                                       /* initialize graphics */
initgraph( &driver, &mode, "c:\\tc\\bgi" );
                                       /* set viewport dimensions */
setviewport( left, top, right, bot, clip );
                                       /* draw rectangle on viewport */
rectangle( left, top, right, bot );
line( x1, y1, x2, y2 );                /* draw line */
circle( xC, yC, radius );              /* draw circle */
getche();                              /* wait for keypress */
closegraph();                          /* shut down graphics system */
}
```

The viewport is created with the **setviewport()** function.

The clipping parameter determines whether an image will be clipped (not displayed) beyond the boundaries of the viewport. Normally this is set to a nonzero value to provide clipping. The **graphresult()** function will return −11 if invalid input is supplied to this function.

Set Viewport Dimensions

```
void far setviewport( left, top, right, bottom, clip )
int left;      /* dimensions of viewport */
int top;
int right;
int bot;
int clip;      /* 0=no clipping, !0=clipping */
```

Viewports can be used in any situation where it is desirable to restrict the area occupied by an image. In a program that produced both text and graphics, for example, the viewport could be used to place the graphics in one area, while the **window()** function would confine the text to a different area. The size of the viewport and the text window could be controlled by the user, thus providing a capability like Microsoft Windows or the Presentation Manager.

The function **clearviewport()** erases the image from the viewport, leaving the rest of the screen untouched, and **getviewsettings()** returns the dimensions and clipping status of the viewport.

Relative Drawing

So far the graphics functions we've seen have used *absolute* screen coordinates, relative to the top left corner of the screen. Several graphics functions use a *relative* coordinate system. In this system, drawing is done relative to a movable point called the *current position* or CP.

Currently the line is the only graphics element that can be drawn using the relative coordinate system. The program that follows includes a function, **square()** (which is part of the program—not a library function), whose purpose is to draw a box. This function uses the **linerel()** library function, which draws a line relative to the CP.

Draws Line from Current Position

```
void far linerel( dx, dy )
    int dx;      /* horizontal distance from CP */
    int dy       /* vertical distance from CP */
```

The **linerel()** function draws the line, and advances the CP to the end of the line.

Since the **square()** function is not concerned with absolute coordinates, it can be used to draw a box anywhere on the screen. The program makes use of this fact to create a checkerboard, using repeated calls to **square()**, and advancing the CP to the appropriate place with the library function, **moveto()**, which moves the CP to an absolute position on the screen. (Actually this position is not truly absolute: it is relative to the current viewport, if one is in use.)

Move Current Position

```
void far moveto( x, y )
    int x;      /* absolute (or viewport) position */
    int y;      /*     for CP */
```

Here's the example. The main part of the program consists of one loop nested inside another. The inner loop moves the CP across 8 screen positions, calling **square()** to draw a square at each position. The outer loop moves the CP down through the 8 rows.

```
/* checker.c */
/* draws checkerboard, demonstrates relative motion */
#include <graphics.h>
#define MAX    160          /* size of board */
#define GRID   20           /* separation of grid points */
#define SIDE   18           /* size of square */
```

```
void square(int side);            /* prototype */

void main(void)
{
    int driver, mode;
    int x, y;

    driver = CGA;                 /* CGA driver */
    mode = CGACO;                 /* palette 0 */
                                  /* initialize graphics */
    initgraph( &driver, &mode, "c:\\tc\\bgi" );
    for( y=0; y<MAX; y+=GRID )    /* move down rows */
        for( x=0; x<MAX; x+=GRID )/* move across columns */
            {
            moveto( x, y );       /* move current position */
            square(SIDE);         /* draw a square there */
            }
    getche();                     /* wait for keypress */
    closegraph();                 /* remove graphics system */
}

/* square() */
/* function to make square */
void square(int side)
{
    linerel( side, 0 );           /* top, left to right */
    linerel( 0, side );           /* right side, top to bottom */
    linerel( -side, 0 );          /* bottom, right to left */
    linerel( 0, -side );          /* left side, bottom to top */
}
```

Figure 12-10 shows the output of the program.

Many drawing activities are more easily carried out using relative coordinates rather than absolute coordinates. Some systems (such as the "turtle graphics" approach in the Logo programming language) contain a more complete group of relative functions. However, the relative functions in Turbo C will be useful in situations where a simple line drawing is needed.

Related functions are **lineto()**, which draws a line from CP to absolute position x, y, and **moveto()**, which moves the CP relative to the old CP.

The Aspect Ratio Problem

In many graphics modes the pixels are not *square*. In other words, each pixel is higher than it is wide (or vice versa). If you magnified a single pixel, it would look like a rectangle, not a square. (Or, if the pixels on your display are round,

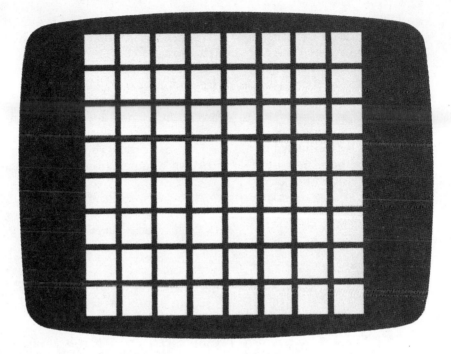

Figure 12-10. Output of the checker.c Program

it would look like an ellipse instead of a circle.) The ratio of a pixel's height to its width is called its *aspect ratio*. A square pixel has an aspect ratio of 1.0.

The fact that pixels are not square leads to some complexities in creating graphics images. When square pixels are used to create a circle, for instance, the circle can be 100 pixels high and 100 pixels wide, and it will look like a circle. However, when pixels have an aspect ratio that differs from 1.0, a 100 pixel by 100 pixel circle will look like an ellipse. If the pixels are too narrow for their height, for instance, the circle will also be too narrow for its height. Similarly, a 100 pixel by 100 pixel square will look like a tall but narrow rectangle.

The typical video screen has a width 4/3 (or 1.3333) times its height. To achieve square pixels there should be 1.3333 times as many pixels per line as there are horizontal lines. This is the case in VGA graphics, which has 640 pixels per line and 480 lines (640/480 = 1.3333). In VGA the pixels are square, with an ideal aspect ratio of 1.0. Both EGA and CGA deviate from this ideal ratio. The ratio in EGA is 1.8286 (640/350), and in CGA it is 1.6 (320/200). Other graphics standards have different ratios.

To compensate for the nonideal aspect ratio of a pixel, Turbo C may take liberties when drawing shapes. Suppose you're in CGA graphics, and you use the **circle()** function to draw a circle, using an argument of 100 as the radius of the circle. You would expect the circle to be 200 pixels high and 200 pixels wide. However, to make it look round, Turbo C makes it only 83 pixels from the center to the top (and from the center to the bottom), although it is 100 pixels from the center to the left or right.

Our next example demonstrates this situation. It draws two circles. The first is created as described, with a radius half the height of the screen. However, this circle does not come close to the top of the screen.

Suppose we want to draw a circle that does just touch the top and bottom of the screen. We could calculate the radius of the circle, which is 100 times 1.3333 divided by 1.6, but it's easier to let the program do it. A Turbo C function **getaspectratio()** returns two numbers from which the aspect ratio of the pixels can be derived.

Gets Pixel Aspect Ratio

```
void far getaspectratio( addrXaspect, addrYaspect )
int far *addrXaspect;    /* address for X part of ratio */
int far *addrYaspect;    /* address for Y part of ratio */
```

This function returns two numbers. The Y part is always 10,000. Dividing the X part, which is less than this (8333 for CGA), by the Y part gives the desired ratio. In our example we use this approach to find the radius to use for the second circle, which will just touch the top and bottom of the screen. Here's the listing:

```
/* aspect.c */
/* shows use of getaspectratio() */
#include <graphics.h>
#define LEFT      0          /* screen borders */
#define TOP       0
#define RIGHT     319
#define BOT       199
#define HEIGHT   (BOT-TOP+1)     /* height and width of screen */
#define WIDTH    (RIGHT-LEFT+1)
#define XC       (WIDTH/2)       /* center of circle */
#define YC       (HEIGHT/2)

void main(void)
{
    int driver, mode;
    int radius;                  /* radius of circle */
    int xAspect, yAspect;        /* for getaspectratio() */
    float ratio;                 /* aspect ratio */
```

```
driver = CGA;                       /* CGA */
mode = CGAC0;                       /* palette 0 */
initgraph( &driver, &mode, "c:\\tc\\bgi" );
                                    /* draw rectangle */
rectangle( LEFT, TOP, RIGHT, BOT );
radius = HEIGHT/2;                  /* naive radius */
circle( XC, YC, radius );           /* draw circle */

getaspectratio( &xAspect, &yAspect );  /* get aspect ratio */
ratio = (float)yAspect / (float)xAspect;   /* calculate it */
radius = radius * ratio;            /* find real radius */
circle( XC, YC, radius );           /* draw corrected circle */
getche();                           /* wait until keypress */
closegraph();                       /* close graphics system */
}
```

Figure 12-11 shows the output of this program. The inner circle uses a radius of 100, but is too small; the outer circle, using a radius derived from **getaspectratio()**, is just right.

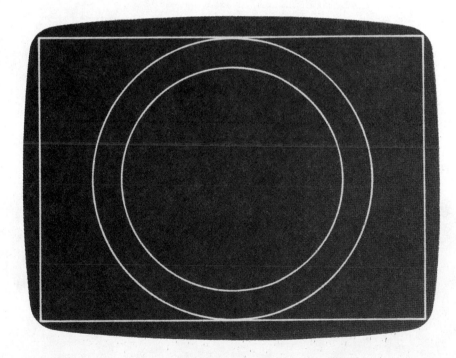

Figure 12-11. Output of the aspect.c Program

The aspect ratio problem also arises when drawing arcs. (An arc is a part of a circle, like an unfilled pie slice.) Suppose you wanted to create a box with rounded corners. It's natural to use quarter-circle arcs to connect the lines and create the corners. However, without special care, the arcs will not meet up correctly with the lines on the top and bottom of the box. Figure 12-12 shows what will happen.

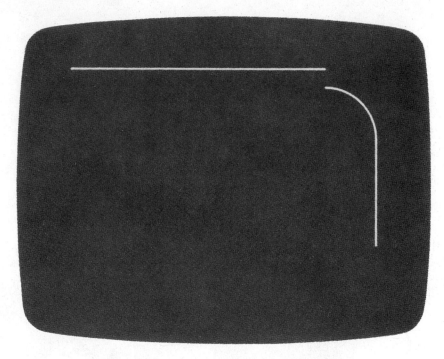

Figure 12-12. Incorrect Connection of Arc and Line

Our next program uses the **arc()** function to draw an arc connecting a vertical and a horizontal line.

Draws Arc

```
void far arc( xA, yA, stAngle, endAngle, radius )
int xA;            /* center of arc */
int yA;
int stAngle;       /* starting and ending angles */
int endAngle;
int radius;        /* radius of arc */
```

This function must be given the coordinates of the center of the arc, the starting and ending angles (measured from the 3 o'clock position in degrees), and the radius.

The program uses a new function, **getarccoords()**, to find out where the arc has actually been drawn.

Get Arc Coordinates

```
void far getarccoords( addrStr )
struct arccoordstype far *addrStr;    /* address of structure */
```

This function fills in a structure whose address has been provided to it as an argument. The structure is defined in graphics.h as

```
struct arccoordstype  {
    int x, y;
    int xstart, ystart, xend, yend;
};
```

The **x** and **y** members of the structure are the center of the arc (which the program probably knows anyway), while **xstart**, **ystart**, **xend** and **yend** are the actual coordinates of the starting and ending points of the arc. The program uses these coordinates to decide where to put the vertical and horizontal lines that connect to the arc, as shown in Figure 12-13.

```
/* arc.c */
/* draws rounded corner, using arc */
#include <graphics.h>
void main(void)
{
    int driver, mode, error;
    int L1x1, L1y1, L1x2, L1y2;   /* 1st line */
    int L2x1, L2y1, L2x2, L2y2;   /* 2nd line */
    int xA, yA, radius;           /* for arc */
    int stAngle, endAngle;        /* arc start and end angles */
    struct arccoordstype ai;      /* structure for arc info */

    driver = CGA;                 /* CGA driver */
    mode = CGAC0;                 /* palette 0 */
                                  /* initialize graphics */
    initgraph( &driver, &mode, "c:\\tc\\bgi" );

    xA = 100;    yA = 50;         /* center of arc */
```

```
radius = 50;                    /* radius of arc */
stAngle = 0; endAngle = 90;  /* arc angles */
arc( xA, yA, stAngle, endAngle, radius );  /* draw arc */

getarccoords( &ai );            /* get arc coordinates */
L1x1 = 0;          L1y1 = ai.yend;    /* horiz line */
L1x2 = ai.xend;    L1y2 = ai.yend;    /*    along top */
L2x1 = ai.xstart;  L2y1 = ai.ystart;  /* vert line */
L2x2 = ai.xstart;  L2y2 = 199;        /*    on right */
setcolor( 2 );
line( L1x1, L1y1, L1x2, L1y2 );  /* draw 1st line */
line( L2x1, L2y1, L2x2, L2y2 );  /* draw 2nd line */
getche();                        /* keep figure until keypress */
closegraph();                    /* shut down graphics system */
}
```

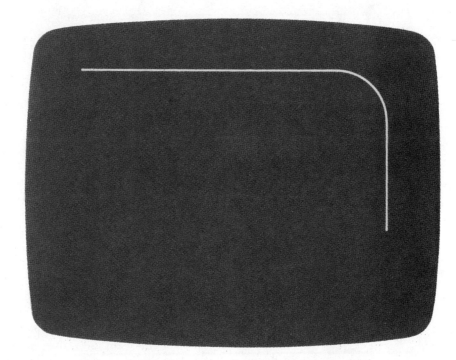

Figure 12-13. Output of the arc.c Program

Pixels

Individual pixels can be plotted using the **putpixel()** function. This is useful when graphing mathematical functions, and in "draw" or "paint" type programs that enable the user to create complex images.

Places a Pixel on the Screen

```
void far putpixel( x, y, color )
int x;      /* coordinates of pixel */
int y;
int color;  /* color to make pixel */
```

Our example program uses **putpixel()** to plot the **sin()** function.

```
/* plot.c */
/* plots function, demonstrates putpixel() */
#include <graphics.h>
#include <math.h>             /* for sin() */
#define CGACO_YELLOW 3        /* in CGA palette 0 */
void main(void)
{
    int driver, mode;        /* graphics driver and mode */
    double angle, sinofA;    /* angle and sin of angle */
    int x, y;                /* screen coordinates */

    driver = CGA;            /* CGA driver */
    mode = CGACO;            /* palette 0 */
                    /* initialize graphics */
    initgraph( &driver, &mode, "c:\\tc\\bgi" );

    line( 0, 100, 200, 100 );   /* line along x-axis */
    for( x=0; x<200; x++ )
      {
      angle = ((double)x / 200) * (2 * 3.14159265);
      sinofA = sin( angle );
      y = 100 - 100*sinofA;
      putpixel( x, y, CGACO_YELLOW );
      }
    getche();                   /* keep figure until keypress */
    closegraph();               /* shut down graphics system */
}
/* angle 0.0,  1.6,  3.1,  4.7,  6.2 */
/* sin   0.0   1.0   0.0  -1.0   0.0 */
/* x     0     50    100   150   199 */
/* y     100   200   100   0     96 */
```

The angle used as input to the **sin()** function is expressed in radians. (There are 2 times pi radians in a circle, so 1 radian is about 57 degrees.)

We'll let the angle in our program vary from 0 to 360 degrees, which is from 0 to 2 times pi radians, or about 6.3 radians. On the screen, the x coordinate rises to 1.0 at about 1.6 radians, goes back to 0 at 3.1 radians, down to −1.0 at 4.7 radians, and is finally back to 0 at 6.3 radians. We plot the x axis (where y=0) at 100 pixels, and x varies between 0 and 199 pixels. Figure 12-14 shows the result.

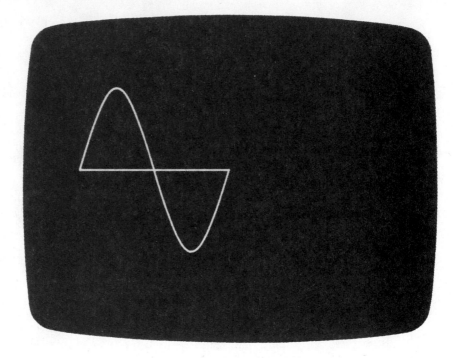

Figure 12-14. Output of the plot.c Program

Another function, **getpixel()**, can be used to find the color of a pixel at a particular point.

Bit Images and Animation

A rectangular area of the screen image can be stored in memory. However it was created—whether from lines, circles, or the elements—the image consists of pixels. Storing an image in memory means storing the color of each pixel, in a known order. An image stored in memory can be written back to the screen, either in the same location or at a different location.

Why would one want to save and restore graphics images? One use of this technique is in animation. In animation, an image moves on the screen. It may change its position, as in the image of a car moving from left to right. Or the image may change its shape; for example, a coin spinning so it appears first as a circle, then as an ellipse, and then—edge on—as a line. In either case images must be drawn quickly to simulate continuous motion.

In these cases, drawing the image from scratch may be too time-consuming. Drawing all the details of a car, for instance, may require many calls to graphics functions for headlights, doors, wheels, and other shapes. It is often faster to draw the image once, then store it in memory, and transfer the complete image back onto the screen in different places.

Our example program is a variation of the bounce.c program from Chapter 11. A ball is set in motion. Each time it hits the edge of the screen, it bounces off in a new direction. The image of the ball is created with **circle()** and stored in memory with **getimage()**.

Places Graphics Image in Memory

```
void far getimage( left, top, right, bottom, addrBuff )
int left;          /* coordinates of region to be saved */
int top;
int right;
int bottom;
void far *addrBuff;  /* address of memory buffer for image */
```

This function needs the coordinates of the rectangular region that is to be saved to memory, and the address in memory where the image will be saved. Since the image size is often not known in advance, there is a function to figure it out, called **imagesize()**.

Returns Number of Bytes Needed for Image

```
unsigned far imagesize( left, top, right, bottom )
int left;        /* coordinates of image */
int top;
int right;
int bottom;
```

The size returned by this function can be passed to **malloc()**, which allocates memory space (as described in Chapter 9). The resulting pointer is then used as an argument to **getimage()**.

Once the image is stored in memory, the program enters a loop in which the image is read back from memory to different places on the screen. The image is restored using the function **putimage()**.

Restores Graphics Image from Memory to Screen

```
void far putimage( left, top, addrBuff, putop )
int left;            /* location to place image */
int top;
void far *addrBuff;  /* address of memory buffer holding image */
int putop;           /* interaction between new and old pixels */
```

This function is given the top left-hand corner of the area where the image will go, the address in memory holding the image, and an operator value. The possible values for this operator, as defined in graphics.h, are:

Value	Constant	Comment
0	COPY_PUT	Replaces old image with new
1	XOR_PUT	XOR old and new images
2	OR_PUT	OR old and new images
3	AND_PUT	AND old and new images
4	NOT_PUT	Replace with inverse of new image

putop

The operator can be used to achieve different effects. Typically a new image is drawn with the operator set to COPY_PUT, and the old image is erased with it set to XOR_PUT. The effect of XORing one image with the same image is to erase it.

```
/* image.c */
/* bouncing ball created from bit image */
#include <graphics.h>
#define LEFT     0
#define TOP      0
#define RIGHT    319
#define BOTTOM   199
#define RADIUS   8
#define CGACO_LIGHTGREEN 1

void main(void)
{
    int driver, mode;               /* for initgraph() */
    int x, y, dx, dy, oldx, oldy;   /* ball coordinates */
    void *ballbuff;                 /* pointer to buffer */
    unsigned size;                  /* size of buffer */
```

```
        driver = CGA;
        mode = CGAC0;                       /* set graphics mode */
        initgraph( &driver, &mode, "c:\\tc\\bgi" );
                                            /* draw boundary */
        rectangle( LEFT, TOP, RIGHT, BOTTOM );
        x = y = RADIUS+10;                  /* create image of ball */
        setcolor( CGAC0_LIGHTGREEN );
        setfillstyle( SOLID_FILL, CGAC0_LIGHTGREEN );
        circle( x, y, RADIUS );
        floodfill( x, y, CGAC0_LIGHTGREEN );
                                            /* get size of image */
        size = imagesize( x-RADIUS, y-RADIUS, x+RADIUS, y+RADIUS );
        ballbuff = (void *)malloc( size );  /* get memory for image */
                                            /* place image in memory */
        getimage( x-RADIUS, y-RADIUS, x+RADIUS, y+RADIUS, ballbuff );

        dx = 2;                             /* set speed of ball */
        dy = 1;
        while ( !kbhit() )                  /* exit on keypress */
           {                                /* memory image to screen */
           putimage( x-RADIUS, y-RADIUS, ballbuff, COPY_PUT );
           oldx = x; oldy = y;              /* remember where it was */
           x += dx;  y += dy;               /* move its coordinates */
                                            /* reflect it at edges */
           if( x<=LEFT+RADIUS+2 || x>=RIGHT-RADIUS-2 )
              dx = -dx;
           if( y<=TOP+RADIUS+1 || y>=BOTTOM-RADIUS-1 )
              dy = -dy;                      /* erase old image */
           putimage( oldx-RADIUS, oldy-RADIUS, ballbuff, XOR_PUT );
           }
        closegraph();
        }
```

p511

Text with Graphics

Turbo C makes available functions that will draw text characters in graphics mode. These functions can be used to mix text and graphics in the same image. They also make it possible to change text fonts and vary the size of text, much as if one were using a graphics-oriented system like the OS/2 Presentation Manager.

Writing in Different Fonts

A *font* is a set of characters in a particular style. The function **settextstyle()** is used to select different fonts, and to specify the orientation (vertical or horizontal) and size of the type.

Specify Text Font, Orientation, Size

```
void far settextstyle( font, direction, charsize )
int font;        /* which font to use */
int direction;   /* horizontal or vertical */
int charsize;    /* size of characters */
```

There are currently five fonts available (although it's easy to add others to the system). These are:

Value	Constant	File	Comment
0	DEFAULT_FONT	built in	Bit-mapped, 8x8
1	TIPLEX_FONT	TRIP.CHR	Stroked (Times-Roman style)
2	SMALL_FONT	LITT.CHR	Stroked (for small letters)
3	SANS_SERIF_FONT	SANS.CHR	Stroked (sans-serif style)
4	GOTHIC_FONT	GOTH.CHR	Stroked (gothic style)

font

The DEFAULT_FONT is a *bit-mapped font*. This means that the characters are defined using bit patterns. Bit-mapped characters expand into exact replicas of their normal-size versions; each pixel is enlarged. So using this font in larger sizes produces letters made up of blocks—the "computer look."

The other fonts are *stroked* fonts. These are created from a number of lines and arcs, or strokes. When these characters are expanded they maintain their clean, detailed look; the pixels don't expand into blocks as in the bit-mapped font. These are the preferred fonts for most graphics applications.

The disadvantage of stroked fonts is that they require more storage space. For this reason, the stroked fonts are kept in separate files with the extension .chr, as shown in the table, and only loaded into memory when needed. To use the stroked fonts, the file for each font must be available in a directory where the system can find it (in the \TC\BGI directory, for example).

Loading these files at run time takes time and also means that an application must consist of multiple files. To avoid these problems, it is possible to link the .chr files with your application. We discuss this in the last section of this chapter.

The **direction** argument to **settextstyle()** can have one of two values:

Value	Constant	Comment
0	HORIZ_DIR	From left to right
1	VERT_DIR	From bottom to top

Horizontal is the default. When VERT_DIR is used, the message is written from bottom to top; it looks like the horizontal message rotated 90 degrees.

When the **charsize** argument is 1, the characters are the smallest size. A value of 2 doubles the size, 3 triples it, and so on. There are no fractional sizes; if small type is needed, use the SMALL_FONT, which starts out with smaller characters than the other fonts.

Our example program generates all the fonts, using a **charsize** of 4. The CGA mode is used in this program, so it will work with any graphics adaptor. The output from the program is shown in Figure 12-15.

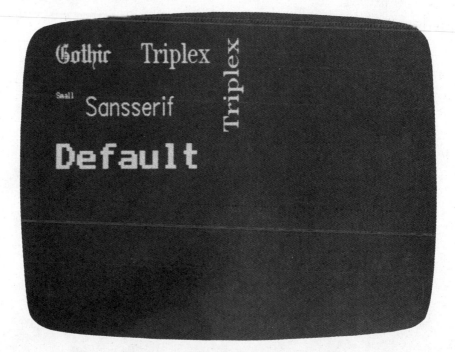

Figure 12-15. Output of the stroke.c Program

```
/* stroke.c */
/* tests stroked characters */
#include <graphics.h>
#define FONT_SIZE  4
void main(void)
```

```
{
    int driver, mode;

    driver = CGA;
    mode = CGAC0;
    initgraph(&driver, &mode, "\\tc\\bgi" );

    settextstyle( GOTHIC_FONT, HORIZ_DIR, FONT_SIZE );
    outtext("Gothic   ");

    settextstyle( TRIPLEX_FONT, HORIZ_DIR, FONT_SIZE );
    outtext("Triplex");

    moveto( 0, 60 );
    settextstyle(SMALL_FONT, HORIZ_DIR, FONT_SIZE );
    outtext("Small    ");

    settextstyle(SANS_SERIF_FONT, HORIZ_DIR, FONT_SIZE );
    outtext("Sansserif");

    moveto( 0, 120 );
    settextstyle(DEFAULT_FONT, HORIZ_DIR, FONT_SIZE );
    outtext("Default");

    moveto( 250, 0 );
    settextstyle( TRIPLEX_FONT, VERT_DIR, FONT_SIZE );
    outtext("Triplex");

    getche();
    closegraph();
}
```

The text is placed at the current position (CP), so the function **moveto()** is used to move the CP to the desired place on the screen prior to printing. The text is written to the screen with the **outtext()** function, which takes as its only argument the string to be displayed.

Display Text in Graphics Mode

```
void far outtext( addrString )
char far *addrString;  /* address of string to be displayed */
```

The **outtext()** function displays the string using the font, orientation, and size specified by **settextstyle()**.

Another function, **outtextxy()**, is similar to **outtext()**, but displays text at a particular location rather than at the current CP.

Normal C functions like **printf()** do not operate with different fonts and are not appropriate in graphics mode.

Justifying and Sizing Text

The term *justification* means (at least in Turbo C) how a text string will be placed relative to the CP. A text string is normally placed so the CP is at its top left hand corner. This can be altered using the **settextjustify()** function.

Set Text Justification (Position Relative to CP)

```
void far settextjustify( horiz, vert )
int horiz;  /* horizontal justification constant */
int vert;   /* vertical justification constant */
```

The horizontal justification constant can have one of three values:

Value	Constant	Description
0	LEFT_TEXT	CP at left of text (default)
1	CENTER_TEXT	CP in horizontal center of text
2	RIGHT_TEXT	CP at right of text

The vertical justification constant is similar to the horizontal:

Value	Constant	Description
0	BOTTOM_TEXT	CP at bottom of text
1	CENTER_TEXT	CP in vertical center of text
2	TOP_TEXT	CP at top of text (default)

Our example program prints messages on a grid of lines so that the effect of different justifications can be seen, as shown in Figure 12-16.

```
/* justify.c */
/* tests stroked characters */
#include <graphics.h>
#define CL        150      /* center line */
#define LEAD       40      /* vertical space between lines */
#define FONT_SIZE   3
```

```
void main(void)
{
    int driver, mode, j;

    driver = CGA;
    mode = CGACO;
    initgraph(&driver, &mode, "\\tc\\bgi" );

    settextstyle( TRIPLEX_FONT, HORIZ_DIR, FONT_SIZE );
    line( CL, 0, CL, 200 );
    for(j=0; j<LEAD*5; j+=LEAD)
        line( 0, j, 300, j );

    moveto( CL, 0 );
    outtext("Default");

    moveto( CL, LEAD );
    settextjustify( LEFT_TEXT, TOP_TEXT );
    outtext("Left-Top");

    moveto( CL, LEAD*2 );
    settextjustify( RIGHT_TEXT, TOP_TEXT );
    outtext("Right-Top");

    moveto( CL, LEAD*3 );
    settextjustify( CENTER_TEXT, TOP_TEXT );
    outtext("Center-Top");

    moveto( CL, LEAD*4 );
    settextjustify( CENTER_TEXT, BOTTOM_TEXT );
    outtext("Center-Bottom");

    getche();
    closegraph();
}
```

The size and also the proportions of stroked characters can be varied with the **setusercharsize()** function.

This function provides two factors for the width of the character, and two factors for the height. Each pair of factors forms a fraction which is multiplied by the normal size of the character. For instance, if **multx** is 3 and **divx** is 2, the resulting characters will be 3/2 times as wide as normal.

When **setusercharsize()** is used, the **settextstyle()** function should have previously set the **charsize** variable to USER_CHAR_SIZE, or 0. This is equivalent to a character size of 4, and permits **setusercharsize()** to scale the characters.

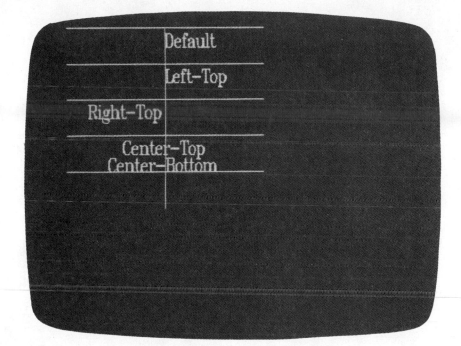

Figure 12-16. Output of the justify.c Program

Change Character Size and Proportions

```
void far setusercharsize( multx, divx, multy, divy )
int multy;    /* multiplies height of character */
int divx;     /* divides width of character */
int multx;    /* multiplies width of character */
int divy;     /* divides height of character */
```

The example program generates text in a variety of sizes, as shown in Figure 12-17.

```
/* charsize.c */
/* uses different character sizes */
#include <graphics.h>
void main(void)
{
    int driver, mode;
    int multx, divx, multy, divy;    /* factors for text size */
```

```
driver = CGA;
mode = CGACO;
initgraph(&driver, &mode, "\\tc\\bgi" );

settextstyle( SANS_SERIF_FONT, HORIZ_DIR, USER_CHAR_SIZE );
outtext("Normal");

moveto( 0, 60 );                    /* twice as wide */
setusercharsize( multx=2, divx=1, multy=1, divy=1 );
outtext("Wider");

moveto( 0, 120 );                   /* 3/2 as tall */
setusercharsize( multx=1, divx=1, multy=3, divy=2 );
outtext("Taller");

moveto( 0, 180 );                   /* half size */
setusercharsize( multx=1, divx=2, multy=1, divy=2 );
outtext("Half as wide and tall");
getche();
closegraph();
}
```

Figure 12-17. Output of the charsize.c Program

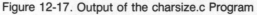

An Annotated Bar Graph

Let's put together what we've learned about text and graphics to create an annotated bar chart. This example is an enhancement of the bargraph.c program shown earlier. Tick marks have been added, the horizontal axis is labelled with the 12 months of the year, and the vertical axis is labelled with numbers. In addition, the graph sports a title. The result is shown in Figure 12-18.

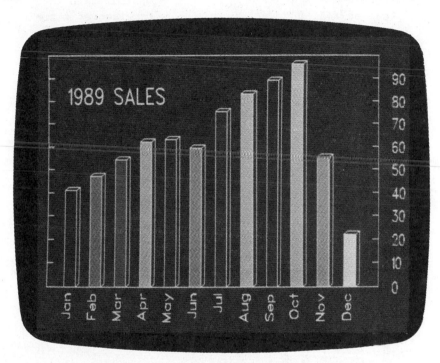

Figure 12-18. Output of the barega.c Program

Text in graphics modes is considerably clearer in EGA (and VGA) modes than it is in CGA, so this program is written for the EGAHI mode. It could easily be modified to run in CGA (or other modes) by varying the **#define** dimensions at the start of the program.

```
/* barega.c */
/* generates bar graph, uses EGA graphics */
#include <graphics.h>
#define N        12          /* number of values to graph */
#define BWIDTH   20          /* width of each bar */
#define SEP      24          /* separation between bars */
#define SHFT     30          /* between border and 1st bar */
```

```
#define LEFT       5              /* left side of graph */
#define DEPTH      6              /* depth of bar */
#define TOPFLAG    1              /* put 3-D top on bar */
#define BOT      300              /* bottom of graph */
#define TOP        5              /* top of graph */
#define TICKS     10              /* number of tick marks */
#define TWIDTH    10              /* width of tick marks */
#define MAXDATA  100              /* maximum data units */
#define XTITLE    40              /* location of title */
#define YTITLE    40
#define FONT    SANS_SERIF_FONT   /* font for labels */
#define DI      (BWIDTH+SEP)      /* distance from bar to bar */
#define WIDTH   ( (N+1) * DI )    /* width of chart */
                                 /* pixels between ticks */
#define PBT ( (float)(BOT-TOP ) / TICKS )
                                 /* pixels per data unit */
#define PPD ( (float)(BOT-TOP) / MAXDATA )
void main(void)
{
   int driver, mode, j;
   char string[40];
                            /* data to display */
   int data[N] = { 41, 47, 54, 62, 63, 59,
           75, 83, 89, 96, 55, 22 };
   char months[12][4] =
       { "Jan", "Feb", "Mar", "Apr", "May", "Jun",
         "Jul", "Aug", "Sep", "Oct", "Nov", "Dec"  };

   driver = EGA;                 /* initialize graphics */
   mode = EGAHI;
   initgraph(&driver, &mode, "\\tc\\bgi" );

                            /* draw border */
   rectangle( LEFT, TOP, LEFT+WIDTH, BOT );
                            /* draw title */
   setusercharsize( 4, 3, 4, 3 );
   settextstyle( FONT, HORIZ_DIR, 0 );
   moveto( XTITLE, YTITLE );
   outtext("1989 SALES");

   setusercharsize( 2, 3, 2, 3 );
   settextstyle( FONT, HORIZ_DIR, 0 );
   for( j=0; j<TICKS; j++ )      /* draw ticks and numbers */
      {
      line( LEFT,              BOT-j*PBT,      /* left tick */
```

```
            LEFT+TWIDTH,         BOT-j*PBT );
      line( LEFT+WIDTH-TWIDTH, BOT-j*PBT,        /* right tick */
            LEFT+WIDTH,         BOT-j*PBT );
      moveto( LEFT+WIDTH+SEP,   BOT-j*PBT-PBT/3 );
      itoa( j*(MAXDATA/TICKS), string, 10 );     /* number */
      outtext( string );
      }
   settextstyle( FONT, VERT_DIR, 0 );
   for( j=0; j<N; j++ )              /* draw bars and months */
      {
      setfillstyle( SOLID_FILL, j );
      bar3d( LEFT+SHFT+j*DI,         BOT-data[j]*PPD,  /* bar */
             LEFT+SHFT+j*DI+BWIDTH, BOT, DEPTH, TOPFLAG );
      moveto( LEFT+SEP+j*DI, BOT+5 );                  /* month */
      outtext( months[j] );
      }
   getche();                     /* keep picture until keypress */
   closegraph();                 /* remove graphics */
}
```

A different number of data items can be graphed by changing the constant **N** and the values in the arrays **data[]** and **months[]**. The data items graphed here lie in the range from 0 to 100. Different ranges of data can be graphed by changing the MAXDATA constant.

Example Programs

This section contains several programs that demonstrate Turbo C graphics in interesting ways. The first program is short and simple, but creates a dazzling and hypnotic display. The second program generates the Mandelbrot set. This mathematical construct can produce some of the most astonishing displays seen on a computer screen.

Bouncing Lines

This example works on a simple principle. Two points bounce around the screen, as the ball did in the image.c program. At each position a line is drawn between the two points. The resulting series of lines is displayed, as the two points, which move at different speeds, bounce around the screen. The color of the line changes every few hundred lines, resulting in colored shapes drawn on top of each other in an ever-changing kaleidoscopic pattern. Surprisingly, curved and wavelike shapes are produced.

The effect is much more dazzling in EGA graphics, with its higher resolution and 16 colors, than it is in CGA, so the example is written in EGAHI mode. It can easily be converted to other modes. Because the effect of this program depends so much on color and the rapid changing of the design, a figure cannot do it justice. A rough idea can be gained from Figure 12-19.

Figure 12-19. Output of the linerega.c Program

```
/* linerega.c */
/* bouncing line creates abstract patterns */
#include <graphics.h>
#define LEFT      0           /* screen borders */
#define TOP       0
#define RIGHT    639
#define BOTTOM   349
#define LINES    200          /* lines per color change */
#define MAXCOLOR 15           /* maximum color value */
void main(void)
{
   int driver, mode, error;
   int x1, y1;                /* one end of line */
   int x2, y2;                /* the other end of line */
   int dx1, dy1, dx2, dy2;    /* increments to move points */
   int count=0;               /* how many lines drawn */
```

```
int color=0;                    /* color being used */

driver = EGA;
mode = EGAHI;                   /* EGA hi res */
initgraph( &driver, &mode, "c:\\tc\\bgi" );
x1 = x2 = y1 = y2 = 10;         /* start points */
dx1 = dy1 = 2;                  /* point 1: 2 pixels per cycle */
dx2 = dy2 = 3;                  /* point 2: 3 pixels per cycle */
while ( !kbhit() )              /* terminate on keypress */
   {
   line( x1, y1, x2, y2 );          /* draw line */
   x1 += dx1;  y1 += dy1;           /* move points */
   x2 += dx2;  y2 += dy2;
   if( x1<=LEFT || x1>=RIGHT )      /* if points are */
      dx1 = -dx1;                   /*    off the screen, */
   if( y1<=TOP || y1>=BOTTOM )      /*    reverse direction */
      dy1 = -dy1;
   if( x2<=LEFT || x2>=RIGHT )
      dx2 = -dx2;
   if( y2<=TOP || y2>=BOTTOM )
      dy2 = -dy2;
   if( ++count > LINES )            /* every LINES lines, */
      {                             /* change color */
      setcolor( color );           /* MAXCOLOR colors */
      color = (color >= MAXCOLOR)  ?  0  :  ++color;
      count = 0;
      }
   }
closegraph();
}
```

This program will run until a key pressed.

The Mandelbrot Program

In the past few years a mathematical construct called the Mandelbrot set has
emerged as one of the most fascinating—and beautiful—objects in mathematics. The set consists of those points on a two-dimensional plane that
satisfy certain characteristics. The boundary of the set, which occupies the
area between about -2 and $+0.5$ on the x axis, and $+1.25$ and -1.25 on the y
axis, is astonishingly complex. Looked at in its entirety, the boundary consists
of several rounded shapes with other rounded shapes attached to them, and
strange lighteninglike filaments radiating from them. If one then "zooms in"
on small areas of this boundary, details can be seen—more rounded shapes,
fernlike curlicues, spirals. It turns out that the boundary is a fractal. Each time

you zoom in to a smaller area, more details and more astonishing shapes are revealed. There is no end to how far you can zoom in. It is quite easy to zoom down to a detail never before seen by human eyes.

The mandel.c program shown here enables you to explore the Mandelbrot set. You can view the complete set, or, by changing parameters in the program, zoom in for more detailed views.

The program contains two nested loops. The outer one steps down from line to line, and the inner one steps across from pixel to pixel on each line. At each pixel location the program calculates whether the point corresponding to that screen location is a member of the Mandelbrot set. If it is, the pixel is drawn as black. If not, the pixel is colored. How are the colors chosen? This has to do with how the set is defined. Before we get into that, here's the listing:

```
/* mandel.c */
/* generates the mandelbrot set */
#include <graphics.h>
#define XMAX 100                 /* change these to change size */
#define YMAX 100                 /*    of picture */
#define MAXCOUNT 16              /* number of iterations */
void main(void)
{
    int x, y;                    /* location of pixel on screen */
    float xscale, yscale;        /* distance between pixels */
    float left, top;             /* location of top left corner */
    float xside, yside;          /* length of sides */
    float zx, zy;                /* real and imag parts of z */
    float cx, cy;                /* real and imag parts of c */
    float tempx;                 /* briefly holds zx */
    int count;                   /* number of iterations */
    int driver, mode;            /* graphics driver and mode */

    left = -2.0;                 /* coordinates for entire */
    top = 1.25;                  /*    mandelbrot set */
    xside = 2.5;                 /*    change to see details */
    yside = -2.5;                /*    of set */
    xscale = xside / XMAX;       /* set scale factors */
    yscale = yside / YMAX;
    driver = EGA;                /* set driver and mode */
    mode = EGAHI;
    initgraph(&driver, &mode, "\\tc\\bgi" );
    rectangle( 0, 0, XMAX+1, YMAX+1 );

    for(y=1; y<=YMAX; y++)       /* for each pixel column */
        {
```

```
    for(x=1; x<=XMAX; x++)       /* for each pixel row */
        {
        cx = x*xscale+left;          /* set c to pixel location */
        cy = y*yscale+top;
        zx = zy = 0;                 /* set z = 0 */
        count = 0;                   /* reset count */
                                     /* size of z < 2 */
        while( zx*zx+zy*zy<4 && count<MAXCOUNT )        z x z̄ < 4
            {
            tempx = zx*zx - zy*zy + cx;  /* set z = z*z + c */
            zy = 2*zx*zy + cy;
            zx = tempx;
            count++;                 /* another iteration */
            }
        putpixel(x, y, count); /* color is count */            p 465

        if( kbhit() )                /* to abort program */
            exit(0);                 /* before picture finished */
        } /* end for(x) */
    } /* end for(y) */
getche();                            /* keep picture until keypress */
closegraph();                        /* close graphics system */
}
```

The program runs in EGA graphics, which provides a far more satisfactory picture than CGA. As shown, the program generates a picture 100 pixels high and 100 pixels wide. This is a small part of the EGA screen. The reason for using a small picture is that it takes the program a considerable time to generate its output. The 100 by 100 pixel picture takes several minutes. (It will be much faster if you have a math coprocessor in your system.) A good way to use the program is to generate a small picture to preview what you want to see. When you like the image, expand the picture size by changing XMAX and YMAX to (say) 400 by 300, and let the program run all night. The effect is shown in Figure 12-20. Unfortunately, the figure cannot do justice to the intricate colored image produced by the program.

A description of the algorithm used to generate the Mandelbrot set is beyond the scope of this book. Very roughly, a point is in the set if a certain iterated calculation performed on it does not escape to infinity. If the calculation does escape to infinity, the point is outside the set, and the speed with which it escapes determines the color of the pixel at that point. Refer to the Mathematical Recreations column in *Scientific American* for August 1985 and November 1987 for a very lucid presentation. (These articles are reprinted in *The Armchair Universe* by A.K. Dewdney, W. H. Freeman Company, 1988.)

Almost any spot on the boundary provides an interesting place to start

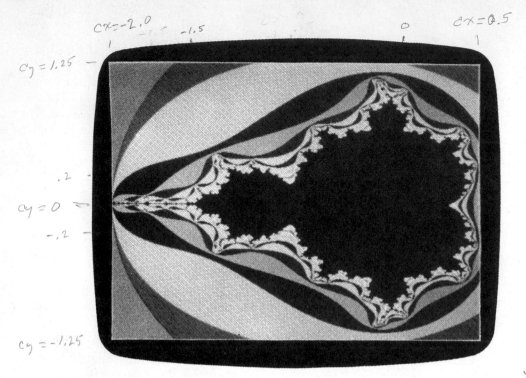

Figure 12-20. Output of the mandel.c Program

exploring the details of the Mandelbrot set. For instance, try the following settings:

```
left = -1.5;
top = -0.2;
xside = 0.25;
yside = 0.4;
```

Creating Stand-Alone Executables

The example programs in this chapter have required that the appropriate BGI file, such as EGAVGA.BGI, be installed in a known directory in the system, a directory specified by an argument to the **initgraph()** function. Also, if fonts are used, the font file, such as GOTH.CHR, must be available in the same directory.

Although this approach is convenient for a C development environment, it is not so satisfactory for applications destined for release to the outside world. Users like to load as few files as possible, and don't want to worry about directory structures. It would be nice if there were a way to link the .BGI and

.CHR files together with the program file, creating a single complete .EXE file. Fortunately, this is possible, although there are several steps involved.

First, the .BGI and .CHR files must be converted to .OBJ files. Second, new library functions are used in the program to register the *public names* of these .OBJ files. Finally, a project file must be created that contains the names of the various program components. The use of project files is an advanced topic. However, if you read the relevant sections in Chapter 14, you'll be ready for the following brief discussion.

As an example, let's create a self-contained .EXE file from the barega.c example described earlier.

Converting the .BGI and .CHR Files

The first step is to convert any .BGI or .CHR files used by the program into .OBJ files that the linker can deal with. The BGIOBJ utility is used for this purpose.

Our example program uses the EGAVGA.BGI file as a graphics driver, and the SANS.CHR file to supply the sans serif font for adding captions to the graph. Enter the following command (don't use the file extension):

```
C>bgiobj egavga
```

The utility will tell you that EGAVGA.OBJ has been created. It will also tell you the public name of this file: **_EGAVGA_driver**. Now enter

```
C>bgiobj sans
```

This creates SANS.OBJ, and gives it a public name of **_sansserif_font**. These public names will be used in the next step.

Registering the Public Names

The program must be modified to tell the graphics system that the .BGI and .CHR files are linked to the program.

```
/* baralone.c */
/* generates bar graph, uses EGA graphics */
#include <graphics.h>
#define N        12              /* number of values to graph */
#define BWIDTH   20              /* width of each bar */
#define SEP      24              /* separation between bars */
#define SHFT     30              /* between border and 1st bar */
#define LEFT      5              /* left side of graph */
#define DEPTH     6              /* depth of bar */
#define TOPFLAG   1              /* put 3-D top on bar */
```

```
#define BOT      300              /* bottom of graph */
#define TOP        5              /* top of graph */
#define TICKS     10              /* number of tick marks */
#define TWIDTH    10              /* width of tick marks */
#define MAXDATA  100              /* maximum data units */
#define XTITLE    40              /* location of title */
#define YTITLE    40
#define FONT    SANS_SERIF_FONT   /* font for labels */
#define DI      (BWIDTH+SEP)      /* distance from bar to bar */
#define WIDTH   ( (N+1) * DI )    /* width of chart */
                                  /* pixels between ticks */
#define PBT ( (float)(BOT-TOP ) / TICKS )
                                  /* pixels per data unit */
#define PPD ( (float)(BOT-TOP) / MAXDATA )
void main(void)
{
    int driver, mode, j;
    char string[40];
                                    /* data to display */
    int data[N] = { 41, 47, 54, 62, 63, 59,
            75, 83, 89, 96, 55, 22 };
    char months[12][4] =
        { "Jan", "Feb", "Mar", "Apr", "May", "Jun",
          "Jul", "Aug", "Sep", "Oct", "Nov", "Dec"  };

    registerbgidriver(EGAVGA_driver);  /* register driver */
    registerbgifont(sansserif_font);   /* and fonts */

    driver = EGA;                       /* initialize graphics */
    mode = EGAHI;
    initgraph(&driver, &mode, "" );     /* note: null pathname */

                                        /* draw border */
    rectangle( LEFT, TOP, LEFT+WIDTH, BOT );
                                        /* draw title */
    setusercharsize( 4, 3, 4, 3 );
    settextstyle( FONT, HORIZ_DIR, 0 );
    moveto( XTITLE, YTITLE );
    outtext("1989 SALES");

    setusercharsize( 2, 3, 2, 3 );
    settextstyle( FONT, HORIZ_DIR, 0 );
    for( j=0; j<TICKS; j++ )             /* draw ticks and numbers */
      {
      line( LEFT,              BOT-j*PBT,      /* left tick */
```

```
            LEFT+TWIDTH,         BOT-j*PBT );
    line( LEFT+WIDTH-TWIDTH, BOT-j*PBT,        /* right tick */
            LEFT+WIDTH,          BOT-j*PBT );
    moveto( LEFT+WIDTH+SEP,  BOT-j*PBT-PBT/3 );
    itoa( j*(MAXDATA/TICKS), string, 10 );   /* number */
    outtext( string );
    }
  settextstyle( FONT, VERT_DIR, 0 );
  for( j=0; j<N; j++ )            /* draw bars and months */
    {
    setfillstyle( SOLID_FILL, j );
    bar3d( LEFT+SHFT+j*DI,        BOT-data[j]*PPD,  /* bar */
           LEFT+SHFT+j*DI+BWIDTH, BOT, DEPTH, TOPFLAG );
    moveto( LEFT+SEP+j*DI, BOT+5 );                  /* month */
    outtext( months[j] );
    }
  getche();                        /* keep picture until keypress */
  closegraph();                    /* remove graphics */
}
```

The essential lines from this program are:

```
registerbgidriver(EGAVGA_driver);  /* register driver */
registerbgifont(sansserif_font);   /* register font */
- - - - - - - -
initgraph(&driver, &mode, "");     /* pathname is null */
```

The **registerbgidriver()** and **registerbgifont()** functions register the driver and font, and the **initgraph()** function is modified to have a null string as the driver path.

Creating the Project File

To learn how to create project files, read Chapter 14. The project file is called baralone.prj. You need the following files on the project list in this file:

```
BAREGA.C
EGAVGA.OBJ
SANS.OBJ
```

After the project list is complete, select Make .EXE File from the Compile menu. Turbo C will generate the the barega.exe file. This is a completely stand-alone file, which can be loaded into any machine and executed. Using a similar technique, you can make your own stand-alone applications.

Summary

This chapter focused on the graphics functions built into Turbo C++ in Versions 1.5 and later. There are two major divisions to these functions: text mode and graphics mode. Text-mode functions deal mostly with writing text to a window. Graphics mode involves images such as lines, circles, and filled areas. A graphics driver such as cga.bgi must be available to the system if graphics mode is used. This driver can be linked dynamically to the program at run time. Appendix E shows how it can be permanently combined with the program. Graphics mode functions also require the file graphics.lib to be available to the system.

Special functions exist to write text in graphics mode, so graphs and drawings can be labelled. These functions normally use stroke fonts, which require a font file to be available to the system. Like graphics drivers, font files can be linked to the application dynamically, or permanently at link time.

Questions

1. What are the advantages of the Turbo C graphics functions over using ROM BIOS or direct memory access?

2. What are the advantages of direct memory access over the Turbo C graphics functions?

3. True or false: you can draw circles and lines in Turbo C Text mode.

4. A window is a screen area in which
   a. colors can be confined
   b. text can be confined
   c. graphics can be confined
   d. both text and graphics can be confined

5. To use text mode, the file _____ must be **#include**d in your program.

6. The function **gotoxy()** places the following item at x, y:
   a. the current position (CP)
   b. the text about to be written
   c. the next line to be drawn
   d. the cursor

7. Each character saved in memory by **savetext()** requires _____ bytes of storage.

8. True or false: a Turbo C graphics function can be used to determine if a particular program requires text or graphics mode.

9. The data type **void *** indicates
    a. nothing is returned by a function
    b. a null pointer
    c. a function takes no arguments
    d. a pointer to any data type

10. What files must be available to your program if you want to draw lines and circles?

11. What utility do you use to change .BGI files to .OBJ files?

12. True or false: the same video driver works for all display types.

13. Graphics mode is initialized with the _____ function.

14. Errors in graphics functions like **initgraph()** can be determined by
    a. examining the function's parameters
    b. examining the return value of the function
    c. calling the function **graphresult()()**
    d. hoping for a sudden inspiration

15. True or false: a Turbo C library function can select the highest resolution graphics mode available with the attached equipment.

16. Dashed circles can be drawn using the function _____ .

17. In Turbo C the angles for arcs, pie slices, and parts of ellipses are measured starting at
    a. 0 degrees
    b. the 12 o'clock position
    c. the 3 o'clock position
    d. 180 degrees

18. A viewport is a screen area in which
    a. colors can be confined
    b. text can be confined
    c. graphics can be confined
    d. both text and graphics can be confined

19. Functions that perform relative line drawing do so relative to
    a. the cursor position
    b. the last text written
    c. the last relative line drawn
    d. the current position (CP)

20. Square pixels
    a. have an aspect ratio of 1.0
    b. have the same height and width
    c. cause no distortion of images
    d. are often really round

Exercises

1. Revise the ezedit.c program to allow the insertion and deletion of individual characters. Use only Turbo C graphics functions, such as **movetext()**. Don't worry about wordwrap when inserting and deleting. Hint: keep in mind which functions use absolute coordinates, and which are relative to the window.

2. Write a program that allows the user to draw on the screen, using the cursor keys. At each position the program should draw a dot, so that patterns of vertical and horizontal lines can be created. Use only Turbo C graphics functions; no ROM BIOS calls or direct memory access.

3. Write a program that creates the animated image of a coin rotating about its vertical axis, as if it were spinning on a table top. Use only Turbo C graphics functions. **getimage()** and **putimage()** are appropriate.

13

Files

- Standard file I/O *p 539*
- Character, string, and formatted I/O
- Block I/O
- Binary and text modes *p 556*
- System-level I/O *p 574*
- Standard files and redirection

13

Most programs need to read and write data to disk-based storage systems. Word processors need to store text files, spreadsheets need to store the contents of cells, and databases need to store records. In this chapter we explore the facilities that C makes available for input and output (I/O) to a disk system.

Disk I/O operations are performed on entities called *files*. A file is a collection of bytes that is given a name. In most microcomputer systems, files are used as a unit of storage primarily on floppy-disk and fixed-disk data storage systems (although they can be used with other devices as well, such as CD-ROM players, RAM-disk storage, tape backup systems, and other computers). The major use of the MS-DOS or PC DOS operating system is to handle files: to manage their storage on the disk, load them into memory, list them, delete them, and so forth.

A C-language program can read and write files in a variety of different ways. In fact, there are so many options that sorting them all out can prove rather confusing. So in the first section of this chapter we'll discuss the various categories of disk I/O. Then we'll examine the individual techniques.

Types of Disk I/O

A group of objects can be divided into categories in more than one way. For instance, automobiles can be categorized as foreign or domestic; cheap or expensive; four, six, or eight cylinders; and so on. A car will fit into more than one category at the same time; it might be a cheap foreign car with four cylinders, for example. Similarly, the various ways file I/O can be performed in C form a number of overlapping categories. In this section we'll give a brief overview of the most important of these categories: a view of the forest before we enter the trees.

Standard I/O Versus System I/O

Probably the broadest division in C file I/O is between *standard I/O* (often called *stream I/O*), and *system-level* (or *low-level I/O*). Each of these is a more or less complete system for performing disk I/O. Each has functions for reading and writing files and performing other necessary tasks, and each provides variations in the way reading and writing can be performed. In many ways these two systems are similar, and in fact, most I/O tasks can be handled by either system. But there are also important differences between the two.

Standard I/O, as the name implies, is the most common way of performing I/O in C programs. It has a wider range of commands, and in many respects is easier to use than system I/O. Standard I/O conceals from the user some of the details of file I/O operations, such as buffering, and it automatically performs data conversion (we'll see what this means later). If there were only one system available for disk I/O in C, standard I/O probably would be it.

System I/O provides fewer ways to handle data than standard I/O, and it can be considered a more primitive system. The techniques it employs are very much like those used by the operating system. The programmer must set up, and keep track of, the buffer used to transfer data, and the system does not perform any format translations. Thus, in some ways, system I/O is harder to program than standard I/O. Since it is more closely related to the operating system, however, it is often more efficient, both in terms of speed of operation and the amount of memory used by the program.

Character, String, Formatted, and Record I/O

The standard I/O package makes available four different ways of reading and writing data. (System-level I/O, by contrast, only uses one of these ways.) Happily, three of these four ways of transferring data correspond closely to methods you've already learned for reading data from the keyboard and writing it to the display.

First, data can be read or written one character at a time. This is analogous to how such functions as **putchar()** and **getche()** read data from the keyboard and write it to the screen.

Second, data can be read or written as strings, as such functions as **gets()** and **puts()** do with the keyboard and display.

Third, data can be read or written in a format analogous to that generated by **printf()** and **scanf()** functions: as a collection of values that may be mixed characters, strings, floating point, and integer numbers.

And fourth, data may be read or written in a new format called a *record*, or *block*. This is a fixed-length group of data, and is commonly used to store a succession of similar data items, such as array elements or structures.

We'll look at each of these ways to transfer data in the section on standard I/O. Figure 13-1 shows the relationship of standard and system I/O to these four categories and the functions used to read and write data for each one.

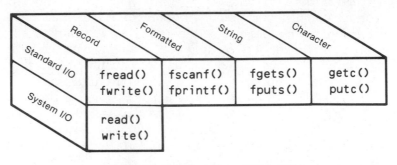

Figure 13-1. Categories of Disk I/O

Text Versus Binary

Another way to categorize file I/O operations is according to whether files are opened in *text mode* or *binary mode*. Which of these two modes is used to open the file determines how various details of file management are handled; how newlines are stored, for example, and how end-of-file is indicated. The reason that these two modes exist is historical: UNIX systems (on which C was first developed) do things one way, while MS-DOS does them another. The two modes are, as we'll see, an attempt to reconcile the standards of the two operating systems.

Just to confuse matters, there is a second distinction between text and binary: the *format* used for storing numbers on the disk. In text format, numbers are stored as strings of characters, while in binary format they are stored as they are in memory: two bytes for an integer, four for floating point, and so on, as we learned in Chapter 2. Some file I/O functions store numbers as text, while others store them as binary.

> Text versus binary *mode* is concerned with newline and EOF translation; text versus binary *format* is concerned with number representation.

These two formats arise not from different operating system standards (as with text versus binary modes), but because different formats work more conveniently in different situations. We'll have more to say about both these text-versus-binary distinctions later on.

At this point we'll narrow our focus from an overview of I/O categories to the details of the various techniques.

Standard Input/Output

Standard I/O is probably the easier to program and understand, so we'll start with it, leaving system-level I/O for later in the chapter.

Of the four kinds of standard I/O, we'll explore the first three in this section: character I/O, string I/O, and formatted I/O. (We'll save record I/O for a later section.) We'll initially look at these three approaches using text mode; later we'll see what differences occur when binary mode is used.

Character Input/Output

Our first example program will take characters typed at the keyboard and, one at a time, write them to a disk file. We'll list the program and show what it does, then dissect it line by line. Here's the listing:

```c
/* writec.c */
/* writes one character at a time to a file */
#include <stdio.h>                /* defines FILE */
void main(void)
{
    FILE *fptr;                    /* ptr to FILE */
    char ch;

    fptr = fopen("textfile.txt","w"); /* open file, set fptr */
    while( (ch=getche()) != '\r' )  /* get character */
        putc(ch,fptr);              /* write it fo file */
    fclose(fptr);                   /* close file */
}
```

p40

In operation the program sits there and waits for you to type a line of text. When you've finished, you hit the [Return] key to terminate the program. In this chapter you'll probably find it easier to execute the examples from DOS rather than Turbo C's IDE, since DOS commands will be used frequently. Here's a sample run (with a phrase from the nineteenth-century poet William Blake):

```
C>writec
Tiger, tiger, burning bright / In the forests of the night
C>
```

What you've typed will be written to a file called textfile.txt. To see that the file has in fact been created, you can use the DOS TYPE function, which will read the contents of the file:

```
C>type textfile.txt
Tiger, tiger, burning bright / In the forests of the night
C>
```

Now that we know what the program does, let's look at how it does it.

Opening a File

Before we can write a file to a disk, or read it, we must *open* it. Opening a file establishes an understanding between our program and the operating system about which file we're going to access and how we're going to do it. We provide the operating system with the name of the file and other information, such as whether we plan to read or write to it. Communication areas are then set up between the file and our program. One of these areas is a C structure that holds information about the file.

This structure, which is defined to be of type **struct FILE**, is our contact point. When we make a request to open a file, what we receive back (if the request is indeed granted) is a pointer to a particular FILE structure. Each file we open will have its own FILE structure, with a pointer to it. Figure 13-2 shows this process.

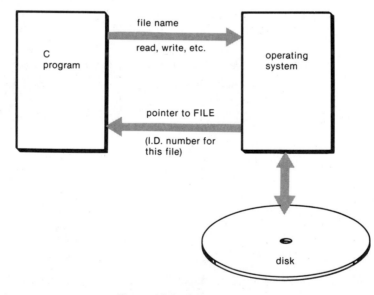

Figure 13-2. Opening a File

The FILE structure contains information about the file being used, such as its current size and the location of its data buffers. The FILE structure is declared in the header file stdio.h (for "standard I/O"). It is necessary to **#include** this file with your program whenever you use standard I/O (but not system-level I/O). In addition to defining the FILE structure, stdio.h also defines a variety of other identifiers and variables that are useful in file-oriented programs; we'll come across some of them later.

In the writec.c program we first declare a variable of type **pointer-to-FILE**, in the statement:

```
FILE *fptr;
```

Then, we open the file with the statement

```
fptr = fopen("textfile.txt","w");
```

This tells the operating system to open a file called "textfile.txt". (We could also have specified a complete MS-DOS pathname here, such as \samples\jan \textfile.txt.) This statement also indicates, via the "w", that we'll be writing to the file. The **fopen()** function returns a pointer to the FILE structure for our file, which we store in the variable **fptr**.

The one-letter string "w" (note that it is a string and not a character; hence the double- and not single-quotes) is called a *type*. The "w" is but one of several types we can specify when we open a file. Here are the other possibilities:

"r"	Open for reading. The file must already exist.
"w"	Open for writing. If the file exists its contents will be written over. If it does not exist it will be created.
"a"	Open for append. Material will be added to the end of an existing file, or a new file will be created.
"r+"	Open for both reading and writing. The file must already exist.
"w+"	Open for both reading and writing. If the file exists its contents are written over.
"a+"	Open for both reading and appending. If the file does not exist it will be created.

In this section we'll be concerned mostly with the "r" and "w" types.

Writing to a File

Once we've established a line of communication with a particular file by opening it, we can write to it. In the writec.c program we do this one character at a time, using the statement:

```
putc(ch,fptr);
```

The **putc()** function is similar to the **putch()** and **putchar()** functions. However, these functions always write to the console (unless redirection is employed), while **putc()** writes to a file. What file? The file whose FILE structure is pointed to by the variable **fptr**, which we obtained when we opened the file. This pointer has become our key to the file; we no longer refer to the file by name, but by the address stored in **fptr**.

The writing process continues in the **while** loop; each time the **putc()** function is executed another character is written to the file. When the user types [Return], the loop terminates.

Closing the File

When we've finished writing to the file we need to close it. This is carried out with the statement

```
fclose(fptr);
```

Again we tell the system what file we mean by referring to the address stored in **fptr**.

Closing the file has several effects. First, any characters remaining in the buffer are written out to the disk. What buffer? We haven't said much about a buffer before, because it is invisible to the programmer when using standard I/O. However, a buffer is necessary even if it is invisible. Consider, for example, how inefficient it would be to actually access the disk just to write one character. It takes a while for the disk system to position the head correctly and wait for the right sector of the track to come around. On a floppy disk system the motor actually has to start the disk from a standstill every time the disk is accessed. If you typed several characters rapidly, and each one required a completely separate disk access, some of the characters would probably be lost. This is where the buffer comes in.

When you send a character off to a file with **putc()**, the character is actually stored in a buffer—an area of memory—rather than being written immediately to the disk. When the buffer is full, its contents are written to the disk all at once. Or, if the program knows the last character has been received, it forces the buffer to be written to the disk by closing the file. A major advantage of using standard I/O (as opposed to system I/O) is that these activities take place automatically; the programmer doesn't need to worry about them. Figure 13-3 shows this "invisible" buffer.

Another reason to close the file is to free the communications areas used by that particular file so they are available for other files. These areas include the FILE structure and the buffer itself.

Reading from a File

If we can write to a file, we should be able to read from one. Here's a program that does just that, using the function **getc()**:

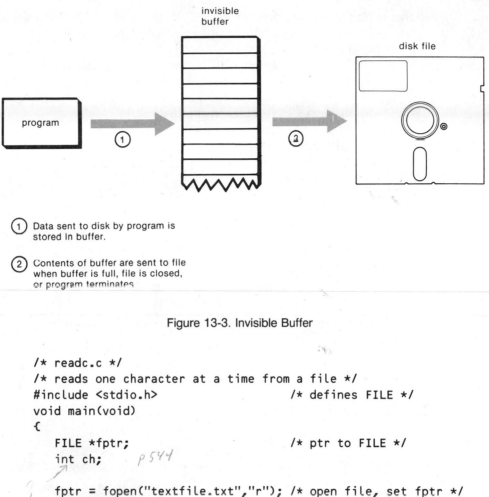

① Data sent to disk by program is
   stored in buffer.

② Contents of buffer are sent to file
   when buffer is full, file is closed,
   or program terminates

Figure 13-3. Invisible Buffer

```
/* readc.c */
/* reads one character at a time from a file */
#include <stdio.h>                  /* defines FILE */
void main(void)
{
   FILE *fptr;                      /* ptr to FILE */
   int ch;          p 544

   fptr = fopen("textfile.txt","r"); /* open file, set fptr */
   while( (ch=getc(fptr)) != EOF )   /* get char from file */
      printf("%c", ch);             /* print it */
   fclose(fptr);                    /* close file */
}
```

As you can see, this program is quite similar to writec.c. The pointer to FILE
is declared the same way, and the file is opened and closed in the same way.
The **getc()** function reads one character from the file "textfile.txt"; this function is the complement of the **putc()** function. (When you try this program,
make sure that the file has already been created by writec.c.)

End-of-File

A major difference between this program and writec.c is that readc.c must be
concerned with knowing when it has read the last character in the file. It does

543

this by looking for an end-of-file (EOF) signal from the operating system. If it tries to read a character, and reads the EOF signal instead, it knows it's come to the end of the file.

What does EOF consist of? It's important to understand that it is *not a character*. It is actually an integer value, sent to the program by the operating system and defined in the stdio.h file to have a value of −1. No character with this value is stored in the file on the disk; rather, when the operating system realizes that the last character in a file has been sent, it transmits the EOF signal. (We'll have more to say about how the operating system knows where the file ends when we look at binary mode files later on.)

> The EOF signal sent by the operating system to a C program is not a character, but an integer with a value of −1.
>
> *binary all 1's*   *FFFF*

So our program goes along reading characters and printing them, looking for a value of −1, or EOF. When it finds this value, the program terminates. We use an *integer* variable to hold the character being read so we can interpret the EOF signal as the integer −1. What difference does it make? If we used a variable of type **char**, the character with the ASCII code 255 decimal (FF hex) would be interpreted as an EOF. We want to be able to use all the character codes from 0 to 255—all possible 8-bit combinations, that is; so by using an integer variable we ensure that only a 16-bit value of −1, which is not the same as any of our character codes, will signal EOF.   *FFFF*

Trouble Opening the File

The two programs we've presented so far have a potential flaw; if the file specified in the **fopen()** function cannot be opened, the programs will not run. Why couldn't a file be opened? If you're trying to open a file for writing, it's probably because there's no more space on the disk. If for reading, it's much more common that a file can't be opened; you can't read it if it hasn't been created yet.

Thus it's important for any program that accesses disk files to check whether a file has been opened successfully before trying to read or write to the file. If the file cannot be opened, the **fopen()** function returns a value of 0 (defined as NULL in stdio.h). Since in C this is not considered a valid address, the program infers that the file could not be opened.

Here's a variation of readc.c that handles this situation:

```
/* readc2.c */
/* reads one character at a time from a file */
/* checks for read error */
#include <stdlib.h>                          /* for exit() */
```

```
#include <stdio.h>                  /* defines FILE */

int main(void)                      /* returns type int */
{
   FILE *fptr;                      /* ptr to FILE */
   char ch;

   if( (fptr=fopen("textfile.txt","r"))==NULL )  /* open file */    p541, 544
      {
      printf("Can't open file textfile.txt.");
      exit(1);                      /* error return value */
      }
   while( (ch=getc(fptr)) != EOF )  /* get char from file */
      printf("%c", ch);             /* print it */       int?
   fclose(fptr);                    /* close file */
   return(0);                       /* normal return value */
}
```

Here the **fopen()** function is enclosed in an **if** statement. If the function
returns NULL, then an explanatory message is printed and the **exit()** is executed, causing the program to terminate immediately, and avoiding the em-
barrassment of trying to read from a nonexistent file.

Since we use the **exit()** function to return a value, we also use **return** for
a normal program termination, returning a value of 0 rather than 1, which
indicates an error.

Counting Characters

The ability to read and write to files on a character-by-character basis has
many useful applications. For example, here's a variation on our readc.c program that counts the characters in a file:

```
/* charcntf.c */
/* counts characters in a file */
#include <stdio.h>
int main( int argc, char *argv[] )     ← command line argoments
{                                           p299
   FILE *fptr;
   char string[81];  ─── ? not used
   int count=0;

   if(argc != 2)                     /* check # of args */
      { printf("Format: C>charcntf filename"); exit(1); }
   if( (fptr=fopen(argv[1], "r")) == NULL)  /* open file */
      { printf("Can't open file %s.", argv[1]); exit(1); }
```

```
      while( getc(fptr) != EOF )          /* get char from file */
         count++;                         /* count it */
      fclose(fptr);                       /* close file */
      printf("File %s contains %d characters.", argv[1], count);
      return(0);
   }
```

p 299

In this program we've used a <u>command-line argument</u> to obtain the name of the file to be examined, rather than writing it into the **fopen()** statement. We start by checking the number of arguments; if there are two, then the second one, **argv[1]**, is the name of the file. For compactness, we've also placed the two statements following the **if** on one line.

The program opens the file, checking to make sure it can be opened, and cycles through a loop, reading one character at a time and incrementing the variable **count** each time a character is read.

If you try out the charcnt.c program on files whose length you've checked with a different program—say the DOS DIR command—you may find that the results don't quite agree. The reason for this has to do with the difference between text and binary mode files; we'll explore this further in the section on string I/O.

Counting Words

It's easy to modify our character-counting program to count words. This can be a useful utility for writers or anyone else who needs to know how many words an article, chapter, or composition comprises. Here's the program:

```
/* wordcntf.c */
/* counts words in a file */
#include <stdio.h>
int main( int argc, char *argv[] )      p 299
{
   FILE *fptr;
   char ch, string[81];
   int white=1;                         /* whitespace flag */
   int count=0;                         /* word count */

   if(argc != 2)                        /* check # of args */
      { printf("Format: C>wordcntf filename"); exit(1); }
   if( (fptr=fopen(argv[1], "r")) == NULL)  /* open file */
      { printf("Can't open file %s.", argv[1]); exit(1); }

   while( (ch=getc(fptr)) != EOF )      /* get char from file */
      {
      switch(ch)
```

```
        {
        case ' ':                      /* if space, tab, or */
        case '\t':                     /* newline, set flag */
        case '\n':
            white++; break;
        default:                       /* non-whitespace, and */
            if(white) { white=0; count++; }  /* flag set, */
        }                              /* count word */
        }
    fclose(fptr);                      /* close file */
    printf("File %s contains %d words.", argv[1], count);
    return(0);
    }
```

What we really count in this program is the *change* from whitespace characters (spaces, newlines, and tabs) to actual (nonwhitespace) characters. In other words, if there's a string of spaces or carriage returns, the program reads them, waiting patiently for the first actual character. It counts this transition as a word. Then it reads actual characters until another whitespace character appears. A "flag" variable keeps track of whether the program is in the middle of a word or in the middle of whitespace; the variable **white** is 1 in the middle of whitespace, 0 in the middle of a word. Figure 13-4 shows the operation of the program.

This program may not work accurately with files produced by some word processing programs, such as WordStar in document mode, which use nonstandard characters for spaces and carriage returns. However, it will work with standard ASCII files.

The wordcntf.c program shows the versatility of character I/O in C. For many purposes, character I/O is just what's needed. However, in other situations, different functions may be more efficient: for instance, in reading and writing whole strings of characters at a time, which is our next topic.

String (line) Input/Output

Reading and writing strings of characters from and to files is almost as easy as reading and writing individual characters. Here's a program that writes strings to a file, using the string I/O function **fputs()**.

```
/* writes.c */
/* writes sentences typed at keyboard, to file */
#include <stdio.h>
void main(void)
{
    FILE *fptr;                        /* declare ptr to FILE */
    char string[81];                   /* storage for strings */
```

p213, 215

```
    fptr = fopen("textfile.txt", "w"); /* open file */
    while(strlen( gets(string) ) > 0)   /* get string from keybd */
        {
        fputs(string, fptr);                /* write string to file */
        fputs("\n", fptr);                  /* write newline to file */
        }
    fclose(fptr);                           /* close file */
    }
```

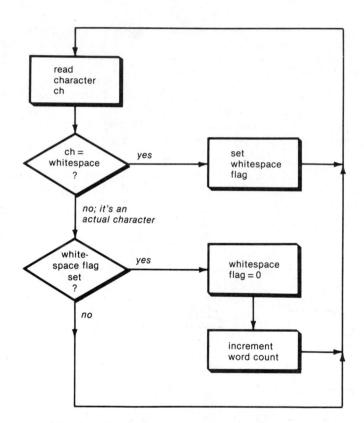

Figure 13-4. Operation of the wordcntf.c Program

The user types a series of strings, terminating each by hitting [Return]. To terminate the entire program, the user hits [Return] at the beginning of a line. This creates a string of zero length, which the program recognizes as the signal to close the file and exit.

We've set up a character array to store the string; the **fputs()** function then writes the contents of the array to the disk. Since **fputs()** does not automatically add a newline character to the end of the line, we must do this explicitly to make it easier to read the string back from the file.

Note that—for simplicity—in this and the next program we have not included a test for an error condition on opening the file, as we did in previous examples. This test should be included in any serious program.

Here's a program that reads strings from a disk file:

```
/* reads.c */
/* reads strings from file */
#include <stdio.h>
void main(void)
{
   FILE *fptr;                             /* ptr to FILE */
   char string[81];                        /* stores strings */

   fptr = fopen("textfile.txt", "r");      /* open file */
   while( fgets(string,80,fptr) != NULL )  /* read string */
      printf("%s", string);                /* print string */
   fclose(fptr);                           /* close file */
}
```

The function **fgets()** takes three parameters. The first is the address where the string is stored, and the second is the maximum length of the string. This parameter keeps the **fgets()** function from reading in too long a string and overflowing the array. The third parameter, as usual, is the pointer to the FILE structure for the file.

Here's a sample run (again courtesy of William Blake), showing the operation of both writes.c and reads.c:

```
C>writes
I told my love, I told my love, CR
I told her all my heart, CR
Trembling, cold, in ghastly fears, CR
Ah! she did depart! CR

C>reads
I told my love, I told my love,
I told her all my heart,
Trembling, cold, in ghastly fears,
Ah! she did depart!
```

The Newline Problem

Earlier we mentioned that our charcntf.c program might not always return the same results as other character-counting programs, such as the DOS DIR command. Now that we can write a file containing several strings, let's investigate this further.

Here's what happens when we try to verify the length of the four-line William Blake excerpt shown above:

```
C>dir textfile.txt
TEXTFILE TXT        116   10-27-87    2:36a

C>charcntf textfile.txt
File textfile.txt contains 112 characters.
```

Using DIR we find 116 characters in the textfile.txt file, whereas using our homemade charcntf.c program we find 112.

This discrepancy occurs because of the difference in the way C and MS-DOS represent the end of a line. In C the end of a line is signalled by a single character: the *newline* character, '\n' (ASCII value 10 decimal). In DOS, on the other hand, the end of a line is marked by *two* characters, the carriage return (ASCII 13 decimal), and the linefeed (which is the same as the C newline: ASCII 10 decimal).

> The end of a line of text is represented by a single character in C (the newline), but by two characters in MS-DOS files (carriage return and linefeed).

When your program writes a C text file to disk, Turbo C causes all the newlines to be translated into the carriage return plus linefeed (CR/LF) combination. When your program reads in a text file, the CR/LF combination is translated back into a single newline character. Thus, DOS-oriented programs such as DIR will count two characters at each end of line, while C-oriented programs, such as charcntf.c, will count one. In our example there are four lines, so there is a discrepancy of four characters.

As we'll see later, binary mode files handle this translation differently from text files.

Reproducing the DOS TYPE Command

As a practical use for string I/O, we can reproduce the DOS TYPE command, as demonstrated in this example:

```
/* type2.c */
/* reads strings from file */
#include <stdio.h>
int main( int argc, char *argv[] )
{
```

```
        FILE *fptr;
        char string[81];

        if(argc != 2)
           { printf("Format: C>type2 filename"); exit(1); }
        if( (fptr=fopen(argv[1], "r")) == NULL)
           { printf("Can't open file %s.", argv[1]); exit(1); }
        while( fgets(string, 80, fptr) != NULL )   /* read string */
           printf("%s",string);                    /* print string */
        fclose(fptr);                              /* close file */
        return(0);
    }
```

This program takes the content of a text file and displays it on the screen, just as the DOS TYPE command does. The advantage of using a homemade command is that you can customize it; you could, for example, add line numbers to your printout or interpret certain characters differently.

Printer Output

There are several ways to send output to the printer. In this section we'll look at two approaches that use standard I/O. The first approach uses standard file handles, and the second uses standard file names.

Standard File Handles

We've seen several examples of obtaining handles that refer to files. MS-DOS also predefines five standard handles that refer to devices rather than files. These handles are accessed using names defined to be of type *FILE in the stdio.h file. They are:

Number	Handle	Device
0	"stdin"	Standard input (keyboard, unless redirected)
1	"stdout"	Standard output (screen, unless redirected)
2	"stderr"	Standard error (screen)
3	"stdaux"	Auxiliary device
4	"stdprn"	Printer

The standard input and standard output normally refer to the keyboard and screen, but they can be redirected (we discussed redirection in Chapter 8). Standard error, which is where errors are normally reported, always refers to the screen. The auxiliary device can be assigned when the system is set up;

it is often used for a serial device. The standard printer handle is what we want for printing.

Because these standard handles are opened by the system, we don't need to open them before using them. Our example program sends the contents of a text file to the printer, using an approach similar to the reads.c and writes.c examples. It opens the file to be read in the usual way, but the printer is not opened. To write to the printer, **fputs()** is used with a filename of "stdprn".

```
/* print.c */
/* prints file on printer -- uses standard handle */
#include <stdio.h>
int main( int argc, char *argv[] )
{
   FILE *fptr;
   char string[81];

   if(argc != 2)                           /* check args */
      { printf("Format: print filename"); exit(1); }
   if( (fptr=fopen(argv[1], "r")) == NULL)   /* open file */
      { printf("Can't open file %s.", argv[1]); exit(1); }
   while( fgets(string, 80, fptr) != NULL )  /* read string */
      {
      fputs(string, stdprn);                /* send to printer */
      putc('\r', stdprn);                   /* with return */
      }
   fclose(fptr);                            /* close file */
   return(0);
}
```

We'll see an example later in this chapter where, with system-level I/O, you use predefined handle *numbers* rather than names for standard devices.

Standard File Names

You can also refer to devices by names, rather than handles. These names are used very much like file names. For instance, you probably know that you can create short text files by typing

```
C>copy con readme.txt
This is a short text file. CR
^Z
```

The CON file name used above refers to the console, which is the keyboard or screen, depending on whether input or output is intended. Similarly, the standard auxiliary device can be called AUX, and the standard printer can be called PRN. DOS

Here's an example that uses the PRN file name to access the printer. Because this is a name, and not a handle, the device must be opened before it is used.

```
/* print2.c */
/* prints file on printer -- uses standard file name */
#include <stdio.h>
int main( int argc, char *argv[] )
{
   FILE *fptr1, *fptr2;
   char string[81];

   if(argc != 2)                             /* check args */
      { printf("Format: C>print2 filename"); exit(1); }
   if( (fptr1=fopen(argv[1], "r")) == NULL)   /* open file */
      { printf("Can't open file %s.", argv[1]); exit(1); }
   if( (fptr2=fopen("PRN", "w")) == NULL)      /* open printer */
      { printf("Can't access printer."); exit(); }
   while( fgets(string, 80, fptr1) != NULL )  /* read string */
      fputs(string,fptr2);                    /* send to printer */
   fclose(fptr1); fclose(fptr2);              /* close files */
   return(0);
}
```

This approach is advantageous if you use more than one printer. The name LPT1 is (usually) a synonym for PRN, but if you have additional printers, you can send output to them using the file names LPT2, LPT3, and so on.

Formatted Input/Output

So far we have dealt with reading and writing only characters and text. How about numbers? To see how we can handle numerical data, let's take a leaf from our secret agent dossier in Chapter 9. We'll use the same three items we used there to record the data for an agent: name (a string), code number (an integer), and height (a floating point number). Then we'll write these items to a disk file.

This program reads the data from the keyboard, then writes it to our "textfile.txt" file. Here's the listing:

```
/* writef.c */
/* writes formatted data to file */
#include <stdio.h>
void main(void)
```

```
        {
            FILE *fptr;                          /* declare ptr to FILE */
            char name[40];                       /* agent's name */
            int code;                            /* code number */
            float height;                        /* agent's height */

            fptr = fopen("textfile.txt", "w"); /* open file */
            do {
                printf("Type name, code number, and height: ");
                scanf("%s %d %f", name, &code, &height);
                fprintf(fptr, "%s %d %f", name, code, height);
                }
            while(strlen(name) > 1);             /* no name given? */
            fclose(fptr);                        /* close file */
        }
```

file-print-formatted   The key to this program is the **fprintf()** function, which writes the ~~values~~ *formatted*
of the three variables to the file. This function is similar to **printf()**, except
that a FILE pointer is included as the first argument. As in **printf()**, we can
format the data in a variety of ways; in fact, all the format conventions of
printf() operate with **fprintf()** as well.

For simplicity this program requires the user to indicate that input is
complete by typing a one-letter agent name followed by dummy numbers; this
avoids using extra program statements to check if the user is done, but it's not
very user-friendly. Here's some sample input:

```
C>writef
Type name, code number, and height: Bond 007 74.5
Type name, code number, and height: Salsbury 009 72.25
Type name, code number, and height: Fleming 999 69.75
Type name, code number, and height: x 0 0
```

This information is now in the "textfile.txt" file. We can look at it there with
the DOS TYPE command—or with type2.c—although when we use these
programs all the output will be on the same line, since there are no newlines in
the data. To format the output more conveniently, we can write a program
specifically to read textfile.txt:

```
/* readf.c */
/* reads formatted data from file */
#include <stdio.h>
void main(void)
{
    FILE *fptr;                          /* declare ptr to FILE */
    char name[40];                       /* agent's name */
```

```
    int code;                          /* code number */
    float height;                      /* agent's height */

    fptr = fopen("textfile.txt", "r"); /* open file */
    while( fscanf(fptr, "%s %d %f", name, &code, &height) != EOF )
       printf("%s %03d %.2f\n", name, code, height);
    fclose(fptr);                      /* close file */
}
```

This program uses the **fscanf()** function to read the data from the disk. This function is similar to **scanf()**, except that, as with **fprintf()**, a pointer to FILE is included as the first argument.

We can now print out the data in a more readable format, using **printf()**:

```
C>readf
Bond 007 74.50
Salsbury 009 72.25
Fleming 999 69.75
x 000 0.00
```

Of course, we can use similar techniques with **fprintf()** and **fscanf()** for other sorts of formatted data: any combination of characters, strings, integers, and floating point numbers.

Number Storage in Text Format

It's important to understand how numerical data is stored on the disk by **fprintf()**. Text and characters are stored one character per byte, as we would expect. Are numbers stored as they are in memory, two bytes for an integer, four bytes for floating point, and so on? No. They are stored as strings of characters. Thus, the integer 999 is stored in two bytes of memory, but requires three bytes in a disk file, one for each '9' character. The floating point number 69.75 requires four bytes when stored in memory, but five when stored on the disk: one for each digit and one for the decimal point. Numbers with more digits require even more disk space. Figure 13-5 shows how this looks.

Numbers with more than a few significant digits require substantially more space on the disk using formatted I/O than they do in memory. Thus, if a large amount of numerical data is to be stored on a disk file, using text format can be inefficient. The solution is to use a function that stores numbers in binary format. We'll explore this option in the section on record I/O.

We've now described three methods in standard I/O for reading and writing data. These three methods write data in text format. The fourth method, record I/O, writes data in binary format. When writing data in binary format it is often desirable to use binary mode, so we'll investigate the differences between binary and text modes before discussing record I/O.

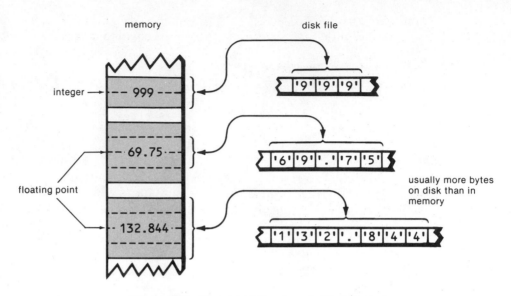

Figure 13-5. Storage of Numbers in Text Format

Binary Mode and Text Mode

As we noted at the beginning of this chapter, the distinction between text and binary can be applied to two different areas of disk I/O. On the one hand, there is the question of how numbers are stored; this is the distinction between text versus binary _format_. On the other hand, we can talk about how files are opened and the format interpretations this leads to; this can be called text versus binary _mode_. It's this second distinction we want to examine in this section.

The need for two different modes arose from incompatibilities between C and the MS-DOS operating system. C originated on UNIX systems and used UNIX file conventions. MS-DOS, which evolved separately from UNIX, has its own, somewhat different, conventions. When C was ported over to the MS-DOS operating system, compiler-writers had to resolve these incompatibilities. The solution decided on by Borland (but not by all C compiler-writers on the PC) was to have two modes. One, the text mode, made files look to C programs as if they were UNIX files. The other, binary mode, made files look more like MS-DOS files.

> Text mode imitates UNIX files, while binary mode imitates MS-DOS files.

There are two main areas where text and binary mode files are different: the handling of newlines and the representation of end-of-file. We'll explore these two areas here.

Text Versus Binary Mode: Newlines

We've already seen that, in text mode, a newline character is translated into the carriage return-linefeed (CR/LF) combination before being written to the disk. Likewise, the CR/LF on the disk is translated back into a newline when the file is read by the C program. However, if a file is opened in binary mode, as opposed to text mode, these translations will not take place.

As an example, let's revise our charcntf.c program to open a file in binary mode and see what effect this has on the number of characters counted in the file. As you may recall, charcnt.c counted fewer characters in a file than did the DOS command DIR, because DIR counted each end-of-line as two characters, while charcnt.c counted it as one. Perhaps we can eliminate this discrepancy. Here's the listing:

p 545

```
/* charcnt2.c */
/* counts characters in a file opened as binary */
#include <stdio.h>
int main( int argc, char *argv[] )
{
   FILE *fptr;
   char string[81];
   int count=0;

   if(argc != 2)                         /* check # of args */
      { printf("Format: C>charcnt2 filename"); exit(1); }
   if( (fptr=fopen(argv[1],"rb")) == NULL)  /* open file */
      { printf("Can't open file %s.", argv[1]); exit(1); }
   while( getc(fptr) != EOF )             /* get char from file */
      count++;                            /* count it */
   fclose(fptr);                          /* close file */
   printf("File %s contains %d characters.", argv[1], count);
   return(0);
}
```

There is only one difference between this program and the original charcntf.c; we have introduced the letter "b" as part of the type string, following the "r":

```
fptr=fopen(argv[1], "rb")
```

The "b" means that the file should be opened in binary mode. (We could also use a "t" to specify text mode, but since this is the default for character I/O, this is not normally necessary.)

557

Now if we apply charcnt2.c to our earlier example of the William Blake poem, we'll get the same character count we got using the DOS DIR command—116 characters; while with the text mode charcntf.c we got 112 characters:

```
C>charcnt2 textfile.txt
File textfile.txt contains 116 characters.

C>charcntf textfile.txt
File textfile.txt contains 112 characters.
```

There are four carriage return-linefeed combinations in the file. Each counts as one character in the text mode program charcntf.c, but as two characters in the binary mode program charcnt2.c; hence the difference of four characters. In binary mode the translation of the CR/LF pair into a newline does not take place: the binary charcnt2.c program reads each CR/LF as two characters, just as it's stored on the file.

Text Versus Binary Mode: End-of-File

The second difference between text and binary modes is in the way end-of-file is detected. Both systems actually keep track of the total length of the file and will signal an EOF when this length has been reached. In text mode, however, a special character, 1A hex (26 decimal), inserted after the last character in the file, is also used to indicate EOF. (This character can be generated from the keyboard by typing [Ctrl] [z]and is often written ^Z.) If this character is encountered at any point in the file, the read function will return the EOF signal (−1) to the program.

This convention arose in the days of CP/M, when all files consisted of blocks of a certain minimum length. To indicate that a file ended in the middle of a block, the ^Z character was used, and its use has carried over into MS-DOS.

There is a moral to be derived from the text-mode conversion of 1A hex to EOF. If a file stores numbers in binary format, it's important that binary mode be used in reading the file back, since one of the numbers might well be the number 1A hex (26 decimal). If this number were detected while we were reading a file in text mode, reading would be terminated (prematurely) at that point.

Also, when writing in binary format, we don't want numbers that happen to have the value 10 decimal to be interpreted as newlines and expanded into CR/LFs. Thus, both in reading and writing binary format numbers, we should use binary mode when accessing the file.

Figure 13-6 shows the differences between text and binary mode.

Text mode *UNIX like*

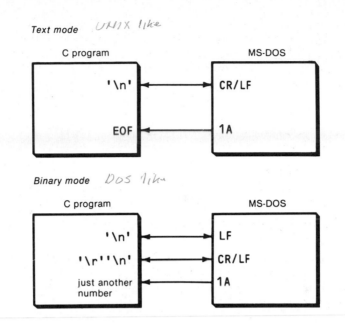

Binary mode *DOS like*

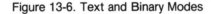

Figure 13-6. Text and Binary Modes

Binary Dump Program

Before leaving the subject of binary versus text modes, let's look at a program that uses binary mode to investigate files. This program looks at a file byte-by-byte, in binary mode, and displays what it finds there. The display consists of two parts: the hexadecimal code for each character and—if the character is displayable—the character itself. This program provides a sort of x-ray of a disk file. It is modelled after the "dump" function in the DEBUG utility in MS-DOS.

Here's the listing:

```
/* bindump.c */
/* does binary dump of disk file */
/* each line is ten ASCII codes followed by ten characters */
#include <stdio.h>
#define LENGTH 10
#define TRUE 0
#define FALSE -1

int main( int argc, char *argv[] )
{
    FILE *fileptr;                      /* pointer to file */
    int ch;
```

↑ *so FFFF is not used as EOF*

```
    int j, not_eof;
    unsigned char string[LENGTH+1];      /* buffer for chars */

    if(argc != 2)                        /* check arguments */
       { printf("Format: C>bindump filename"); exit(1); }
    if( (fileptr=fopen(argv[1],"rb"))==NULL )   /* binary read */
       { printf("Can't open file %s", argv[1]); exit(1); }
    not_eof = TRUE;                      /* not EOF flag */
    do
       {
       for (j=0; j < LENGTH; j++)        /* chars in one line */
          {
          if ( (ch=getc(fileptr)) == EOF ) /* read character */
             not_eof = FALSE;            /* clear flag on EOF */
          printf( "%3x ", ch );          /* print ASCII code */
          if (ch > 31)
             *(string+j) = ch;           /* save printing char */
          else                           /* use period for */
             *(string+j) = '.';          /* non-printing char */
          }
       *(string+j) = '\0';               /* end string */
       printf("   %s\n", string);        /* print string */
       }
    while ( not_eof == TRUE );           /* quit on EOF */
    fclose(fileptr);                     /* close file */
    return(0);
    }
```

To use this program, you type the name of the program followed by the name of the file to be investigated. If the file is too big to fit on one screen, scrolling can be paused with the [Ctrl] [s] key combination.

Earlier we wrote a William Blake poem to the file textfile.txt. Let's see what happens when we apply bindump.c to that file.

```
C>bindump textfile.txt
 49  20  74  6f  6c  64  20  6d  79  20    I told my
 6c  6f  76  65  2c  20  49  20  74  6f    love, I to
 6c  64  20  6d  79  20  6c  6f  76  65    ld my love
 2c   d   a  49  20  74  6f  6c  64  20    ,..I told
 68  65  72  20  61  6c  6c  20  6d  79    her all my
 20  68  65  61  72  74  2c   d   a  54     heart,..T
 72  65  6d  62  6c  69  6e  67  2c  20    rembling,
 63  6f  6c  64  2c  20  69  6e  20  67    cold, in g
 68  61  73  74  6c  79  20  66  65  61    hastly fea
 72  73  2c   d   a  41  68  21  20  73    rs,..Ah! s
```

buffer padding to
end of sector
TCCR p206

```
68   65   20   64   69   64   20   64   65   70      he did dep
61   72   74   21    d    a ffff ffff ffff ffff      art!..~~~~
```

In each row the numbers correspond to the characters printed on the right: 49 hex is 'I', 20 is a space, 74 is 't', and so on. Notice that the CR/LF combination is represented as D hex followed by A hex. If we had opened the file in text mode, we would have seen only the A's. Also, if the program encounters the number 1A hex, it will print it out just like any other number; it will not be interpreted as EOF, as it would have been in text mode.

At the end of the file, the program starts to read real EOFs, which are printed as ffff hex. The program reads until the end of a line, even if it has found an EOF, so the rest of the line is filled out with ffff. With a modest increase in complexity, the program could be rewritten to terminate on the first EOF. Also, if you prefer decimal to hexadecimal output, changing the format specifier in the **printf()** statement will do the trick.

> Binary mode is ordinarily used for binary format data and text mode for text format data, although there are exceptions.

Now that we know something about binary mode, let's investigate the fourth method of performing standard I/O: record I/O.

Record Input/Output

Earlier we saw how numbers can be stored using the formatted I/O functions **fscanf()** and **fprintf()**. However, we also saw that storing numbers in the format provided by these functions can take up a lot of disk space, because each digit is stored as a character. Formatted I/O presents another problem; there is no direct way to read and write complex data types such as arrays and structures. Arrays can be handled, but inefficiently, by writing each array element one at a time. Structures must also be written piecemeal.

In standard I/O, one answer to these problems is *record I/O*, sometimes called *block I/O*. Record I/O writes numbers to disk files in binary (or "untranslated") format, so that integers are stored in two bytes, floating point numbers in four bytes, and so on for the other numerical types—the same format used to store numbers in memory. Record I/O also permits writing any amount of data at once; the process is not limited to a single character or string or to the few values that can be placed in a **fprintf()** or **fscanf()** function. Arrays, structures, structures of arrays, and other data constructions can be written with a single statement.

Writing Structures with *fwrite()*

Taking the structure used for secret agent data in Chapter 9, we'll devise a pair of programs to read and write such structures directly. The first one, listed here, will write a file consisting of a number of agent records, each one consisting of the structure **agent** defined in the program.

```
/* writer.c */
/* writes agent's records to file */
#include <stdio.h>                    /* for FILE, etc. */
#include <stdlib.h>                   /* for atof(), etc. */
int main(void)
{
    struct                           /* define structure */
       {
       char name[40];                /* name */
       int agnumb;                   /* code number */
       double height;                /* height */
       } agent;
    char numstr[81];                 /* for numbers */
    FILE *fptr;                       /* file pointer */

    if( (fptr=fopen("agents.rec","wb"))==NULL )  /* open file */
       { printf("Can't open file agents.rec"); exit(1); }
    do
       {
       printf("\nEnter name: ");      /* get name */
       gets(agent.name);
       printf("Enter number: ");      /* get number */
       gets(numstr);
       agent.agnumb = atoi(numstr);         p 298
       printf("Enter height: ");      /* get height */
       gets(numstr);
       agent.height = atof(numstr);         p 327
                                      /* write struct to file */
       fwrite(&agent, sizeof(agent), 1, fptr);
       printf("Add another agent (y/n)? ");
       }
    while(getche()=='y');
    fclose(fptr);                     /* close file */
    return(0);
}
```

This program will accept input concerning name, number, and height of each agent, and will then write the data to a disk file called "agents.rec". Any number of agents can be entered. Here's a sample interaction:

```
C>writer
Enter name: Holmes, Sherlock
Enter number: 010
Enter height: 73.75
Add another agent (y/n)? y
Enter name: Bond, James
Enter number: 007
Enter height: 74.5
Add another agent (y/n)? n
```

Most of this program should be familiar to you from Chapter 9 and from earlier examples in this chapter. Note, however, that the agents.rec file is opened in binary mode.

The information obtained from the user at the keyboard is placed in the structure **agent**. Then the following statement writes the structure to the file:

```
fwrite(&agent, sizeof(agent), 1, fptr);
```

The first argument of this function is the address of the structure to be written. The second argument is the size of the structure. Instead of counting bytes, we let the program do it for us by using the **sizeof()** function. The third argument is the number of such structures we want to write at one time. If we had an array of structures, for example, we might want to write the entire array all at once. This number could then be adjusted accordingly, as we'll see shortly. In this case, however, we want to write only one structure at a time. The last argument is the pointer to the file we want to write to.

Writing Arrays with *fwrite()*

The **fwrite()** function need not be restricted to writing structures to the disk. We can use it (and its complementary function, **fread()**, which we'll examine next) to work with other data as well. For example, suppose we wanted to store an integer array of 10 elements in a disk file. We could write the 10 items one at a time using **fprintf()**, but it is far more efficient to take the following approach:

```
/* warray.c */
/* writes array to file */
#include <stdio.h>
int table[10] = { 1, 2, 3, 4, 5, 6, 7, 8, 9, 10 };

void main(void)
{
    FILE *fptr;                          /* file pointer */
```

```
        if( (fptr=fopen("table.rec","w"))==NULL )  /* open file */
           { printf("Can't open file agents.rec"); exit(1); }
        fwrite(table, sizeof(table), 1, fptr);      /* write array */
        fclose(fptr);                            /* close file */
     }
```

This program doesn't accomplish anything useful, but it does demonstrate that the writing of an array to the disk is similar to the writing of a structure. (We'll soon see an example of writing an array of structures.)

Reading Structures with *fread()*

To read the structure written by writer.c, we can concoct another program, similar to writer.c:

```
/* readr.c */
/* reads agent's records from file */
#include <stdio.h>                            /* for FILE, etc. */
int main(void)
{
   struct
     {
     char name[40];                            /* name */
     int agnumb;                               /* code number */
     double height;                            /* height */
     } agent;
   FILE *fptr;

   if( (fptr=fopen("agents.rec","rb"))==NULL )
      { printf("Can't open file agents.rec"); exit(1); }
   while( fread(&agent,sizeof(agent),1,fptr)==1 )
      {                                         /* read file */
      printf("\nName: %s\n", agent.name);       /* print name */
      printf("Number: %03d\n", agent.agnumb);   /* print number */
      printf("Height: %.2lf\n", agent.height);  /* print height */
      }
   fclose(fptr);                                /* close file */
   return(0);
}
```

The heart of this program is the expression

```
      fread(&agent,sizeof(agent),1,fptr)
```

This causes data read from the disk to be placed in the structure **agent**; the format is the same as **fwrite()**. The **fread()** function returns the number of items read. Ordinarily this should correspond to the third argument, the number of items we asked for—in this case, 1. If we've reached the end of the file, however, the number will be smaller—in this case, 0. By testing for this situation, we know when to stop reading.

The **fread()** function places the data from the file into the structure; to display it, we access the structure members with **printf()** in the usual way. Here's how it looks:

```
C>readr

Holmes, Sherlock
010
73.75

Bond, James
007
74.50
```

In record I/O, numerical data is stored in binary mode. This means that an integer always occupies two bytes, a floating point number always occupies four bytes, and so on. Figure 13-7 shows the relationship of data stored in memory and on the disk in binary format. As you can see, record I/O, because it makes use of binary format, is more efficient for the storage of numerical data than functions that use text format, such as **fprintf()**.

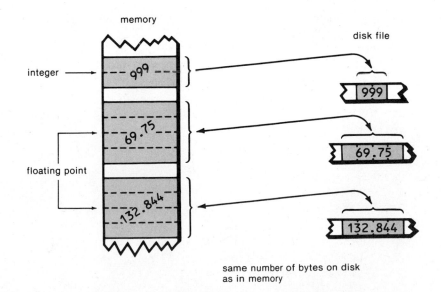

Figure 13-7. Storage of Numbers in Binary Format

Since data is stored in binary format, it's important to open the file in binary mode. If it were opened in text mode, and should the number 26 decimal be used in the file (as an agent number, for instance), the program would interpret it as an EOF and stop reading the file at that point. We also want to suppress the conversion of newlines to CR/LFs.

A Database Example

For a more ambitious example of record I/O at work, we'll add disk reading and writing capability to our agent.c program from Chapter 9. The resulting program will allow data for up to 50 agents to be entered into an array of structures in memory. Then a single command will write the entire array to disk, thus saving the database for future access. Another command reads the array back in again.

Here's the listing:

```c
/* agentr.c */
/* maintains list of agents in file */
#include <stdio.h>
#include <stdlib.h>
#define TRUE 1
void listall(void);             /* prototypes */
void newname(void);
void rfile(void);
void wfile(void);

struct personel                 /* define data structure */
   {
   char name [40];              /* name */
   int agnumb;                  /* code number */
   double height;               /* height in inches */
   };
struct personel agent[50];      /* array of 50 structures */
int n = 0;                      /* number of agents listed */
char numstr[40];

void main(void)
{
   while ( TRUE )
      {
      printf("\n'e' enter new agent\n'l' list all agents");
      printf("\n'w' write file\n'r' read file\n'q' exit: ");
      switch ( getche() )
         {
         case 'e': newname(); break;
```

```
            case 'l': listall(); break;
            case 'w': wfile(); break;
            case 'r': rfile(); break;
            case 'q': exit(0);
            default:                        /* user mistake */
               puts("\nEnter only selections listed");
            }  /* end switch */
         }  /* end while */
   }  /* end main */


/* newname() */
/* puts a new agent in the database */
void newname(void)
{
   printf("\nRecord %d.\nEnter name: ", n+1); /* get name */
   gets(agent[n].name);
   printf("Enter agent number (3 digits): "); /* get number */
   gets(numstr);
   agent[n].agnumb = atoi(numstr);
   printf("Enter height in inches: ");        /* get height */
   gets(numstr);
   agent[n++].height = atof(numstr);
}


/* listall() */
/* lists all agents and data */
void listall(void)
{
   int j;
   if (n < 1)                               /* check for empty list */
      printf("\nEmpty list.\n");
   for (j=0; j < n; j++)                     /* print list */
      {
      printf("\nRecord number %d\n", j+1);
      printf("   Name: %s\n", agent[j].name);
      printf("   Agent number: %03d\n", agent[j].agnumb);
      printf("   Height: %4.2lf\n", agent[j].height);
      }
}


/* wfile() */
/* writes array of structures to file */
void wfile(void)
{
   FILE *fptr;
```

```
      if(n < 1)
         { printf("\nCan't write empty list.\n"); return; }
      if( (fptr=fopen("agents.rec","wb"))==NULL )
         printf("\nCan't open file agents.rec\n");
      else
         {
         fwrite(agent, sizeof(agent[0]), n, fptr);
         fclose(fptr);
         printf("\nFile of %d records written.\n", n);
         }
   }


/* rfile() */
/* reads records from file into array */
void rfile(void)
{
   FILE *fptr;
   if( (fptr=fopen("agents.rec","rb"))==NULL )
      printf("\nCan't open file agents.rec\n");
   else
      {
      while( fread(&agent[n],sizeof(agent[n]),1,fptr)==1 )
         n++;                    /* count records */
      fclose(fptr);
      printf("\nFile read. Total agents is now %d.\n", n);
      }
}
```

Using this program, we can enter a number of secret agents, using the 'e' option:

```
C>agentr

'e' enter new agent
'l' list all agents
'w' write file
'r' read file: e
Record 1.
Enter name: Mike Hammer
Enter agent number (3 digits): 004
Enter height in inches: 74.25
```

We can continue this process for as many names as we want. Once we've entered the names, we write them to disk with the 'w' option. Then we can quit the program, turn off the computer, whatever; it doesn't matter if the array in memory is destroyed. When we run the program again, we can read the list back in from the disk. The following sequence shows that there is nothing in the list until we read the file; then we can list the contents:

```
C>agentr4

'e' enter new agent
'l' list all agents
'w' write file
'r' read file: l
Empty list.

'e' enter new agent
'l' list all agents
'w' write file
'r' read file: r
File read. Total agents is now 3.

'e' enter new agent
'l' list all agents
'w' write file
'r' read file: l

Record number 1
    Name: Mike Hammer
    Agent number: 004
    Height: 74.25

Record number 2
    Name: Lew Archer
    Agent number: 026
    Height: 71.50

Record number 3
    Name: Sam Spade
    Agent number: 492
    Height: 71.75
```

The new capabilities of this program are in the functions **wfile()** and **rfile()**. In **wfile()** the statement

```
fwrite(agent, sizeof(agent[0]), n, fptr);
```

causes the entire array of n structures to be written to disk all at once. The address of the data is at **agent**; the size of one record is **sizeof(agent[0])**, which is the size of the first record; the number of such records is **n**; and the file pointer is **fptr**.

When the function **rfile()** reads the data back in, it must do so one record—that is, one structure—at a time, since it doesn't know in advance how many agents are in the database. Thus, the expression

```
fread(&agent[n],sizeof(agent[n]),1,fptr)
```

is embedded in a **while** loop, which waits for the **fread()** function to report that no bytes were read, indicating end-of-file. This expression causes the data in the structure to be stored at address **&agent[n]**, and to have the size of **agent[n]**. It causes one such structure to be read at a time, from the file pointed to by **fptr**.

> The **fread()** and **fwrite()** functions work with any kind of data, including arrays and structures, and store numbers in binary format.

This program, although it deals with secret agents, could serve as a skeleton for all sorts of database applications, from recipes and stamp collecting to employee records and inventory control.

Random Access

So far all our file reading and writing has been sequential. That is, when writing a file we've taken a group of items—whether characters, strings, or more complex structures—and placed them on the disk one at a time. Likewise, when reading, we've started at the beginning of the file and gone on until we came to the end.

It's also possible to access files "randomly." This means directly accessing a particular data item, even though it may be in the middle of the file.

The following program allows random access of the file agents.rec, created with the agentr.c program above.

```
/* randr.c */
/* reads one agent's record from file */
#include <stdio.h>
int main(void)
{
   struct
     {
     char name[40];                          /* name */
```

```
        int agnumb;                         /* code number */
        double height;                      /* height */
        } agent;
FILE *fptr;
int recno;                                  /* record number */
long int offset;                            /* must be long */
                                            /* open file */
if( (fptr=fopen("agents.rec","r"))==NULL )
   { printf("Can't open file agents.rec"); exit(1); }

printf("Enter record number: ");           /* get record num */
scanf("%d", &recno);
offset = (recno-1) * sizeof(agent);        /* find offset */
if(fseek(fptr, offset, 0) != 0)            /* go there */
   { printf("Can't move pointer there."); exit(1); }

fread(&agent,sizeof(agent),1,fptr);        /* read record */
printf("\nName: %s\n", agent.name);        /* print name */
printf("Number: %03d\n", agent.agnumb);    /* print number */
printf("Height: %.2lf\n", agent.height);   /* print height */
fclose(fptr);                              /* close file */
return(0);
}
```

And here—assuming the same database exists that we created with the agentr.c program earlier—is what it looks like if we use randr.c to ask for the second record in the file:

```
C>randr
Enter record number: 2

Name: Lew Archer
Number: 026
Height: 71.50
```

File Pointers

To understand how this program works, you need to be familiar with the concept of *file pointers*. A file pointer is a pointer to a particular byte in a file. The functions we've examined in this chapter all made use of the file pointer: each time we wrote something to a file, the file pointer moved to the end of that something—whether character, string, structure, or whatever—so that writing would continue at that point with the next write function.

When we closed a file and then reopened it, the file pointer was set back to the beginning of the file, so that if we then read from the file, we would

571

start at the beginning. If we had opened a file for append (using the "a" type option), then the file pointer would have been placed at the end of an existing file before we began writing.

> The file pointer points to the byte in the file where the next access will take place. The **fseek()** function lets us move this pointer.

The function **fseek()** gives us control over the file pointer. Thus, to access a record in the middle of a file, we use this function to move the file pointer to that record. In the program above the file pointer is set to the desired value in the expression:

```
if(fseek(fptr, offset, 0) != 0)
```

The first argument of the **fseek()** function is the pointer to the FILE structure for this file. (As you know, this is also referred to as a "file pointer," but it is something quite different from the file pointer that indicates where we are in the file. We have to trust to context to indicate which file pointer we mean.)

The second argument in **fseek()** is called the *offset*. This is the number of bytes from a particular place to start reading. Often this place is the beginning of the file; that's the case here. (We'll see other possibilities in a moment.) In our program the offset is calculated by multiplying the size of one record—the structure **agent**—by the number of the record we want to access. In the example we access the second record, but the program thinks of this as record number 1 (since the first record is 0) so the multiplication will be by 1. It is essential that the offset be a *long* integer.

The last argument of the **fseek()** function is called the mode. There are three possible mode numbers, and they determine where the offset will be measured from.

Mode	Offset is measured from
0	beginning of file
1	current position of file pointer
2	end of file

Once the file pointer has been set, we read the contents of the record at that point into the structure **agent** and print out its contents.

For simplicity we've demonstrated random access to the agents.rec file as a separate program, but it could easily be incorporated into agentr.c as a function, becoming another option for the user.

Another function, **ftell()**, returns the position of the file pointer.

Error Conditions

In most cases, if a file can be opened, it can be read from or written to. There are situations, however, when this is not the case. A hardware problem might occur while either reading or writing is taking place, a write operation might run out of disk space, or some other problem might occur.

In our programs so far, we have assumed that no such read or write errors occur. But in some situations, such as programs where data integrity is critical, it may be desirable to check explicitly for errors.

Most standard I/O functions do not have an explicit error return. For example, if **putc()** returns an EOF, this might indicate either a true end-of-file or an error; if **fgets()** returns a NULL value, this might indicate either an EOF or an error, and so forth.

To determine whether an error has occurred we can use the function **ferror()**. This function takes one argument: the file pointer (to FILE). It returns a value of 0 if *no error* has occurred, and a nonzero (TRUE) value if there is an error. This function should be reset by closing the file after it has been used.

Another function is also useful in conjunction with **ferror()**. This one is called **perror()**. It takes a string supplied by the program as an argument; this string is usually an error message indicating where in the program the error occurred. The function prints out the program's error message and then goes on to print out a system-error message.

Here's how we could rewrite the earlier writef.c program to incorporate these two error-handling functions:

```
/* writef2.c */
/* writes formatted data to file */
/* includes error-handling functions */
#include <stdio.h>
int main(void)
{
   FILE *fptr;                         /* declare ptr to FILE */
   char name[40];                      /* agent's name */
   int code;                           /* code number */
   float height;                       /* agent's height */
                                       /* open file */
   if( (fptr=fopen("textfile.txt","w"))==NULL )
      { printf("Can't open textfile.txt"); exit(1); }
   do {
      printf("Type name, code number, and height: ");
      scanf("%s %d %f", name, &code, &height);
      fprintf(fptr, "%s %d %f", name, code, height);
      if( ferror(fptr) )               /* check for error */
```

573

```
            {
            perror("Write error");        /* write message */
            fclose(fptr);                  /* close file */
            exit(1);
            }
      }
   while(strlen(name) > 1);               /* no name given? */
   fclose(fptr);                          /* close file */
   return(0);
}
```

In the event that, for example, there is a disk error, **ferror()** will return a nonzero value and **perror()** will print out the following message:

```
Write error: Bad data
```

The first part of this message is supplied by the program and the second part, from the colon on, is supplied by the system.

Explicit error messages of this type can be informative both for the user and for the programmer during development.

We've completed our exploration of standard I/O so we're ready to move into the second type of C-language input/output: system-level I/O.

System-Level Input/Output

System-level (sometimes called low-level) I/O parallels the methods used by MS-DOS for reading and writing files. In system-level I/O, data cannot be written as individual characters, or as strings, or as formatted data, as is possible using standard I/O. There is only one way data can be written: as a buffer full of bytes.

Writing a buffer full of data resembles record I/O in the standard I/O package. However, unlike standard I/O, the programmer must set up the buffer for the data, place the appropriate values in it before writing, and take them out after reading. Figure 13-8 shows that the buffer in system I/O is part of the program, rather than being invisible as in standard I/O.

There are advantages to system-level I/O. Because it parallels the methods that MS-DOS uses to write to the disk, system-level I/O is more efficient than standard I/O. The amount of code used by the C library routines is less than with standard I/O, so programs can be smaller. Finally, because there are fewer layers of routines to go through, system I/O can also operate faster. Actually, because it is the more basic system, system I/O routines are used by many compiler writers to create the standard I/O package.

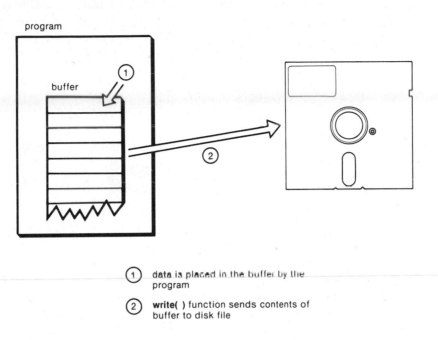

① data is placed in the buffer by the program

② write( ) function sends contents of buffer to disk file

Figure 13-8. Visible Buffer

Reading Files in System I/O

Our first example is a program that reads a file from the disk and displays it on the screen. We've seen several examples of how this operation is carried out in standard I/O, so this program will point out the differences between the two approaches.

As an example of the program's operation, we'll use it to display its own source file:

```
c>sysread sysread.c
/* sysread.c */
/* reads and displays file */
#include <fcntl.h>                         /* needed for oflags */
#define BUFFSIZE 512                       /* buffer size */
char buff[BUFFSIZE];                       /* buffer */
int main( int argc, char *argv[] )
{
    int inhandle, bytes, j;
    if(argc != 2)                          /* check arguments */
        { printf("Format: C>search filename"); exit(1); }
                                           /* open file */
```

```
if( (inhandle = open(argv[1], O_RDONLY | O_BINARY)) < 0)
    {printf("Can't open file %s.", argv[1]); exit(1); }
                                    /* read one buffer */
while( (bytes = read(inhandle,buff,BUFFSIZE)) > 0)
    for(j=0; j<bytes; j++)          /* print buffer */
        putch(buff[j]);
close(inhandle);                    /* close file */
return(0);
}
```

Setting Up the Buffer

The first difference you'll notice in this program is that we declare a character buffer with the statements:

```
#define BUFFSIZE 512
char buff[BUFFSIZE];
```

This is the buffer in which the data read from the disk will be placed. The size of this buffer is important for efficient operation. Depending on the operating system, buffers of certain sizes are handled more efficiently than others. In MS-DOS, the optimum buffer size is a multiple of 512 bytes. As we'll see later, the absolute size of the buffer is also important. In some cases a large buffer is more efficient, so multiples of 512, such as 2048 or 4096, should be used.

sectors

Opening the File

As in standard I/O, we must open the file before we can access it. This is done in the expression

```
if( (inhandle = open(argv[1], O_RDONLY | O_BINARY)) < 0)
```

We open the file for the same reason we did in standard I/O: to establish communications with the operating system about the file. We tell the system the name of the file we want to open—in this case, the name placed in the command-line array **argv[1]** by the user. We also indicate whether we want to read or write to the file and whether we want the file opened in binary or text mode. However, the method used to indicate this information is different in system I/O. Each characteristic is indicated by a constant called an *oflag*. A list of oflags is shown in Table 13-1.

Some of the possibilities listed in Table 13-1 are mutually exclusive: you can't open a file for read-only and read-write at the same time, for example.

In our sysread.c program we open a file using the oflags O_RDONLY and O_BINARY. We'll see examples of other oflags in use as we go along. The oflags are defined in the file fcntl.h, so this file must be **#include**d in pro-

Table 13-1. *System-Level Oflags*

Oflag	Meaning
O_APPEND	Place file pointer at end of file
O_CREAT	Create a new file for writing (has no effect if file already exists)
O_RDONLY	Open a new file for reading only
O_RDWR	Open file for both reading and writing
O_TRUNC	Open and truncate existing file to 0 length
O_WRONLY	Open file for writing only
O_BINARY	Open file in binary mode
O_TEXT	Open file in text mode ← *default*

grams using system I/O. (Note, though, that the stdio.h file, which was necessary in standard I/O, is not necessary here.)

When two or more oflags are used together, they are combined using the bitwise OR operator (|).

File Handles

Instead of returning a pointer, as **fopen()** did in standard I/O, **open()** returns an integer value called a *file handle*. This is a number assigned to a particular file, which is used thereafter to refer to the file.

If **open()** returns a value of −1 rather than a valid file handle (which must be greater than 0), an error has occurred. (We can find out more about the error by using another function, as we'll see in the next example.)

> The system-level function **open()** returns a file handle, which is not a pointer, but simply a reference number to identify a file.

Reading the File into the Buffer

The following statement reads the file—or as much of it as will fit—into the buffer:

```
bytes = read(inhandle,buff,BUFFSIZE)
```

The **read()** function takes three arguments. The first is the file handle. The second is the address of the buffer—in this case, the variable **buff**. The third argument is the maximum number of bytes we want to read. In this case we'll allow the function to fill the entire buffer, but in some situations reading fewer bytes might be desirable. Reading more bytes than the buffer can hold is not, of course, recommended.

The **read()** function returns the number of bytes actually read. This is an important number, since it may very well be less than the buffer size, and we'll need to know just how full the buffer is before we can do anything with its contents. We assign this number to the variable **bytes**.

Once the buffer is full we can print it out. We do this with a **for** loop running from 0 to **bytes**, printing one character at a time.

Closing the File

No surprises here: we use the **close()** function to close the file. This releases the communications areas and the file handle for use by other files.

Error Messages

As with standard I/O, it is possible in system I/O to query the system about what went wrong in the event that an error condition is encountered when an **open()** or other file operation is attemped. A return value of −1 indicates an error, and the type of error can be determined with the function **perror()**. This function, as we saw earlier, uses as its argument an error message from the program and, when executed, prints not only the program's message, but also the system-error message.

Here's a modification of sysread.c that incorporates this function to check for errors on opening the file:

```
/* sysread2.c */
/* reads and displays file, uses perror()  */
#include <fcntl.h>                        /* needed for oflags */
#define BUFFSIZE 512                      /* buffer size */
char buff[BUFFSIZE];                      /* buffer */
int main( int argc, char *argv[] )
{
    int inhandle, bytes, j;

    if(argc != 2)                         /* check arguments */
       { printf("Format: C>sysread2 filename"); exit(1); }
                                          /* open file */
    if( (inhandle = open(argv[1], O_RDONLY | O_BINARY)) < 0)
       { perror("Can't open input file"); exit(1); }
                                          /* read one buffer */
    while( (bytes = read(inhandle,buff,BUFFSIZE)) > 0)
       for(j=0; j<bytes; j++)             /* print buffer */
          putch(buff[j]);
    close(inhandle);                      /* close file */
    return(0);
}
```

Here's a sample of the program's operation when the user attempts to operate on a nonexistent file:

```
C>sysread2 nofile.xxx
Can't open input file: No such file or directory
```

The first part of the message is the program's, the second comes from the system.

This technique can be used to provide information about read and write errors as well as errors in opening a file.

Buffer Operations

Putting the contents of a file in a buffer has certain advantages; we can perform various operations on the contents of the buffer without having to access the file again. There are several functions that can speed up operations on buffered data, as our next example demonstrates. This program searches a text file for a word or phrase typed by the user.

```
/* fsearch.c */
/* searches file for phrase */
#include <fcntl.h>                        /* needed for oflags */
#include <stdio.h>                        /* needed for NULL etc */
#include <string.h>                       /* needed for memchr() */   + memcmp
#define BUFFSIZE 1024                     /* buffer size */
void search(char *, int);                 /* prototype */
char buff[BUFFSIZE];                      /* buffer */

int main( int argc, char *argv[] )
{
   int inhandle, bytes;

   if(argc != 3)                          /* check arguments */
      { printf("Format: C>fsearch filename phrase"); exit(1); }
                                          /* open file */
   if( (inhandle = open(argv[1], O_RDONLY )) < 0)
      { printf("Can't open file %s.", argv[1]); exit(1); }
                                          /* read file */
   while( (bytes = read(inhandle,buff,BUFFSIZE)) > 0)
      search(argv[2],bytes);              /* search for phrase */
   close(inhandle);                       /* close file */
   printf("Phrase not found");
   return(0);
}
```

```
/* search() */
/* searches buffer for phrase */
void search(char *phrase, int buflen)
{
    char *ptr, *p;

    ptr = buff;
    while( (ptr=memchr(ptr,phrase[0],buflen)) != NULL)
        if( memcmp(ptr,phrase,strlen(phrase)) == 0)
            {
            printf("First occurrence of phrase:\n.");
            for(p=ptr-100; p<ptr+100; p++)
                putchar(*p);
            exit(0);
            }
        else ptr++;
}
```

p294

This program requires the user to type two arguments on the command line (in addition to the program name): the name of the file to be searched and the phrase to be searched for. The program then finds the first occurrence of this phrase. To show where the phrase is in the file, the characters on each side of the phrase are printed out so that it can be seen in context.

Here's an example of the program searching the manuscript version of Chapter 9 of this book for the word "aside":

```
C>fsearch chp9.ms aside
First occurrence of phrase:

list of prices.
3. The purpose of declaring a structure type is to
      a. set aside the appropriate amount of memory
      b. define the format of the structure
      c. specify
```

The main part of this program is similar to sysread.c. One difference is that the file has been opened in text mode. This is the default when no mode is specified, and we did not include the O_BINARY oflag. This means that CR/LFs will be translated into newlines when we read the file.

Buffer Manipulation Functions

The function **search()**, called by the main program, makes use of several buffer manipulation functions. The first such function is **memchr()**. This function searches a buffer for a specific character. In our example, the expression

```
ptr=memchr(ptr,phrase[0],buflen)
```

shows the three arguments necessary for **memchr()**. The first is the address of the buffer. Here we've assigned the address to the pointer variable **ptr**. The second argument is the character to be searched for—in this case, the first character of the phrase typed by the user, argv[2]. This is passed to the function **search()** and stored in the variable **phrase**. The third parameter is the length of the buffer to be searched.

The **memchr()** function returns a NULL if the character is not found; otherwise it returns a pointer to the character in the buffer. Here it assigns the pointer to the variable **ptr**.

The **search()** function then enters an **if** statement to see if the character actually marks the beginning of the sought-after phrase. This comparison is handled by the function **memcmp()**, in the expression

```
if( memcmp(ptr,phrase,strlen(phrase)) == 0)
```

This function also takes three arguments: a pointer to the place in the buffer where the comparison should begin, the address of the phrase to be compared, and the length of the phrase. The function then compares the phrase with the characters in the buffer; if they match, it returns 0.

If a match is found, the **search()** function prints the characters on both sides of the match and exits. Otherwise, the process is repeated until **memchr()** can no longer find the character in the file.

The buffer manipulation functions require that the string.h file be **#include**d with the program.

Writing Files in System I/O

Writing a file in system I/O is somewhat more complicated than reading a file. As an example, let's look at a program that copies one file to another; that is, it imitates the DOS COPY command.

To use this function, the user types the name of the source file (which should already exist) and the destination file (which will be created) on the command line.

```
C>copy2 source.txt dest.txt
```

Since the files are opened in binary, any file can be copied, whether a text file or a binary file such as an executable program.

Here's the listing:

```
/* copy2.c */
/* copies one file to another */
#include <fcntl.h>                       /* needed for oflags */
#include <sys\stat.h>                     /* needed for permiss */
#define BUFSIZ 4096                       /* buffer size */
char buff[BUFSIZ];                        /* buffer */


int main( int argc, char *argv[] )
{
   int inhandle, outhandle, bytes;

   if(argc != 3)                         /* check arguments */
     { printf("Format: C>copy2 source destination"); exit(1); }
                                         /* open files */
   if( (inhandle = open(argv[1], O_RDWR | O_BINARY)) < 0)
     {printf("Can't open input file %s.", argv[1]); exit(1); }
   if( (outhandle = open(argv[2],
       O_CREAT | O_WRONLY | O_BINARY, S_IWRITE)) < 0)
     { printf("Can't open output file %s.", argv[2]); exit(1); }
                                         /* copy file */
   while( (bytes = read(inhandle,buff,BUFSIZ)) > 0)
     write(outhandle,buff,bytes);
   close(inhandle);                      /* close files */
   close(outhandle);
   return(0);
}
```

Two files are opened. One is the source file, whose handle is assigned to the variable **inhandle**. The other is the destination file, whose handle will be in **outhandle**. The expression that opens the source file should look familiar from previous examples. The one that opens the destination file, though, has some unfamiliar features:

```
if( (outhandle = open(argv[2],
    O_CREAT | O_WRONLY | O_BINARY, S_IWRITE)) < 0)
```

This expression is so large it must be written on two lines. To create a nonexistent file, we use the O_CREAT oflag. We want to write and not read to this file, so we also use O_WRONLY. And we want to use binary mode, so we use O_BINARY.

Whenever the O_CREAT oflag is used, another variable must be added to the **open()** function to indicate the read/write status of the file to be created. These options are called the "permiss" (for "permission") arguments. There are three possibilities:

Permiss	Meaning
S_IWRITE	Writing permitted
S_IREAD	Reading permitted
S_IREAD ¦ S_IWRITE	Reading and writing permitted

If the permiss flags are to be recognized, the file sys\stat.h must be **#include**d with the source file for this program, along with fcntl.h.

The **write()** function is similar in format to **read()**. Like **read()**, it takes three arguments: the handle of the file to be written to, the address of the buffer, and the number of bytes to be written.

To copy the file, we use both the **read()** and **write()** functions in a **while** loop. The **read()** function returns the number of bytes actually read; this is assigned to the variable **bytes**. This value will be equal to the buffer size until the end of the file, when the buffer probably will be only partially full. The variable **bytes** therefore is used to tell the **write()** function how many bytes to write from the buffer to the destination file.

Notice that we've used a larger buffer size in this program than in previous examples. The larger the buffer, the fewer disk accesses the program must make, so increasing the size of the buffer significantly speeds up the operation of the program; it copies an 80K file twice as fast with a buffer size of 4096 as it does with 512. You can experiment with buffer size to see which works best in your particular application.

When large buffers are used they must be made global variables, otherwise stack overflow occurs.

Writing to the Printer in System I/O

You can easily write to the printer using system level I/O functions. As we saw earlier, there are five predefined file handles. The file handle argument supplied to **write()** is a number (unlike the handles used in standard I/O), so we use the numbers from 0 to 4 to select one of the predefined handles. The number for the printer is 4.

Here's a program that prints the contents of a file whose name is typed on the command line by the user.

```
/* print3.c */
/* prints file to printer -- using standard file numbers */
#include <fcntl.h>                       /* needed for oflags */
#include <sys\stat.h>                    /* needed for permiss */
#define BUFSIZ 4096                      /* buffer size */
char buff[BUFSIZ];                       /* buffer */
int main( int argc, char *argv[] )
{
    int inhandle, bytes;
```

583

```
    if(argc != 2)                        /* check arguments */
       { printf("Format: C>print3 sourcefile"); exit(1); }
                                         /* open input file */
    if( (inhandle = open(argv[1], O_RDWR | O_BINARY)) < 0)
       {printf("Can't open file %s.", argv[1]); exit(1); }
                                         /* send file to printer */
    while( (bytes = read(inhandle,buff,BUFSIZ)) > 0)
       write(4, buff, bytes);            /* standard handle is 4 */
    close(inhandle);                     /* close file */
          return(0);
  }
```

p553

This program is similar to the print2.c example shown before. No file needs to be opened for the printer, because we already know the handle number.

Redirection

In Chapter 8 we discussed redirection: the capability built into DOS and the C runtime system to redirect output to a disk file that would normally go to the screen and to take input from a disk file that would normally come from the keyboard.

It is also possible to modify disk-oriented programs, such as those in this chapter, so that they make use of redirection. This can be helpful if the programs are to be used, UNIX-style, in such a way that they act as *filters*, taking input from one program via indirection, modifying it, and passing it on to another program, again via indirection. (For more on filters and the related subject of pipes, see your DOS manual, or the other books listed in the bibliography.)

Let's see how we would modify the copy2.c program to use indirection. Essentially we rewrite the program so that its input, instead of coming from a file, comes from the keyboard, and it's output, instead of going to a file, goes to the display. Then, when the program is used, indirection can be employed to specify that input should again come from a file and that output should also go to a file (or be piped to another program).

The simplest way to invoke this new version of the program would be:

```
C>copy3 <source.ext >dest.ext
```

where source.ext is the file we want to copy and dest.ext is the destination file. However, if we wanted to copy the output of another program, say prog1, and send the copied file to a third program, say prog2, we could write:

```
C>prog1 ¦ copy3 ¦ prog2
```

A fringe benefit of using redirection is that the programming is somewhat simplified. Here's the modified version of copy2.c:

```
/* copy3.c */
/* copies one file to another */
/* uses redirection; format is C>copy3 <source.xxx >dest.xxx */
#include <fcntl.h>                    /* needed for oflags */
#define inhandle 0                    /* stdin file */
#define outhandle 1                   /* stdout file */
#define BUFSIZ 4096                   /* buffer size */
char buff[BUFSIZ];                    /* buffer */

void main(void)
{
    int bytes;

    setmode(inhandle, O_BINARY);      /* set file mode */
    setmode(outhandle, O_BINARY);     /*    to binary */
                                      /* copy file */
    while( (bytes = read(inhandle,buff,BUFSIZ)) > 0)
        write(outhandle,buff,bytes);
}
```

We use the predefined handle numbers 0 and 1 for standard input and output, so we don't need to open any files.

Since we don't open files, we can't use the **open()** function to specify which mode—text or binary—we want the file to be in. However, there is another way to do this: the **setmode()** function. **Setmode()** can take one of two arguments: O_TEXT and O_BINARY. You'll recognize these from our discussion of the **open()** function; they're defined in the file fcntl.h.

The actual reading and writing of the files is done the same way in this program as in the earlier copy2.c.

When to Use What

Because of the multiplicity of functions available for file access in C, it's sometimes hard to know which method to use.

Standard I/O is probably most valuable where it's natural to handle data as characters, strings, or formatted **printf()** style form. System I/O is more natural in situations where blocks of data, such as arrays, are to be handled. In many cases, standard I/O is simpler to program, while system I/O usually generates more efficient code, both in terms of speed and the size of the executable file.

It's important not to mix standard and system-level I/O. If a file has been opened with **fopen()**, don't try to use **read()** or **write()** with it, and vice versa. Thus, while system-level I/O would usually be used for reading blocks of data, for compatibility, **fread()** and **fwrite()** might be used if the file is already being used by other standard I/O functions.

Text mode is usually used with files containing text, and binary mode is used for files that may contain numbers other than ASCII codes. This avoids translation problems that would corrupt numerical data. However, as in the bindump.c program, it is occasionally useful to use binary mode on text files.

Summary

The subject of file input/output in Turbo C is a rich and complex one. In this chapter we've only covered the highlights. But you probably have enough of a head start to finish the exploration of files on your own.

We've shown that there are two main families of file-handling functions: standard I/O and system-level I/O. Standard I/O can deal with data in a larger variety of ways, but system I/O is generally the more efficient. In standard I/O we showed examples of the four ways to handle data: as characters, as strings, as formatted data in the style of **printf()**, and as fixed-length records or blocks. We saw that the first three of these ways store data—whether text or numbers—as ASCII characters, while the fourth way, record I/O, causes numerical data to be stored in binary format.

We also explored the difference between text and binary modes (not to be confused with text and binary formats). In text modes C newlines are translated into the MS-DOS CR/LF pair, and the character 1A indicates an EOF; in binary mode neither of these is true.

We finished the chapter with a look at system-level I/O. This family of commands requires that the programmer set up a buffer for the data and use only one system for reading and writing; data is always considered to consist of a block of bytes. Buffer manipulation functions can help with operations on the data in the buffer.

Questions

1. The two main systems of I/O available in C are _____ I/O and _____ I/O.

2. A file must be opened so that

a. the program knows how to access the file

b. the operating system knows what file to access

c. the operating system knows if the file should be read from or written to

d. communications areas are established for communicating with the file

3. A file opened with **fopen()** will thereafter be referred to by its
_____.

4. The function **fopen()** can specify which of the following?
   a. The file may be opened for appending.
   b. The file may be opened in binary mode.
   c. The file may be given read-only status.
   d. Numbers in the file will be written in binary format.

5. In standard I/O the function used to close a file is _____.

6. When reading one character at a time, which of the following functions is appropriate?
   a. **fread()**
   b. **read()**
   c. **fgets()**
   d. **getc()**

7. True or false: closing a file after writing to it is optional.

8. Text and binary mode have to do with
   a. the way numbers are stored on the disk
   b. the way numbers are stored in memory
   c. the way newlines are handled
   d. the way EOFs are handled

9. To examine every single byte of a file, is text or binary mode more suitable?

10. Which of the following are valid parts of standard input/output?
    a. record I/O

b. structure I/O

c. character I/O

d. array I/O

e. string I/O

f. formatted I/O

11. When writing numbers to disk, the file should usually be opened in _____ mode.

12. To write a small number of mixed string and integer variables to a file, the appropriate function is
    a. **fputs()**
    b. **fgets()**
    c. **fprintf()**
    d. **fwrite()**

13. True or false: since files must be read sequentially, there is no way to read data from the middle of a file without starting at the beginning.

14. Whenever a file is open, a number indicates at what position in the file the next access will be made. This number is called the
    a. read/write status (type int)
    b. file handle (type int)
    c. file pointer (type pointer to char)
    d. file pointer (type long int)
    e. file handle (type long int)

15. To write a block of data to a file in standard I/O, the appropriate function is _____.

16. The offset is the number of _____ from a certain point in a file.

17. The function **fseek()**
    a. finds a given word or phrase in a file
    b. finds the correct file
    c. helps access records in the middle of a file
    d. moves the file pointer to the desired location

18. A file opened by **open()** will thereafter be referred to by its file
    _____.

19. Which of the following describes system I/O?
    a. closer to DOS methods
    b. slower
    c. more data formats
    d. smaller executable programs

20. In system-level I/O, the function used to read from a file is
    _____.

21. When a predefined file handle is used, text or binary mode may be
    specified using the _____ function.

22. Which of the following functions will search a block of data for a specific
    character?
    a. **search()**
    b. **strchr()**
    c. **memchr()**
    d. **buffcmp()**

23. True or false: a system-level file can be opened for reading and writing at
    the same time.

24. An oflag can
    a. signal when a file is unreadable
    b. specify if a file should be read or written
    c. signal when EOF is detected
    d. specify binary mode

25. If O_CREAT is used, the _____ argument must be added
    to indicate the read/write protection mode for the file.

26. If data is to be treated in large blocks, the _____ I/O
    system is usually more appropriate.

27. The advantage of using redirection is that the input to a program may
    then come from

a. the keyboard

b. pipes

c. filters

d. other programs

28. Write a DOS command to use indirection to read input data from the file file1.txt to the program encrypt, and then write the output of this program to the file file2.txt.

29. If a system-level program employs redirection, it should
    a. use standard file handles for keyboard and display
    b. open files in binary mode
    c. set binary mode using the **setmode()** function
    d. use the **redir()** function

30. True or false: there is only one right way to do things in the world of C files.

Exercises

1. Write a program that will read a C source file and verify that the number of right and left braces in the file are equal. Use a command-line argument for the name of the file and the **getc()** function to read in the file.

2. It is sometimes desirable to store a group of strings of different lengths in the same file. It is also sometimes desirable to access these strings randomly—that is, to read only the desired one, without starting at the beginning of a file. To do this, the offset of each string can be placed in a table. To compile the table of offsets, one can use the function **ftell()**, which returns the current offset, taking only the file pointer (**fptr**) as an argument.

   Write a program that uses string I/O, enabling the user to type a group of phrases, and that tells the user the offset of each phrase typed in, like this:

```
C>writedex
Open the pod bay doors, Hal.
Offset=0

Klingons attacking!
```

```
Offset=29

Your fuel is dangerously low.
Offset=49

Unknown craft approaching at warp factor 7.
Offset=79
```

3. Write a function that can be added to the agentr.c program, so that an agent's record can be deleted from the database. The file is first read in, the deletion is made in memory, then the revised list of agents is written out to the file.

14

Larger Programs

- Separate compilation
- External variables and separately compiled files
- Modular programming and separate compilation
- Conditional compilation using #if
- Memory models

14

The C language is particularly rich in tools for creating large, sophisticated programs. However, in this book our program examples have, of necessity, been comparatively small. In this chapter we'll examine some of the techniques used when programs become larger and more complex.

In particular, we'll discuss how sections of larger programs can be compiled separately and linked together using Turbo C's Project option; and we'll explore the related issue of how data can be shared by such separately compiled modules. We'll show how parts of a source file can be compiled under some circumstances but not others, and finally we'll discuss memory models, which permit programs and data to occupy very large amounts of memory.

Separate Compilation

So far in this book we have always written, compiled, and linked one program at a time. The program might have had several functions in it, but they were all treated as a single entity for the purpose of compilation. However, it is possible to break a program apart into separate *files*, each file consisting of one or more functions. These files can be compiled separately and then linked together to form the final executable program.

Let's examine some simple examples of this process; then we'll discuss why we might want to use separate compilation.

Here's a complete C source file, called mainprog.c.

```
/* mainprog.c */
/* main program to test separate compilation */
int formula(int, int);    /* prototype */

void main(void)
```

```
{
    int a, b, ans;

    printf("Type two integers: ");
    scanf("%d%d", &a, &b);
    ans = formula(a,b);
    printf("The sum of the squares is %d.", ans);
}
```

This is a variation of a program from Chapter 5, multifun.c, which calculates the sum of the squares of two numbers. However, part of the multifun.c program is missing here. We'll see where it went in a moment.

Type in the source file for this program with the Turbo C editor, and save it by pressing [F2]. Now you have a file called mainprog.c. Why shouldn't you compile and link the file? The linker would give an error message when it encountered the reference to the function **formula()**:

```
ans = formula(a,b);
```

In a similar manner, type in and save the following program:

```
/* formula.c */
/* function returns sum of squares of arguments */
int formula(int x, int y)
{
    return( x*x + y*y );
}
```

This creates a file called formula.c. This file contains, as you can see, the missing function, **formula()**.

How do we turn these two source files—mainprog.c and formula.c—into a complete program?

Using Turbo C's Project Feature

With most C compilers, there are two ways to combine several source files into one executable program. The process can either be done "by hand," by typing command-line messages to compile each source file and to link them together, or the process can be turned over to a Make utility.

Make is a program that automates the compiling and linking process. Why is this necessary? Suppose you have a large program with a dozen source files. You need to compile each one, then link the resulting .obj files to create a final .exe file. When you change a source file, you need to recompile it and relink everything, but it's not necessary to recompile those source files that haven't been changed. With so many files, it's difficult to keep track of which have been compiled since the last link and which haven't.

That's where the Make utility comes in. You tell it the name of the source files (and library files too, if necessary), and it keeps track of which source files must be recompiled to produce the final .exe file. It also automates the whole compile-and-link process, so that one command suffices to perform all the steps necessary to generate the final .exe file.

In Turbo C a Make utility is incorporated into the IDE, so it isn't necessary to invoke a separate program to perform the Make operation. This results in a convenient process.

Creating the .PRJ File

At the heart of the Project process is a file with the .PRJ extension. This file contains the names of all the files that will be combined into a single program. Turbo C will use this file as a guide to creating your program.

You don't need to create the .PRJ file list yourself by typing it in. Turbo C creates it automatically. However, you must tell Turbo C what files to put on the list. Here's how to do it.

To begin, you must have created all the source (.C) files for the project. There may also be already compiled files, such as .LIB or .OBJ files. Make sure all these files are in the current directory. Now call up Turbo C, and select Open Project from the Project menu. Type the name of the project file in the Load Project File box and give it the .PRJ file extension; for example, sumsqr.prj. The name you use here will be given to the .EXE file that is the end result of the process; in our case, sumsqr.exe.

Press [Enter] when you've typed the project file name. The Load Project File box will disappear, and a window called Project: SUMSQR (or whatever name you gave the project file) will appear at the bottom of the screen. This window will show the files used in the project, but it will be blank until you specify the files. To do this, use the keys shown at the bottom of the screen. To add a file, press [Insert]. A box called "Add Item to Project List" appears. It displays all the .C files in the current directory. To add one of these files to the project list, select it with the mouse and click on the Add button (or select it with the arrow keys and press [Enter]). For our example, you'll need mainprog.c and formula.c. As each program is added to the project list, you'll see it appear in the Project window. If you must add .LIB or .OBJ files (as you do when creating stand-alone programs that use Turbo C graphics functions), type them into the Name field.

When the project list is complete, press [F10] to return to the main menu. Choose Make from the Compile menu (or press the [F9] key). You'll see Turbo C compiling the various files—mainprog.c and formula.c in our example—and linking the resulting .obj files together into sumsqr.exe. You can run the resulting program in the usual way, either from Turbo C (select Run from the Run menu), or by exiting to DOS and invoking sumsqr.exe directly. Here's some sample output:

```
Type two integers: 3 4
The sum of the squares is 25
```

If you now make a change in one of your source files, you can rebuild your whole project quickly. Select Open Project from the Make File, and select the previously created .PRJ file from the Files box. The Project window with the source files—already filled in—will appear. Now select Make from the Compile menu, and Turbo C will rebuild your project. It will recompile only those files that have been changed since the last rebuild.

Note how convenient Turbo C's multiwindow capability is when working with multiple source files. You can keep a window open on each of several source files at the same time, so you can see, for example, whether the arguments you are passing to a function in a different file are what the function expects to receive. Try this with mainprog.c and formula.c, for example. Simply select Open from the File menu to open a second file.

Another approach to using Project is to compile (but not link) each source file as you create it, using Compile in the Compile menu. When you're debugging, this may be a more efficient method, as it lets you correct errors on each file separately. When all the files compile correctly, you can use Project to link them. This happens automatically when Make is invoked: source files that have already been compiled will not be compiled again (unless they've been changed since the last compile).

The Linking Process

What does the linker do with the .obj files? It merges the two files together. When it sees the reference in mainprog.obj to **formula()**, it looks for this function in any other files being linked; in this case, there is only one: formula.c. Finding the function in this file, it makes the appropriate connection. The result is an executable file called sumsqr.exe, which contains both functions **main()** and **formula()**, almost as if you had typed them into the same file. Figure 14-1 shows this process.

Advantages of Separate Compilation

Now that we've shown how to generate a single .exe file from two source files, what have we accomplished? With a program this small, not much. But when programs start to get larger, with many functions and hundreds or thousands of lines of code, then separate compilation starts to have some real advantages. Why?

One reason is that compile time is proportional to the size of the file being compiled. And, usually, a programmer is only working on one part of a program at a time. So to minimize compile time, a programmer compiles only those parts of a program that have been changed since the last compilation. The parts of the program that are already working and debugged are not

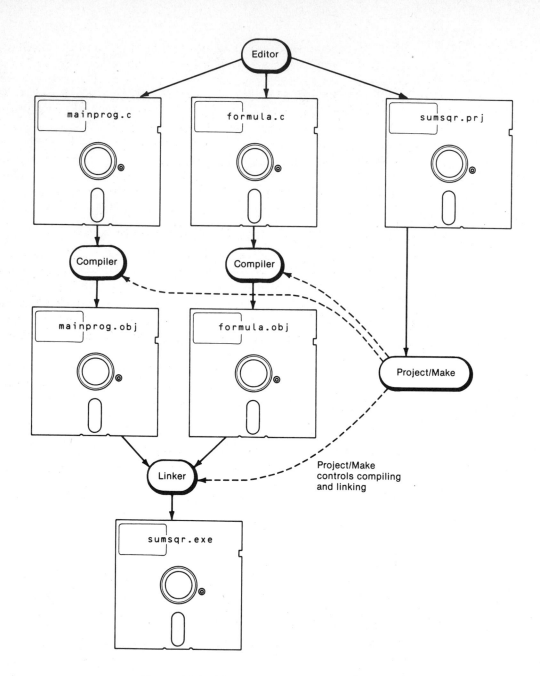

Figure 14-1. Separate Compilation of Functions

recompiled; they form a group of permanent object files. Each time a new version of the current file—the part of the program that is being written and debugged—is compiled, it can be linked with the previously compiled files.

Using this approach, only a small part of the program need be compiled at any one time; the rest already exists in the form of .obj files. If several programmers are working on a project, they can share previously developed object files. Since a module need not be recompiled after it is developed and debugged, there is less chance that it will be inadvertently modified or that two programmers will be using different versions of one function.

A more important reason for using separate compilation is that it enables you to write well-structured, modular programs. Finally, separate compilation allows you to use library files. We'll say more about these topics later. Now let's look at how functions in separately compiled files share data.

External Variables and Separately Compiled Files

In our example, in which **mainprog()** and **formula()** were linked, two numbers were passed from **mainprog()** to **formula()** using arguments, and the result from **formula()** was returned to **mainprog()** with a **return** statement. This kind of data communication between separately compiled functions is easy to implement; it requires no special statement in either function. But suppose we wanted functions in separately compiled files to have access to the same *external* variable?

A function in one file can access an external variable located in another file if it declares the variable using the keyword **extern**. To show how this works, we'll rewrite the **mainprog()** and **formula()** functions this way:

```
/* mainpro2.c */
/* main program to test separate compilation */
int formula(void);  /* prototype */

int a, b;           /* definition of external variables */

void main(void)
{
   int ans;

   printf("Type two integers: ");
   scanf("%d%d", &a, &b);
   ans = formula();
   printf("The sum of the squares is %d.", ans);
}
```

This is similar to the mainprog.c file shown earlier, except that we've moved the variables **a** and **b**, which hold the two integers the user types in, to a position outside the function. They are now external variables. Now when mainpro2.c calls **formula2**, it no longer needs to pass any arguments.

Here's the revised formula.c file:

```
/* formula2.c */
/* function returns sum of squares of arguments */
/* uses global variables for input */

int formula(void)
{
    extern int a, b;    /* declaration of external variables */

    return( a*a + b*b );
}
```

Here you can see that we no longer need to declare any variables as formal arguments to the function, but that we do declare the two variables **a** and **b** to be of type **extern int**. What does this mean?

The word **extern** is an example of a *storage class*, which we'll discuss in detail in Chapter 15. For the moment, what we need to know is that, for an external variable to be visible in a file other than the one in which it's defined, it must be declared using the **extern** keyword. This keyword tells the compiler: "Somewhere in another file we've defined these variables. Don't worry that they aren't defined in this file, but let the linker know about them." When the linker gets the message from the compiler that these variables are external, it looks for them in different files. When it finds them, it makes the appropriate connections. From then on, references in **formula2()** to **a** and **b** will be correctly linked to the **a** and **b** defined in the mainpro2.c file. Figure 14-2 shows an external variable declared in two different files.

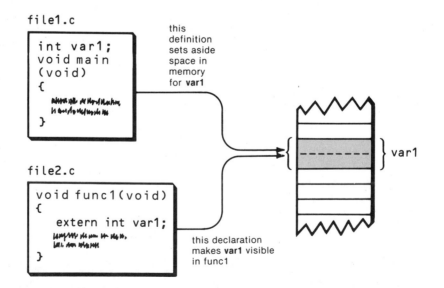

Figure 14-2. External Variable Declared in Different Files

To combine these two files, create a project file called sumsqr2.prj, whose contents are mainpro2.c and formula2.c. Then make your project as described above.

Library Files

We've seen how a number of functions constituting a program can either be kept together in a single file or divided among several files that are compiled separately and linked together. There is a third possibility we should mention here. Functions can also be included in a special kind of file called a *library*. A library is a file consisting of a number of functions. The functions are combined into groups called modules, which have a special characteristic; when you link a program with the library, only those modules containing functions that are actually referenced by the program will be included in the resulting .exe file.

You've already used library files, perhaps without thinking much about it. Every time you use a C library function, such as **printf()**, it is a library file that supplies the actual code for the function. The object files of whatever C functions you referenced are linked with your program to generate the final .exe file. But not all the functions in the library file are added to your program; this would make every C program huge. The linker extracts only those functions you need and links them with your object file. This is an important characteristic of C, since it helps to minimize the size of the final program.

Most C programmers will purchase specialized libraries of functions not available in the standard C library. Commercially available libraries include those for window and menu creation, statistical functions, database handling, specialized I/O, and many others. Also, programmers will develop their own libraries, which will include families of functions they use frequently. For a working programmer such libraries can significantly increase speed and productivity.

A detailed discussion of how to create and use a library file is beyond the scope of this book, but you should be aware of the possibility so that when your programs become larger and more complex you can make use of this facility.

Modular Programming and Separate Compilation

Perhaps the most important reason for using separate compilation is that it is an important aid in writing well-structured, modular programs. Let's examine the relation of C to modular programming.

Dividing a program into separately compiled files can help make it modular.

You probably know that it isn't considered good programming practice to write a large program as a single unit. Instead, the program should be broken down into smaller, easily understood parts. A C program usually consists of a **main()** function which calls several other functions to carry out the important tasks of the program. Each of these functions in turn calls other functions, and so on, until the functions being called are so simple that they need not make further calls.

Each function should carry out a single, clearly defined task. At the upper level, a function might calculate a payroll, for example. This function might call another function to calculate withholding tax. This function might call still another function to look up tax rates in a table. The important points are these: first, the role of a function should be clearly defined, and second, the function should not be too large. Some programmers use a rule of thumb that no function should exceed one page in length, but of course many functions should be smaller.

How does separate compilation fit into modular programming? Using separate files gives us a different size building block to use when constructing programs. A program can be broken down into files and each file can be broken down into functions, as shown in Figure 14-3.

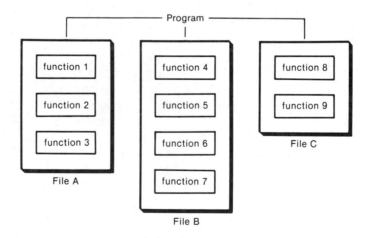

Figure 14-3. Separate Compilation and Modular Programming

As we'll see in Chapter 15, it's possible to restrict variables, not only to one function (as we've seen earlier with automatic variables), but to only one *file* as well. This ability to *hide* data from parts of the program is another aid to modular programming, since it is important that the variables in one part of a program not have access to variables in another part unless it is absolutely necessary.

Program Design

C provides the tools for designing well-structured programs, but it's up to the programmer to use them effectively.

Any large program should be planned in considerable detail before a single line of code is written. Each function should be specified. The specification should include the purpose of the function, the arguments to be passed to it and returned by it, and the functions it will call. Most programmers recommend a "top down" approach. This means specifying the most general functions—probably starting with **main()**—first, and working down to the specific functions that perform low-level tasks, such as putting a character on the screen. In some situations, however, low-level functions must be planned concurrently with the higher-level ones.

Data storage should also be thoroughly specified before code is written. Special care must be given to large data items such as arrays and structures. External variables should be used only when absolutely necessary. As we have noted, external variables are vulnerable to being altered inadvertently by functions that shouldn't be accessing them. Care should be given to the naming of external variables, so that their names do not conflict with other variables. Long, descriptive names are better than short ones. For instance, the variable names **a** and **b**, used earlier in this chapter, would not be appropriate in a large program; it would be too easy to confuse them with other variables. Names like **SystemTemperature** and **GlobalErrorStatus** would be better. Automatic variables should be given meaningful names as well, but it's less critical.

The programmer must decide how to divide the program into different files. Major sections of the program, or those to be worked on by different programmers, might be placed in different files. A group of routines that can be used with other programs as well as the one under development might be placed in a library file to facilitate its use in different situations.

If a program is thoroughly specified before the code is written, it is possible to write almost any individual function before those functions that it calls, and that call it, are written. Dummy functions can supply it with data, so it can be tested and debugged independently from the other parts of the program. Once all the functions have been tested and shown to work independently, it's far more likely that they will work together in the final program.

Conditional Compilation Using #if

A situation may arise where it is useful to compile parts of a source file under some circumstances but not others. This capability is often used in larger programs, but let's first look at an application that can be used in programs of any size.

Suppose you want to measure the speed of a section in your program.

You insert statements that will print "start" and "stop" messages at the beginning and end of the crucial section of code. This way, you can time the execution of the code with a stopwatch (assuming the program is slow enough). However, you only want these messages to be printed when you're testing the program, not when it's running normally.

> The directive **#if**, along with other directives, permits sections of a program to be compiled in some circumstances but not others.

You could simply insert statements to print the "start" and "stop" messages each time you wanted to test the program and then remove them and recompile the program when testing was over. However, if there are a lot of such messages in a program, or they are complex, this could be inconvenient. A better way is to use a combination of preprocessor directives: **#define**, **#if**, and **#endif**. Using this system, you can keep your test statements in the listing at all times, but activate them only when you wish—by changing one **#define** statement at the beginning of the program. You will still need to recompile your program to activate or deactivate the test mode, but the rewriting of code is minimized.

Here's an example:

```
/* define.c */
/* demonstrates #if, #else, #endif */
#define TIMER                        /* remove if no test */
void main(void)
{
   int j, k;

   #if defined(TIMER)                /* executed only if */
      printf("Starting test\n");     /* TIMER is defined */
   #endif

   for(j=0; j<3000; j++)             /* main part of program */
      for(k=0; k<1000; k++)          /*    lengthy loop */
         ;

   #if defined(TIMER)                /* executed only if */
      printf("Ending test\n");       /*    timer is defined */
   #else                             /* executed only if */
      printf("Done\n");              /*    timer is not defined */
   #endif
}
```

In this program we want to test how long a timing loop, consisting of two nested **for** loops, takes to execute. We insert a statement to print "Starting test" at the beginning of the loop and another to print "Ending test" at the end of the loop. By enclosing these statements in the **#if #endef** combination, we ensure that they will be executed only if the directive **#define TIMER** is executed. If the program is compiled and executed as shown above, it will print

```
C>define
Starting test
Ending test
```

with a delay of several seconds between the two messages. If we remove the **#define TIMER** directive, or make it into a comment like this,

```
/* #define TIMER */
```

our "test" statements will not be executed. The program will run, but without the test messages.

The *#if* and *#endif* Directives

The **#if defined (TIMER)** directive tells the compiler to compile the statements that follow it, only if TIMER is **#defin**ed. The **#endif** indicates that this conditional part of the compilation is over, and the compiler can go back to the normal mode of compiling all statements. Thus, **#define** acts as a switch, while **#if** and **#endif** act as delimiters for the section of code switched by **#define**.

The *#else* Directive

In the program above, if TIMER is *not* **defin**ed, another message ("Done") will be printed out when the loop is over. This is arranged with the **#else** directive. It fulfills a role analogous to the **else** in a normal C **if . . . else** statement: whatever follows it is compiled only when the matching **#define** directive has *not* been executed.

Other Uses for Conditional Compilation

There are many other circumstances in which conditional compilation might prove useful. For instance, you might need two versions of a program: one to run on the IBM AT, for example, and one to run on the PS/2 series. Instead of creating two complete source files, you could group those statements in the program that varied from one version to another and enclose them by appropriate **#if**, **#else**, and **#endif** statements. Then, inserting a single statement at the beginning of the program, such as

```
#define AT
```

would convert the program from the PS/2 version to the AT version.

The *#undef* Directive

Another related preprocessor directive is the **#undef** directive, which cancels the action of a previous **#define** directive. For example, if at some point in your program you insert the directive

```
#define TEST
```

and later in the program you insert

```
#undef TEST
```

then at this point TEST will no longer be defined. You can use this directive to make conditional compilation specific to certain sections of the program.

Another use for **#undef** is to "turn off" macros that you have previously defined with a **#define** directive. This might be useful in a large and complex program where the same name is used for different macros in different parts of the program, and you want to avoid the possibility of conflict. Turning off a macro with **#undef** makes your macro a "local" macro, known only in a limited section of the program.

Memory Models

In Turbo C a *memory model* is the specification for how much memory different parts of the program can occupy. Turbo C specifies six possible options: tiny, small, compact, medium, large, and huge. So far we have used only the small memory model. This is the default model—what you get if you don't specify otherwise. What are memory models, and why might you want to use one besides small?

To appreciate the necessity for different memory models, it's important to understand the way the microprocessor used in the PC computer family addresses memory. We discussed the topic of segments and segment/offset addressing in Chapter 10. Let's review the situation to see how it applies to memory models.

Segment/Offset Addressing

The Intel 80x86 microprocessor uses 16-bit registers for addresses. A register this size can hold an address up to FFFF hex, which is 65,536 decimal, or 64K. This amount of memory is called a segment. To access addresses outside of this segment, the processor must use two registers. One, called the segment register, holds a number that is the starting address of a 64K segment. The other holds the offset address, which is the number of bytes from the start of the segment. To find the "real" or absolute address, the number in the segment register is multiplied by 16 (shifted left four bits) and added to the offset address. (See Chapter 10 if any of this is unclear.) This permits addressing FFFFF hex (1,048,576 decimal) bytes (although with MS-DOS, only 640K bytes are available for the user's program).

Two Kinds of Microprocessor Instructions

The machine-language program generated by the C compiler uses two different techniques for referring to data in memory locations: if the location is *within* the 64K segment already specified in a segment register, the program can use a single instruction to access data. This approach, which corresponds to using **near** pointers in C, executes quickly. On the other hand, if the program needs to refer to an address in a segment *outside* the segment register, it must first alter the segment register, then perform the appropriate action using the offset address, and, finally, restore the segment register to its former value. This corresponds to using **far** pointers in C and is comparatively slow to execute. Turbo C also uses a third kind of pointer, **huge** pointer, which is a different form of the **far** pointer. The **huge** pointer avoids certain problems in performing comparisons on **far** pointers, but is slower in operation.

We can categorize machine-language instructions in a different way. There are instructions that deal with addresses in the *program code* itself, such as jumps and calls to functions, and there are instructions that reference *data*, such as fetching a data item from memory and placing it in a register. Instructions that refer to program code can be either **near** or **far**, and instructions that refer to data can also be either **near** or **far**. So we can think of four different types of microprocessor instructions: **near** instructions for program control and for data, and **far** instructions for program control and data.

Compact, Small, Medium, and Large Models

These four possibilities for microprocessor instructions correspond to four of the six memory models available in Turbo C, as shown in Figure 14-4. If the code for your program fits inside one 64K segment and the data fits inside another 64K segment, you can use the small memory model. Most programs don't require more program or data space than this. If the code for your program is larger than 64K but the data fits inside 64K, you should use the medium model. If the code is less than 64K but the data is larger, the

Model	References to code	References to data
small	near	near
medium	far	near
compact	near	far
large	far	far

Figure 14-4. Four Memory Models

compact model is appropriate. If both code and data require more than 64K, the large model is necessary.

Note that these models all involve a trade-off; **far** instructions take longer to execute than **near** instructions, so programs written in memory models other than **small** will take longer to execute. The moral is, don't use a larger model than you need.

The Tiny Model

The tiny memory model is used in special cases where the amount of memory available for code and data *together* is limited to 64K. It is rare today for a PC's memory to have only 64K, so this model is seldom used. It can be used to generate a kind of executable file called a .com file, which is in some ways simpler than a .exe file, but is used only in special circumstances.

The Huge Model

The huge model is provided for the case of a single data item, usually an array, that by itself is larger than 64K. (If you think this is unlikely, imagine an array of structures used for storing a database; for many applications, such an array could profitably use all available memory.)

Compiler Options

In the Turbo C IDE the choice of memory model is specified by choosing one of six selections from the Code Generation menu, which is accessed from the Compiler selection in the Options menu. The selections are summarized in Figure 14-5.

Once a memory model is selected, the compiler specifies the type of addressing instructions to be used in the program. Also, since the library routines must be accessed with the same kind of instructions as the rest of the program, a set of C library functions is provided for each of the memory models (except tiny, which uses the small model's routines). The IDE ensures that the correct set of routines is linked to the program.

Model	Total Segments	Code Segments	Data Segments	Segments for One Data Item
tiny	1	(1 shared)		1
small	2	1	1	1
medium	many	many	1	1
compact	many	1	many	1
large	many	many	many	1
huge	many	many	many	many

Figure 14-5. Memory Models and Compiler Options

Fine Tuning

We've already seen that, when using the small memory model, it is possible to use the **far** keyword when a variable is outside the normal data segment. Similarly, if we use the compact or large models, we can declare a **near** data type to refer to variables that we know are in the normal 64K data segment. This can reduce the time needed to access these variables.

By combining memory models and **near** and **far** data references in different ways, it's possible to achieve just the right compromise between execution speed and program size.

Summary

In this chapter we've reviewed some of the techniques that can be used when programs become large and complex. We've covered separate compilation of program files and discussed how external variables can be shared between such files using the **extern** keyword. We also mentioned library files and explored the advantages of separate compilation to speed up the compiling process and contribute to modular programming.

We examined conditional compilation, which uses the **#define**, **#if**, **#else**, and **#endif** preprocessor directives to permit selective compiling of various parts of a source file under different circumstances. And finally we discussed the use of different memory models, which permit a program to expand beyond the normal bounds of two 64K segments.

With these techniques you should be able to construct programs of almost any size, up to the limit of the memory in your computer.

Questions

1. One advantage of separate compilation of program modules is
   a. the resulting program will be more modular
   b. compilation time can be faster
   c. program modules can be protected from inadvertent alteration during program development
   d. the program will run faster

2. Separately compiled modules are combined using the _____ _____.

3. For a variable to be visible in a file other than that where it was defined, it must be _____ using the _____ keyword.

4. Which of the following are ways to pass information from one function to another function in a separately compiled file?
   a. as arguments
   b. as static variables
   c. as external variables
   d. as automatic variables

5. True or false: when a library file is linked to a program, all the functions in the library file are used in the final program.

6. Separate compilation is an aid to modular programming because
   a. functions cannot access variables in other files
   b. only functions relating to the same program can be combined in one file
   c. external variables can be restricted to one file
   d. related functions can be combined in a file

7. Conditional compilation is used to
   a. compile only those programs that are error free
   b. compile some sections of programs and not others
   c. remove comments and compress the source file
   d. none of the above

8. The _____ preprocessor directive is used as a switch to turn compilation on and off.

9. The preprocessor directive **#if define (ADV)** causes the code that follows it to be compiled only when
   a. ADV is an integer
   b. ADV is equal to a predefined constant
   c. ADV is TRUE
   d. ADV is **#define**d

10. Using different memory models is useful when a program or data becomes too _____.

11. The *medium* memory model permits
    a. more than one code segment
    b. more than one data segment
    c. only one code segment
    d. only one data segment

12. True or false: selecting the correct memory model determines the size of the stack segment.

13. Memory models are necessary because of the
    a. stack-based architecture of the microprocessor
    b. segmentation of memory
    c. large size of the data or code in some programs
    d. need to keep programmers guessing

14. True or false: different memory models cannot be selected from within the IDE.

15. The disadvantage of using a memory model that is larger than necessary is
    a. memory is wasted
    b. simple data type cannot be used
    c. program files are harder to link
    d. program instructions take longer to execute

15

Advanced Variables

- Storage classes
- Lifetime and visibility
- Enumerated data types
- **typedef**
- Identifiers and naming classes
- Type conversion and casting

15

Although we have been using variables all along in this book, we have, to avoid complicating the explanations of other topics, made certain assumptions about variables and their usage. We have also alluded to various properties of variables without explaining these properties in detail. In this chapter we'll take a more careful look at variables and investigate some of the advanced features the C language makes available for variable usage.

Storage Classes

Every C variable possesses a characteristic called its *storage class*. The storage class defines two characteristics of the variable: its *lifetime*, and its *visibility* (or *scope*). We've mentioned these characteristics before; now let's take a closer look.

First, why are storage classes necessary? The answer is that by using variables with the appropriate lifetime and visibility we can write programs that use memory more efficiently, run faster, and are less prone to programming errors. Correct use of storage class is especially important in large programs.

Lifetime

The lifetime of a variable is the length of time it retains a particular value. In terms of their lifetime, variables can be divided into two categories: *automatic* variables have shorter lifetimes than do *static* and *external* variables. We'll look at these cases in turn.

Lifetime of Automatic Variables

Automatic variables are the most commonly used in C; the majority of the variables we've used so far have been of this class. In a program's source file, automatic variables are written inside the braces that serve as delimiters for a function. They are created (that is, memory space is allocated to them) when the function containing them is called, and destroyed (their memory space is "deallocated") when the function terminates. In the following function,

```
func()
{
    int alpha;
    auto int beta;
    register int gamma;
}
```

all three variables are created when the function **func()** is called and disappear when it has finished and control returns to the calling function. Such variables are called "automatic" because they are created and destroyed automatically. (Automatic variables are stored on the stack.)

> Variables of type **auto** and **register** are created when the function containing them is called and destroyed when control returns to the calling program.

The variable **alpha** is automatic by default, while **beta** has been made automatic explicitly, using the **auto** keyword. The effect is exactly the same, but the keyword **auto** is sometimes used to avoid confusion. The **gamma** variable is a special kind of automatic variable called a **register** variable; the compiler will assign it to one of the CPU registers—leading to faster operation—provided a register is available. We'll show an example of register variables later in this chapter.

Lifetime of Static and External Variables

If we want a variable to retain its value after the function that defines it is terminated, we have several choices. First, the variable can be defined to be of type **static**, as shown in this example.

```
func()
{
    static int delta;
}
```

A static variable is known only to the function in which it is defined, but, unlike automatic variables, it does not disappear when the function terminates. Instead it keeps its place in memory and therefore its value. In the example above, even after the function **func()** has terminated, **delta** will retain the value it was given in the function. If program control returns to the function again, the value of **delta** will be there for the function to use.

Another way to ensure that a variable retains its value throughout the course of a program is to make it *external*, as we've mentioned in earlier chapters. This is done by placing the variable outside of any function, as **zeta** is in this example:

```
int zeta;
main()
{
}

func()
{
}
```

Like static variables, external variables exist for the life of the program. The difference between them has to do with their visibility, which we'll examine in the next section.

> Variables of type **external**, **static**, and **external static** exist for the life of a program.

Reasons for Different Lifetimes

Why do some variables have longer lifetimes than others? The advantage of eliminating a variable when the function containing it terminates is that the memory space used for the variable can be freed and made available for other variables. Depending on the program, this can result in a considerable saving in memory. This is a good reason for using automatic variables whenever possible.

Static variables can be used in those situations when a variable in a function must retain its value between calls to the function.

Visibility

The visibility (or scope) of a variable refers to which parts of a program will be able to recognize it. There are more distinctions involved in visibility than there are in lifetime: a variable may be visible in a block, a function, a file, a group of files, or an entire program. In this section we'll examine these possibilities in more detail.

Visibility of Automatic and Static Variables

An automatic variable is only recognized within the function in which it is defined; therefore, it is sometimes called a "local" variable. For instance, in this example:

```
main()
{
}

func()
{
    int eta;
}
```

the variable **eta** is recognized only in the function **func()**, not in **main()**. In fact, we could have another variable called **eta** in **main()**; the two would be completely different.

The same is true of static variables (unless they're external, a possibility we'll examine later). They are visible only in the function where they are defined.

Blocks

The visibility of automatic and static variables can be restricted even further; they can be defined inside a *block*. A block is a section of code set off by braces. Here's an example of a block within a function:

```
main()
{
    int epsilon;
    {
        int pi;
    }
}
```

In this example the variable **pi** is visible only within the inner set of braces, while **epsilon** is visible throughout the function **main()**. The braces used to group statements in an **if** or **while** construction form blocks; variables defined within such blocks won't be visible outside of the block.

It is not common practice to define variables within blocks, but in some complicated functions it can provide increased flexibility. Two variables with the same name could be used in the same function, for example.

Visibility of External Variables

To create a variable that is visible to more than one function, we must make it external. As noted above in the discussion of lifetime, this means defining the variable outside of any function. Thus, in the example

```
int theta;
main()
{
}

func()
{
}
```

the variable **theta** will be visible to both **main()** and **func()**, or to any functions placed after the definition of **theta** in this file.

An external variable (unless it is declared elsewhere) is visible only to those functions that *follow* it in the file. If we rearranged our example like this:

```
main()
{
}

int theta;

func()
{
}
```

the variable **theta** will be visible to the function **func()**, but it will be invisible to **main()**.

In Chapter 14 we discussed how separate files, each containing part of a program, can be compiled separately and linked together to create a final program. As we saw there, it is possible for an external variable to be visible in files other than the one in which it is defined, provided it is declared in the other files with the keyword **extern**. We'll pursue this topic in a moment, but first let's clarify some definitions.

Defining and Declaring

A variable can be declared in a particular function without being defined. A declaration is an announcement that a variable with a particular name and type exists. The variable is defined, meaning that memory is set aside for it, elsewhere. Typically, a variable is defined in one file and then declared in every other file in which it will be used. In the multifile program example in Chapter 14, two variables **a** and **b** were defined (in the file containing mainpro2.c) with the statement

```
int a, b;          /* external variables defined in one file */
```

and declared (in the file containing formula2.c) with the statement

```
    extern int a, b;     /* and declared in another file */
```

A variable can be defined only once (since it can only exist in one place in memory), but it must be declared in any file that wishes to access it.

So we can say that external variables are visible only in the file in which they are defined, unless they are declared in other files. Figure 15-1 shows the visibility of a variety of different variables.

The declaration of variables using the **extern** keyword follows the same visibility rules as the definition of variables. In Figure 15-1, the variables **uno**, **dos**, **tres**, and **quatro** are all defined at the same place in File 1, but they all have different visibilities in File 2, depending on where they are declared.

Register Variables

Another storage class specifier is **register**. This specifier is like **auto** in that it indicates a variable with a visibility and a lifetime limited to the function in which it is defined. The difference is that the compiler, if possible, will assign a register variable to one of the microprocessor's registers instead of storing it in memory. Registers can be accessed much faster than memory locations, so using the **register** class for variables that are frequently accessed can result in significantly increasing a program's speed.

There are also drawbacks to the use of register variables. Only a few variables can be register variables in a given program. The exact number is determined by the compiler, and it depends on how many registers the program needs for other purposes. When you define a variable to have the storage class **register**, you're making a *request* to the compiler; it will honor it if it can, but you have no guarantee your request will be carried out. However, with the Turbo C++ compiler, you can normally count on two registers being free for register variables.

Also, not all types of variables can be register variables. The Turbo C++ compiler only guarantees register storage of type **int** and normal pointer types (not **far** pointers).

What variables should be made register variables? The obvious candidates are those variables the program spends the majority of its time operating on. This may be hard to figure out, but if your program has loops, a good guess is to make the loop variables the register variables. If there are nested loops, the variables in the innermost loop will be executed most often.

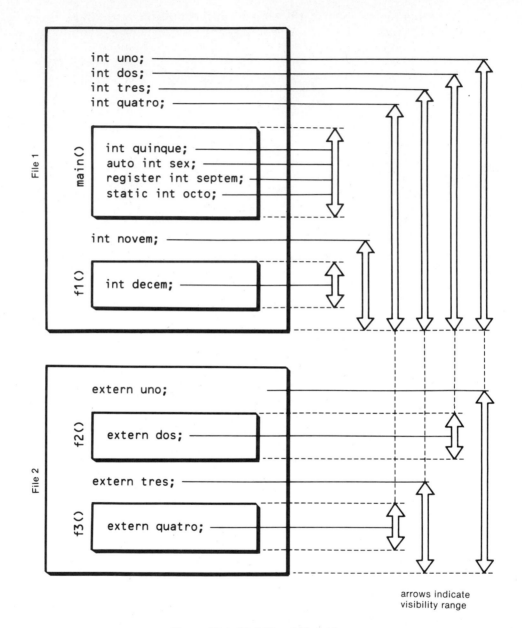

arrows indicate
visibility range

Figure 15-1. Visibility of Variables

One area where execution speed is important is graphics. As you learned in Chapter 10, many graphics operations require large numbers of pixels to be written to the screen in the shortest possible time. Thus graphics operations are a natural place for the use of register variables. We'll revise our dfill2.c program from Chapter 10 to use register variables for the loop variables and and see what speed increase this gives.

Since **register** is a storage class specifier, it precedes the variable type, as in the expression:

```
register int x, y;
```

The revision of dfill2.c uses register variables for the loop variables **col** and **row**.

```
/* dfillreg.c */
/* uses direct memory access to fill screen */
/* tests register variables */
#define ROMAX 25
#define COMAX 80
void main(void)
{
    int far *farptr;
    register int col, row;          /* register variables */
    char ch;

    printf("Type character to start, type again to change");
    farptr = (int far *) 0xB8000000;  /* (B0000000 for mono) */
    while( (ch=getche()) != '\r' )
        {
        for(row=0; row<ROMAX; row++)
            for(col=0; col<COMAX; col++)
                *(farptr + row*COMAX + col) = (int)ch | 0x0700;

    }
}
```

This change results in a 20 percent speed increase over the old version. While not as dramatic as the improvement provided by using direct memory access instead of the C library function **putch()**, it's not bad considering that only one word needed to be added to the program.

You can also let the compiler decide when to use register variables. Select Register Optimization from the Optimization Options box in the Options/ Compiler/Optimization submenu.

Summary of Storage Classes

Table 15-1 summarizes the lifetime and visibility of various types of variables.

The first three variable types shown in the table are local variables: those defined within a function. Their visibility is confined to that function, and

Table 15-1. *Storage Classes*

Where Declared	Keyword	Lifetime	Visibility (scope)
function	auto (default)	function	function
function	register	function	function
function	static	program	function
external	static	program	one file only
external (not decl)	—	program	one file
external (declared)	extern	program	multifile

their lifetime—except for static variables—is also the same as that of the function. These first three variable types can also be defined within a block (a pair of braces); in that case, they will only be visible within the block.

The second group of three variable types are defined external to any function.

The first case, that of an external static variable, is confined to a single file; the **extern** keyword cannot be used to reference it from other files. We use this storage class when we wish to hide the variables in one file—a library file, for instance—from other files.

The second case of external variables is probably the most common; the variable is defined externally but is not declared in any other files. The visibility of such a variable is confined to a single file. In this case (and in the case of external static variables) the variable is visible only from the place in the file where it's defined to the end of the file. It is invisible to functions occurring before it in the file.

In the third case, a variable is defined in one file, but also declared in other files. In this case, its visibility will extend to the appropriate parts of all the files in which it is declared.

By using the correct storage class for a variable, the programmer can economize on memory requirements by restricting the lifetime of the variables, and help maintain a modular, well-structured program by allowing access to variables only to those files and functions that need it. The number of ways to vary the visibility and lifetime of variables is an important reason for C's popularity with developers of large programs and systems.

Enumerated Data Type

Let's examine another data type, one we haven't seen before. The enumerated (**enum**) type gives you the opportunity to invent your own data type and specify what values it can take on. This can help to make listings more readable, which can be an advantage when a program gets complicated or when more than one programmer will be working on it. Using enumerated types can also help you reduce programming errors.

For example, one could invent a data type called **birds** which had as its possible values **sparrow**, **robin**, **eagle**, and **egret**. Don't confuse these values with variable names; **sparrow**, for instance, has the same relationship to the variable **birds** that the value 12 has to an integer variable.

The format of the **enum** definition is similar to that of a structure. Here's how the preceding example would be implemented:

```
enum birds {                          /* declare data type */
    sparrow,                          /* specify values */
    robin,
    eagle,
    egret };
enum birds thisbird, thatbird;        /* define variables */
```

The first statement declares the data type itself—type **enum birds**—and specifies its possible values, which are called *enumerators*. The second statement defines one or more variables—**thisbird** and **thatbird**—to be of this type. Now we can give values to these variables:

```
thisbird = sparrow;
thatbird = egret;
```

We can't use values that aren't in the original declaration. The expression

```
thisbird = magpie;
```

would cause an error.

Internally, the compiler treats enumerated variables as integers. Each value on the list of permissible values corresponds to an integer, starting with 0. Thus, in the **birds** example, sparrow is stored as 0, robin as 1, eagle as 2, and egret as 3.

This way of assigning numbers can be overridden by the programmer by initializing the enumerators to different integer values, as shown in this example:

```
enum birds {                          /* declare data type */
    sparrow = 10,                     /* specify and */
    robin = 20,                       /* initialize values */
    eagle = 30,
    egret = 40 };
enum birds thisbird, thatbird;        /* define variables */
```

In some compilers, the following expressions are illegal, but they work in Turbo C.

```
            thisbird = 1;
            num = eagle;
            thisbird = 2*sparrow;
            if(thisbird<thatbird)
            if(thisbird<eagle)
            magpie++;
```

In other words, you can treat enumerated variables pretty much as if they were integers.

Using the Enumerated Data Type

Enumerated variables are usually used to clarify the operation of a program. For instance, if we need to use a group of employee categories in a payroll program, it makes the listing easier to read if we use values like **management** and **clerical** rather than integer values like 0 and 2.

Here's a short example that makes use of enumerated variables, and also points out one of their weaknesses. (This approach would ordinarily be part of a larger program.)

```
/* enums.c */
/* uses enumerated variables */
void main(void)
{
    enum empcats { management, research, clerical, sales };
    struct {
       char name[30];
       float salary;
       enum empcats category;
    } employee;

    strcpy(employee.name, "Benjamin Franklin");
    employee.salary = 118.50;
    employee.category = research;

    printf("Name = %s\n", employee.name);
    printf("Salary = %6.2f\n", employee.salary);
    printf("Category = %d\n", employee.category);

    if(employee.category==clerical)
       printf("Employee category is clerical.\n");
    else
       printf("Employee category is not clerical.\n");
}
```

We first declare the type **enum empcats** (for "employee categories") and specify four possible values: management, research, clerical, and sales. A variable of type **enum empcats**, called **category**, is then defined in a structure. The structure, **employee**, has three variables containing employee information.

The program first assigns values to the variables in the structure. The expression

```
employee.category = research;
```

assigns the value research to the **employee.category** variable. This is much more informative to anyone reading the listing than a statement like

```
employee.category = 1;
```

The next part of the program shows the weakness of using enum variables: there is no way to use the enum values directly in input and output functions such as **printf()** and **scanf()**. Here's the output of the program:

```
C>enums
Name = Benjamin Franklin
Salary = 118.50
Category = 1
Employee category is not clerical.
```

The **printf()** function is not sophisticated enough to perform the translation; the category is printed out as "1", not as "research". Of course we could write a routine to print out the correct enumerated values, using a table or a **switch** statement, but that would decrease the clarity of the program.

Even with this limitation, however, there are many situations in which enumerated variables are a useful addition to the C language.

Renaming Data Types with *typedef*

Let's look at another technique which in some situations can help to clarify the source code for a C program. This is the use of the **typedef** declaration, whose purpose is to redefine the name of an existing variable type. Its use can result in clearer programs because the name of a type can be shortened and made more meaningful.

For example, consider the following statement in which the type **unsigned char** is redefined to be of type BYTE:

```
typedef unsigned char BYTE;
```

Now we can declare variables of type **unsigned char** by writing

```
BYTE var1, var2;
```

instead of

```
unsigned char var1, var2;
```

Our assumption here is that **var1** and **var2** will be used in a context in which declaring them to be of type BYTE is more meaningful than declaring them to be of type **unsigned char** (for example, they might be values to be placed in a one-byte register during a ROM BIOS call). Using the name BYTE suggests to anyone reading the program that the variables are used in one-byte registers. Uppercase letters are often used to make it clear that we're dealing with a renamed data type.

> The **typedef** declaration causes the compiler to recognize a different name for a variable type.

While the increase in readability is probably not great in this example, it can be significant when the name of a particular type is long and unwieldy, as it often is with structure declarations.

For example, the passtwo2.c program in Chapter 14 contained the declaration:

```
typedef struct personnel  {     /* define data structure */
   char name [30];              /* agent name */
   int agnumb;                  /* agent number */
};
```

Using **typedef**, we could rewrite this:

```
typedef struct personnel AGENT; /* new name for this type */
AGENT  {                        /* define data structure */
   char name [30];              /* agent name */
   int agnumb;                  /* agent number */
};
```

Subsequent references to **struct personnel** can now be replaced with AGENT throughout the program, for example:

```
AGENT agent1;               /* declare structure variable */
AGENT agent2;               /* declare another one */
```

typedef looks something like the **#define** directive, but it actually works in a different way. Using **#define** causes the preprocessor to perform a simple substitution of one phrase for another throughout the program. Using **typedef**, on the other hand, causes the compiler to actually recognize a new name for a specific type. This can make a difference when pointers are concerned, as the following statement demonstrates:

```
typedef struct personnel *PTRAGENT;
```

This statement defines PTRAGENT to be a synonym for the data type "pointer to **struct personnel**." Now we can use the declaration

```
PTRAGENT agent1, agent2;
```

which is equivalent to

```
struct personnel *agent1, *agent2;
```

A **#define** directive could not have been used in this situation, since the asterisks are repeated for each variable.

By reducing the length and apparent complexity of data types, **typedef** can help to clarify source listings.

Identifiers and Naming Classes

So far we've named variables and functions without saying too much about what the restrictions are on such names. In this section we'll mention these restrictions, and then go on to show how the same name can be used, under some circumstances, for different elements in a program.

The names given to variables and functions (and various other programming elements) are called *identifiers*. Allowable characters in identifiers are the letters from A to Z (in both upper- and lowercase), the digits from 0 to 9, and the underscore character (_). The identifier must begin with a letter or an underscore. C distinguishes between upper- and lowercase, so the compiler will treat

```
BigVar
```

as a different variable from

```
bigvar
```

Identifiers can have any number of characters, but only the first 31 will be recognized by the compiler. It's not clear why anyone would want to use more than 31 characters anyway. For those of us who wrote programs in early versions of BASIC, which only recognized variable names of 2 characters, 31 is the ultimate in luxury.

As in most other computer languages, identifiers in C cannot be the same as certain keywords used in the language itself. Fortunately, there are fewer keywords in C than in many languages. In Turbo C these keywords fall into two classes. Those used for defining data are **auto**, **char**, **const**, **double**, **enum**, **extern**, **far**, **float**, **huge**, **int**, **long**, **near**, **register**, **short**, **signed**, **static**, **struct**, **typedef**, **union**, **unsigned**, **void**, and **volatile**. Those used for program control are **asm**, **break**, **case**, **cdecl**, **continue**, **default**, **do**, **else**, **for**, **goto**, **if**, **interrupt**, **pascal**, **return**, **sizeof**, **switch**, and **while**.

Naming Classes

The various program elements that are named with identifiers, such as functions and variables, are divided into *naming classes*. Within a naming class, each item must have a distinct identifier (in other words, you can't have two variables with the same name). However, you can use the same name for different elements if the elements are in different naming classes. The five naming classes are described next.

1. Variables and Functions

A variable cannot have the same name as a function in which it is visible. A function's formal parameters also fall into this naming class, so they cannot have the same name as any of the variables used in the function. (However, as we discussed in the section on storage classes, several variables within a function can have the same name if they are in separate blocks.) Enumeration constants are also part of this naming class; you can't use the same name for an enumeration constant as for a variable (unless they have different visibilities).

2. Tags

As you may recall, structures, unions, and classes of enumeration variables are named with a tag. For instance, in the structure definition

```
struct ex1 {
    int intnum;
    float fltnum;
    } svar1;
```

the identifier **ex1** is the tag, while **svar1** is a variable name. Tags form their own naming class, so it would be legal, for instance, to change the variable name **svar1** to **ex1** in this example, since the same identifier can be used for two elements if they are in different naming classes.

3. Members

Members of structures and unions, such as **intnum** and **fltnum** in our example, form a separate naming class. They must be distinct from other members of the same structure or union, but they can be the same as other identifiers in the program.

In the following example the identifier **apple** is used in three different places. Since each use is a different naming class, the compiler will find this perfectly acceptable.

```
struct apple {       /* 'apple' names a tag */
    int apple;       /* 'apple' names a member */
    float pear;      /* could not be 'apple' here */
} apple;             /* 'apple' names a variable */
```

4. Statement Labels

Statement labels form a distinct naming class. Within a function, statement labels must all have distinct names, but these can be the same as those of variables or members of other naming classes. We'll discuss labels further at the end of this chapter.

5. typedef Names

The names of types defined with **typedef** are treated by the compiler as if they were keywords. Thus, once a name has been defined in a **typedef** statement, no other program elements, no matter what naming class they are in, can use the same identifer.

Of course, none of the rules about naming classes alter the rules about visibility. If the visibility of two program elements is different, then they can have the same identifier, even if they are in the same naming class (for example, two automatic variables in different functions).

Type Conversion and Casting

You have probably noticed by this time that it's possible to mix data types in C expressions. Thus the following program will elicit no error message from the compiler (as a similar construction would in Pascal, for instance):

```
void main(void)
{
    int intnum = 2;              /* integer type */
```

```
        float fltnum = 3.3;        /* floating point type */
        double ans;                /* double precision type */
        ans = intnum + fltnum;     /* mixed expression is legal */
    }
```

There are dangers involved in mixing types; that's why some languages make such mixing illegal. But the philosophy in C is that it's better to give the programmer the freedom to mix types, which often leads to simpler code, than to try to keep the programmer out of trouble by flagging type mismatches as an error. Of course, with the freedom to mix data types comes the responsibility to make sure that such mixing is not the result of a mistake, such as assuming a variable is of one type when it really is of another.

When data types are mixed in an expression, the compiler converts the variables to compatible types before carrying out the intended operation. In these conversions, variables of lower rank are converted to the rank of the higher-ranking operand. The ranking corresponds roughly to how many bytes each type occupies in memory. This is shown in Figure 15-2.

```
lower  ◄─────────────────────────►  higher
rank                                 rank

char < int < long < float < double
```

Figure 15-2. Ranking of Data Types

As an example, consider the following program:

```
void main(void)
{
    char ch;
    int intnum;
    long longnum;
    float fltnum;
    double doubnum;
    int answer;
    answer = (ch * intnum) +  (ch * longnum) + (fltnum * doubnum);
}
```

Before each operator is applied to the appropriate pair of variables, the variable with the lower rank is converted to the rank of the higher-ranking variable. This process is shown in Figure 15-3.

Promotion, or moving from a lower rank to a higher rank, usually doesn't cause problems. Demotion, however, can easily result in a loss of precision or even yield a completely incorrect result. Table 15-2 details what happens when demotion occurs.

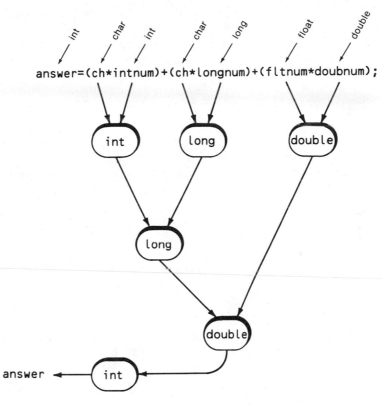

Figure 15-3. Data Type Conversion

Table 15-2. *Data Type Demotion*

Demotion	Result
int to **char**	low-order byte is used
long to **char**	low-order byte is used
float to **char**	**float** converted to **long** and low-order byte used
double to **char**	**double** converted to **float, float** to **long,** and low-order byte used
long to **int**	low-order word (two bytes) used
float to **int**	**float** converted to **long** and low-order word used
double to **int**	**double** converted to **float, float** to **long,** and low-order word used
float to **long**	truncate at decimal point; if result is too large for **long,** it is undefined
double to **long**	truncate at decimal point; if result is too large for **long,** it is undefined

Generally, if a number is too large to fit into the type to which it is being demoted, its value will be corrupted. Some loss of precision can even occur in the *promotion* of **long** to **float**, since these two types both use four bytes.

The moral is, avoid type conversions unless there's a good reason for them, and be especially careful when demoting a variable, since you may lose data.

Typecasting

Typecasting provides a way to force a variable to be of a particular type. This overrides the normal type conversions we just described. The mechanism for typecasting is to precede the variable by the desired type, enclosed in parentheses. For example, in this statement

```
answer = (int)fltnum;
```

the typecast will cause the value of **fltnum** to be converted to an integer value before being assigned to **answer**, no matter what type **fltnum** is.

Typecasting is often used to ensure that a value passed to a function is of the type the function is expecting. For instance, suppose we have a variable **intnum** of type **int** and we want to take its square root. However, the square root function requires a variable of type **long**. We could use the expression

```
sqroot( (long)intnum )
```

and the effect would be to pass a variable of type **long** to the function.

Typecasting can also ensure that a constant has the right type. This is especially useful for pointer types, as we saw in Chapter 10, where we used the expression

```
farptr = (int far *) 0xB000000;
```

Without the typecast, the compiler becomes confused about the type of the constant and issues error messages; with the cast, we can specify that the constant is a **far** pointer and that it points to an integer.

Labels and the *goto* Statement

We have deliberately put off a discussion of the **goto** statement until the end of the book. There is seldom a legitimate reason for **goto**, and its use is one of the leading reasons that programs become unreliable, unreadable, and hard to debug. And yet many programmers (especially those accustomed to BASIC) find **goto** seductive. In a difficult programming situation it seems so easy to throw in a **goto** to get where you want to go. Almost always, however, there is a more elegant construction using an **if** or **switch** statement or a loop. Such constructions are far easier to understand than **goto** statements. A **goto** statement can cause program control to end up almost anywhere in the program, for reasons that are often hard to unravel.

We trust that, by getting this far in the book without using a **goto**, we have provided proof that, at least in most cases, its use can be avoided. If you turned to this page from the index, desperate to use a **goto**, try very hard to employ another approach.

For completeness, however, here's how **goto** is used. Consider the following program fragment:

```
- - -
if(temp>max)
  goto scramble;              /*goto label*/
- - -
scramble:                     /*note colon after label */
  printf("Emergency!");
- - -
```

The **goto** statement transfers control to the label **scramble**, causing the **printf()** statement to be executed immediately after the **goto**. The **goto** must specify a label, and the label must exist or a compiler error will result. Since the compiler doesn't care about whitespace, the label, which must be followed by a colon, can be on a separate line or on the same line as another statement.

```
scramble: printf("Emergency!");
```

Labels are used only with **goto** statements. Other statements on the same line as a label will operate as if the label didn't exist. As we noted earlier in this chapter, labels form a naming class and are formed in the same way as other identifiers.

Summary

This chapter has covered some of the less common aspects of variables. We've examined storage classes, which permit control of the lifetime and visibility of a variable; enumerated data types, which permit the programmer to define a data type and its values; and **typedef**, which lets the programmer give a new name to an existing data type. We've also examined the conventions used for naming variables and other elements in C programs, and we've seen how these names or identifiers apply to different categories of program elements called naming classes. We've seen how variables are converted automatically from one type to another and how this conversion can be overridden with type-casting. Finally we looked at labels and their use with the **goto** statement.

Questions

1. The storage class of a variable is related to
   a. the amount of memory space the variable occupies
   b. the quality of the memory space occupied
   c. how long the variable will occupy a space in memory
   d. what parts of the program can "see" the function

2. For a variable to be visible in a file other than the one where it is defined, it must be _____ using the _____ keyword.

3. A variable definition differs from a declaration in that
   a. the declaration sets aside storage space
   b. the declaration specifies the name and type of the variable
   c. the definition sets aside storage space
   d. the definition specifies the name and type of the variable

4. An *automatic* variable is one that is automatically c_____ and d_____.

5. A *static* (nonexternal) variable can be seen only within
   a. a block
   b. a function
   c. a file
   d. many files

6. True or false: an external variable is always visible throughout the file in which it is defined.

7. To restrict the visibility of an external variable to one file, it must be of type _____ _____.

8. In an enumerated data type, the programmer can define
   a. whether the new type will be integer or floating point

    b. the number of bytes used by variables of the new type

    c. the values of the new type d.many types of the same storage class

9. If **fish** has already been defined to an enumerated data type, what statement will define the variable **gamefish** to be of this type?

10. The **typedef** declaration is used to
    a. declare a new data type
    b. perform a **#define**-style substitution of one identifier for another
    c. define a new data type
    d. give a new name to a data type

11. Identifiers are the _____ given to variables and other elements in a program.

12. A naming class is
    a. a category of variables of the same type
    b. a place to learn how to name variables
    c. a category in which identifiers must be distinct
    d. the category of functions and variables

13. True or false: the same identifier can be used for a structure and a member of that structure.

14. The rank of a variable in data conversions is roughly indicated by the number of _____ _____ used by the character.

15. A typecast is used to
    a. force a value to be of a particular variable type
    b. define a new data type
    c. rename an old data type
    d. provide harder than usual data

16

C++ and Object-Oriented Programming

- Object-oriented programming
- Useful C++ features
- Classes and objects
- Constructors and destructors
- Inheritance
- Function and operator overloading

16

Turbo C incorporates extensions to the C language that enable programmers to write programs in C++. C++ is a superset of C: that is, it incorporates all the operators and syntax of ordinary C, but adds additional features. The primary reason for these additional features is to facilitate object-oriented programming, but there are other new capabilities as well.

In this chapter, we'll first describe object-oriented programming (OOP) in general. Then we'll discuss a few of the new features of C++, such as the stream I/O functions and the new comment style, that will be used in the programming examples to follow. Next come examples that demonstrate how the new C++ features are used to write complete object-oriented programs. We'll close with several more complex programs that use multiple objects.

This chapter is by no means a complete primer in C++ programming; that would require an entire book. Instead we want to give you a feeling for what OOP is and how C++ supports it.

Object-Oriented Programming

It's important understand that object-oriented programming is an approach to *organizing* programs. It is not primarily concerned with the details of program code; its focus is the overall structure of the program. For this reason, we will start our discussion of OOP, not with specific program examples, but with a general discussion of how programs are organized. You may be eager to see and write specific examples, but be patient. A prerequisite for writing object-oriented programs is understanding the philosophy of OOP. Without the philosophy, the specifics are meaningless.

OOP is not applicable to all programs. Because it applies to program organization, OOP becomes increasingly helpful as programs grow larger. In many cases, there isn't any reason to use OOP in one- or two-function programs. It's when an application requires dozens or hundreds of functions that

OOP has the greatest potential for simplifying program conceptualization, coding, debugging, and maintenance. Because it imposes a certain overhead, OOP may also not be ideal for hardware-oriented tasks such as device drivers and some kinds of system software.

Organizing Programs with Functions

In previous chapters—notably the chapter on larger programs—we discussed the mechanisms that classic C provides to aid in program organization. We discussed how C *functions* are used to organize the program in well-defined sections. Each function has (or should have) a clearly defined purpose, and clearly defined communications with other functions. We also discussed how functions can be combined into separate *source files* to provide a higher level of organization. Both levels of organization are based on organizing functions. This organizational approach helps the programmer to write the program, and aids in debugging and maintenance.

Procedure-Oriented Organization

Statements in the C language cause the program to do something, such as adding two numbers or printing a result. Each function is built up from statements, and it also performs a specific action, such as reading a disk file, printing a string, calculating an average, sorting a file, and so on. Notice that the emphasis is on the *verb* in these phrases: "*sort* the data." When we say that a function should have a clearly defined purpose, the purpose we define is an *action*.

Programming in C thus consists of writing a list of instructions for the computer to follow, and organizing these instructions into groups, and these groups into larger groups. C is called a *procedural* language: it describes a procedure—a list of instructions—for solving a problem. The whole philosophy (or *paradigm*, which means "conception" or "model") in C is to organize the actions taken by the program. When we draw a typical program flowchart, the boxes represent actions and the lines connecting the boxes represent the flow of control from one action to the next.

What About the Data?

The attentive reader may have noticed that while our descriptions of computer actions, such as "Sort the data," start with a verb, they also contain a noun; in this case "data." We've been focusing on the action, and forgetting about the thing *acted on*. What happens to the data when you organize your program into functions? Organizationally, the data is a second-class citizen. You plan your program along procedural lines, and hope the data will work out.

But data is much more important than the procedural paradigm would lead you to believe. After all, the point of executing all the statements in a program is to operate *on* data. The important thing in an inventory program isn't the instructions in the program, it's the inventory itself. The *data* is the reason for the program's existence, yet the program organization focuses on *instructions*. This can lead to problems in conceptualizing problems, and in writing robust, error-free code.

Vulnerable Data

One problem is that important data structures may need to be external variables, because they must be accessed by many major functions. But (as we've noted in earlier chapters) there are problems with external variables. They are subject to being changed inadvertently by any function. Also, it's difficult to tell from looking at a normal C source listing what functions access a particular external data structure. Revising a data structure requires rewriting every function that interacts with it.

Figure 16-1-a shows the relationship of data and functions in traditional C.

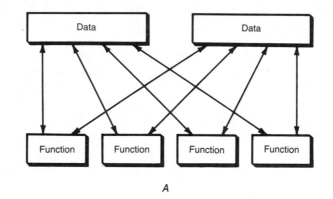

A

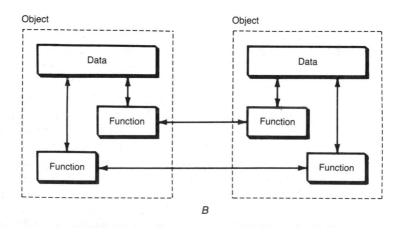

B

Figure 16-1. OOP Versus Procedural Organization

Representing the Real World

Another problem with the procedural approach is that it's not a good match for many situations in the real world. In an accounting system, for example, the major conceptual items are data: a list of accounts receivable, a list of accounts payable, a payroll list, an inventory, and so on. C functions, being actions, don't correspond well with the elements of the problem.

Object-Oriented Organization

Object-oriented programming attempts to solve some of the problems of the procedural approach. OOP gives data a more central position in program organization, and ties the data more closely to the functions that act on it. In the procedural approach, the organizational units are functions. In OOP, the organizational units contain both the data and the functions that act on that data. These units are called (as you may have guessed) *objects*.

Point of View

OOP is essentially a *point of view*. It does not really depend on particular language features. In fact, it's possible to write an object-oriented program using classic C. (many Microsoft Windows and OS/2 Presentation Manager applications are at least partially written this way.) The extensions to C embodied in C++ are intended to make it easier to write object-oriented programs, but they aren't indispensable for the purpose and they are not the heart of OOP. A general understanding of OOP doesn't require learning any new programming operators or syntax; it does require looking at program organization in a new way.

Objects

In OOP, a program is organized into objects. As we noted, an object consists of data and the functions that operate on that data. In a typical situation, only the functions in the object can access the object's data; it cannot be accessed by functions in other objects.

For example, you might have an object that is an inventory consisting of a list of automobile parts. This object might contain functions to add and delete items from the inventory, read items from the inventory, and print out the inventory. The inventory data is usually **private**: no functions other than those within the inventory object can access it. On the other hand, the functions within an object are usually **public**. They can be accessed by other functions in the program, including functions in other objects. That's how other functions and objects access the data in an object: by using the functions that are part of the object. The organization of OOP programs is shown schematically in Figure 16-1-b.

A New Vocabulary

Object-oriented programming has its own vocabulary for some of the concepts we've talked about. The functions in an object are called *methods*. They do something to the object's data. The binding together of the data with the functions that operate on it is called *encapsulation*. The fact that the data in an object cannot be accessed by other objects is called *data hiding*. Encapsulation and data hiding are key elements in OOP.

Classes

In OOP, objects are members of *classes*. Let's see what this means.

In ordinary C, as we discussed in the chapter on advanced variables, we distinguish between declaring and defining a variable. Let's say we declare a structure like this:

```
struct easy
    {
    int num;
    char ch;
    };
```

This declaration doesn't cause any code to be generated; it tells the compiler, "This is how structures of type **struct easy** look. Memorize it; we'll refer to it later." Later in the listing we might define two variables of this type with the statement

```
struct easy ez1, ez2;
```

This statement causes the compiler to generate code to actually set aside areas of memory for two structures of this size, and associate these memory areas with the names **ez1** and **ez2**.

Remember that the declaration of **struct easy** is only a *specification*. It doesn't set aside any memory. It is the definitions of **ez1** and **ez2** that create real variables based on this specification.

A class in OOP has the same relationship to an object that the declaration of **struct easy** has to the variables **ez1** and **ez2**. The class is a specification for any number of objects. Specifying the class doesn't create the objects, it merely describes the form such objects will take when they are created. When we actually define an object, specifying that it is of a certain class, we cause memory to be set aside to hold its data, and code for its functions to be created. We say we've created an *instance* of the class.

Inheritance

An important feature of C++ is *inheritance*. Inheritance means making objects out of other objects. Suppose you've created an object that represents an automobile parts inventory. It contains a list of parts, with their characteristics and prices, and functions for storing and deleting items, listing them, and so on. This inventory object is debugged, and it works. Now suppose you want an object that represents a pharmacy inventory. It's similar to the car parts inventory, but requires a few new items, such as a category for the expiration date of the drug. In C++ you can use the car parts inventory object *without changing it in any way*. You declare a new object, the pharmacy inventory object, which incorporates the car parts inventory and adds the new data items and functions. You can use the old functions—created for the car parts—to operate on the drugs, and the new functions as well. This is shown in Figure 16-2.

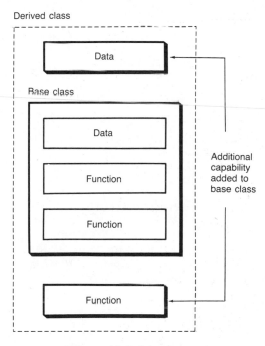

Figure 16-2. Inheritance

In normal C you would need to rewrite the car inventory functions to adapt them to the pharmacy inventory. You could probably salvage some of the code, but you would still need to create new data structures and functions. This would require debugging everything from the beginning. In C++ you can define a new object that has all the characteristics of an existing object, plus some new ones. There's no need to touch the code for the existing object. This is a great time saver in developing applications, because you don't need to rewrite and debug the existing object.

We'll soon see program examples that demonstrate classes and objects and their characteristics. First, we'll look at some less central features of C++.

Some Useful C++ Features

C++ brings a variety of additions and improvements to C that are not related to OOP. In this section, we'll discuss several of the most useful of these features. We'll be using them in the OOP programs that follow, so you need to know what they look like.

Comments

Perhaps the most common—and the simplest—improvement provided by C++ is the one-line comment. This new comment style requires only an initial double slash (//). It is terminated by the carriage return at the end of the line. The double slash can appear at the beginning of the line, or following a program statement.

```
// this is a comment on its own line
error = 666;        // this is a comment following a statement
```

This new comment style does away with the problem in traditional C of forgetting to insert the closing */ symbol. It's also easier to type. The old comment style, delimited by /* and */, can still be used in C++, and may be more convenient for long multiline comments.

The Stream I/O Functions

One of the most programmer-friendly innovations in C++ is a new I/O function library. Using this library helps to avoid the perverse formatting requirements of such functions as **printf()** and **scanf()**.

These stream functions use the header file IOSTREAM.H, so if you want to use them, the directive

```
#include <iostream.h>
```

should appear at the beginning of your program. As in normal C, the header file contains function prototypes and various definitions used with a group of functions. (Other C++ compilers may use a file named STREAM.H for this purpose.)

Output

Here's a statement that prints a string:

```
cout << "This string will be printed";
```

The **cout** identifier (pronounced "C out") represents the standard output stream. The << operator, called "put to," causes the string on its right to be passed to the standard output stream on its left. When this statement is executed, the string will appear on the standard output device, which is usually the screen (unless the output has been redirected).

Note the absence of any formatting information. The operator is smart enough to examine the type of the variable whose value is being output, and print strings as strings, integers as integers, and so on.

The "put to" operator can be used more than once in a statement. The following statement will output a string, an integer, and another string:

```
cout << "Mars is " << miles << " from the sun.\n";
```

Input

A similar construction is used for input. The following statement reads an integer from the keyboard and places it in the variable **size**.

```
cin >> size;
```

The **cin** identifier (pronounced "C in") represents the standard input device. The >> operator, called "get from," takes the input from the device on its left and places it in the variable on its right. Again, the function is smart enough to interpret the input according to the data type of the variable that will receive it. If **size** is an integer, and the user types "27", the integer value 27 will be placed in **size**. If **size** is a string, the string "27" will be placed in it.

Overloading

If you read the section on the bitwise operators in Chapter 10, you may be wondering how it's possible to use the >> and << operators both to direct input and output as we've shown here, and to shift bits as shown in that chapter. C++ uses a concept called *overloading* to make it possible for a function or operator to perform more than one job. We'll discuss overloading later in this chapter.

Variable Definitions and Scope

In classic C, all local variables used in a function must be defined at the beginning of the function, before any executable statements. In C++ this rule is relaxed. Executable statements can precede variable definitions. This makes it possible to define variables close to the point at which they are used, which can—in some circumstances—make the listing more readable.

For example, the following construction is allowed:

```
for(int j=0; j<7; j++)
    cout << j << "\n";
```

Here **j** is defined within the **for** statement.

Remember that (as we mentioned in Chapter 15) the scope of a variable is the block in which it is defined, where a *block* is delimited by a curly bracket pair. For example, in the following program fragment, the variable **j** is visible everywhere, while **k** and **beta** are visible only within the block delimited by the curly brackets.

```
for(int j=0; j<7; j++)
    {
    int beta=10;
    for(int k=0; k<11; k++)
        cout << j*k*beta << "\n";
    }
```

Remember this block definition limitation when taking advantage of variable definitions inside the program.

C++ has many other new features, but these few will be enough to get you started understanding our example OOP programs.

Classes and Objects

In this section, we'll start looking at examples of object-oriented programs written in C++. Our first example demonstrates a class and an object. It models a simple expense ledger. Imagine you're running a lemonade stand, and every time you buy supplies you write down the amount: $10.50 for lemons, $4.12 for paper cups, and so on. Our program lets you record such expenses on your computer. You would probably want to record the date and a description of the item, but for simplicity the program records only the dollar amount, expressed as a floating point number.

Data

The central data structure in this program is an array of floating point numbers to hold the expenses. The array size is fixed; we assume it is large enough to hold all the entries likely to be made.

Actions on the Data

What actions do we want to perform on this list of expenses? First, we need to be able to enter new items into the list. We also want to print the total of all the items. One can imagine other useful actions, such as printing out the entire list of expenses, or deleting an entry if we make an mistake, but to keep the program simple we'll restrict ourselves to making an entry and displaying the total.

To calculate the total expenses, we need to keep a count of how many items are in the array; this requires another data item besides the array. At the beginning of the program we'll need to initialize this count to 0 to signify that no entries have been made. This is another necessary action. Thus we must handle two data items and three methods (functions).

Declaring a Class

We mentioned that declaring a class is somewhat like declaring a structure. It specifies what objects of this class will look like. Here's the declaration of class **ledger**:

```
class ledger                    // declaration of class ledger
{
   private:
      float list[100];          // define array for items
      int count;                // define number of items entered
   public:
      void initCount(void);     // declare method
      void enterItem(void);     // declare method
      void printTotal(void);    // declare method
};
```

The first line of the declaration uses the keyword **class** to specify that we're declaring a class called **ledger**. The body of the declaration is delimited with curly brackets and terminated with a semicolon. Within the class, the variables **list** and **count** are declared. So far this is very much like a classic C language structure. However, in a **class**, we can declare functions as well as variables. Remember that the functions in a class are called methods. We declare the methods **initCount()**, **enterItem()**, and **printTotal()**. In this case we didn't place the complete method in the class declaration, only a method declaration or prototype. The methods themselves will appear later in the listing.

Some of the members of the class **ledger** are private, and some are public. As it happens, the data items are all private and the methods are all public. This is a common situation, although it need not always be the case. Data or methods designated **public** can be accessed from outside the object, but those marked **private** can be accessed only from within the object.

We did not really need to include the keyword **private** in the class declaration shown above, since this is the default. It is commonly omitted from class declarations, but including it avoids the possibility of confusion.

Remember that the declaration of **ledger** shown above does not define any objects of class **ledger**. It only specifies what such objects will contain if they are defined.

Defining Methods

In the class shown above, we declared three methods. That is, we specified they would be a part of the class **ledger**. However, we did not specify what they were. Here are the definitions for the methods **initCount()**, **enterItem()**, and **printTotal()**.

```
///////////////////////////////////////////////////////////
void ledger::initCount(void)   // a function in class ledger
{                              // initializes count to 0
   count = 0;
}
///////////////////////////////////////////////////////////
void ledger::enterItem(void)   // a function in class ledger
{                              // puts entry in list
   cout << "\nEnter amount: ";
   cin >> list[count++];
}
///////////////////////////////////////////////////////////
void ledger::printTotal(void) // a function in class ledger
{                              // prints total of all entries
   float total=0.0;
   for(int j=0; j<count; j++)
     total += list[j];
   cout << "\n\nTotal is: " << total << "\n";
}
///////////////////////////////////////////////////////////
```

The first method, **initCount()**, simply sets the variable **count** to 0 to indicate that the array **list[ ]** is empty. The second method, **enterItem()**, prints a prompt to the user, and then assigns the amount typed by the user to the array member **list[count]**. The third method, **printTotal()**, finds the total of all the entries in **array[ ]** and displays it.

How do we tell the compiler that these methods are part of the **ledger** class? We use the *scope resolution* operator, represented by two side-by-side colons (::). This operator specifies the area of the program—or scope—where a method will be visible. Thus the line

```
void ledger::initCount(void)
```

indicates that we are defining the function **initCount()** to be a method of class **ledger**. (The **void**s specify in the usual way that the function takes no arguments and has no return value.)

Although in this example the methods are only declared in the class, it's also possible to put the code for simple methods completely inside the class declaration, as we'll see later.

The Theory of the *ledger* Class

Now that we've declared the class **ledger**, how do we go about creating objects of this class? Here's a declaration of two such objects:

```
ledger expense, income;
```

This defines two objects, **expense** and **income**, to be of class **ledger**. This definition causes actual memory space to be set aside for the components of the two objects. Each object contains an array and the methods for acting on that array. You can define as many objects of a given class as you want.

Compiling C++ in Turbo C++

We are (at long last) about to introduce our first complete C++ example program. Before we do, however, you should know how to use Turbo C++ to create a C++ executable program from a source listing. Actually the process is very similar to creating a standard C program. The major difference is that your source file is given the .CPP extension, rather than the .C extension. Here are the steps:

1. Type in your C++ source file. Save it with the .CPP file extension.
2. Select Compile or Make from the Compile menu, just as with a normal C program.

When Turbo C++ knows that a source file has the .CPP extension, it compiles it as a C++ program, rather than a C program. If you attempt to compile a C++ program that has a .C extension, you'll get numerous compiler errors, since Turbo C++ won't recognize the C++ syntax.

The expense.cpp Example

Let's put the C++ components we discussed above into a complete C++ program. This example program permits the user to record amounts in the list, and print out the total.

```
/////////////////////////////////////////////////////////////////
// expense.cpp
// object oriented expense ledger

#include <iostream.h>          // for cout, cin, etc.
/////////////////////////////////////////////////////////////////
class ledger                   // declaration of class ledger
{
   private:
```

```
            float list[100];        // array for items
            int count;              // number of items entered
        public:
            void initCount(void);   // declare function
            void enterItem(void);   // declare function
            void printTotal(void);  // declare function
    };
    //////////////////////////////////////////////////////////////////
    void ledger::initCount(void)  // a function in class ledger
    {                             // initializes count to 0
        count = 0;
    }
    //////////////////////////////////////////////////////////////////
    void ledger::enterItem(void)  // a function in class ledger
    {                             // puts entry in list
        cout << "\nEnter amount: ";
        cin >> list[count++];
    }
    //////////////////////////////////////////////////////////////////
    void ledger::printTotal(void)  // a function in class ledger
    {                              // prints total of all entries
        float total=0.0;
        for(int j=0; j<count; j++)
            total += list[j];
        cout << "\n\nTotal is: " << total << "\n";
    }
    //////////////////////////////////////////////////////////////////
    ledger expenses;                // an instance of class ledger
    //////////////////////////////////////////////////////////////////
    main()                          // main -- handles user interface
    {                               //    uses object "expenses"
        char option;
        expenses.initCount();       // initialize count
        do
            {                       // display options
            cout << "\nOptions are:  e -- enter expense"
                 << "\n              E -- print total expenses"
                 << "\n              q -- quit (terminate program)"
                 << "\nType option letter: ";
            cin >> option;          // get option from user
            switch (option)
                {                   // act on option selected
                case 'e': expenses.enterItem(); break;
                case 'E': expenses.printTotal(); break;
                case 'q': break;
```

```
        default: cout << "\nUnknown command\n";
        }
    } while(option != 'q');
} // end main
```

The elements in this listing, up to the **main()** function, should be familiar to you. There is the same **ledger** class declaration here that we discussed earlier. There is only one object of this class: it's called **expenses**.

The user-interface part of the program takes place in the **main()** function. A list of choices is printed for the user's edification, and the user's selection, indicated by a single typed character, is used in a **switch** statement to determine the program's action. Here's some sample output (which assumes other expense amounts have already been entered):

```
Options are:  e -- enter expense
              E -- print total expenses
              q -- quit (terminate program)
Type option letter: e
Enter amount: 10.97

Options are:  e -- enter expense
              E -- print total expenses
              q -- quit (terminate program)
Type option letter: E
Total is: 99.44
```

Accessing the Methods

Note that you can't put statements in **main()** that access **list[]** or **count** directly, since they were declared **private**. To access these variables, you must call the methods contained in a particular object. The format for these calls requires the dot operator (.). The object's name precedes the dot, and the method's name follows it. Thus the line

```
    expenses.enterItem();
```

calls the **enterItem()** method in the **expenses** object, as shown schematically in Figure 16-3. The other methods are called similarly.

OOP Benefits

You may be thinking that you could write a program with the same functionality more concisely in ordinary C. This is probably true. However, notice how conceptually tight the program is. The data is safely hidden away in the object. Only the object's methods can access this data. We can be sure that no matter what egregious programming errors we make, the data will not be corrupted by

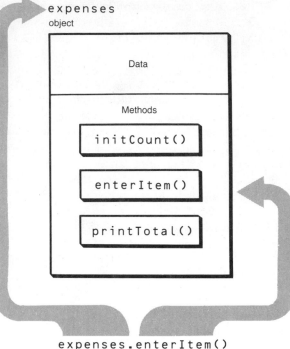

Figure 16-3. Accessing Methods

methods that are not part of **ledger**. Also, the program is easy to read. Any-one looking at the listing can see at a glance exactly what methods have access to the data.

Constructors and Memory Allocation

Let's look at some C++ language features that increase the functionality of objects. Although these features are not essential to object-oriented program-ming, they can be a considerable convenience for C++ programmers, and they are commonly used.

Constructors

In the expense.cpp example we needed to initialize the variable count, which recorded the number of entries in the array. We did this by calling the method **initCount()** at the start of **main()**, in the line

```
expenses.initCount();
```

This is an inconvenience. If we had dozens of objects of a particular class we would need statements to initialize each one of them. It would be nice if an object could initialize itself, and in fact C++ incorporates just such a mechanism.

A **constructor** is a method (function) that is executed whenever an object is first created. It is declared within a class in a way similar to other methods, but with some differences. The key feature of a constructor is that it has the same name as the class.

We could have written a constructor in the expenses example to perform exactly the same task as the **initCount** method. It would have been declared this way in the class declaration:

```
ledger();
```

Note that the method's name is the same as the class name. The definition for this method would be

```
ledger::ledger()
{
    count = 0;
}
```

If we substitute this constructor for the **initCount()** method, we can remove the statement from **main()** that calls **initCount()**. Nor do we need to write any calls to **ledger()**, since it is executed *automatically* whenever an object of class **ledger** is defined. No matter how many objects of class **ledger** there are, each will be initialized to 0 when it is created.

A Time Example

In the next program we'll show another way to use constructors. This example also demonstrates how methods can be be defined inside the class declaration, rather than externally.

This example uses objects in a somewhat different way than did the expense.cpp example. In expense.cpp, the important data was an array of numbers. In a more ambitious program, this array could be expanded into an array of structures, each of which contained, not only a money amount, but a text description, date, and so on. Such objects can be fairly large and complex.

However, the important data in an object can also be very simple, consisting of only a few variables. An object could represent a point on a two-dimensional plane, for example. The only two items of data in such an object would be the X and Y coordinates of the point. Using an object to model data in this way is almost like creating a new data type. It's similar to the way you create new data types using structures, but using an object brings in all the other advantages of OOP. Other potential examples of such programmer-defined data types are complex numbers (with imaginary and real parts), three-dimensional coordinates, strings (since there is no true sting type in C or C++), dates, times, and so on.

In this example we'll create a class called **time**. The private variables in the class consist of integers representing seconds, hours, and minutes. Methods in the **time** class allow these time values to be set and accessed. Another method allows you to add two time values.

Here's the listing for time0.cpp. (We can't use the name **time** because it would conflict with the MS-DOS system function of the same name.)

```cpp
// time0.cpp
// creates a class for a new data type: time

#include <iostream.h>                    // for cout, etc.
#include <stdio.h>                       // for printf(), scanf()
/////////////////////////////////////////////////////////////////
class time                              // declaration of class time
{
   private:
      int hrs;                          // hours
      int mins;                         // minutes
      int secs;                         // seconds
   public:
      time()                            // constructor
         { secs=0; mins=0; hrs=0; }     // initialize to 0:00:00

      void printTime(void)              // print time
         { printf("%d:%02d:%02d", hrs, mins, secs); }
      void readTime(void)               // read time from keyboard
         { scanf("%d:%d:%d", &hrs, &mins, &secs); }

      void addTime(time t)              // add time t to this time
         {
         secs += t.secs;                        // add secs
         if(secs > 59) { secs -= 60; ++mins; }  // carry secs
         mins += t.mins;                        // add mins
         if(mins > 59) { mins -= 60; ++hrs; }   // carry mins
         hrs += t.hrs;                          // add hrs
         }
};
/////////////////////////////////////////////////////////////////
main()
{
   time t1, t2, tAnswer;                // declare time objects
```

```
cout << "\nEnter first time period (format hh:mm:ss): ";
t1.readTime();                        // read t1

cout << "\nEnter second time period (format hh:mm:ss): ";
t2.readTime();                        // read t2

cout << "\nt1 = ";                    // print t1
t1.printTime();
cout << "\nt2 = ";                    // print t2
t2.printTime();

tAnswer.addTime(t1);                  // add t1 to tAnswer
tAnswer.addTime(t2);                  // add t2 to tAnswer
cout << "\nSum of time periods = ";   // print tAnswer
tAnswer.printTime();
}
```

We have, in effect, created a new data type: one that consists of three integer values. Here's the output when you run the program:

```
Enter first time period (format hh:mm:ss): 5:32:30
Enter second time period (format hh:mm:ss): 4:27:30
t1 =  5:32:30
t2 = 4:27:30
Sum of time periods = 10:00:00
```

If you were writing an application that dealt extensively with time, you might find the **time** class useful. You could simply copy it in your program, define the appropriate **time** objects, and operate on them almost as if they were normal C variables.

Of course you could achieve a similar functionality in classic C, using a structure to hold the **hrs**, **mins**, and **secs** data. However, variables of this type would not be protected from alteration by unauthorized functions, and the conception and use of the data type would not be as clear. More importantly, some of the simplifications made possible by operating overloading—which we'll discuss soon—would not be possible.

Defining Methods Within a Class

In time0.cpp, all the methods are defined inside the class, instead of being declared inside and then defined outside, as in expense.cpp. This is appropriate for short, simple methods. Defining long and complex methods inside the class makes the class declaration hard to understand; and some constructions, such as **for** loops, are not allowed in methods defined in the class. Often both approaches are used: short methods are defined inside the class, and more complex ones are defined outside.

The Constructor in time0.cpp

The constructor in time0.cpp is the method **time()**. It is executed automatically whenever an object of class **time** is created. This happens in the statement

```
time t1, t2, tAnswer;
```

This statement not only creates the three objects with the names shown, it also—using the constructor—initializes these objects to the value 0:00:00. The definition of these objects looks very much like the definition of variables of a normal C data type. As we'll see when we discuss operator overloading, you can model new data types that can be used almost exactly as if they were a part of the language.

Modifying the expense.cpp Example

Let's modify the expense.cpp example to use some additional C++ language features. This example demonstrates *destructors*, which are the opposite of constructors, and the **new** and **delete** keywords, which allocate and free memory.

```
//////////////////////////////////////////////////////////////////
// expense2.cpp
// expense ledger -- with destructor, 'new' and 'delete'

#include <iostream.h>            // for cout, cin, etc.
//////////////////////////////////////////////////////////////////
class ledger                    // declaration of class ledger
{
   private:
      float *list;              // pointer to items
      int count;                // number of items entered
   public:
      ledger()                  // constructor
         {
         count = 0;             // set list to empty
         list = new float[100]; // get memory for list
         }
      void enterItem(void)      // put entry in list
         {
```

```
            cout << "\nEnter amount: ";
            cin >> list[count++];
            }
        void printTotal(void);  // print total of all entries


        ~ledger()               // destructor
            { delete list; }    // release memory for list
};
////////////////////////////////////////////////////////////////
void ledger::printTotal(void) // print total of all entries
{
    float total=0.0;
    for(int j=0; j<count; j++)
        total += list[j];
    cout << "\n\nTotal is: " << total << "\n";
}
////////////////////////////////////////////////////////////////
ledger expenses;                // an instance of class ledger
////////////////////////////////////////////////////////////////
main()                          // main -- handles user interface
{                               //         uses object "expenses"
    char option;
    do
        {                           // display options
        cout << "\nOptions are:  e -- enter expense"
            << "\n               E -- print total expenses"
            << "\n               q -- quit (terminate program)"
            << "\nType option letter: ";
        cin >> option;          // get option from user
        switch (option)
            {                       // act on option selected
            case 'e': expenses.enterItem(); break;
            case 'E': expenses.printTotal(); break;
            case 'q': break;
            default: cout << "\nUnknown command\n";
            }
        } while(option != 'q');
}  // end main
```

Destructors

Constructors are automatically executed when an object is created. It's also useful to have methods that are automatically executed when an object is destroyed. Such a function is called a *destructor*. Like a constructor, it uses the same name as the class, but preceded by a tilde ($\sim$), like this:

```
~onexit()    // tilde indicates destructor
{
    // statements here will be executed when object is destroyed
}
```

Constructors and destructors should not return a value, and should not use the **return** statement. A constructor can take arguments, but a destructor cannot.

In expense2.cpp, a destructor is defined in the lines

```
~ledger()               // destructor
   { delete list; }     // release memory for list
```

We'll see what this destructor accomplishes in the next section.

The *new* and *delete* Keywords

In ordinary C, memory can be obtained from the heap with **malloc()** and similar functions. C++ introduces a simpler way to obtain memory: the **new** keyword. This keyword is followed by the data type that the memory will be used for, and optionally by an array size.

In the constructor for the **ledger** class in expense2.cpp, we use this approach to obtain memory for the list of expenses. Instead of declaring a fixed size array variable **list[ ]** as we did in expense.cpp, we declare **list** to be a pointer instead, and use **new** in the constructor to obtain the memory, in the line

```
list = new float[100];    // obtains memory for 100 float variables
```

The variable **list** can be used in the same way in expense2.cpp as it was in expense.cpp, but it is now a pointer rather than an array address.

The **delete** keyword is used to deallocate the memory when it's no longer needed. In the above example the line

```
    delete list;
```

returns the memory occupied by **list** to the heap, where other objects can access it. In the example this takes place in the destructor. Thus each time an object of class **ledger** is created, an array of 100 **floats** is assigned to it, and each time the object is destroyed, this array is returned to the heap. Returning unused memory to the heap makes it available for other objects or for other applications in the system. In the expense2.cpp example it doesn't really matter that we allocate memory dynamically, because there is only one object, **expenses**, that uses memory. But in complicated programs with many objects, intelligent memory management can substantially improve system efficiency.

Inheritance

One of the most powerful features of C++ is *inheritance*. Inheritance lets you increase the functionality of previously defined classes without having to re-write the original class declaration. This can be a great time-saver in writing applications. If you have a class that works well but to which you want to add additional features, you don't need to alter the original class. You simply incorporate it into a new class. This saves you from having to rewrite and debug the code in the original class.

To demonstrate inheritance, we'll add to our previous time0.cpp example the capability to subtract two time intervals, creating a new example timesub.cpp. To do this we don't rewrite our original **time** class. Instead we define a new class, **time2**, that inherits all the variables and methods of **time**, and adds the capability to subtract time values. The original **time** class is called the *base* class, and its descendant **time2** is called the *derived* class. Here's the listing for timesub.cpp:

```
// timesub.cpp
// adds derived class to subtract times

#include <iostream.h>           // for cout, etc.
#include <stdio.h>              // for printf(), scanf()
//////////////////////////////////////////////////////////////
class time
{
    protected:                  // note: not private
        int hrs;                // hours
        int mins;               // minutes
        int secs;               // seconds
    public:
        time()                  // constructor
            { secs=0; mins=0; hrs=0; }

        void printTime(void)    // print time
            { printf("%d:%02d:%02d", hrs, mins, secs); }

        void readTime(void)     // read time from keyboard
            { scanf("%d:%d:%d", &hrs, &mins, &secs); }

        void addTime(time t)    // add time to this time
            {
            secs += t.secs;
            if(secs > 59) { secs -= 60; ++mins; }
            mins += t.mins;
            if(mins > 59) { mins -= 60; ++hrs; }
```

```
                    hrs += t.hrs;
                    }
};
///////////////////////////////////////////////////////////////
class time2 : public time          // declare new class time2
{
   public:
      time2() : time()             // constructor calls
         { }                       // time constructor

      void subTime(time2 t)        // new function
         {
         if(secs < t.secs) { secs += 60; --mins; }
         secs -= t.secs;
         if(mins < t.mins) { mins += 60; --hrs; }
         mins -= t.mins;
         hrs -= t.hrs;
         }
};
///////////////////////////////////////////////////////////////
main()
{
   time2 t1, t2, tAnswer;          // declare time variables
                                   // (note time2 class)
   cout << "\nEnter first time interval (format hh:mm:ss): ";
   t1.readTime();                  // read t1

   cout << "\nEnter second time interval (format hh:mm:ss): ";
   t2.readTime();                  // read t2

   cout << "\nt1 = ";              // print t1
   t1.printTime();
   cout << "\nt2 = ";              // print t2
   t2.printTime();

   tAnswer.addTime(t1);            // add t1 to tAnswer
   tAnswer.subTime(t2);            // subtract t2 from tAnswer
   cout << "\nDifference = ";      // print tAnswer
   tAnswer.printTime();
}
```

Note that the time objects **t1**, **t2**, and **tAnswer** in **main()** are defined to be of class **time2**, not **time** as in previous versions of the program. Because **time2** inherits the characteristics of **time**, these objects can use the methods specific to the **time2** class as well as those inherited from **time**.

Declaring a Derived Class

A derived (descendant) class must be declared in a special way. Here's the declaration of **time2**:

```
class time2 : public time          // declare new class time2
```

The beginning is what you would expect: **class time2** declares the new class. But the colon is new. The single colon, followed by the class name **time**, causes **time** to be inherited by **time2**. (We'll see what the keyword **public** does in a moment.) The **time2** class will have all the capabilities of **time**, plus a new one: it can subtract two time values. There are no new variables in this class, but there are two new methods: a constructor called **time2()** and the function **subTime()**.

The constructor simply calls the **time()** constructor in **time**. This is indicated by the colon and the name **time** in its declaration. We could add additional statements to the **time2()** constructor if we needed them.

The **subTime()** method works like the **addTime()** method in **time**, subtracting **secs**, **mins**, and **hrs** in turn, carrying if necessary before each subtraction.

public, *private*, and *protected* Class Members

We've made a small change in the original **time** class. The variables **hrs**, **mins**, and **secs** no longer have **private** scope; instead they are **protected**. This means that, while they still cannot be accessed directly from **main()**, they can be accessed from derived classes; in particular, the derived class **time2**. This change is necessary because we want the methods in the derived class **time2**, such as **subTime()**, to be able to directly access the **hrs**, **mins**, and **secs** variables in the base class **time**, in such statements as

```
if(secs < t.secs) { secs += 60; --mins; }
```

Introducing the **protected** keyword rounds out the three possible categories of visibility that members of C++ classes can have. They are summarized in the following table:

Keyword used within class	Visibility of class members
public	Unrestricted from within and outside the class
protected	Unrestricted from within the class and derived classes
private	Unrestricted only from within the class, not from derived classes

public, *private*, and *protected* Class Declarations

We promised we would discuss the **public** keyword in the declaration of the derived class **time2**. To understand its purpose, ask yourself whether, in an object of a derived class, you can access members of the base class. For example, examine the following statement in timesub.cpp:

```
t1.readTime();
```

The object **t1** is of the derived class **time2**. The method **readTime()** is a member of the base class **time**. Is this a valid expression? For it to be valid, two conditions must be met. First, as we've just discussed, the members of the base class must be **public**, otherwise they will not be visible outside the base class and its descendants. Second, the derived class, of which the object is an instance, must also be declared to be **public**. Here's the line where that happens:

```
class time2 : public time          // declare new class time2
```

There are only two options here. The other is the keyword **private**(which is the default). If we had used **private** in this statement, the members of the base class, no matter what visibility they had been given within that class, would have been inaccessible to objects of class **time2** in **main()** and other functions in the outside world.

The following program example shows the possibilities:

```
//////////////////////////////////////////////////////////////
// scope.cpp
// investigates scope of class members
#include <iostream.h>
//////////////////////////////////////////////////////////////
class base
{
   private:
      int base_priv;
   protected:
      int base_prot;
   public:
      int base_publ;
};
//////////////////////////////////////////////////////////////
class pub_derv : public base      // declares class derived
{                                 // from base as public
};
```

```
//////////////////////////////////////////////////////////////
pub_derv pub_derv1;              // an object of class pub_derv
//////////////////////////////////////////////////////////////
class prv_derv : private base    // declares class derived
{                                // from base as private
};
//////////////////////////////////////////////////////////////
prv_derv prv_derv1;              // an object of class prv_derv
//////////////////////////////////////////////////////////////
main()
{
// can objects from publicly derived class
// access members of base class?
   pub_derv1.base_priv = 1;      // error: not accessible
   pub_derv1.base_prot = 1;      // error: not accessible
   pub_derv1.base_publ = 1;      // accessible!

// can objects from privately derived class
// access members of base class?
   prv_derv1.base_priv = 1;      // error: not accessible
   prv_derv1.base_prot = 1;      // error: not accessible
   prv_derv1.base_publ = 1;      // error: not accessible
}
```

Notice that of the six possible combinations of private, protected and public variables in the base class, and derived classes declared to be public or private, only one leads to a member of the base class being accessible from an object of the derived class. The others (if you are unwise enough to write them) cause compiler errors.

Judicious use of **public** and **private** in class declarations provides another way to hide those variables that need not be accessed in the outside world, while making accessible those that should be.

The taxable.cpp Example

Here's a somewhat more involved example of inheritance. Imagine that you record all income received in your lemonade stand, but that you must pay state sales tax on some income amounts but not others. (Perhaps those cups of lemonade mailed out of state are exempt.) We're going to create a class called **ledgerTax**, which is derived from the base class **ledger**, last seen in the expense.cpp example. This new class will be used to record not only income amounts (a capability already built into **ledger**) but also the tax status of these amounts.

The new class contains an array called **taxStatus[]**. For every amount entered in the array **list[]** in class **ledger**, a status value (taxable or not) is entered in **taxStatus[ ]**. A constructor initializes all the elements of this array to nontaxable. If an item is taxable, the appropriate element of **taxStatus[ ]** is set to taxable, otherwise it's left alone. The relation of the two arrays is shown in Figure 16-4.

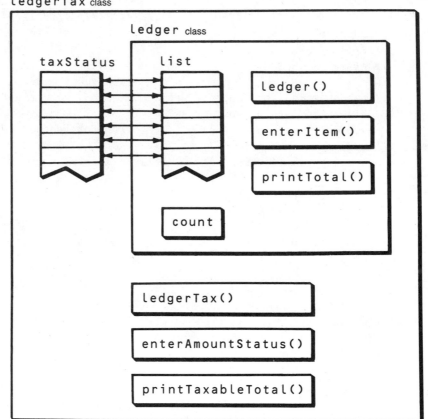

Figure 16-4. Relation of *list[ ]* and *taxStatus[ ]* Arrays

The method **enterAmountStatus()** in **ledgerTax** lets the user enter an income amount and a tax status. Another method, **printTaxableTotal()**, prints out the total of the taxable items. The old method **printTotal()** in the base class **ledger** still works admirably for printing the total of all items. Here's the listing for taxable.cpp:

```
/////////////////////////////////////////////////////////////////
// taxable.cpp
// object-oriented income ledger; includes tax status of income
```

```
#include <iostream.h>           // for cout, cin, etc.
//////////////////////////////////////////////////////////////
class ledger                    // declaration of class ledger
{
   protected:                   // can be accessed by descendants
      int count;                // number of items entered
      float list[100];          // array for items
   public:
      ledger(void)              // constructor
         { count=0; }           //    sets list to empty
      void enterItem(void)      // puts entry in list
         { cout << "\nEnter amount: "; cin >> list[count++]; }
      void printTotal(void);    // print total from list
};
//////////////////////////////////////////////////////////////
void ledger::printTotal(void)   // print total from list
{
   float total=0.0;
   for(int j=0; j<count; j++)
      total += list[j];
   cout << "\nTotal is: " << total << "\n";
}
//////////////////////////////////////////////////////////////
enum taxable {tax, notax};      // taxable status
//////////////////////////////////////////////////////////////
class ledgerTax : public ledger // declares ledgerTax class
{                               // derived from 'ledger' class
   private:                     //    adds taxable status
      taxable taxStatus[100];   // array holds tax status values
   public:
      ledgerTax(void);          // constructor
      void enterAmountStatus(); // enter amount and tax status
      void printTaxableTotal(); // print total of taxable items
};
//////////////////////////////////////////////////////////////
ledgerTax::ledgerTax(void) : ledger()   // calls ledger
{                                       //    constructor
   for(int j=0; j<100; j++)             // set all items to
      taxStatus[j] = notax;             //    nontaxable
}
//////////////////////////////////////////////////////////////
void ledgerTax::enterAmountStatus(void) // enter amount and
{                                       //    its tax status
   char ch;                             // use ledger function
   enterItem();                         //    to get amount
```

```
                                                    // enter tax status
   cout << "\nEnter tax status (t/n): "; cin >> ch;
   taxStatus[count-1] = ( ch=='t' ) ? tax : notax;
}
//////////////////////////////////////////////////////////////////
void ledgerTax::printTaxableTotal(void)  // print total of
{                                        //     taxable items
   float total=0.0;
   for(int j=0; j<count; j++)                // include in total
      if ( taxStatus[j]==tax )               //     only if taxable
         total += list[j];
   cout << "\nTaxable total is: " << total << "\n";
}
//////////////////////////////////////////////////////////////////
ledgerTax income;                    // an object of class ledgerTax
//////////////////////////////////////////////////////////////////
main()                               // handles user interface
{

     char option;
        do
          {                              // display options
          cout << "\nOptions are:  i -- enter income"
               << "\n               I -- print total income"
               << "\n               T -- print total taxable income"
               << "\n               q -- quit (terminate program)"
               << "\nType option letter: ";
          cin >> option;               // get option from user
          switch (option)
             {                              // act on option selected
             case 'i': income.enterAmountStatus(); break;
             case 'I': income.printTotal(); break;
             case 'T': income.printTaxableTotal(); break;
             case 'q': break;
             default : cout << "\nUnknown command\n";
             }
          } while(option != 'q');
     } // end main
```

The overall construction of the program is similar to expense.cpp. The possible values to place in the **taxStatus** array are given in the **enum** declaration as **tax** and **notax**. As in the previous timesub.cpp example, the variables in the base class are given protected visibility so they can be accessed from the derived class, and the derived class is declared to be public so that the methods in the base class can be accessed from **main()**.

Methods in the derived class can make use of methods in the base class. The constructor **ledgerTax()** calls the constructor in **ledger** to initialize the count of entries to 0, and also sets all the entries in **taxStatus[ ]** to **notax**. The **enterAmountStatus()** method calls the **enterItem()** method from **ledger** to store the amount, then executes its own statements to prompt the user and obtain the tax status.

Advantages of Inheritance

We've seen two examples where inheritance is used to provide additional funtionality to existing classes. What have we gained by using inheritance, instead of simply rewriting code? In these short examples the gain may not be obvious. Inheritance starts to pay dividends in large projects where a class may consist of dozens of methods and data items, with thousands of lines of code. In such projects debugging may contribute a significant portion—or even a majority—of the time and expense of creating the class, which may easily run to thousands of man-hours and tens of thousands of dollars. If the code in the class is changed, the debugging process must be repeated, with resulting time loss and expense.

Using inheritance, we can add functionality to a class without compromising its integrity. If we don't rewrite any code in the class, we can assume we don't need to debug it again. Only the additional code needs to be developed and debugged.

Large and complex classes can become standard building blocks for many different projects. For example, imagine a class that models a window, as used for the user interface in Microsoft Windows, the Presentation Manager, and on the Macintosh. This class comes complete with scroll bars, sizing borders, the ability to move about the screen, and other capabilities. Developing such a class is a major project. However, once it's developed, it can be given or sold to other developers, who can customize it by using inheritance to add additional capabilities.

Function Overloading

In standard C, if you declare two functions with the same name, you'll get a compiler error. In C++ you can declare two functions with the same name, provided they can be distinguished by the number or types of arguments they take. This is called *function overloading*. Function overloading is an example of *polymorphism*, which means one thing serving several purposes. Function overloading is commonly used for functions that perform closely related actions but take different parameters. One common use of function overloading is to provide multiple constructors in a class.

Here's our time0.cpp example modified to have two constructors; the result is timecon.cpp. The first constructor is the same as before: it initializes the time to 0:00:00. The second lets you initialize a time to an arbitrary value.

```cpp
// timecon.cpp
// uses two constructors to show function overloading

#include <iostream.h>              // for cout, etc.
#include <stdio.h>                 // for printf(), scanf()
#include <stdlib.h>                // for atoi()
#include <string.h>                // for strtok()
////////////////////////////////////////////////////////////////
class time
{
   private:
      int hrs;                     // hours
      int mins;                    // minutes
      int secs;                    // seconds
   public:
      time()                       // constructor
         { secs=0; mins=0; hrs=0; } // takes no arguments

      time(char *string)           // overloaded constructor
         {                         // sets time to string argument
         hrs =  atoi( strtok(string, ":") );
         mins = atoi( strtok(NULL, ":") );
         secs = atoi( strtok(NULL, ":") );
         }
      void printTime(void)         // print time
      { printf("%d:%02d:%02d", hrs, mins, secs); }

      void readTime(void)          // read time from keyboard
      { scanf("%d:%d:%d", &hrs, &mins, &secs); }

      void addTime(time t)         // add time to this time
         {
         secs += t.secs;
         if(secs > 59) { secs -= 60; ++mins; }
         mins += t.mins;
         if(mins > 59) { mins -= 60; ++hrs; }
         hrs += t.hrs;
         }
};
////////////////////////////////////////////////////////////////
main()
{
   time t1("9:27:30"), t2, tAnswer;  // declare time variables
```

```
        cout << "\nEnter time (format hh:mm:ss): ";
        t2.readTime();                  // read t2

        cout << "\nt1 = ";              // print t1
        t1.printTime();
        cout << "\nt2 = ";              // print t2
        t2.printTime();

        tAnswer.addTime(t1);            // add t1 to tAnswer
        tAnswer.addTime(t2);            // add t2 to tAnswer
        cout << "\nSum  = ";            // print tAnswer
        tAnswer.printTime();
    }
```

The constructor **time(char *string)** is called with a string argument: "9:27:30" in the example. It uses the C library function **strtok()** to break this string down into three separate strings ("9", "27", and "30"), and the function **atoi()** to convert these substrings to integers.

You can call either constructor. If you call with no arguments, you'll get **time()**; if you call with a string argument, you'll get **time(char *string)**. Both calls are used when defining the objects for the program. Notice how much more natural it is to use the same name for functions that perform closely related tasks. In normal C, two different function names would be necessary: **time1()** and **time2()**, for example.

Here's some output from the program:

```
Enter time (format hh:mm:ss): 10:10:10
t1 =  9:27:30
t2 = 10:10:10
Sum  = 19:37:40
```

There are two ways to implement function overloading. The approach depends on when the choice is made as to which of the several overloaded functions will actually be executed. If the compiler makes the choice at compile time, it is called *early binding*. That's what we've shown in our examples. If, on the other hand, the choice is not made until run time, it is called *late binding*. A different kind of function, the *virtual* function, is used to implement late binding. Function overloading is a powerful feature of C++, but further exploration of these concepts is beyond the scope of this chapter.

Operator Overloading

The normal C-language operators, such as +, −, *, /, ++, −−, and many others (although not all), can be overloaded so they can be used to operate on programmer-defined classes as well as on traditional C data types such as **int** and **float**. Actually, these operators are already overloaded in C: as you know, the (+) sign works for both integer and floating point numbers, although different routines are employed depending on the data type.

Overloading Unary Operators

For our first example of operator overloading, we'll overload the standard C unary operator (++). This operator is normally used to increment a number. We'll overload it so that it can also be used to increment an object of class **time**.

Let's see first how a normal increment method (function) would look, as a member of the **time** class.

```
void incTime(void)          // add 1 sec to this time
   {
   secs++;
   if( secs > 59 )  { secs -= 60; ++mins; }
   if( mins > 59 )  { mins -= 60; ++hrs; }
   }
```

To increment a time **t1**, we would call this method in the usual way:

```
t1.incTime();             // increment t1
```

In the example we use this same method, but now it's invoked using the ++ operator rather than the name **incTime()**.

```
// timeinc.cpp
// uses overloaded ++ operator to increment objects of class time

#include <iostream.h>            // for cout, etc.
#include <stdio.h>              // for printf(), scanf()
////////////////////////////////////////////////////////////////////
class time
{
   private:
      int hrs;                  // hours
      int mins;                 // minutes
      int secs;                 // seconds
   public:
      time()                    // constructor
         { secs=0; mins=0; hrs=0; }  // initializes time to 0:00:00

      void printTime(void)      // print time
```

```
        { printf("%d:%02d:%02d", hrs, mins, secs); }

    void readTime(void)          // read time from keyboard
        { scanf("%d:%d:%d", &hrs, &mins, &secs); }

    void operator ++ (void)      // add 1 sec to this time
        {
        secs++;
        if( secs > 59 )  { secs -= 60; ++mins; }
        if( mins > 59 )  { mins -= 60; ++hrs; }
        }
};
///////////////////////////////////////////////////////////////////
main()
{
    time t1;                     // declare time variable

    cout << "\nEnter time (format hh:mm:ss): ";
    t1.readTime();               // read t1

    cout << "\nt1 =  ";          // print t1
    t1.printTime();

    ++t1;                        // increment t1 (or use t1++)

    cout << "\nAfter increment, t1 = ";   // print t1 again
    t1.printTime();
}
```

Instead of using the name **timeInc()** to define the method, we use the keyword **operator** followed by the operator itself:

```
void operator ++ (void)
```

Now we can increment **t1**, an object of class **time**, with the natural expression

```
++t1;
```

We don't need the dot (.) operator, and the ++ can be written either before or after the object name (it has the same effect in both locations; there is no prefix versus postfix distinction). We can continue to use ++ to increment normal variables in the usual way. It now serves two purposes: it's overloaded.

Here's some sample output from the program:

```
Enter time (format hh:mm:ss): 9:59:59
t1 =  9:59:59
After increment, t1 = 10:00:00
```

Overloading Binary Operators

We've seen the **addTime()** method used in the **time** class in several examples. In the next example we'll convert this method so it can be accessed with the + operator.

```cpp
// timeplus.cpp
// demonstrates operator overloading, using '+' to add times

#include <iostream.h>              // for cout, etc.
#include <stdio.h>                 // for printf(), scanf()
/////////////////////////////////////////////////////////////////
class time
{
   private:
      int hrs;                     // hours
      int mins;                    // minutes
      int secs;                    // seconds
   public:
      time()                       // constructor
         { secs=0; mins=0; hrs=0; }   // initialize to 0:00:00

      void printTime(void)         // print time
         { printf("%d:%02d:%02d", hrs, mins, secs); }

      void readTime(void)          // read time from keyboard
         { scanf("%d:%d:%d", &hrs, &mins, &secs); }

      time operator + (time t)     // add two times
         {                         // to tmp time
         time tmp;
         tmp.secs = secs + t.secs;
         if(tmp.secs > 59) { tmp.secs -= 60; ++tmp.mins; }
         tmp.mins += mins + t.mins;
         if(tmp.mins > 59) { tmp.mins -= 60; ++tmp.hrs; }
         tmp.hrs += hrs + t.hrs;
         return( tmp );            // return tmp time
         }
};
/////////////////////////////////////////////////////////////////
```

```
main()
{
   time t1, t2, tAnswer;           // declare time variables

   cout << "\nEnter first time (format hh:mm:ss): ";
   t1.readTime();                  // read t1

   cout << "\nEnter second time (format hh:mm:ss): ";
   t2.readTime();                  // read t2

   cout << "\nt1 =  ";             // print t1
   t1.printTime();
   cout << "\nt2 = ";              // print t2
   t2.printTime();

   tAnswer = t1 + t2;              // overloaded + operator
   cout << "\nSum  = ";            // print tAnswer
   tAnswer.printTime();
}
```

Notice the very natural expression in **main()** that performs addition on **time** object:

```
tAnswer = t1 + t2;        // add t1 and t2, place result in tAnswer
```

This is far handier and easier to grasp than the previous

```
   tAnswer.addTime(t1);       // add t1 to tAnswer
   tAnswer.addTime(t2);       // add t2 to tAnswer
```

To facilitate the use of the + operator, we've modified the method that does the actual addition. First we declare a temporary object of class **time**. To see why do we need this additional object, ask yourself this question: Of what object is the + operator a member method? It turns out it's a member of the **t1** object. If it used its own **secs**, **mins**, and **hrs** variables, it would trash the value in **t1** (which is itself). In this case it wouldn't matter, because the answer would be correct; but usually when we perform addition, we want the variables that are being added to retain their original values, so we must use another object for temporary storage.

A similar approach could be used to subtract one time interval from another, multiply a time interval by an integer, decrement a time, and so on. An object of class **time** could be given any necessary functionality by using familiar arithmetic or C operators.

Towers of Hanoi

We'll end this chapter with a game program that models the Towers of Hanoi puzzle. This is a somewhat more frivolous example than those we've looked at so far, but it shows how OOP can simplify the conceptualization of a programming problem.

In this puzzle there are three towers (or posts). On one tower there are a number of disks. In the original version of the puzzle there were said to be 64 disks made of solid gold, but we'll assume there are just nine disks. The program displays them on the screen, as shown in Figure 16-5.

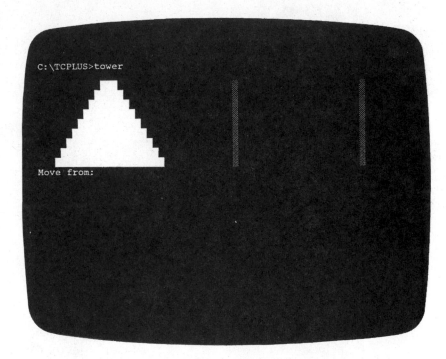

Figure 16-5. Towers of Hanoi: Initial Position

The object is to move the disks, one at a time, from the left tower to the right tower. The catch is a rule that no disk can ever be placed on a smaller disk. As you can see, the intermediate post is necessary if the disks are to be transferred without violating this rule.

The user types instructions to the program to move the disks. The towers are numbered 1, 2, and 3. Entering "1" and then "3" transfers the topmost disk on tower 1 to tower 3. If there is a smaller disk on tower 3, or if tower 1 is empty, the program displays "Illegal move" (since you can't put a larger disk on a smaller disk, and you can't move a nonexistent disk).

The computer doesn't compete against you or try to solve the puzzle, it simply records your moves and displays the current state of the towers. Figure 16-6 shows the situation after a few dozen moves.

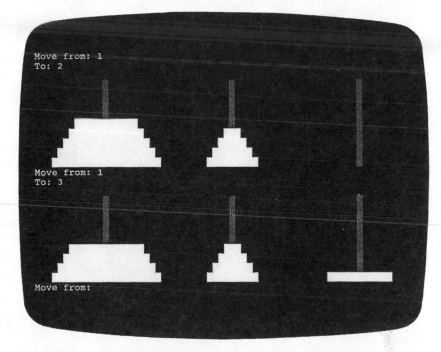

Figure 16-6. Towers of Hanoi: Partially Solved

Program Organization

Figuring out how to divide a programming problem into objects is one of the challenges in OOP program design. In this example we decided to use one class: **tower**, and three objects in this class, each representing one of the towers. One can imagine other approaches, such as making each disk an object.

The class **tower** contains two private data variables: a pointer **stack** to an array, and the integer **top**, which tells how many disks are on the tower. The array index corresponds to the position on the tower (0 at the bottom and 8 at the top) where a disk may be placed. The value of an array element represents the size of the disk (from 1 to 9) at each level. A value of 0 means there is no disk at that level. Thus

```
stack[8] = 1;
```

would place a disk of size 1 on level 8, the top of the tower. (In fact, this is the only size disk you can place at the very top.) Figure 16-7 shows how the disks are numbered.

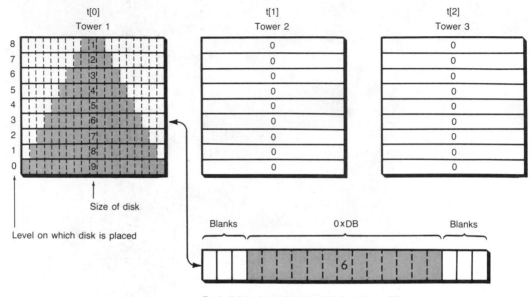

Figure 16-7. Disk Numbering

Methods in the **tower** class allow a disk to be placed on the tower or removed from it. This is similar to placing data in a software stack, and the method names **push()** and **pop()** reflect this. The methods **height()** and **read()** return the number of disks on a tower and the size of the disk at a particular level. The method **display()** displays the disk at a level specified by an argument. A constructor allocates memory for the tower and initializes all levels to 0, and a destructor deallocates memory.

Here's the listing for tower.cpp:

```
////////////////////////////////////////////////////////////////
// tower.cpp -- Towers of Hanoi puzzle

#include <iostream.h>
const int maxtop=9;
////////////////////////////////////////////////////////////////
class tower                          // declare tower class
{
    private:
        int *stack;                  // element value is size of disk
        int top;                     // indicates place for next disk
```

```
public:
   tower(void);                      // constructor
   ~tower()                          // destructor
      { delete stack; }              //    deallocate stack
   void push(int size)               // put disk on tower
      { stack[top++] = size; }
   int pop(void)                     // take disk off tower
      {
      int size=(stack[--top]);       // get size of disk
      stack[top]=0;                  // remove disk
      return(size);                  // return size of disk
      }
   int read(void)                    // find disk size, top of tower
      { return(stack[top-1]); }
   int height(void)                  // find how many disks on tower
      { return(top); }
   void display(int);                // display disk at any level
};
//////////////////////////////////////////////////////////////////
tower::tower(void)                   // constructor
{
   stack = new int[maxtop];          // allocate memory for stack
   for(int j=0; j<maxtop; j++)       // initialize tower to 0s
      stack[j] = 0;
   top = 0;                          // no disks on the tower
}
//////////////////////////////////////////////////////////////////
void tower::display(int level)       // display disk at given level
{
   if(stack[level] != 0)             // if there is a disk
      {                              // spaces to start of disk
      for(int k=0; k < maxtop-stack[level]; k++)
         cout << " ";
                                     // disk itself (size 1 disk is
      for(k=0; k < 2*stack[level]+1; k++)    // 3 chars wide)
         cout.put(0xDB);
                                     // spaces following disk
      for(k=0; k < maxtop-stack[level]; k++)
         cout << " ";
      }
   else                              // no disk, just spaces & tower
      {
      cout << "         ";           // 9 spaces (if maxtop=9)
      cout.put(0xB1);                // 1 char for tower (halftone)
      cout << "         ";           // 9 spaces
```

```
        }
    }
//////////////////////////////////////////////////////////////////
tower t[3];                       // define array of 3 towers
//////////////////////////////////////////////////////////////////
main()
{
    for(int j=0; j < maxtop; j++)  // push disks on left tower
        t[0].push(maxtop-j);       // sizes from 9 to 1

    while(1)
        {                          // print configuration
        for(int level=maxtop-1; level>=0; level--)
            {                      // from top to bottom level
            cout << "\n";          // new line for each level
            for(int j=0; j<3; j++) // each tower in turn
                {                  // from left to right
                cout << "   ";     // spaces to next tower
                t[j].display(level); // display disk (or no disk)
                }
            }
        int from, to;              // source and destination towers
        cout << "\nMove from: ";   // get from and to tower indexes
        cin >> from;               // user types 1, 2, or 3
        if(from==0) break;         // exit if user enters 0
        cout << "To: ";
        cin >> to;                 // user types 1, 2, 3
        from -= 1; to -= 1;        // indexes are 0, 1, or 2
                                   // check if legal move
        if( t[from].height() > 0 &&  // if disk on source stack, and
            ( t[from].read() < t[to].read() ||  // smaller on larger
              t[to].height() == 0 ) )  // (or dest empty),
            t[to].push( t[from].pop() );  // then move disk
        else
            cout << "\nIllegal move\n";
        }
}
```

Program Operation

The **main()** function starts by putting the initial set of nine disks on the first tower, **t[0]**, using the **push** method. The size 9 disk goes on first (on the bottom) and the size 1 disk last (at the top). Then, in a **while** loop, the program displays the current configuration, and then queries the user for the number of the tower to move a disk from, and the number of the tower to move the disk to. From the user's perspective the towers are numbered from 1 to 3.

We've used a new function in the program: **cout.put(0xB1)**. This is a member function of **cout**, and permits outputting of values as single characters.

For a move to be legal, several conditions must be met. First, the **from** tower must not be empty. That is, the expression

```
t[from].height() > 0
```

must be true. Second, either the topmost disk in the **from** tower must be smaller than the topmost disk in the **to** tower, or the **to** tower must be empty. Thus either

```
t[from].read() < t[to].read
```

or

```
t[to].height() == 0
```

must be true.

If these conditions are met, then the disk is transferred from the **from** tower to the **to** tower with the statement

```
t[to].push( t[from].pop() );
```

That is, the size of the disk is popped off the **from** tower and used as the argument to the **push** method in the **to** tower.

The program can be terminated by entering a zero value for the **from** tower value.

Summary

C++ was created to make object-oriented programming easier. An object contains both data and functions (called methods) that act on that data. Data and methods in the object can be hidden from functions outside the object. Classes have the same relation to objects that data types have to variables: objects are instances of classes.

A class, called the derived class, can inherit the characteristics of another class, called the base class. This makes it easy to create new objects. Calling a function can invoke different functions depending on the argument type. This is called function overloading. Operators such as + can also be overloaded. Function and operator overloading are examples of polymorphism.

There is much more to learn about C++. In this introduction, we have omitted **friend** functions, which can access private members of a class; the **this** pointer, which implicitly points to the current object; multiple inheritance, wherein a class can inherit characteristics of several other classes, and many other details. However, we hope this chapter has given you the flavor of the topics involved in OOP, and a headstart in C++ programming.

Appendices

- A. Reference
- B. Hexadecimal Numbering
- C. Bibliography
- D. ASCII Chart
- E. Turbo C Graphics
- F. The Turbo C Editor

A

Reference

This appendix provides a reference for some of the more fundamental constructions in the C programming language. Our goal is not to cover the entire language; the manuals that accompany your compiler perform that task. Rather, we want to present, in an easily accessible format, those aspects of the language that will be most useful for readers of this book.

Wherever possible we've used examples, as this is the quickest and most easily grasped way to communicate particular formats. For more detailed explanations, see the relevant sections of the book. Note that the examples only demonstrate format; they are not intended as working programs. Also, they are not intended to cover all possible situations, only the most general ones.

A. Control Constructions

In the following examples, the word "statement" represents any suitable program statement.

1. Structure of Simple C Program

```
void main(void)
{
   statement;
   statement;
}
```

2. The for Loop

```
for(j=0; j<10; j++)       /* single-statement loop */
   statement;

for(j=0; j<10; j++)       /* multistatement loop */
```

```
      {
      statement;
      statement;
      }

   /* multiple initialization and increments */
   for(j=0, other=0; j<20; j++, other++)
      statemaccount;
```

3. The while Loop

```
   while (ch != 'X')          /* single-statement loop */
      statement;

   while (y < 10)             /* multistatement loop */
      {
      statement;
      statement;
      }

   while (getche() != 'X')        /* function used as variable */
      statement;

   while ((ch=getche()) != 'X')   /* assignment statement used */
      statement;                  /* as variable */
```

4. The do while Loop

```
   do                 /* single-statement loop */
      statement;
   while (ch != 'X');

   do                 /* multistatement loop */
      {
      statement;
      statement;
      }
   while (x <= 42);
```

5. The if and if . . . else Statements

```
   if(x==42)          /* single statement if */
      statememnt;
```

```
if(x < 19)          /* multistatement if */
   {
   statement;
   statement;
   }

if(ch=='a')         /* if-else */
   statement;
else
   statement;

if(x < 10)          /* nested ifs */
   if(y > 5)
      statement;

if(ch=='a')         /* "else-if" construct */
   statement;
else if(ch=='b')
   statement;
else if(ch=='c')
   statement;

if(x > 5)           /* else paired with second of two ifs */
   if(y < 10)
      statement;
   else
      statement;

if(x > 5)           /* else paired with first of two ifs */
   {                /* (braces are necessary) */
   if(y < 10)
      statement;
   }
else
   statement;
```

6. The break Statement

```
while(ch != "X")
   {
   statement;
   if( count>MAX )
      break;        /* causes exit from loop */
   statement;
   }
```

7. The continue Statement

```
while(ch != 'X')
   {
   if(ch==SPACE)
      continue;      /* skip other loop statements, */
   statement;        /*    go to start of loop */
   statement;
   }
```

8. The switch Statement

```
switch (j)          /* integer switch */
   {
   case 1:
      printf("j is 1");
      break;
   case 2:
      printf("j is 2");
      statement;
      break;
   default;
      printf("j is anything else");
   }

switch (ch)         /* character switch */
   {
   case 'a':
   case 'b':
      printf("ch is 'a' or 'b'.");
      break;
   case 'c':
      printf("ch is 'c'.");
   }
```

B. Function Formats

1. Simple Function

```
void fun1(void);            /* prototype */
void main(void)             /* define main */
{
   puts("\nMain program.")
```

```
        fun1();                 /* call function */
    }

    void fun1(void)             /* define function */
    {
        puts("\nFunction.");    /* body of function */
    }
```

2. Returning a Value from a Function

```
    int always7(void);          /* prototype */
    void main(void)             /* define main */
    {
        printf("Value returned is %d.", always7() );
    }

    int always7(void)           /* define function */
    {
        return(7);              /* return statement */
    }
```

3. Passing Arguments to a Function

```
    void sum(int, int);       /* prototype */
    void main(void)
    {
        int x=2, y=3;          /* pass any number of values */
        printf("Sum of x and y is %d.", sum(x,y) );
    }

    void sum(int xf, int xy) /* declare function with arguments */
    {
        return(xf+yf);       /* return only one value */
    }
```

4. Passing Arguments Using Pointers

```
void sumarray(int *);                      /* prototype */
void main(void)
{
    static int list[3] = { 25, 36, 42 };   /* declare array */
    printf("Sum = %d.", sumarray(list) );  /* pass it to func */
}
```

```
void sumarray(int *ptr)                       /* define func */
{
  return( *(ptr) + *(ptr+1) + *(ptr+2) ): /* elemnts of array */
}
```

C. Data Constructions

1. Arrays

```
void main(void)        /* defining arrays */
{
   int list[3];           /* one-dimensional array; 3 items */
   char table[4][3];   /* 2-dimen array, 4 rows, 3 columns */
   list[2] = 333;         /* referring to array elements */
   table[1][3] = 'c';
}
```

```
/* initializing arrays */
int lista[3] = { 23, 34, 45 };   /* initialize as external var */
void main(void)
{
   static int listb[2][3] =     /* initialize as static var */
            { { 2, 4, 6 },
              { 3, 5, 7 } };
}
```

2. Strings

```
char name[30];                      /* string is char array */
static char salute[] = "Greetings!"; /* initialize string */
static char *salute = "Greetings!";  /* initialize string */
puts(salute);                       /* refer to string */
salute[2]=='e'                      /* character in string */
static char names[3][30] =          /* array of strings */
            { "Katrina", "Sam", "Rodney" };
static char *names[30] =            /* array of strings */
            { "Nancy", "Robert", "Laurie" };
puts(&names[2][0]);                 /* ref to string in array */
```

3. Pointers

```
/* initializing pointers */
int *ptr;                           /* pointer to int (or int array) */
```

```
char *charptr;              /* pntr to char (or char array) */
/* other variables used in example below */
int numb;                   /* integer variable */
int table[3] = {5, 6, 7};   /* array */

/* using pointers */
ptr = &numb;                /* assign address to pointer */
*ptr = 8;                   /* assign 8 to numb */
prt=table;                  /* assign array address to pointer */
printf("%d", *ptr );        /* print first element of array */
printf("%d", *(ptr+1) );    /* print second element of array */
```

4. Structures

```
struct employee            /* declare structure of type employee */
   {
   int empno;              /* three items in this structure */
   float  salary;
   char name[40];
   };
struct employee clerks;    /* define clerks to be variable of */
                           /*    type struct employee */
struct employee staff;     /* define other variables */
                           /* reference elements of structure */
printf("Clerk's employee number is %d", clerks.empno );
printf("Clerk's salary is %f", clerks.salary );

/* shorthand way to define a structure variable */
struct                     /* no need to name structure type */
   {
   int empno;
   float  salary;
   char name[40];
   } clerks;               /* define clerk var of type struct */
```

5. Unions

```
union intflo               /* declare union */
   {                       /* memory location can be referred to */
   int intnum;             /* as either float or int */
   float fltnum;
   } unionex;              /* define union variable */
unionex.intnum;            /* reference to two-byte int */
unionex.fltnum;            /* reference to four-byte float */
```

D. Operators

1. Arithmetic Operators

Symbol	Operator	Example
+	addition	a+b
−	subtraction	a-b
*	multiplication	a*b
/	division	a/b
%	remainder	a%b

2. Increment and Decrement Operators

Symbol	Operator	Example
++	increment	a++ or ++a
−−	decrement	a−− or −−a

3. Relational Operators

Symbol	Operator	Example
<	less than	a<b
>	greater than	a>b
<=	less than or equal	a<=b
>=	greater than or equal	a>=b
==	equal	a==b
!=	not equal	a!=b

4. Logical Operators

Symbol	Operator	Example
&&	AND	a<b && c>d
¦¦	OR	a<b ¦¦ c>d
!	NOT	!(a<b)

5. Bitwise Operators

Symbol	Operator	Example
&	AND	a & b
¦	inclusive OR	a ¦ b
^	exclusive OR	a ^ b
~	complement	~a
>>	right shift	a >> 2
<<	left shift	b << 3

6. Assignment Operators

=	equal	a = b
+=	addition	a += b (same as a=a+b)
−=	subtraction	a −= b (same as a=a-b)
*=	multiplication	a *= b (same as a=a*b)
\=	division	a /= b (same as a=a/b)
%=	remainder	a %= b (same as a=a%b)
&=	bitwise AND	a &= b (same as a=a&b)
¦=	bitwise inclusive OR	a ¦= b (same as a=a¦b)
^=	bitwise exclusive OR	a ^= b (same as a=a^b)
<<=	left shift	a <<= 2 (same as a=a<<2)
>>=	right shift	a >>= 3 (same as a=a>>3)

7. Conditional Operator

```
result = (expression) ? value1 : value2;      max = (a>b) ? a : b;
```

8. Address and Indirection Operators

&	address	addr = &var
*	indirection	value = *addr

9. Sizeof Operator

```
sizeof()                          sizeof(int), sizeof(struct emp)
```

10. Precedence and Associativity of Operators

Operators	Type	Associativity
() [] . −>	groups, membership	left to right
− ~ ! * &	unary	right to left
++ −− sizeof casts	unary	right to left
* / %	multiplicative	left to right
+ −	additive	left to right
<< >>	shift	left to right
< > <= >=	relational	left to right
== !=	equality	left to right
&	bitwise AND	left to right
^	bitwise excl OR	left to right
¦	bitwise incl OR	left to right

Operators	Type	Associativity
&&	logical AND	left to right
¦¦	logical OR	left to right
?:	conditional	right to left
= *= /= %= += −=		
<<= >>= &= ^= ¦=	assignment	right to left
,	comma (series)	left to right

E. Data Types

1. Integer (int)

On the PC, in Turbo C, integers occupy two bytes, and have a range from
−32,768 to 32,767 (−8,000 to 7FFF hex). Unsigned integers have a range
from 0 to 65,535 (0 to FFFF hex). On other machines, integers may occupy
different amounts of memory (as may the other data types shown here).

```
int x;              /* define integer variable */
int y = 12;         /* initialize integer variable */
unsigned int c;     /* define unsigned integer variable */
12                  /* decimal constant (do not use initial 0) */
0x0C                /* hex constant (must use initial 0x) */
014                 /* octal constant (must use initial 0) */
```
                                                          └ zero

2. Character (char)

Characters occupy one byte, and have a range from −128 to 127 (−80 to 7F
hex). Unsigned characters have a range from 0 to 255 (0 to FF hex).

```
char ch;                /* define character variable */
unsigned char k;        /* define unsigned character variable */
char c1 = 'a';          /* initialize character variable */
char c2 = 97;           /* initialize using decimal value */
char c3 = 0x61;         /* initialize using hexadecimal value */

/* special character constants */
'\n'    /* newline (linefeed); 0x0A */
'\b'    /* backspace; 0x08 */
'\r'    /* carriage return; 0x0D */
'\f'    /* formfeed; (0x0C) */
'\t'    /* tab; 0x09 */
'\v'    /* vertical tab; 0x0B */
```

```
'\\'    /* backslash 0x5C */
'\''    /* single quote 0x27 */
'\"'    /* double quote; 0x22 */
'\0'    /* null; 0x00 */
```

3. Short Integer (short)

On the PC, in Turbo C, short integers are the same as integers.

4. Long Integer (long)

Long integers occupy <u>four bytes</u> in memory and have a range from −2,147,483,648 to 2,147,483,647 (−80000000 to 7FFFFFFF hex). Unsigned long integers have a range from 0 to 4,294,967,295 (0 to FFFFFFFF hex).

```
long int bignum;     /* define long integer */
long bignum;         /* alternative form */
long bn1 = 12L;      /* initialize long integer */
10L                  /* decimal constant */
0x0AL                /* hexadecimal constant */
012L                 /* octal constant */
```

5. Floating Point (float)

Floating point numbers occupy <u>four bytes</u> of memory. The exponent has a range of 10^{-38} to 10^{38}. The mantissa has up to <u>six digits</u> of precision.

```
float flnumb;        /* define floating point number */
float fnb = 37.42;   /* initializing floating point number */
99.99                /* constant in decimal notation */
9999E-2              /* constant in exponential notation */
/* floating point constants always have type double */
```

6. Double-Precision Floating Point (double)

Double-precision floating point numbers occupy <u>eight bytes</u> of memory. The exponent has a range of 10^{-308} to 10^{308}. The mantissa has up to <u>15 digits</u> of precision.

```
double verybig;       /* define double precision fp number */
long float verybig;   /* alternative form for declaration */
double vb = 7.1416;   /* initializing double precision number */
320000.0              /* constant in decimal notation */
3.2E5                 /* constant in exponential notation */
```

7. Long Double Floating Point

Type **long double** stores an 80-bit floating point number.

```
long double verybig;        /* define long double */
long double verybig=1.33; /* initialize long double */
```

8. Strings (Array of Type char)

Strings are arrays of characters, terminated with the null character ('\0').
They occupy as many bytes as there are characters in the string, plus one for
the null.

```
char name[30];          /* define character array for string */
char phrase[] = "Error.";  /* initialize string as array */
char *phrase = "Error.";   /* initialize string as pointer */
"Greetings!\n"             /* string constant */
```

9. Void (for Functions)

Type **void** has three uses. It may be used to declare functions that do not
return any value.

```
void noreturn()
```

It may indicate that a function taxes no arguments.

```
int noargs(void)
```

It may define a pointer to *any* data type (rather than to a specific type).

```
void *ptr;
```

10. Enumeration Types

Creates a new type with a limited, user-defined set of values. (Actual values
are stored as integers.)

```
enum change           /* creates new type */
  { penny, nickel,    /* specifies allowable values */
    dime, quarter };
enum change ch1;      /* define variable of type change */
ch1 = penny;          /* give value to variable */
```

11. Typecasts

Changes the type of a variable.

```
long num = 12L;                /* num starts off as type long */
printf("%d", (int)num );       /* is cast as type int before use */
```

12. Typedef

Specifies a new name for a data type.

```
typedef long big;     /* renames type long to be type big */
big num;              /* declares num to be of type big (long) */
```

13. Logical Types

There is no specific logical or binary type in C. An integer with a value of 0 represents false, and an integer with a value of 1 (or any other nonzero value) represents true.

Examples of printf() Format Specifiers

```
/* colons show margins of field */
printf("%d", num);       /* :25:        decimal */
printf("%7d", num);      /* :      25:  specify field width */
printf("%-7d", num);     /* :25      :  left-justify */
printf("%07d", num);     /* :0000025:  leading zeros */
printf("%f", fnum);      /* :7.333333: floating point */
printf("%7.2f", fnum);   /* :   7.33:  decimal places */
```

p 320 →

Hexadecimal Numbering

The hexadecimal numbering system is widely used on PC (and many other) computer systems. In essence, this is because hexadecimal is closer to the binary system than is decimal. Let's see why binary is important, and then see how it relates to hexadecimal.

The Binary System

A numbering system can be defined by how many distinct digits are available in the system. In the decimal system there are 10: the digits from 0 to 9. After using 10 digits in the one's column, the ten's column must be employed to express larger numbers, such as 10 and 11. In the binary system there are only 2 digits: 0 and 1. After using only 2 digits in the one's column, the next column over—the two's column—must be used. After two more numbers are counted, the four's column comes into play. Thus counting in binary looks like this: 0, 1, 10, 11, 100, 101, 110, 111, 1000, and so on.

Binary is a natural system for computers because the circuits used to store numbers can be in one of only two states: off or on. These two states can be represented by the binary digits 0 or 1. Two such circuits then represent the four binary numbers 00, 01, 10, and 11. Three such circuits can represent eight numbers (from 000 to 111), eight circuits can represent 256 numbers (from 00000000 to 11111111), and so on.

Binary is not convenient for humans, however, since it's hard to read long strings of 0s and 1s. Another system is needed, and as it turns out, hexadecimal is that more convenient system.

The Hexadecimal System

Hexadecimal (or hex) is a numbering system that uses 16 digits. Since there are only 10 digit-symbols on most computers, letters are used for the remaining digits, so counting in hex looks like this: 0, 1, 2, 3, 4, 5, 6, 7, 8, 9, A, B, C,

D, E, F, 10, 11, 12, and so on. You can count up to F (15 decimal) in the one's column before needing to use the next column.

To see why hexadecimal is more closely related to binary than is decimal, examine Table B-1.

Table B-1.

Decimal	Binary	Hexadecimal	Decimal	Binary	Hex
0	0	0	16	10000	10
1	1	1	17	10001	11
2	10	2	18	10010	12
3	11	3	....	....	....
4	100	4	255	11111111	FF
5	101	5	256	100000000	100
6	110	6	....	....	....
7	111	7	4095	111111111111	FFF
8	1000	8	4096	1000000000000	1000
9	1001	9	....	....	....
10	1010	A	65535	1111111111111111	FFFF
11	1011	B	65536	10000000000000000	10000
12	1100	C			
13	1101	D			
14	1110	E			
15	1111	F			

The key point to notice here is that one hexadecimal digit is exactly represented by four binary digits. When the shift is made from one to two hex digits (from F to 10 hex), a corresponding shift is made from four to five binary digits. Likewise, when the shift is made from two to three hex digits, the binary digits go from eight to nine. There is no such easy correspondence between binary and decimal: when the decimal digits shift from one to two (from 9 to 10), the binary digits remain at four, and when the binary digits go from three to four (from 111 to 1000), the decimal digits remain at one (going from 7 to 8).

Thus it is convenient to arrange binary digits into groups of four, and represent each group by a hexadecimal number. The binary number 1111001101111100, for example, can be divided into groups of four (1111 0011 0111 1100) and translated by sight into the hex number F37C.

Translating large numbers back and forth between decimal and hexadecimal is not easy, and is best left to a computer program. We show how this is done in the text.

C

Bibliography

There are hundreds of books on various aspects of C available. This bibliography covers only a very few of them—those we like and find especially useful for programming in C on the PC.

Because C was originally developed on UNIX systems, many books on it assume a UNIX environment. This assumption is not ideal for those working in MS-DOS on the PC, but it is not fatal either. Here are some UNIX-oriented C books that are nevertheless very helpful for the PC C programmer.

Bolski, M. I., *The C Programmer's Handbook*, Prentice Hall, 1985. A well-organized small reference book, packed full of brief examples and explanations. A useful place to look something up in a hurry.

Feuer, Alan, *The C Puzzle Book*, Prentice Hall, 1982. Using this book will hone your programming ability to a fine edge. If you can answer all the questions it poses you're ready for anything.

Gehani, Narain, *Advanced C: Food for the Educated Palate*, Computer Science Press, 1985. A literate exploration of some of the finer points of C. This book is fun to read after you've digested the fundamentals.

Kernighan, Brian, and Dennis Ritchie, *The C Programming Language*, Prentice Hall, 1978. This book defined the C language, at least for the UNIX-based systems on which C was originally developed. In C, the watchword still is: when in doubt, follow Kernighan and Ritchie. This is not a beginner's book, but it is useful and interesting and it covers C thoroughly. Serious C programmers will want to own a copy. A second edition, copyright 1988, is ANSI-compatible.

Waite, Mitchell, Steven Prata, and Donald Martin, *C Primer Plus*, Howard W. Sams & Co., 1987. A classic generic C tutorial, clearly written and easy to learn from, full of valuable insights about C.

Many recent books deal specifically with C in the PC environment. We've listed some of these here. We've also included several books which, although they don't deal with C specifically, may be of interest to the C programmer working in the PC environment.

Chesley, Harry, and Mitchell Waite, *Supercharging C with Assembly Language*, Addison Wesley, 1987. This book explores ways to squeeze the last ounce of speed and capability from your C program. A principal method is the use of assembly language routines in critical places in the program.

697

Jordain, Robert, *Programmer's Problem Solver*, A Brady Book (Prentice Hall Press), 1986. This book is crammed full of examples of how to get the PC to do what you want. Examples are in BASIC and assembly, and explanations are sometimes cryptic, but it's an extremely useful book for serious PC programmers.

Lafore, Robert, *Assembly Language Primer for the IBM PC and XT*, New American Library, 1984. People tell us that this is still one of the best books for learning assembly language from scratch, should you want to incorporate AL routines into your C programs. It works on the AT as well as the PC and XT.

Norton, Peter, *The Peter Norton Programmer's Guide to the IBM PC*, Microsoft Press, 1985. This is essentially a guide to the ROM BIOS routines built into the IBM, although other topics are covered as well. This book is a must for system-level programmers on the PC.

Prata, Stephen, *Advanced C Primer++*, Howard W. Sams & Co., 1986. Dr. Prata provides an in-depth exploration of C on the PC, including a very readable description of using assembly language routines with C programs.

D

ASCII Chart

see p280 for extended codes

Table D-1. IBM Character Codes

DEC	HEX	Symbol	Key	Use in C
0	00	(NULL)	Ctrl 2	
1	01	☺	Ctr-A	
2	02	●	Cul B	
3	03	♥	Ctrl C	
4	04	♦	Ctrl D	
5	05	♣	Ctrl E	
6	06	♠	Ctrl F	
7	07	●	Ctrl G	Beep
8	08	▣	Backspace	Backspace
9	09	○	Tab	Tab
10	0A	■	Ctrl J	Linefeed (newline)
11	0B	♂	Ctrl K	Vertical Tab
12	0C	♀	Ctrl L	Form Feed
13	0D	♪	Enter	Carriage Return
14	0E	♫	Ctrl N	
15	0F	☼	Ctrl O	
16	10	▶	Ctrl P	
17	11	◀	Ctrl Q	
18	12	↕	Ctrl R	
19	13	‼	Ctrl S	
20	14	¶	Ctrl T	
21	15	§	Ctrl U	
22	16	▬	Ctrl V	
23	17	↨	Ctrl W	
24	18	↑	Ctrl X	
25	19	↓	Ctrl Y	
26	1A	→	Ctrl Z	
27	1B	←	Esc	Escape
28	1C	∟	Ctrl \	

Table D-1 (cont.)

DEC	HEX	Symbol	Key
29	1D	↔	Ctrl]
30	1E	▲	Ctrl 6
31	1F	▼	Ctrl -
32	20	*space*	SPACE BAR
33	21	!	!
34	22	"	"
35	23	#	#
36	24	$	$
37	25	%	%
38	26	&	&
39	27	'	'
40	28	(	(
41	29	)	)
42	2A	*	*
43	2B	+	+
44	2C	,	,
45	2D	—	—
46	2E	.	.
47	2F	/	/
48	30	0	0
49	31	1	1
50	32	2	2
51	33	3	3
52	34	4	4
53	35	5	5
54	36	6	6
55	37	7	7
56	38	8	8
57	39	9	9
58	3A	:	:
59	3B	;	;
60	3C	<	<
61	3D	=	=
62	3E	>	>
63	3F	?	?
64	40	@	@
65	41	A	A
66	42	B	B
67	43	C	C
68	44	D	D
69	45	E	E
70	46	F	F

Table D-1 (cont.)

DEC	HEX	Symbol	Key
71	47	G	G
72	48	H	H
73	49	I	I
74	4A	J	J
75	4B	K	K
76	4C	L	L
77	4D	M	M
78	4E	N	N
79	4F	O	O
80	50	P	P
81	51	Q	Q
82	52	R	R
83	53	S	S
84	54	T	T
85	55	U	U
86	56	V	V
87	57	W	W
88	58	X	X
89	59	Y	Y
90	5A	Z	Z
91	5B	[	[
92	5C	\	\
93	5D	]	]
94	5E	^	^
95	5F	_	_
96	60	`	`
97	61	a	a
98	62	b	b
99	63	c	c
100	64	d	d
101	65	e	e
102	66	f	f
103	67	g	g
104	68	h	h
105	69	i	i
106	6A	j	j
107	6B	k	k
108	6C	l	l
109	6D	m	m
110	6E	n	n
111	6F	o	o
112	70	p	p

Table D-1 (cont.)

DEC	HEX	Symbol	Key
113	71	q	q
114	72	r	r
115	73	s	s
116	74	t	t
117	75	u	u
118	76	v	v
119	77	w	w
120	78	x	x
121	79	y	y
122	7A	z	z
123	7B	{	{
124	7C	¦	¦
125	7D	}	}
126	7E	~	~
127	7F	Δ	Ctrl ←
128	80	Ç	Alt 128
129	81	ü	Alt 129
130	82	é	Alt 130
131	83	â	Alt 131
132	84	ä	Alt 132
133	85	à	Alt 133
134	86	å	Alt 134
135	87	ç	Alt 135
136	88	ê	Alt 136
137	89	ë	Alt 137
138	8A	è	Alt 138
139	8B	ï	Alt 139
140	8C	î	Alt 140
141	8D	ì	Alt 141
142	8E	Ä	Alt 142
143	8F	Å	Alt 143
144	90	É	Alt 144
145	91	æ	Alt 145
146	92	Æ	Alt 146
147	93	ô	Alt 147
148	94	ö	Alt 148
149	95	ò	Alt 149
150	96	û	Alt 150
151	97	ù	Alt 151
152	98	ÿ	Alt 152
153	99	Ö	Alt 153
154	9A	Ü	Alt 154

Table D-1 (cont.)

DEC	HEX	Symbol	Key
155	9B	¢	Alt 155
156	9C	£	Alt 156
157	9D	¥	Alt 157
158	9E	P$_t$	Alt 158
159	9F	ƒ	Alt 159
160	A0	á	Alt 160
161	A1	í	Alt 161
162	A2	ó	Alt 162
163	A3	ú	Alt 163
164	A4	ñ	Alt 164
165	A5	Ñ	Alt 165
166	A6	a̲	Alt 166
167	A7	o̲	Alt 167
168	A8	¿	Alt 168
169	A9	⌐	Alt 169
170	AA	¬	Alt 170
171	AB	½	Alt 171
172	AC	¼	Alt 172
173	AD	¡	Alt 173
174	AE	«	Alt 174
175	AF	»	Alt 175
176	B0	░	Alt 176
177	B1	▒	Alt 177
178	B2	▓	Alt 178
179	B3	│	Alt 179
180	B4	┤	Alt 180
181	B5	╡	Alt 181
182	B6	╢	Alt 182
183	B7	╖	Alt 183
184	B8	╕	Alt 184
185	B9	╣	Alt 185
186	BA	║	Alt 186
187	BB	╗	Alt 187
188	BC	╝	Alt 188
189	BD	╜	Alt 189
190	BE	╛	Alt 190
191	BF	┐	Alt 191
192	C0	└	Alt 192
193	C1	┴	Alt 193
194	C2	┬	Alt 194
195	C3	├	Alt 195
196	C4	─	Alt 196

Table D-1 (cont.)

DEC	HEX	Symbol	Key
197	C5	$+$	Alt 197
198	C6	⊨	Alt 198
199	C7	⊩	Alt 199
200	C8	⊔	Alt 200
201	C9	⊏	Alt 201
202	CA	⊥	Alt 202
203	CB	⊤	Alt 203
204	CC	⊩	Alt 204
205	CD	$=$	Alt 205
206	CE	⊹	Alt 206
207	CF	⊥	Alt 207
208	D0	⊥	Alt 208
209	D1	⊤	Alt 209
210	D2	⊤⊤	Alt 210
211	D3	⊔	Alt 211
212	D4	⊢	Alt 212
213	D5	⊨	Alt 213
214	D6	⊓	Alt 214
215	D7	⧺	Alt 215
216	D8	⧻	Alt 216
217	D9	⌟	Alt 217
218	DA	⌜	Alt 218
219	DB	■	Alt 219
220	DC	▬	Alt 220
221	DD	▐	Alt 221
222	DE	▌	Alt 222
223	DF	▬	Alt 223
224	E0	α	Alt 224
225	E1	β	Alt 225
226	E2	Γ	Alt 226
227	E3	π	Alt 227
228	E4	Σ	Alt 228
229	E5	σ	Alt 229
230	E6	μ	Alt 230
231	E7	τ	Alt 231
232	E8	Φ	Alt 232
233	E9	Θ	Alt 233
234	EA	Ω	Alt 234
235	EB	δ	Alt 235
236	EC	∞	Alt 236
237	ED	φ	Alt 237
238	EE	ε	Alt 238

Table D-1 (cont.)

DEC	HEX	Symbol	Key
239	EF	∩	Alt 240
240	F0	≡	Alt 241
241	F1	±	Alt 242
242	F2	≥	Alt 243
243	F3	≤	Alt 244
244	F4	⌠	Alt 245
245	F5	⌡	Alt 246
246	F6	÷	Alt 246
247	F7	≈	Alt 247
248	F8	°	Alt 248
249	F9	•	Alt 249
250	FA	.	Alt 250
251	FB	√	Alt 251
252	FC	η	Alt 252
253	FD	²	Alt 253
254	FE	■	Alt 254
255	FF	(blank)	Alt 255

Those key sequences consisting of "Ctrl" are typed in by pressing the CTRL key, and while it is being held down, pressing the key indicated. These sequences are based on those defined for PC Personal Computer series keyboards. The key sequences may be defined differently on other keyboards.

IBM Extended ASCII characters can be displayed by pressing the Alt key and then typing the decimal code of the character on the keypad.

E

Turbo C Graphics Reference

This appendix summarizes the Turbo C graphics functions used (or mentioned) in this book. If you can't remember the name of a function, or its parameters, you can look it up here. It also lists structures and constants used by the functions. Part A covers text-mode functions, part B graphics-mode functions, and part C functions for text in graphics mode. Part D contains structures and definitions used by the functions. The summary does not specify the data types of function arguments, but they are almost all type **int**. For more detail on specific functions, check the summary boxes in Chapter 12.

A. Text-Mode Graphics Functions

1. Header File

```
#include <conio.h>            /* graphics.h not needed */
```

2. Setting Text Mode

```
textmode( mode )             /* BW40, C40, BW80, C80, MONO */
```

3. Creating Text Window

```
window( left, top, right, bottom )
```

4. Reading and Writing to Text Window

```
cprintf( string, arg, ...)   /* like printf, but to window */
cputs( string )              /* like puts, but to window */
putch( ch )                  /* uses window coordinates */
ch = getche()                /* echo to window coordinates */
```

5. Cursor

```
gotoxy( x, y )              /* moves cursor to x, y */
x = wherex()               /* returns cursor col (1 to 80) */
y = wherey()               /* returns cursor row (1 to 25) */
```

6. Screen Control

```
clrscr()                   /* clear screen */
clreol()                   /* clear to end of line */
delline()                  /* delete line */
insline()                  /* insert line */
```

7. Text Blocks: Move on Screen, to and from Memory

```
movetext( left, top, right, bottom, newleft, newtop )
gettext( left, top, right, bottom, destinAddr )
puttext( left, top, right, bottom, sourceAddr )
```

8. Attributes

```
textcolor( color )         /* number or name, 16 choices */
textbackground( color )    /* number or name, 8 choices */
textattr( attrWord )       /* set attr bits individually */
highvideo()                /* high intensity characters */
lowvideo()                 /* low intensity characters */
normvideo()                /* reset original intensity */
```

9. Query: Window and Screen Size, Attributes, Mode, Cursor

```
gettextinfo( addrStruc )   /* address of text_info struct */
```

B. Graphics-Mode Functions

1. Header and Library Files

```
#include <graphics.h>
graphics driver (cga.bgi, etc.) must be available
graphics.lib library file must be available
```

2. Graphics System

```
detectgraph(&driver, &mode)        /* finds best driver, mode */
initgraph(&drive, &mode, drivePath) /* sets graphics system */
closegraph()                       /* removes graphics system */
error = graphresult()              /* gets latest error */
messagePtr=grapherrormsg(error)    /* returns error message */
```

3. Screen

```
cleardevice()              /* clears screen, homes CP to 0,0 */
maxx = getmaxx()           /* maximum x pixel coordinate */
maxy = getmaxy()           /* maximum y pixel coordinate */
```

4. Viewport

```
setviewport( left, top, right, bottom, clipflag )
getviewsettings(addrStruc)  /* struc viewporttype */
clearviewport               /* clears viewport, homes CP */
```

5. Bit Images

```
getimage(left, top, right, bottom, imageAddr)
putimage(left, top, imageAddr, op)    /* op = COPY_PUT, etc */
unsigned size = imagesize( left, top, right, bottom )
```

6. Pixels

```
putpixel( x, y, color )
color = getpixel( x, y )
```

7. Drawing

```
arc( x, y, startAngle, endAngle, radius )
circle( x, y, radius )
ellipse( x, y, startAngle, endAngle, xRadius, yRadius )
line( x0, y0, x1, y1 )
rectangle( left, top, right, bottom )
drawpoly( numpoints, addrPoints )    /* addr of x,y list */
```

8. Moving and Drawing Relative to Current Position (CP)

```
moveto( x, y )             /* moves CP to x, y */
moverel( dx, dy )          /* moves CP relative to old CP */
```

```
linerel( dx, dy )              /* draws line, relative to old CP */
lineto( x, y )                 /* draws line, updates CP */
```

9. Queries

```
getarccoorrds(addrStruc )      /* struc arccoordstype */
getaspectratio(&xasp, &yasp)   /* xasp=10,000, yasp<10,000 */
getlinesettings( addrStruc )   /* struc linesettingstype */
setlinestyle( style, unsigned pattern, thickness )
```

10. Filling

```
setfillstyle( pattern, color )
getfillsettings( addrStruc )   /* struc fillsettingstype */
fillpoly( numPoints, addrPoints )  /* addr of x, y list */
floodfill( x, y, borderColor )
```

11. Graphs

```
bar( left, top, right, bottom )
bar3d( left, top, right, bottom, depth, topflag )
pieslice( x, y, startAngle, endAngle, radius )
```

12. Set Colors

```
setcolor( color )              /* foreground color */
setbkcolor( color )            /* background color */
setpalette( paletteNumber, color )
setallpalette( addrStruc )     /* struc palettetype */
```

13. Query Color Info

```
color = getcolor()             /* foreground color */
color = getbkcolor()           /* background color */
getpalette( addrStruc )        /* struc palettetype */
maxcolor = getmaxcolor()       /* maxcolor = paletteSize-1 */
```

14. Registering Drivers and Fonts

```
registerbgidriver( driverName )  /* use driver and font */
registerbgifont( fontName )      /*   names from BGIOBJ */
```

C. Text in Graphics Mode

1. Set Text Style, Justification

```
settextstyle( font, direction, charsize )
settextjustify( horiz, vert )
```

2. Save Old Text Style and Justification

```
gettextsettings( addrStruc )    /* struc textsettingstype */
```

3. Write String to Display

```
outtext( string )               /* displays string at CP */
outtextxy( x, y, string )        /* displays string at x, y */
```

4. Scale Default Character Size (Width Factor = multx/divx, etc.)

```
setusercharsize( multx, divx, multy, divy )
```

5. Find Height and Width of String (in Pixels)

```
height = textheight( string )
width = textwidth( string )
```

D. Graphics Lists and Structures

1. Colors (for getbkcolor, setbkcolor, getcolor, setcolor, etc.)

Number	Name
0	BLACK
1	BLUE
2	GREEN
3	CYAN
4	RED

Number	Name
5	MAGENTA
6	BROWN
7	LIGHTGRAY
8	DARKGRAY
9	LIGHTBLUE
10	LIGHTGREEN
11	LIGHTCYAN
12	LIGHTRED
13	LIGHTMAGENTA
14	YELLOW
15	WHITE

2. Fill Types

Name	Number	Result
EMPTY_FILL	0	sold background
SOLID_FILL	1	solid
LINE_FILL	2	horiz lines
LTSLASH_FILL	3	///// thin lines
SLASH_FILL	4	///// thick lines
BKSLASH_FILL	5	\\\\\ thick lines
LTBKSLASH_FILL	6	\\\\\ thin lines
HATCH_FILL	7	light hatch
XHATCH_FILL	8	heavy cross-hatch
INTERLEAVE_FILL	9	interleaved lines
WIDE_DOT_FILL	10	wide-spaced dots
CLOSE_DOT_FILL	11	close-spaced dots
USER_FILL	12	user-defined pattern

3. Operators for putimage()

Name	Number	Result
COPY_PUT	0	copy source to screen
XOR_PUT	1	xor source with screen
OR_PUT	2	or source with screen
AND_PUT	3	and source with screen
NOT_PUT	4	copy inverse of source to screen

4. Line Settings for getlinesettings(), etc.

Linestyles	Number	Result
SOLID_LINE	0	solid
DOTTED_LINE	1	dotted
CENTER_LINE	2	centered
DASHED_LINE	3	dashed
USERBIT_LINE	4	user-defined

Thickness	Number	Result
NORM_WIDTH	1	1 pixel wide
THICK_WIDTH	3	3 pixels wide

```
struct linesettingstype {        /* for getlinesettings() */
    int linestyle;               /* see list */
    unsigned upattern;           /* applies only if linestyle=4 */
    int thickness;               /* see list */
}

struct fillsettingstype {        /* for getfillsettings() */
    int pattern;
    int color;
}
```

5. EGA/VGA Colors for getpalette(), setpalette()

Number	Name
0	EGA_BLACK
1	EGA_BLUE
2	EGA_GREEN
3	EGA_CYAN
4	EGA_RED
5	EGA_MAGENTA
20	EGA_BROWN
7	EGA_LIGHTGRAY
56	EGA_DARKGRAY
57	EGA_LIGHTBLUE
58	EGA_LIGHTGREEN
59	EGA_LIGHTCYAN
60	EGA_LIGHTRED

Number	Name
61	EGA_LIGHTMAGENTA
62	EGA_YELLOW
63	EGA_WHITE

```
struct palettetype  {          for getpalette()
   unsigned char size;
   signed char colors[MAXCOLORS+1];
};
```

6. Text Structure for gettextinfo()

```
struct text_info  {
   unsigned char winleft;     /* left window coordinate */
   unsigned char wintop;      /* top window coordinate */
   unsigned char winright;    /* right window coordinate */
   unsigned char winbottom;   /* bottom window coordinate */
   unsigned char attribute;   /* text attribute */
   unsigned char normattr;    /* normal attribute */
   unsigned char currmode;    /* BW40, BW80, C40, C80 */
   unsigned char screenheight;   /* screen dimensions */
   unsigned char screenwidth;
   unsigned char curx;        /* cursor coordinates in window */
   unsigned char cury;
};
```

7. Text Settings for settextjustify()

Name	Number	Result
LEFT_TEXT	0	horizontal, left
CENTER_TEXT	1	horizontal and vertical
RIGHT_TEXT	2	horizontal, right
BOTTOM_TEXT	0	vertical, bottom
TOP_TEXT	2	vertical, top

8. Font Names for settextstyle()

Name	Number	Result
DEFAULT_FONT	0	8x8 bit-mapped
TRIPLEX_FONT	1	stroked triplex

Name	Number	Result
SMALL_FONT	2	stroked small
SANS_SERIF_FONT	3	stroked sans-serif
GOTHIC_FONT	4	stroked gothic

9. Text Direction for settextstyle()

Name	Number	Result
HORIZ_DIR	0	left to right
VER_DIR	1	bottom to top

```
struct textsettingstype  {    /* for gettextsettings() */
   int font;
   int direction;
   int charsize;
   int horiz;
   int vert;
};


struct viewporttype  {         /* for getviewport() */
   int left, top, right, bottom;
   int clipflag;
};
```

10. Drivers and Modes for initgraph(), etc.

Driver	Mode	Value	Resolution	Colors	Pages
CGA	CGAC0	0	320x200	palette 0	1
	CGAC1	1	320x200	palette 1	1
	CGAC2	2	320x200	palette 2	1
	CGAC3	3	320x200	palette 3	1
	CGACHI	4	640x200	2 colors	1
EGA	EGALO	0	640x200	16 colors	4
	EGAHI	1	640x350	16 colors	2
VGA	VGALO	0	640x200	16 colors	2
	VGAMED	1	640x350	16 colors	2
	VGAHI	2	640x480	16 colors	1

11. CGA Colors

Mode	0	1	2	3
CGAC0	BLACK	LIGHTGREEN	LIGHTRED	YELLOW
CGAC1	BLACK	LIGHTCYAN	LIGHTMAGENTA	WHITE
CGAC2	BLACK	GREEN	RED	BROWN
CGAC3	BLACK	CYAN	MAGENTA	LIGHTGRAY

F

The Turbo C++ Editor

In this appendix we'll summarize the operation of the Turbo C++ editor. We don't cover all details of the editor; instead we provide enough quick and easy information for you to type in the programs in this book and perform a few other simple operations. For a complete list of features, see the Turbo C++ documentation.

We'll assume you've had experience with some kind of word processor. If you've used other Borland editors before—such as those for Turbo BASIC or Turbo Pascal—you'll find this one essentially the same. If you're familiar with the classic WordStar commands, you'll also feel right at home. However, the Turbo C++ editor is easy to learn, even without this experience.

You may also want to review Chapter 1, which has some comments about the operation of windows, menus, and the mouse.

Getting Started

The Turbo C++ editor is part of the Integrated Development Environment (IDE). To call up this program, type **tc** at the DOS prompt.

Opening an Edit Window

After the IDE display appears, you must open an Edit window into which you can type your program. There are two approaches to this. First, you can type your program name as a command-line argument when you invoke Turbo C:

```
C>tc myprog.c
```

If myprog.c doesn't exist, a file will be created for it. If it exists already, the file will be opened. An Edit window will also be opened and labelled MYPROG.C.

You can also open an Edit window by selecting New from the File menu. This Edit window will be given the title NONAME00.C.

If you're already in the IDE and you want to open a file that already exists, select Open . . . from the File menu. A dialog window will appear. Type in the name of the file in the Name field, or select it from the list displayed. Note that only source files—those with the .C extension—are listed.

Making a Window Active

Before you can type into an Edit window it must be active. An active window has a double-line border, while an inactive window has a single-line border. If the menu bar, or another window, is active, you can cause your Edit window to be active by clicking on it with the mouse, or by pressing the [F6] key.

Exiting from the Editor

Before exiting from the IDE, you should close the Edit window containing the file your're working on. If you don't, this window will appear whenever you start up the IDE, even if you're working on another program. To close the Edit window, click on the square in the upper left corner (the *close box*), select Close from the Window menu, or press [Alt] [F3].

To exit from the IDE, select Quit from the File menu, or type [Alt] [X]. If you have not saved the file you're working on, a dialog box will prompt you to do so.

Basic Editor Commands

The most important commands in any editor are those that move the cursor on the screen and insert and delete text. If you haven't used the editor before, you might want to type in some sample text at this point so you can experiment with these commands. The following summary shows some of the most common commands for the Turbo C++ editor.

[left arrow]	Move one character left
[right arrow]	Move one character right
[Ctrl] [left arrow]	Move one word left
[Ctrl] [right arrow]	Move one word right
[up arrow]	Move up one line
[down arrow]	Move down one line
[Home]	Go to start of line
[End]	Go to end of line
[PgUp]	Go up one screen
[PgDn]	Go down one screen

[backspace]	Delete character to left of cursor
[Del]	Delete character at cursor position
[Ins]	Toggle insert mode on/off
[Enter]	Insert CR/LF, move to next line down

To insert text, move the cursor to the insertion point, and start typing. The existing text will shift right to make room. If you want to type over existing text, toggle insert mode off using the [Ins] key. To return to normal insertion mode, press [Ins] again.

The editor differs in several ways from an ordinary word processor. There is no wordwrap. When you reach the end of the line, you just keep typing, and the line scrolls left; you don't automatically drop down to the next line. You can type up to 249 characters on one line (although it's not clear why you would want to; usually you want the entire line to be visible on the screen). When you end one line and are ready to move down to the next line, press [Enter].

In the Turbo C++ editor (unlike most word processors) you can move the cursor anywhere in the blank area at the right of a line or below the last line. This makes it easier to place material in columns (to line up comments, for example) without having to type a lot of spaces or tabs.

The Turbo C++ editor does not insert nonstandard control characters into the file, the way word processors like WordStar and WordPerfect do. Such characters cannot be read by the Turbo C compiler.

Window Handling

Windows in Turbo C++ are areas for typing in text or reading messages from the system. They have some surprisingly versatile features.

Scrolling

If your file is too long to fit in the window, you can scroll its contents up and down with the cursor keys. If a line is too long, you can scroll it with the left and right cursor keys.

Windows have *scroll bars* on the right and bottom edges. These allow you to scroll the window contents with the mouse. To scroll one line up or down, click on the triangle-shaped arrows on the scroll bar. To scroll faster through the file, drag the scroll box—the highlighted box-in-a-box character situated on the scroll bar. ("Dragging" means to position the mouse pointer on an object, hold down the left mouse button, move the pointer, and release the button.) You can scroll one page at a time by clicking on the shaded areas above and below the scroll box.

Resizing and Moving Windows

You can change the size of a window by dragging the lower right corner. You can move a window by dragging the *title bar*—the double-line at the top of the window that contains the file name.

Opening Multiple Windows

Turbo C++ can have many Edit windows on the screen at once. This is a powerful feature. You can open windows on two files at the same time to compare them, or to copy text from one to the other. (This is described in the section on block commands.) You can even open different windows on the same file, but at different places in the file. This enables you to do such things as looking at the call to a function, and at the function itself, at the same time, or copying text from one part of a file to another.

To open a second Edit window, simply select Open . . . (or New) from the File menu, just as you would when opening the first Edit window. When you have several windows on the screen you may need to make them smaller, and move them around, so you can see the relevant parts of all of them at the same time.

File Handling

Files are manipulated from the File menu. We've already discussed the Open . . . and New commands.

Saving Files

To save a file, select Save or Save as . . . from the File menu. (Save as . . . is only visible if you toggle Full menus in the Options menu to Yes.) These commands will save the file shown in the *active window*. Files in other windows won't be affected. The Save option saves the file under the name shown in the title bar. If you want to change the name, use the Save as . . . option. This invokes a dialog box containing a field into which you can type the new file name. The Save all option saves all open files.

Although the editor in the IDE is used primarily to edit C and C++ programs, it can be used to generate other kinds of text files. This is useful if you don't have a word processor program, or if your word processor is too ponderous to use for short files. C programs must have the extension .C, but you can create files with any name and extension. You can create .BAT batch files, .CPP files for C++, .TXT text files, and so on. All you need to do is type them in, and save them under the appropriate file name and extension.

Changing Directories

You can change the current directory by selecting the Change dir . . . option from the File menu. (This also requires Full menus from the Options menu.) Once you've changed directories, Open will list the source files in the new directory. When you exit TC, you'll be in the new directory.

Printing

To send the contents of the file in the active window to the printer, select Print from the File menu.

DOS Shell

You can call up a copy of DOS by selecting DOS shell from the File menu. In DOS you can delete or list files, change directories, and perform any other DOS command. To return to the IDE, enter the word "exit" at the DOS prompt.

Invoking the DOS shell is a useful way to position the cursor at the beginning of the line of the output screen.

Block Commands

You can mark a block of text in an Edit window, then move it to another place in the same window, or to a different window. You can also perform other operations on marked text. We'll first see how to mark a block of text; then we'll find out what you can do with it.

Marking a Text Block

To mark a block of text with the mouse, position the mouse pointer at the beginning of the block, hold down the left button, and drag the pointer to the end of the block. The marked block will be highlighted. To unmark the block, click anywhere.

To mark a block from the keyboard, position the cursor at the beginning of the block, hold down the [Shift] key, and use the cursor keys to move the cursor to the end of the block

You can also use the old WordStar-style commands to mark blocks and carry out operations on them, but they are harder to learn.

Cut, Copy, Paste, and Clear

Once a block is marked, you can perform various operations on it. These operations can be invoked from the Edit menu, or by typing key combinations. They make use of an internal text buffer called the *clipboard*. The following table summarizes the possibilities.

Selection from Edit menu	Shortcut keystrokes	Action
Cut	[Shift][Del]	Delete block and write it to clipboard
Copy	[Ctrl][Ins]	Copy block to clipboard
Paste	[Shift][Ins]	Insert block from clipboard at cursor
Clear	[Ctrl][Del]	Delete block, don't write to clipboard

To move a block of text, mark it, and then select Cut or Copy. The text will be written to the clipboard, replacing whatever was there before. Then position the cursor where you want the block to go, and select Paste. The block will be written at that location.

You can also copy text from the help file examples to the clipboard using the Copy examples option in the Edit menu, and from there paste this text to your listing.

Reading and Writing Blocks to Disk

Once you've marked a block, you can write it to disk. To do this you'll need to use a WordStar key combination. Press [Ctrl] and [K] at the same time, then press [W].

To read a file into a document at the cursor location, press [Ctrl] [K] and then [R].

Search and Replace

You can search your text file for a string of up to 30 characters. To do this, select Find . . . from the Search menu, and type in the string in the "Text to Find" field in the resulting dialog box. Options in the box let you specify the direction and origin of the search. Alternately, you can position the cursor on an instance of the word to be searched for, and then invoke Find . . . from the Search menu. The word will appear automatically in the "Text to Find" field.

Select Search Again from the Search menu to find the next instance of the same search string.

To do a search and replace operation, select Replace . . . from the Search menu. Type in the text to find and the text to replace it with.

Other Commands

Here are some miscellaneous editor commands that you may find useful.

Restore Line

One of the most useful commands is Restore line in the Edit menu. This is a one-line "undo" feature. If the cursor is still on the line you have altered, this selection will restore the line to the state it was in when you first moved the cursor to it.

Matching Braces

When programs get complicated, you can lose track of which closing brace matches which opening brace. To sort things out, Turbo C++ provides a pair-matching facility. Position the cursor on the brace you want to match. Now, type [Ctrl] and [Q] together, and type [[] (the open bracket key). The cursor will immediately jump to the brace that Turbo C++ thinks matches the one the cursor was on. If it jumps somewhere else, you've made a mistake somewhere. You can jump from a closing brace to an opening brace with [Ctrl] [Q] []] (the close bracket key).

The same keystrokes will find matching pairs of brackets and parentheses. In fact it will find a match for double quotes ("), single quotes ('), angle brackets (< and >), and comment symbols (/* and */). For the comment symbols, make sure you place the cursor on the first of the two characters in the symbol: the (/) for an open comment, and the (*) for a close comment.

Jump to Last Cursor Position

To return to the previous cursor position, type [Ctrl] [Q] followed by [P].

G

The Turbo C Debugger

One of the most innovative and useful features of Turbo C++ is the integration of debugging facilities into the IDE. In Chapter 1 we described how easy it is to correct syntax errors. But Turbo C++ goes far beyond this form of debugging. Using menu selections and function keys in the IDE, you can also single step through programs, watch variables change as the program runs, execute sections of the program at full speed and stop where you want, and change the value of variables in the middle of a program.

In this appendix we'll explain the major debugging features that Turbo C++ makes available. We'll use short program examples with obvious bugs. The bugs are not very realistic, in that most beginners to C can spot them easily. However, our aim is not to provide a play-by-play description of a search for a bug in a long and obscure program. Rather we want to quickly familiarize you with the tools Turbo C makes available for debugging (so you can apply them yourself to your own long and obscure programs).

The debugger does not work with the command-line version of Turbo C++, called TCC. You must be in the IDE.

Single Stepping

Even when your program compiles perfectly, it still may not work. Panic! What's the matter with it? Will you ever be able to find the problem?

Before you do anything, look through the listing very carefully. Mentally review the program's operation, line by line. Often the mistake will be obvious, especially after a little thought. If the mistake is still obscure, you'll need some assistance. Fortunately, this assistance is close at hand.

One Step at a Time

The first thing the debugger can do for you is slow down the operation of the program. One trouble with finding errors is that a typical program executes in a few milliseconds, so all you can see is its final state. By invoking Turbo

C++'s single-stepping capability, you can execute just one line of the program at a time. This way you can follow where the program is going.

Here's a small example program:

```
/* errelse.c */
/* demonstrates single stepping */
void main(void)
{
    int number, answer = -1;

    number = -50;              /* test value */
    if(number < 100)
  if(number > 0)
  answer = 1;
    else
  answer = 0;
    printf("answer is %d\n", answer );
}
```

Type in the program and compile it in the usual way by selecting Make EXE File from the Compile menu.

Our intention in this program is that when **number** is between 0 and 100, **answer** will be 1, when **number** is 100 or greater, **answer** will be 0, and when **number** is less than 0, **answer** will retain its initialized value of −1. This relationship is summarized in the following table:

Number	Answer
number<0	−1
0<number<100	1
number=>100	0

Unfortunately, when we run the program as shown with a test value of −50 for **number**, we find that **answer** is set to 0 at the end of the program, instead of staying −1. What's wrong? (You may see the problem already, but bear with us.)

Perhaps we can understand where the problem is if we single step through the program. To do this, simply press the [F7] key (or select Trace Into from the Run menu). Alternatively you can also press [F8] (or select Step Over from the Run menu); this operates the same way as [F7] unless functions are involved. The first line of the program will be highlighted. This high-lighted line is called the *run bar*. Press [F7] again. The run bar will move to the next program line. The run bar appears on the line *about to be executed*. You can execute each line of the program in turn by pressing [F7]. Eventually you'll reach the first if statement:

```
if(num < 100)
```

This statement is true (since **number** is −50); so, as we would expect, the run bar moves to the second **if** statement:

```
if(num > 0)
```

This is false. Because there's no **else** matched with the second **if**, we would expect the run bar to move to the **printf()** statement. But it doesn't! It goes to the line

```
answer = 0;
```

Now that we see where the program actually goes, the source of the bug should dawn on us: the **else** goes with the last **if**, not the first **if** as the indenting would lead us to believe. So the **else** is executed when the second **if** statement is false, which leads to the erroneous results. We need to put braces around the second **if**, or rewrite the program in some other way. We've successfully used the single stepping feature to track down a simple bug.

In this short example, single stepping may not be necessary to discover the bug, but in a more complex program, with multiple nested **if**s, loops, and functions, it's often an essential technique. Try single stepping through some programs containing loops and complex **if** statements.

Pressing [F7] or [F8] for the first time starts a debugging session. During debugging the IDE is in a somewhat different state than it is normally. For example, the Inspect option in the Debug menu, which is normally not selectable, becomes selectable during a debugging session. If the .EXE or .OBJ versions of the program do not exist or are not up to date when you press the [F7] key, the system will recompile and relink your program.

Resetting the Debugger

Suppose you've single stepped part way through a program, and want to start over at the beginning. How do you place the run bar back at the top of the listing? You can reset the debugging process and initialize the run bar by selecting the Program Reset option from the Run menu.

Watches

Single stepping is usually used with other features of the debugger. The most useful of these is the *watch* (or *watch expression*). This is a sort of magic microscope that lets you see how the value of a variable changes *as the program runs*.

Here's another short program. This one is intended to calculate the factorial of a number entered by the user. It's similar to the factor.c program in Chapter 3, but uses a **for** loop instead of a **while** loop.

```
/* errloop.c */
/* doesn't calculate factorials */
/* demonstates watchpoints */
void main(void)
{
    long number, j, answer;

    printf("Enter number: ");
    scanf("%D", &number );
    answer = 1;
    for( j=0; j<number; j++ )
        answer = answer * j;
    printf("Factorial of %ld = %ld\n", number, answer );
}
```

Unfortunately, no matter what number we enter when we run this program, it always prints the same result:

```
Factorial of 5 is 0
```

The factorial of 5 should be 120. Can we find the problem with the debugger? Single stepping by itself isn't much help, as the program seems to go around the loop the correct number of times (5 in this case). Let's see if Watches can cast more light on the problem.

We'll assume that you've typed in the program and successfully compiled it. Position the cursor on name **number** in the variable definition. Select Watches from the Debug menu, and select Add Watch from the resulting submenu (or use the [Ctrl] [F7] shortcut key combination). You'll see **number** in the "Watch expression" field in the resulting dialog box. Click on "Ok" or press [Enter]. You'll see a new window, the Watch window, open at the bottom of the screen. This window will contain the line

```
number: undefined symbol 'number'
```

The variable is undefined because we have not yet executed the statement that defines it.

Repeat this process for **j** and **answer**. Similar lines for these variables will appear in the Watch window.

Now, make the Edit window active, and then single step through the program, using the [F7] key. You'll see the run bar move down through the listing as before. You'll also see the values of the variables change in the Watch window. (You may need to resize the Edit window to bring the Watch window into view.) When you execute the program line where the variables are defined, the Watch window will change to something like this:

```
number: -43234244
j: 72319873
answer: 930986876
```

The variables are defined, but have garbage values because they have not yet been initialized. When you execute the **scanf()** statement, the output screen will appear. Enter a small number, like 5. Continue single stepping through the program. In the Watch window you'll see **number** acquire the value 5, and **answer** the value 1. When you enter the loop, **j** becomes 0.

When you execute the loop, you'll see that the run bar highlights the line with the **for** statement only on the first time through the loop. After that, only the single statement in the loop body,

```
answer = answer * j;
```

is executed when you press [F7], so the run bar doesn't appear to move from this line. However, the program is going around the loop. You can tell this because the values in the Watch window change.

Can you figure out what the bug is? The variable **answer** is initialized to 1, but on the first cycle through the loop, it becomes 0, as you can see in the Watch window. From then on it remains 0, since anything times 0 is still 0. Why did it become 0? As we can also see in the Watch window, **j** is 0 the first time through the loop, and the program multiplies **j** by **answer**. The bug is that we start **j** at 0 instead of 1. To fix this, we must change **j=0** to **j=1** in the **for** loop, and **j<number** to **j<=number**. When we make these changes, the program works correctly.

If you no longer need to watch a particular variable, you can delete it from the Watch window. Click on the variable name in the Watch window and then select Delete Watch from the Watches submenu of the Debug menu. You can also edit an existing Watch, or delete all Watches, using other options in this submenu.

Breakpoints

It often happens that you've debugged part of your program, but must deal with a bug in another section, and don't want to single-step through all the statements in the first part to get to the section with the bug. Or you may have a loop with many iterations that would be tedious to single step through.

Here's an example. This program attempts to average the integers from 0 to 499.

```c
/* errbreak.c */
/* demonstrates breakpoints */
void main(void)
{
    int j, total=0, average;

    for( j=0; j<500; j++ )
        total += j;
    average = total / j;
    printf("average = %d\n", average );
}
```

When we run the program, it says the average is −12. This doesn't look right; the average should be around 250. To figure out what's wrong, set up Watches for **j**, **total**, and **average**. Now try single stepping into the loop. Everything looks good for the first dozen or so cycles: **j** starts at 0 and is incremented each time, and **total** starts at 0 and is increased by whatever **j** is. We could go on stepping through the loop, but 500 iterations is too time-consuming. We want to stop the program just after the loop, so we can check the variables at that point.

The way to do this is with a *breakpoint*. A breakpoint marks a statement where the program will stop. If you start the program with [Ctrl] [F9], it will execute all the statements up to the breakpoint, then stop. You can now examine the state of the variables at that point using the Watch window.

Installing Breakpoints

To set a breakpoint, first position the cursor on the appropriate line; in this case

```c
average = total / j;
```

Now select Toggle breakpoint from the Debug menu (or press [Ctrl] [F8]). The line with the breakpoint will be highlighted (differently from the run bar).

To run the program down to the breakpoint, press [Ctrl] [F9] (or select Run from the Run menu). All the instructions in the loop will be executed. The program stops on the line with the breakpoint. Now look at the Watches. The **total** variable is −6322. A large negative number often results from the overflow of a positive number, so perhaps at this point we can guess that we've exceeded the capacity of signed integers. In fact the actual total is 499 times 250, or 124,750, which is far larger than the 32,767 limit of type **int** 0. The cure is to use variables of type **long int**.

You can install as many breakpoints in a program as you want. This is useful if the program can take several different paths, depending on the result of **if** statements or other branching constructs. You can block all the paths with breakpoints, then see where it stops.

Removing Breakpoints

You can remove a single breakpoint by positioning the cursor on the line with the breakpoint and selecting Toggle breakpoint from the Debug menu (just as you did to install the breakpoint). The breakpoint highlight will vanish.

The Breakpoints Window

Calling up Breakpoints . . . from the Debug menu opens a window that gives you several other breakpoint options. When you call up this option, you'll see a list of all the currently set breakpoints, with their line numbers. Buttons at the bottom allow you to select various options. Two of the most interesting options are selected with the "Edit" button. This button allows you to set a *pass count* and a *condition* for each breakpoint.

The pass count modifies a breakpoint so that it doesn't stop the program flow the first time it's reached. It specifies how many times the program will pass this breakpoint before it stops. To set up this option you must have already installed a breakpoint. In the errbreak.c example, try placing one on the line

```
total +=j;
```

Suppose we want to see what happens just before the end of the loop; we want to stop when **j** is 498. Call up Breakpoints . . . from the Debug menu. Click on the Edit button. You'll see a dialog box with various fields. Type the number 498 into the "Pass count" field and press [Enter]. Click on "Ok". Now when you run the program (resetting first if necessary) it will stop with **j** at 497, allowing you to single-step through the final few cycles of the loop.

In a similar way you can set a *condition* by entering it into the "Condition" field in the dialog box called up from the Edit button. A condition is an expression with a true or false value. In the current example, instead of using a pass count, you could use a condition of **total < 200**. This lets you stop the program when a variable reaches a certain value.

The Go To Cursor Option

If you only need to install one breakpoint, you can take a shortcut approach: the Go To Cursor option. Position the cursor on the line where you want the program to stop. Now run the program by selecting Go To Cursor from the Run menu, or pressing [F4]. (Don't use the normal Run option or

[Ctrl] [F9].) The effect is the same as if you had installed a breakpoint on the line with the cursor, but there is no breakpoint to remove later.

Function Debugging

When one function calls another, certain complexities arise in the debugging process. In this section we'll see how the Turbo C debugger handles these function-related situations.

Trace Into Versus Step Over

Suppose you're single stepping through the **main()** function, and it calls another function, say **func()**. Do you want to single step *into* **func()**, stepping through the lines of code that constitute the function, or do you want to step over it, treating it as a single line of code? The answer is, it depends: sometimes you want to single step into (or *trace into*) a function, and sometimes you want to execute it as a single line of code, or *step over it*.

This is the purpose of the [F7] and [F8] keys. Both these keys provide single stepping, but the [F7] traces into any functions it encounters, while the [F8] key skips over them. By selecting the appropriate key at each step, you can determine whether you trace into or step over a particular function.

For example, consider the following example program.

```
/* errfunc.c */
/* demonstrates trace, step, call stack */
void func1(void);
void func2(void);

void main(void)
{
   func1();
   func1();
}

void func1(void)
{
   func2();
}

void func2(void)
{
}
```

Try single stepping through this program with the [F8] key. You'll see the run bar go from the line **main()** to the first **func1()** call, to the second **func1()** call, and then to the closing brace of **main()**. It never goes to the functions themselves.

Now reset the debugger with the Program Reset option, and use [F7] to trace into the functions. The run bar goes to the first line of **main()**, then to the call to **func1()**, then to first line of **func1()** itself, then to the call to **func2()**, then to the first line of **func2()**, and so on. All the code in all the functions, no matter how deeply nested, will be traced into.

Even using the [F7] key you can't trace into a Turbo C library routines such as **printf()**. For one thing the source file needs to be available for tracing to take place, and the source files for the library routines are not included in the system. Also, these routines are presumably bug-free, so there is no need to debug them.

The Call Stack Option

When tracing into several levels of functions, it's easy to forget where you came from. You may know you're in a particular function, but you've forgotten which function called the function you're in.

Turbo C provides a handy way to see the whole chain of function calls that led to your present location in the program.

For instance, suppose you're single stepping through the errfunc.c program, using the [F7] key to trace into every function. The **main()** function has called **func1()**, and **func1()** has called **func2()**. To see the function calls that have taken place up to this point, select the Call Stack . . . option from the Debug menu. The Call Stack list will look like this:

```
func2()
func1()
main()
```

It would be nice to watch new functions being added to and removed from the Call Stack list as you single stepped through a program, but this is not possible. You can't leave the Call Stack list on the window as you single step. Call Stack is a snapshot, not a movie. However, it can remind you where you've come from if you get lost.

If a call to a function has arguments, the values of the arguments will also be shown on the Call Stack list.

Using the Call Stack window, you can cause the listing in the Edit window to scroll to a particular function. Select the function name from the Call Stack list and press [Enter]. The Call Stack window will vanish, and the Edit window will display that function, with the cursor marking the currently executing statement.

The Evaluate/Modify Window

You can use the Turbo C debugger to change the values of variables while a program is running. This can be useful if you've single stepped to a certain point and realize that a variable has an incorrect value, but want to see what would happen if you continued with the correct value. Or you might want to generate different values to test the operation of certain routines, without actually inputting these values to the program.

The feature that makes it possible to change variable values is called the *Evaluate/Modify window*. You can call up this window by choosing the Evaluate/Modify option from the Debug menu, or by pressing the hot key combination [Ctrl] [F4].

Evaluating Simple Variables

p 726

Let's try the Evaluation window with the faulty errloop.c example from earlier in this chapter.

Call up errloop.c, and set Watches for **number**, **j**, and **answer**, as described earlier. Now trace through the program with [F7], inputting the value 5 to the **scanf()**. Go slowly when you step into the **for** loop. The first time through the loop you'll see **answer** go to 0. This is the bug: once it's 0, this variable remains 0 no matter what it's multiplied by.

Suppose at this point we want to see whether the program would work correctly if **answer** started with the correct value. To change its value, select Evaluate/Modify from the Debug menu. You'll see a window with three fields: "Expression", "Result", and "New Value".

The "Expression" field may already contain a word; it will repeat whatever word the cursor is resting on in the Edit window. If it does (and if it's the wrong word), backspace over it. Now type in the name **answer**. When you press [Enter] you'll see the value of this variable (it should be 0) show up in the "Result" field.

To change the value, move the cursor down to the "New Value" field. Enter the new value: 1. You'll see the value of **answer** in the "Result" field change from 0 to 1.

When you leave the Evaluate window by pressing [Esc] you'll see the value of **answer** change in the Watch window as well.

Now you can continue single stepping through the program. This time **answer** will grow as expected, from 1 to 2 to 6 to 24. The program stops at this point—before it has calculated the correct value of 120—because we haven't changed the upper limit in the **for** loop from **j<number** to **j<=number**. However, we have seen that starting with a nonzero value of **answer** will solve the problem.

Evaluating Expressions

You can use the Evaluate/Modify window to find the values of *expressions* as well as simple variables. In the example above, single step the first few lines until the program gives **answer** the value 1. Now call up the Evaluate window, and type **answer*3** into the Evaluate field. When you press [Enter] the Result field will show the value 3 (the result of 1*3). The entire expression has been evaluated.

You can use all sorts of expressions in the Evaluate field. They can involve one or more variable names, and various operators. One common use for this feature is finding the values of array elements and the contents of pointers, such as **list[2]**, ***(ptr+7)**, or ***(ptr+index)**.

The Evaluate window won't handle functions, like **sin()** or **sqrt()**, or anything created with a **#define** or **typedef**.

Inspecting Data

Another way to look at data is with the Inspect . . . option in the Debug menu. This is a more technical capability, best suited to looking at complex data like structures, unions, arrays, arrays of structures, and so on. It shows you all the elements of such variables, displaying them in a window so you can scroll through them if they are too large to see all at once.

To use this option, you must first press [F7] or [F8] to put the IDE into debugging mode. This will activate the Inspect option. Now position the cursor on the variable you want to inspect. Select Inspect . . . from the Debug menu. The variable name should appear in the "Inspect" field in the resulting dialog box. If it doesn't, type it in. Press [Enter] and a window will appear containing the contents of the variable. If it's a structure or array you may need to scroll the window to see all of it.

In this appendix we haven't covered all the debugging features, but what we've said should be enough to get you started debugging your program and learning about the debugger's capabilities.

Answers to Questions and Exercises

Chapter 1

Answers to Questions

1. b
2. compiled, linked, and executed
3. a and c are both correct
4. automate
5. The parentheses following **main()** indicate that "main" is a function and provide a place to put arguments.
6. a and b
7. False: only the semicolon signals the end of a statement.
8. Here's what's wrong with the example:
   a. no parentheses following **main**
   b. parentheses used instead of braces around body of program
   c. "print" used instead of "printf"
   d. no parentheses surrounding **printf()**'s argument
   e. no semicolon at the end of the statement
   f. program statement not indented
9. On the left there is a string which will be printed; on the right is a series of constants (or variables) which will be placed in the string.
10. The output is:

```
one
two
three
```

Chapter 1
Suggested Answers to Exercises

Exercise 1

Here's one possibility, although there are others:

```
void main(void)
{
    printf("Mr. %s is %d,\n", "Green", 42);
    printf("Mr. %s is %d.",   "Brown", 48);
}
```

Exercise 2

```
void main(void)
{
    printf("%c, %c, and %c are all letters.", 'a', 'b', 'c');
}
```

Chapter 2
Answers to Questions

1. a, b, and c are correct.
2. character (**char**), integer (**int**), floating point (**float**), long integer (**long**), and double-precision floating point (**double**)
3. a, b, and d are correct; there is no type "double float," except in ice cream parlors. However, **long float** is the same as **double**.
4. True
5. four
6. −32768 to 32767
7. d
8. False: it can hold numbers 65,536 times as large.
9. b and c are correct
10. '\x41' prints 'A' and '\xE0' prints the Greek letter alpha.
11. *decimal*   *exponential*
    a. 1,000,000   1.0e6
    b. 0.000,001   1.0e−6

c. 199.95   1.9995e2

d. −888.88   −8.8888e2

12. *exponential*   *decimal*

    a. 1.5e6   1,500,000

    b. 1.5e-6   0.000,001,5

    c. 7.6543e3   7,654.3

    d. −7.6543e−3 −0.007,654,3

13. There's no address operator preceding the **years** variable in the **scanf()** function.

14. d

15. True

16. a and c

17. `number++;`

18. `usa += calif;`

19. '\t' is the tab character, '\r' is the return character which prints a carriage return (but no linefeed), not to be confused with the newline character, '\n', which prints both a carriage return and a linefeed.

20. d

21. False

22. b

23. a. 1 > 2   false

    b. 'a' < 'b'   true (the ASCII codes are compared)

    c. 1 == 2   false

    d. '2' == '2'   true

24. b

25. No. The begin-comment symbol (/*) can't be used within a comment.

Chapter 2
Suggested Answers to Exercises

Exercise 1

```
/* age2.c */
/* calculates age in minutes */
void main(void)
```

```c
{
    float years, minutes;

    printf("Please type your age in years: ");
    scanf("%f", &years);
    minutes = years * 365 * 24 * 60;
    printf("You are %.1f minutes old.\n", minutes);
}
```

Exercise 2

```c
/* square.c */
/* finds square of typed-in number */
void main(void)
{
    float square, number;

    printf("Type in number to be squared: ");
    scanf("%f", &number);
    square = number * number;
    printf("Square is %f", square);

}
```

Exercise 3

```c
/* box2.c */
/* draws 4x4 box */
void main(void)
{
    printf("\xC9\xCD\xCD\xBB\n");    /* top line */
    printf("\xBA  \xBA\n");          /* two spaces in the middle */
    printf("\xBA  \xBA\n");          /* ditto */
    printf("\xC8\xCD\xCD\xBC\n");    /* bottom line */
}
```

Chapter 3
Answers to Questions

1. initialize, test, increment
2. d

3. semicolon

4. b

5. commas

6. a

7. False

8. b

9. deeply

10. value

11. a, b, c, and d are all correct

12. True

13. b

14. b

15. False: it causes a return to the beginning of the loop.

Chapter 3
Suggested Answers to Exercises

Exercise 1

```
/* square2.c */
/* prints out the squares of the first 20 integers */
void main(void)
{
   int n;

   for(n=1; n<21; n++)
      printf("The square of %2d is %3d\n", n, n*n);
}
```

Exercise 2

```
/* charcnt3.c */
/* counts characters in a phrase typed in */
/* until period is typed */
void main(void)
{
   int count=0;
```

```
      printf("Type in a phrase:\n");
      while ( getche() != '.' )
         count++;
      printf("\nCharacter count is %d", count);
}
```

Exercise 3

```
/* between.c */
/* tells how many letters between two letters */
void main(void)
{
    char ch1, ch2;

    while( ch1 != '\r' )
       {
       printf("\nType first character: ");
       ch1 = getche();
       printf("\nType second character: ");
       ch2 = getche();
       printf("\nThere are %d characters between.", ch2-ch1-1);
       }
}
```

Chapter 4
Answers to Questions

1. b and c are both correct
2. Yes, except for the keyword **then**, which doesn't exist in C.
3. False
4. c
5. a—there is no conditional expression following **else**.
6. Yes: the compiler doesn't care if you put multiple statements on one line, although it is more difficult to read.
7. False
8. b
9. d
10. b
11. No: colons must be used after the **case** statements, and **break** statements are needed after the **printf()** statements.

12. False: **break** statements are not used if two **case**s trigger the same set of statements.

13. No: variables, such as **temp**, cannot be used in **case** expressions.

14. d

15. 0

Chapter 4
Suggested Answers to Exercises

Exercise 1

```
/* speed.c */
/* prints appropriate responses to user's speed */
void main(void)
{
   int speed;

   printf("Please type the speed you normally ");
   printf("travel in a 55 mph zone: ");
   scanf("%d", &speed);
   if(speed > 75)
      printf("I'm taking you to headquarters, buddy.");
   else
      if(speed > 55)
         printf("I'll let you off with a warning, this time.");
      else
         if(speed>45)
               printf("Have a good day, sir.");
            else
               printf("Can't you get the lead out, buddy?");
}
```

Exercise 2

```
/* checker2.c */
/* draws a checkerboard on the screen */
void main(void)
{
   int x, y, z;

   for(y=1; y<=8; y++)                    /* stepping down screen */
```

```
            for(z=1; z<=3; z++)              /* 3 lines per square */
            {
                for(x=1; x<=8; x++)          /* stepping across screen */
                    if( (x+y) % 2 == 0 )     /* even-numbered square? */
                                             /* print 6 rectangles */
                        printf("\xDB\xDB\xDB\xDB\xDB\xDB");
                    else
                        printf("            ");   /* print 6 blank spaces */
                    if(y * z < 24)           /* print newline, */
                        printf("\n");         /* except on last line */
            }
        }
```

Exercise 3

```
/* linesX2.c */
/* prints four crossed lines on screen */
void main(void)
{
    int x, y;

    for(y=1; y<24; y++)                      /* step down screen */
        {
        for(x=1; x<24; x++)                  /* step across screen */
            if( x==y || x==24-y || x==12 || y==12 )
                printf("\xDB");              /* print solid color */
            else
                printf("\xB0");              /* print gray */
        printf("\n");                        /* next line */
        }
}
```

Chapter 5
Answers to Questions

1. All except b are valid reasons for using functions. Functions don't run faster than inline code or macros.

2. True

3. No: the call to the function must be terminated with a semicolon.

4. False: you can return from a function by simply "falling through" the closing brace.

5. False: you can only return one data item with a function using **return()**.

6. No: first, the declarator should not be terminated with a semicolon. Second, the definition of the argument **num** should take place within the declarator. Third, the declarator should specify a return type of **int**.

7. a and c

8. False: functions commonly use local variables which are accessible only to the function in which they're defined.

9. b and c, although we won't learn about c until the chapter on pointers (Chapter 7).

10. a, b, d, and e

11. No: the argument passed to the function is type **int** in the calling program but type **float** in the function.

12. a

13. many

14. d

15. c

16. c

17. substituted

18. No: you can't have spaces in the left-hand part of the statement (the identifier).

19. "EXP" is the identifier and "2.71828" is the text.

20. a and b are both correct.

21. a, b, and d

22. No: the macro expands into the incorrect

```
postage = rate*l + w + h
```

23. inserted

24. b, c, and d

25. INCLUDE

Chapter 5
Suggested Answers to Exercises

Exercise 1

```
/* maximum.c */
/* prints largest of two numbers typed in */
```

```
int max(int, int);        /* prototype */

void main(void)
{
    int num1, num2, ans;

    printf("Type in two numbers: ");
    scanf("%d %d", &num1, &num2);
    printf("Largest one is %d.", max(num1,num2) );
}

/* max() */
/* returns largest of two integers */
int max(int n1, int n2)
{
    return( n1>n2 ? n1 : n2 );
}
```

Exercise 2

```
/* times.c */
/* calculates difference between two times */
#include <stdio.h>        /* for printf(), etc. */
float getsecs(void);      /* prototype */

void main(void)
{
    float secs1, secs2;    /* declare variables */

    printf("Type first time (form 12:22:55): ");
    secs1 = getsecs();
    printf("Type second (later) time: ");
    secs2 = getsecs();
    printf("Difference is %.0f seconds.", secs2-secs1);
}

/* getsecs() */
/* gets time from kbd in hours-minutes-seconds format */
/* returns time in seconds */
float getsecs(void)
{
    float hours, minutes, seconds;
```

```
        scanf("%f:%f:%f", &hours, &minutes, &seconds);
        return ( hours*60*60 + minutes*60 + seconds );
}
```

Exercise 3

```
/* timesM.c */
/* calculates difference between two times */
/* uses macro */
#define HMSTOSEC(hrs,mins,secs) (hrs*3600 + mins*60 + secs)

void main(void)
{
    float secs1, secs2;    /* declare variables */
    float hours, minutes, seconds;

    printf("Type first time (form 12:22:55): ");
    scanf("%f:%f:%f", &hours, &minutes, &seconds);
    secs1 = HMSTOSEC(hours, minutes, seconds);
    printf("Type second (later) time: ");
    scanf("%f:%f:%f", &hours, &minutes, &seconds);
    secs2 = HMSTOSEC(hours, minutes, seconds);
    printf("Difference is %.2f seconds.", secs2-secs1);
}
```

Chapter 6
Answers to Questions

1. c
2. d
3. type, name, size
4. No: brackets are used in array declarations, not parentheses.
5. The fifth element
6. b
7. d
8. No: use **j<MAX**, and **&prices[j]**.
9. No: must use brackets following the name.
10. c
11. d

12. **external, static**
13. c and d
14. sure
15. array[1][0]
16. address
17. a
18. a and c, which are the same thing.
19. False: the function doesn't move the values stored in the array.
20. c, although some other choices aren't clearly false.
21. string, character.
22. c
23. null '\0'.
24. **gets()**
25. 9 (space must be left for the '\0' character).
26. True
27. a
28. **&string[5]**
29. You can't use assignment statements with strings.
30. **strlen(name)**

Chapter 6
Suggested Answers to Exercises

Exercise 1

```
/* temp2.c */
/* averages one week's temperatures */
/* prints them out along with average */
void main(void)
{
   int temper[7];             /* array definition */
   int day, sum;

   for (day=0; day<7; day++)     /* put temps in array */
      {
      printf("Enter temperature for day %d: ", day);
      scanf("%d", &temper[day]);
```

```
            }
        sum = 0;                        /* calculate average */
        for (day=0; day<7; day++)       /* and print temperatures */
            {
            printf("Temperature for day %d is %d.\n", day, temper[day]);
            sum += temper[day];
            }
        printf("Average is %d.", sum/7);
    }
```

Exercise 2

```
        /* fltemp3.c */
        /* averages arbitrary number of temperatures */
        #define LIM 100
        void main(void)
        {
            float temper[LIM];              /* array declaration */
            float sum=0.0;
            int num, day=0;

            printf("Enter temperature for day 0: ");
            scanf("%f", &temper[0]);

            while ( temper[day++] > 0 )     /* put temps in array */
                {
                printf("Enter temperature for day %d: ", day);
                scanf("%f", &temper[day]);
                }
            num = day-1;                    /* number of temps entered */
            for (day=0; day<num; day++)     /* calculate average */
                sum += temper[day];
            printf("Average is %.1f", sum/num);
        }
```

Exercise 3

```
/* insert.c */
/* inserts a character into a string */
#include <stdio.h>                  /* for printf(), etc. */
#include <string.h>                 /* for strcpy() */
void strins(char[], char, int);     /* prototype */
```

```
void main(void)
{
   char charac;
   char string[81];
   int position;

   printf("Type string [Return], character, position\n");
   gets(string);
   scanf("%c %d", &charac, &position);
   strins(string,charac,position);
   puts(string);
}

/* strins() */
/* inserts character into string */
void strins(char str[], char ch, int n)
{
   char scratch[81];                  /* temporary space */

   strcpy( scratch, &str[n] );   /* save 2nd half in scratch */
   str[n] = ch;                  /* insert character */
   strcpy( &str[n+1], scratch ); /* shift 2nd half right */
}
```

Chapter 7
Answers to Questions

1. b and c
2. a and c
3. True
4. False: we learned how to pass the addresses of arrays to functions in the last chapter.
5. False: when a value is passed to a function, the value itself (not its address) is stored in the function's memory space.
6. d
7. c
8. addresses, declare, indirection
9. b

10. Both a and d will work (provided they are known to the function where the reference is made).

11. c

12. *pointvar = *pointvar / 10;

13. b and d

14. In the function's memory space

15. ptrj = &j;

16. No: it should be **scanf("%d", ptrx);**

17. a

18. No: you can't increment an address, which is a pointer constant.

19. Print the array elements: "4 5 6".

20. 2

21. Print the addresses of the array elements.

22. Print the array elements: "4 5 6".

23. Almost: the second creates a pointer as well as an array.

24. The same amount, different amounts

25. "I come not to bury Caesar"

    "I come not to bury Caesar"

    "to bury Caesar"

26. 13 bytes: 11 for the string plus null character and 2 for the pointer to the string.

27. False: every *row* of a two-dimensional array can be considered to be a *one*-dimensional array.

28. arr7[1][1], *(*(arr+1)+1)

29. d

30. *(*(arr7+x)+y)

Chapter 7
Suggested Answers to Exercises

Exercise 1

```
/* zerovars.c */
/* tests function which zeros three variables */
#include <stdio.h>              /* for printf() */
void zero(int *, int *, int *); /* prototype */
```

```
void main(void)
{
   int x=4, y=7, z=11;

   zero( &x, &y, &z );
   printf("x=%d, y=%d, z=%d.", x, y, z);
}

/* zero() */
/* puts zero in three variables in calling program */
void zero(int *px, int *py, int *pz)
{
   *px = 0;
   *py = 0;
   *pz = 0;
}
```

Exercise 2

```
/* zeroarr.c */
/* tests function to zero array elements */
#include <stdio.h>              /* for printf() */
void zero(int *, int);          /* prototype */
#define SIZE 5                  /* size of array */

void main(void)
{
   static int array[SIZE] = { 3, 5, 7, 9, 11 };
   int j;

   zero(array, SIZE);              /* call funct to insert 0s */
   for (j=0; j<SIZE; j++)          /* print out array */
      printf("%d  ", *(array+j) );
}

/* zero() */
/* zeros out elements of array in calling program */
void zero(int *ptr, int num)
{
   int k;
   for(k=0; k<num; k++)
```

```
                    *(ptr+k) = 0;
        }
```

Exercise 3

```
/* zerostr.c */
/* tests function which puts null character in string */
#include <stdio.h>              /* for printf() */
void zero(char *);              /* prototype */

void main(void)
{
   char *phrase = "Don't test the river with both feet";

   printf("Phrase=%s.\n", phrase);
   zero(phrase);
   printf("Phrase=%s.\n", phrase);
}

/* zero() */
/* function to put null character at start of string */
void zero(char *str)
{
   *str = '\0';
}
```

Chapter 8
Answers to Questions

1. b and c
2. 256
3. 2
4. False: key combinations such as [Alt] [z] can be represented as well.
5. d
6. b and c
7. a, b, and c
8. a. The CONFIG.SYS file must be in the main directory and must contain the line DEVICE=ANSI.SYS. The ANSI.SYS file must be in the system.

9. d is the most correct, although a case could be made for c.
10. "\x1B[2J"
11. False: it can be moved immediately to any location.
12. bold, blinking, underlined, reverse video
13. "\x1B[C"
14. False: it causes an exit from the entire program.
15. num=atoi(str);
16. True
17. b and d
18. strcpy(str,"steeple");
    strcat(str,"chase");
19. a, c, and d
20. C>prog1 <f1.c >f2.c

Chapter 8
Suggested Answers to Exercises

Exercise 1

```
/* backsp.c */
/* prints letters, backspaces with left arrow key */
#define C_LEFT "\x1B[D"              /* move cursor left */
#define L_ARRO 75                    /* left arrow key */
void main(void)
{
    char key;

    while ( (key=getch()) != '\r' )  /* read keyboard */
        if( key == 0 )               /* if extended code, */
            {
            if( getch() == L_ARRO )  /* read second code */
                {                    /* if left arrow */
                printf(C_LEFT);      /* move cursor left */
                printf(" ");         /* print space over char */
                printf(C_LEFT);      /* reset cursor */
                }
            }
        else
```

```
            putch(key);                      /* not ext code, print char */
    }
```

Exercise 2

```
/* decihex.c */
/* translates decimal number into hexadecimal */
/* uses command-line arguments */
void main( int argc, char *argv[] )
{
    unsigned int num;

    if( argc != 2 )
        printf("Example usage: decihex 128");
    else
        {
        num = atoi( *(argv+1) );
        printf("Hex=%x", num );
        }
}
```

Exercise 3

```
/* braces.c */
/* checks numbers of right and left braces are equal */
/* uses redirection for input file */
#include <stdio.h>      /* for EOF definition (-1) */
void main(void)
{
    int left=0, right=0;
    char ch;

    while( (ch=getchar()) != EOF )
        {
        if( ch=='{' )
            left++;
        if( ch=='}' )
            right++;
        }
    if (left != right)
        printf("\n\nMismatched braces\n");
}
```

Chapter 9

Answers to Questions

1. same type, different types
2. False: arrays are more appropriate for elements of the same type.
3. b, c, and d are all correct
4. ```
   struct xxx
      {
      char string[10];
      int num;
      };
   ```
5. c
6. type, variable, value
7. `struct vehicle car;`
8. `jim.arms = 2;`
9. ```
   struct body
      {
      int arms;
      int legs;
      }jim;
   ```
10. Yes, at least in modern compilers.
11. a and b
12. ```
    struct partners
       {
       struct body sandy;
       struct body pat;
       };
    ```
13. True (in modern compilers)
14. `struct book *ptrbook;`
15. a and d. This expression will also work.

    `(*addweath).temp`
16. a free section of memory
17. memory
18. next structure
19. False: the **sizeof()** function returns the size of a *data type*.
20. d
    ```

21.
```
union intstr
  {
  char string[10];
  int num;
  };
```

22. Read-Only Memory Basic Input/Output System

23. d

24. True

25. d

26. AX, BX, CX, DX

27. AH, AL, BH, BL, CH, CL, DH, DL

28. b and c

29. d

30. False: there is a ROM service routine that returns the memory size.

Chapter 9
Suggested Answers to Exercises

Exercise 1

```
/* date.c */
/* demonstrates structure to hold date */
void main(void)
{
   struct date
     {
     int month;
     int day;
     int year;
     };
   struct date today;

   today.month = 12;
   today.day = 31;
   today.year = 91;

   printf("date is %d/%d/%d",
            today.month, today.day, today.year );
}
```

Exercise 2

```
/* date2.c */
/* demonstrates passing structure to function */
#include <stdio.h>          /* for printf() */

struct date                 /* structure definition */
   {
   int month;               /* structure members */
   int day;
   int year;
   };

void prindate(struct date mmddyy);    /* prototype (follows */
                                      /*     struct def) */
void main(void)
{
   struct date today;       /* structure variable */

   today.month = 12;        /* give values to */
   today.day = 31;          /*     structure variables */
   today.year = 91;
   prindate(today);         /* print date from structure */
}

/* prindate() */
/* prints date passed via structure */
void prindate(struct date mmddyy)
{
   printf("date is %d/%d/%d",
             mmddyy.month, mmddyy.day, mmddyy.year );
}
```

Exercise 3

```
/* pos2.c */
/* demonstrates ROM 'cursor position' service */
#include <dos.h>                 /* for REGS */
#define CLEAR "\x1B[2J"          /* clear screen */
#define ERASE "\x1B[K"           /* erase line */
#define VIDEO 0x10
#define SETC 2
```

```
void main(void)
{
   union REGS regs;
   int row=1, col=1;

   printf(CLEAR);                    /* clear screen */
   while ( !(row==0 && col==0) )     /* terminate on row=0, col=0 */
      {
      regs.h.ah = SETC;             /* 'set cur pos' service */
      regs.h.dh = 22;               /* row in DH */
      regs.h.dl = 0;                /* column in DL */
      int86(VIDEO, &regs, &regs);   /* call video services */
      printf(ERASE);                /* erase line */
      printf("Type row and column number (form 10,40): ");
      scanf("%d,%d", &row, &col);   /* get coordinates */
      regs.h.ah = SETC;             /* 'set cur pos' service */
      regs.h.dh = row;              /* row in DH */
      regs.h.dl = col;              /* column in DL */
      int86(VIDEO, &regs, &regs);   /* call video services */
      printf("*(%d,%d)", row, col);    /* print coordinates */
      }
}
```

Chapter 10
Answers to Questions

1. a. 00000001,
   b. 11111000,
   c. 0001001000110100,
   d. 1111110000001010
2. b
3. False: the bitwise operators treat variables as sequences of bits.
4. c
5. mask
6. c
7. d (since the sign bit will be shifted in on the left)
8. combine
9. segment, offset
10. b

11. a and b are equivalent and both are correct

12. absolute

13. four

14. d

15. True

16. faster

17. b

18. False: the pointer must be typecast:

    ```
    farptr = (int far *) 0xA1001234;
    ```

19. a, b, c, and d are all correct

20. True

21. c and d are both true

22. bits, groups of bits

23. a, c, and d are all correct

24. 0xB0000, 0xB0F9F

25. a, b, c, and d are all correct

Chapter 10
Suggested Answers to Exercises

Exercise 1

```
/* exortest.c */
/* demonstrates bitwise EXCLUSIVE OR operator */
void main(void)
{
   unsigned int x1, x2;

   while( x1 !=0 || x2 != 0 )    /* terminate on 0 0 */
      {
      printf("\nEnter two hex numbers (ff or less, example 'cc 7'): ");
      scanf("%x %x", &x1, &x2);
      printf("%02x ^ %02x = %02x\n", x1, x2, x1 ^ x2 );
      }
}
```

Exercise 2

```c
/* bintohex.c */
/* converts binary number typed by user to hex and decimal */
void main(void)
{
   int count, ans=1;
   char ch;

   while( ans != 0 )        /* terminate on 0 decimal */
      {
      printf("Enter binary number: \n");
      count=0; ans=0;
      while( count++ < 16 )
         {
         if( (ch=getche()) == '0' )
            ans <<= 1;
         else if( ch == '1')
            ans = (ans << 1) + 1;
         else break;
         }
      printf("= %x (hex) = %u (dec)\n\n", ans, ans );
      }
}
```

Exercise 3

```c
/* ddraw.c */
/* moves cursor on screen,leaves trail */
/* uses direct display memory access */
#include <conio.h>                    /* for getch() */
#define COMAX 80                      /* max columns */
#define ROMAX 25                      /* max rows */
#define L_ARRO 75                     /* extended codes */
#define R_ARRO 77
#define U_ARRO 72
#define D_ARRO 80
#define ACROSS 205                    /* graphics characters */
#define UPDOWN 186
#define BOX 219
int far *farptr;                      /* pointer to memory */
int col=40, row=12;                   /* insert position */
void insert(char);                    /* prototypes */
void clear(void);
```

```
void main(void)
{
   char ch;

   farptr = (int far *)0xB8000000;  /* start of screen mem */
   clear();               /* clear screen */
   while( (ch=getch()) == 0 )       /* quit on normal char */
      {
      switch( getch() )             /* read extended code */
      {
      case R_ARRO: if(col<COMAX) ++col; ch=ACROSS; break;
      case L_ARRO: if(col>0)     --col; ch=ACROSS; break;
      case D_ARRO: if(row<ROMAX) ++row; ch=UPDOWN; break;
      case U_ARRO: if(row>0)     --row; ch=UPDOWN; break;
      default: ch=BOX;              /* rectangle at corners */
      }
      insert(ch);                   /* insert char */
      }
}

/* insert() */
/* inserts character at cursor position */
void insert(char ch)
{
   *(farptr + COMAX*row + col) = (ch & 0x00FF) | 0x0700;
}

/* clear() */
/* clears screen using direct memory access */
void clear(void)
{
   int j;

   for(j=0; j<2000; j++)            /* fill screen memory */
      *(farptr + j) = 0x0700;       /* with 0's (attr=07) */
}
```

Chapter 11
Answers to Questions

1. resolution, text/graphics, number of colors, monitor type, display adaptor type, memory size, number of pages, memory starting address

2. d

3. 4, 8

4. b

5. ROM BIOS routine, direct memory access

6. blue, green, red, intensity

7. all four choices

8. 4

9. d

10. b

11. sixteen (including black)

12. a

13. False

14. b and c

15. color

16. a

17. On each bit plane, eight.

18. None is correct; a single bit plane cannot represent cyan.

19. bit

20. d

21. read

22. c

23. False

24. b

25. move

Chapter 11
Suggested Answers to Exercises

Exercise 1

```
/* fillco.c */
/* fills screen with color */
#include <stdio.h>

void main(void)
{
```

```
   char far *farptr;                    /* to hold screen address */
   int j;
   char cocon, color[20];

   printf("Type cyan, magenta, white, or black: ");
   gets(color);
   switch ( color[0])                   /* check first char */
      {
      case 'c': cocon = 0x55; break; /* set cocon to color */
      case 'm': cocon = 0xAA; break;
      case 'w': cocon = 0xFF; break;
      default:  cocon = 0;    break;
      }
   farptr = (char far *)0xB8000000;  /* set ptr to screen addr */
   for(j=0; j<0x3F3F; j++)              /* for all bytes */
      *(farptr+j) = cocon;             /* insert constant */
}
```

Exercise 2

```
/* conrect2.c */
/* draws concentric rectangle of different colors */

void rect(int, int, int, int, unsigned char);  /* prototypes */
void putpt(int, int, unsigned char);

void main(void)
{
   int z;

   for(z=50; z>=10; z-=10)           /* draw series of rectangles */
      rect(100-z, 100+z, 160-z, 160+z, (z/10)%4);
}

/* rect() */
/* draws rectangle on screen using putpt() */
void rect(int top, int bot, int left, int rite,
                                      unsigned char color)
{
   int x, y;

   for(y=top; y<=bot; y++)
      for(x=left; x<=rite; x++)
         putpt(x,y,color);
```

```
    }

/* putpt() */
/* displays point at location col, row */
#define BYTES 40                        /* (bytes per row) / 2 */
#define PIX    4                        /* pixels per byte */
void putpt(int col, int row, unsigned char color)
{
    int addr, j, bitpos;
    unsigned int mask=0xFF3F;           /* 11111111 00111111 */
    unsigned char temp;
    unsigned char far *farptr;          /* to hold screen address */

    farptr = (char far *)0xB8000000; /* set ptr to screen addr */
    /* calculate offset address of byte to be altered */
    addr = row*BYTES + col/PIX;          /* calculate address */
    if(row & 1)                          /* if odd row number */
       addr += 8152;                     /* use 2nd memory bank */

    /* shift two-bit color & mask to appropriate place in byte */
    color <<= 6;                         /* put color on left */
    bitpos = col & 0x03;                 /* get lower 2 bits */
    for(j=0; j<bitpos; j++)              /* shift mask & color */
       {                                 /*    to right */
       mask >>= 2;                       /*    bitpos times */
       color >>= 2;
       }

    /* put two color bits in screen memory location */
    temp = *(farptr+addr) & (char)mask; /* and off color bits */
    *(farptr+addr) = temp | color;       /* or on new color */
}
```

Exercise 3

```
/* ediag.c */
/* draws diagonal lines on screen.  Use mode 13 (320x200) */
/* (uses EGA write mode 2) */
#include <conio.h>                 /* for outportb() */
#define BLUE 0x01                  /* ega colors */
#define YELLOW 0x0E
#define RED 0x04
#define BLACK 0
void putpte(int, int, unsigned char);  /* prototype */
```

```c
void main(void)
{
    int x;

    for(x=0; x<200; x++)
        {
        putpte(x,x,BLUE);              /* diagonal line */
        putpte(x,199-x,YELLOW);        /* diagonal line */
        putpte(x,100,RED);             /* horizontal  line */
        putpte(100,x,BLACK);           /* vertical line */
        }
}

/* putpte() */
/* displays colored pixel at location col, row */
/* uses EGA write mode 2 */
#define MAXR 200                    /* rows */
#define MAXC 320                    /* columns */
#define PIX  8                      /* pixels per byte */
#define MAXB (MAXC/PIX)             /* bytes in a row */

void putpte(int col, int row, unsigned char color)
{
    static unsigned char table[8] = { 0x80, 0x40, 0x20, 0x10,
                                       0x08, 0x04, 0x02, 0x01 };
    char far *farptr;
    int addr, bitpos;
    unsigned char temp;

    farptr = (char far *) 0xA0000000;  /* set ptr to EGA mem */
    outportb(0x3CE,5);                 /* select mode register */
    outportb(0x3CF,2);                 /*     set to mode 2 */
    outportb(0x3C4,2);                 /* select map mask register */
    outportb(0x3C5,0xF);               /* activate all bit planes */

    addr = row*MAXB + col/PIX;         /* calculate address */
    bitpos = col & 7;                  /* lower 3 bits are bitpos */
    outportb(0x3CE,8);                 /* select bit mask reg */
    outportb(0x3CF,table[bitpos]);     /* set bit to be changed */
    temp = *(farptr+addr);             /* read byte into latches */
    *(farptr+addr) = color;            /* send color to address */

    outportb(0x3CE,8);                 /* select bit mask reg */
    outportb(0x3CF,0xFF);              /* make all bits writeable */
    outportb(0x3CE,5);                 /* select mode register */
```

```
        outportb(0x3CF,0);                    /* set write mode 0 */
    }
```

Chapter 12
Answers to Questions

1. Turbo C library functions are more convenient.
2. Direct memory access is generally faster and more flexible.
3. False. You must use graphics mode.
4. b
5. canio.h
6. b and d
7. 2
8. False
9. d
10. graphics.lib, a graphics driver like cga.bgi, and graphics.h.
11. BGIOBJ.EXE
12. False
13. **initgraph()**
14. b and c
15. True
16. There is no such function.
17. a and c
18. c and d
19. c and d
20. a, b, c and d

Chapter 12
Suggested Answers to Exercises

Exercise 1

```
/* ezedit.c */
/* mini editor works in window */
/* allows deleting of char with backspace, and insertion */
```

```
#include <conio.h>              /* needed for text functions */
#define LEFT   10               /* left side of window */
#define TOP     8               /* top of window */
#define RIGHT  50               /* right side of window */
#define BOT    21               /* bottom of window */
#define WIDTH  (RIGHT-LEFT+1)   /* width of window */
#define HEIGHT (BOT-TOP+1)      /* height of window */
#define ESC    27               /* escape key */
#define BACKSP  8               /* backspace key */
#define L_ARRO 75               /* cursor control keys */
#define R_ARRO 77
#define U_ARRO 72
#define D_ARRO 80
#define INS    82               /* other extended code keys */
#define DEL    83
int linebuff [WIDTH];           /* line buffer for backspace */

void main(void)
{
    int x, y;
    char key;

    clrscr();                       /* clear entire screen */
    window( LEFT, TOP, RIGHT, BOT ); /* define window */
    x = 1; y = 1;                   /* position cursor */

    while( (key=getch()) != ESC )   /* if [Esc], exit loop */
      {
      if( key == 0 )                /* if extended code, */
        {
        switch( getch() )           /* read second character */
          {
          case L_ARRO:              /* move cursor left */
            if( x > 1 )
            gotoxy( --x, y );
            break;
          case R_ARRO:              /* move cursor right */
            if( x < WIDTH )
            gotoxy( ++x, y );
            break;
          case U_ARRO:              /* move cursor up */
            if( y > 1 )
            gotoxy( x, --y );
            break;
```

```
                case D_ARRO:                /* move cursor down */
                    if( y < HEIGHT )
                    gotoxy( x, ++y );
                    break;
                case INS:                   /* insert new line */
                    insline();
                    break;
                case DEL:                   /* delete line */
                    delline();
                    break;
                } /* end switch */
            } /* end if */
            else                            /* not extended code */
            {
            if( key == BACKSP )         /* if [Backspace] */
                {                           /* & cursor not at left */
                if( x > 1 )             /* move chars from cursor */
                    {                       /* to end of line, left */
                    movetext( LEFT+x-1, TOP+y-1, RIGHT, TOP+y-1,
                            LEFT+x-2, TOP+y-1 );
                    gotoxy( WIDTH, y );   /* go to end of line */
                    putch( ' ' );         /* write blank */
                    gotoxy(--x, y);       /* move cursor left */
                    }
                }
            else                        /* insert normal char */
                {                           /* move chars right */
                movetext( LEFT+x-1, TOP+y-1, RIGHT-1, TOP+y-1,
                        LEFT+x,   TOP+y-1 );
                putch( key );           /* print normal char */
                x = wherex();           /* update cursor */
                y = wherey();
                }
            } /* end else (not extended code) */
        } /* end while */
}
```

Exercise 2

```
/* paint.c */
/* permits user to draw, using cursor */
#include <graphics.h>
#define ESC    27                           /* escape key */
```

```
#define L_ARRO 75                          /* cursor control keys */
#define R_ARRO 77
#define U_ARRO 72
#define D_ARRO 80


void main(void)
{
    int driver=CGA, mode=CGAC0;
    int x, y, width, height;
    char key;
                                           /* initialize graphics */
    initgraph( &driver, &mode, "c:\\tc\\bgi" );
    width = getmaxx();                     /* get screen dimensions */
    height = getmaxy();
    x = width/2;                           /* put dot in middle */
    y = height/2;
    putpixel(x, y, WHITE);
    while( (key=getch()) != ESC )          /* if [Esc], exit loop */
        {
        if( key == 0 )                     /* if extended code, */
            {
            switch( getch() )              /* read second character */
                {
            case L_ARRO:                   /* move cursor left */
                if( x > 0 )
                    --x;
                break;
                case R_ARRO:               /* move cursor right */
                if( x < width )
                    ++x;
                break;
                case U_ARRO:               /* move cursor up */
                if( y > 0 )
                    --y;
                break;
                case D_ARRO:               /* move cursor down */
                if( y < height )
                    ++y;
                break;
                }  /* end switch */
            putpixel(x, y, WHITE);         /* draw dot */
            }  /* end if */
        }  /* end while */
```

767

```
        closegraph();                         /* shut down graphics */
}
```

Exercise 3

```
/* coin.c */
/* displays a coin rotating about vertical axis */
#include <graphics.h>
#define CGACO_LIGHTGREEN 1         /* cga color */
#define XC 160                     /* center of ellipse */
#define YC 100
#define RAD 25                     /* vertical radius */
#define N  8                       /* number of views */
#define DELAY 20                   /* delay between views */

void main(void)
{
   int xRad;
   void *buff[N];                  /* pointers to buffers */
   unsigned size;                  /* size of buffer */
   int j, mode;
   int driver = DETECT;
                                   /* set graphics mode */
   initgraph( &driver, &mode, "c:\\tc\\bgi" );
                   /* get image size */
   size = imagesize( XC-RAD, YC-RAD, XC+RAD, YC+RAD );
   setcolor( CGACO_LIGHTGREEN );
   for( j=0; j<N; j++ )            /* make and store */
      {                            /*    images of ellipses */
      xRad = j * RAD / (N-1) ;     /* find x radius */
      if( j==0 )  xRad = 1;        /* vertical line */
      cleardevice();               /* get rid of old images */
      ellipse( XC, YC, 0, 360, xRad, RAD );  /* draw ellipse */
      buff[j] = (void *)malloc(size);  /* get memory for image */
                                   /* place image in memory */
      getimage(XC-RAD, YC-RAD, XC+RAD, YC+RAD, buff[j]);
      }
   while( !kbhit() )               /* draw ellipses */
      {                            /*    until keypress */
      for( j=0; j<N; j++ )         /* increasing width */
         {                         /* draw image */
         putimage( XC-RAD, YC-RAD, buff[j], COPY_PUT );
```

```
         delay ( DELAY );              /* delay, erase image */
         putimage( XC-RAD, YC-RAD, buff[j], XOR_PUT );
         }
      for( j=N-1; j>0; j--)           /* decreasing width */
         {                            /* draw image */
         putimage( XC-RAD, YC-RAD, buff[j], COPY_PUT );
         delay ( DELAY );             /* delay, erase image */
         putimage( XC-RAD, YC-RAD, buff[j], XOR_PUT );
         }
      } /* end while */
   closegraph();
}
```

Chapter 13
Answers to Questions

1. standard I/O and system I/O
2. a, b, c, and d are all correct
3. file pointer
4. a and b
5. **fclose()**
6. d
7. False: a file that is written to but not closed may lose data when the program is terminated.
8. c and d
9. binary mode
10. a, c, e, and f
11. binary, unless using formatted I/O
12. c
13. False
14. d (not to be confused with c)
15. **fwrite()**
16. bytes
17. c and d
18. handle
19. a and d
20. **read()**

21. **setmode()**
22. c
23. True
24. b and d
25. permiss
26. system-level
27. d
28. C>encrypt <file1.txt >file2.txt
29. a and c
30. False

Chapter 13
Suggested Answers to Exercises

Exercise 1

```
/* braces2.c */
/* checks if numbers of right and left braces are equal */
#include <stdio.h>

int main( int argc, char *argv[] )
{
   FILE *fptr;
   int left=0, right=0;
   char ch;

   if( argc != 2)                        /* check args */
      { printf("Syntax: braces2 filename"); exit(1); }

   if( (fptr=fopen(argv[1], "r")) == NULL)  /* open file */
      { printf("Can't open file %s.", argv[1]); exit(1); }

   while( (ch=getc(fptr)) != EOF )           /* get character */
      {
      if( ch=='{' )  left++;               /* count lefts */
      if( ch=='}' )  right++;              /* count rights */
      }
   if (left != right)                        /* check if equal */
      printf("\nMismatched braces\n");
```

```
   else
      printf("\nBraces match.\n");
   fclose(fptr);                              /* close file */
   return(0);
}
```

Exercise 2

```
/* writedex.c */
/* writes strings typed at keyboard, to file */
/* prints offset for each phrase */
#include <stdio.h>
void main(void)
{
   FILE *fptr;                       /* declare ptr to FILE */
   char string[81];                  /* storage for strings */

   fptr = fopen("textfile.txt","w");  /* open file */
   while(strlen(gets(string)) > 0)    /* get string from keybd */
      {
      printf("Offset=%ld\n\n", ftell(fptr) );  /* print offset */
      fputs(string, fptr);           /* write string to file */
      fputs("\n", fptr);             /* write newline to file */
      }
   fclose(fptr);                     /* close file */
}
```

Exercise 3

Make appropriate changes to the interface part of the program, and add this
routine:

```
/* agentr2.c */
/* maintains list of agents in file */
/* permits deletion of one record */
#include <stdio.h>              /* for FILE, etc. */
#include <conio.h>              /* for getche(), etc. */
#include <stdlib.h>             /* for atof() */
#define TRUE 1
void newname(void);             /* prototypes */
void listall(void);
void wfile(void);
void rfile(void);
```

```
void delrec(void);

struct personel                    /* define data structure */
   {
   char name [40];                 /* name */
   int agnumb;                     /* code number */
   float height;                   /* height in inches */
   };
struct personel agent[50];         /* array of 50 structures */
int n = 0;                         /* number of agents listed */

int main(void)
{
   while (TRUE)
      {
      printf("\n'e' enter new agent\n'l' list all agents");
      printf("\n'w' write file\n'r' read file");
      printf("\n'd' delete record\n'q' quit: ");
      switch ( getche() )
         {
         case 'e': newname(); break;
         case 'l': listall(); break;
         case 'w': wfile();   break;
         case 'r': rfile();   break;
         case 'd': delrec();  break;
         case 'q': exit(0);
         default:              /* user mistake */
            puts("\nEnter only selections listed");
         }  /* end switch */
      }  /* end while */
}  /* end main */

/* newname() */
/* puts a new agent in the database */
void newname(void)
{
   char numstr[81];              /* temporary string storage */

   printf("\nRecord %d.\nEnter name: ", n+1); /* get name */
   gets(agent[n].name);
   printf("Enter agent number (3 digits): "); /* get number */
   gets(numstr);
   agent[n].agnumb = atoi(numstr);
   printf("Enter height in inches: ");        /* get height */
```

```
       gets(numstr);
       agent[n++].height = (float)atof(numstr);
   }

/* listall() */
/* lists all agents and data */
void listall(void)
{
   int j;
   if (n < 1)                    /* check for empty list */
      printf("\nEmpty list.\n");
   for (j=0; j < n; j++)         /* print list */
      {
      printf("\nRecord number %d\n", j+1);
      printf("    Name: %s\n", agent[j].name);
      printf("    Agent number: %03d\n", agent[j].agnumb);
      printf("    Height: %4.2f\n", agent[j].height);
      }
   }

/* wfile() */
/* writes array of structures to file */
void wfile(void)
{
   FILE *fptr;
   if(n < 1)
      { printf("\nCan't write empty list.\n"); return; }
   if( (fptr=fopen("agents.rec","wb"))==NULL )
      printf("\nCan't open file agents.rec\n");
   else
      {
      fwrite(agent, sizeof(agent[0]), n, fptr);
      fclose(fptr);
      printf("\nFile of %d records written.\n", n);
      }
   }

/* rfile() */
/* reads records from file into array */
void rfile(void)
{
   FILE *fptr;
   if( (fptr=fopen("agents.rec","rb"))==NULL )
      printf("\nCan't open file agents.rec\n");
```

```
        else
            {
            while( fread(&agent[n],sizeof(agent[n]),1,fptr)==1 )
                n++;                    /* count records */
            fclose(fptr);
            printf("\nFile read. Total agents is now %d.\n", n);
            }
    }

    /* delrec() */
    /* deletes selected record */
    void delrec(void)
    {
        int recno, j;
        printf("\nEnter record number to be deleted: ");
        scanf("%d", &recno);
        if(recno<1 || recno>n)
            { printf("Invalid record number.\n"); return; }
        for (j=--recno; j<n-1; j++)  /* write each structure */
            agent[j] = agent[j+1];   /*   over preceding one */
        n--;                         /* one less structure */
    }
```

Chapter 14
Answers to Questions

1. a, b, and c
2. linker
3. declared, **extern**
4. a and c
5. False: only modules containing functions referred to in the program are included.
6. c and d
7. b
8. **#define**
9. d
10. large
11. a and d
12. False: except that the stack segment can share the data segment.

13. b and c
14. False
15. d

Chapter 15
Answers to Questions

1. c and d
2. declared, **external**
3. c
4. created and destroyed
5. a and b
6. False: it is only visible from the point where it is defined onward.
7. **external static**
8. c
9. **enum fish gamefish;**
10. d
11. names
12. c
13. True
14. bytes of memory
15. a

Index

? conditional operator 130,690 (handwritten)

strcat 301
sqrt 336

Mandelbrot 525

The Waite Group's
C Programming Using
Turbo C++

Waite Group Reader Feedback Card
Help Us Make A Better Book

To better serve our readers, we would like your opinion on the contents and quality of this book. Please fill out this card and return it to *The Waite Group*, 100 Shoreline Hwy., Suite A-285, Mill Valley, CA, 94941 (415) 331-0575.

Name _____

Company _____

Address _____

City _____

State _____ ZIP _____ Phone _____

1. How would you rate the content of this book?

- ☐ Excellent
- ☐ Very Good
- ☐ Good
- ☐ Fair
- ☐ Below Average
- ☐ Poor

2. What were the things you liked *most* about this book?

- ☐ Pace
- ☐ Content
- ☐ Writing Style
- ☐ Accuracy
- ☐ Examples
- ☐ Listings
- ☐ Appendixes
- ☐ Design
- ☐ Cover
- ☐ Index
- ☐ Quizzes
- ☐ Size
- ☐ Price
- ☐ Illustrations
- ☐ Construction

3. Please explain the one thing you liked *most* about this book. _____

_____

_____

4. What were the things you liked *least* about this book?

- ☐ Pace
- ☐ Content
- ☐ Writing Style
- ☐ Accuracy
- ☐ Examples
- ☐ Listings
- ☐ Appendixes
- ☐ Design
- ☐ Cover
- ☐ Index
- ☐ Quizzes
- ☐ Size
- ☐ Price
- ☐ Illustrations
- ☐ Construction

5. Please explain the one thing you liked *least* about this book. _____

_____

6. How do you use this book? For work, recreation, look-up, self-training, classroom, etc?

_____

_____

_____

_____

7. What would be a useful follow-up book to *C Programming Using Turbo C++* for you?

_____

_____

8. Where did you purchase this particular book?

- ☐ Book Chain
- ☐ Small Book Store
- ☐ Computer Store
- ☐ Other: _____
- ☐ Direct Mail
- ☐ Book Club
- ☐ School Book Store

_____

9. Can you name another similar book you like better than this one, or one that is as good, and tell us why?

_____

_____

10. How many Waite Group books do you own? _____

11. What are your favorite Waite Group books?

_____

12. What topics or specific titles would you like to see The Waite Group develop?

_____

_____

_____

13. What programming languages do you know?

_____

14. Do you own an earlier edition of this book?

_____

15. Any other comments you have about this book or other Waite Group titles?

_____

_____

_____

_____

_____

16. ☐ Check here to receive a free Waite Group catalog.

22737

Tables
Format Specifiers   p 36, 44
Escape Sequences   p 40
Operators   p 53, 56

Fold Here

- -

From:

_____

_____

_____

The Waite Group, Inc.
100 Shoreline Highway, Suite A–285
Mill Valley, CA 94941

Staple or tape here

22737